THE POCKET

WINE

ENCYCLOPEDIA

THE POCKET
WINE
ENCYCLOPEDIA

BARNES & NOBLE BOOKS
NEW YORK

Managing Director	Cheryl Perry
Publishing Manager	Sarah Anderson
Art Director	Stan Lamond
Managing Editor	Susan Page
Editors	Dannielle Doggett
	Fiona Doig
	Alan Edwards
	Kate Etherington
	Mary Halbmeyer
Cover Design	Dee Rogers
Designers	Joy Eckermann
	Andrew Davies
Typesetting	Dee Rogers
Picture Research	Alan Edwards
Photo Library	Alan Edwards
Index	Heather McNamara
Publishing Assistant	Cara Codemo
Foreign Rights	Dee Rogers
Production	Bernard Roberts

This edition published by Barnes & Noble, Inc,. by arrangement with Global Book Publishing

2006 Barnes & Noble Books ·

Text © Global Book Publishing Pty Ltd 2002
Maps © Global Book Publishing Pty Ltd 2002
Photographs from the Global Photo Library
© Global Book Publishing Pty Ltd 2002

Produced by Global Book Publishing Pty Ltd
Level 8,15 Orion Road, Lane Cove, NSW,2066, Australia
Phone: +61 2 9967 3100 Fax: +61 2 9967 5891
Email: rightsmanager@globalpub.com.au

First published in 2002

M 10 9 8 7 6 5 4 3 2 1

ISBN 0-7607-8029-3

Printed in Hong Kong by Sing Cheong Printing Co. Ltd, Hong Kong
Film separation Pica Digital Pte Ltd, Singapore

Captions for images in the preliminary pages

Page 1 Barrels have been used for the past 2,000 years to store wine.

Page 2/3 Vineyards with an old stone building, near Tain, in the Rhône Valley, France.

Page 4/5 Vineyards, Greece.

Page 7 Regular early morning mists contribute to the formation of botrytis, Sauternes, France.

Page 9 Piles of wooden stakes lie ready to be used to support new plantations of vines.

Page 11 Just a portion of the wines stored in the underground cellars of Cellier Le Brun, Marlborough, New Zealand.

Page 12 A harvest worker takes a moment to reflect while waiting for the truck, Mendoza, Argentina.

All captions for pictures in the introduction to each chapter can be located on the last page of the book.

Contributors

Dr. Patrick Farrell M.W., a medical doctor by training, is one of a handful of Masters of Wine living in the U.S. He has followed California's wine-producing regions carefully since moving to the Golden State in 1988. He is a past program and professional session chairman of the Society of Wine Educators and actively teaches about wine. Patrick has judged wine competitions internationally and keeps a busy schedule visiting the world's wine regions. He is currently combining his wine and medical training in writing a book on wine and health.

Catherine Fallis M.S. is the fifth woman in the world to have earned the title of Master Sommelier; she is also a student in the U.K.-based Master of Wine program. In January 2000, she opened Planet Grape, an international wine consultancy (www.PlanetGrape.com). She is wine director at Aqua, a restaurant in San Francisco, and has recently coauthored a wine encyclopedia. Her articles on wines, spirits, cigars, food, travel, and lifestyle appear in a variety of trade and consumer publications and websites, including *The Epicurean Traveler*, OntheRail.com, *Restaurant Hospitality*, *Santé*, and *Wine Business Monthly*. She is currently developing a book and television series with an irreverent approach to good living.

Rebecca Chapa is a San Francisco-based wine consultant whose clients include some major hotels. She is a contributing editor for *Wine & Spirits* and writes freelance for *Santé*, www.SpiritsUSA.com, and has a bimonthly column in *SOMA* magazine. She was coprogram chair of the Society of Wine Educators Conference in San Jose, California, in August 2000. She has completed the Higher Certificate towards the Master of Wine degree given by the Wine and Spirits Education Trust in England and is one of a handful of Americans to have completed the Diploma course of study.

Peter Forrestal was the founding editor of *The Wine Magazine* and is now its associate editor. As a freelance wine and food writer, he has written *A Taste of the Margaret River*, coauthored *The Western Table*, and edited *Discover Australia: Wineries*. He is a former president of the Wine Press Club of Western Australia, a member of the Circle of Wine Writers, and the Australian Society of Wine Educators. He has been wine correspondent for the *West Australian*, the *Western Review*, and the *Perth Weekly*.

Maureen Ashley M.W. started tasting wine as a hobby in the 1970s and entered the wine trade in 1979. She became a Master of Wine in 1984, also attaining the Tim Derouet Award for the excellence of her results. She became a freelance writer in 1986. One of the foremost Italian wine experts, she now lives in Rome. Maureen has written three books in the Touring in Wine Country series as well as *Italian Wines*, in the Sainsbury's Regional Wine Guides series. She writes widely for international audiences, leads wine tours in Italy, and gives talks and tutored tastings.

Tony Aspler, based in Toronto, is the editor of *Winetidings* magazine, wine columnist for the *Toronto Star*, and creator of the Air Ontario Wine Awards. He is a member of the Advisory Board for Masters of Wine (North America). Tony contributed to Jancis Robinson's *Oxford Companion To Wine*, and the *Larousse Encyclopedia of Wine*. He is himself the author of several books on wine, including *Guide to New World Wines*, *Vintage Canada*, *Travels With My Corkscrew*, *The Wine Lover's Companion*, and *The Wine Lover Dines*. He also writes murder mysteries about a wine writer/detective. His website is at www.tonyaspler.com.

James Aufenast writes for *Harpers Wine & Spirit Weekly*, the U.K.'s major wine trade magazine, on emerging wine areas including the south of France, Israel, and Canada. He specializes in Eastern Europe, and has visited Romania and Bulgaria to investigate the wine industries in those countries. He also writes for *The Times* Weekend section on food and drink, and reviews restaurants for the *Who Drinks Where Crushguide*, a London restaurant guide. James has written a cocktail book for Quarto Publishing. He lives in London.

Helena Baker, a native of Prague, holds a Diploma from the Wine and Spirit Education Trust in London, is one of the founders of the Prague Wine Society and the Slow Food Convivium of Prague, a freelance wine writer, columnist, wine taster at international wine competitions, consultant, and lecturer. She has translated the *Encyclopedia of Czech and Moravian Wines*, by professor Vilém Kraus, and published her own *Pocket Guide 2000 to the Wines and Winemakers of the Czech Republic*, which she is currently translating into English. She lives in a country house just outside Prague.

Jeffrey Benson spent the last 30 years traveling to virtually every wine growing country in the world as buying director for a large wine importing company. Specializing in wines from outside Europe, he was instrumental in developing new export markets for such countries as India, Canada, and Zimbabwe. He has coauthored three books on his favorite wines, *Sauternes*, *Saint Emilion/Pomerol*, and *The Sweet Wines of Bordeaux*. He is now a wine consultant to various hotel groups around the world and travels extensively lecturing and contributing articles to various international wine publications.

Stephen Brook worked as an editor in the U.S. and Britain before becoming a freelance writer specializing in travel and wine. His *Liquid Gold: Dessert Wines of the World* won the Andre Simon Award in 1987. Other awards include the Bunch Award for wine writer of the year in 1996. He is the author of *Sauvignon Blanc and Sémillon* and the *Wine Companion to Southern France, Sauternes and the Other Sweet Wines of Bordeaux*, and *The Wines of California*. He lives in London, where he is a regular contributing editor for *Decanter* and writes on wine for *Condé Nast Traveller*.

Jim Budd started writing about wine in 1988, having previously taught English in London. He contributes to a number of specialty drinks magazines, including *Wine & Spirit International*, *Decanter*, and *Harpers Wine & Spirit Weekly*, and contributes to a number of internet sites, including decanter.com and madaboutwine.com.

He wrote *Appreciating Fine Wines*, and contributed to *Oz Clarke's Pocket Wine Book*, the Oz Clarke CD ROM, and *Oz Clarke's Encyclopedia of Wine*. In 1997 he won Le Prix du Champagne Lanson Noble Cuvée for investigating bogus Champagne investment schemes. Jim now has a website (www.investdrinks.org) about drinks investments.

Steve Charters M.W. qualified as a lawyer in the U.K., but was seduced by the allure of wine, and worked in retail and wine education in both London and Sydney. He is one of only 240 members of the Institute of Masters of Wine in the world, and one of only 12 in Australia, having passed its rigorous theory and tasting examination in 1997. Steve now lectures in Wine Studies at Edith Cowan University, in Perth, Australia. His courses cover the understanding and appreciation of wine, its varying worldwide styles, and marketing and selling wine.

Michael Fridjhon is chairman of the South African Wine Industry Trust and an international wine judge. He is the convenor of the South African Airways selection panel, a regular columnist for *Business Day*, and a contributor to the *Financial Mail*, *Wine*, *Wine & Spirit International*, *Harpers Wine & Spirit Weekly*, and *Decanter*. He wrote *The Penguin Book of South African Wine*, is coauthor of *Conspiracy of Giants— An Analysis of the South African Liquor Industry*, and a contributor to the *John Platter South Africa Wine Guide*, *The Complete Book of South African Wine*, *Hugh Johnson's Wine Companion*, and the new *Oxford Companion to Wine*.

Ken Gargett, based on the Gold Coast in Queensland, Australia, is a practicing lawyer as well as a senior writer for *Vine, Wine & Cellar* and a contributor to *The Wine Magazine*, *Discover Australia: Wineries*, and other publications. He is a wine educator for the Wine Society in Queensland and conducts training and consults within the industry, as well as judging. He was the 1993 winner of the Vin de Champagne Award and has conducted numerous Australian wine promotions, seminars, and Master of Wine classes internationally.

Harold Heckle pursued his love of romance languages and literature at the universities of Bristol and King's College (England). After working with the British Council in Perú and a subsidiary of the Bank of England, he became a theater producer, then went on to research, write, and broadcast for BBC Radio. One feature, *The Grape Debate*, led to wine journalism. He has chaired The Wine Club since its inception. Today, Harold writes for *Wine & Spirit International* and *Decanter*, and is columnist for the Spanish newspaper, *El Mundo*. He lives in England and grows his own organic vegetables.

Brian Jordan became interested in wine in the early 1980s when he purchased a hotel restaurant in Britain's west country, and subsequently was twice winner and twice runner-up for the best wine list in the U.K. He began writing about wine in the 1990s, subsequently expanding into international judging, consultancy, photography, lecturing, broadcasting, and organizing wine competitions. As a freelance wine writer, his articles have appeared in every significant wine-oriented magazine in the U.K. as well as several in other countries.

James Lawther M.W., based in Bordeaux, France, cut his teeth in the wine trade retailing wine at Steven Spurrier's Caves de la Madeleine in Paris, and as a lecturer at the Académie du Vin. He was the first Englishman to pass the Master of Wine examination while resident in France (1993). He is now an independent wine consultant, writer, and contributing editor to *Decanter*. He is the author of the *Bordeaux Wine Companion* and has contributed to the recent edition of *The Wine Atlas of France*. James also leads tours in the French wine regions.

Alex Liddell has lived in France, Portugal, and Italy and travels the wine countries of the world for six months of the year. He is the author of *Port Wine Quintas of the Douro*, and *Madeira*. Alex is currently working on a book about the wines of Hungary. He is a member of the Circle of Wine Writers and contributes to Australia's *The Wine Magazine*.

Wink Lorch has worked in the world of wine for over 20 years, in the last 15 as a writer and educator. She was one of the two contributing editors for Williams-Sonoma's *The Wine Guide*, published by Time-Life in 1999. She currently writes for trade and consumer magazines in the U.K. Wink is a founding member of the Association of Wine Educators in the U.K. and regularly leads tutored tastings and wine courses. She divides her time between her chalet in the French Alps (close to Savoie, Jura, and Swiss vineyards) and a *pied-à-terre* in England.

Nico Manessis, born on the island of Corfu, has been active in the international wine business for over 20 years in Europe and the U.S. His first book, *The Greek Wine Guide*, published in 1994, has been instrumental in bringing quality Greek wine to international attention. More recently, he has written *The Illustrated Greek Wine Book*. He also regularly contributes to newspapers and *Decanter*, and lectures frequently on the new wines of his native country, appearing often at the Université de Vin in France. He is a member of l'Académie Internationale du Vin and lives in Geneva, Switzerland.

Sally Marden is a professionally trained journalist who cut her writing teeth on regional U.K. newspapers. She turned to drink in 1990 when she joined leading trade publication *Off Licence News*. She has traveled extensively to wine regions throughout Europe, the U.S., Chile, and Australia, and, as well as writing for a range of wine publications in the U.K., has co-presented a food and drink television series for Channel 4 in the U.K. In 1998 she moved to the Barossa, where she now writes and consults for a specialist wine marketing company, as well as contributing regularly to publications, including *The Wine Magazine* and *Le Vigneron.*

Giles MacDonogh is a historian and the author of several books on Germany, including lives of Frederick the Great and the Kaiser and histories of Prussia and Berlin. He is also a wine writer, contributing a regular column to the *Financial Times* and *Punch*, as well as writing occasional articles for

Decanter, *Wine*, and other specialized magazines. He is the author of three books on wine, two of them on Austria: *The Wine and Food of Austria* and *New Wines from the Old World*. He is currently writing a book on Portuguese wines.

Kate McIntyre learned firsthand about vineyards and wineries growing up from the age of nine on her family's estate on Victoria's Mornington Peninsula. She began her career in the wine industry at Philip Murphy Wine and Spirits in 1996. In 1998 she was the inaugural winner of the Negociants Working with Wine Fellowship. She is now studying for the Master of Wine exam and is a regular contributor to *The Wine Magazine*. In 1999 she was wine writer for *Women's Weekly* and is an occasional contributor to *Divine* magazine. She was also a contributor to *Discover Australia: Wineries*.

Alex Mitchell credits her involvement in the 1998 Negociants Working With Wine program as being the turning point in her career in wine. It exposed her to an unprecedented range of imported wines and winning its prestigious Wine Writing Prize has led to her writing regularly for *The Wine Magazine*. After many years of nursing and four years in wine retail, she now has her own business. She has taught wine studies at Swinburne University and has contributed to two books. She plans to complete a Bachelor of Oenology and intends to become a winemaker.

Jasper Morris M.W. joined the U.K. wine trade in 1979 and founded his company, Morris & Verdin Ltd, two years later. The plan was to import wines from all over France but he rapidly developed a heavy bias towards Burgundy. He has also developed a strong second string in Californian wines. Since becoming a Master of Wine in 1985, he has been much in demand as a writer and lecturer. He regularly contributes to *Decanter* magazine and was responsible for the Burgundy entries in the *Oxford Companion to Wine*.

Jeremy Oliver is an independent Australian wine writer, broadcaster, author, and speaker. Since 1984, when

he became the world's youngest published wine author, he has written nine books and has contributed wine columns to dozens of magazines and newspapers. In addition to his self-published annual guide to Australian wine, *The OnWine Australian Wine Annual*, and his bimonthly newsletter, *Jeremy Oliver's OnWine Report*, he currently contributes to *The Wine Magazine*, *Personal Investment*, and *The Australian Way*. He is also a speaker and master of ceremonies at wine presentations and has a comprehensive and independent wine website at www.onwine.com.au.

Anthony Peregrine, who comes from Lancashire in Northern England, studied political sciences before working as a teacher in Mexico City. On his return to England, he wrote for several newspapers before moving to France in 1988. He now lives near Montpellier in the Languedoc region where he freelances for the British press, covering wine, food, and travel. His work appears in the *Daily Telegraph*, the *Daily Mail*, *Decanter*, *Wine & Spirit International*, and on BBC Radio 4.

John Radford has been writing about wine professionally since 1977, after an earlier career in the wine trade. He has a special interest in the wines of Spain and Portugal and contributed chapters on Iberia to the *Larousse Encyclopedia of Wine* and *Hugh Johnson's Wine Companion*. His book, *The New Spain*, won the Glenfiddich, Lanson, and Versailles Cookbook Fair prizes in 1999. He cowrote the *Mitchell Beazley Pocket Guide to Fortified and Sweet Wines* and writes for *Decanter*, *Wine*, and other specialty magazines in the U.K. He lives on the south coast of England.

Margaret Rand has been writing about wine for 20 years. She has edited *Wine*, and *Wine & Spirit International*, is wine editor of *Oz Clarke's Wine Guide*, and was founding editor of *Whisky Magazine*. She contributes to a wide range of publications, including *The Sunday Times* (U.K.), the *Daily Telegraph*, and *Wine*. She wrote the audio guide for Vinopolis, London's major wine exhibit, and is currently working with Oz Clarke on a book about grape varieties. A recent publication includes an introductory guide to wine, which she coauthored with Robert Joseph.

Michele Round was an art teacher before pursuing her fascination for food and wine as a consultant, writer, and commentator. She is a regular contributor to *The Wine Magazine*, writes a weekly food column for a Tasmanian newspaper, and has written about wine for a variety of national publications. Through her work in gastronomy as a cook, writer, and teacher, she is passionate about the synergy between food and wine. Born and raised in Tasmania, Michele became well known as a champion of the developing island wine industry through a weekly ABC Radio wine segment.

Joanna Simon is an award-winning wine writer for *The Sunday Times* (U.K.), for which she writes a weekly column, and a contributor to many other publications worldwide. She is a former editor of two leading U.K. wine magazines, *Wine* and *Wine & Spirit International*, and is author of *Wine with Food* and *Discovering Wine*. She is also a broadcaster, presenting *The Bottle Uncorked* in 1999, BBC Radio 4's first series devoted to wine. When not writing, tasting, talking about wine, or visiting the world's vineyards, she escapes from London to a beautiful and remote part of France.

Marguerite Thomas is the author of *Wineries of the Eastern States*. She is travel editor of *The Wine News* and she writes "Tastings," a food and wine column for the *Los Angeles Times* Syndicate International. She is a regular contributor on food and wine to various U.S. publications, including *Saveur*, *Country Home*, and *Time Out New York*. She was raised in France and California, and now resides in New York, where she has been nominated to receive the prestigious James Beard Award for wine journalism.

Joelle Thomson is a freelance wine writer in Auckland, New Zealand. She started writing about wine for the weekly arts newspaper, *Capital Times*, in the mid-1990s and worked full-time in food and design magazines in New

Zealand prior to her freelance career. She published her first book, *Joelle Thomson's Under $15 Wine Guide*, in 1999 and has since written *Weekends for Wine Lovers*. She is currently wine writer for the *Christchurch Press*, *Grocer's Review*, *SHE*, and *NZ Home & Entertaining*, and a regular contributor to *The Wine Magazine*.

Roger Voss, one of Britain's leading wine and food writers, is European editor for the New York-based *Wine Enthusiast* magazine and writes for U.K. magazines such as *Decanter* and *Harpers Wine & Spirit Weekly*. He has been an editor of the Consumers' Associations' *Which? Wine Guide* for four years and has also written *Wine and Food of France* and *The Wines of the Loire*, as well as guides to port and sherry, and chardonnay and cabernet. Upcoming publications include a fifth edition of his guide to the wines of the Loire, Alsace, and the Rhône. He lives in the Bordeaux region of France.

Dr. Paul White, originally from Oregon, captained the Oxford University Blind Wine Tasting Team while completing a doctorate at Oxford University. He developed his analytical skills further as a judge at London's International Wine Challenge. Based in Wellington, he is currently a columnist for the *New Zealand Herald*, and contributes to the *Oregonian* and other media throughout Australasia, the U.S., and Europe. He also publishes an online wine tasting guide at www.winesense.co.nz. His senior judging credits include London's International Wine Challenge, the Sydney International Top 100, and Sydney Royal Easter Show.

Simon Woods, a former electronics design engineer, picked up the wine bug while traveling in Australia in 1988 and has hardly put a glass down since. He spent the early 1990s coordinating London's International Wine Challenge, the world's largest wine competition, and is now coeditor of *Which? Wine Guide*, as well as being a regular columnist for *Wine*. He has judged at wine competitions in France, England, and Australia and has also appeared on radio and television both at home and abroad. He lives in the Pennines in the North of England.

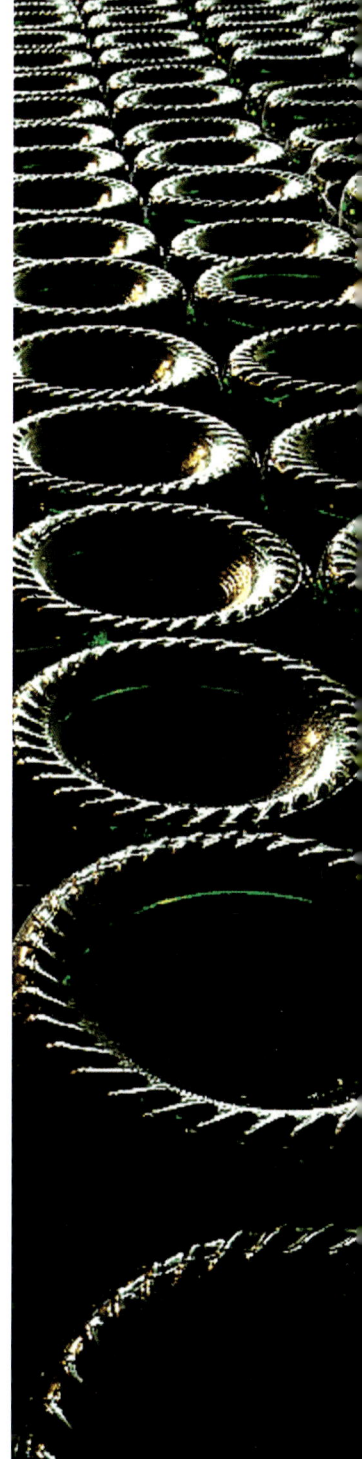

Contents

The World of Wine

The History of Wine

More than any other beverage across the world, wine fascinates, entices, and seduces. It was most likely first made in the region of the Caucasus Mountains, roughly in present-day Georgia or Kurdistan, perhaps 8,000 years ago. The usual hypothesis is that a few bunches of wild grapes were stored in a clay pot and forgotten for a few days. They began to ferment, probably by carbonic maceration. As juice ran out, yeast fermentation may have begun. After a few days, the owner of the pot remembered the grapes and, perhaps feeling thirsty, she drank the juice that

had accumulated at the bottom. Although it may not have been very pleasant, she found that it made her feel strangely euphoric. Thus the first wine, perhaps the first alcoholic drink, was born.

WINE AS A COMMODITY

As Neolithic society became more developed with the more efficient cultivation of crops, so it began to create surplus product and afford certain individuals the opportunity to trade that surplus. The climate around cities like Ur and Babylon, among the earliest centers of civilization in the Middle East, was too hot for production of the balanced grapes needed to produce good wine, but places such as these had the wealth to purchase it, and in this way, wine became a commodity.

The first wine trader might have lived in one of the cities of Sumer, in what is now southern Iraq. Located on major rivers like the Tigris and Euphrates, these cities irrigated their crops, and became arteries of trade. Wine producers there would load up reed boats with large pots of the magic liquid and float it downstream to the great centers of the south.

Wine spread rapidly throughout the Mediterranean world. It was produced by the Egyptians, though only for their rich, and then later by the Greeks, who produced it for all classes. The austere early Romans were suspicious of it, but wine had become popular well before the time of Caesar, and was again a huge source of wealth for those who produced it (using slave labor) on a large scale.

The wine drunk in the ancient world would not have resembled most of the wines we drink today. The taste then was for sweeter wine. It may well have had a lower alcohol level, and would regularly

Barrels were the technological change needed to spread cheap, mass-produced wine. They were resilient, held more, and were stackable.

have been mixed with other substances such as honey, spices, and sometimes even seawater!

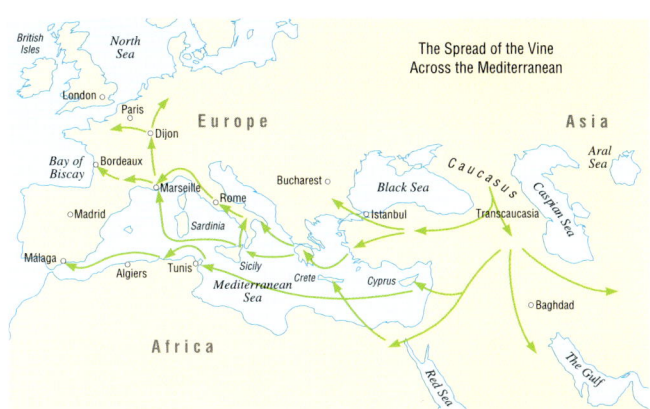

The Roman Empire, and its efficient transport network, encouraged not only the trade of wine but also the spreading of the vine. Even before Roman arrival, Greek traders had brought the vine to the southern areas of France, but then the *pax Romana* spread it throughout all of France and Spain—and possibly encouraged the use of wild vines in Germany. By the end of the third century AD, wine was being made in many of the places we now see as its traditional home: Bordeaux, Burgundy, the Mosel valley, and Jeréz. Eventually, these areas started to send wine back to Rome itself.

Critical to this spread was a revolution in the method of transporting wine. The early storage of all liquids, including wine, was in long thin clay jars, called *amphorae*. However, a new form of container appeared from France, in the second century AD. Barrels, invented by the Celts, were the technological advance necessary to distribute cheap, mass-produced wine to the burgeoning masses of the Roman Empire.

THE INFLUENCE OF THE CHURCH

As Europe entered the Middle Ages, the trade in wine that declined during the Dark Ages began to resume. Rich and heady Mediterranean wines such as malmsey, which was a sweet wine from Greece, became particularly popular in northern Europe. Meanwhile the Church became important in both the production and distribution of wine. In the monasteries, monks observed and studied the natural world, and these observations and studies led to an understanding of, and later skills in, viticulture.

This medieval carving from Catalonia in Spain appears above a castle door and shows a hand and a bunch of grapes.

The Abbey of Citeaux, founded by the Cistercian order in 1098, sits just outside the Côte d'Or, the heartland of the Burgundy wine region. Originally seeking simple, austere lives, the monks later became wealthy as the laity bequeathed property (including vineyards) to the abbey. By the end of the twelfth century the Church owned much of the land in the village of Vougeot. Visitors sampled the wines and the monks' reputation spread, stimulating demand for their produce. Their influence lasted until the French Revolution of 1789.

A new era in wine followed Columbus' voyage to the Americas in 1492. By the end of 1521, there were vineyards in Mexico, by 1548 they could be found in Chile; by 1769 they were in California. The Dutch made wine in the Cape of Good Hope in 1659, and vine cuttings were taken from there by the first European settlers traveling to the new lands of Australia and New Zealand.

Wine production and consumption

The chart detailing consumption trends in three different countries shows that, in a typical southern European wine-producing country such as Portugal, consumption has halved over about 35 years. In Germany, on the other hand, a country which makes and imports wine,

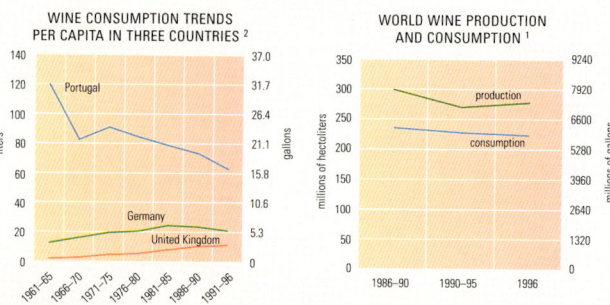

there has been a steady growth in the amount drunk. From the small base in the United Kingdom, there has been rapid growth, particularly in the last ten years. Worldwide, in the long term, if markets in China and the United States grow, then overall consumption may increase. In the

countries of Southeast Asia recently there has been a dramatic increase in the consumption of red wine.

1 Figures from the Wine Institute, California, based on information from the Organisation for Wine and the Vine, Paris.
2 Based on Berger, Anderson and Stringer, "Trends in the World Wine Market," 1961–96, CIES, Adelaide, 1998.

THE SCIENTIFIC REVOLUTION

The seventeenth and eighteenth centuries saw both the scientific and industrial revolutions. In this period, empirical work allowed the development, in Champagne, of the greatest sparkling wine in the world, and subsequently more growth in the wine trade. At the same time, the rising middle classes provided ever-expanding markets for what until then had still been largely consumed in the regions that produced it. The spread of railways ushered in this next development. When wines from Italy or the south of France could be delivered in Berlin or London or Paris within 24 hours, producers no longer needed to seek a market only in the nearest towns and cities.

One other important legacy of the nineteenth century was the work of Louis Pasteur. He contributed substantially to our ability to control the processes involved in winemaking—and thus our ability to make good wine. Pasteur showed that microscopic organisms were responsible for fermentations. When he was commissioned by the

French government to investigate wine spoilage, he discovered the various bacteria that cause it and offered means of preventing their activity. It was due to this man more than any other that winemaking became a science, and that the drink we now enjoy can be produced so reliably and also so cheaply.

What had been a golden age came to an end in the 1860s when the pest phylloxera arrived from North America. It ravaged vineyards, first in France, then through the rest of Europe, until the solution of grafting was discovered. At the same time, the widening trade in wine provoked widespread fraud, as producers of cheap wine tried to pass their product off as *grand vin*. The response to the fraud problem in Europe was to develop a system to protect the producers of quality wine by guaranteeing its origin. This process, which developed into the French Appellation system, also gave rise to the European idea of labeling "quality" wine, which has a specific demarcated origin, and "table" wine, which does not.

Grapes and Viticulture

In producing wine, there's a tension between what occurs "naturally" and what results from human intervention. For a commercial wine that is made on a large scale and sells for less than U.S. $8, the essential element is the ability of the winemaker to maximize the character of the variety. For more expensive, high-quality wines the varietal character should shine through, but the winemaker may also need enough restraint to reveal the environmental influences.

THE ENVIRONMENT FOR GROWING GRAPES

Vines need to grow in temperate climates, and generally flourish best between 30 and 50 degrees latitude in the northern hemisphere and between 30 and 40 degrees in the southern hemisphere (due to its greater maritime influence). Altitude reduces the average temperature by 2°F (0.6°C) for each 330 feet (100 m), so vines tend to be planted at lower levels except in the warmest climates. In addition, vines must have access either to reasonable rainfall levels, ideally concentrated in winter, or to some form of irrigation.

The French term, *terroir*, related to *terre*, meaning soil, is more correctly translated as "region." The term encompasses the entire natural environment of the vine—the topography, climate, soil, and site of the vineyard where it grows. Diehard *terroiristes* claim that wine must reflect the specific site on which the grapes are grown. Their opponents retort that all you need to grow wine grapes is a decent climate and a regular supply of water (irrigation, if necessary).

The reality is that most winemakers don't limit their production to grapes from single regions. At the end of the 1990s, even in France—the bastion of *terroir*-based wines—around 50 percent of all wine sold was *vin de table*, which is not marketable under a region of origin. However, in California and many southern hemisphere wine regions, many producers continue to claim that the specific topographies and soils which characterize their own particular vineyards make their wines distinctive.

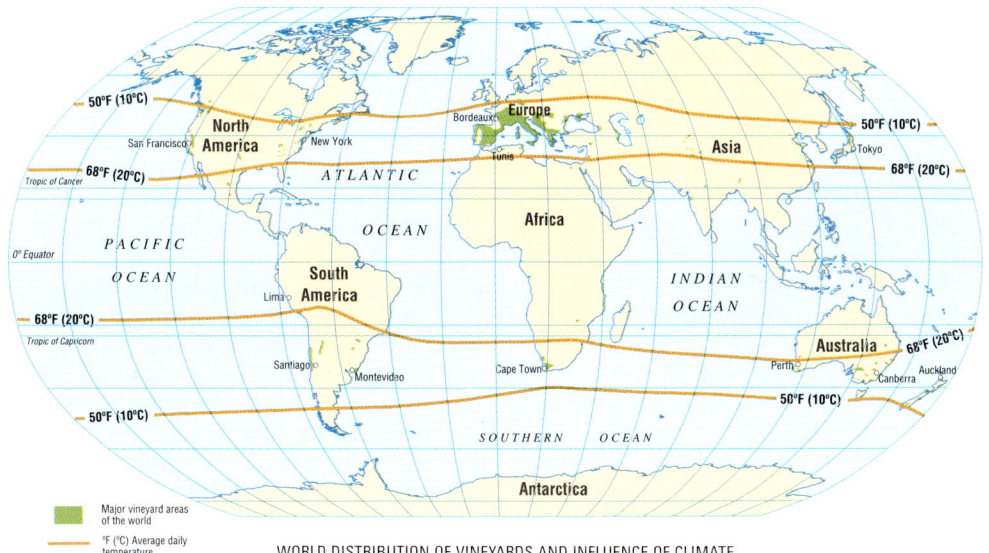

WORLD DISTRIBUTION OF VINEYARDS AND INFLUENCE OF CLIMATE

Left: *Flat vineyards in the hot wine regions found in southern California*
Below left: *Grapevines in winter, Soave, Italy; snow is not a problem, but spring frosts can be.*

Climate

Climate includes temperature, sunshine, rainfall, frost, and the impact of wind.

Vines are dormant below about 50°F (10°C), and ripening occurs only above about 63°F (17°C). Vine function diminishes above 75°F (24°C), and the vine may shut down entirely at temperatures higher than about 90°F (32°C). Sunny days well into fall are crucial, as harvest may take place late in September, or even into October (translating to March or April in the southern hemisphere).

A vine needs about 20 inches (500 mm) of water per year in cool climates, rising to about 30 inches (750 mm) in the warmest regions. In traditional regions where irrigation is banned, this may mean that it is difficult to obtain a good vintage in drought years (though most of the places that refuse to irrigate are temperate with a good rainfall). Where irrigation is practiced, rainfall levels become less important—as long as river flow or dam water levels are maintained.

Frost affects the quantity of wine more than the quality. Winter frosts are rarely a problem, but a frost late in spring can literally nip a crop in the bud by burning off the spring shoots. Frost impact can be mitigated by good site selection, or by artificial means. One of the most basic of these involves the use of hot braziers in the vineyards to raise the temperature, while one of the more technologically advanced methods is aspersion—spraying the shoots with water, which freezes and, paradoxically, insulates the vines against the worst extremes of the cold.

Winds may cool or burn the vines and at their worst can rip leaves off. While it is not a general problem, it may be recurrent in specific regions such as the Rhône valley, where the Mistral can whip down towards the Mediterranean, stressing the vines and impeding ripening. Winds can also be beneficial in a warm climate, as in the Hunter region in Australia, where the valley funnels in sea breezes to moderate the heat of the sun.

Soil

The most important benefit offered by soil, often overlooked, is anchorage. The ability to root the vine into the ground is essential. Beyond that, however, the key element is drainage. Vines don't like to be waterlogged and respond badly in those conditions. Additionally, if drainage is poor and there is heavy rain near harvest, the grapes are likely to soak up extra water and dilute their other components, reducing the quality of the resulting wine. Drainage can be modified.

Climatic variables in four major wine-growing regions[3]

One can roughly categorize wine regions in four ways—maritime, continental, Mediterranean and hot inland. The following charts give examples of each, using four wine regions—Bordeaux, the Rheingau, Provence, and the Riverland in Australia. The information covers just four of the many variables: sunshine hours during summer, the mean July temperature (January for the Riverland), the mean winter temperature, and annual rainfall.

From this, it becomes apparent that Bordeaux and the Rheingau have broadly similar summer temperatures (the former is a bit hotter,

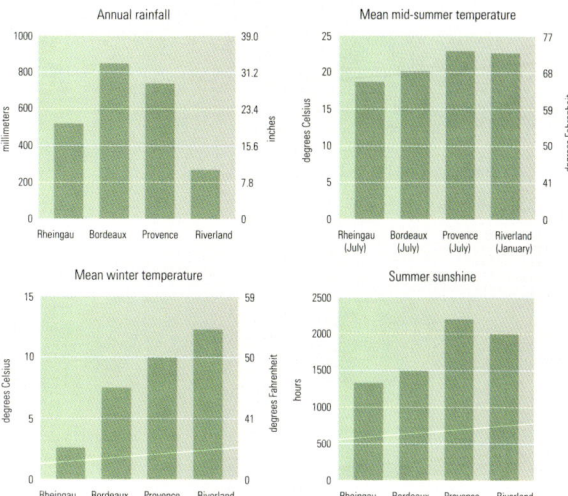

and has marginally more sunshine), but the continental climate is markedly colder in winter. The Mediterranean and hot inland climates are both warmer in summer, and noticeably warmer in winter. The maritime climate, with its proximity to the ocean, is the wettest, but the Mediterranean is also quite wet (though it is in fact rather drier in summer, which is why it has the highest number of sunshine hours). The inland region has the least rainfall, and irrigation is essential here.

It is impossible to use climatic modeling to predict exactly what varieties will be used, and which

wines will be made, but the wines of each of these nominated regions shows something about their climate:

Rheingau produces delicate, light but intensely flavorful white wines, based on riesling.

Bordeaux has a range of full whites, from fine cabernet and merlot-based reds to dessert wines.

Provence boasts robust but flavorful reds, and some tasty rosés.

Riverland produces some good wines, but it concentrates on the production of bulk wine.

3 Based on J. Gladstones, "Viticulture and Environment," Winetitles, Adelaide, 1992.

Left: *Lush German vineyards on the riverside.*
Far left: *Mature vines found in the warmer Mediterranean climate of southern France.*

The world-famous "Terra Rossa" (red soil) of Coonawarra, Australia, provides excellent drainage.

Site and topography

The site of a vineyard mediates between the pre-dominant soil and the overall climate of the area. By dint of a particular aspect, the climate may have, say, a more south-facing aspect than is general, or the soil may be modified by erosion. The winding Mosel valley offers many sites; the best are those with a southerly aspect on a hillside. The flatter parts of the region, on the other hand, make less fine, less intense wine.

Other factors can also be decisive. Isolated hills encourage airflow, thus reducing the chance of frosts in late spring. Rivers also reduce the chance of frosts because they tend to raise the prevailing temperature slightly through airflow. Altitude can also be decisive; a rise of 330 feet (100 m) reduces the average temperature by 2°F (0.6°C). Sites can be modified by human intervention. Trees are often planted to act as wind-breaks, and eroded soil can be removed from the foot of a slope and taken back up to the top.

VINE AND VARIETY

The grape

The grape variety is of vital importance in shaping wine styles. At its most basic, it determines the color of the wine. After that, choice of grape influences the levels of acidity, alcohol and (in red wines) tannin, as well as the body and style of the wine. The variety also determines how the winemaker will approach the wine. Few winemakers would age riesling in oak or put it through malo-lactic fermentation. Conversely, no winemaker is going to prevent the malolactic fermentation in cabernet sauvignon, and most will also give it some oak treatment.

The typical wine grape is quite small. Even with white wines, some flavor comes from the skin, and a low juice-to-skin ratio enhances those characters. In black grapes (also known as red grapes), the skin gives the wine its tannin and color. Thicker skins and/or smaller grapes mean deeper color and more tannic wine.

Vines can tolerate quite a wide range of soil pH levels, from about 5.5 (acidic) to around 8.5 (alkaline), although it may be better to adjust the soil at either end of the spectrum, and particular rootstocks may be required to cope with extreme situations. Nutrient content is also critical. Vines need a supply of various elements, most notably nitrogen, but also phosphorus, potassium, and various metals. However, excessive fertilizer—particularly too much nitrogen—promotes more vigorous vine canopy growth that may shade the bunches of grapes and inhibit ripening. Likewise, too much potassium in the soil will reduce the acid level in juice resulting in a less balanced and stable wine, and reducing its aging potential.

The myth should be dispelled that soil conveys flavor to the wine, as there is no evidence for this. Mosel wines may be described as "slatey," or chablis as "flinty," but that is not because slate or flint in the soil imparts flavor. However, although unproven, it is possible that chemical components of the soil may influence nuances of taste.

The variety, of course, also gives the wine its core flavors. Each variety may have a range of typical aromas and tastes—its "flavor spectrum." No wine will display all of these flavors, but a reasonably good wine should show at least one or two flavors to give good varietal character, and a complex wine will display more.

The vine

The grapevine *Vitis vinifera*, originally native to east Asia, is now the most commonly cultivated species across the world, with possibly as many as 10,000 varieties although few of them are used to make wine. Only 200 are recorded as being significant in France.

Most viticultural attention these days is focused not on new varieties, but rather on the genetic manipulation of existing varieties. It should be possible, for example, to exclude from chardonnay the genes that make it prone to rots and other fungal diseases, thus reducing the costs of cultivating the grapes as well as ensuring a more regular quality.

The most important part of the vine's cycle is the process of ripening, which is what creates the final wine —and it is particularly important in the period following *véraison* (the key stage at which grape skins begin to turn black, or to become translucent if they are white grapes). After *véraison*, when the vine normally has enough reserves of sugar, the surplus is sent into the grapes. This surplus sugar is eventually converted into alcohol, and thus grape juice can be made into wine.

Ripening, however, is crucial for more than just sugar accumulation. Developing grapes are quite high in acidity, but the relative acid levels drop during the ripening process,

allowing a balanced wine to develop. Ripening also allows the various flavor components of the grape to develop. At the same time, the phenolic compounds that give red wines their color and tannin also increase, with the tannins developing from green and coarse to ripe and smooth.

Right: *A grapevine leaf during fall in California's famous Napa Valley wine region.*
Below: *Vineyards slope gracefully down hillsides lining the side of Lake Geneva in Switzerland.*

Top row, from left: *Cabernet franc—almost ripe; cabernet sauvignon; grenache; malbec; petit verdot; pinot noir.*
Bottom row, from left: *Syrah; tannat; tempranillo; zinfandel.*

Red grape varieties

Barbera Widely planted in Italy and California but only makes characterful wines in Piedmont.

Cabernet franc Contributes a lot to Bordeaux wines, and makes interesting, underrated wines in the Loire valley.

Cabernet sauvignon The most ubiquitous red variety in the world. Bordeaux is its heartland, with upstarts now found in California, Tuscany, and Australia.

Gamay Makes fruity wines in Beaujolais, whose wines are much misunderstood.

Grenache The most planted red variety in the world, but concentrated in France and Spain. Only makes great wine in Châteauneuf-du-Pape.

Lambrusco You have to search out the best examples. Otherwise, it's a frothy, sweet, insubstantial wine for cola drinkers.

Malbec A minor player in southwest France, but the major player in Argentina.

Merlot The "other" great red variety of Bordeaux, but responsible for its priciest wines. Now relocating to California.

Mourvèdre Little-known grape from southern France and Spain, often useful in giving a tannic backbone to blends.

Nebbiolo High acid, high tannin variety which makes complex and long-lived wines in northwest-Italy's Piedmont region.

Petit verdot A minor but high-quality component in the bordeaux mix; also being investigated in emerging wine regions.

Pinotage South Africa's own variety, a crossing of the productive cinsault and exacting pinot noir.

Pinot meunier Least well known but most widely planted grape in Champagne. Krug is proud of pinot meunier's role in its wine.

Pinot noir The classic red grape of Burgundy, but one of the fussiest varieties to manage. Only New Zealand and parts of the U.S. seem to be making headway with it.

Sangiovese Widely planted in Italy, and capable of making great savory wines in Tuscany.

Syrah/shiraz Makes stunning wines in the northern Rhône and Australia. An increasingly popular variety, sometimes to blend, in other parts of the world.

Tannat Hard tannic variety in southwest France that, with age, turns in some complex, interesting wines.

Tempranillo The great grape of Rioja, also producing good wines in other parts of Spain and northern Portugal.

Touriga naçional Portugal's great indigenous variety. A key component of port, but also used for increasingly good table wines.

Zinfandel California's own variety. Makes juicy, brambly, powerfully alcoholic wines.

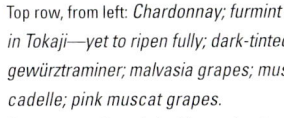

Top row, from left: *Chardonnay; furmint in Tokaji—yet to ripen fully; dark-tinted gewürztraminer; malvasia grapes; muscadelle; pink muscat grapes.*
Bottom row, from left: *Pinot gris; riesling; sémillon to be processed; viognier.*

White grape varieties

Chardonnay The most desired grape variety in the world. Makes full-bodied, often potentially complex wines.

Chenin blanc Makes great wine in the Loire valley and much ordinary wine in South Africa. Often used as an anonymous base in California.

Colombard A good workhorse variety in the south of France; it is also widely planted in South Africa, California, and Australia.

Furmint Described as "fiery," this grape is the great variety of Hungarian tokay and has potential for table wine.

Garganega Neutral variety, but can make wines of great texture and character in Soave.

Gewürztraminer A most distinctive variety, with lychee and rose-petal characters. Its best examples are found in Alsace.

Malvasia Heavy but interesting variety, little known but widely planted in southern Europe.

Marsanne Mainstay of white wines in the northern Rhône valley, and surprisingly concentrated in central Victoria, Australia.

Melon de bourgogne The variety of muscadet. Neutral and light.

Müller-thurgau Widely planted, early ripening, but mediocre "flowery" variety. Planted mainly in Germany but now also has an outpost in New Zealand.

Muscadelle Generally a minor supporting variety, but the grape behind the great fortified tokays of Australia.

Muscat A wide family of grapes, but at its best (*muscat blanc à petits grains*) responsible for dry aromatic wines in Alsace, good sparkling wine in Asti and great fortified wines in southern France and Australia.

Palomino Boring variety, but it does make exciting sherry.

Pinot blanc Restrained variety, at its best in Alsace and Italy.

Pinot gris Makes full-bodied, slightly aromatic wines. Best in Alsace, but also used in Italy and central Europe.

Riesling The world's greatest white variety, based partly on its longevity, it makes stunning, focused wines (from dry to very sweet) in Alsace, Germany, Austria and Australia.

Sauvignon blanc A classic in the central Loire and New Zealand.

Sémillon Makes great wines in Bordeaux (especially botrytized dessert wines) and the Hunter valley.

Trebbiano The world's most widely planted and boring white grape variety. Ideal for cognac.

Viognier Makes full-bodied and aromatic white centered on the northern Rhône, but now attracting attention in California.

Planting a grafted vine in a stony Spanish vineyard.

IN THE VINEYARD

Site selection

Before a vine is even planted, the choice of site for the vineyard is crucial. In addition to factors such as guaranteeing adequate drainage, and avoiding frosts—there are economic factors to consider. Is the vineyard able to be harvested mechanically? Is there ready access to a market? If a cellar door is planned, will there be substantial passing trade? What does the land cost? You will pay much more per acre in Champagne, for example, than you would in Languedoc.

Rootstocks

In Europe and California, and often in other parts of the world, grapevines will invariably be grafted on to other rootstocks before planting. The technique of grafting has been known to horticulturists for centuries, and essentially is the insertion of the shoot of one species into the branch of another. In viticulture, it allows shoots from various *Vinifera* vines species to be grafted onto the roots of other vine species, often in order to gain resistance to pests, disease, or other conditions.

Planting

The orientation within which vines will be planted is done with two—sometimes contradictory— aims. The first is to optimize the angle to sun; to be at 90° to the midday sun is most generally considered to be ideal. However, it is better to plant along a slope rather than down it, as rows of vines down a slope will facilitate erosion. In Europe, vines are traditionally close-spaced, sometimes as

many as 4,000 plants per acre (10,000 per ha). The theory is that this increases the pressure on the vines, limiting yields, and thus guaranteeing quality. In practice, much less dense planting is used in many regions, especially where machines are used for harvesting and other forms of vineyard management.

Pruning and training

Pruning allows the viticulturist to determine how productive the vine is to be for the next season, offering the opportunity for a greater or lesser yield. It is also the precursor to training the vine, creating the "architecture" of the canopy to allow for various forms of management. Training may be along a wire, with just one cane or cordon or a number of them, or it may be in bush form, which is excellent for conserving the vine's resources in arid regions, but is not such a good shape for mechanized vineyards. Canopy management techniques both open grapes up to sunlight, as well as encouraging airflow to inhibit those diseases which stem from humidity.

Irrigation

Perhaps the oldest, simplest method of irrigation, known since ancient times, was flood irrigation. This eventually evolved into irrigation by furrow, which channels water along rows beside the vines, but which needs flattish land to work effectively. Spray irrigation was developed over

Mountainside vineyards, growing alongside bananas in Madeira in Spain. Care must be taken to avoid erosion on sloping sites.

the last 40 years (often with mobile sprinklers), and then drip irrigation, with a pipe along each row of vines dropping water into the soil, was introduced. There are many advantages to this system, among them precision, simplicity, and the ability to apply other products such as liquid fertilizer along with the water.

Soil management

A midrow crop inhibits soil erosion and makes it easier to get mechanical access without churning up the soil. Careful choice of the crop (grass, rye, or clover) allows the cutting or digging-in of the greenery to create a nutritious mulch. This is more natural than inorganic fertilizers, which are still widely used. Soil compacts with time, so it may

be necessary to plough or even deep-rip it to facilitate airflow and drainage. Unfortunately, loosening the soil can also promote erosion.

Diseases and disorders

Fungal diseases of the vine include rots, oidium, and peronospera. Rot starts from dead material (often dead flowers from late spring) and needs humidity to develop. It is controlled by sprays and pre-empted by good canopy management. Oidium is a powdery mildew that splits berries and inhibits bunch growth. It is now easily inhibited by dusting with sulfur if caught early. Peronospera is a downy mildew that is easily controlled with copper-based sprays. The most virulent bacterial disease is Pierce's Disease,

which kills vines and is incurable, and is a particular problem in the U.S. Spread by small insects called leafhoppers, it occurs especially in vineyards near streams. Viral diseases, including fanleaf virus and leafroll virus, are of recent origin (from about 1890) when rootstocks began to be used. Tending to be spread via cuttings from infected plants, they may still be passed on by insects like nematodes. The only effective treatment is to heat-treat vine stock to create virus-free material. Other vine disorders, including chlorosis, *millerandage*, and also *coulure* occur. These are not diseases, instead they are environmental problems that can afflict vines at different times.

Vine pests

Phylloxera arrived in France in the early 1860s, probably from an imported vine from North America, and started spreading from a vineyard in Marseilles. This small louse, native to North America, lives on the roots of native vine species. Here, vines have become tolerant to the insect and, as it feeds off the roots, they callous over with no lasting damage. However, in other parts of the world vines have no natural defense against this pest and it has caused great destruction. In France it had reached all parts within 30 years before then spreading on throughout Europe. Hundreds of thousands of acres of vine were lost, never to be replanted, and the viticultural map of Europe was altered forever. Phylloxera still exerts an influence in some regions of the world. It is active in New Zealand and in the Australian state of Victoria, though other parts of Australia have been effectively quarantined. Paradoxically, it has also just spread through the vineyards of California, necessitating complete replanting there.

Age of vines

Vines reach maximum productivity at about seven years. Productivity usually declines after 20 to 30 years. Regular replanting is necessary to maintain the yields for those making a mass-produced wine from high yields. On the other hand, a producer seeking higher quality may welcome lower yields of older vines, which often leads to a more concentrated flavor and more depth in the resulting wine. In such cases, they are more likely to simply replace vines as they die rather than replant entire vineyards, thus maintaining relatively high average ages for the grapevines of such vineyards.

Cleaning buckets to prevent the spread of disease, Maximin Grünhaus Estate, Saar, Germany.

Winemaking

HARVEST AND CRUSHING

The first stage in the process of making wine is to harvest the grapes. This can be done either by machine or by hand. Mechanical harvesting is usually fine on flat or undulating vineyard sites. It generally preserves the fruit quality almost as well as hand-picked fruit. Handpicking does, however, allow more selectivity and can ensure that you pick whole bunches without any of the juice starting to run, which is all but inevitable with the vigorous harvesters.

Most vineyards are near to the wineries that serve them, but transporting of the grapes can become an issue when they are some distance away. Adding sulfur dioxide so as to inhibit the oxidation process, and then blanketing them under an inert gas in a closed container allows them to be shipped over long distances without significant damage. Large producers will often have their white grapes pressed and simply transport them to a winery as juice. In Champagne, where grapes need to be dealt with quickly in order to guarantee a good base wine, they are often pressed at press houses to be found in the middle of the vineyards themselves.

The first stage, once the grapes are at the winery, is to destem and crush them. Crushing is not aimed at pressing the juice out of the grapes, but is merely meant to split open the skins, and to encourage some juice to run out naturally.

Mechanical harvesters straddle the vines, and rapidly vibrating beaters shake the plant's trunk, dislodging the grapes.

Presses

Presses come in different forms. The most traditional type is the basket press, which is still used in Champagne, and by anyone who wants a fast but gentle press. A more recent development is the vaslin press, comprising a cylinder with plates at each end that are pulled together by metal chains, thus compressing the grapes. The movement of the heavy chains as the press compacts and opens breaks up the cake of skins, making repressing easier.

Today the most common style of press is probably the air-bag (bladder) press. A thick rubber membrane lies in a cylinder that is filled with grapes. The membrane is then blown up, compacting the grapes and extracting the juice.

Above right: Mats used to contain the grapes in a basket press, drying after use.
Right: A traditional "basket" press in Spain, with the marc (pressed grape skins and residue) spilling out after a pressing.

WHITE WINE FERMENTATION

White grapes are pumped from the crusher to the press, initially without any pressure. The grapes merely sit (or get turned if it is a rotary press) to encourage juice to flow out naturally. This is the "free-run juice" that provides the freshest, most delicate wine. After it has been allowed to run out, pressure is applied, and a number of pressings will probably be carried out. The juice, or must, can be modified to ensure that the resulting wine is well structured. Modification includes:

Enrichment This increases the sugar content of the must, which increases the final alcohol content (but not the sweetness) of the wine.

Acidification In warm areas, acid can be added to the must, which both maintains its freshness and protects it from bacterial spoilage.

Deacidification In cooler areas, acid can be removed from the must.

RED WINE FERMENTATION

A key element in the production of red wine is the extraction of the phenolics, a process which happens mainly during maceration of the grape must and skins. The fermentation temperature for red wines is generally higher than for whites. This is necessary to help extract the color and tannin from the skins, but the heat sacrifices some of the

WHITE WINE FERMENTATION

Crushing and destemming

Tank or barrel maturation followed by racking if not previously done

Malolactic fermentation —probably in barrel

Pressing in a cylindrical air-bag press

Blending

Racking off the yeast lees

Tank fermentation

Fining

Cold stabilization in a tank with chilling coils

Settling the free-run juice and racking off to a fermentation vessel

Bottling

Filtering and stabilization

aromatic elements which are therefore less likely to show in red wines. Winemakers have several methods to aid the uptake of phenols in the wine:

Pumping must over This involves taking wine from the bottom of the fermentation tank and spraying it over the cap.

Plunging Pushing the cap down into the must to enable more contact.

Header boards A series of boards held at right angles to each other that are used to keep the cap constantly submerged below the top of the must.

Rotofermenting The modern method, this is essentially a fermentation tank tipped on its side that can rotate occasionally to tumble the cap.

Following the end of fermentation, the red wine is pumped off the skins, which are then run into a press. The resulting red press wine is usually much harsher than the other wine because the process of pressing extracts more tannins, though such resulting wine may be quite deep-colored and also quite flavorful.

A second process—called "malolactic fermentation"—may also be used on the wine. Almost all red wines undergo this, as may some more full-bodied whites. This results due to the activity not of yeasts, but of bacteria. The activity of lactic bacteria converts the malic acid into much softer, creamier lactic acid.

RED WINE FERMENTATION

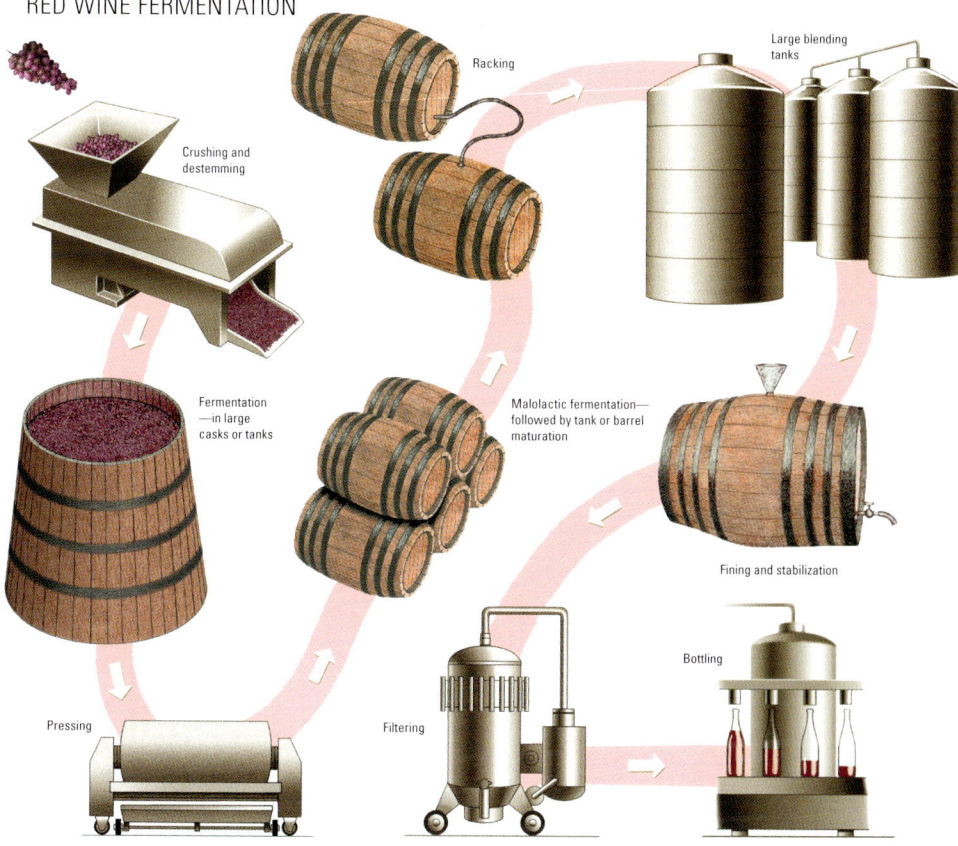

Crushing and destemming

Racking

Large blending tanks

Fermentation —in large casks or tanks

Malolactic fermentation— followed by tank or barrel maturation

Fining and stabilization

Pressing

Filtering

Bottling

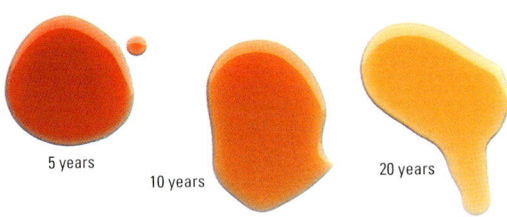

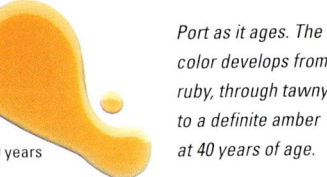

5 years

10 years

20 years

40 years

Port as it ages. The color develops from ruby, through tawny, to a definite amber at 40 years of age.

MATURATION

All wine needs a period to settle down following fermentation, during which it may undergo some treatments. For light, fresh wines, this period of maturation may only be a few weeks, but can last up to three years for some wines before bottling takes place. There are different ways in which such maturation can occur.

Barrel Barrels may be made of usually oak or chestnut—occasionally of some other woods. Oak allows minute oxygen contact with the wine via the staves, which helps it to stabilize naturally and develops the flavor components.

Tank Large stainless steel tanks are completely inert so that wine can be stored for a fairly long period without losing its freshness.

Bottle Wine is rarely stored for long in bottle. The economics of production mean that wine is usually out on the wine store shelves as soon as possible after bottling.

Racking

Racking generally refers to the process of moving juice, must or wine from one container to another. Racking is used to aerate the wine when a small amount of oxygen contact is deemed beneficial.

FINISHING

Almost all wines, including the most expensive vintages in the world, are blended in some form or other. What is essential is that any blend should be better balanced and more complex than the sum of its parts. More often than not, wines are blended from a number of vineyards and/or varieties. It is also critical to stabilize a wine; and a number of operations may be included in this process.

Fining This process uses substances with one electrical charge to attract substances that are suspended in the wine with the opposite charge.

Filtration This extracts solids, often of minute size, including yeast cells and also some bacteria.

Additives Almost all wine has some chemical addition to ensure its freshness, and sometimes to act against bacterial or yeast spoilage.

Cold stabilization Chilled wine tends to deposit crystals of potassium bitartrate. These are harmless, but consumers tend to find them unsightly. Most treatments involve chilling the wine so the tartrates

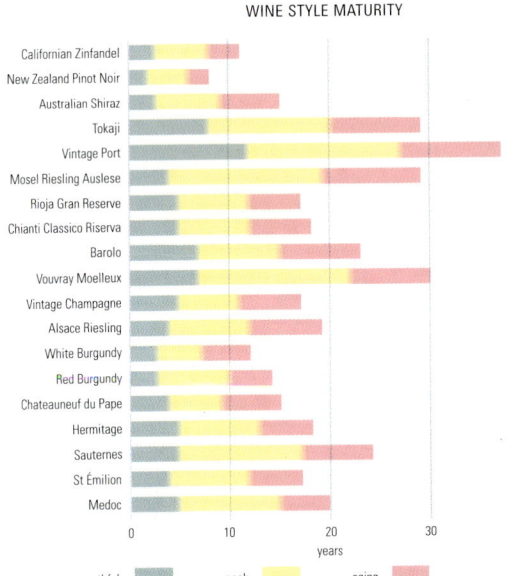

WINE STYLE MATURITY

Californian Zinfandel
New Zealand Pinot Noir
Australian Shiraz
Tokaji
Vintage Port
Mosel Riesling Auslese
Rioja Gran Reserve
Chianti Classico Riserva
Barolo
Vouvray Moelleux
Vintage Champagne
Alsace Riesling
White Burgundy
Red Burgundy
Chateauneuf du Pape
Hermitage
Sauternes
St Émilion
Medoc

0   10   20   30   40
years

youthful   peak   aging

precipitate out in order that they might be subsequently filtered out of the finished product.

BOTTLING

The bottling process is mechanized these days, and large companies have their own bottling lines which are in constant use. There is much debate currently about how bottles should be closed. Cork—a flexible and effective stopper—has been used for at least 300 years. Its problem is that it can lead to cork taint. Because this affects between 2 and 5 percent of all wine bottled, there is potentially one bottle in each case of wine that you buy which could be tainted. To avert this, many wine companies are exploring other options, such as synthetic corks and even crown seals.

AGING

The development of wine in bottle is still little understood. It is basically a slow oxidation. The danger in this is that the oxidizing process will reduce the wine to a dull liquid, or even a vinegar. The first precondition for aging wine, therefore, is a component to slow down its oxidative development. With both white and red wines, acidity performs this function by preserving freshness. With white wine, the impact of time is to deepen its color through lemon to gold and finally to amber. The reverse is true with red wine: with age, it moves from deep purple, via ruby and mahogany to tawny. In both cases, if the wine is brown the process has gone too far and the wine is oxidized, unless it is a fortified wine, in which case brown may be an acceptable color.

Above: *For much of the last 2,000 years, barrels have been the most widespread way of storing, and thus aging, wine.*
Right: *Bottles of wine lie in the cellar of a Spanish restaurant, undergoing the slow process of aging.*

The second requirement for aging wine is that it has sufficient flavor complexity to make it worth keeping. A U.S. $9 cabernet sauvignon from almost anywhere in the world may have enough tannin to allow it to age, but it will lose its fruitiness with time, and develop no interesting new flavors to make it enjoyable. Some quite expensive wines are deliberately made to be drunk young and are all the more enjoyable for it, for they will seem little different, and certainly no better, even should they be aged for some years.

The World's Best Reds

Red wine is made in many different places around the world, with varying levels of success. Some regions have been recognized as producers of top quality wines for many years, while other areas have only attained that status much more recently.

For example, in Burgundy the vineyard of Clos de Vougeot was enclosed sometime in the 1300s. It is classified as Grand Cru, the very highest level in Burgundy's appellation system. (In Bordeaux the highest ranking is Premier Cru, in a classification system which was compiled in 1855. This ranking is exemplified by the superb Chateau Latour.)

By comparison, Stag's Leap 1973 Cabernet Sauvignon, ranked as best in the world by French judges, comes from the

much younger winemaking region of California's Napa Valley. The first commercial winery was built here as relatively recent as 1861.

Australia is also regarded as part of winemaking's New World. That country's most acclaimed red, Penfold's Grange Hermitage from the Barossa Valley in South Australia, was inspired by the best wines of Bordeaux, and is much sought after.

Left to right: *Patrizi Barolo; Domaine Jacques Prieur Clos Vougeot; Chateau Latour Grand Vin; Robert Mondavi Cabernet Sauvignon; Alejandro Fernandez Pesquera; Puente Alto Don Melchor; Penfolds Grange Hermitage.*

Reflecting Italy's long and fragmented history, the wines from each region are highly individual, using specific indigenous grape varieties. Nebbiolo, for example, is emblematic of Piedmont, with the Barolo and Barbaresco zones recognized as being the producers of the best quality wines.

Spain is another European country with a long tradition of winemaking. The wines from Ribera del Duero, in Castilla-León, are some of the most prestigious, exemplified by Pesquero, a wine made entirely from tempranillo grapes.

Spain also introduced red wine to Chile. Their wine industry is a rapidly expanding one, with the Maipo Valley region near Santiago probably best known. Concha y Toro is one of the most outstanding winemakers here.

The World's Best Whites

White wines, as with reds, are produced the world over, and greatly vary in quality. Various regions of the Old World, long renowned for particular wines, now find themselves rivals in the far more recently established estates to be found in the New World.

Perhaps most synonymous the world over with celebration and superlative wine is the Champagne region of France. Located here is the Veuve Clicquot-Ponsardin estate, and La Grande Dame is its prestige cuvée. A wine of great finesse and balance, it still displays the famed yellow label devised by Madame Clicquot herself.

The greatest rieslings originate in the Mosel-Saar-Ruwer region of Germany, and the most expensive and renowned of these are from the famous vineyards of the Bernkastel district, where

Left to right: *Veuve Clicquot-Ponsardin La Grande Dame; Domaine Jacques Prieur Montrachet; Chateau d'Yquem Sauternes; Lauerburg Berncastler Doctor; Marcarini Moscato d'Asti; Leeuwin Estate Art Series Chardonnay; Cloudy Bay, and Stag's Leap Chardonnay.*

around a dozen different producers make and sell Bernkasteler Doctor riesling auslese.

Italy's finest moscato originates near Asti, in the Piedmont region. Moscato d'Asti is a light and elegant beverage, excellent with desserts. Among dessert wines, however, France's Chateau d'Yquem, of the sauternes-specializing Graves district south of Bordeaux, is regarded as one of the world's best.

Western Australia's Margaret River region is said to be "for wine lovers who seek class and finesse." Here the Leeuwin Estate, renowned for wines of great complexity, produces Art Series Chardonnay, regarded as one of Australia's best.

Marlborough is New Zealand's best known wine region, famed for its sauvignon blanc. The highly regarded Cloudy Bay winery produces a Sauvignon Blanc that has achieved something of a cult-status since its release in 1985, and its Chardonnay is also much vaunted.

California's most famous wine region is Napa Valley, one of the greatest districts being the Stags Leap District. Though renowned for a legendary Cabernet Sauvignon, the Chardonnay of Stag's Leap Wine Cellars is also excellent.

How to Taste Wine

There are four senses used in tasting: sight, smell, taste, and touch. In wine jargon, the terms used are "appearance," "nose," and "palate" (which covers both taste and touch). Before you even take a sip, you may, using these criteria, be able to determine the wine's likely age, possible origin, and the grape variety used, as well as the climate the grapes were produced in and how the wine was most probably made and stored.

Sight

The first part of the process is to look carefully at the wine. Is its appearance cloudy or hazy? If it is, then it may be out of condition—although a slight haze on some red wines may merely mean that the winemaker has chosen not to filter too harshly. A sediment in the bottom of the glass does not count as a haze, and is a perfectly normal part of the development of the wine in the bottle.

The depth of color gives clues about the wine. A deep red suggests a thick-skinned variety such as cabernet sauvignon or syrah. A paler color may simply a variety like pinot noir or gamay. As red wines get older their color also fades, so this will give you more information about the wine. A pale, almost watery color in white wines hints at grapes grown in a cool area. A deep gold may be the result of a warmer climate, though it could also suggest some age on the wine and/or the use of oak as part of the aging process.

The hue of a wine is also important. A youthful red wine will probably have a purple-crimson character. With age, the wine progresses through shades of cherry or plum (still revealing some youth), through ruby to garnet and tawny. With white wines the reverse is true: the older the wine, the deeper its color becomes, and the lemon (and sometimes green) of youth becomes gold, then old-gold and amber. In any wine (other than fortified wines), a brown shade indicates the wine is too old.

Particularly useful in observing red wines is the hue of the wine's rim. (Hold it at a 45° angle against a white background and look at the edge of the wine.) A terra-cotta color can be an early indication that the wine is developing some age.

With sparkling wines, it is also important to observe the bead (the bubbles) and the mousse (the foam on the surface). There should be multiple, persistent

Changing color with age

Below: Penfold's Grange 1993 (left) and 1981 (right). The young red wine has a deep plum color and vibrant pink-crimson rim. The color of the older vintage Grange (1981) is no longer as deep: the hue has changed more to ruby, and there is a distinct brick tone about the rim, a clear sign of age.

Bottom: Trimbach Riesling, cuvée "Frederic Emile" 1994 (left) and 1983 (right). The younger white wine has a very pale lemon hue, with a tinge of green (common in white wines from a cooler climate). The older wine (1983) has developed a distinct gold-amber hue, betraying the impact of oxygen as it ages.

beads of small bubbles trailing up to the surface of the wine, forming a regular mousse.

Smell

Generally, if a wine is faulty or
oxidized, it will be evident on the
nose. After that, the nose should
give the taster a sense of the age and
maturity of the wine. The two are
not the same. A three-year-old sauvignon blanc may be getting a bit
tired perhaps, whereas a three-year-
old cabernet may be barely hitting its
straps. Broadly speaking, however, the
fresher the wine smells, the younger it is.
Aroma is used to describe the smell of a
young, fresh wine, whereas bouquet is a term
for an older wine, one less fresh but which is possibly more complex.

Yet another key aspect of assessing wine is the
intensity of the smell. Generally, the more intense
the smell, the better the quality of the wine. Some
wines have a fragrance that leaps from the glass;
other wines, usually described as "dumb," have
barely a whiff at all.

Numerous methods have been used to classify
what we smell and taste in wine. The most widely
accepted currently is the aroma wheel. This tool is
undoubtedly helpful as a prompt when trying to
work out what it is
that you are smell-
ing. The danger in
this is that it can
lead to a tendency
among tasters to
believe that they
should all be smell-
ing and also tasting

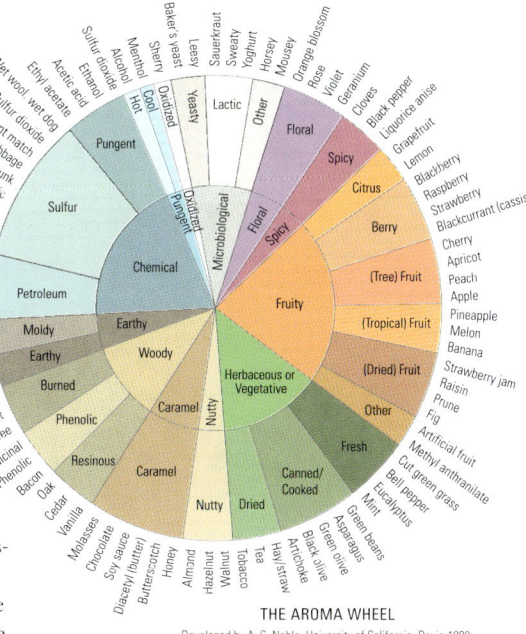

THE AROMA WHEEL
Developed by A. C. Noble, University of California, Davis, 1990:
http://wineserver.ucdavis.edu/acnoble/home.html

exactly the same characters in a wine, when this
is not necessarily the case.

Taste

At this point, both the sense of taste and that of
touch come into play. Generally speaking, the
tongue can only taste compounds that are sweet,
sour (or acidic), salty, and bitter. All the other
descriptors that are used for wine are an extension
of the sense of smell, which is why smelling the
wine is so important before drinking it.

Sugar Wines are classified as dry (that is, with
no detectable sugar) through to sweet, with many
gradations in between. Sugar is not the only cause
of sweetness in wine, however. Alcohol itself is a
sweet liquid, so that wines with a higher alcohol
level may give a hint of sweetness. Many fruity
wines can give an impression of sweetness—of
mangos, peaches, strawberries, or other similarly
luscious fruit. When tasting these wines it becomes
important to learn to distinguish the fruit sweetness from sugar sweetness.

*Assessing sparkling
wine—bubbles
showing regular and
persistent bead in a
glass of Champagne.*

The rules for tasting

- DO NOT INTRODUCE INTRUSIVE SMELLS
  No perfume or aftershave: it really can distract
  your and other people's ability to smell and
  assess wine.
- ENSURE THERE IS GOOD LIGHTING
  It is the only way to get a really good idea of the
  appearance of the wine.
- BE QUIET
  Talking may disturb others.
- DO NOT DISCUSS THE WINES WITH OTHERS
  This may prejudice them or you, and cause you
  to reach faulty conclusions. You can compare
  notes at the end.
- WRITE NOTES
  To aid memory.
  To act as a reminder—especially if later
  decisions have to be made about it.
  To monitor the progress of the wine.
- ALWAYS SPIT IF TASTING MORE THAN A FEW WINES
  To avoid getting drunk.
- THINK CAREFULLY ABOUT THE WINE
  Start by analyzing the structure.
  Don't get sidetracked by the fruit aromas
  and flavors.
  Evaluate the quality and maturity of
  the wine.
  This is not primarily a case of whether or not you
  like it, but how good it is.
- KEEP YOUR GLASSES CLEAN
  Even detergent may affect the character
  of the wine.

Bitterness Bitterness should only be present in wines in very limited amounts, and in white wines should ideally be avoided altogether. It tends to be sensed at the back of the tongue and the back of the throat, and is most generally associated with high tannin levels.

Acidity Acidity is the tart character one can sense in food and drinks. Fresh and delicate white

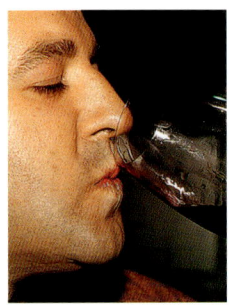

A big sniff gets the full aroma of the wine.

wines—rieslings, sauvignon blancs, and chenin blancs—will have the highest levels of acidity. Red wines generally possess less acid, and a fortified red wine, like a port, will have among the lowest acidity component.

Salt In minute doses, salt may be noticed from the trace minerals in wine, but any wine that has an obviously salty character is unpleasant and likely to be badly made. Salt tends to be detected at the center of the tongue.

Touch

ALCOHOL

Although we register only four components of taste on the tongue, we can also pick up on other sensations in the mouth associated with what we feel. Alcohol is a key factor here. It gives a weight and body that is essential to the full experience of both tasting and drinking wine.

BODY

Body is a quality that one feels as a sense of weight on the tongue. Just as olive oil feels fuller in the mouth than water, so different wine styles have different weights, from a light Mosel riesling to a weighty vintage port.

TANNIN

Tannin is also registered by what we feel in the mouth. Tannin is the drying sensation that covers the teeth, cheeks, and gums when red wine is drunk or tasted. Red wines have varying levels of tannins in them, and these tannins can come in different forms. Some are coarse and sandy, which is not generally so attractive; some—even with wines that display high tannin levels—seem fine and smooth. Tannin is often, although not invariably, associated with bitterness in wine.

TEXTURE

Wine also has mouthfeel, or texture. Again, this is connected to weight, but is not identical, and it is also related to acidity and the form of tannin. A big condrieu (a wine made from viognier grapes in the Rhône valley in France) will seem viscous, even almost oily or buttery, in the mouth. A sancerre on the other hand, made from sauvignon blanc, feels much less smooth. Just as sparkling wines require attention to the appearance of the bead, so it is necessary, when tasting them, to think about the mousse in the mouth. The ideal mouthfeel should be smooth, almost creamy.

The concept of structure

The structure of the wine includes acidity, sugar, bitterness (occasionally), tannin (in red wines), alcohol, weight, and mouthfeel and mousse (in sparkling wines), as well as the intensity of the fruit flavor. All of these components should be in balance—they are not just viewed in isolation, but in relationship to each other. Thus, wines of high sugar levels need crisp acidity to avoid becoming too cloying. Higher tannin levels require a fuller body and overt alcohol so as to avoid becoming too aggressive. All of the components must be in an equilibrium with the intensity of the fruit flavor. When a balance has been achieved, the wine can be described as being harmonious.

Buyers tasting wine before bidding at the most famous wine auction in the world, the Hospices de Beaune, in Burgundy.

Judging wine quality

While the quality of a wine is often referred to, it is rarely defined. Experienced tasters have their own varying ways of analyzing the excellence of what they drink, but the following are some good rules of thumb.

Intensity of flavor Ideally, a wine should have a good hit of fruit flavor on the palate, and in turn this should fruit flavor should be balanced by a concentrated aroma.

Balance The structural elements of a wine should be in balance. This is often most generally referred to as "harmony."

Length Mediocre wines will fade fast, but a good wine has a flavor that will go on for about 15 seconds or longer.

Complexity Complexity refers to the layers of flavor in the wine. A simple syrah will only have one or two distinctive flavors—black fruit, for instance. A more complex one could also exhibit spice, coffee, cedar, black olive, and tar. Complex wines also tend to have flavor patterns that then develop and change in the mouth, starting with fruit dominating, adding coffee and cedar, and ending on spice and tar, without the fruit flavor ever entirely being lost.

France

Roubaix
Lille
Somme
Amiens
Le Havre
Rouen
Seine
Caen
Oise
Reims
Metz
Moselle
PARIS
Marne-la-Vallée
Marne
Champagne
Nancy
Seine
Champagne
Strasbourg
Guernsey
Channel Is.
(U.K.)
Jersey
Gulf of St-Malo
Brest
Rennes
Le Mans
Burgundy
Vosges
Alsace
Mulhouse
Belle-Île
Nantes
Angers
Loire
Tours
The Loire
Cher
Loire
Dijon
Besançon
Saône
Burgundy
Lake Geneva
Jura, Savoie,
Bugey
F R A N C E
Île de Ré
Beaujolais
Rhône
Mt Blanc
15770 ft
(4808 m)
Île d'Oléron
Cognac
Limoges
Clermont-Ferrand
Lyon
Cognac
Puy de Sancy
6186 ft (1886 m)
St-Étienne
The
Rhône
Grenoble
Dordogne
Plomb du Cantal
6094 ft (1858 m)
Mt Mézenc
5753 ft (1754 m)
Barre des Écrins
13455 ft (4102 m)
A L P S
Bordeaux
Bordeaux
Southwest
France
Lot
Mt d'Aubrac
4824 ft (1471 m)
Rhône
Garonne
Southwest
France
Cévennes
The Rhône
Durance
Nice
Mon
MON
Southwest
France
Toulouse
Montpellier
Nîmes
Provence
Marseilles
Toulon
P y r e n e e s
Garonne
Languedoc-
Roussillon
Gulf of
Lion
LIGURIAN
Perpignan
SEA

NORTH

60 miles
(96 kilometers)

France

Few would disagree that, when it comes to wine, France is the leader. It produces more wine than any other country and, despite having the world's second-highest per-capita level of consumption, heads the table of exporters. But there is more to its status than size. France was pre-eminent even when Italy's output was greater in the early 1990s, and it remains so even though Spain continues to have a larger acreage under vine. Its supremacy rests on the fact that it produces more great wines than any other country; as a consequence, its wines serve as a model for the rest of the winemaking world.

This doesn't mean that France produces only wines of enviable quality. Although winemaking standards have improved enormously in the last two decades—control of fermentation temperatures allowing the harvesting of riper grapes, for example—the French continue to be responsible for some very poor wines. This is partly the result of certain cultural factors—mainly the combined forces of ignorance and complacency—but it is also attributable to the country's highly variable climate.

Corsica
Île de Beauté
jACCIO

Enormous variations in climate and soil in France are expressed in the diversity of individual wine styles made there.

The classic French wine regions—including Bordeaux, Burgundy, and Champagne—are all close to the geographical limits of successful vine-growing. In poor years, the grapes just don't see enough sun and warmth to get perfectly ripe. In other years, all might be progressing well when devastating hail tears through the vineyards, as occurred in part of St-Émilion in 1999.

France has an extraordinary range of terrain and weather patterns, which is why its winemaking practices are so complex and its wines so diverse. Bordeaux, for example, on the west coast, has a maritime climate; the prevailing dampness can cause disease, bringing disaster to some winemakers, yet be a boon for the sweet-wine producers of Sauternes. Burgundy, inland to the north and east, is cooler than Bordeaux; its continental climate places it at the northern limit for red wines. But, at their best, those wines have fragrance, complexity of flavor, and silkiness of texture. The Loire Valley lies even farther north, but vines still thrive there as a result of the moderating influences of moist Atlantic breezes and the expansive river system. Champagne is so far north that the grapes barely ripen each year, but high-acid, fairly low-sugar grapes are perfect for the finest sparkling wines.

More than climate, however, what counts is *terroir*, the complete package of soil and subsoil, aspect and altitude, climate and mesoclimate. The soils and geology of French vineyards are varied: Burgundy and Jura have limestone, Beaujolais and the northern Rhône sit on granite, Champagne has chalk and the Médoc has gravel. While no single soil type produces the best wine, the one characteristic France's finer vineyards share is poor soils on which little else will thrive—particularly on slopes that can retain some water without becoming waterlogged. Thus, in some regions the best vineyards (often called *crus*) tend to be on the hillsides.

These are, however, generalizations as there is no such thing as a single-soil region. Most of the important French winegrowing areas have been divided into subregions based on the characteristics of their *terroirs*. Such distinctions form the basis of France's national classification system of appellations.

The appellation system

Testing a new vintage.

The appellation system was created in 1935 to protect the authenticity of wines and the livelihoods of producers. It does this by defining boundaries and, within each area, stipulating the permitted grape varieties, yields, and also alcohol content; cultivation, vinification, and maturation practices; and labeling procedures. Fine distinctions may result in numerous subregions. In Bordeaux, for example, within the generic appellation, there are 56 smaller appellations; Burgundy has 98.

Appellation d'origine contrôlée guarantees the origin and style of a wine but not its quality. The appellation authorities have sometimes shown themselves to be pointlessly intractable. In Provence, for example, the leading estate, Domaine de Trévallon, was refused appellation status on the grounds that its blend contained "too much" cabernet sauvignon. A lack of flexibility makes it difficult for dynamic winemakers to innovate, improve their wines, or even label them differently. Consequently, some producers opt for the less prestigious but far less restrictive *vin de pays* (VDP) classification, an intermediate category between *vin de table*, the most basic of French wine, and AC. It includes wines labelled by grape variety (*vin de cépages*). The French tend to be dismissive of varietal wines, insisting that wine is far more than mere grapes—it is *terroir*— but these wines are successful. So *vins de pays* now compete with varietal wines from countries like Australia, Chile, and Argentina.

Although the system is quite complicated, *appellation d'origine contrôlée* has spawned many similar appellation systems around the world, and it has also played a critical role in protecting both the identity and the reputation of French wines.

Right: Harvest at Chateau Ausone. Below: Fall vines at Château Latour.

Champagne

Champagne's effervescent charm has signaled celebrations of every kind. The sound of champagne corks popping is heard at weddings, births, and anniversaries. Champagne originates from the province of the same name, which is 100 miles (160 km) east of Paris, centered on the towns of Reims and Épernay, where most of the champagne houses are based. It was in the seventeenth century that the natural process that gives rise to the bubbles began to be understood, but it was only in the nineteenth century that sparkling wine became Champagne's principal product. Today, only wines made following the local appellation laws and originating in the viticultural region of Champagne are allowed to use that name.

History

Pope Urban II, pontiff from 1088–99, declared that there was never a better wine than that produced in Aÿ—although, given that he was a Champenois, he might just have been a little biased. In the *Bataille des Vins*, written around 1200, Henri d'Andelys

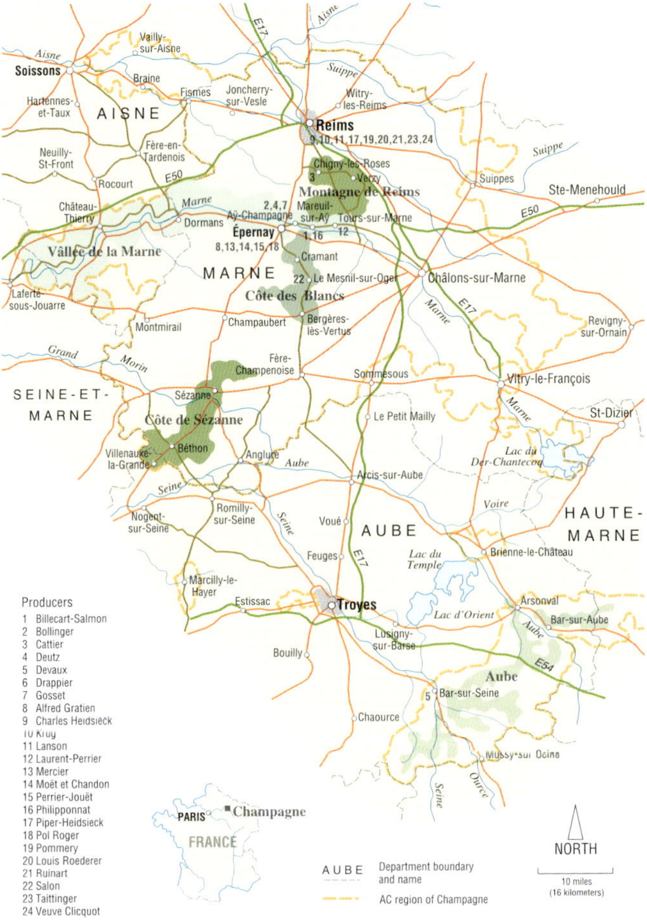

Producers
1 Billecart-Salmon
2 Bollinger
3 Cattier
4 Deutz
5 Devaux
6 Drappier
7 Gosset
8 Alfred Gratien
9 Charles Heidsieck
10 Krug
11 Lanson
12 Laurent-Perrier
13 Mercier
14 Moët et Chandon
15 Perrier-Jouët
16 Philipponnat
17 Piper-Heidsieck
18 Pol Roger
19 Pommery
20 Louis Roederer
21 Ruinart
22 Salon
23 Taittinger
24 Veuve Clicquot

AUBE   Department boundary and name
        AC region of Champagne

NORTH

10 miles
(16 kilometers)

rated the wines of Épernay, Reims, and Hautvillers among the best in Europe.

Around the first half of the sixteenth century, Pope Leo X, Charles V of Spain, François I of France, and Henry VIII of England all owned vineyards in Champagne. A batch of *vin d'Aÿ* sent to Henry VIII's chancellor, Cardinal Wolsey, in 1518, was the first recorded shipment of wine from Champagne to England. Henri IV (1553–1610) became the first French king to introduce wine from Champagne to his court.

The first notable producer of champagne as we know it, was Ruinart, founded in 1729 (though Gosset had been producing still wine since at least 1584 and remains the oldest Champagne house operating today). Others were established soon afterward, including the houses now known as Taittinger (in 1734), Moët et Chandon (in 1743), later followed by Veuve Clicquot (in 1772).

Demand grew mostly in the late nineteenth century, which was a glorious time for Champagne. The dawn of the twentieth century saw unrest among growers from the Aube district, who had been excluded from Champagne, and simmering discontent erupted in 1911 when 5,000 Aube growers marched on Champagne. Eventually the Aube was incorporated into the region of Champagne.

Since World War II, the region has prospered. Recently, the industry has been rationalized and there have been amazing improve-

Champagne bottles are stored in angled racks to make the sediment fall into the neck.

ments in the yield and quality of the harvest. Yet, at the same time, the distinctive character of champagne remains much as it was in the late nineteenth century.

Flutes used for drinking champagne are designed to preserve the bubbles.

Landscape and climate

The marginal conditions at the northern limits of the wine-producing world are highly appropriate for the production of champagne: the cool temperatures produce high levels of acidity that are perfect for sparkling wine, and subregional variations result in distinctive styles that lend themselves to blending. However, only in certain areas do soil, topography, aspect, and other factors, such as the presence of forests, create a *terroir* fit for ripening vines. Thick belemnite chalk subsoils are believed to be the source of much of the fineness and lightness that characterize champagne. They provide excellent drainage and adequate moisture retention, and they absorb heat from the sun, slowly releasing it at night, thus warming the vines at the coldest times.

Vineyards and classifications

The boundaries of the viticultural area of Champagne were legally defined in 1927. There are five major wine-producing districts: Côte des Blancs, Montagne de Reims, Vallée de la Marne, Côte de Sézanne, and the Aube. The top villages in Champagne are ranked as either Grand Cru or Premier Cru, from a system known as the *échelle des crus* (cru ladder), introduced in 1919. The very finest villages are deemed to be Grand Cru and awarded an *échelle* of 100 percent. Premier Cru villages receive an *échelle* of

Méthode champenoise

England was the first country to develop a taste for sparkling wine. During the period following the Restoration of 1660, young wines from Champagne were usually imported in barrels during winter, by which time the cold climate had arrested fermentation. Once spring arrived, however, the wine, by now transferred to bottles, would warm again and the yeasts would be reactivated. Fermentation would then restart, producing carbonic gas. In France, this usually caused the bottle to open or shatter; in England, however, cork stoppers and much stronger glass were already in widespread use, so the wine could develop further.

The process of secondary fermentation probably began to be understood in France soon afterward. This discovery is traditionally attributed to Dom Pérignon but contrary to legend, he did not invent champagne. However, he did make several significant contributions to its development.

Champagne must be served chilled.

Riddling bottles to shake the yeast into the neck.

For a long period, the still wines of Champagne remained in greater demand. This situation only changed following several technical innovations in the early nineteenth century, including the process of *remuage* (or riddling), which allowed producers to remove the sediment that forms during secondary fermentation without emptying the bottle.

The production process is strictly regulated. Once the beginning date for harvesting is announced, usually mid-September, hand-picked grapes go to nearby press houses. The juice goes through *débourbage*, or settling out, followed by fermentation. After racking, the *assemblage*, or blending, takes place, then bottling, when the *liqueur de tirage* (a solution of yeast and sugar) is added to initiate secondary fermentation. Bottles are sealed with a crown cap or the traditional agrafe cork and placed in cellars to spend time on lees and build complexity. Dead yeast cells are worked down to the top of the inverted bottle (known as *remuage*), which is then dipped in freezing brine. The cap is then removed and the frozen plug of sediment flies out (*dégorgement*). A small quantity of wine plus sugar (the *liqueur d'expedition*) is then added, with the amount of sugar determining the eventual sweetness of the champagne. Levels range from brut (very dry) through extra sec (dry), sec (semisweet), and demisec (sweet) to doux (very sweet). Finally, the cork is inserted and the bottle is labeled.

Veuve Clicquot champagne has a distinctive foil.

between 90 and 99 percent; others are rated as low as 50 percent, though this was modified in 1985 to a minimum of 80 percent. Villages can receive different ratings for different varieties.

The *échelle* system was used to dictate growers' payments. A price would be struck and Grand Cru vineyards would receive 100 percent of that price; others would receive the percentage represented by their village's *échelle*. A free-market system now operates, but the villages still retain their ratings.

In 1919, laws entitling the Champagne region to its own appellation were passed. Legislation in 1927 made Champagne one of the earliest appellations in France; it is still the only one permitted to omit the phrase *appellation d'origine contrôlée* or the initials AC or AOC from its labels.

Vines and wines

Only three kinds of grape variety are permitted in the Champagne appellation. Pinot noir gives champagne structure, weight, power, and backbone, plus a richness of flavor. Pinot meunier is an undervalued grape that few houses admit to using (though most do); it provides fruit flavor in the midpalate and sometimes a slightly earthy character. It is particularly useful in cold years due to its ripening ability. Chardonnay is the only variety that is used regularly on its own in a champagne, the *blanc de blancs*. At its best, the grape is characterized by elegance, delicacy, finesse, and refinement. It also contributes to the acidity of the wine and is essential to the length of the finish.

Around 80 percent of champagnes are non-vintage blends—which is why the name of the producer rather than the vineyard appears on the label. The Champenois are master blenders, skillfully combining wines from different grapes, vineyards, and vintages. Wine from a poor vintage can be turned into an outstanding product by blending with wines from superior vintages. In doing so, the blenders add their own signatures to the wines.

Beyond celebrations

The explosive pop of the cork, the shimmering bubbles, and market image of champagne all point to the world's celebratory wine *par excellence*. One of the best kept secrets in the world of wine is how wonderful champagne can be with food. From omelets to caviar to smoked salmon to chicken with a cream sauce, champagne is a joy. If one is to drink wine with sushi, champagne (nonvintage) is the only choice. Blue cheese with champagne is an earthly delight. With the added weight of pinot noir and skin contact, rosé champagne can take on a surprising array of red meats! An evening of joy can arise from piecing together a meal pairing different champagnes with all courses encountered.

Because the *terroir* here is so variable, grape varieties will have different characteristics when they are grown in different vineyards. For example, chardonnay grown on the Côte des Blancs has a steely backbone, yet on the Montagne de Reims and in some parts of the Vallée de Marne, it produces a much fuller wine. This can be useful in creating a blend.

The best vineyards, such as these in the commune of Verzenay, near Verzy, are classified as Grand Cru.

Around 1870, some houses started bottling particularly good years separately, thus creating vintage champagnes. Today, these are released, on average, four or five times a decade. Other styles of champagne include rosé, *blanc de blancs*, and the unusual *blanc de noirs*, which is made only from black grapes. Most houses also issue prestige cuvées, a practice that began when Moët et Chandon released the 1921 Dom Pérignon in 1937. The Champagne region also makes small quantities of still reds, rosés, and whites, as well as ratafia and eaux-de-vie.

Producers

BOLLINGER   *Established* 1829 *Owner* NA *Vineyard area* 356 acres (144 ha)

Bollinger champagne is distinctive: rich, complex, and heavily reliant on pinot. The prestige R.D. (*récemment dégorgé*) is effectively the vintage wine (Grande Année) given additional time on lees to develop further complexity. The Grande Année is also mixed with still pinot noir to produce a particularly powerful rosé.

A great champagne needs a stylish flute.

MOËT ET CHANDON   *Established* 1743 *Owner* LVMH *Vineyard area* 1,520 (615 ha)

The largest of the Champagne houses, Moët's vintage champagnes are admirable, their bold citrus flavors and strong acidity ensuring that they mature superbly. The outstanding flagship, Dom Pérignon, displays delicate, lemon citrus flavors; rich, creamy texture; great finesse and balance; and gentle acidity.

KRUG   *Established* 1843 *Owner* LVMH *Vineyard area* 49 acres (20 ha)

The Krugs are traditionalists who ferment in 54-gallon (205-l) oak casks and allow no malolactic fermentation or filtration. Substantial reserves enable them to blend close to 50 wines from numerous vintages to produce their Grande Cuvée. Vintage Krug is one of the world's great wines, exhibiting delicacy and finesse with a tight structure, steely backbone, and great richness and depth of flavor. The classy 100 percent chardonnay Clos du Mesnil, with its creamy texture and underlying strength, is a rarity.

POL ROGER   *Established* 1849 *Owner* NA *Vineyard area* 210 acres (85 ha)

Pol Roger produces an impressive range. The prestige cuvée, Sir Winston Churchill, displays power and finesse, accompanied by layers of flavor that linger on the palate. White Foil nonvintage is medium-bodied with some floral characters and persistent flavors; the vintage is pristine, intense, and tightly

Some of the world's most prestigious champagnes come from the house of Bollinger.

Above: *Statue of legendary champagne-maker Dom Pérignon, who introduced the use of cork stoppers, outside Moët et Chandon.*

structured when young, and develops a biscuity toastiness with age. The Blanc de Chardonnay combines lemony freshness, an exquisitely creamy texture, and impressive intensity.

POMMERY *Established* 1856 *Owner* LVMH *Vineyard area* 759 acres (307 ha)

Remarkable chalk cellars and wall carvings are found at Pommery. The company has extensive vineyard holdings—a great asset. The house style tends toward finesse and delicacy, with the vintage wines notable for their body and depth of flavor. The prestige Cuvée Louise displays even greater intensity, a tighter structure, and yet more power.

LOUIS ROEDERER *Established* 1760 *Owners* Roederer family *Vineyard area* 470 acres (190 ha)

Louis Roederer is another great house. The Brut Premier, with its tight structure, power, and biscuity, yeasty flavors, is one of the top nonvintage champagnes. The vintage is also outstanding, showing finesse, balance, and intensity of flavor. The pinnacle is the superb Cristal, the embodiment of elegance—subtle, yet powerful; delicate, but intense; restrained, yet opulent; with a soft, creamy texture, and gentle, lingering acidity.

RUINART *Established* 1729 *Owner* LVMH *Vineyard area* 37 acres (15 ha)

Founded by a friend of Dom Pérignon, Ruinart is now a part of a worldwide enterprise. However, it still manages to retain its identity as a small, quality-oriented house. The flagship wine, Dom Ruinart, a *blanc de blancs*, is outstanding.

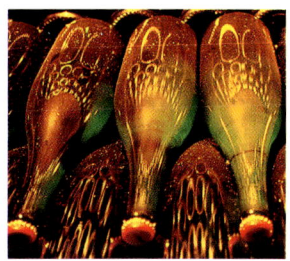

Right: *Sealed with crown caps, these cellared bottles of Moët et Chandon are undergoing their secondary fermentation.*

VEUVE CLICQUOT *Established* 1772 *Owner* LVMH *Vineyard area* 702 acres (284 ha)

Veuve Clicquot is best known for its rich pinot-dominated champagnes, including the distinctive Yellow Label Brut nonvintage. The vintage is consistently excellent: delicate, yet intense; balanced, yet powerful; crisp and dry, yet soft and refreshing. The prestige cuvée, La Grande Dame, is a wine of great finesse and balance with firm structure and biscuity, yeasty flavors.

Other recommended producers in Champagne include Gosset, Perrier-Jouët, Philipponnat, Salon, Billecart-Salmon, Charles Heidsieck, Cattier, Deutz, Devaux, Drappier, Alfred Gratien, Lanson, Laurent-Perrier, Mercier, Piper-Heidsieck, and Taittinger. See the map on page 48 for the locations of the producers listed here.

The Loire

The French have a saying: "The Loire is a queen and the kings of France have loved her." It's a good description of the intimate relationship that France has with its longest river, which flows from the mountains of the Massif Central to the Atlantic Ocean, past characteristic French landscape. Once a major transport artery for French agricultural and

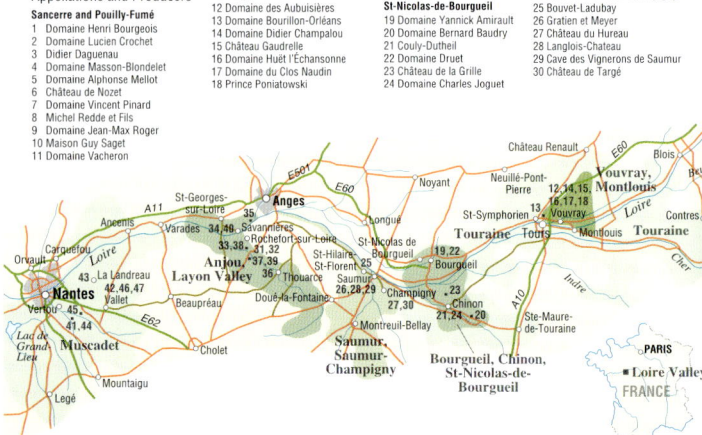

Appellations and Producers

Sancerre and Pouilly-Fumé	Vouvray, Montlouis and Touraine	Bourgueil, Chinon and St-Nicolas-de-Bourgueil	Saumur and Saumur-Champigny
1 Domaine Henri Bourgeois	12 Domaine des Aubuisières	19 Domaine Yannick Amirault	25 Bouvet-Ladubay
2 Domaine Lucien Crochet	13 Domaine Bourillon-Orléans	20 Domaine Bernard Baudry	26 Gratien et Meyer
3 Didier Daguenau	14 Domaine Didier Champalou	21 Couly-Dutheil	27 Château du Hureau
4 Domaine Masson-Blondelet	15 Château Gaudrelle	22 Domaine Druet	28 Langlois-Chateau
5 Domaine Alphonse Mellot	16 Domaine Huët l'Échansonne	23 Château de la Grille	29 Cave des Vignerons de Saumur
6 Château de Nozet	17 Domaine du Clos Naudin	24 Domaine Charles Joguet	30 Château de Targé
7 Domaine Vincent Pinard	18 Prince Poniatowski		
8 Michel Redde et Fils			
9 Domaine Jean-Max Roger			
10 Maison Guy Saget			
11 Domaine Vacheron			

industrial products, today it is the last natural, undammed great river of Europe. The language spoken in the regions of Anjou and Touraine, through which the river flows, is regarded as the purest, clearest form of French. The great cities of Orléans, Tours, Nantes, and Angers, and their grand châteaux for which the Loire Valley is most famous, are a reminder of the country's glorious past.

The River Loire also provides a mild meso-climate for wine production. The valleys of the river's main tributaries are just those few vital degrees warmer in summer and winter, allowing grapes to flourish. There are few hills in the region, so moist, warm air from the Atlantic Ocean can spread far up into the interior, moderating the climate.

The wine region extends from Montbrison in the Côtes du Forez all the way to the Atlantic Ocean. Throughout that region, vineyards line the river and its tributaries—the Allier, Cher, Indre, Vienne, Sèvre Nantaise, and Loir.

Vintage counts

Vintage affects the Loire Valley wines more than those from other regions of France. The very cool climate coupled with varieties that are not easily ripened make for a challenge. Under-ripe vintages are common, yet can produce "food friendly" wines. Sauvignon blanc is then lighter in color, more acidic, and less fruity. Mineral notes become more pronounced. Cabernet franc is also lighter and crisper, having a more weedy aromatic profile. Riper vintages have deeper color, especially the cabernet franc. Sauvignon becomes rounder while still crisp. Mineral notes give way to lime fruit. Cabernet franc, when riper is more deeply colored (a relative term in the Loire) and less astringent. Aromas and flavors shift to raspberries and lead pencil. Vintage counts, especially in the Loire, so be careful.

Wines and grapes

Loire wines cover every style imaginable—dry and sweet white, light red and rich red, dry and sweet sparkling—and include 60 different appellations. But all share certain characteristics, including freshness, fruitiness, and zing, and all are very much northern, cool-climate wines.

Twenty odd years ago Loire wines were not as well known as they are today. Nowadays wines such as the sauvignon blancs of Pouilly-Fumé and Sancerre serve as benchmarks. Some experts predict the sweet wines of Anjou and the red wines of Chinon and Bourgueil will be equally acclaimed.

The finest Loire wines are produced from three grape varieties that never seem to achieve such quality elsewhere in France: chenin blanc, cabernet franc, and sauvignon blanc. The great whites of the Coteaux du Layon, Vouvray, Savennières, and Montlouis are all based on chenin blanc. The intense cabernet franc is able to strut its stuff in the quartet of red-wine appellations of Saumur-Champigny, St-Nicolas-de-Bourgueil, Bourgueil, and Chinon. Sauvignon blanc's spiritual home is in the vineyards of Sancerre and Pouilly-sur-Loire. Of these three grapes, only one, chenin blanc, is native to the Loire. Three other major grape varieties are encountered in the Loire: muscadet or melon de bourgogne, pinot noir, and gamay—all imports from eastern France.

The list of obscure Loire grapes is fascinating and almost endless. The tressallier of Saint-Pourçain; the romorantin of Cour-Cheverny; the pineau d'aunis, pineau menu, and groslot of Touraine; the gros plant of the Pays Nantais—all are rare species that make unusual, exotically flavored wines.

Loire wines, when young, are fresh and fruity, but they age well, especially the chenin-blanc-based wines from Savennières, Coteaux du Layon, and Vouvray. The sauvignon-blanc-based wines of Pouilly-Fumé, for example, do not begin to show their true character until they are around three years old. Sancerre whites mature and fade

Château Azay-la-Rideau is one of many magnificent chateaux found in the Loire Valley.

more quickly, as does muscadet, although in the best vintages the top cuvées will develop and mature. Loire reds can also develop well; better wines from Chinon and Bourgueil age as well as many Bordeaux reds, and the lighter wines of Saumur-Champigny and St-Nicolas-de-Bourgueil will continue to develop for at least ten years.

APPELLATIONS

The Loire's 60-odd appellations include some famous names and some rarities. Among the latter are the scattered VDQS areas of Château-meillant (red and rosé wines), Coteaux di Giennois, (red, rosé, and white wines), Vin de l'Orléanais (red, rosé, and white wines), and Vin du Thouarsais (more red, rosé, and white wines).

There are two major Loire-wide appellations. Crémant de Loire applies to traditional method sparkling wines with a generally higher level of quality than those of Saumur, and Vin de Pays du Jardin de la Loire applies to varietally labelled wines (in particular chardonnay). Otherwise, the Loire's appellations can be conveniently grouped under five main headings of Sancerre, Pouilly-Fumé, and the vineyards of the Center; Vouvray, Montlouis, and Touraine; Bourgueil, Chinon, and St-Nicolas-de-Bourgueil; Saumur and Saumur-Champigny; and Anjou and the Layon Valley.

Sancerre, Pouilly-Fumé, and the vineyards of the Center

Sauvignon-blanc and pinot noir are the two stars in these vineyards. The two principal appellations are Sancerre (whites, reds, and rosés) and Pouilly-Fumé (whites only). Menetou-Salon, Quincy, and Reuilly are lesser appellations. All these wines combine richness, freshness, and acidity.

DOMAINE LUCIEN CROCHET   *Established* NA
Owners Crochet family   *Vineyard area* 84 acres (34 ha)

The sancerres here are concentrated and full-bodied. The *négociant* wines, made from purchased grapes, are pleasant but the true emphasis is on *domaine* wines, from vineyards that include parts of some of the best in Bué. The Le Chêne cuvée comes from the Chêne Marchand vineyard, and the Sancerre Prestige is a blend from the best lots.

DIDIER DAGUENEAU   *Established* 1980s   *Owner* Didier Dagueneau   *Vineyard area* 28.4 acres (11.5 ha)

Didier Dagueneau's wines are among the great white wines of France. The range of different cuvées, many of which are wood-aged, begins with Cailloux, and moves through increasingly complex, long-lasting wines: Le Bois Renard (formerly known as Le Bois Menard), Silex, Pur Sang, and, most remarkable of all, Astéroïde.

CHÂTEAU DE NOZET   *Established* NA
Owners de Ladoucette family   *Vineyard area* 257 acres (104 ha)

Based in a nineteenth-century château, the de Ladoucettes are the biggest players in Pouilly. Its top cuvée is Pouilly-Fumé Baron de L. The rest of the Nozet range is made from purchased grapes and is generally of good standard.

Historic Sancerre, where eleventh century monks began the production of wine on abbey-owned land.

MICHEL REDDE ET FILS *Established* 1800s
Owners Redde family *Vineyard area* 87 acres (35 ha)

The Reddes run a smart operation that turns out a wide range of excellent quality pouilly-fumé. The top cuvée, Cuvée Majorum, is made only in the best years. It has excellent ripeness and depth. On the other hand, the light cuvée, La Moynerie (which is named after the estate), is spicier and less complex. The Reddes also make sancerre and les tuilières wines, as well as the rare, chasselas-based Pouilly-sur-Loire.

DOMAINE VACHERON *Established* NA *Owners* Vacheron family *Vineyard area* 89 acres (36 ha)

The Vacheron cellars issue a range that includes what is possibly the best red cuvée in the area, a wine that is one of the few to justify the fuss made about Sancerre reds. Aged in *barriques*, it also develops well in the bottle—10- and even 15-year-old examples are still in their early maturity. The whites are generally fresh, clean, and minerally. The Vacherons have made wine for generations, and Jean-Louis, Denis, and Jean-Dominique have continually updated their production methods, filling the ancient cellars with modern equipment.

Above: *Saumur is one of many attractive winery towns situated along the Loire River's long, winding journey.* Right: *Alphonse Mellot the nineteenth tests wine in his cellars at Domaine Alphonse Mellot.*

Vouvray, Montlouis, and Touraine

Vouvray and Montlouis produce only white wines from chenin blanc. However reds, rosés, and whites are produced from a wide range of grapes in the vineyards of Touraine.

DOMAINE DIDIER CHAMPALOU *Established* 1984 *Owners* Didier and Catherine Champalou *Vineyard area* 47 acres (19 ha)

Didier and Catherine Champalou favor the *sec-tendre* style—off dry, with a touch of residual sugar. They make two blends in this style, as well as some superb sweet botrytized wines (including Cuvée CC), and an excellent dry sparkling wine.

A mansion in Saumur, where a single appellation produces about 12 million bottles of sparkling wine a year.

Bourgueil, Chinon, and St-Nicolas-de-Bourgueil

Also in Touraine, these three appellations form a red wine (cabernet franc) enclave in a predominantly white-wine region.

DOMAINE HUËT L'ÉCHANSONNE (LE HAUT LIEU)
Established NA *Owner* Gaston Huet *Vineyard area* 87 acres (35 ha)

This is the most famous vineyard in Vouvray. It was formerly run by owner and noted winemaker Gaston Huët, but his son-in-law Noël recently took charge. Noël has totally transformed the estate into an impressive biodynamic vineyard, and the great wines have gone from strength to strength. The new approach produces a great purity of fruit and a fine expression of the *terroir*. Stars of the Huët range include the single-vineyard wines from the Clos du Bourg, which are made in dry, medium-dry, and sweet styles. The *domaine* also makes one of the best sparkling wines in Vouvray.

The best use of bad wine is to drive away poor relations.

French proverb

PRINCE PONIATOWSKI   *Established* 1707
Owners Poniatowski family *Vineyard area* 30 acres (12 ha)

The ancient Vouvray estate of Clos Baudoin has been in the Poniatowski family for about 70 years. The wines, which are on the dry side, emphasize elegance and finesse, and take several years to develop. Clos Baudoin is the name of the main still wines, whereas the Aigle Blanc label is used for still and sparkling wines. Like many other properties in Vouvray, the winery is set into the cliff so that part of the house is actually a cave.

DOMAINE COULY-DUTHEIL   *Established* 1921
Owners Couly family *Vineyard area* 210 acres (85 ha)

This *négociant* firm dominates winemaking in Chinon. Estate wines such as the single-vineyard Clos de l'Écho, Clos de l'Olive, and Les Gravières are among the best wines in the appellation, full of supermature fruit that provides great richness. Bertrand Couly also makes the other cuvées such as Domaine René Couly, as well as the *négociant* wines that come from Chinon, Bourgueil, and St-Nicolas-de-Bourgueil.

DOMAINE CHARLES JOGUET
Established NA *Owner* Charles Joguet *Vineyard area* 91 acres (37 ha)

This estate produces some of the best wines in Chinon. In ascending order of power and richness, Joguet's cuvées are: Chinon Terroir, Cuvée du Clos de la Cure, Cuvée Clos du Chêne Vert, Les Varennes du Grand Clos, and Clos de la Dioterie. All wines exhibit suppleness and ripeness of the tannins.

DOMAINE BERNARD BAUDRY   *Established* 1975
Owner NA *Vineyard area* 69 acres (28 ha)

Bernard Baudry has vines in Cravant-les-Coteaux in Chinon. He vinifies the grapes from each parcel of land separately, producing Les Granges, Le Domaine, La Croix Boissée, and Les Grezeaux. All Baudry wines are aged in a mix of old and new barrels, adding complexity to great fruit.

Saumur and Saumur-Champigny

The westernmost vineyards of Anjou comprise these appellations, which produce still whites and reds, and sparkling wines under the Saumur Mousseux appellation.

GRATIEN ET MEYER   Established 1864
Owners Gratien family   *Vineyard area* 49 acres (20 ha)

One of the largest producers of sparkling saumur, Gratien et Meyer has recently shown a definite hike in quality. Wines such as Cuvée Flamme, vintage Cuvée de Minuit and Crémant de Loire Cuvée Royale are the result of significant financial investment and working with contract growers to improve the quality of the fruit. A new departure for this company was the development of a range of still wines from the estate, under the name Château Gratien.

LANGLOIS-CHATEAU   *Established* 1885
Owner Bollinger   *Vineyard area* 161 acres (65 ha)

Drawing on vineyards in Saumur, Saumur-Champigny, and Sancerre, this company makes a range of still wines, of which the most exciting are the red Saumur and Saumur-Champigny. Following the traditions of its parent company, the firm also makes sparkling wine, but instead of making the local saumur, it produces crémant de loire to a high standard. The best is Cuvée Quadrille.

These vines above Bourgueil are protected from prevailing winds by the wooded plateau beyond.

CAVE DES VIGNERONS DE SAUMUR
Established 1957   *Owner* 300-member cooperative
Vineyard area 3,460 acres (1,400 ha)

Using huge state-of-the-art vinification and press rooms, this cooperative makes a range of wines from all over the Saumur and Saumur-Champigny appellations, as well as rosé de Loire and some sparkling wines. The most successful wines here are the red and white saumur, and the deliciously fruity rosés.

Anjou and the Layon valley

An enormous variety of wines come under the Anjou banner. The principal grapes chenin blanc (for sweet and dry whites) and cabernet franc (for reds). The jewels of the Layon valley are the many sweet-wine appellations concentrated there.

A stainless steel spittoon, designed to avoid splashes.

DOMAINE DES BAUMARD   *Established* NA   *Owners* Baumard family   *Vineyard area* 99 acres (40 ha)

Florent Baumard makes the Layon valley's best and most consistent range at the sixteenth-century family home in Rochefort-sur-Loire. The

Quarts de Chaume has the characteristic intensity of this great sweet wine and develops beautifully after ten years in the bottle. The two savennières, Clos St-Yves and Clos du Papillon, are lighter than some wines from this appellation and therefore more appealing when young. Clos Ste-Catherine is a deliciously balanced coteaux du layon. The Baumards also make red anjou and a crémant de loire.

CHÂTEAU D'EPIRÉ   *Established* NA   *Owners* Bizard family   *Vineyard area* 25 acres (10 ha)

This *domaine* has been owned by the Bizard family for over a century. Based in a fine château in the village of Epiré, it includes 20 acres (8 ha) of chenin blanc for savennières and 5 acres (2 ha) of cabernet franc for an Anjou rouge, Clos de la Cerisaie. The traditional technique of using old wood for fermentation was abandoned in favor of stainless steel, but much of the white wine is still aged in barrels. The wines are designed for long-term aging, and the savennières is at its best after 10 years. The chateau also produces medium-dry and sweet wines in good years.

CHÂTEAU DE FESLES   *Established* NA   *Owner* Bernard Germain   *Vineyard area* 87 acres (35 ha)

The benchmark *domaine* for the ultrasweet bonnezeaux, Château de Fesles has landed in the lap of Bernard Germain, whose family owns 11 estates in Bordeaux as well as others in the Coteaux du Layon. The Bonnezeaux of Château de Fesles is the star of the range, which also includes a rosé d'Anjou, an Anjou rouge, and an Anjou villages.

DOMAINE OGEREAU   *Established* Early 1900s   *Owner* Vincent Ogereau   *Vineyard area* 57 acres (23 ha)

Vincent Ogereau believes in making wines with balance. From his vineyards in the Coteaux du Layon village of St-Lambert-du-Lattay, he is able to conjure wines that combine lightness and elegance with sweet, sometimes botrytized flavors. Whole-cluster maceration before fermentation adds concentration to the likes of the Coteaux du Layon St-Lambert and the top-of-the-range Prestige. Half the production is good-quality Anjou Rouge and Anjou Villages.

CLOS DE LA COULÉE DE SERRANT   *Established* Twelfth century   *Owners* Joly family   *Vineyard area* 35 acres (14 ha)

Nicolas Joly is a passionate, articulate advocate for biodynamic cultivation. In addition, Joly also has to deal with the responsibility of making wine in one of just three single-vineyard appellations in the whole of France. The white wine, which is made from chenin blanc, comes from a precipitous 17-acre (7-ha) slope in the savennières vineyards. Recent vintages have revealed enormously rich, dry, full-bodied wines, which last seemingly forever. Among the other wines originating from the Joly family cellars, the Savennières Roches aux Moines and the minerally Savennières Becherelle stand out.

Quarts de Chaume vineyard in Anjou is known for exceptional sweet white wines.

Muscadet

The main grape grown is the melon de bourgogne, used to produce the popular white, muscadet.

DOMAINE DE LA LOUVETRIE   *Established* NA
Owner J. Landron *Vineyard area* 62 acres (25 ha)

Joseph Landron makes several muscadets, each one from grapes grown in a particular soil type. The lightest and freshest, Cuvée Amphibolite, is bottled without any chaptalization or filtration. Hard, rocky orthogneiss soils are used to produce the fatter Hermine d'Or, as well as the old-vine Fief du Breuil wines.

CHÂTEAU DE LA RAGOTIÈRE   *Established* NA
Owners Couillauds *Vineyard area* 161 acres (65 ha)

The Couillaud brothers own two Muscadet properties; from this one comes classic, rich, fat muscadet, including one cuvée, Auguste Couillaud, aged in wood. The other, Château la Moriniere, issues a *vin de pays* from chardonnay, which in warm years seems akin to chablis. Top of the range here is a superb bottling of the best selection from Château de la Ragotière, which is aged on, and racked straight off, the lees.

SAUVION ET FILS   *Established* 1965 *Owners*
Sauvion family *Vineyard area* 74 acres (30 ha)

This is one of the best-known names in Muscadet. The vineyards near Vallet produce a reserve

Above: *Winters can be chilly in the Loire, which is at the limit of winegrowing in western France.*
Right: *A winemaker samples late-harvest grapes that will be used to make sweet, northern, cool-climate wine.*

wine. The other top cuvée is Cardinal Richard, which is made from wines selected by a panel of tasters from the best lots during the spring following the harvest. The Découverte range consists of *négociant* wines. The Sauvions also make Allégorie, a barrel-fermented muscadet, which has a distinctive vanilla-and-toast taste.

Other good producers in the Loire are Domaine Henri Bourgeois, Domaine Masson-Blondelet, Domaine Alphonse Mellot, Domaine Vincent Pinard, Domaine Jean-Max Roger, Maison Guy Saget, Domaine des Aubuisières, Château de la Grille, Château Gaudrelle, Domaine Bourillon-Orléans, Domaine du Clos Naudin, Domaine Yannick Amirault, Domaine Druet, Bouvet-Ladubay, Château du Hureau, Château de Targé, Château Bellerive, Domaine Cady, Chateaux Pierre Bise, Domaine Jo Pithon, Domaine Cherau-Caré, Domaine des Dorices, Domaine de l'Écu, Domaine Gadais et Fils, and Domaine du Closel.

Cognac

The cognac tradition began in the early 1600s, when Dutch traders pioneered distillation at Charentes, and by 1700 "cogniack brandy," as it was known in England, had become popular. In the eighteenth century, the English and Irish came to Cognac to exploit the region's potential, setting up businesses that still exist today. The production area was defined in 1909, and 25 years later the six constituent *crus* were recognized.

The *crus* were divided on the basis of climate and soil. The soils with the heaviest concentrations of chalk resemble those of Champagne, and are therefore known as Grande Champagne and Petite Champagne. (Fine Champagne is a mix of these *crus*, including at least 50 percent Grande Champagne.)

Cognac's growing popularity attracted the attention of multinationals in the 1970s and 1980s. Yet the cognac industry was in turmoil as the twenty-first century began.

> *A man, fallen on hard times, sold his art collection but kept his wine cellar. When asked why he did not sell his wine, he said, "A man can live without art, but not without culture."*
>
> ANONYMOUS

Export sales had plummeted, overproduction was running at 25 percent, and prices paid to grape growers had plunged. To combat the crisis, new styles of cognac are being added, aimed at women and younger customers.

Cognac production and producers

Once vinified, cognac wine is double-distilled in copper pot-stills. Afterward, it measures 70 percent alcohol, so it has to be diluted during aging, usually with distilled water. The length of aging varies, but can last for decades. As a result of evaporation during aging, each year about 2 percent of the cognac in the region's storehouses simply disappears into thin air—this is known locally as "the angels' share."

Although single-vintage and single-*cru* cognacs are becoming fashionable, most cognacs are made from different *crus* and vintages. The traditional

Boutiers-St-Trojan
Tourtrat
Nercillac
+2
3 Cognac
5
6
Les Métairies
St-Brice
Charente
Bourg-Charente
Jarnac
Nt41
+1
Châteaubernard
La Pallue
Gensac-la-Pallue
NORTH   1 mile (1.6 kilometers)
Mainxe

Producers
1 Courvoisier
2 Croizet
3 Hennessy
4 Hine
5 Martell
6 Rémy Martin

PARIS
FRANCE
Cognac
Segonzac   +4

A vineyard and winery in Grande Champagne, Cognac's most important cru.

cognac classifications relate to the length of aging. VS (Very Special) or three stars means that the youngest brandy in the blend has been aged for at least 3 years; the youngest brandy in a VSOP (Very Superior Old Pale) blend has been aged for 4 years. A Napoléon has had a minimum aging of 6 years, though it is more usually 7 to 15 years. This is the stepping stone from VSOP to XO (Extra Old), whose youngest component must have been aged for 6 years, though it is not unusual for the actual minimum to be nearer 25 years.

Above: *The township of Biard lies in the heart of cognac country, which is divided into six* crus.

HINE   *Established* 1763   *Owner* LVMH

This house was established by an Englishman, Thomas Hine, in the eighteenth century. It still retains its unbeatable reputation for cognacs of delicacy, elegance, and great age. Rare & Delicate is just as its name suggests, but rounded out with structured mellowness, while Antique bal-

ances light and shade, and displays floral notes as well as hints of leather.

HENNESSY   *Established* 1765   *Owner* LVMH

Since Christophe Navarre took over in 1998, Cognac's biggest producer has consolidated its hold in the United States, created three single-distillery cognacs (Camp Romain, Izambard, and Le Peu), and produced one of the most interesting of the "young-generation" cognacs, the Pure White. This house has also enhanced its reputation for complex premium cognacs with the top-end Grande Champagne XO.

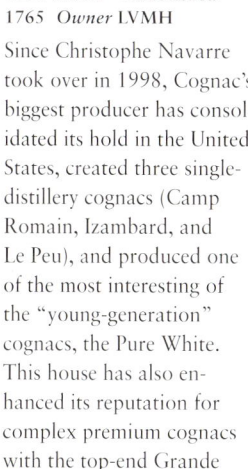

RÉMY MARTIN   *Established* 1724   *Owner* Rémy Cointreau

Although this is the only house whose produce is all at least Fine Champagne, Rémy has nevertheless affixed its centaur emblem to new-era cognacs—notably, the floral and spicily fruity Trek. Meanwhile, Rémy Silver (cognac premixed with vodka and a "secret ingredient") is a shot at the cocktail market. But Rémy Martin's most notable achievement still remains the Louis XIII: a Grande Champagne of astonishingly rich, concentrated aromas made from eaux-de-vie at least 50 and up to 100 years old. Purchasers will, of course, need particularly deep pockets.

COURVOISIER   *Established* 1805   *Owner* Allied Domecq

Napoleon visited Courvoisier's operation in 1811, thus initiating the link between the emperor and cognac. The house continues to justify its imperial connections with a range as fine and aromatic as any. From a VS with fruit and flower tones, it runs through the complexity of the flagship Napoleon to an XO Impérial of almost exotic character.

Two other recommended Cognac producers are Croizet (established in 1805) and Martell (established in 1715).

Bordeaux

Bordeaux's reputation rests squarely on a group of illustrious châteaux and their sought-after and increasingly expensive wines. The likes of Lafite, Margaux, and Pétrus turn out benchmark products—firm, long-lived, finely balanced, and, for the most part, red. But they represent just 5 per-

cent of Bordeaux's production, which includes a vast range of wines, including excellent-value offerings from the petites appellations as well as a large quantity of far-from-consistent generic bordeaux. About 85 percent of the region's output is red; the rest is mainly dry and sweet white, with a little rosé, clairet, and sparkling crémant.

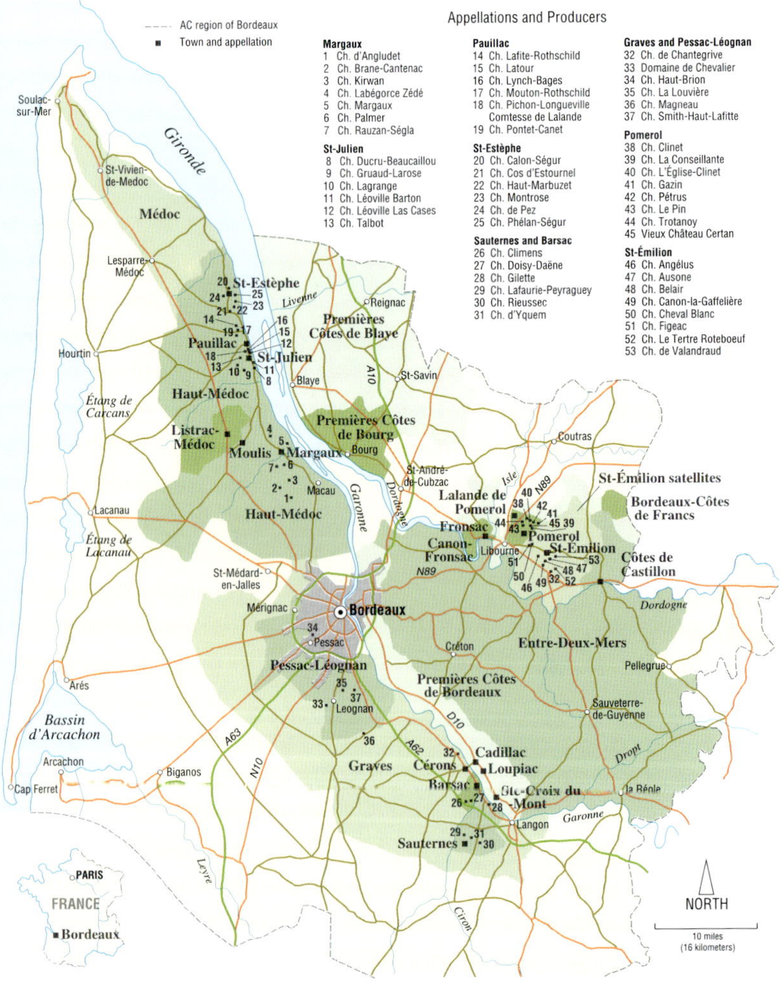

Appellations and Producers

Margaux
1 Ch. d'Angludet
2 Ch. Brane-Cantenac
3 Ch. Kirwan
4 Ch. Labégorce Zédé
5 Ch. Margaux
6 Ch. Palmer
7 Ch. Rauzan-Ségla

St-Julien
8 Ch. Ducru-Beaucaillou
9 Ch. Gruaud-Larose
10 Ch. Lagrange
11 Ch. Léoville Barton
12 Ch. Léoville Las Cases
13 Ch. Talbot

Pauillac
14 Ch. Lafite-Rothschild
15 Ch. Latour
16 Ch. Lynch-Bages
17 Ch. Mouton-Rothschild
18 Ch. Pichon-Longueville
    Comtesse de Lalande
19 Ch. Pontet-Canet

St-Estèphe
20 Ch. Calon-Ségur
21 Ch. Cos d'Estournel
22 Ch. Haut-Marbuzet
23 Ch. Montrose
24 Ch. de Pez
25 Ch. Phélan-Ségur

Sauternes and Barsac
26 Ch. Climens
27 Ch. Doisy-Daëne
28 Ch. Gilette
29 Ch. Lafaurie-Peyraguey
30 Ch. Rieussec
31 Ch. d'Yquem

Graves and Pessac-Léognan
32 Ch. de Chantegrive
33 Domaine de Chevalier
34 Ch. Haut-Brion
35 Ch. La Louvière
36 Ch. Magneau
37 Ch. Smith-Haut-Lafitte

Pomerol
38 Ch. Clinet
39 Ch. La Conseillante
40 Ch. L'Église-Clinet
41 Ch. Gazin
42 Ch. Pétrus
43 Ch. Le Pin
44 Ch. Trotanoy
45 Vieux Château Certan

St-Émilion
46 Ch. Angélus
47 Ch. Ausone
48 Ch. Belair
49 Ch. Canon-la-Gaffelière
50 Ch. Cheval Blanc
51 Ch. Figeac
52 Ch. Le Tertre Roteboeuf
53 Ch. de Valandraud

The Bordeaux wine trade is unique in that it has its own marketplace, the Place de Bordeaux, where wines are sold in bulk and bottle, and as futures. Producers sell to *négociants*, who then sell to French distributors or importers overseas.

History

The Romans may have been the first to cultivate the vine in Bordeaux, but it was under English rule that trade in wine initially developed, and Bordeaux enjoyed its first golden period. During the seventeenth century, the Dutch became a major force, initiating a number of changes in wine styles and channels of distribution. Whereas the demand from the English was for the rather thin, light-red *clairet* (hence the term "claret" for red bordeaux), the Dutch taste ran to dry and semisweet white wines.

From Holland, these products soon spread into other parts of northern Europe. The eighteenth century provided Bordeaux's second golden era. A new, powerful moneyed class, the *noblesse de robe*, were keen to invest in vineyards. Wines from individual estates were increasingly recognized and sought out by wealthy Europeans, some of whom set up their own merchant houses.

In 1855, a classification system was introduced, which ranked the wines from the top châteaux in the Médoc and Sauternes according to their market price. (The most expensive were classed as Premiers Crus, then came Deuxièmes Crus, and so on.) Then disaster: phylloxera in the 1870s and downy mildew toward the end of the century devastated the region's vineyards. Viticulturalists used American rootstock to reconstruct, and it was probably around this time that cabernet sauvignon, cabernet franc, merlot, sémillon, sauvignon blanc, and muscadelle became the principal Bordeaux grape varieties.

The twentieth century saw many setbacks—war, depression, the oil crisis—but there were also positives. In 1936, the system of *appellation contrôlée* was established, which delimited boundaries, defined work practices and, to a degree,

Above: *The St-Émilion region, being cool and humid, is best-suited to early-ripening grapes; merlot is dominant here.* Left: *Deep in the cellars of Château Lafite-Rothschild there are still some bottles of wine held from very old vintages.*

Right versus left banks

The communes of the Médoc are among the most classified and reported wine regions of the world. A more basic and, perhaps more useful, distinction is the difference in taste characteristics between the cabernet sauvignon-dominated wines of the Médoc (left bank of the Garonne) and the merlot/cabernet franc-dominated wines of Pomerol and St-Émilion (right bank). Left bank soils tend toward more gravel while the right bank soils have more clay. In the glass, both are deeply colored and often kissed with toasty new French oak. Left bank wines are more apt to have cassis notes in youth and cedar notes with age. Right bank wines tend toward plum, cherry, and fruit-cake in youth and smoky notes with time. Textural differences are often more apparent with the cabernet sauvignon-dominated left bank wines being tighter, more acidic, and more astringently tannic. The right bank counters with somewhat more round wines, which can be silky with age. As apparent as the differences are on paper, many a master of wine has confused "classic" left and right bank wines while blind tasting.

set standards of quality. The 1960s saw châteaux owners and *négociants* financing development by selling wines as futures *(en primeur)*, and in the 1970s the practice of bottling wines at the châteaux became compulsory.

Landscape and climate

The Bordeaux region is in the Gironde department of southwestern France, extending from the Pointe de Grave in the northwest to Langon in the southeast, and is crossed by the Dordogne and Garonne rivers. The vineyards are situated along these waterways in an area known as the Entre-Deux-Mers. Most of Bordeaux is flat or undulating and, generally, soil types determine which variety of grape is planted. On the "left

bank" (the Médoc and Graves), the soils are composed mainly of pebbles, gravel, and sand and are generally poor, but retain heat and have good filtration properties, ideal for late-ripening cabernet sauvignon. On the "right bank" (St-Émilion, Pomerol, and Fronsac), the soils are composed mainly of clay, limestone, sand, and small pockets of gravel, and are cooler, making them more suited to early-ripening merlot.

Bordeaux has a temperate maritime climate made milder by the warming influence of the Gulf Stream. Rainfall is abundant, summers are warm, and winter rarely drops below freezing. The absence of extremes means that the grapes ripen only to a certain level of intensity, resulting in wines that are subtle and reserved. Cold winter snaps and spring frosts are a danger, but July to early September is the critical period for ripening. Often it coincides with a rainy spell, creating a nail-biting finish to the growing season. In fall, morning mists provoke the onset of noble rot *(Botrytis cinerea)* needed for sweet white wines.

Vines and wines

The production of red wines has increased dramatically over the last 30 years, with merlot being the most widely planted grape. Its supple fruit and higher alcohol content add weight and substance to a blend, while its softness can make a wine more approach-able. It adapts well to the cooler clay-limestone soils of the right bank and Entre-Deux-Mers, where it is dominant.

Cabernet sauvignon is probably Bordeaux's most famous red variety, being most firmly associated with the great wines of the Médoc and Graves: it is less sensitive to spring frosts than merlot, and it ripens later, but it needs the assistance of warmer soils to come to full maturity. Its small, thick-skinned grapes provide color, tannin, and a firm but finely edged texture and bouquet.

Cabernet franc also plays a particularly significant role on the right bank, where it partners merlot in St-Émilion and Pomerol blends. When fully ripe, it adds elegance and a fruity complexity. Other red varieties include petit verdot and malbec.

Unlike wines made here in the past, the great red wines of Bordeaux today are quite capable of aging for several decades, and become gradually more harmonious and complex with time.

White grape varieties now make up only around 15 percent of Bordeaux's vineyards. Sémillon is still the principal variety, particularly in the sweet-wine appellations. A productive grape, it makes wines with a citrus flavor and aroma when vinified dry; however, because it is particularly susceptible to noble rot, it is more widely used to make sweet wines that are rich, unctuous, and redolent of honey, raisins, and tropical fruits.

Sauvignon blanc is the only white variety that is planted more widely now than in the past. Small amounts are blended with sémillon in sweet wines to supply added zest and aroma.

Right: *Harvest time in Bordeaux usually runs from early September to mid-October.*
Below: *Excellent drainage in the Graves area is largely due to the pebbly soils, which retain heat very well.*

French regional cuisine

Local producers sample a variety of foods and wines at an informal picnic in the Pays Nantais region.

Much wine is at its best when drunk with food. The rich, robust, rustic cuisine of south-western France is a good match for its sturdy wines: foods like confit of duck, foie gras from the Gers, ham and chocolate from Bayonne, and prunes from Agen. Gascony is known for *garbure*, a rich vegetable soup, and for sheep's cheese. The east is home to the hearty and filling dish known as cassoulet, a stew of beans, confit of duck, and sausage.

Bordeaux's regional fare is rich, warm, and hearty, and red bordeaux, with its fresh, tannic edge, is a natural foil. Red meat, duck, and game often feature. Typical dishes include foie gras, *entrecôte* steak grilled over vine cuttings, and milk-fed Pauillac lamb. In fall, cèpe mushrooms are sought-after; spring is asparagus season. A crisp white wine from the Graves or Entre-Deux-Mers is the perfect accompaniment to fish or seafood dishes, such as oysters and lampreys.

The Mediterranean climate strongly influences Languedoc-Roussillon's local cuisine. Here, fish soups are a specialty as is creamed salt cod, *brandade de morue*. Game is eaten when in season, and vegetables, in particular, aubergines, peppers, and tomatoes, are important year round. Meat and fish are usually grilled. Roussillon displays a strong Catalan influence, with grilled pepper salad and crème catalan, a form of crème brulée, among the local specialties.

Jura has a strong gastronomic tradition that has been integral to the success of its wines, which demand food. Poulsard, a very pale red wine, can be surprisingly good when combined with the right dish, such as smoked Morteau sausage. Comté is a cheese with a strong, nutty flavor perfect for *vin jaune*. Bresse's chicken in a cream and *vin jaune* sauce is a local specialty.

Alsace's French and German cultural mix is seen in its gastronomy. The emphasis is a blend of German heartiness and French refinement: spicy sausages, foie gras, rich stews, and *choucroute* (like sauerkraut). Alsatian gewürztraminers are excellent with many rich local dishes or Munster cheese. Tokay (pinot gris) is often drunk with foie gras, which it complements perfectly.

Right: *Even a simple meal is enhanced by a glass or two of wine.*

Below: *An uncommon but very French meal: snails with red burgundy.*

A cellarmaster selects wines for the blend during the maturation process.

Winemaking

Each grape variety is vinified separately, as are grapes from different parcels of land if sufficient tank space is available. The fruit is destemmed and crushed, and then pumped or gravity-fed into fermentation tanks or *cuves*. The tanks may be made of cement, stainless steel, or wood. Each material has its own attributes and champions: for example, Pétrus is vinified in cement, Haut-Brion in stainless steel, and Margaux in wood. Sulfur dioxide (SO_2) is widely used as an additive to protect against oxidation and bacteria.

Alcoholic fermentation lasts an average of eight to ten days. Natural yeasts are used and, if necessary, a yeast starter, or *pied de cuve*, may be taken from one tank and added to the others. Following fermentation and maceration, the free-run wine is drained off and the remaining marc is pressed. The press wine is retained for blending purposes, with between 5 and 10 percent being used in the final blend. The wine then undergoes malolactic fermentation either in tank or, increasingly, in new oak barrels. The wine is then aged for anything up to 24 months in French oak barrels or *barriques*. A choice of oak is available (Limousin, Nièvre, or Allier) and producers often buy from a number of cooperages, both to ensure supply and to increase complexity. American oak is used at some châteaux, but rarely by the top producers. During the aging process, the wine is racked off its lees into a fresh barrel every three or four months. It is also clarified or fined using egg whites or a similar albumin preparation. Prior to bottling, the wine normally undergoes a light filtration.

A bottle in the traditional claret shape.

An important task during the early stages of barrel maturation is the selection and blending for the principal wine. The selection process has become steadily more rigorous, with the *grand vin* now representing as little as 30 to 40 percent of total production at top estates.

The procedure for making dry white wines generally follows principles employed around the world. Variations practiced in Bordeaux include hand harvesting into perforated plastic containers, and machine harvesting and barrel fermentation.

The sweet, rich wines of the best estates in Sauternes and Barsac—and occasionally across the river in Cadillac, Loupiac, and Ste-Croix-du-Mont—are made from grapes affected by noble rot. After selective harvesting, the grapes are pressed and then fermented, either in stainless steel, or, increasingly at the top estates, in new or relatively new oak barrels. The fermentation process is necessarily long and slow. When the wine has reached the desired alcohol-sugar balance, the fermentation process is halted by reducing the temperature, racking, and adding sulfur dioxide. Aging in barrel then continues for another two or three years.

Margaux

Margaux is the most southerly and extensive of the communal appellations in the Médoc, with its vineyards spread through five communes. Margaux's gravel and sand soils account for the area's generally lighter-bodied and more fragrant style of red wine. Conditions suit late-ripening cabernet sauvignon and petit verdot.

CHÂTEAU MARGAUX *Owners*

Mentzelopoulos family and associates
Vineyard area 193 acres (78 ha)

This magnificent estate, with its nineteenth-century colonnaded château, has probably been the most consistent of the Premiers Crus since 1977. In recent years, the selection process has become more rigorous, with only 50 percent of the production going into the *grand vin* and the rest into the second wine, Pavillon Rouge. Both of these wonderful wines combine power and elegance with a purity of fruit and finely honed structure. The château also produces a decent white wine, Pavillon Blanc, made from barrel-fermented sauvignon blanc.

A meal without wine is like a day without sunshine.
ANTHELME BRILLAT-SAVARIN
(1755–1826)

CHÂTEAU PALMER *Owner* SCI Château Palmer
Vineyard area 112 acres (45 ha)

Established in the early nineteenth century, this estate has regularly surpassed its Troisième Cru classification. The wines have been remarkably consistent, and in the 1960s and 1970s were perhaps the best in the Margaux appellation. The large quantity of merlot grown on the estate accounts for Château Palmer's famous velvety texture, and with only one-third new oak barrels used for aging, the oak always remains discreet.

CHÂTEAU RAUZAN-SÉGLA
Owner Wertheimer family *Vineyard area* 121 acres (49 ha)

Château Rauzan-Ségla has begun to realize its full potential since it was acquired by the Wertheimer family, owners of Chanel, in 1994. Vineyards have been drained and replanted, cellars renovated, new equipment installed, and the proportion of new oak barrels increased to about 70 percent. Production from the estate's younger vines now goes into a second wine called Ségla.

The high percentage of merlot in the main blend (up to 40 percent) endows Rauzan-Ségla with the body and texture to complement its elegant bouquet.

Other recommended Margaux producers include Kirwan, d'Angludet, Brane-Cantenac, La Gurgue, Dauzac, Durfort-Vivens, d'Issan, Ferrière, Giscours, Labégorce Zédé, Lascombes, Siran, du Tertre, Malescot-St-Exupéry, Monbrison, and Prieuré-Lichine.

Château Margaux is the appellation's most productive winery. The building was restored in the late 1970s.

St-Julien

St-Julien has been the most consistent appellation in Bordeaux for many years. Its success is aided by a superior location and highly committed producers. The appellation's vineyards are on two plateaus located between Pauillac to the north and the Haut-Médoc to the south, and close to the warming influence of the waters of the Gironde Estuary. Local conditions enhance the ripening cycle, contributing to a mellow fruit character in the red wines that is backed by a firm structure with great potential for aging.

CHÂTEAU DUCRU-BEAUCAILLOU *Owner* Borie family *Vineyard area* 123 acres (50 ha)

This Deuxième Cru occupies a prime location, close to the Gironde Estuary at the southern end of the appellation. The estate's fortunes were revived during the 1950s by Jean-Eugène Borie, with the assistance of enologist Émile Peynaud, and their work is continued by Borie's son, François-Xavier. Wood contamination in the cellars caused some irregularity in late-1980s vintages, but various improvements have seen Ducru-Beaucaillou return to top form. The wines are rich, ripe, and elegant, but need at least ten years to develop.

CHÂTEAU GRUAUD-LAROSE *Owners* Merlaut family *Vineyard area* 203 acres (82 ha)

Gruaud Larose probably has the most full-bodied, fruity and muscular wine in St-Julien, partly due to its heavier soils. The Merlaut family have improved the drainage, added new machinery, a weather station, and 14 new wooden vats. During vinification, the wines are pumped over and undergo a long period of maceration. The estate uses only 30 percent new oak barrels for aging.

CHÂTEAU LÉOVILLE BARTON *Owner* Anthony Barton *Vineyard area* 116 acres (47 ha)

This vineyard has a high percentage of old vines but no château or cellars, so the wine is made at Troisième Cru Château Langoa Barton. Wooden vats are used for vinification, and the wine is then aged in 50 percent new oak barrels. Anthony Barton and manager Michel Raoult have made the winemaking process steadily more rigorous, and the resulting wines are now rich, full, and firmly structured.

Other noteworthy St-Julien producers include Beychevelle, Branaire, La Bridane, Glana, Gloria, Lalande-Borie, Langoa Barton, Léoville Poyferré, St-Pierre, Lagrange, Léoville Las Cases, and Talbot.

Right: *Château Branaire's head winemaker outside this historic winery in St-Julien.*

Below: *A vine worker tends the vines at Château Léoville Las Cases, St-Julien.*

Pauillac

Pauillac has the quintessential wine of the Médoc: firm and powerful, slightly austere in youth, made for aging, and with a distinct scent of blackcurrant and cigar box. Significantly, this appellation is home to three Premiers Crus—Lafite, Mouton-Rothschild, and Latour—as well as 15 other classified estates.

CHÂTEAU LAFITE-ROTHSCHILD   *Owners* **Barons de Rothschild** *Vineyard area* **247 acres (100 ha)**

The most northerly of Pauillac's three Premiers Crus, most of the vineyard is planted on an undulating gravel knoll which faces the Gironde Estuary. Lafite has always been lighter in style than either Mouton or Latour, and possesses a greater elegance; it also has a huge capacity for aging. Since 1995, manager Charles Chevallier and his team have refined their viticulture, resulting in a wine of greater weight and structure. The estate's second wine is known as Carruades.

CHÂTEAU LATOUR   *Owner* **François Pinault** *Vineyard area* **160 acres (65 ha)**

Château Latour is the epitome of a classic Pauillac wine: deep color; blackcurrant, cedar, and mineral bouquet; subdued power; and firm structure for long aging. The vineyard has a high proportion of cabernet sauvignon, a southeasterly exposure, deep gravel soils, and close proximity to the warming influence of the Gironde Estuary. Wines for the Grand Vin de Château Latour are produced from this area, while the excellent second

A seventeenth-century tower is a highlight at the exquisite Château Latour, which has extensive vineyards.

wine, Les Forts de Latour, and a third wine, simply labelled Pauillac, are produced from other parcels of land.

CHÂTEAU MOUTON-ROTHSCHILD   *Owner* **Baronne Philippine de Rothschild** *Vineyard area* **185 acres (75 ha)**

Classified as a Deuxième Cru in 1855, this vineyard was upgraded to Premier Cru in 1973 thanks to Baron Philippe de Rothschild, who took over the estate in 1922, and generally improved the quality and dimensions of the wines. Mouton has the power and concentration of Pauillac but an opulence and panache that sets it apart from Lafite, whose vineyard has the same geological profile. A second label, Le Petit Mouton, was introduced in the 1990s and a small quantity of white wine, L'Aile d'Argent, is also produced.

Other Pauillac producers of note include d'Armailhac, Batailley, Clerc Milon, Duhart-Milon, Fonbadet, Grand-Puy-Ducasse, Grand-Puy-Lacoste, Haut-Bages-Libéral, Haut-Batailley, La Fleur Milon, Pibran, Pichon-Longueville (Baron), Lynch Bages, Pontet Canet, and Pichon-Longueville Comtesse de Lalande.

St-Estèphe

Variations in St-Estèphe's soil structure influence the choice of grape varieties and add certain nuances to the area's wines. Cabernet sauvignon is still the most common variety grown here, but given the preponderance of cooler soils, merlot has gained favor and now represents 35 percent of production. St-Estèphe wines are generally fruity and full-bodied but with a firm tannic edge. This edge can be a little aggressive, though modern wine-making methods and grape selection have greatly alleviated this problem.

CHÂTEAU CALON-SÉGUR   *Owner* Madame Capbern-Gasqueton *Vineyard area* 136 acres (55 ha)

Calon is one of the appellation's oldest estates, dating back to Gallo-Roman times. The wines are firm, powerful, and rich in the better vintages, but have tended toward leanness at other times. Fortunately recent changes have been made, including work in the vineyard, a new vat-room, the introduction of partial malolactic fermentation in barrel, and an increase in the percentage of new oak for aging. All these have gone some way to remedying the problem.

CHÂTEAU COS D'ESTOURNEL   *Owners* Merlaut family and Cavas de Santa Maria *Vineyard area* 161 acres (65 ha)

Cos, which in the old Gascon tongue means "hill of pebbles," was founded in 1811 by Louis Gaspard d'Estournel, who constructed this distinctive pagoda-like winery. The wines are dark, rich, and opulent, the high percentage of merlot adding an uncharacteristic (for the appellation) suavity and the well-judged oak an exotic, spicy nuance. The second wine is Les Pagodes de Cos.

Above: *Château Pichon-Longueville's elegant spires are reflected in an ornamental lake.* Right: *One of the grapes- and wine-themed artworks held by Château Mouton-Rothschild.*

CHÂTEAU MONTROSE   *Owner* Jean-Louis Charmolüe *Vineyard area* 168 acres (68 ha)

The vineyard of this Deuxième Cru has deep gravel soils, southeasterly exposure, and close proximity to the Gironde Estuary. The wines are firm and powerful, dominated by cabernet sauvignon, and have great potential for aging. In recent years, later picking of riper grapes has mellowed what used to be a rather tough exterior. The estate's second wine, La Dame de Montrose, is also worth seeking out.

Other St-Estèphe producers include Haut-Marbuzet, Le Boscq, Cos Labory, Le Crock, Lilian-Ladouys, Marbuzet, Les Ormes de Pez, Tour de Pez, de Pez, and Phélan-Ségur.

Sauternes and Barsac

Near Bordeaux, these communes make the rich, opulent wines known as sauternes and barsac. These wines result from a unique combination of climatic influences. During fall, mists form that provoke the onset of noble rot, or *Botrytis cinerea*, a fungus that increases sugar, acidity, and flavor. Grapes are hand-picked selectively, so the wines are costly. In certain years the top châteaux are unable to declare a vintage. Sémillon is the principal grape variety; a little sauvignon blanc is normally added to increase aroma and acidity, and occasionally muscadelle. Barsac is generally a lighter wine than sauternes.

The vineyards of Château d'Yquem in Sauternes are on a tiny knoll that provides excellent ripening conditions.

CHÂTEAU LAFAURIE-PEYRAGUEY, SAUTERNES
Owner Domaines Cordier *Vineyard area* 99 acres (40 ha)

This property in Haut-Bommes includes a thirteenth-century château. In 1978, the estate again began using oak casks for fermentation; it has since increased the proportion of new oak to around 50 percent. Also, picking has become increasingly selective. Since the notable 1983 vintage, Lafaurie-Peyraguey has consistently turned out wines that are rich, full, and balanced, and have wonderful fruit expression.

CHÂTEAU D'YQUEM, SAUTERNES *Owners* Group LVMH and Lur-Saluces family *Vineyard area* 262 acres (106 ha)

Singled out as a Premier Cru Supérieur in the 1855 classification, Yquem owes its status to the owners, who run the *domaine* with precision, and a geographical situation that provides excellent ripening conditions. Yields here

Quintessential Barsac: Château Climens offers wines of unparalleled finesse and delicacy.

rarely exceed 0.5 tons per acre (9 hl per ha), or about one glass of wine per vine. The wines are fermented and aged for three-and-a-half years in 100 percent new oak barrels, and are the richest and most powerful in the appellation. Their capacity to age is legendary.

CHÂTEAU RIEUSSEC, SAUTERNES *Owners* Barons de Rothschild *Vineyard area* 185 acres (75 ha)

Rieussec almost rivals its neighbor Yquem for the concentration and power of its wines. Since the Rothschilds of Château Lafite purchased this Premier Cru in 1985, fine-tuning has yielded greater finesse and fruit flavor. The selective harvesting has become more precise, the aging in barrel has been lengthened from 15 months to two-and-half years, and in 1996 the estate once again began fermenting the wines in barrel.

A number of other noteworthy Sauternes and Barsac producers include Climens, Doisy-Daëne, Gilette, Bastor-Lamontagne, de Malle, Clos Haut-Peyraguey, Coutet, Cru Barréjats, Doisy-Védrines, Fargues, Guiraud, Rayne Vigneau, Haut-Bergeron, les Justices, de Myrat, Nairac, Rabaud-Promis, Raymond-Lafon, Sigalas-Rabaud, Suduiraut, and La Tour Blanche.

The Graves and Pessac-Léognan

The Graves is Bordeaux's oldest viticultural zone, with vineyards dating back to at least the Middle Ages. Cabernet sauvignon is the dominant red variety; there is also merlot. The dry whites, made from sauvignon blanc and sémillon, have a citrus and mineral nuance. Pessac-Léognan, the northern sector of Graves, became a separate appellation in 1989.

CHÂTEAU DE CHANTEGRIVE, GRAVES
Owners Françoise and Henri Lévèque *Vineyard area* 220 acres (90 ha)

Françoise and Henri Lévèque built this estate in 1967 and have steadily expanded it to the point where it is now the largest in the Graves. The regular white wine is crisp and fruity, but of most interest is the Cuvée Caroline, a special bottling of barrel-fermented sémillon and sauvignon blanc. In certain years it can stand alongside the best from Pessac-Léognan. The red has been of less interest, but the yields have been reduced and the wines now appear richer and riper.

CHÂTEAU HAUT-BRION, PESSAC-LÉOGNAN
Owner Domaine Clarence Dillon *Vineyard area* 114 acres (46 ha)

Haut-Brion is *the* great estate of the region. Slightly higher average temperatures here allow the grapes to attain much greater levels of maturity than in the Médoc. They are vinified in a modern, purpose-built *cuverie*. The red wine is always finely textured with smooth tannins, ripe fruit and a slightly burnt, roasted note. The white is full and complex.

CHÂTEAU SMITH-HAUT-LAFITTE, PESSAC-LÉOGNAN
Owners Daniel and Florence Cathiard *Vineyard area* 136 acres (55 ha)

No expense has been spared to improve the wines: a reorganized vineyard, reduced yields, organic methods, modernized facilities, and oak barrels from the estate's own cooperage. The barrel-fermented white is rich and aromatic, and contains a tiny percentage of sauvignon gris. The red has gained in both density and finesse.

Recommended Graves producers are Magneau, de Chevalier, Archambeau, d'Ardennes, Olivier, and Bichon-Cassignols. Other noteworthy producers in Pessac-Léognan include Les Carmes Haut-Brion, La Louvière, Carbonnieux, de Fieuzal, de France, La Garde, Haut-Bergey, Larrivet Haut-Brion, and Haut-Bailly.

Château Olivier has Grande Cru Classé for both its red and white wines.

Pomerol

The tiny appellation of Pomerol produces some of the finest and most sought-after wines in the world. Dominated by merlot, the best are rich, sweet, and unctuous, the layered fruit extract adding gloss to a firm, tannic structure. Pomerol is on a gently sloping plateau northeast of the town of Libourne. The clay and gravel soils of the center and east produce the richest wines, while the sandy soils to the west and south yield wines that are lighter in style.

CHÂTEAU CLINET   *Owners* Jean-Michel Arcaute and associates *Vineyard area* 22 acres (9 ha)

Rich, powerful, and intense, Clinet is one of the most outstanding producers in Pomerol. Its style changed in the 1980s and the grapes are now picked extremely ripe and given a long period of maceration for maximum extract. The wine is aged in new oak barrels for at least 24 months.

At the Château Certan-de-May in Pomerol, a worker brings in the harvest by hand.

CHÂTEAU PÉTRUS   *Owners* Ets Jean-Pierre Moueix and Madame Lily Lacoste *Vineyard area* 27 acres (11 ha)

Pétrus makes Bordeaux's most expensive wine. It is produced almost entirely from merlot, which thrives on a high plateau. It is big, powerful, and brooding, with layers of rich extract and firm but fine tannins, and ages extremely well. A team of pickers harvests the grapes at optimum ripeness in just half a day. After the wines are vinified in cement tanks they are aged in 100 percent new oak barrels.

CHÂTEAU LE PIN   *Owner* Jacques Thienpont *Vineyard area* 5 acres (2 ha)

Its limited volume, velvety texture, and almost Burgundian intensity of raspberry and cherry fruit have made Le Pin one of the region's biggest—and most expensive—sensations. Grown in sand and gravel soils, with low yields, the grapes are vinified in temperature-controlled stainless steel vats, and the wine run off into 100 percent new oak barrels, where it undergoes malolactic fermentation and matures for up to 18 months.

VIEUX CHÂTEAU CERTAN   *Owners* Thienpont family *Vineyard area* 33 acres (13.5 ha)

The high percentage of cabernet gives this wine a distinctive style. The sixteenth-century property is ideally located on the high plateau, where a complexity of soils includes pure clay, gravel, clay-gravel, and sand. Each parcel of the vineyard is worked according to soil type, grape variety, and age of vine.

Other Pomerol producers of note include La Conseillante, L'Église-Clinet, Gazin, Trotanoy, Beauregard, Le Bon Pasteur, Bourgneuf-Vayron, Certan de May, Clos l'Église, La Croix de Gay, La Croix du Casse, L'Évangile, La Fleur-Pétrus, Gombaude-Guillot, Lafleur, Latour à Pomerol, Mazeyres, Montviel, Petit Village, La Pointe, and de Sales.

St-Émillion producer Château Figeac's vineyards are classified as Premiers Grands Crus Classés B.

St-Émilion

St-Émilion is Bordeaux's most historic wine region—vine cultivation has occurred here since Gallo–Roman times. Located around nine villages or communes, including St-Émilion, the whole area is a World Heritage site. There are 13,340 acres (5,400 ha) under production and two appellations within the same region, St-Émilion and St-Émilion Grand Cru.

Merlot is the dominant grape variety followed by cabernet franc, but there is a wide variety of wine styles. For example, in the northwest, adjacent to Pomerol, a pocket of gravelly soils provides elegant, cabernet-dominated wines, while on the limestone plateau and *côtes*, the merlot-dominated wines are full-bodied, fresh, and made for long aging. The properties are generally small family-run affairs, and the local cooperative is also a major producer.

CHÂTEAU ANGÉLUS   *Owner* **Boüard family**
Vineyard area **58 acres (23 ha)**

Angélus is St-Émilion's modern success story. Since the 1980s new practices in the vineyard and cellars transformed the château from a middling Grand Cru Classé into a top estate. It set the standard for a more contemporary style of St-Émilion: deeper in color, richer, and more concentrated. A second wine, Carillon de l'Angélus was launched to improve the selection.

the estate's soil types (ancient gravel, sand, and clay) and the high percentage of cabernet franc in the blend. The vineyard was first cultivated in the eighteenth century and the first cabernet franc grapes were planted late in the nineteenth century. In 1998 the estate was sold to Albert Frère and Bernard Arnault. Manager Pierre Lurton has ensured a high degree of continuity during the last decade. Yields are kept very low, and a second wine, Le Petit Cheval, permits further selection.

Above: *The vineyard at Château Cheval Blanc has an unusual mix of gravel, sand, and clay, which contributes to its distinctive style of wine.*
Left: *The rich colors of vine leaves during fall brighten the landscape of Bordeaux.*

CHÂTEAU AUSONE *Owner* Vauthier family
Vineyard area 17 acres (7 ha)

Ausone is designated as Premier Grand Cru Classé A. The château is located on the steep southern slopes of St-Émilion. The southeasterly exposure of the vineyard and the limestone, clay, and sand soils shape the character of the wine—powerful but fine, and slow to mature. Since Alain Vauthier took charge of production in 1996, the wines have gained in color, weight, and fruit expression.

CHÂTEAU CHEVAL BLANC *Owners* Albert Frère and Bernard Arnault *Vineyard area* 89 acres (36 ha)

Known for its silky, elegant style, and long aging potential, Cheval Blanc has been St-Émilion's top wine for over 50 years. It owes its originality to

CHÂTEAU FIGEAC *Owner* Thierry Manoncourt
Vineyard area 99 acres (40 ha)

The origins of Figeac date back to the Gallo–Roman period. A large part of the vineyard is located on ancient gravel soils, and when the present owner started replanting in 1947, the nature of the *terroir* led him to select an unusually high proportion of cabernet franc and cabernet sauvignon. These produce a wine that is more of a Médoc style, displaying elegance, balance, and depth of fruit in good years, a slight herbaceousness in mediocre vintages, and a deceptive ability to age.

Other excellent St-Émilion producers include Belair, Canon-la-Gaffelière, Tertre Roteboeuf, Valandraud, L'Arrosée, Balestard-la-Tonnelle, Beau-Séjour-Bécot, Canon, Clos Fourtet, La Dominique, Faugères, Fleur Cardinale, Grand Mayne, La Gaffelière, Grand Pontet, Larcis-Ducasse, Larmande, Laroze, Magdelaine, La Mondotte, Monbousquet, Moulin St-Georges, Pavie, Pavie-Decesse, Pavie-Macquin, Pipeau, Soutard, La Tour Figeac, and Troplong-Mondot.

Minor appellations

The Médoc appellation has more than 600 vine growers, two-thirds of whom belong to the co-operative system. The wines, uniquely red, are generally fruity and forward. The Haut-Médoc appellation's gravelly soils have the potential to produce red wines of Classed Growth standard, as demonstrated by Château Sociando-Mallet. The wines of the Listrac-Médoc are firm and slightly austere, but the tendency of late has been to plant and use a higher proportion of merlot in order to soften them. Moulis produces cabernet sauvignon-dominated wines that are of a high quality, as well as a light and fruity merlot.

Sweet white wine appellations include Cérons, with rare wines that can be elegant and concentrated; Cadillac, with wines that vary from fresh, fruity, and semisweet to richly botrytized; Loupiac, with consistent, fresh, fruity, and sweet wines; and Ste-Croix-du-Mont, which can produce rich, concentrated wines, but the quality tends to vary—their best is very good indeed.

Premières Côtes de Bordeaux produces some sweet white wine, but the merlot-dominated reds have a bright, aromatic fruit character, and are either firm or lightly structured. A beautiful part of Bordeaux, it is also one of the best value-for-money appellations.

The Entre-Deux-Mers region produces quite a large volume of generic red bordeaux and also a dry white wine produced from sauvignon blanc, sémillon, and muscadelle. The Côtes de Castillon's merlot-based wines are

solid and fruity. Neighboring Bordeaux-Côtes de Francs has some good red and dry white wines. Wines can be a little rustic in the St-Émilion "satellites," and Fronsac and Canon-Fronsac.

The Côtes de Bourg has full-bodied red wines with good color and structure; the best are aged in oak. A little dry white Côtes de Bourg is produced. Premières Côtes de Blaye's wines are less substantial than those of Bourg.

The Bordeaux and Bordeaux Supérieur appellations produce 50 percent of the region's wine. Quality varies, and styles range from light and fruity wines to richer, oak-aged offerings. Red wine is the main product.

The vineyards at Château Loudenne in the Médoc appellation, a distinctively rural appellation with a mix of soil types.

The Southwest

The vineyards of southwestern France stretch from the edge of Sauternes in Bordeaux to Toulouse in the southeast and down to the Spanish border. The area encompasses the Atlantic-influenced mesoclimates of the Dordogne and the Landes, the warmer river gorges of the Cevennes, and the sheltered valleys of the Pyrenean foothills. There are around 30 appellations in all, mostly in isolated pockets of vineyards. The region produces some distinctive wines, often using grape varieties found nowhere else. Among the local white varieties are the petit manseng and gros manseng of Jurançon; the petit courbu from Irouléguy, Jurançon, and Pacherenc du Vic Bilh; the mauzac from Gaillac; and the loin-de-l'œil, also from Gaillac.

Sheep are farmed for milk to make cheeses that are a fine match for the region's wines.

The reds include duras from Gaillac; fer servadou, found in Madiran, Côtes de St-Mont, and Irouléguy. The once-rare tannat is the leading variety in Madiran. Malbec is the most significant variety in Cahors.

The Bordeaux "satellites"

These areas lie close to the Bordeaux vineyards, grow a similar mix of grape varieties, and make comparable wines that often represent better value than their Bordeaux equivalents. The whites are made principally from sémillon, sauvignon blanc, and a little muscadelle; the reds are normally a blend of merlot, cabernet sauvignon, and cabernet franc. Pécharmant's reds are some of the best in the region and age well, while Bergerac's standard has improved considerably. Côtes de Montravel, Haut-Montravel, Saussignac, and Monbazillac are sweet-wine appellations; the best Monbazillac is a rich, honeyed mouthful.

Montravel is mainly for dry whites as is the Côte de Duras, both places are best suited to dry whites, in particular sauvignon blanc. Most of the Côtes du Marmandais's production is red. Buzet's production is dominated by red wines; the remainder is white and rosé.

The Garonne

Winemaking on the northernmost tributary of the Garonne, the Lot, centers on Cahors, an area once known for its "black wine." Although Cahors produces some light, easy-drinking red wines, the best producers favor concentrated, powerful fare that needs time in oak and then bottle. Farther up the Lot Valley, the Aveyron department produces powerful, rustic reds,

Producers
1 Château de Bachen
2 Domaine Brana
3 Alain Brumont
4 Domaine Cauhapé
5 Domaine de Mouréou
6 Plaimont Cooperative
7 LaTour de Gendres
8 Château de Triguedina
9 Clos Uroulat

NORTH

20 miles
(32 kilometers)

The climate tends to be mild and wet in the winegrowing regions near the southwest coast of France.

mainly from fer servadou. North of Toulouse, the Côtes du Frontonnais appellation uses négrette, a red variety of grape, which is blended with syrah, gamay, cabernet franc, cabernet sauvignon, malbec, and mauzac. The wines range from soft and light to those that need two or three years' aging. Northwest of Frontonnais, Côtes du Brulhois and Lavilledieu produce mainly red wines. To the east lies Gaillac, a curiously amorphous appellation that produces an enormous array of styles from a wide range of grapes.

The Landes, Gascogne, and the Pays Basque

This area is home to some of the most dynamic producers in all of Southwest of France. The best of the wines, particularly those from Madiran, are powerful and robust.

Tursan produces mainly red or rosé; the white is made from baroque, which is found only in Tursan. To the southeast lie Madiran, a red-wine appellation, and the much smaller dry- and sweet-wine appellation of Pacherenc. The

chief red grape here is tannat, a decidedly robust and tannic variety that is capable of producing complex, powerful wines; these need around a decade of aging. Grapes include arrufiac, petit and gros manseng, bordelais, sauvignon, and sémillon. In Côtes de St-Mont the reds are made mainly from tannat but they are considerably softer than Madiran's.

The best from Jurançon is among the country's most elegant and complex whites. It is made from three varieties: petit manseng, gros manseng, and petit courbu (gros manseng is the chief variety used.) While traditionally this is a sweet wine, a dry wine—jurançon sec—was created in the middle of the nineteenth century. Both styles of jurançon can age well.

The reds and rosés of the small Pyrenean appellation of Irouléguy are made from cabernet franc, cabernet sauvignon, and tannat. They tend to be less muscular versions of madiran, best after several years' aging. The whites are made from petit courbu, and gros and petit manseng, and are usually crisp and lemony.

There is much lush farmland in southwestern France, and the vineyards occupy the less fertile pockets.

Producers

DOMAINE BRANA, IROULÉGUY *Established* 1985 *Owners* Brana family *Vineyard area* 54 acres (22 ha)

When Étienne Brana died in 1992, his son Jean took over the winemaking, and his daughter Martine became the distiller. Both red and white irouléguy are made. The red is a blend of cabernet franc, cabernet sauvignon, and tannat, and is aged in oak for 12 months. The white is made from petit courbu and gros manseng.

CHÂTEAU DE TRIGUEDINA, CAHORS *Established* 1830 *Owners* Baldès family *Vineyard area* 99 acres (40 ha)

The vineyards here are planted on gravel with merlot, tannat, and auxerrois. The wines, made by Jean-Luc Baldès, are among the best in Cahors. Prince Probus comes from old vines and is aged in new oak. Deep-colored when young, its concentration and power usually require a good five years in bottle.

DOMAINE CAUHAPÉ, JURANÇON *Established* 1980 *Owner* Henri Ramonteau *Vineyard area* 62 acres (25 ha)

Henri Ramonteau has done much to raise the international profile of Jurançon with his excellent range. There are four dry whites: three from 100 percent gros manseng and one from 100 percent petit manseng fermented in new oak. The sweet-wine range is headed by Noblesse de Petit Manseng and Quintessence, which are made exclusively from petit manseng, and the Vieilles Vignes, which is half petit manseng and half gros manseng.

CHÂTEAU DE BACHEN, VDQS TURSAN *Established* 1988 *Owner* Michel Guérard *Vineyard area* 42 acres (17 ha)

Chef Michel Guérard bought Château de Bachen in 1983, built an impressive winery in Palladian style and produced his first vintage in 1988. The wines include an unoaked Château de Bachen and the Baron de Bachen, which is fermented and aged in new oak. The latter is more concentrated, and complex, and benefits from two to three years in bottle. The former should be drunk young and goes well with shellfish.

PLAIMONT COOPERATIVE, MADIRAN *Established* 1970 *Owner* Plaimont Producers *Vineyard area* NA

This cooperative in the Adour Valley has done much, under the leadership of André Dubosc, to develop both VDQS Côtes de St-Mont and VDP des Côtes de Gascogne, and to help local growers. It was Dubosc who foresaw the decline of Armagnac and realized that Gascogne could yield easy-drinking, everyday white wines. The Plaimont range includes some Madiran, but it's the red Côtes de St-Monts that offer the greatest interest and value, particularly the top of the range, Château de Sabrezan.

DOMAINE DE MOURÉOU, MADIRAN *Established* 1968 *Owner* Patrick Ducournau *Vineyard area* 35 acres (14 ha)

Patrick Ducournau makes elegant, powerful, and well-balanced wines, especially Chapelle Lenclos, which is made from pure tannat and ages well—at least ten to fifteen years after good vintages. He is best known as the inventor of the micro-oxygenation system. Initially developed to help soften tannat's powerful tannins, it is being used increasingly to soften and round out wines without using costly barrels.

LA TOUR DE GENDRES, BERGERAC *Established* NA *Owner* SCEA de Conti *Vineyard area* 100 acres (40 ha)

Luc de Conti's vineyards are run mainly on organic principles. The white wines range from La Tour de Gendres, a good-value, pure sémillon, to Moulin des Dames, a blend of sémillon and sauvignon, and the rich, barrel-fermented Anthologia, which is mainly sauvignon blanc and always expensive. The red wines include La Gloire de Mon Père, which is chiefly merlot, and Moulin des Dames, a blend of cabernet sauvignon, cabernet franc, and merlot.

CLOS UROULAT, JURANÇON *Established* 1983 *Owner* C. Hours *Vineyard area* 18.5 acres (7.5 ha)

Charles Hours makes just two wines: Cuvée Marie (a jurançon sec) and the sweet Clos Uroulat; both fermented in barrel. The vineyard is planted with petit courbu and the two mansengs, and yields are kept low, which explains the concentration and complexity that supports a thrilling purity of flavor in all Hours's wines.

Other producers of note in the Southwest include Alain Brumont (Madiran) and Domaine Brana (Irouléguy).

The peaks of the Pyrenees in the distance as seen from Massat, with parallel ranges between.

Languedoc-Roussillon

Situated between the Rhône delta and the Spanish border at Banyuls, Languedoc-Roussillon is the world's largest wine region. After 150 years devoted to producing mainly cheap red table wine made principally from alicante boucher and aramon, there has been a recent shift toward Mediterranean specialties and major international varietals.

Roussillon is dominated by the Pyrenees and its vineyards are located mainly in narrow valleys. In contrast, Languedoc's vines are planted largely on the broad coastal plains. Languedoc-Roussillon has a Mediterranean climate, with most of its rain falling in winter and very little occurring between the beginning of May and mid-August. The plains of Languedoc are the hottest and most arid areas of France.

Generally, Languedoc-Roussillon remains best suited to the production of red wines, as well as rosés for summer drinking; the whites tend to lack acidity and freshness.

History

Along with those of Provence, the vineyards of Languedoc-Roussillon are the oldest in France. Vines were first planted here by the Greeks near Narbonne during the fifth century BC. During the eighteenth and early nineteenth centuries, the area had a reputation for quality wine, most of which came from the *coteaux*, or hillsides, where the soils are poorer and the temperatures more moderate than elsewhere in the region.

With the arrival of industry—and thirsty workers—in the nineteenth century, Languedoc was in an ideal position to supply northern France with plentiful cheap red wine—known as *le gros rouge*. The focus on these wines continued until the late twentieth century. As the yields were high, the wine was usually thin and had to be bolstered by more full-bodied reds from Algeria.

Various changes in French lifestyle during the 1970s caused the demand for cheap red wine to collapse; a trend that has continued. By 1998, per capita consumption of wine in France had declined to around 16 gallons (60 l), from around 30 gallons (112 l) in 1970.

Producers
1 Domaine Cazes
2 Mas de Daumas Gassac
3 Daniel and Patricia Domergue
4 Château des Estanilles
5 Domaine Ferrer-Ribière
6 Domaine Gauby
7 Domaine de l'Hortus
8 Mas Jullien
9 Domaine de la Rectorie
10 Cave du Sieur d'Arques
11 Val d'Orbieu-Listel
12 Château de la Voulte-Gasparets

Corbiéres was promoted to appellation status in 1985, one of six red-wine appellations in Languedoc-Roussillon.

Vines and wines

Over the last 15 years, there has been a dramatic move toward higher quality wine and also a shift to international varieties, which include cabernet sauvignon, chardonnay, merlot, and syrah.

On the *coteaux*, new grape varieties, mainly from the Rhône, such as mourvèdre, vermentino, grenache, syrah, and viognier, have been planted for use as flavor boosters *(cépages améliora-teurs)* in blends. The great potential of the *coteaux* has, however, been realized over the past decade, with producers now turning out wines of concentra-tion and character, often interwoven with the scents—especially rosemary and thyme—of the region's characteristic vegetation, the scrubby *garrigue*.

Notable wine-producing regions on the hill-sides include the Pic St-Loup, some 15 miles (25 km) north of Montpellier; the schistose hills of Faugères; and nearby St-Chinian. To the west, significant areas include the terraces of the Minervois, which overlook the valley of the Aude, and the vineyards of the dramatically var-ied Corbières region, which extends from the shores of the Mediterranean to the gentle slopes of the Aude Valley and upward into the moun-tains. Another important area is the coastal bluff of La Clape, which is close to Narbonne.

Appellations

Most of the appellation wines are red and tend to be blends chosen from grenache, carignan, mourvèdre, syrah, and occasionally cinsault. Although appellation restrictions have limited the excessive planting of cabernet sauvignon, chardonnay, and merlot, they have, at the same time, prevented growers from experimen-ting with different varieties of grapes.

Roussillon is also noted for its fortified wines, known locally as *vins doux naturels*; however, the sweetness is not natural but is due to the addition of pure alcohol. Among the most impor-tant fortified-wine appellations are Rivesaltes and

> *Drink wine, drink poetry, drink virtue.*
>
> Attributed to
> **CHARLES BAUDELAIRE**
> (1821–1867)

The Castle of Puilaurens in the rugged escarpments of Corbières has a long and interesting history.

Muscat de Rivesaltes; however, Banyuls is the best known. At one time, the production of various proprietary brands of aperitif, such as Dubonnet, was a significant activity.

Producers

CAVE DU SIEUR D'ARQUES, LIMOUX, LANGUEDOC   *Established* 1946 *Owner* Cooperative of 500 members *Vineyard area* 12,350 acres (5,000 ha)

Sieur d'Arques makes around 90 percent of the wine produced in the Limoux area. It offers a wide range of varietal *vin de pays* from chardonnay, chenin, mauzac, cabernet sauvignon, and merlot. It also produces a barrel-fermented Toques et Clochers Chardonnay, as well as individual-vineyard, barrel-fermented AC Limoux chardonnays. In addition, it makes 90 percent of all sparkling blanquette de limoux and crémant de limoux, plus some small quantities of *méthode ancestrale* sparkling wine.

DOMAINE CAZES, RIVESALTES, ROUSSILLON   *Established* NA *Owners* André and Bernard Cazes *Vineyard area* 395 acres (160 ha)

This estate has recently begun converting its entire vineyard to the biodynamic system. Once this is completed, the estate may be the largest biodynamic winemaker in the world. It currently produces 20 different wines, ranging from *vins de pays* through Côtes du Roussillon and Côtes du Roussillon Villages to some very fine *vins doux naturels*. Aimé Cazes, their top fortified wine, is made from grenache blanc and is aged for more than 20 years before release. Although it is a *vin de pays*, Le Credo is the estate's top red; it is made from a blend of merlot, cabernet sauvignon, and syrah.

DOMAINE DE L'HORTUS, COTEAUX DU LANGUEDOC (PIC ST-LOUP), LANGUEDOC   *Established* 1981 *Owner* Jean Orliac *Vineyard area* 74 acres (30 ha)

Jean Orliac is among the top producers in the Pic St-Loup. He and his wife, Marie-Thérèse, have vineyards mainly planted with mourvèdre, syrah, and grenache. The Cuvée Classique, a blend of these three red varieties, is matured in stainless steel vats, whereas the Grande Cuvée is made from mourvèdre and syrah, and spends 15 months or so in new oak. Orliac also makes a promising barrel-fermented white (Grande Cuvée), a blend of chardonnay and viognier. Pic St-Loup's high-altitude makes it well suited to white-wine production.

DOMAINE GAUBY, CÔTES DU ROUSSILLON VILLAGES, ROUSSILLON   *Established* NA *Owner* Gérard Gauby *Vineyard area* 87 acres (35 ha)

Run on organic principles, these vineyards' wines have softened since the early 1990s, allowing the fruit to come to the fore. The pick of the range are a powerful Côtes de Roussillon Villages; the white Cuvée Centenaire, a rich wine displaying fruit and honey flavors, made from grenache blanc; and La Muntada, made from syrah. Most Gauby whites are now designated *vin de pays* as they invariably exceed the low 12.5 percent limit on alcohol content set for Côtes du Roussillon.

DOMAINE DE LA RECTORIE, COLLIOURE AND BANYULS, ROUSSILLON *Established* NA *Owners* Marc and Thierry Parcé *Vineyard area* 54 acres (22 ha)

Marc and Thierry Parcé are well established as this appellation's top winemakers. Their Banyuls Cuvée Parcé Frères can be enjoyed young, but the impressive Collioure will repay long aging. The Cuvée Leon Parcé, which is aged in oak for 18 months, has a robust structure and also ages well. An outstanding *vin de pays*, Cuvée l'Argile, is made from grenache gris.

MAS DE DAUMAS GASSAC, VDP DE L'HÉRAULT, LANGUEDOC *Established* 1974 *Owners* Aimé and Véronique Guibert *Vineyard area* 87 acres (35 ha)

It was only when the special qualities of their soil were pointed out to Aimé and Véronique Guibert that they decided to plant vines, producing their first vintage in 1978. The red is mainly cabernet sauvignon, malbec, merlot, and syrah; the white is mainly viognier, chardonnay, and muscat. Collaborating with the local cooperative they produce ranges of cheaper wines sold under names such as Figaro and Terrasses de Guilheim.

Other producers in this region are Val d'Orbieu-Listel, Mas Jullien, Daniel and Patricia Domergue, Ferrer-Ribière, des Estanilles, and de la Voulte-Gasparets.

Right: *The region's arid, gravelly soils are ideal for growing vines.* Below: *Minerve, in the Minervois appellation, is on the River Cesse.*

Provence

Provence is France's oldest wine region and one of the country's prettiest places. For years its mainly rosé wines had a merely playful reputation, which began in the 1930s with the advent of paid leave in France—producers suddenly had droves of undemanding sundrenched vacationers, happy to be there and ready to drink any light fare. And that's what the locals served them.

It's only in the last two decades that producers felt the need to improve standards—with excellent results. Without sacrificing any of their characteristic freshness, the rosés (which make up 75 percent of production) have gained a gastronomic legitimacy—most notably within the context of high-tone Provençal cuisine, but also as accompaniments to East Asian dishes.

Warm summers and relatively mild winters provide good conditions for grape-growing. But there are many nuances, for Provence is a disparate region. In the Alpine foothills winters can be tough. However, the region's summers can be very hot, particularly in the inland areas, though nearer the coast, the torrid conditions are softened by moist sea breezes.

Provence's *terroirs* are also varied: though mainly limestone and arid, they range from the terraced slopes overlooking the sea at Bandol and Cassis to the Var uplands, where the pebbly soil is colored red by iron oxide.

Wines and vines

While Provençal wines remain fun, these days they display far greater depth, substance, and consistency. Besides fresh, fruity rosé, the region also offers dry, aromatic whites from areas such as Cassis, and elegant, powerful reds, capable of long aging, from Bandol. The range of quality produce is now huge, as is the permitted range of grape varieties. Across the region, the main rosé

Producers
1 Domaine de la Bastide Neuve
2 Mas de Cadenet
3 Domaines Ott
4 Château de Pibarnon
5 Domaine Rabiéga
6 Château Roubine
7 Domaine St-André-de-Figuière
8 Châteaux Elie Sumeire
9 Domaine de Trévallon
10 Château Vignelaure

Bandol exemplifies the diversity of Provence: vineyards climb up mountains near the sea.

and red grape varieties are grenache, mourvèdre, cinsault, carignan, the local tibouren, and syrah. Of late, cabernet sauvignon has also crept in. White wine, which makes up 5 percent of the total, comes mainly from clairette, ugni blanc, the wonderfully aromatic rolle, bourboulenc, sémillon, and sauvignon.

Producers

DOMAINES OTT, CÔTES DE PROVENCE
Established 1912 *Owners* Ott family *Vineyard area* 420 acres (170 ha)

In 1912 Marcel Ott founded one of the region's finest family-run winemaking empires. Later the Otts added the white-producing Clos Mireille (also Côtes de Provence) and Château Romassan in Bandol to the stable, while building an unbeatable reputation for quality and consistency. The rosé, Cœur de Grain, has been their worldwide calling card, and the Blanc de Blancs and Bandol reds justify prices that are somewhat above the Provençal average.

CHÂTEAU DE PIBARNON, BANDOL
Established 1978 *Owners* de St-Victor family *Vineyard area* 111 acres (45 ha)

If Bandol is the most prestigious of Provençal appellations, it's because it is known for red wines, with thanks due to a small group of quality-minded trailblazers keen to restore mourvèdre to primacy. The limestone soils of this estate now harness the power of mourvèdre to produce wines with finesse and structure; they represent an exemplary combination of *terroir*, grape variety and exceptional winemaking. The rosé is powerful, spicy and fresh, and quite the equal of the outstanding reds.

DOMAINE DE TRÉVALLON, LES BAUX-DE-PROVENCE
Established 1973 *Owners* Durrbach family *Vineyard area* 49 acres (20 ha)

Eloi Durrbach fashioned his vineyard from the limestone of the northern Alpilles hills. His idiosyncratic, organic-influenced ideas create rich, tannic, but wonderfully elegant wines that age for years. Made with low-yielding cabernet sauvignon and syrah, fermented for an extended period, and aged for 18–22 months, these are world-class reds. Falling foul of appellation rules, they are sold as *vin de pays*, yet the wines are the undoubted stars of Provence, and expensive.

CHÂTEAU VIGNELAURE, COTEAUX D'AIX-EN-PROVENCE
Established 1995 *Owners* O'Brien family *Vineyard area* 148 acres (60 ha)

This estate has a reputation for bordeaux-tinged reds. These incorporate beautifully balanced cabernet sauvignon, syrah, and grenache, and are barrel-aged for 18 months, creating a concentrated wine that will age splendidly beyond ten years. The headline wine is AC, but, due to their high cabernet content, the other cuvées are classified VDP Côteaux du Verdon. Vignelaure also produces a fine rosé.

Other noteworthy producers in Provence are de la Bastide Neuve, Mas de Cadenet, Rabiéga, St-André-de-Figuière, and Châteaux Elie Sumeire.

The Rhône

The Rhône Valley is an area of classical French rural scenery and industrial sprawl, of steep, stark slopes in the north and generous rolling hills in the south, of the splendor of outstanding estate-grown Châteauneuf-du-Pape and the shame of mass-produced, inferior examples. Wine lovers have been somewhat reticent in embracing this area; their experience is perhaps

The town of Tain lies on the Rhône River, surrounded by a sea of vineyards.

based on that staple of French café life, côtes du rhône. But just taste the finest wines from Châteauneuf and from other appellations such as Côte Rôtie and Hermitage, and see why the

Producers
1 Chapoutier
2 Chave
3 Clape
4 Clusel-Roch
5 Jean-Luc Colombo
6 Yves Cuilleron
7 Delas Frères
8 Pierre Dumazet
9 Bernard Faurie
10 Jean-Michel Gerin
11 Alain Graillot
12 Jean-Louis Grippat
13 Guigal
14 Paul Jaboulet Aîné
15 Jean-Paul &
   Jean-Luc Jamet
16 André Perret
17 René Rostaing
18 Marc Sorrel
19 Georges Vernay
20 Noel Verset
21 François Villard
22 Alain Voge
23 Château de Beaucastel
24 Henri Bonneau
25 Les Cailloux
26 Domaine de la
   Charbonnière
27 Clos des Papes
28 Domaine Font de Michelle
29 Château Fortia
30 Domaine Gramenon
31 Domaine de la Janasse
32 Domaine de Marcoux
33 Domaine de la Mordorée
34 Château de la Nerthe
35 Domaine du Pégaü
36 Château Rayas
37 Domaine Santa Duc
38 Domaine de la
   Soumade
39 Tardieu Laurent
40 Domaine du Vieux
   Télégraphe

NORTH

6 miles
(10 kilometers)

Rhône deserves the same recognition as Bordeaux and Burgundy. Indeed, at its best, the Rhône offers the authority and longevity of the former with the sensual pleasures of the latter, and usually undercuts both in price.

From a winemaking point of view, the region known as the Rhône begins in eastern central France near Vienne to the south of Lyon and then spreads southward toward the Mediterranean, finishing in a rather sprawling fashion around Avignon. The region splits conveniently into two distinct subregions. The northern Rhône is home to red wines of power and elegance made from the syrah grape. Whites are very much in the minority here, but the best, made from viognier, marsanne, and rousanne, can be every bit as compelling as the reds. In the southern Rhône, too, red wines vastly outnumber whites, although grenache is the principal variety. In general the whites do not approach the quality of the reds, although this is the home of France's best and most famous *vin doux naturel*, Muscat de Beaumes de Venise.

No flying saucers

In 1954, the wine producers issued an extraordinary decree, which was translated by John Livingstone-Learmonth in his book, *The Wines of the Rhône* (Faber & Faber, 1992) as follows:

"Article 1. The flying overhead, landing and taking off of aeronautical machines called 'flying saucers' or 'flying cigars,' of whatever nationality they may be, is strictly forbidden on the territory of the commune of Châteauneuf-du-Pape."

"Article 2. Any aeronautical machine—'flying saucer' or 'flying cigar'—that lands on the territory of the commune will be immediately taken off to the pound."

History

This area has a very long history of winemaking—its wines were praised by Pliny the Elder in AD 71. It was after Louis XIII (1601–43) visited Tain that hermitage of both colors rose in popularity throughout Europe. The red wine was then also much in demand in Bordeaux for "improving" the local produce, and wines that had been *hermitagé* (hermitaged) sold for higher prices than unblended clarets. In 1787 Thomas Jefferson, then U.S. Ambassador to France, eulogized both red and white hermitage. He praised the red for "its full body" and "exquisite flavor," while he declared the white to be the world's finest. By the end of the nineteenth century, phylloxera caused havoc, then wars and depression meant the Rhône

Winery and vineyards in the Rhône Valley near Tain.

Vines are protected from the ferocity of the winds by being planted in terraces angled to the hillside.

entered the last half of the twentieth century in a pitiful state. However, things did change. In 1978, the first release of Marc Guigal's Côte Rôtie La Landonne, arguably the finest of the company's stunning trio of single-vineyard wines, set new standards for the Rhône and established it as a fully fledged fine wine region.

Since then there have been other new winemakers of excellence, such as the Chapoutiers, who have produced excellent prestige cuvées. Improved techniques and the additional number of winemakers in the area are likely to see the southern Rhône continue to rise in prominence.

Landscape and climate

The vine-growing regions in the northern sector are generally cooler, wetter, and steeper than those of the southern sector, the *Méridionale*. Indeed, the only common factors in the two regions are the river and the often vicious winds which rip branches from vines, so trees are often planted as windbreaks; however, the winds also dry the vines and protect them from spring frosts. The climate in the north is continental and the best sites, such as those in Côte Rôtie and Hermitage, are steep slopes angled south or southeast and often overlooking the river so that the vines

benefit from reflected as well as direct heat. In the warmer southern region, some of the vineyards face south to avoid too much heat.

Viticulture

Producers fall roughly into three different camps. Traditionalists do things as they have always been done, modernists use the latest gizmos and techniques, and pragmatists weigh up the pros and cons of each approach and use what they think will work best for them. They all agree that the lower the yields in the vineyards, the better the quality of the wine.

Stainless steel, old wooden vats, and concrete are all used for fermenting syrah in the north, the choice being a personal preference on the part of the producer. Fermentation temperatures are generally high, while total maceration times vary from a few days to up to three weeks after fermentation has stopped. Traditional southern producers follow a similar method, but others prefer to put some or all of the fruit through carbonic maceration, which produces lighter and fruitier wines.

Traditionalists age their wines in large, old barrels; modernists often prefer new oak, although relatively few do so. Commercial pressures often mean that wines are bottled earlier than a producer would prefer. Also, while quantities produced in most northern Rhône cellars allow wines to be bottled in just one batch, this is not

Above: *Parts of the Rhône have granite subsoils, which retain heat and thus promote ripening.* Right: *Red and white hermitage, both produced by the Chapoutier winery.*

the case at many southern *domaines*, where some wines are still bottled to order over a period of many months. This practice, which sees huge variation between bottles, is becoming less prevalent.

Advances in vinification technology have had a particularly beneficial effect on Rhône white wines. Dull, heavy, oversulfured, and downright faulty whites are disappearing. Some producers now choose to make different batches of wine and blend them. So a fresh, aromatic, fruity portion that has been fermented at a low temperature in stainless steel might be blended with a barrel-fermented and aged cuvée that has less fruitiness but greater weight and more complex, nutty flavors.

A wax-patching dish, which is used to repair the wax lining of tanks.

Northern producers

CHAPOUTIER　*Established* 1808　*Owners* Chapoutier family　*Vineyard area* 173 acres (70 ha)

The extensive Chapoutier family domaines are biodynamically farmed, and the cuvées made here—Ermitage Le Pavillon (red), Hermitage Cuvée de l'Orée (white), St-Joseph Les Granits (red and white), Crozes-Hermitage Les Varonniers (red), Côte Rôtie La Mordorée, and Châteauneuf-du-Pape Barbe Rac—are each among the top half-dozen wines made in each appellation. The regular releases from Côtes du Rhône and Côtes du Ventoux levels upward are also reliably good.

DELAS FRÈRES　*Established* 1835　*Owner* Louis Roderer　*Vineyard area* 35 acres (14 ha)

With Jacques Grange (ex-Chapoutier and Colombo) in charge of the cellars, there has been a much-

Left: *An oak barrel sealed with a glass bung.* Below: *A vineyard in Rasteau, one of the 16 villages in the Côtes du Rhône appellation.*

needed surge in quality here. Hermitage Les Bessards remains the finest wine, but whereas it used to be necessary to choose carefully from the rest of the range, everything is now of a high standard.

CHAVE　*Established* 1481　*Owners* Gérard and Jean-Louis Chave　*Vineyard area* 37 acres (15 ha)

Chave makes exemplary hermitage, both red and white, with each being capable of lasting for 20 years or longer. Since 1990, good vintages have seen a small parcel of the wine being given a sojourn in new oak and the result is the superb but rare Cuvée Cathelin. There are also small quantities of a ripe, supple St-Joseph and, from the 1997 vintage onward, rather larger amounts of a distinctly affordable Côtes du Rhône called Mon Cœur.

RENÉ ROSTAING　*Established* 1971　*Owner* René Rostaing　*Vineyard area* 20 acres (8 ha)

René Rostaing's Côte Rôties are now beginning to get the attention they deserve. From a selection of vineyards, which includes vines more than 80 years old, he makes four cuvées: regular, Côte Blonde, La Viallière, and La Landonne—all richly fruited and supple. Rostaing also produces small amounts of fine condrieu.

MARC SORREL　*Established* 1928　*Owner* Marc Sorrel　*Vineyard area* 10 acres (4 ha)

Marc Sorrel makes fine and underrated hermitage, as well as some delicious crozes-hermitage. The top red is the dense, sweet Hermitage Le Gréal, made from a mixture of fruit from the Le Méal and Les Greffieux vineyards. The top white is the powerful, alcoholic, and long-lived, 100 percent marsanne Hermitage Les Rocoules.

Vineyards near Tain, in the Rhône Valley, where a visit by Louis XIII caused a boom in hermitage sales in Europe.

GUIGAL *Established* 1946 *Owner* Marcel Guigal
Vineyard area 35 acres (14 ha)

The Côte Rôties are fine wines with high prices. La Mouline has the most viognier and is the lightest and most perfumed, La Turque has more muscle, and La Landonne is the massive tannic monster built for the very long haul. The less pricey Côte Brune et Blonde cuvée is a lovely wine. Château d'Ampuis cuvée sits in between. From holdings in Condrieu comes delicious wine, with the partly barrel-fermented and aged La Doriane cuvée ranking as one of the stars.

GEORGES VERNAY *Established* 1953 *Owner* Christine Vernay *Vineyard area* 40 acres (16 ha)

This is the reference point for condrieu. The aim is to accentuate viognier's peach and apricot characters, so the harvest is late. Stainless steel and oak are used for fermentating and aging. A regular cuvée is bottled when young, but the two top wines, Les Chaillées de l'Enfer (The Terraces of Hell) and Coteau de Vernon, spend extra time in cask on their lees. Both emerge in fat, aromatic splendor, and drink well for up to five years.

PAUL JABOULET AÎNÉ *Established* 1834 *Owner* Jaboulet family *Vineyard area* 260 acres (105 ha)

This company's monumental Hermitage La Chapelle is a selection of the best of the vintage from Jaboulet's holdings in Hermitage. The other stars are the Crozes-Hermitage from Domaine de Thalabert—"poor man's La Chapelle," as some call it—and the Domaine St-Pierre Cornas.

Other northern producers are Clape, Pierre Dumazet, Clusel-Roch, Jean-Luc Colombo, Yves Cuilleron, Delas Frères, Bernard Faurie, Jean-Michel Gerin, Alain Graillot, Jean-Louis Grippat, Jean-Paul and Jean-Luc Jamet, André Perret, Noel Verset, François Villard, and Alain Voge.

Southern producers

HENRI BONNEAU   *Established* 12 generations ago
Owner Henri Bonneau   *Vineyard area* 15 acres (6 ha)

Old grenache vines and low yields are just two of the factors that make this one of the best addresses for fans of Châteauneuf, but Henri Bonneau is not likely to divulge the other secrets of his huge, sumptuous, and long-lived wines. For a fabulous tasting begin with the (far from) basic cuvée then work up through the Cuvée Marie Beurrier to the stupendous Réserve des Célestins.

DOMAINE DE LA CHARBONNIÈRE   *Established* 1912   *Owner* M. Maret   *Vineyard area* 54 acres (22 ha)

Michel Maret sprang to prominence in the 1990s for his ripe, herby Châteauneufs. Mourvèdre plays a prominent part—as much as 25 percent—in most of his wines, although the finest cuvée, the Vieilles Vignes, is mostly grenache. The *domaine* also makes fine Vacqueyras.

TARDIEU LAURENT   *Established* 1996   *Owner* Michel Tardieu   *Vineyard area* None

This joint venture of Dominique Laurent and Michel Tardieu is based in Lourmarin in the southern Rhône, although the company sources wine from throughout the Rhône Valley. Quantities are small but the quality is high, as are the prices. The Côtes du Rhône Cuvée Guy Louis is an admirable introduction to a fine range.

Tavel is a rosé-only district; it makes juicy, fresh wines.

DOMAINE FONT DE MICHELLE   *Established* 1950
Owners Jean and Michel Gonnet   *Vineyard area* 74 acres (30 ha)

Jean and Michel Gonnet make a crisp, fruity white and a modern-style, smoky, spicy red with cherry and berry flavors. In homage to their father, they make Cuvée Étienne Gonnet, the red a deliciously aromatic and full-bodied wine, the white fleshy and perhaps slightly overoaked.

CHÂTEAU FORTIA   *Established* Eighteenth century
Owner Baron Le Roy de Boiseaumarie   *Vineyard area* 67 acres (27 ha)

It was Baron Pierre Le Roy de Boiseaumarie of Château Fortia who in 1923 drew up the rules that eventually developed into France's system of *appellation contrôlée*. Since 1994, his grandson Bruno, with Jean-Luc Colombo, has been making ripe, concentrated, but supple wines.

DOMAINE GRAMENON   *Established* 1979
Owners Philippe and Michèle Laurent   *Vineyard area* 54 acres (22 ha)

Philippe Laurent is one of the finest producers of Côtes du Rhône. Several red cuvées are made, all of them rich, concentrated, and far superior to the average Châteauneuf-du-Pape. The finest are Les Ceps Centenaires (from a 100-year-old grenache vineyard) and Cuvée des Laurentides (grenache plus 30 percent syrah). Gramenon recently introduced a late-harvest Cuvée Pascal and a full-bodied white, heavy with viognier.

DOMAINE DE MARCOUX   *Established* Thirteenth century   *Owner* SCEA Armenier   *Vineyard area* 45 acres (18 ha)

Philippe Armenier runs this estate on biodynamic viticulture principles. The old vines and low yields give his wines great intensity of spicy, plummy, blackcurrant-and-cherry flavors, even in less than favorable vintages. The Vieilles Vignes cuvée is spectacularly good, while the white, in which the fleshy roussanne makes its presence felt, is also excellent.

The Château des Fines Roches, in Châteauneuf-du-Pape appellation.

DOMAINE DU PÉGAÜ
Established Late seventeenth century *Owners* Paul and Laurence Feraud *Vineyard area* 45 acres (18 ha)

Paul and Laurence Feraud make traditional Châteauneuf from scattered vineyards. The reds are fermented and aged in large old oak barrels. These thick, spicy, fruity wines need eight years to show their best and will drink well for at least a decade after that. New wood is used with some rich, waxy, grenache blanc-based white.

CHÂTEAU RAYAS   *Established* 1890
Owner Emmanuel Reynaud *Vineyard area* 30 acres (12 ha)

A policy of miserly yields and almost 100 percent grenache established the sweet and stylish Rayas in the top league of Châteauneufs. Pignan, from a separate vineyard, is a fine wine, and cheaper; the two côtes du rhônes from Domaine Fon salette, one a blend of 50 percent grenache with mourvèdre and syrah, the other a thick, smoky, long-lived 100 percent syrah, are also relative bargains.

DOMAINE SANTA DUC   *Established* NA *Owner* Yves Gras *Vineyard area* 47 acres (19 ha)

Old vines, low yields, and ultraripe fruit result in wines with powerful structures and fruit flavors; they need several years in bottle to soften. In good vintages, Santa Duc produces a Cuvée Prestige des Hautes Garrigues which spends time in new oak and contains a high proportion of mourvèdre. Bargain hunters should look for the stylish Côtes du Rhône.

Wines from southern producer Domaine de la Janasse.

DOMAINE DE LA SOUMADE   *Established* 1979
Owner André Romero *Vineyard area* 64 acres (26 ha)

André Romero makes two cuvées of *vin doux naturel*, but it is his three Côtes du Rhône-Villages reds that really merit attention. The basic wine is soft and friendly and is best drunk in the first five years of its life, whereas the Cuvée Prestige is more serious, full-bodied, and slightly leathery. The top wine is Cuvée Confiance, a wonderfully juicy blend of ancient grenache with about 20 percent syrah.

DOMAINE DU VIEUX TÉLÉGRAPHE
Established 1900 *Owners* Daniel and Frédéric Brunier *Vineyard area* 178 acres (72 ha)

This estate produces one of the more restrained Châteauneufs, a wine with lovely cherry and raspberry fruit infused with the aromas of Provençal herbs. The 1993 vintage saw a new second label, Vieux Mas des Papes; a prestige cuvée, Hippolyte, appeared in 1994. Vieux Télégraphe, a white, is a fresh, floral wine best drunk young.

Other Southern Rhône producers are Les Cailloux, Clos des Papes, Domaines de la Janasse and de la Mordorée, and Châteaux de Beaucastel and de la Nerthe.

Beaujolais

From the gluggable, tooth-staining *nouveau* wines dispatched to the far reaches of the globe each November, to the serious, cellarworthy selections from the region's best *crus*, Beaujolais wines are, almost without exception, red, soft, fruit-driven, and light—truly, wines with a universal appeal.

On a cusp between the cold north and the sunny Mediterranean, and classified as a part of Burgundy, Beaujolais' wines are vastly different. Indeed, Beaujolais first distinguished itself from Burgundy in the late fourteenth century by specializing in wine made mainly from gamay. This affordable quaff soon found favor with the thrifty Lyonnais. By the mid-twentieth century, it had seduced the Parisians; then it won over the British, Americans, Japanese, and Europeans. Today, Germany is the leading importer, followed by Switzerland and Japan.

Beaujolais is the Burgundy region's largest producer, most originating from the flatter

The town of Beaujeu was founded in the tenth century, and is the town for which Beaujolais is named.

southern half and sold most often as beaujolais nouveau. The northern half is particularly hilly, with granite-based subsoils and easy-draining sandy topsoils, on which gamay grapes thrive. Its climate is generally temperate and sunny. Thirty-nine communes, or villages, in the north qualify for the superior Beaujolais-Villages appellation, and an additional ten communes are singled out as *crus*. These *crus* are considered the jewels of the region.

Wines and vines

Ninety-eight percent of Beaujolais is planted with gamay noir à jus blanc, a gamay grape not grown elsewhere. Two percent is planted with chardonnay, used mainly for beaujolais blanc. Aligoté is also allowed, but rarely planted.

Beaujolais is a good introduction to red wines. Fans of whites and rosés enjoy this fruity, smooth, silky, perfumed wine, especially when drunk chilled. Beaujolais nouveau is the best known (but the least impressive)—it has to be drunk young. Beaujolais-villages can be good and keeps for up to two years.

The most characterful wines are from the *crus*. The ten *crus* show how differing *terroirs* alter the character of similar wines: Chiroubles is delicate,

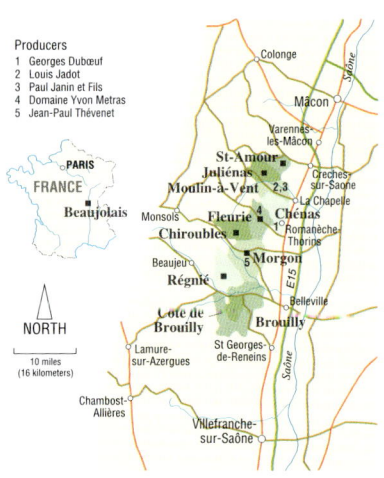

Brouilly is full-flavored, Côte-de-Brouilly is earthy, Julienas has wild aromatics, Fleurie is elegant and full-bodied, St-Amour is less fruity, Chenas is ageworthy, and Morgon and Moulin-à-Vent are powerful, solid, and ageworthy. Regnie is still establishing its identity. After three to five years, the top *crus* take on the characteristics of well-aged softer Rhine or Cotes de Beaune wines.

Producers

GEORGES DUBŒUF   *Established* 1964
Owners Georges Dubœuf and family
Vineyard area NA

The king of Beaujolais, Georges Dubœuf works with over 600 growers to produce a dizzying array of wines that are always around, affordable, and reliable. His *cru* bottlings are top of their class; the Morgon, for example, is lean and juicy with cranberry and licorice flavors, becoming softer and more subtle after three to four years in bottle.

DOMAINE YVON METRAS   *Established* NA
Owner Yvon Metras *Vineyard area* 3.75 acres (1.5 ha)

Metras' vineyard is known locally as Grille Midi, or "roasting at midday," a reference to its sunny location. It produces inky, concentrated Fleurie, which is rarely chaptalized and shows floral, raspberry, and cherry flavors and a lush texture, with enough acid and tannins for aging. Metras belongs to a group of growers known as the Gang of Four, which follows organic principles and avoids using sulfur or yeast during fermentation.

LOUIS JADOT   *Established* 1859 *Owner* Kobrand *Vineyard area* NA

For many, the wines of Jacques Lardière are the first taste of Burgundy; they are good value and reliable. Lardière's passion comes through in the Château des Jacques' Moulin-à-Vent—it has great intensity of fruit when young and ages superbly. His trusty Beaujolais-Villages should be on the required drinking list of every aspiring connoisseur.

Above: *The church in Fleurie village occupies a prominent position amid local vineyards.* Right: *After three to five years in bottle, top* cru *wines become seamless, rich, and velvety, and display distinctive earthy characters.*

PAUL JANIN ET FILS   *Established* 1925
Owners Paul Janin and family *Vineyard area* 25 acres acres (10 ha)

Janin's vineyard, Domaine des Vignes du Tremblay, is on granite-based hillsides in Moulin-à-Vent and was planted by his grandparents; it is now farmed biodynamically. The wine is bold and characterful: after four to five years it displays aromas and flavors of incense, cigar box, cranberries, and orange rind; a lithe, soft texture; and a long finish.

JEAN-PAUL THÉVENET   *Established* 1870
Owners J. Thévenet *Vineyard area* 13 acres (5 ha)
Jean-Paul Thévenet makes two Morgon cuvées: Tradition and Vieilles Vignes. The latter is made from 70-year-old vines and aged in oak for six to eight months. Intense, cedary, and grapey when young, it is more elegant after two or three years.

Burgundy

Burgundy produces some of the greatest red and white wines of the world. It is a region steeped in tradition, yet is equipped with modern research stations. The word itself is tremendously evocative, suggesting a deep red color (though many of the wines are a light, bright cherry red). It conjures images of stone cellars, small villages dominated by churches, and peasants working among the vines. The wines of Burgundy can be the most majestic of all—a resurgence of quality is particularly noticeable in the region's red wines.

Burgundy was once a great independent duchy, nearly a separate kingdom, that stretched from the foothills of the Alps all the way to Flanders. Today, it is a province of France, where it is known as Bourgogne. It is to some of the smaller towns, such as Beaune and Nuits-St-Georges, and certain large villages, that the studious wine seeker must go. Beaune is the capital of vinous Burgundy, with scores of wine shops, cafés, restaurants, and museums, as well as the medieval grandeur of the Hôtel Dieu. For all

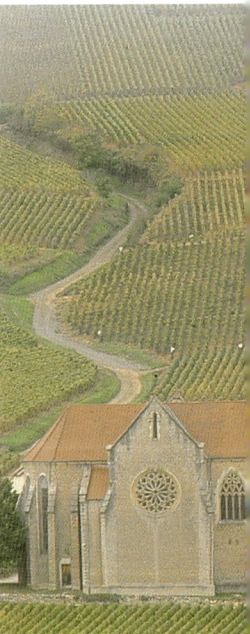

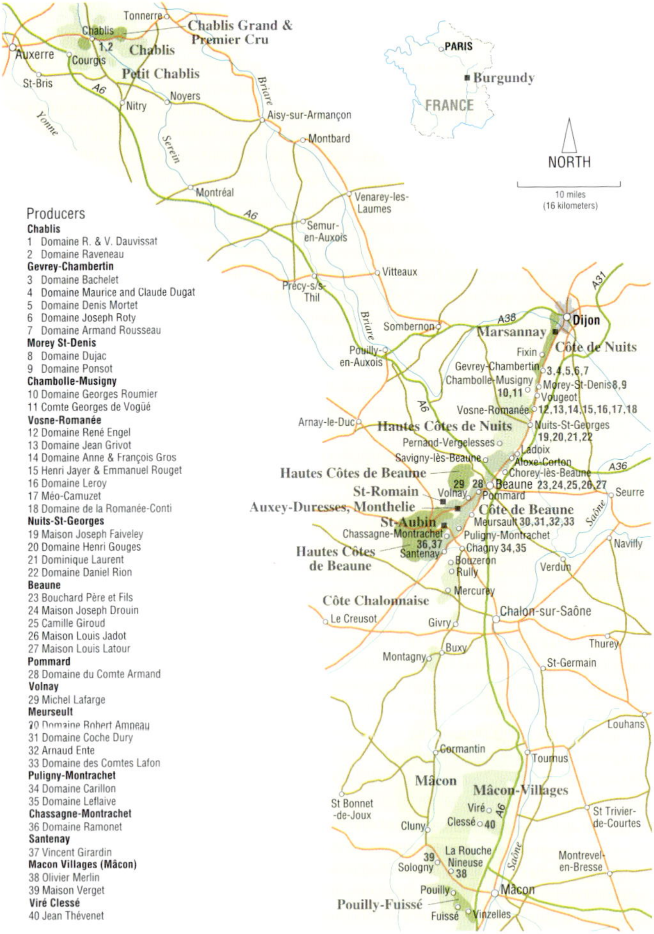
Producers
Chablis
1 Domaine R. & V. Dauvissat
2 Domaine Raveneau
Gevrey-Chambertin
3 Domaine Bachelet
4 Domaine Maurice and Claude Dugat
5 Domaine Denis Mortet
6 Domaine Joseph Roty
7 Domaine Armand Rousseau
Morey St-Denis
8 Domaine Dujac
9 Domaine Ponsot
Chambolle-Musigny
10 Domaine Georges Roumier
11 Comte Georges de Vogüé
Vosne-Romanée
12 Domaine René Engel
13 Domaine Jean Grivot
14 Domaine Anne & François Gros
15 Henri Jayer & Emmanuel Rouget
16 Domaine Leroy
17 Méo-Camuzet
18 Domaine de la Romanée-Conti
Nuits-St-Georges
19 Maison Joseph Faiveley
20 Domaine Henri Gouges
21 Dominique Laurent
22 Domaine Daniel Rion
Beaune
23 Bouchard Père et Fils
24 Maison Joseph Drouin
25 Camille Giroud
26 Maison Louis Jadot
27 Maison Louis Latour
Pommard
28 Domaine du Comte Armand
Volnay
29 Michel Lafarge
Meursault
30 Domaine Robert Ampeau
31 Domaine Coche Dury
32 Arnaud Ente
33 Domaine des Comtes Lafon
Puligny-Montrachet
34 Domaine Carillon
35 Domaine Leflaive
Chassagne-Montrachet
36 Domaine Ramonet
Santenay
37 Vincent Girardin
Macon Villages (Mâcon)
38 Olivier Merlin
39 Maison Verget
Viré Clessé
40 Jean Thévenet
PARIS
Burgundy
FRANCE
NORTH
10 miles
(16 kilometers)
Tonnerre
Chablis Grand & Premier Cru
Chablis
1,2
Auxerre
Courgis
Petit Chablis
St-Bris
A6
Nitry
Noyers
Yonne
Serein
Briare
Aisy-sur-Armançon
Montbard
Montréal
Venarey-les-Laumes
Semur-en-Auxois
Vitteaux
Précy-s/s-Thil
Sombernon
Pouilly-en-Auxois
A38
A31
Dijon
Marsannay
Côte de Nuits
Fixin
Gevrey-Chambertin 3,4,5,6,7
Chambolle-Musigny 10,11
Morey-St-Denis 8,9
Vougeot
Vosne-Romanée 12,13,14,15,16,17,18
Arnay-le-Duc
Hautes Côtes de Nuits
Nuits-St-Georges 19,20,21,22
Pernand-Vergelesses
Ladoix
Savigny-lès-Beaune
Aloxe-Corton
Chorey-lès-Beaune
A36
Hautes Côtes de Beaune
29 28
Beaune 23,24,25,26,27
St-Romain
Volnay
Pommard
Seurre
Auxey-Duresses, Monthelie
Côte de Beaune
St-Aubin
Meursault 30,31,32,33
Chassagne-Montrachet
Puligny-Montrachet
36,37
Santenay
Hautes Côtes de Beaune
Chagny 34,35
Navilly
Bouzeron
Rully
Verdun
Saône
Mercurey
Côte Chalonnaise
Le Creusot
Chalon-sur-Saône
Givry
Thurey
Buxy
Montagny
St-Germain
Louhans
Cormantin
Tournus
Mâcon
Mâcon-Villages
St Bonnet -de-Joux
Viré
Clessé 40
St Trivier-de-Courtes
Cluny
La Rouche Nineuse
39
38
Sologny
Montrevel-en-Bresse
Pouilly
Mâcon
Pouilly-Fuissé
Fuissé
Vinzelles

Mist shrouds the vineyards surrounding the village of Fuissé in the Mâconnais.

its pageantry, Burgundy remains a proud rural area where vineyards seldom come up for sale. Producers owe their fortunes to the soil.

Landscape and climate

Located in eastern central France, Burgundy has a generally continental climate, with cold winters, warm summers, and short falls. Overall, the temperature is cooler than in maritime Bordeaux, so Burgundy is very much at the northern limit of red-wine-producing regions.

Most of Burgundy is underpinned by limestone and some of the best soils for winemaking are the Kimmeridgian limestones found in Chablis and the oolitic limestones of the Côte d'Or. The best vineyards of the Mâconnais are found where Bajocian and Bathonian limestone crop up.

Burgundy is the region that best exemplifies the French concept of *terroir*, and it is fascinating to sample the difference between one vineyard and another only 50 yards (46 m) away. Besides

Burgundy is home to numerous cooperages offering a wide choice of barrel types.

soil, the wine's flavor is determined by such factors as the vineyard's exposure to the sun, its slope, aspect, lay of the land, and drainage—all these variables play a part in creating a wine even before human intervention, in the form of varying viticultural practices, further shapes the style.

Vines and wines

The two great grapes of Burgundy are chardonnay for white wines and pinot noir for reds, both of which have an affinity for the local limestone soils. Chardonnay is certainly the most sought-after grape in the world, and it is native to Burgundy. It has many advantages: it is relatively easy to grow, can set a reasonable crop without obvious detriment to quality, ripens more often than not, produces a full-bodied wine that appeals to both experts and beginners alike, and it can be made in a variety of different styles.

The Yonne accounts for just under a third of Burgundy's whites, most of which is chablis. The Saône et Loire, which incorporates the Côte Chalonnaise and the Mâconnais, produces over half the whites. The most famous part of Burgundy, the Côte d'Or, represents only 15 percent of white wine production, but it supplies the best quality—Puligny-Montrachet, Chassagne-Montrachet, Corton-Charlemagne, and Meursault make Burgundy's great white wines.

Wanted: ethereal, perfumed, and silky

Great red burgundy seduces with its perfumed, floral aromatics, silky mouthfeel, and ethereal character. Once so seduced, one is set on a lifetime search for the ultimate expression of the pinot noir grape. A difficult quest, as only the better sites and best producers regularly deliver this ideal of beauty, and even then, not always. Great vintages make the hunt easier, though the fragmentation of growers and producers (some having just two rows of vines) makes the hunt challenging at best. Here's where specialty knowledge on the part of one's wine merchant can save the consumer time, money, and disappointment. Ethereal red burgundy is usually worth the hefty price. Insipid, charmless red burgundy, acquired from a lesser producer, though still at substantial cost, can be a terrible disappointment. Yet, the lifetime of seduction and hunting continues.

Other white grapes are also used in Burgundy, and the most important of these is aligoté, which is traditionally used to make a light, tart wine that is served by the *pichet* (jug) in cafés. This wine is light and tart, with a little too much acidity for its body to be of any interest except as a refreshing, lowish-alcohol drink.

After chardonnay, the most significant white-wine grapes are members of the pinot family, particularly pinot gris and pinot blanc. These are mutations of the original red grape (pinot noir).

Pinot noir is much more difficult to grow than chardonnay and, although Burgundy is generally thought to be ideal for this grape, even here success is not guaranteed. Because pinot skins are relatively thin, tannin generally plays a lesser part in burgundy's ability to age than acidity. Certain years do have high tannin levels but

Chablis is a historic town in the department of the Yonne, in Burgundy.

in some instances the fruit never comes into balance with the dryness of the tannin. Only some vintages offer the perfect combination of rich, fully ripe fruit and a decent structure for long-term aging.

Since a wine's color is in part derived from the grape's skin, red burgundy tends to be pale. Winemakers who macerate for maximum color often also extract coarser tannins.

The hallmark of great pinot noir is its beguiling fragrance, which, when the wines are young, covers a whole register of red fruits, from cherries of different sorts through red currants to raspberries, strawberries, and plums. As the wines age, the details of the fragrance emerge. At Premier Cru level or above, it should be multilayered: a wonderful bouquet should slowly unfold, its core of fruit edged by a decadent leafy, gamey, or truffley aroma of decay. Above all, there should be a long, graceful, and lingering finish.

The most important of the minor red grapes of Burgundy are gamay and césar. César is mostly used to add color; gamay was more significant but is losing ground.

Viticulture and winemaking

The vineyards of Burgundy are quite densely planted. Vines are always grafted onto rootstocks, and there are many examples of vineyards with 60- or 80-year-old vines in fruitful production.

Viticultural practices tend to vary. The traditional method was to spray chemically against weeds, pests, and diseases while adding fertilizer, but many growers have switched to organic methods. A handful of estates, including some of

the region's flagship names (Lafon, Leflaive, and Leroy), have espoused biodynamic principles.

The harvest takes place between mid-September and early October, varying with the area. After harvest, the white grapes are pressed, left overnight to settle (a process known in French as *débourbage*), then run off into tanks or barrels for fermentation. Throughout the region, white wines are still allowed to ferment using natural yeasts. Most cellars are warmed slightly to encourage fermentation. In the last few years, most producers have returned to the formerly standard practice of lees stirring (*bâtonnage*), which nourishes the wine, fleshes it out a bit, and ensures that the natural antioxidant function of the yeast cells acts on all the wine. White wines almost always undergo malolactic fermentation, then the wines are racked and left on fine lees in barrel or tank until bottling.

Red grapes may be lightly sulfured when they leave the vineyard, and in warm years they may

A vineyard worker trimming chardonnay vines following the annual harvest.

need to be cooled on arrival at the cellar so that the juice can macerate on the skins for a few days before fermentation begins. Fermentation usually takes place in open-topped vats and is accompanied by regular punching down (*pigeage*). The

Vineyards in the Côte de Beaune appellation.

The first *négociants*, or merchant houses, were established in the eighteenth century. The leading *négociants* sell Burgundian wines made with fruit from their own vineyards, and with grapes and wine bought from other suppliers.

Appellations

Almost all the vineyards of Burgundy fall within *appellation contrôlée* regulations. At the bottom level are the generic appellations— Bourgogne Blanc and Rouge, Bourgogne Aligoté and Passetoutgrains, Hautes Côtes de Nuits and Côtes de Beaune, and Mâcon. At the next level are the communal or village appellations, which include such famous names as Gevrey-Chambertin and Puligny-Montrachet. Excepting the Mâconnais district, the best vineyards of each village are classifieds as Premiers Crus. The very best vineyards are classified as Grand Cru. However, the status of any given wine depends on the potential quality of the patch of vineyard from which it came. Appellation laws also specify where vines can be planted, which grape varieties are allowed, how they must be pruned, what yields are permitted, and minimum sugar levels.

wine remains in vat for fermentation and maceration for between one and four weeks; it is then run off into barrel, where malolactic fermentation takes place, for further maturation. One racking is performed after the malolactic fermentation; another if the wine needs subsequent aeration. Barrels vary in age and provenance—lesser red wines go into older barrels.

Growers, cooperatives, and merchants

The label on a bottle of burgundy gives the name of the producer but you may have to dig a little deeper to find out if the wine has come from an individual grower, a cooperative, or a merchant (*négociant*). Growers' wines are normally identified by words such as *propriétaire-récoltant* (owner-grower) or *mise en bouteilles au domaine* (bottled at the estate), whereas a merchant's wines usually bear the words *négociant-éleveur*. Wines from cooperatives are sometimes disguised as if they were from individual producers, but normally the label will refer to a *cave cooperative*, *producteurs réunis*, or *groupement de producteurs*.

   Far more burgundy is marketed by cooperatives and *négociants* than by individual growers.

After the vines have shed their leaves in early winter, they are cut back to encourage new growth.

THE YONNE

The most northerly of Burgundy's departments, the Yonne is home to one of the most famous of all white wines, chablis. In Chablis chardonnay grapes give a lean, dry wine. The Yonne is also the logical place in Burgundy for a major production center of sparkling wine. The principal producer in the region, Caves de Bailly, has cellars near the Yonne River, just south of Auxerre.

Bourgogne is in the area surrounding Chablis, where there are scattered vineyards. The best areas are Irancy (for reds), and Côtes d'Auxerre, Epineuil, Coulanges-La-Vineuse, Chitry, and a bit farther afield, Vézelay and Côte St-Jacques (for reds and whites). The village of Chitry is also locally well known for its Bourgogne Aligoté.

Sauvignon-de-St-Bris is the only wine in Burgundy made from sauvignon blanc; the best grower is J.-H. Goisot.

DOMAINE RAVENEAU, CHABLIS *Owner*
Jean-Marie Raveneau *Vineyard area* **20 acres (8 ha)**

Like his father, Jean-Marie Raveneau still uses old barrels to make fascinating, rich, complex chablis from the Grands Crus of Valmur, Les Clos, and Blanchots, and Premiers Crus such as Chapelots and Fôrets. Twenty- or thirty-year-old wines from Raveneau *père* are still fabulous.

Chablis

The key to chablis is its Kimmeridgian soil, a limestone-clay mix, full of tiny marine fossils, which gives the wine its energetic, flinty character. Another, fossil-free, local soil produces wines without the authentic chablis character. There was almost civil war in Chablis in the early 1970s when a group of vignerons set about expanding the appellation to include slopes on this soil. Eventually they won.

Most straight chablis wines can be drunk fairly young, though some producers make them to keep. Premier Cru wines usually benefit from two or three years in bottle. Chablis Grand Cru wines, the highest classification, are powerful and concentrated, and need to be kept for five or more years—not something you usually think of doing with chablis.

A number of other producers in the Yonne are recommended and these include Domaines R. & V. Dauvissat, Adhémar Boudin, Defaix, Droin, Grossot, Laroche, Michel, Picq, and Vocoret, and also the cooperative La Chablisienne.

Looking toward Chablis from the Grande Crus vineyards in Valmur.

CÔTE DE NUITS

Côte de Nuits is one half of the department of the Côte d'Or (the slope of gold), which is somewhat romantically named for the vine-covered escarpment that rises from the valley of the Saône below. The Côte de Beaune is the other half. The Côte de Nuits makes Burgundy's greatest red wines from a variety of villages.

Appellations

Marsannay's reputation was built on its rosé wines, although reds and whites are also produced. The wines of Fixin are much more substantial—deeper in color, with greater depth of fruit and noticeably more tannin. Twelfth-century Cistercian monks identified Vougeot as prime vineyard land; today wines vary widely, from young and unseductive to deep, powerful, and concentrated, with a fairly tannic structure. The wines of Gevrey-Chambertin (one of the famous

Left: *A sign indicates an outer limit of the town of Nuits-St-Georges.*
Below: *Vineyards at Nuits-St-Georges in the Côte de Nuits.*

Burgundy villages) can be among the longest-lived burgundies—deep in color, full-bodied, with fruit sometimes masked by tannin. The pride of Morey St-Denis is the range of Grands Crus; the wines have some of the elegance of chambolle with some of the structure of Gevrey-Chambertin but a touch more rustic.

A typical Chambolle-Musigny is the most elegant wine in Burgundy. The wines tend not to be deep-colored nor especially full-bodied but have an exquisite, lacy delicacy, and a sublime fragrance. Vosne-Romanée wines have a striking elegance on top of a brilliantly concentrated structure, without ever seeming heavy. Village-level Vosne-Romanée is fine, balanced, and attractive quite early; the Grands Crus are exceptionally long-lived. The Grand Cru vineyards of Richebourg make a wonderfully rich, profound wine, and Romanée-St-Vivant yields a wine that is a touch lighter and very stylish. Anne Gros, Grivot, and Méo-Camuzet produce excellent examples of Richebourg; very fine Romanée-St-Vivant can be found *chez* Drouhin and Arnoux. The capital of the Côte de Nuits, Nuits-St-Georges produces wines that are deep-colored, full-bodied, sturdy, and tannic. All are worth aging. Half a dozen *domaines* produce white Nuits-St-Georges. The less-favored communes of the Côte de Nuits use the general label of Côte de Nuits Villages; most produce light, refreshing red wines made for early drinking.

Producers

DOMAINE DENIS MORTET, GEVREY-CHAMBERTIN *Owner* **Denis Mortet** *Vineyard area* **25 acres (10 ha)**

Despite having inherited a *domaine* with a modest reputation, Denis Mortet has risen to fame with his deeply colored,

The historic Clos de Vougeot Grand Cru vineyard has at least 80 registered owners.

quite heavily extracted wines made from a range of village Gevrey-Chambertin vineyards and a tiny bit of Le Chambertin. The most recent vintages indicate that he is searching for a touch more refinement along with the power.

DOMINIQUE LAURENT, NUITS-ST-GEORGES
Owner Dominique Laurent *Vineyard area* None

This former pastry chef turned *mini-négociant* specializes in small batches of red wines sourced from low-yielding, old vines. Laurent is a devotee of new oak, and has been celebrated by some for using what has been described as "200 percent new wood"—meaning that he racks his wine from one new barrel into another brand new one. The wines are certainly concentrated and can be fabulous, but sometimes the taste of the vineyard is lost behind the style of vinification and maturation.

HENRI JAYER & EMMANUEL ROUGET, VOSNE-ROMANÉE
Owner Emmanuel Rouget *Vineyard area* 17 acres (7 ha)

Now in retirement, Henri Jayer became the most famous of all growers for his wonderfully rich, perfumed, and marvellously harmonious red wines. His nephew, Emmanuel Rouget, is his heir both to the vineyards and the style. The wines include Echézeaux, Vosne-Romanée Les Beaumonts, Vosne-Romanée Cros Parentoux, Vosne-Romanée, and Nuits-St-Georges.

DOMAINE DUJAC, MOREY ST-DENIS
Owner Jacques Seysses *Vineyard area* 28 acres (11.5 ha)

Dujac's controversial wines are frequently light in color when young and carry the aroma of the stalks, which are not removed—a rarity. After a few years in bottle, however, a magnificent perfume transcends any youthful awkwardness.

Comte de Vogüe's vineyards in winter: a tiny quantity of very expensive and good white Musigny is made here.

COMTE GEORGES DE VOGÜÉ, CHAMBOLLE-MUSIGNY Owner Baronne de Ladoucette *Vineyard area* 30 acres (12 ha)

This rather impressive *domaine* is a particularly important one in Chambolle-Musigny. It makes grand Le Musigny, Bonnes Mares, Chambolle-Musigny Les Amoureuses, Chambolle-Musigny, and also a little white Musigny. Nowadays the reds have an immense concentration of fruit, which seems to come from the vineyard—there is no sense of overextraction or of coarse use of oak here. Naturally massive, the wines should be kept for many years. Avoid most vintages of the 1970s and 1980s, but even the lesser vintages of the 1990s have been most impressive.

DOMAINE JOSEPH ROTY, GEVREY CHAMBERTIN
Owner Joseph Roty *Vineyard area* 20 acres (8 ha)

Joseph Roty's forceful personality shows through in the character of his wines, which were dark, concentrated and oaky even in the early 1980s, when such a style was rare in Burgundy. Roty's range of single-vineyard Gevrey-Chambertin wines is supplemented by tiny amounts of Griottes-Chambertin, Mazy-Chambertin, and a wonderful Charmes-Chambertin made from very old vines and labelled *très vieilles vignes*.

DOMAINE LEROY, VOSNE-ROMANÉE *Owner* Lalou Bize-Leroy *Vineyard area* 56 acres (22.5 ha)

In 1998, Domaine Leroy purchased Domaine Charles Noellat, which included Richebourg, Romanée-St-Vivant, Clos de Vougeot, Vosne-Romanée Beaumonts, Vosne-Romanée Les Brulées, and Nuits-St-Georges Boudots. More recent acquisitions have added Le Musigny, Le Chambertin, Latricières Chambertin, Clos de la Roche, and Volnay-Santenots. The Leroy estate is run biodynamically with tiny yields; the wines have extraordinary concentration and longevity—and astronomical prices.

MAISON JOSEPH FAIVELEY, NUITS-ST-GEORGES
Owner François Faiveley *Vineyard area* 285 acres (115 ha)

Though technically a *négociant*, Faiveley actually has sufficient vineyards of his own to supply most of the winery's needs. The red wines made here are quite deep in color and sometimes rather tannic, making them a trifle ungainly in their youth, but they are certainly capable of long aging. The range includes a fine selection of Grands Crus, a bevy of Nuits-St-Georges, including the whole production of Clos de la Maréchale, and a major holding of Mercurey in the Côte Chalonnaise. A handful of white wines are also produced here, including Mercurey Blanc and a little rather exquisite Corton-Charlemagne.

MÉO-CAMUZET, VOSNE-ROMANÉE *Owner* Jean and Jean-Nicolas Méo *Vineyard area* 37 acres (15 ha)

This estate produces Corton Clos Rognet, Clos de Vougeot, Richebourg, Vosne-Romanée Cros Parantoux, Vosne-Romanée Les Brulées, Vosne-Romanée Les Chaumes, Nuits-St-Georges Aux Boudots, Nuits-St-Georges Aux Murgers, Vosne-Romanée, and Nuits-St-Georges. The wines have gained great acclaim for their power and structure, although for some people the oak is a little too dominant.

DOMAINE DE LA ROMANÉE-CONTI, VOSNE-ROMANÉE *Owners* de Villaine and Leroy families *Vineyard area* 63 acres (25.5 ha)

This is the grandest *domaine* of them all, making nothing but Grand Cru wines, and the only estate in Burgundy permitted to be named for a single vineyard. The wines are Richebourg, Romanée-St-Vivant, Grands Echézeaux, Echézeaux, and Le Montrachet. Yields are kept low and less-than-perfect grapes are eliminated during the late harvest. Even the most modest of the wines is wonderfully perfumed, silky, and gracious. The top wines have the same delicacy, to which they add a massive, powerful framework that requires years of bottle age to reach perfection.

DOMAINE HENRI GOUGES, NUITS-ST-GEORGES *Owners* Christian and Pierre Gouges *Vineyard area* 36 acres (14.5 ha)

Following a less impressive spell, the grandsons of the original Henri Gouges have carefully nurtured this *domaine* back to the top league. Even now, Gouges wines are not always appreciated because they are made for the long term and sometimes lack youthful appeal. But the superb range of Nuits-St-Georges Premiers Crus, notably Les St-Georges, Vaucrains, Clos des Porrets St-Georges, and Pruliers, will reward long aging. The *domaine* also makes a small quantity of interesting white Nuits-St-Georges from pinot blanc.

DOMAINE DANIEL RION, NUITS-ST-GEORGES *Owners* Patrice Rion and brothers *Vineyard area* 46 acres (18.5 ha)

This is a steadily developing *domaine* situated in Prémeaux, which is near the town of Nuits-St-Georges. It makes comparatively modern, structured wines from Hauts Pruliers, Clos des Argillières, and Vignes Rondes in Nuits-St-Georges, as well as several cuvées of Vosne-Romanée, and some Grand Cru Echézeaux and Clos de Vougeot. In recent years, the quality of the fruit has blossomed, which better supports the wines' firm structures.

There are many other particularly good producers to be found in the prestigious Côte de Nuits region, and those that are highly recommended include the following: Domaines Bachelet, Maurice and Claude Dugat, Armand Rousseau, Ponsot, Georges Roumier, René Engel, Jean Grivot, Anne and François Gros, and Dominique Laurent.

Right: *Burgundy's cool, sunny climate is ideal for growing pinot noir—the thin-skinned grape can be scorched in extreme heat.* Below: *The entrance to one of the many holdings in the historic Clos de Vougeot Grand Cru.*

CÔTE DE BEAUNE

The Côte de Beaune is an excellent source of red wines, although none can match the greatest reds of the Côte de Nuits. The outstanding wines here are the whites from the Montrachet, Meursault, and Corton-Charlemagne vineyards.

Places and Wines

Pernand-Vergelesses, as part of the Grand Cru Corton-Charlegmagne, produces one of Burgundy's most thrilling white wines, and its Premier Cru Les Vergelesses vineyard yields the Côte de Beaune's best red wines. Some reds and whites can be rather angular. The village and Premier Cru wines of Aloxe-Corton are a little expensive for their quality. The local jewels are the Grand Crus Corton-Charlemagne (white) and Corton (mostly red). Savigny-lès-Beaune is a sound bet for good-quality, affordable red burgundy that ages well.

Close Vouget from Domaine Jacques Prieur.

The Côte de Beaune's most elegant wines are produced in Volnay. They lack deep color but are wonderfully perfumed, subtle, and complex; and, despite their appeal when young, can age very well.

Chorey-lès-Beaune mostly produces red consisting of a fruity, Côte-de-Beaune-style burgundy, best drunk quite young. Monthelie reds have a slightly harder edge and not quite the same depth of fruit as Volnay's wines. "Duresses" refers to a certain hardness found in both red and white wines of the village Auxey-Duresses. They are good value only in warm years.

The village of Pernand-Vergelesses is tucked into a side valley off the main slope.

The style of St-Romain's reds and whites also tends to be lean. Maranges produces mostly red wine; it can be deep in color and full of fruit but is usually tannic and somewhat rustic. St-Aubin is best known for its white wines, but makes much fruity, if sometimes lean, red wines.

The capital of winegrowing Burgundy, Beaune is home to most of the major *négociants*. It offers wines that are sound, middle-of-the-road examples of red burgundy. Pommard wines fetch the highest prices in the Côte de Beaune after Corton, despite their relatively high tannin content. These are firm, deep wines that are slow to mature.

The largest great white-wine village of the Côte d'Or, Meursault, offers full-bodied, round, satisfying wine. Mature meursault (five to ten years old) is buttery and nutty. Three of Meursault's Premier Cru vineyards stand out. Genevrières yields wines with a thrilling, racy, mineral quality, abundant finesse, and not too much weight. Charmes has a soft, rich texture. Perrières combines the best of both these two, but outdoes both, approaching Grand Cru in quality. Another of Meursault's great strengths is its village wine.

In Côte de Beaune's Domaine Robert Ampeau, the dead wood is burnt off in fall.

Puligny-Montrachet is the most famous of the Côte de Beaune's white wine villages. The Grand Cru Montrachet vineyard has been considered the most sublime of Burgundy's white-wine vineyards since the early eighteenth century. Only the extraordinarily rich can afford a bottle. The Grand Cru of Chevalier-Montrachet can be impressive. The wines of the various Bâtards are a little more approachable but slightly less fine.

The international fame of Chassagne-Montrachet rests on its white wines. Fine Chassagne-Montrachet has the steely backbone of Puligny-Montrachet and slightly more weight, but lacks the floral character and, often, the elegance. The reds do not come close to the best whites.

Santenay's red wines, while generally full-bodied, tend toward the rustic. White Santenay can be interesting.

Côte de Beaune Villages is a catch-all appellation for red wines coming from 14 villages within the Côte de Beaune. These are either major white-wine producers that also make some red wine, or else villages of lesser fame.

Producers

DOMAINE COCHE DURY, MEURSAULT
Owner Jean-François Coche Dury *Vineyard area* 22 acres (9 ha)

Dury makes hyper-elegant, fine, and exciting Meursault from Les Perrières (Premier Cru), Les Narvaux, and Les Rougeots, among other vineyards, in addition to a tiny amount of Grand Cru Corton-Charlemagne. These wines have a near-perfect delineation of detail and much more power than the attractive floral bouquet would suggest. There are also some increasingly good reds being made here.

MICHEL LAFARGE, VOLNAY   *Owner* Michel Lafarge *Vineyard area* 25 acres (10 ha)

The wines here continue to be the finest in Volnay—perhaps in the Côte de Beaune. They are not overextracted or overoaked, yet are dark in color and intense in flavor. Lafarge produces Beaune Grèves and Pommard Les Pézérolles, plus a fine range of Volnays, topped by a superb Clos des Chênes, a benchmark for Volnay.

DOMAINE LEFLAIVE, PULIGNY-MONTRACHET
Owner Leflaive family *Vineyard area* NA

Great whites are made here—sensual yet refined, concentrated yet appealing—from Le Montrachet, Chevalier-Montrachet, Bâtard-Montrachet,

Bienvenues-Bâtard-Montrachet, Puligny-Montrachet Les Pucelles, Puligny-Montrachet Les Combettes, Puligny-Montrachet Folatières, Puligny-Montrachet Clavoillon, and Puligny-Montrachet. There was a weak period late last century but biodyamic methods have helped the *domaine* return to top form.

VINCENT GIRARDIN, SANTENAY   *Owner*
Vincent Girardin *Vineyard area* NA

Having established a reputation for the quality of his red and white wines, mostly in Santenay, Vincent Girardin has satisfied growing demand by also setting up as a *négociant*. The wines, which are generally oaky but still full of fruit, include an impressive Chassagne-Montrachet.

DOMAINE RAMONET, CHASSAGNE-MONTRACHET   *Owner* Ramonet family
Vineyard area 42 acres (17 ha)

Now run by the late Pierre Ramonet's grandsons, this estate's wines develop outstanding concentration and complexity with bottle age. They include extraordinary whites from Le Montrachet, Bâtard-Montrachet, Bienvenues-Bâtard-Montrachet; Premier Cru Chassagne-Montrachet from Les Ruchottes, Les Caillerets, Les Chaumées and Morgeot; and reds from Premiers Crus Morgeot, Clos de la Boudriotte, and Clos St-Jean.

DOMAINE DU COMTE ARMAND, POMMARD
Owner Comte Armand *Vineyard Area* NA

Comte Armand is noted for its immensely rich, black, tannic Pommard Clos des Epeneaux, to which it has sole rights, and which for a long time was its only wine. Now it has additional red wines from Auxey-Duresses and Volnay, along with a little white wine. The high standards are maintained by new winemaker Benjamin Leroux.

MAISON LOUIS JADOT, BEAUNE   *Owner* Kopf
family *Vineyard area* 148 acres (60 ha)

Maison Louis Jadot makes powerful wines including very good Beaune Clos des Ursules, Beaune Grèves, and Beaune Boucherottes and Corton-Pougets, plus such Grands Crus from the Côte de Nuits as Chambertin Clos de Bèze and Le Musigny. Particularly impressive are the Chevalier-Montrachet Les Demoiselles, Corton-Charlemagne, Chassagne-Montrachet, and, at an inexpensive level, Rully.

Other producers in Côte de Beaune include Maison Louis Latour, Domaine des Comtes Lafon, Bouchard Père et Fils, Maison Joseph Drouhin, Camille Giroud, Domaine Robert Ampeau, Arnaud Ente, and Domaine Carillon.

Beaune's wine cellars form a labyrinth of tunnels covering around 3 acres (1.2 ha).

Limestone soils predominate in the Côte Chalonnaise, and in most of Burgundy.

CÔTE CHALONNAISE

Five villages make up this area south of Chagny, where the escarpment that provides the great wines of the Côte d'Or peters out and the vineyards start to become more fragmented. Both red and white wines are produced here, mostly for early consumption.

Bouzeron is a small village noted for its aligoté, made from the lesser and thinner of the Burgundian white grapes, attractive in its youth for its firm, tangy character. In Rully, the white wines are light and fruity but generally do not age well. The red wines are medium-bodied and rely on fruit rather than structure, yet they can be pleasing. The best and most ageworthy red wines of this region are to be found in Mercurey, though they need a soft hand during vinification; white Mercurey can be quite full-bodied. Givry reds usually have good fruit backed by a reasonably tannic structure. Montagny produces whites that can be brisk and steely rather than soft and round; drink young.

MÂCONNAIS

On the limestone hills west of the city of Mâcon, most of the production is white and inexpensive, save for fashionable Pouilly-Fuissé, and made from chardonnay. Red Mâcon and Mâcon Supérieur are made from the gamay grape, while wines made from pinot noir are labeled Bourgogne Rouge.

The Mâconnais produces mainly white wines.

Wines of Pouilly-Fuissé, the top appellation, are generally rich, full-bodied, heady, and powerful but vary enormously. Most white Mâcon wines are labeled Mâcon Villages. They are mostly inexpensive but unremarkable chardonnay, although some growers may soon produce fine white burgundy. The adjacent villages of Viré and Clessé are known for making some of the richest and most appealing wines. Not all of St-Véran is well-suited to chardonnay, so choose carefully.

Village producer Oliver Merlin has established a reputation as one of the most serious producers of high-quality barrel-aged Mâcon, while Maison Verget makes excellent albeit sometimes expensive wines, though he does an inexpensive Mâcon. Clessé-based Jean Thévenet's specialty is late-picked wines, sometimes botrytis affected, as in the Cuvée Levoutée.

Jura, Savoie, and Bugey

Located on the eastern fringes of France, in the foothills of the Alps, the wine regions of Jura, Savoie, and Bugey are somewhat out on a limb. Yet their isolation is at least in part responsible for the distinctive and intriguing nature of their wines.

Outside of the growing season, Jura producers must protect vines against frost.

JURA

The vineyards of Jura produce one of France's most curious, sought-after wines, the sherry-like *vin jaune* (yellow wine) as well as luscious, sweet *vin de paille* (straw-wine), and dry whites, reds and sparkling wines from both burgundian, and rare, indigenous grape varieties. Today, the industry centers on the town of Arbois, once home to Louis Pasteur, who was significant to the wine industry for his work on fermentation.

Jura is both the name of the department and of the mountain range that straddles France and Switzerland. The landscape is dramatic and gentle and vineyards are sited, sometimes steeply, on the southern and southwestern slopes.

Traditionally, Jura red wines were blends, but today many are single varietals. Poulsard is the most widely planted red grape, followed by pinot noir and trousseau. Producers recommend aging

Vin de paille, a Jura specialty, is made from grapes that have been dried on straw mats.

for all reds for several years. Trousseau provides the most interesting red, displaying structure and almost animal flavors combined with dark red fruits.

Most Jura white winemakers prefer to make wines that have the slightly oxidized or nutty flavors associated with aging in old wood. Wines are usually varietal chardonnays or savagnins, or a blend. Like the reds, whites are sold with at least two years' cellar aging. Crémant du Jura is usually made with chardonnay and is similar to a delicate crémant de bourgogne, the best being creamy and fruity with well-integrated bubbles. Good examples of *vin de paille* rate among the finest sweet wines. *Vin jaune* is the apogee of Jura winemaking; distinctly yellow, dry, and concentrated, with flavors of spice and nuts— it can resemble old dry sherry. It ages well.

Winemaker Alain Baud of Domaine Baud Père et Fils makes a fine Cuvée Tradition; a blend of savagnin and chardonnay, it is a nutty white wine. He also makes two great *vins jaunes*. At Domaine Rolet Père et Fils, in Arbois, the Arbois Trousseau is notable for its powerful structure. The whites are of a traditional style, and the *vin jaune* is exemplary.

SAVOIE AND BUGEY

Savoie wines are inextricably linked with images of snow-capped mountains and wooden chalets. Yet the region's vineyards, on south-facing slopes, are in fact, confined to lower altitudes that rarely have snow. Indeed, some vines enjoy an almost Mediterranean climate, with peach and almond trees thriving in the area.

Bugey, whose vineyards lie west of the River Rhône in the Ain department, is less influenced by alpine weather.

Savoie is planted with 80 percent white grapes, the most important of which is jacquère; its whites are fresh, with a flowery fruitiness, and should be drunk young. Altesse, chasselas, chardonnay, roussanne (known as bougeron here), gringet, and molette are other white varieties. The reds are gamay, pinot noir, and mondeuse. André and Michel Quenard, Chignin, are consistently good producers of chignin bergeron (a local specialty) and other whites and reds.

The best Savoie white is altesse, sold as Roussette de Savoie. This wine is a specialty of Edmond Jacquin et Fils, Jongieux (and their marestel is a concentrated, fruity style balanced by lively acidity). With a similar structure to chardonnay, altesse is made in various styles: with residual sugar, old-oak aging, or dry and fresh with a nutty, fruity character. In Bugey, chardonnay is the most successful white; some is light and fresh, some is vinified in oak.

Savoie's growers plant mainly white grape varieties, with jacquère being the most significant.

Most Savoie reds are simple and fruity, particularly those from gamay and pinot noir. Mondeuse has an earthy flavor, allied with blackberry and blueberry, and a spicy touch not unlike syrah, even when unoaked. Vin du Bugey reds—generally made from gamay, pinot noir, or mondeuse—are light, early-drinking fare.

Sparkling wines are also made in Savoie, especially in Seyssel. In the *cru* of Ayze, gringet provides a more aromatic sparkling wine. Bugey sparklers include *méthode traditionnelle* wines.

Alsace

The Alsatian wine country is a picture-book landscape, and traveling the region's wine route is enchanting. Medieval houses cluster at the base of the hills, and are surrounded by vines that climb up the hillsides. Above the vines, the heavily wooded slopes of the lower Vosges stretch up toward towering peaks.

When you sample Alsatian wines, you get a snapshot of central European history. The bottle is Germanic—tall and fluted; the grapes (riesling, gewürztraminer, and sylvaner) are Germanic as are the surnames (Hugel, Dopff, Humbrecht). Yet the labels are French, and so is the style of the wine.

This is the only part of France that is permitted to plant riesling. Alsace is predominantly a white-wine region—the most important in France, with 32,000 acres (13,000 ha) of vines producing over 140 million bottles annually.

That vast majority of Alsation wines are dry. They may have Germanic grape names, but the sugar in the wonderfully ripe grapes is all converted into alcohol. That means that some of the

Dining table gems

Most consumers underappreciate the wonderful, food-friendly white wines of Alsace. Don't be put off with tall, skinny bottles that conjure images of inexpensive German wines from decades past. Alsace produces French styled wines from, largely, Germanic varieties. Gewürztraminer is the most distinctive with its bold aromatics of roses and lychees. Delightful alone, it is one of the few wines capable of standing up to spicy Asian or fusion cooking. Pinot gris, pinot blanc, and riesling should be at the top of "ABC" (anything but chardonnay) lists as these wines are unoaked, deliver acidity, balance, and flavor, and are complementary to food across the board. Gewürztraminer, riesling, and pinot gris can age beautifully, though they are apt to be found prematurely on the dining table for their grace and flexibility.

wines—gewürztraminer and the tokay pinot gris for example—are relatively high in alcohol, at around 13.5 or 14 percent. Alsatian wines are labelled varietally.

Landscape and climate

Alsace's situation makes it a perfect place for grape growing. Facing east and south across the Rhine toward Germany, the vineyards lie on the leeward side of the Vosges Mountains. This lofty range shields Alsace from the Atlantic weather systems that spread eastward across France. Consequently, Alsace's rainfall is among the lowest in the country; rainclouds can be

Many Alsatian towns have historic houses and wine cellars open for tastings; canal cruising is also an option.

The Trois Châteaux d'Eguisheim crowns the hill above Husseren-les-Châteaux.

seen over the Vosges at almost any time, but they rarely come over the Alsatian vines, which are on the drier, eastern side of the mountains.

The best vineyards are located on the mountainsides, either on the flanks of the steep valleys that run deep into the range or on the gentler slopes that face outward onto the flat, alluvial plain that extends toward the Rhine. The Haut-Rhin (High Rhine), to the south, has higher mountains. These afford greater protection from the worst weather, so it has the finest vineyards—and most picturesque villages. To walk the narrow streets of Riquewihr, Ribeauvillé, Bergheim, or Eguisheim is to experience the charm and quaintness of a medieval world. Colmar, the principal town, has retained its historic quarters, including a cluster of charming canals.

Vines and wines

Alsace grape varieties are divided into two categories: the noble varieties—gewürztraminer, riesling, tokay pinot gris, and muscat—and the lesser varieties. Apart from pinot noir, all are white. Gewürztraminer has brought more fame to the region than any other grape variety. In Alsace, the wine has high alcohol and a distinctive, spicy, full, oily taste. Sometimes it also has a bitter finish, and there is a dryness in even the sweetest examples.

Riesling provides the finest wine in Alsace: bone dry, with a flinty, steely taste, it is usually very fresh and frequently acidic when young, but softens with age, developing into a superb wine.

The Alsatians' favorite wine, tokay pinot gris, is full, rich, soft, and well-balanced, with high acidity, a touch of pepper, moderately high alcohol, and an ability to age over a long period.

Alsace muscat is dry, yet with a honeyed tone; a perfect combination of sweetness and lightness, it is delicious as an aperitif wine but it is rare.

Pinot blanc grapes produce some of the region's most drinkable wines. These are relatively low in alcohol, fresh-tasting, and soft, and have a pleasing touch of acidity and not too pro-

DOMAINE MARCEL DEISS
Established 1949　*Owner* Marcel Deiss　*Vineyard area* 49 acres (20 ha)

Marcel Deiss makes extravagant wines from fine vineyards around Bergheim. His greatest success is his riesling, but he also created the Grand Vin d'Altenberg de Bergheim, a blended wine that encapsulates the vineyard more than the grape.

LÉON BEYER　*Established* 1867
Owners Beyer family　*Vineyard area* 173 acres (70 ha)

Léon Beyer is known for its dry, elegant wines, expressed both in the top Cuvée des Comtes d'Eguisheim and in the Léon Beyer and Réserve ranges. It is also noted for its gewürztraminer and Vendange Tardive wines.

DOMAINE ZIND-HUMBRECHT　*Established* 1620　*Owners* Humbrecht family　*Vineyard area* 99 acres (40 ha)

Wonderful vineyards in some of the best Grands Crus produce a vast range of stunning produce. The style is rich, but never sweet (except for the Vendange Tardive and Sélection des Grains Nobles wines). Possibly the finest wines are those from the Grands Crus of Brand and Hengst, and the Clos St-Urbain in Thann. The estate recently converted to biodynamic methods.

MAISON TRIMBACH　*Established* 1626　*Owners* Trimbach family　*Vineyard area* 65 acres (27 ha)

Taste a classic Alsace riesling at Trimbach: from a basic, pure wine to two superb cuvées: Cuvée Frédéric Émile and the single-vineyard Clos Ste-Hune. There is not a trace of residual sugar in these expensive, rare, and beautifully balanced wines, which demand long aging. Don't overlook the wonderful Gewürztraminer Cuvée des Seigneurs de Ribeaupierre and the Tokay Pinot Gris Réserve Personelle.

Above: The steep slopes of Clos St-Landelin provide Domaine René Muré with superb fruit.
Left: One of the region's most common varieties, gewürz-traminer, gives relatively low yields.

nounced a character. Sylvaner is widely planted in Alsace and produces a neutral, reliable wine that is good for quaffing. It has a smoky, herby taste and a soft, low-acid, fruit flavor.

In Alsace, red and rosé wines are all made from pinot noir and some respectable reds are finally being made. Sparkling whites and some sweeter white styles are also produced.

Producers

DOMAINES SCHLUMBERGER　*Established* 1810
Owners Schlumberger family　*Vineyard area* 346 acres (140 ha)

The largest estate in Alsace, Schlumberger's wines are known for their minerally character, derived from the local soil. The two famous cuvées (Cuvée Christine, a Vendange Tardive, and Cuvée Anne, a Sélection des Grains Nobles) are triumphs, although both tend to be rich and full-bodied rather than sweet.

HUGEL ET FILS   *Established* 1639   *Owners* Hugel family   *Vineyard area* 62 acres (25 ha)

A major name in Alsace, the Hugel family helped shape the region's wine styles. However, while its top wines are still among the best, they are no longer at the very pinnacle of Alsace winemaking. The others are more variable, particularly the varietals named Hommage à Jean Hugel. The Tradition range provides excellent wines, especially the tokay pinot gris and riesling.

KUENTZ-BAS   *Established* 1795   *Owners* Bas and Weber families   *Vineyard area* 41 acres (17 ha)

Based in an attractive, rambling cellar complex, Kuentz-Bas makes some of Alsace's most reliable, appealing wines. The style is rich, often opulent, particularly in the gewürztraminer and the wonderful muscats. The top-range Réserve Personelle wines are especially ageworthy.

DOMAINE RENÉ MURÉ   *Established* 1630   *Owner* René Muré   *Vineyard area* 54 acres (22 ha)

With a 40-acre (16-ha) vineyard of Clos St-Landelin at its heart, René Muré's *domaine* is able to produce some of the most impressive riesling in Alsace and a highly successful pinot noir. Another Muré specialty is the riesling-based Crémant d'Alsace, which successfully retains its aromatic character after bottle aging.

DOMAINE OSTERTAG   *Established* 1966   *Owners* Ostertag family   *Vineyard area* 30 acres (12 ha)

André Ostertag's wines sometimes achieve greatness and sometimes fall flat. Successes include the complex Riesling Grand Cru Moenchberg and the Riesling Fronholz. The tokay pinot gris is made in a dense style, more Burgundian than Alsatian.

Grand Cru vineyards surround the small town of Niedermorschwihr.

DOMAINE WEINBACH   *Established* 1898   *Owners* Madame Théo Faller and daughters   *Vineyard area* 59 acres (24 ha)

Based in a former Capuchin monastery, Colette Faller and her daughters Catherine and Laurence produce a bewildering array of wines. The Cuvée Théo, Cuvée Catherine, and Cuvée Laurence ranges include various late-harvest wines, Sélections des Grains Nobles, and the even more concentrated Quintessence. Dry wines include riesling from the Grand Cru of Schlossberg and the gewürztraminer from the Grand Cru of Furstentum. The concentration and purity of fruit in these wines is the result of severe green harvests and almost organic viticulture.

Other excellent producers to be found in the Alsace region are Dopff au Moulin and Domaines Albert Boxler, Hering, and Meyer-Fonné.

Corsica

Corsican wines have come a long way in a short time. Once predominantly rustic products of a mountainous Mediterranean island, in recent years they have improved significantly, worthy of a 2,500-year viticultural tradition.

Corsican wine benefits from the Mediterranean climate and even the wild, tortuous terrain yields some schistose and limestone. Two-thirds of Corsica's vineyards have been restructured under a replanting program with an emphasis on traditional grapes. The dense, tannic nielluccio (known as sangiovese in Tuscany) and the more supple, sophisticated (and indigenous) sciacarello have reassumed their primacy in Corsican reds and rosés, while vermentino once again characterizes the ample dry whites. Simultaneously, winemaking techniques have developed immeasurably, so that even the more modest wines—which once either descaled the throat or passed down it unnoticed—generally, these days, boast freshness and balance.

The island now produces an improving range of *vins de pays* that are usually honest, consistent, and refreshing. Varietal wines are made from the traditional grapes, plus an interesting range of double-variety wines.

Corsica's appellation structure is complex, reflecting the diversity of its vineyards and terrain. The island's appellation wines include reds that are darkly robust, others that are lighter and spicier, and rosés that marry fruitiness and structure. Whites are in the minority.

Producers

Rosés from producer Clos Capitoro combine sophistication and festive fruitiness, while its red wines, from sciacarello grapes, are lighter in color than others but lack nothing in structure or staying power.

The leading producer in the Figari appellation is Domaine de Tanella. Its Cuvée Alexandra comes in all three colors, all regularly cited among the island's top wines. The red, in which syrah has been added to the two traditional Corsican varieties, is a wine of real breeding; it displays a structured elegance and is at once deeply aromatic and built to last.

Domaine Fuimicicoli produces reds (from sciacarello, nielluccio, and grenache) with spicy elegance, strength, and length, and rosés that demonstrate how intense sciacarello can be. Domaine de Torraccia makes a rich, powerful red from a mixture of (mainly) nielluccio and some sciacarello, without losing finesse or balance, and that will age well.

Corsica's most interesting white wines are made from vermentino, an Italian variety.

Vins de Pays

Introduced in September 1979, the *vin de pays* (VDP) classification added another layer to the pyramid of categories used to define wine quality in France. *Vin de pays*, meaning "country wine," occupies a position above basic *vin de table* but below VDQS and *appellation contrôlée*. Found throughout France, *vin de pays* allows producers more freedom than the appellation rules, and it makes up almost 30 percent of French wine.

Vin de pays areas

In the Loire, neighboring VDP departments have merged to form the regional VDP du Jardin de la France. About 45 percent of its production is white, and most are varietal wines that do not comply with individual appellation restrictions. Aquitaine-Charente includes three zonal denominations; the output is largely white. The Midi-Pyrénées' *vins de pays* produce about 65 percent white wine.

Nearly 80 percent of all *vins de pays* are now produced in Languedoc-Roussillon, where many vineyards are being upgraded. Corsican *vin de pays* is labelled "l'Île de Beauté." Provence-Côte d'Azur uses a wide range of varieties as does the Rhône-Alpes region. Both these produce mostly red, with some rosé and white. The East is the least significant *vin de pays* region.

Producers

Domaine de la Chevalière, VDP d'Oc, Languedoc, has planted chardonnay, roussanne, vermentino, viognier, cabernet sauvignon, merlot and syrah, which will eventually be used for prestige cuvées. Fortant de France, VDP d'Oc,

Languedoc, recognized the potential of varietal wines from the Languedoc. There are three product ranges: an unoaked range, a lightly oaked middle range, and a premium range, Fortant F (chardonnay, cabernet sauvignon, and merlot).

Domaine de Tariquet, VDP Côtes de Gascogne in the Southwest, has the Tariquet range, which runs through crisp dry whites with a colombard base to an attractive and complex chardonnay/sauvignon and a late-harvest gros manseng. The estate also produces Domaine de La Jalousie, Domaine de Plantérieu and Domaine de Rieux, as well as a fine range of armagnacs.

Other noteworthy *vin de pays* producers are Ackerman–Laurance (Loire), Domaine de la Baume (Languedoc), and James Herrick (Languedoc).

Right: *The most successful* vin de pays *abroad have been international varietals from the south.*

Below: *The Rhône uses regional, departmental, and zonal* vin de pays *classifications.*

Germany

Germany

A century ago German wine was as highly prized as the finest Bordeaux. Prestigious merchants' wine lists offered bottles from the top vineyards and villages of Germany—Rüdesheim, Marcobrunn, Piesport—at prices comparable to, and sometimes even higher than, first-growth Bordeaux. Nowadays most people find this hard to believe, a sad reflection on the decline in reputation of German wine as a whole. There remains a following for the high-priced and rare specialties—eiswein and trockenbeeren-auslesen from the finest estates—but no wine-producing country can base a reputation, or indeed an industry, on a relatively small quantity produced in exceptional vintages.

Some of the long-term factors that provoked this slump in reputation will be examined in the sections that follow, but the main reason has been the connivance of the regulatory authorities with the production and promotion of dilute sugary wines of poor quality, which at one time captured a sizeable proportion of the world market for cheap wines, but at a terrible cost to Germany's reputation.

No one should be in any doubt that Germany is fully capable of producing some of the world's great white wines. It has glorious rieslings, stern sylvaners, robust pinot blancs, and exquisite sweet wines. Its mainstay is the versatile riesling grape, which in the eyes of many connoisseurs is the world's greatest white wine grape. No other country or region has been able to replicate the ethereal delicacy, the mouth-watering freshness, and grapiness of a Mosel kabinett from a top estate.

History

The great sweet-wine vintages mark the progress of German wine through the past two centuries: 1893 and 1921 were both outstanding years, and bottles of beerenauslese or trockenbeerenauslese from these vintages still surface at times, or are sold at auction for astronomical sums. Some ancient wines, now as dry and pungent as a venerable madeira, are testimony to the long history of German wine production. In the cellars of Bremen's town hall—for centuries a center of the German wine trade in the north—repose some large old casks containing wine dating back to the seventeenth century. Only a select few are allowed to taste the oldest. In Brauneberg and Piesport are vestiges of

Wine rejoices the heart of man and joy is the mother of all virtues.

JOHANN WOLFGANG VON GOETHE (1749–1832)

Roman wineries and other artifacts, and in other parts of Germany there is archaeological confirmation that vineyards have been present for 2,000 years or more.

German wine has always been expensive, and demand for it during periods of prosperity pre-1914 kept prices buoyant. It also encouraged counterfeiters, just as in France, where the amount of Châteauneuf-du-Pape available before strict regulations were introduced always exceeded the quantity of wine the region could conceivably have produced. Wine laws were introduced in 1901 to combat fraud.

Post World War II, new crossed grape varieties ripened early and were genetically selected to produce high sugar levels—a grape-grower's dream: vast crops of very sweet wines. But being heavy and sickly, a proliferation of wines from these new varieties—such as ortega, optima, bacchus, and siegerrebe—did nothing for the reputation of German sweet wine. Subsequently, advances in viticulture and innovations in winery equipment meant that the taste of quality German sweet wine, traditionally due to incomplete fermentations that left residual sugar in the wine, could be replicated by technology.

In the 1980s and 1990s there was a trend toward greater diversity in the wines of Germany. Dry white wines, even from regions better suited to off-dry or sweet wines, became quite fashionable. Much German red wine, even the highly praised spätburgunders from the Rheingau and Ahr, struck outsiders as thin and weedy, although there were exceptions in ripe vintages. But from the 1980s some good, if

Kloster Eberbach, in the Rheingau, has magnificent twelfth-century cellars.

rarely world-class, red wines, usually from spät-burgunder but also from new varieties like the dornfelder, began to be grown in warmer regions.

The choice of styles today is greater than it would have been a century ago, and the experimentation of the 1980s and 1990s has settled down to a steady exploitation of appropriate grapes in appropriate sites.

Landscape and climate

Good German wine is very site-sensitive, and the nuances of site and microclimate count for much. So certain sites have always been acclaimed as especially fine. Except in the Pfalz and in Baden, the German climate is cool, so every nuance of exposition and climate must be exploited to the maximum. This explains why only certain slopes along the Mosel River's banks are planted with vines; along the opposite side the sunshine is too patchy to allow the grapes to ripen.

With such variations come nuances in taste and structure. In the Middle Mosel, the wines of Graach are usually identifiable as a touch broader and more ample than those from neighboring Wehlen. Within the large Brauneberger Juffer vineyard is a central patch that, it has long been acknowledged, usually provides better wines than the rest of the site: this is the parcel honored with its own name of Brauneberger Juffer-Sonnenuhr.

Germany's marginal or extreme climate means grapes do not always ripen easily. Many red wines could be mistaken for rosés; without some balancing residual sugar, the rieslings of the Saar and Ruwer can be uncompromisingly harsh and tart. The acidity that can be so refreshing and zesty in a well-balanced riesling can be tooth-achingly unpleasant in a riesling made from unripe grapes. The greatest German wines have always been made on its climatic edges, though, and a great vintage gives wines that balance fruitiness and acidity.

Terraced plantings of vines at Oberrotweil, Kaiserstuhl, in Baden, follow contours to reduce soil erosion.

Vines and wines

Although riesling is the most popular wine in Germany, there are other wines of note. Eiswein (ice wine) is a relatively new phenomenon and was a freak of nature until the 1970s, when some estates began leaving parcels of vines untouched in corners of the vineyard that were most prone to frost. Strict regulations dictated the depth and longevity of the frost required before the resulting wine could be classified as eiswein. This style of wine remains fashionable, despite very high production costs.

The more traditional, and indeed more complex, beerenauslese and trockenbeerenauslese are often produced in tiny quantities. They might be poured for honored guests or perhaps conserved for a future generation. Sometimes they are offered at auction where high prices win recognition for the estate. Sylvaner has quite a distinguished pedigree in Germany and is best known as a somewhat earthy, vigorous, dry wine, one that is well

A Bohemian decanter dating from 1840.

Riesling

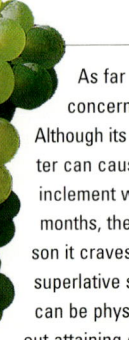

The highly versatile riesling grapes.

As far as Germany is concerned, riesling is king. Although its late-ripening character can cause problems when inclement weather dogs the fall months, the long growing season it craves can yield wines of superlative structure. The grapes can be physiologically ripe without attaining exceptional sugar levels. A great Mosel riesling may have only 7° (or seven percent) of alcohol; a Rheingau or Nahe wine has perhaps 10°. Yet this does not entail any loss of intensity.

As long as yields are kept to a sensible level so that there is no trace of dilution or unripeness, that intensity is provided by the racy acidity allied to the mouthwatering fruitiness of the riesling grape. There is no white variety quite as versatile as riesling. In warmer regions it can produce rich, dry wines of considerable power. The mighty dry rieslings of Alsace and the Wachau in Austria show this to be so, though in some vintages dry rieslings from the Pfalz can come close to matching their power. But the German dry rieslings are more graceful and elegant than those from elsewhere in the world, with the emphasis on finesse, not power.

In the more northerly regions, the wines need some balancing residual sugar. In the Rheingau the estates that formed the Charta Association in the 1970s promoted an off-dry style (known as halbtrocken in German). This wine was intended to be better adapted to consumption with food than the sweeter styles of riesling. Good white wine is all about balance. For example, some rieslings from the Mosel–Saar–Ruwer have surprisingly high levels of residual sugar, yet the wine does not taste especially sweet; this is because of the equally high levels of acidity and extract. The precise balance of any wine is partly the result of the

attributes of the grapes when harvested but is also subject to the choices made by the producer.

Where riesling astonishes most is in its capacity to produce very long-lived and unashamedly sweet wines. It's a risky business, but the top estates will leave grapes on the vine until perilously late in the fall. If they are lucky, the grapes will have shriveled or become botrytized, provoking a concentration of sugar, as well as the production of other chemical compounds such as glycerol. These very late-harvested wines, beerenauslese or trockenbeerenauslese, are so high in sugar that they ferment with difficulty and are often even lower in alcohol than traditional riesling styles. Their acidity is very high too, allowing them to age for decades, becoming gradually more honeyed and unctuous. A great beerenauslesen or trockenbeerenauslesen from a classic vintage, even at 50 or 100 years old, can be a mind-blowing experience, with an infinitely complex range of aromas and flavors. Even a more modest riesling of kabinett quality, if well made, can easily age over 20 years.

Above right: A refractometer is used to test the sugar content of riesling grapes.
Right: The last bottle of riesling from the great 1917 vintage is held at Kloster Eberbach.

suited to accompany food. In southern Germany the pinot varieties do well: spätburgunder (pinot noir), weissburgunder (pinot blanc), and grauer burgunder (pinot gris).

Grauer burgunder is rarely improved by aging in *barriques*, but the German consumer is quite keen on the style. When vinified as a sweet wine, it can give extremely fat, unctuous, figgy wines at beerenauslese and trockenbeerenauslese levels.

In Württemberg, lemberger can make a lively cherryish wine of considerable character. The other common red variety here is trollinger, which produces pallid wines that appeal mostly to local consumers. Pinot meunier, known in Germany as schwarzriesling, is also found in Württemberg and Baden, but as a dry red wine it can be somewhat neutral. There are swathes of portugieser in many southern vineyards; its wine is light, fruity, and innocuous.

With white wines, rieslaner has high acidity and makes brilliant sweet wines that are very close in character to riesling, in regions such as Franken and the Pfalz. Scheurebe yields a some-what grapefruity dry wine, especially in the Pfalz region, and can also make exceedingly good sweet wines.

Chardonnay is a relative newcomer to Germany, but it can give quite good wines in the Pfalz and Baden as long as it is not smothered in new oak.

Some German sparkling wines—such as those from Breuer in the Rheingau, Lindenhof in the Nahe, and Koehler-Ruprecht in the Pfalz, among a number of others—are of very acceptable quality.

The town of Oberrotweil, Kaiserstuhl, in Baden, is surrounded by vineyards.

Viticultural practices

German winemaking procedures are relatively uncontroversial. There is generally near-universal agreement that for varieties such as riesling, müller-thurgau, and sylvaner, *barriques* are anathema. Many traditional estates retain their large oval casks, in which all their wines are fermented and aged. The producers argue that these large casks allow the wine to breathe and mature gracefully without imparting any trace of oakiness. Other producers tend to favor a more reductive approach, and they are more in favor of using stainless steel.

The pinot varieties as well as the red wines benefit from some wood-aging, but the styles of oak-aging vary greatly. In Baden new *barriques* enjoy quite a strong following, sometimes with rather coarse results.

The presence of residual sugar in many German wines means that technical options such as chilling, sterile filtration, or centrifuging are still employed. But dependence on technology is being questioned more these days than it has been in the past, and German wine from top estates is a product of considerable purity.

Mosel–Saar–Ruwer

The Mosel River twists and turns on its leisurely way from Koblenz, heading toward Luxembourg. Vineyards are planted on the best-exposed nearby slatey slopes—and, regrettably, on some flat land stretching away from the river. Despite the size of the region, there is surprising homogeneity in the character of its riesling wines. Although half the vineyards are planted with other varieties, mostly müller-thurgau, the Mosel–Saar–Ruwer is, or should be, pre-eminently riesling territory. Nowhere else in the world does riesling display such razor-sharp intensity of flavor. Although the noble wines from the Rheingau may dispute the claim, many would argue that Mosel rieslings are the finest of all.

The Mosel River itself is divided into the Lower, Middle, and Upper Mosel. The wine heartland lies in the Middle Mosel or Mittelmosel (M-M), where the slatey soils imbue the wines with a characteristic mineral tang. The Lower Mosel has less slate; wines tend to be light and delicate, without the steeliness of the finest rieslings. The Upper Mosel offers sublime sweet rieslings in certain vintages, and müller-thurgau and elbling are often

A 1992 Berncastler Doctor riesling auslese, a classic Mosel wine.

encountered. Most of the estates, especially within the Lower Mosel area, are small; the largest properties were formerly ecclesiastical or educational foundations.

Loading harvested grapes at the Maximin Grünhaus vineyard in the Saar Valley. This estate is renowned for auslesen and eisweins.

MAXIMIN GRÜNHAUS, GRÜNHAUS
Owner Dr. Carl Von Schubert *Vineyard area* 84 acres (34 ha)

This estate is admired within Germany for its dry rieslings, but it is the marvelous auslesen and eisweins that generate the most excitement for everyone else. Von Schubert bottles auslese from individual casks under a rather confusing cask number. The price indicates quality.

FRITZ HAAG, BRAUNEBERG
Owner Wilhelm Haag *Vineyard area* 17 acres (7 ha)

Wilhelm Haag produces some powerful wines of intense flavor and long complex aftertastes. All his best wines come from the Juffer-Sonnenuhr vineyard. The Fritz Haag label has become a guarantee of classic, long-lived riesling. And the sweet wines are sensational.

REICHSGRAF VON KESSELSTATT, TRIER
Owner Annegret Reh-Gartner *Vineyard area* 141 acres (57 ha)

Annegret Reh-Gartner has imposed high standards in the vineyard and winery. Kesselstatt owns vineyards throughout the Mosel–Saar–Ruwer, and wines from Kaseler Nies'chen, Scharzhofberg, Josephshöfer, Piesporter Goldtröpfchen, and Bernkasteler Doctor can be recommended without hesitation.

DR. LOOSEN, BERNKASTEL
Owner Ernst Loosen *Vineyard area* 25 acres (10 ha)

The dynamic Ernst Loosen is focused on quality above all else, ruthlessly cutting yields and harvesting as late as possible. Other estates occasionally surpass Loosen in finesse but few can match the sheer brilliance and concentration of his wines, from the humblest kabinett to his majestic sweet wines.

EGON MÜLLER (SCHARZHOF), WILTINGEN
Owners Egon Müller family *Vineyard area* 20 acres (8 ha)

A legendary estate, distinguished by the astonishing quality of its wines—and astonishing prices. In a beautiful old manor house, the Egon Müllers coax the utmost complexity and refined structure from their incomparable and indestructible sweet wines, although the QbA and kabinett are usually of lesser interest.

J. J. PRÜM, WEHLEN *Owner* Manfred Prüm
Vineyard area 35 acres (14 ha)

Thanks to the gentle prickle of natural carbon dioxide in these wines, they can be deceptively youthful and can age for decades. In great vintages these can be the finest expressions of the Middle Mosel, supremely elegant distillations of the steep slaty soils of the Wehlener Sonnenuhr.

WWE. DR. H. THANISCH–ERBEN THANISCH, BERNKASTEL *Owner* Sofia Thanisch Spier
Vineyard area 15 acres (6 ha)

There are two estates with almost identical names and labels, and this is the better of the two (it sports the VDP logo on its label). It is best known for rich, firm wines of great distinction from the Bernkasteler Doctor vineyard. Buyers pay a handsome premium for the illustrious name.

SELBACH-OSTER, ZELTINGEN *Owner* Johannes Selbach *Vineyard area* 25 acres (10 ha)

All of Johannes Selbach's wines are of good quality, but those from his vineyards in Wehlen, Zeltingen, and Graach are often outstanding. Selbach-Oster demonstrates the high quality of the Zeltingen sites, which can rival those of neighboring Wehlen. The wines are accessible when young, but they age well.

Trittenheim lies along the banks of the Mosel River, in southern Mittelmosel.

ZILLIKEN, SAARBURG *Owner* Hans-Joachim Zilliken *Vineyard area* 25 acres (10 ha)

The cellars are three floors deep, and bottles resting in the lowest level barely age. These wines of great longevity have the steely acidity typical of the Saar, and great concentration of flavor. The wines from Ockfener Bockstein can be very good but the masterpieces come from Saarburger Rausch, notably a breathtaking eiswein.

DR. WEINS-PRÜM, WEHLEN *Owner* Bert Selbach *Vineyard area* 10 acres (4 ha)

Although quite small, the Weins-Prüm estate owns a wide spectrum of vineyards and, in addition to fruity, stylish, and dependable wines from Wehlener Sonnenuhr, there are some succulent sweet wines from Erdener Prälat.

WILLI SCHAEFER, GRAACH *Owner* Willi Schaefer *Vineyard area* 6 acres (2.5 ha)

The outstanding quality of the wines here only became widely recognized in the 1990s. The sweet wines are often the best, marrying grace and elegance with understated power and purity of fruit.

S. A. PRÜM, WEHLEN *Manager* Raimund Prüm *Vineyard area* 25 acres (10 ha)

The wines here are extremely good, especially those from Wehlener Sonnenuhr. The vines are very old, yielding wines of impeccable concentration and fruitiness.

There are many other excellent producers in the Mosel–Saar–Ruwer region; recommended are Christoffel Erben, Von Hövel, Grans-Fassian, Reinhold Haart, Heymann Löwenstein, Karthäuserhof, Heribert Kerpen, Schloss Lieser, Dr. Pauly-Bergweiler, Schloss Saarstein, Max. Ferd. Richter, and Dr. Heinz Wagner.

Left: *The church at Piesport sits on the banks of the Mosel River.*
Right: *A vineyard worker tastes fresh-picked grapes to test them for ripeness and sweetness.*

Nahe

The Nahe, named after a tributary of the Rhine, is one of Germany's more amorphous regions. With its vast geological variation, there is little uniformity of style. Some of the best wines, with fine extract and raciness, come from the volcanic and slatey soils found around Niederhausen and Schlossböckelheim. Other varieties include müller-thurgau, sylvaner, grauer burgunder, and more recent varieties such as kerner. The region has a growing reputation for stunning eiswein and other very sweet styles.

The Nahe's best wines, inevitably, are rieslings, but this variety accounts for less than one third of the area planted. At their best, they have the verve and raciness of good Mosel combined with the weightier structure of the Rheingau. Equally important are some very singular vineyards with remarkable and distinctive soils; when yields are kept low, these vineyards produce wines with a strong personality. All recommended producers are shown on the map below, and some are further detailed next.

Producers
1 Crusius
2 Schlossgut Diel
3 Dönnhoff
4 Emrich-Schönleber
5 Göttelmann
6 Kruger-Rumpf
7 Gutsverwaltung
   Niederhausen-
   Schlossbockelheim

4 miles
(6.5 kilometers)

Plastic sheeting is used to protect riesling grapes from birds in frost-prone corners. These grapes will be made into the stunning eisweins for which Nahe is famous.

CRUSIUS, TRAISEN *Owner* Dr. Peter Crusius
Vineyard area 30 acres (12 ha)

This highly regarded estate's top wine is invariably the riesling from Traiser Bastei, which has a distinctive earthy mineral tone allied to great vivacity and finesse. Almost as fine are the wines from Traiser Rotenfels and from Schlossböckelheimer Felsenberg.

SCHLOSSGUT DIEL, BURG LAYEN *Owner* Armin Diel *Vineyard area* 37 acres (15 ha)

While not abandoning his great fondness for dry wines, Armin Diel has also been making wines in a more classic style from his Dorsheim sites. However, devotees of *barrique*-aged Burgundian varieties will find these here, too. The range is topped by some exceptional but very pricey sweet wines.

DÖNNHOFF, OBERHAUSEN *Owner* Helmut Dönnhoff *Vineyard area* 32 acres (13 ha)

This is the Nahe's most outstanding producer. Some dry wines are produced—pinot blanc and pinot gris as well as riesling—but the glory of this estate is the riesling. These wines show an exceptional balance of fruit and acidity, and develop considerable complexity as they mature. In suitable vintages, Dönnhoff also produces some dazzling sweet wines.

Rheingau

West of the twin cities of Mainz and Wiesbaden, the northern banks of the Rhine are swathed in an almost uninterrupted band of vineyards. The vineyards of Hochheim, just east of Mainz, are also part of the Rheingau.

The Rheingau is quite a small region that has become synonymous with riesling, although around the village of Assmannshausen, spätburgunder (pinot noir) is highly regarded. The region's flagship is the magnificent Kloster Eberbach, buried in the forests just behind the most northerly band of vineyards and long in use as a cultural and educational center. The accessibility of the region from some of Germany's largest and most prosperous cities has made it a focus for gastronomic festivals, which are held in some of the Rheingau's stunning old cellars and monasteries.

JOHANNISHOF, JOHANNISBERG

Owner Johannes Eser *Vineyard area* 44 acres (18 ha)

This property is one of the top estates in Johannisberg. In recent years this estate has expanded by acquiring vineyards in Rüdesheim, which should enhance the quality as well as the quantities of wine available. The style of the wines made here is

A twelfth-century Cistercian monastery houses the wine at Kloster Eberbach, an old winery in the Rheingau.

quite steely, and they benefit from some bottle age before they show at their best.

GEORG BREUER, RÜDESHEIM

Owner Bernhard Breuer *Vineyard area* 57 acres (23 ha)

Bernhard Breuer uses only the names of the top Rüdesheim vineyards on his labels. Anything from less than first-rate sites is bottled as gutsriesling under the estate name. His dry wines are exemplary, never showing harshness or lack of ripeness. And his nobly sweet wines can be extraordinary—and understandably expensive.

AUGUST KESSELER, ASSMANNSHAUSEN

Owner August Kesseler *Vineyard area* 40 acres (16 ha)

Based in the village of Assmannshausen, Kesseler has focused on the red wines that are the mainstay of this area. Indeed, spätburgunder constitutes half the vineyards on this estate. These are not the watery pallid reds that were common here just 20 years ago, but well-structured *barrique*-aged wines that command high prices. Kesseler also makes luscious rieslings from excellent sites in Rüdesheim.

Producers
1 J. B. Becker
2 Georg Breuer
3 Domdechant Werner'sches Weingut
4 Graf von Kanitz
5 Schloss Johannisberg
6 Johannishof
7 August Kesseler
8 Knyphausen
9 Peter Jakob Kuhn
10 Franz Künstler
11 Josef Leitz
12 Schloss Reinhartshausen
13 Balthasar Ress
14 Schloss Vollrads
15 Robert Weil

GERMANY
BERLIN
Rheingau

NORTH

4 miles
(6.5 kilometers)

Schlangenbad
Igstadt
Hofheim
Ranselberg
Rotzheim
Wiesbaden
Breckenheim
Presberg
Rauenthal
Frauenstein
Erbenheim
Wallau
Lorch
Stephanshausen
Eberbach
Kiedrich
Walluf
Delkenheim
Weilbach
Hallgarten
Erbach
Eltville
Massenheim
Niederheimbach
Johannisberg
Hattenheim
Kostheim
Hochheim
Flörsheim
Assmannshausen
Alhausen
Winkel
Oestrich
Heidesheim
Mainz
Biebrich
Rüsselsheim
Rüdesheim
Gelsenheim
A60
Rhine
Weilers
Bingen
Ingelheim
Ginsheim
Waldalgesheim
Gau-Algesheim
Ochenheim
Rheingau
Rhine
Main

Wine auction

Kloster Eberbach, the magnificent twelfth-century Cistercian monastery, has a rich viticultural history as one of the most highly regarded wine estates of the Middle Ages. Now home to the German Wine Academy and Rheingau Wine Society, it hosts the world-renowned *Die Glorige Tage*, a three-day wine auction. *Die Glorige Tage* attracts legions of gourmands and wine industry luminaries such as Michael Broadbent, Jancis Robinson, and Hugh Johnson, who descend upon the abbey to taste, and bid on, charta rieslings and wines with self-imposed restrictions on residual sugar (no more than 3 grams/liter total acidity). There are also blind-tasting elimination rounds for overall quality.

KNYPHAUSEN, ERBACH   *Owner* Gerko Freiherr zu Knyphausen   *Vineyard area* 54 acres (22 ha)

Gerko zu Knyphausen is a charming man, and his ancient home is absolutely beautiful. He produces wines from a range of good sites in Erbach, Kiedrich, and Hattenheim. The wines are not in the very first rank, but are invariably elegant and shapely. These are classic examples of firm Rheingau riesling.

ROBERT WEIL, KIEDRICH
Manager Wilhelm Weil
Vineyard area 131 acres (53 ha)

The vineyards here are outstanding. Wilhelm Weil insists on ripeness levels far above the minimum prescribed by wine laws, so his auslesen are more likely to be declassified beeren-

auslesen. All the wines are good, even the modest kabinett, but the top of the range truly excels, with a simply breathtaking range of nobly sweet, and expensive, wines.

FRANZ KÜNSTLER, HOCHHEIM   *Owner* Gunter Künstler   *Vineyard area* 59 acres (24 ha)

Gunter Künstler ranks with Rheingau's elite producers and is a master of all styles, from dry to ultrasweet. In 1996 he bought the well-known Aschrott estate, also in Hochheim, and expanded his production facilities so he now offers a broader range of wines.

JOSEF LEITZ, RÜDESHEIM   *Owner* Johannes Leitz   *Vineyard area* 15 acres (6 ha)

The use of indigenous yeasts is quite rare among German wine estates—which usually prefer technological certainties to the vagaries of nature—but their use is routine practice at Josef Leitz. Do not discount the splendid potential of the vineyards, which lie in some of the steepest sections of Rüdesheim.

Other excellent producers in the Rheingau are J. B. Becker, Domdechant Werner'sches Weingut, Graf von Kanitz, Schloss Johannisberg, Peter Jakob Kuhn, Schloss Reinhartshausen, Schloss Vollrads, and Balthasar Ress.

In the hills above Winkel, Schloss Vollrads has substantial vineyards and buildings.

Rheinhessen

The vineyards of Rheinhessen cover more than 64,000 acres (26,000 ha) and produce one-quarter of all German wine. The overall quality of wines is distressingly low (bar some from the eastern fringes), and this may be to blame for the decline in Germany's reputation as a great wine-producing country.

Riesling accounts for less than 10 percent of plantings here. About a quarter of the vine-yards are stocked with the often neutral müller-thurgau. Sylvaner, which can deliver very good wines if grown in the right site, is also widely planted. Elsewhere, Rheinhessen is home to the crossings developed to generate high yields of early-ripening grapes (bacchus, kerner, huxelrebe, and many others); some are also frost-resistant, enabling them to be planted in very fertile soils. A small quantity

To enjoy wine . . . what is needed is a sense of smell, a sense of taste, and an eye for color. All else is experience and personal preference.

CYRIL RAY (1908–1991),
Ray on Wine

of somewhat undistinguished red wine is also produced. Yet excellent—and sensibly priced—wine can be found in Rheinhessen. In the north, near Bingen, are some good riesling sites. The most distinctive wines come from the so-called Rheinfront, the string of riverside villages south of Mainz: Nackenheim, Nierstein, and Oppenheim. Sylvaner can be quite delicious here.

Rheinhessen is also the birthplace of Liebfraumilch. Made entirely for export markets, it is produced from müller-thurgau, sylvaner, and kerner, but riesling can also be used in the blend.

For years growers of the Rheinhessen interior made a good living from their overcropped vineyards, but bulk wine prices tumbled in the 1990s

The village of Westhofen sits amid vast vineyards.

and some growers have been losing money, however high their yields. Some of the overproduction disappears into "Euro-blends," but it is increasingly clear that the market for insipid, sugary wine is dwindling.

Villages of the Rheinhessen

Bingen's rieslings bear some resemblance to those from the Rheingau, but they rarely attain the same finesse. Nackenheim's best site is Rothenberg, which is blessed with the zone's famous red soils; Gunderloch is the best-known producer in this Rheinfront village. Nierstein is also famous, but most bottles labeled Nierstein don't contain a drop from this village. Authentic Nierstein riesling or sylvaner can be excellent, so look for the top vineyard names of Oelberg, Brudersberg, Hipping, and Pettental. Another Rheinfront village, Oppen-

Worms, a town marking the southern limit of the Rheinhessen wine region, has an ornate cathedral.

heim, has chalky soils well adapted to riesling, which is well represented here. Only a few of the steepest vineyards are of outstanding quality.

Producers

BALBACH, NIERSTEIN   *Manager/lessee* Fritz Hasselbach   *Vineyard area* 32 acres (13 ha)

Balbach went into a gradual decline in the early 1990s. However, since 1996, lessee Fritz Hasselbach of Gunderloch fame has taken advantage of the excellent vineyards owned by Balbach to revive this property's reputation. Riesling is the dominant variety and he has rightly focused on it.

GUNDERLOCH, NACKENHEIM   *Owner* Fritz Hasselbach   *Vineyard area* 32 acres (13 ha)

Although the estate owns vineyards in Nierstein, its top wines come from the reddish soil of the Nackenheimer Rothenberg site. The standard, off-dry riesling is labeled "Jean-Baptiste" and offers good value, but the top wines are the sweeter styles from Rothenberg. Wines are well-structured and require a few years to open up.

SCHALES, FLÖRSHEIM-DALSHEIM   *Owners* Schales family   *Vineyard area* 119 acres (48 ha)

This estate is typical of the best of the *domaines* inland from the Rhine. The Schales cultivate a huge range of grape varieties and vinify them in many different styles. Although sometimes a bit hit-and-miss, there is good rieslaner and a quite bizarre sparkling eiswein.

Other producers in Rheinhessen that are recommended include Heyl zu Herrnsheim, Keller, Kühling-Gillot, and Sankt Antony.

Pfalz

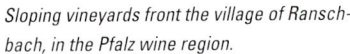

The Pfalz is the largest German wine region after Rheinhessen, which lies to the north. A good deal of mediocre wine is produced in the less-favored localities and for much the same reasons as in Rheinhessen: large vineyards on essentially flat land are planted with high-yielding and early-ripening varieties best suited to bulk wines. Even so, there is a far higher proportion of fine wine made in the Pfalz than in its northern neighbor, and observers presently find it to be the country's most exciting wine region.

The quality heart of the Pfalz lies in the stretch of vineyards just south of Bad Dürkheim, through the villages of Wachenheim, Forst, Deidesheim, and Ruppertsberg. The great estates here are the source of most of the area's greatest wines. Excellent vineyards can also be found just north of Bad Dürkheim in the villages of Kallstadt and Ungstein. Other sectors of the Pfalz are now recognized, notably in the Südliche Weinstrasse in the south around Landau, which are capable of producing wines of high quality, although not all are in the classic riesling mold.

The southern sector in particular is well suited to the classic Burgundian varieties. Chardonnay is permitted as a commercial variety and quite a few estates have planted it. The best reds are spät-burgunder, although the grape is still not as widely planted as portugieser or dornfelder. Portugieser rarely yields wine of much interest or structure and is often vinified as a rosé, but dornfelder can be as enjoyable as a ripe

Vines are trained on wires— this often necessary task is quite labor-intensive.

Beaujolais-type as long as yields are kept under control. There is also a smattering of cabernet sauvignon, but the Pfalz is unsuited to this variety.

Throughout the region riesling combines fruitiness, opulence, and stylishness, especially in its sweeter manifestations.

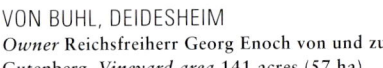
Sloping vineyards front the village of Ranschbach, in the Pfalz wine region.

BASSERMANN-JORDAN, DEIDESHEIM
Owner **Margrit von Bassermann-Jordan**
Vineyard area **104 acres (42 ha)**

Still owned by the founding family after almost three centuries, this grand estate uses only riesling grapes. Although based in Deidesheim, its best vineyards are in Forst and Ruppertsberg. The wines were decidedly dull in the 1980s, but improved after the arrival of a new winemaker.

VON BUHL, DEIDESHEIM
Owner **Reichsfreiherr Georg Enoch von und zu Gutenberg** *Vineyard area* **141 acres (57 ha)**

This estate is at the forefront of Pfalz estates. Winemaker Frank John has produced some dazzling wines, from dry rieslings to sumptuous trockenbeerenauslesen. John's method involves harvesting the fruit later—this ensures high levels of ripeness, but can mean smaller crops.

BÜRKLIN-WOLF, WACHENHEIM *Owner*
Bettina Bürklin-Wolf Guradze *Vineyard area*
235 acres (95 ha)

Bürklin-Wolf's top wines are made by whole-cluster pressing, which delivers cleaner, more aromatic, and more elegant fruit. This large property's dry wines have a following, but its sweeter styles are more popular outside Germany. In exceptional vintages, its nobly sweet wines and eisweins are sensational. Riesling dominates but there are also decent reds made from dornfelder and spätburgunder.

MÜLLER-CATOIR, NEUSTADT *Owner*
Jakob Heinrich Catoir *Vineyard area*
50 acres (20 ha)

Winemaker Hans-Gunter Schwartz
routinely produces exceptional wines.
Riesling is the dominant grape but he
also works his magic with grauer burgunder, muskateller, and scheurebe. His
rieslaner is surely the finest in Germany.
Yields are low, which accounts for
their concentration, but Schwartz's
willingness to trust the wine to make
itself is the key.

PFEFFINGEN, UNGSTEIN *Owner* Doris
Eymael *Vineyard area* 27 acres (11 ha)

As well as rich spicy riesling from Ung-
steiner Herrenberg, this well-regarded
estate produces robust sylvaner and
plump, sappy scheurebe. A little spätburgunder and dornfelder have recently been planted
and these will be *barrique*-aged.

J. L. Wolf 1996 and
1997 Rieslings; the
first vintages under
the management of
Ernst Loosen.

KOEHLER-RUPRECHT, KALLSTADT
Owner Bernd Philippi *Vineyard area* 25 acres (10 ha)

Bernd Philippi, an international wine consultant
as well as a winemaker, is an individualist.
The core of his production remains rieslings
from the splendid Saumagen vineyard,
made in every conceivable style according to the vintage. Powerfully structured
wines, they are capable of great longevity.
Philippi also makes a range of *barrique*
wines, including chardonnay, spätburgunder, and weisser and grauer burgunder,
and his sweet wines—such as the occasional spätburgunder eiswein—can
be extraordinary. To avoid confusion,
barrique wines are sold under the
Philippi label.

Other recommended producers in the
Pfalz region include Friedrich Becker,
Josef Biffar, Christmann, Kurt Darting, Knipser,
Mosbacher, Rebholz, and J. L. Wolf.

Franken

Franken (or Franconia) is a Bavarian region surrounding the stately baroque city of Würzburg. The River Main loops through the region, with most vineyards on steep sites overlooking the river. The soils are varied, but fall into three main types: sandstone, limestone, and marl. These soils influence the varieties planted as well as the flavor and structure of the wines. Franken enjoys an essentially continental climate: winters are cold and prolonged, bringing a risk of spring frosts; summers can be blisteringly hot. Harvesting rarely begins before October and often continues until the end of November. Müller-thurgau is the most widely planted variety, delivering fresh, straightforward wines that can have a light mineral tone and a refreshing acidity. But Franken's specialty is sylvaner, originally brought here from Austria in the seventeenth century. Overcropped sylvaner can be neutral in character, but in Franken it can have a fine mineral edge. Riesling can also be delicious here, but it can be planted only in the best sites because it ripens so late.

For centuries Franken wine has been consigned to a dumpy bottle called the *bocksbeutel*, which has hindered its reputation, despite the fact that its best wines are of extremely high quality. Most are dry, but have the body and structure to keep any harshness at bay. They have an almost earthy mineral quality. There are also some magnificent sweet wines that are intense, structured, and long-lived. Parts of Franken are also well suited to red wines. Spätburgunder is the principal grape in these areas, but a new variety, domina, is also popular. The best reds are aged in *barriques* and command high prices. White Burgundian varieties are also grown and are often fermented and aged in *barriques*, with considerable success.

Vines heavy with huge, nearly ripe bunches of spätburgunder grapes.

Producers

SCHMITTS KINDER, RANDERSACKER
Owner **Karl Martin Schmitt** *Vineyard area* **35 acres (14 ha)**

Sylvaner is the main variety here, but Schmitt also does well with riesling, rieslaner, and even bacchus. For his top wines and for the sweet wines, he likes to use *barriques*, although oaked müller-thurgau is not a great success. Nor are the red wines, but the dry white wines are of the highest quality.

FÜRST LÖWENSTEIN, KREUZWERTHEIM
Owner **Alois Konstantin Fürst zu Löwenstein** *Vineyard area* **67 acres (27 ha)**

Since the 1990s a determined effort has been made to improve this estate's performance. A princely estate, it has vineyards at the Homburger Kallmuth site that produce richly earthy sylvaner. Other than the rare sweet wines, all varieties are vinified in a totally dry style and the top range is bottled under the Asphodel label. There is also some good spätburgunder that is aged in mostly new *barriques*.

Above: *Harvesting spätburgunder grapes in western Franken, where it is the main variety.*

Right: *Collecting the grapes along steep terraces.*

SCHLOSS SOMMERHAUSEN, SOMMERHAUSEN
Owners **Steinmann family** *Vineyard area* **50 acres (20 ha)**

Owned since 1968 by the same family, the Schloss estates produce very good sylvaner and riesling, a wide range of Burgundian varieties, and a well-known range of sparkling wines. The best of these are produced from riesling and auxerrois. In top years there are superb nobly sweet wines made from chardonnay, rieslaner, and scheurebe.

JULIUSSPITAL, WÜRZBURG
Manager **Horst Kolesch** *Vineyard area* **250 acres (100 ha)**

Ancient Juliusspital is currently the best of the large Würzburg estates. Wine production supports this primarily charitable foundation. It has extensive holdings in almost all the best sites in Franken. The quality of its wines is brilliant. Riesling and sylvaner are the star turns, but there are also exceptional wines from weissburgunder and rieslaner. Nobly sweet wines are rarities here, but when they are made they are magnificent.

WIRSCHING, IPHOFEN
Owner **Dr. Heinrich Wirsching** *Vineyard area* **173 acres (70 ha)**

The winemaking here is less interventionist than at most other large estates, and this allows spicy, complex fruitiness to shine forth. Sylvaner and riesling are very good dry wines, and there is attractive traminer and rieslaner in a sweeter style. Wirsching is rightly proud of its low-yielding grauer burgunder, aged for 15 months in *barriques*. The reds are also of above-average quality.

Other good producers in Franken include Castell, Bürgerspital, Rudolf Fürst, Johann Ruck, Horst Sauer, and Staatliche Hofkeller.

Baden

Baden is a state, not a wine region. Its micro-climates and soils are so diverse that it is futile to seek a characteristic that unites this region. Not surprisingly, wine styles vary enormously. In the far north you can find sylvaners sold in the squat *bocksbeutel*; in the Ortenau, Rhine-style rieslings dominate. To the south, the Burgundian varieties thrive, especially spätburgunder, but even on the baking Kaiserstuhl soils, there are rows of riesling and sylvaner vines. Although the climate encourages the production of dry wines, there are areas, such as the Kaiserstuhl, where it is often possible to make botrytis wines of excellent quality. Rich and figgy, they tend to mature much more rapidly than the equivalent wines from the Mosel or Rhine.

This vast range of wines is perpetuated by the 120 cooperatives that dominate Baden's wine production. Some are of very high quality, but even the best offer a huge variety of wines and styles to satisfy local demand. The villages in Baden to look for are Neuweier, Durbach, Sasbach, Ihringen, Oberrotweil, and Königschaffhausen.

HEGER, IHRINGEN *Owner* Joachim Heger
Vineyard area 37 acres (15 ha)

Given the vast range of varieties grown by Joachim Heger and the very low yields he insists upon, it is remarkable how many wines he manages to produce each year. The range is extraordinary: crisp dry rieslings, powerful dry muskatellers, broad spicy grauer burgunder, and the most sumptuous nobly sweet wines. One outstanding site, the Ihringer Winklerberg, is almost solely responsible for this array of glorious wines. Wines from the Heger estate are bottled under

BERLIN
GERMANY
Baden

FRANCE

Benfeld

Rhinau

Marckolsheim

Bischoffingen

Burkheim

Breisach

Bad Krozingen

Gaggenau
Baden Baden
Lichtenau
Neuweier
Rheinau Buhl
Strasbourg
Kehl
Achern
Renchen
Oberkirch
Offenburg Durbach
Fessenbach
Hohberg
Ortenberg
Friesenheim
Baden
GERMANY
Altdorf
Kenzingen
Malterdingen
Sasbach Endingen
Königschaffhausen
Oberrotweil
Ihringen
Freiburg
Ebringen

Müllheim
Mauchen

NORTH

10 miles
(16 kilometers)

Producers
1 Bercher
2 Durbacher Winzergenossenschaft
3 Heger
4 Huber
5 Johner
6 Laible
7 Lämmlin-Schindler
8 Schloss Neuweier
9 Salwey
10 Winzergenossenschaft Königschaffhausen

Oak barrels line the cellars of Bercher, Burkheim, in the Kaiserstuhl area of Baden.

the Dr. Heger label; those from bought grapes or lesser sites are released as cheaper varietal wines under the Weinhaus Joachim Heger label.

HUBER, MALTERDINGEN
Owner Bernhard Huber *Vineyard area* 37 acres (15 ha)

Bernhard Huber left the local cooperative in 1987 and rapidly became one of Baden's most respected producers of Burgundian wines. The chardonnay has sometimes been over-oaked, and a similar defect has unfortunately marred the otherwise excellent spätburgunder, especially the sumptuous reserve bottling. However, with each successive vintage, Huber manages to fine-tune the wines and they now show more finesse as well as richness and power.

A Bohemian colored tumbler with gilt decoration.

LAIBLE, DURBACH   *Owner* Andreas Laible
Vineyard area 15 acres (6 ha)

This Durbach cooperative run by Andreas Laible produces what are perhaps the finest rieslings of Baden. Made from low-yielding grapes grown on steep rocky slopes, these are wines of great fire and extraction. Gewürztraminer and grauer burgunder can also be excellent here, but riesling is definitely the specialty of the house.

SCHLOSS NEUWEIER, BADEN-BADEN
Owner Gisela Joos *Vineyard area* 25 acres (10 ha)

This grand castle estate has been carefully restored by the Joos family, who have also improved the quality of the wines. Almost all the wines are produced from riesling grapes, and the style is generally dry. These wines can be quite austere in their youth and are not to everyone's taste, but they are quite impressive, with shapely acidity, great elegance, and fine concentration. They can be sampled with good food in the castle's restaurant.

WINZERGENOSSENSCHAFT KÖNIGSCHAFFHAUSEN, KÖNIGSCHAFFHAUSEN
Manager Edmund Schillinger (cooperative)
Vineyard area 408 acres (165 ha)

This cooperative produces wines of better quality than many private estates in Baden. Its subtly oaked weisser burgunder is exemplary, and there is a fine range of oaked spätburgunder, too. The cooperative also produces some of the most sumptuous and brilliant nobly sweet wines in Baden, often from the grauer burgunder grape (this is known as ruländer when it is vinified sweet).

Other wine producers found in the Baden area that are highly recommended include Johner, Lämmlin-Schindler, Bercher, Durbacher Winzergenossenschaft, and Salwey.

Other German Regions

WÜRTTEMBERG

Of all the major German wine regions, Württemberg is the least known. Its vineyards are scattered, with the best near Stuttgart and Heilbronn. Although some good, even exceptional, riesling is produced, especially around Stuttgart, this is essentially red-wine country. An unimpressive red grape, trollinger, gives a pale red easily mistaken for rosé. Other varieties cultivated are spätburgunder (pinot noir), schwarzriesling (pinot meunier), lemberger, and the mutation of schwarzriesling known as samtrot. Many of the best examples are aged in small oak barrels and can have surprising richness and extraction.

GRAF ADELMANN, KLEINBOTTWAR

Owner **Michael Graf Adelmann** *Vineyard area* 44 acres (18 ha)

One of the Württemberg region's leading estates, Adelmann harvests as late as possible—so these are wines of richness and great concentration. The dry rieslings are excellent and there is some lovely traminer and muskateller, but the best wines are oak-aged red cuvées. Herbst im Park is supple and lush. More structured is Vignette, an exceptionally elegant blend of lemberger and samtrot.

NEIPPERG, SCHWAIGERN

Owner **Karl Eugen Erbgraf zu Neipperg** *Vineyard area* 77 acres (31 ha)

Riesling is made here, but this is not Neipperg's strength. Instead, he prefers to produce varietal red wines and has little interest in the fashionable blended reds. An enthusiast for local traditions, he also ages his best reds in barrels crafted from oak trees grown in the family's own forests. The top wines are usually lemberger and samtrot.

Pickers enjoying their lunch and wine in the vineyards.

HESSISCHE BERGSTRASSE

This very small region clustered around Bensheim is planted mostly with riesling, but Burgundian varieties also do well. Staatsweingut is an exceptionally consistent producer, and the best wines emerge from Heppenheimer Centgericht. The winery specializes in eiswein. Another reliable estate is Simon-Bürkle, which offers a wide range of red and white wines at reasonable prices. The town of Bensheim also has its own winery, making good riesling and Burgundian wines from its chalky Kalkgasse site.

> *Mixing one's wines may be a mistake, but old and new wisdom mix admirably.*
> BERTOLT BRECHT (1898–1956)

AHR

The River Ahr flows into the Rhine at Linz, to the northwest of Koblenz, its terraced rocky slopes planted with vines. The warming reflections off its craggy cliffs help bring the grapes to maturity. This most northerly region is best known for red wines that are very popular within Germany, largely because the area is exceedingly pretty and studded with inns, making it a pleasant outing for day-trippers.

Spätburgunder (pinot noir) is the focus, with some riesling and portugieser. A handful of estates make pinot noirs that are increasingly rich and Burgundian in style. The best wines in Ahr are quite expensive.

The town of Besigheim, near Stuttgart, is located in the Württemburg wine country.

NELLES, HEIMERSHEIM   *Owner* Thomas Nelles *Vineyard area* 12 acres (5 ha)

Spätburgunder is the base of the best wines here. Bottled without vineyard designation but with an arcane numbering system, these are pinot noirs of substance and elegance. The B-52 is often the best. The prices are less extravagant than those of other estates in the region, and the Rubis bottling offers a lively, simple pinot noir at an affordable price.

MITTELRHEIN

Mittelrhein has some dazzling scenery. Riverside villages crouch beneath steep vineyards and castle-capped cliffs; vineyards are strung out along the Rhine around Koblenz. Wines from vines grown on slaty soils around Bacharach, in the far south, are often among the best. The village of Boppard is capable of occasionally producing notable sweet wines. The Mittelrhein offers racy, pleasurable

rieslings. Their marked acidity gives them a freshness that is appealing when young and helps the wines to age quite well. Prices are reasonable.

TONI JOST, BACHARACH
Owner Peter Jost *Vineyard area* 22 acres (9 ha)

Peter Jost remains Mittelrhein's leading grower, making a full range of wines, from dry to very sweet, all of reliable quality. He is best known for his amazingly sumptuous dessert wines, especially the Riesling Trockenbeerenauslese from Bacharacher Hahn.

SAALE-UNSTRUT

To the west of Leipzig, this is the most northerly wine region in continental Europe. The climate can be harsh, so early-ripening varieties dominate. Devastating spring frosts mean yields in some

years are greatly reduced. Sixteenth-century commentators complained of the wine's sourness and little has changed since. Müller-thurgau is the dominant variety. Astonishingly, the leading estate, Lützkendorf, occasionally succeeds in producing a beerenauslese from sylvaner grapes.

SACHSEN

Here, too, spring frosts can slash yields to uneconomic levels, and Sachsen has yet to establish any reputation for quality. Müller-thurgau is the dominant variety in this region. Riesling is a significant variety, and the white Burgundian varieties, as well as traminer, are also quite widely encountered. The Zimmerling estate bottles all its production as dry table wine. In Meissen there is a "Weingalerie" near the cathedral, where many of the wines can be sampled.

Austria

A small but significant wine producer, Austria makes about the same amount of wine as the Bordeaux region. It is now producing some of the most exciting sweet and dry white wines in Europe, as well as increasingly interesting reds, which make up 20 percent of the output. Grapes were planted in the area we now call Austria as early as Celtic times and wine received another fillip from the Romans. It was the wine-loving Emperor Probus who first encouraged vine-growing in the area when idle soldiers were set to work planting vines on the warm Pannonian plain in the east. The Barbarian invasions naturally set back developments, but by the end of the first millennium Charlemagne's armies had established Christianity on both sides of the Danube. In their wake came the great monasteries and with the monks came the vineyards.

Vineyards at Grinzing, just outside Vienna. The parish church was built by twelve local wine-growers in 1417–1426.

At one time Austrian wines enjoyed a huge reputation, until the popularity of *Heurigen* (the local wine bars run by individual growers) led many growers to concentrate more on bulk than quality. Between the two world wars, Austria established a reputation for hospitality and good cheer that appealed chiefly to the Germans. Sweet, or off-dry wines were the rule, but later Wachau and South Styria developed completely dry white wines, while Burgenland proved its ability to make convincing reds. Production of sweet wines is now chiefly limited to the area around the shallow Neusiedlersee.

Landscape and climate

With a continental climate, Austria has a long growing season. Top growers in the Wachau, for example, may still be picking at the end of November. The Wachau and parts of the Kremstal are composed of steep primary rock soils where grapes grown on horizontal

Ruby red flashing has been used in the design of this Bohemian wine decanter from the late nineteenth century.

terraces produce racy wines. Most vineyards in Lower Austria are found close to the River Danube, on ridges of loess and volcanic rock that provide relief to a largely flat region.

In Burgenland, black grapes, such as cabernet sauvignon, merlot, syrah, and nebbiolo, have little problem achieving good levels of ripeness when grown close to the warm lake of Neusiedlersee. The Leitha Hills to the north and west are chalky and both chardonnay and pinot noir have been successful. Central and Southern Burgenland are predominantly red-wine areas. The chief grape grown here is the blaufränkisch.

Vines and wines

Austria has many indigenous varieties providing a nice distraction from the globalization of tastes. On heavy soils the weinviertel produces sappy, refreshing wines with a distinctly peppery bouquet. On the primary rock soils of the Wachau, however, it is so different in character that tasters often believe they are drinking top white burgundies. Riesling is an important white grape, while chardonnay, known as morillon, has a long tradition in Styria. Weiss- and grauburgunder, or pinots blanc and gris, have a longer tradition and often produce better results.

Neuburger is sometimes claimed as a pinot. Vinified dry or affected by botrytis, it can be superb. In Burgenland and Styria the workhorse grape is welschriesling, which can be excellent when well-vinified and in sweeter styles.

The most widely planted red grape is zweigelt, a crossing of St. Laurent and blaufränkisch. Low yields can produce stunning results. Blaufränkisch is seen as the number-one quality cultivar, but it tends to dry out in *barriques*. In West Styria there is blauer wildbacher, which is generally vinified as an acid rosé called schilcher.

Winemaking

Austrians like wines with a refreshing acidity. Flavors are more angular than those from, say, Australia. Oaking became very common in the late eighties and *barriques* were often used to age quite light, unsuitable wines. Many of Austria's best growers never use *barriques*; riesling and grüner veltliner are generally thought not to need it. In Styria the classical style with sauvignon blanc or morillon (chardonnay) has been to age in oak, concrete or stainless steel. Many reds are also "oak aged."

With very few firms able to supply a large amount of wine of consistent quality, Austria's strength now lies in high-quality niche products.

With the average holding being less than 5 acres (2 ha), most Austrians cannot hope to lay hands on some of the more highly rated wines. Yet even with just 15 acres (6 ha), a grower will make up to half a dozen wines, ranging from dry whites to reds and botrytis-affected whites or eiswein. This means that production is limited, and demand (and prices) for the top quality wines is very high.

At the other end of the scale, in the *Heurige*, wine is drunk very young and it is very cheap. These places are often so profitable that there is little incentive to labor over making good wine. On the other hand, some makers reinvest their profits in properly made wines.

Austrian wines are graded by levels of natural residual sweetness. In some areas there are as yet unofficial classifications of vineyards on the basis of the French *cru* system.

Right: *An experienced winemaker may taste wine grapes in order to assess their readiness. They are very different from the grapes eaten as fruit.*

Right: *At Wolkersdorf, riesling grapes are picked by hand.*

Producers

There are 16 wine-producing regions in Austria: these are Vienna, Thermenregion, Carnuntum, Donauland, Weinviertel, Kamptal, Kremstal, Wachau, Traisental, Neusiedlersee, Neusiedlersee–Hügelland, Central and Southern Burgenland, and also Southeast, West, and South Styria. A selection of producers is outlined below; others that are also recommended for the remaining regions include Fritz Wieninger (Vienna); Hans Pitnauer (Donauland-Carnuntum); Ludwig Neumayer (Traisental); Engelbert Gesellmann (Central Bugenland); Krutzler (Southern Burgenland); Georg Winkler-Hermaden (Southeast Styria); Erich and Walter Polz (South Styria); and Domaine Müller (West Styria).

> *Wine comes in at*
> *the mouth*
> *And love comes in at the eye;*
> *That's all we shall know for truth*
> *Before we grow old and die.*
> WILLIAM BUTLER YEATS (1865–1939),
> *The Green Helmet and Other Poems*
> A Drinking Song

KARL ALPHART, TRAISKIRCHEN *Owner* Karl Alphart *Vineyard area* 25 acres (10 ha)

The Thermenregion derives its name from its warm springs and spas. It is a little suntrap protected by the last outriders of the Alps and grapes ripen a little too well here, meaning either too much sugar, or too much alcohol. Yet Alphart makes it seem easy to make great wine; he uses the curious duo of zierfandler and rotgipfler, two local grapes found pretty much nowhere else. Vinified together and apart, they are imbued with an exciting spiciness. There is also a great riesling from the steep slopes, good chardonnay, and, on occasion, some quite marvelous beerenauslesen and trockenbeerenauslesen.

KARL FRITSCH, KIRCHBERG AM WAGRAM *Owners* Fritsch family *Vineyard area* 17 acres (7 ha)

The Donauland region's Wagram, on a ridge overlooking the Danube, produces some exemplary grüner veltliner. The Fritsch family has built up a huge reputation over the past few years for their whites. They also make a few red wines, but they are best known for the Schlossberg with its redolence of pineapples and grapefruit; or Perfektion (a name that might be asking for trouble), which is a silent auslese, up to 14 percent alcohol, with a huge bouquet of pepper and angelica.

HELMUT TAUBENSCHUSS, POYSDORF *Owner* Helmut Taubenschuss *Vineyard area* 25 acres (10 ha)

Poysdorf provides the base wine for much of Austria's sparkling sekt. While some local wine is very sour, Helmut seems to have no trouble making well-rounded, balanced wines here in the Weinvertel region, on the Czech border. He makes lovely grüner veltliners bursting with flavor, but his best wines are weissburgunders.

WILLI BRÜNDLMAYER, LANGENLOIS *Owners* Bründlmayer family *Vineyard area* 123 acres (50 ha)

In the Kamptal region, Bründlmayer's wines range from superconcentrated grüner veltliner and riesling to an exemplary chardonnay with *barrique* aging but no malolactic fermentation; to a wonderful, buttery, *barrique*-aged grauburgunder, a trio of reds, and one of Austria's best champagne-style sparklers. When the year is up to it, he makes glorious dessert wines.

Pure, clear, Austrian schnapps is a profitable sideline for Austrian wineries. It is made from distilling grape skins, then fermenting the liquid.

Austrian villages are full of delightful surprises, such as this pretty side street in the village of Heiligenstadt.

MARTIN NIGL, SENFTENBERG   *Owner* Martin
Nigl *Vineyard area* 23 acres (9.5 ha)

Nigl is reputedly one of the country's best wine-makers. His grapes grow on the best land in the Krems Valley, in the Kremstal region, on primary rock soils that produce the raciest grüner velt-liners and rieslings imaginable. Mostly bone-dry, every now and then out comes a trockenbeeren-auslese or an eiswein. He makes two wines with less appeal: a semisweet chardonnay, and a trendy, but misguided, sauvignon blanc.

ERNST TRIEBAUMER, RUST   *Owners* Triebaumer
family *Vineyard area* 27 acres (11 ha)

Black grapes ripen superbly on the warm soils in the Neusiedlersee–Hügelland region, producing good dry whites. Ernst Triebaumer makes superb ausbruch, often with high alcohol levels, but in the Marienthal he also makes Austria's best blaufränkisch, a barrel-fermented chardonnay, and a lovely traminer.

LUIS KRACHER, ILLMITZ   *Owner* Luis Kracher
Vineyard area 18 acres (7.5 ha)

Luis Kracher is the pope of Austrian sweet wine and in some years he makes more trockenbeeren-auslesen than Germany. His skill combines with special local conditions in the Neusiedlersee region, where the mists settle on the stagnant ponds and botrytis sets in most years. The wines divide into new-oak fermented Nouvelle Vague and the Zwischen den Seen range.

F. X. PICHLER, LOIBEN   *Owner* F. X. Pichler
Vineyard area 18 acres (7.5 ha)

Austrian winelovers would cite F. X. as their greatest winemaker, yet he produces little wine. F. X. makes great riesling and grüner veltliner on steep sites in the beautiful Wachau. He is an austere, unrelenting man, but his determination shows in the great concentration of the wines. The best of a great year is marked "M" for "monumental." These wines are rarest of all.

Switzerland

The most mountainous country in Europe finds space for more than 37,000 acres (15,000 ha) of vineyards in its valleys and foothills. Surprisingly, few cling to the sides of mountains and most are planted at altitudes common in Alsace and Burgundy. Switzerland has borders with Alsace, Haute Savoie, and Jura in France, with Baden in southern Germany, with western Austria, and with northern Italy, so a number of wine styles are produced. Some grape types that survive from ancient times have names of Latin origin, such as amigne and arvine. The Romans cultivated vines in the canton of Valais on the shores of lakes Geneva, Neuchâtel, Zürich, and Constance, where vineyards still thrive.

NORTH

60 miles
(96 kilometers)

Schaffhausen
Schaffhausen
Constance
Thurgau   Lake
             Constance
Basle
Aargau   Zurich
Zurich   Winterthur
Aarau   St Gallen
Zurich   Lake Zurich   St Gallen
Zurich   Eastern
         Switzerland

La Chaux-
de-Fonds   Bienne
Neuchâtel   Lake Bienne
Neuchâtel   Vully   BERNE   Lucerne
Lake Neuchâtel   Lake Lucerne   Graubunden
Vaud   (Grisons)
                                          Chur
                SWITZERLAND
Thun

Lausanne
La Côte   Lavaux
Mandement   Chablais   Jungfrau
Geneva   Lake   13,638 ft (4158 m)
Genèva   Geneva   Monthey   Valais
         Arve et Lac Valais   Rhône   S
Arve et   Martigny   Saas-Fee   Ticino   Graubunden
Rhône   Zermatt   (Grisons)
         L
         A   Matterhorn   Monte Rosa   Lugano
              14,684 ft (4477 m) 15,199 ft (4634 m)

Rhaetian Alps
St Moritz

Switzerland's vineyards lie between the 45° and 47°N latitudes, potentially ideal for quality viticulture. Generally the climate is temperate or continental, with plenty of sunshine and rainfall at the right time of year, cold winters and warm summers, though with considerable vintage variation. The appearance in some valleys of the *Föhn*, a warm alpine wind, can hasten ripening dramatically. Many soils are of glacial origin and broken-up slate, schist, and large stones are very common. The variety of soil types accounts for the marked differences in character in the chasselas wines.

Wine regions

Wine regions in Switzerland are divided, first into the three main language divisions, French, German, and Italian, and then further into cantons. French-speaking Switzerland accounts for about 77 percent of the total, from which about 83 percent of Switzerland's wine is produced.

Valais has some of the most picturesque vineyards. Some of Europe's highest vineyards are in the Haut-Valais, below the ski resorts of Zermatt and Saas-Fee. The region's greatest density of vineyards is on the south-facing slopes of the

Packers carefully prepare pinot noir grapes for transport; this is a grape the vigneron must treat well.

upper Rhône Valley, which runs east–west between Leuk (Loèche) and Martigny. The wine center and also the capital of the canton is Sion.

Vaud has four main vineyard regions, the three largest close to Lake Geneva, the smallest close to Lake Neuchâtel. Lakes have a most important climatic influence, regulating temperature and increasing the effect of the sun by reflection. The Chablais area may be affected by the *Föhn*.

Geneva is close to three growing areas. Mandement contains Switzerland's largest grape-growing community, Satigny. Geneva's other two areas are Entre Arve et Rhône (between the Arve and Rhône rivers) and Entre Arve et Lac. Viticulture in this canton, with a landscape of rolling hills, is easier and more mechanized than elsewhere. There is plenty of sunshine and the nearby mountains deflect clouds, giving relatively low rainfall. Lake Geneva protects the vineyards from spring frosts and the best vineyards are on hillsides that warm rapidly in the morning sunshine.

Neuchâtel lies on the northern shores of the lakes of Neuchâtel and Bienne and south of the Jura mountains. This area has a fairly dry climate, but lacks the intensity and amount of sunshine enjoyed by more southerly cantons.

German-speaking Switzerland has vineyards scattered across 18 cantons, with significant plantings in Zürich, Schaffhausen, Aargau, Graubünden (Grisons), Thurgau, and St Gallen (by Lake Constance). Here the climate is marginal for viticulture, though proximity to the Rhine River in the north, to various lakes, and the influence of the *Föhn* in the east, help certain vineyards.

Almost all the vineyards in Italian-speaking Switzerland are in Ticino, the country's fourth-largest wine-producing canton. Sopraceneri and Sottoceneri, north and south

Mechanized harvesting is possible in the Geneva region, but steep sites in some other areas prevent its use.

of Monte Ceneri, have scattered plots, mostly on terraces, many currently being reconstructed to aid mechanization. With the climate influenced by the Mediterranean, there are more sunshine hours than anywhere in Switzerland, but the rainfall is higher, too.

Vines and wines

Chasselas is grown widely in the French-speaking cantons, notably in Vaud. The wine's character derives much more from the soil type than from the grape. Malolactic fermentation is used to lower acidity and create a softer, creamier mouth-feel. Almost all chasselas is dry, and fendant (the local name for the grape) from the Valais can vary from soft and fruity (and sometimes lacking in acidity) to a far more intense, mineral or stony flavor.

The Grand Crus of Dézaley and Calamin provide intensity in the first and elegance in the sec-

And Noah he often said to his wife when he sat down to dine, "I don't care where the water goes if it doesn't get into the wine."

G. K. CHESTERTON (1874–1936),
Wine and Water

ond, but nearby villages of Epesses and Saint-Saphorin can produce equally good, structured, and honeyed wines. Yvorne and Aigle, with steep vineyards in Chablais, also produce excellent chasselas. Young chasselas often has a slight spritz and good examples benefit from two or more years aging.

Riesling-sylvaner, known elsewhere as müller-thurgau, is the first recorded vine crossing and is most prevalent in German-speaking parts. This grape produces a dry or medium-dry, flowery wine to be drunk when young.

Sylvaner thrives on steep, stony sites and it produces grapes with considerably higher natural sugar levels than chasselas. Sylvaner can be made into dry, medium, or perfumed late-harvest wines.

Chardonnay does better in Geneva and Neuchâtel where both dry light and elegant styles are made. Oak-matured wines are also made there, less successfully.

Pinot gris has long been grown in Valais. This grape also does well in the warmer parts of Germanic Switzerland.

Marsanne has thrived for many years in the Upper Rhône Valley, yielding wines labeled Ermitage (or Hermitage). Highly alcoholic, these dry or sweet wines develop vivid dried apricot or peach tones.

Pinot noir is especially favored in Germanic Switzerland, where it accounts for 70 percent of plantings. Thermo-vinification (the application of heat before fermentation) is widely practiced to give color but no tannin and this means most wines are lacking in flavor. Where producers with good sites treat pinot better, the results are good. Also important in French Switzerland, it is Neuchâtel's only permitted red grape giving, notably, an excellent dry rosé, Oeil de Perdrix. It is gaining ground in Vaud, especially in La Côte,

and is the most-planted red in Valais, where much of it goes into the dôle and goron blends.

Gamay is grown quite widely in French Switzerland and used almost exclusively for blends in Valais, but Geneva successfully produces a characteristic fruity varietal with good acid balance.

Merlot is now the principal variety in Ticino. Good Ticino merlots show lively acidity, soft tannins, and succulent fruit flavors, but many are light, fruity, and rather thin. A number of producers are making structured merlot, some with oak aging.

Syrah is causing excitement in Valais. Small quantities have been grown there for many years, but not given much attention. There are now about 125 acres (50 ha), mostly in Valais, on prime, steep slopes for maximum sunshine.

Gamaret and garanoir are two red wine crossings with white reichensteiner (itself a crossing) and red gamay in their parentage. They have

proved remarkably successful, and particularly so in Geneva and Vaud. Used sometimes in blends and sometimes pure, these grapes can produce deep-colored reds with good black fruit character and structure to cope with oak aging. In the Valais the crossing diolinoir is now also gaining ground.

Most wines are labeled with the canton, some with the village, too, and usually the grape variety, unless the wine is marketed under one of several "stylistic" appellations that have been in use for many years.

Harvesting chasselas grapes near Geneva–the city is a mere 6 miles (10 km) from the grape-growing region.

Producers

Switzerland has several thousand vineyard owners, many with tiny plots. Most are either part of a wine cooperative, or pass their crop over to a local *négociant*. In Valais alone about 700 producers make and sell their own wine. The following producers make a range that can be recommended, as can Bon Père Germanier and René Favre & Fils, both in Valais.

DOMAINE LES HUTINS, GENEVA   *Established* 1976 *Owners* Jean & Pierre Hutin *Vineyard area* 44 acres (18 ha)

Based in Dardagny, close to the French border, Jean and Pierre Hutin were among the first Swiss to plant sauvignon blanc. They produce both non-oaked and *barrique* versions of sauvignon blanc, chardonnay, and pinot noir, the latter most successfully. Their best chasselas, Le Bertholier, is fresh and creamy. Le Bertholier Rouge, 80 percent gamaret with

Many vineyards, like these near Lake Geneva, benefit from particular microclimates, provided by proximity to water, which reflects warmth.

cabernet sauvignon, is aged partly in new *barriques* giving fabulous depth and complexity. Viognier and merlot are the latest challenge.

DOMAINE DU MONT D'OR, VALAIS   *Established* 1848 *Owners* Domaine du Mont d'Or S. A. (majority Schenk S. A.) *Vineyard area* 50 acres (20 ha)

This rather famous old domaine has vineyards in prime south-facing, steep sites. It has always made very reliable fendant and dôle, but its specialty is late-harvest wine, from several varieties, and, wherever possible, from botrytized grapes. Its signature wine is johannisberg (as sylvaner is known here), which shows a tropical fruit character. The fine Petite Arvine Sous L'Escalier (below the steps) ages superbly.

JEAN & PIERRE TESTUZ, VAUD   *Established* 1845 *Owners* J. & P. Testuz S. A. *Vineyard area* 147 acres (60 ha)

A large firm of growers and *négociants* based in the Grand Cru vineyards of Dézaley in Lavaux, Testuz specializes in chasselas, but also produces a range of other varietals. Run by Jean-Philippe, a thirteenth-generation Testuz, the firm is totally family owned (some of its vineyards are leased) and it takes its chasselas seriously. A wine with a subtly different character, reflecting various soil types and aspects, is produced from each major Lavaux appellation.

Italy

Matterhorn
14,684 ft (4477 m)
Mt Rosa
15,199 ft (4634 m)
Mt Bianco
15,770 ft (4808 m)

Lake Maggiore

Valle d'Aosta

Piedmont

Turin

Asti

Novara

Lake Como

Bolzano

Trentino-Alto Adige

Trento

DOLOMITES

Udine

Friuli-Venezia Giulia

Trieste

Franciacorta

Bergamo

Monza

Milan

Brescia

Lake Garda

Lugana

Verona

Valpolicella

Soave

Vicenza

Padua

Mestre

Venice

Gulf of Venice

Adige

Po

Piacenza

Emilia-Romagna

Parma

Reggio nell'Emilia

Modena

Bologna

Ferrara

Adige

Po

Emilia-Romagna

Piedmont

Genoa

Savona

Liguria

Liguria

La Spézia

APENNINES

Emilia-Romagna

Prato

Florence

Rimini

SAN MARINO

ADRIATIC SEA

Pisa

Livorno

Tuscany

Arezzo

Siena

Lake Trasimeno

Perugia

Umbria

Ancona

Marche

Elba

Tuscany

Orvieto

Terni

Teramo

Pescara

L'Aquila

Abruzzo

Monti dei Frentani

Corsica (France)

Lazio

ROME

Lazio

Molise

Campobasso

Foggia

TYRRHENIAN SEA

Campania

Naples

Torre del Greco

Ischia

Campania

Salerno

Mt Vesuvius
4203 ft (1281 m)

Basilicata

Potenza

Puglia

Bari

Brindisi

Taranto

Sardinia

Sassari

Sardinia

Punta La Marmora
6015 ft (1834 m)

Campania

Mt del Papa
6576 ft (2005 m)

Appennino Lucano

Calabria

Sardinia

Cagliari

Cosenza

Mt Botte Donato
6323 ft (1928 m)

Calabria

Calabria

Catanzaro

Lipari Islands

Calabria

Messina

Reggio di Calabria

Bianco

Palermo

Trapani

Sicily

Sicily

Mt Etna
10,899 ft (3323 m)

Catania

Siracuse

Sicily

Pantelleria

NORTH

60 miles
(96 kilometers)

A L P S

Italy

If it's true that good things come in small packages then Italy, with its multiplicity of often pocket-handkerchief-sized wine zones, must have good things in plenty. However, the profusion of its wines and the vast abundance of the grape varieties making them are both Italy's glory and its downfall. For some, the country's wines are a treasure trove, for others they are just complicated and confusing.

Italy is geographically complex, too. To the north, the well-drained lower slopes of the bordering Alps provide prime grape-growing territory before they give way to the plains of the Po valley, about the only part of Italy where grapes are not consistently grown. This entire northern part has a gently continental climate with marked inconsistencies from year to year, giving pronounced vintage variations.

The long, narrow penin-sular part of the country is defined by the Apennine mountain chain that forms its spine. There are numerous hill ranges and comparatively little flat ground. In some places the mountains fall right to the sea, creating the most dramatic of scenery and growing conditions.

Much of the lack of consistency in Italy's wine production is derived from Italy's history. However, in the mid-1970s the wine industry realized its survival lay in quality, and the resulting Italian wine renaissance hit its peak in the late 1980s. Winemaking was upgraded with new cellar equipment and technical know-how; vineyards were revamped. Most estates had to start from scratch to find the best combinations of rootstock and variety for their heterogeneous terrains, the most suitable clones, and optimal planting density. This takes many years, so the improvements will continue to emerge.

Italy has a wealth of indigenous vines and, while Italians accept international varieties, the future of Italian wine lies in the individuality provided by the indigenous grapes. Dozens of varieties can be considered emblematic of one or more regions—Piedmont's nebbiolo, the tocai of Friuli–Venezia Giulia, nero d'avola in Sicily, for example. Varieties that are found nationwide are the classics—cabernet and chardonnay—which lead the field. Italians tend to be a little coy about revealing the makeup of their wines in those cases where they have added a small amount of chardonnay to an indigenous variety to give it a more international taste; they prefer you to think that such a wine comes from a pure indigene.

It is important to note that in Italy wine is conceived and made as a food accompaniment. Drinking wine on its own is a habit for foreigners.

Barolo traditions

Dining at the home of a top producer in a small but world-recognized wine region is a fascinating experience. The characters behind the famous brands can often leave a longer-lasting impression than the wine. The best hosts and hostesses understand the fine art of making every guest feel important, but one or two attendees may be elevated to the special rank of "guest of honor." In Barolo, these privileged few are treated with the leftover wine! Locals feel that overnight aeration greatly enhances their wine, smoothing out the tannins and allowing more flavor to come through, so they save open, unfinished bottles at the end of the night, reserving them for their special guests the next day.

Consequently, many wines that taste disappointingly harsh or neutral when unaccompanied suddenly spring into life when drunk with food.

Regions and styles

Traditionally Italian wines, if aged at all, were put in large wooden barrels (*botti*) but most estates have replaced or supplemented its *botti* stock with *barriques*—small casks of new oak. A growing voice holds that many Italian grape varieties are not well-suited to the *barrique* treatment. Producers of all sizes are increasingly placing their trust in well-known, highly skilled contract winemakers to guide production. While this does ensure that a wine is competently made, they risk their wines reflecting their enologist's ideas of style and character.

The ancient small town of Poggio Lavarino is situated in Umbria, an important winemaking region in Italy.

Piedmont and North-west Italy

At the center of northwestern Italy, the Piedmont region's heart is the zones of Barolo and Barbaresco, names that for many represent the peak of Italian winemaking. Parts of Piedmont are mountainous but the main wine zones cluster to the south and east of Turin, an area of sharply defined hilly outcrops intersected by flat river valleys.

Most wines are single varietals. Three varieties, all red, stand out: nebbiolo, barbera, and dolcetto. Of these, nebbiolo is the most illustrious, classically making slow-developing wines of intensity, austerity, and great refinement. Barbera is often aged in oak to soften the wine, while dolcetto's fruitiness is usually enjoyed while the wine is young. Other indigenous red grapes of note include grignolino, freisa, brachetto, and croatina.

Leading the white grapes is moscato bianco, the white muscat that here produces the lightest, freshest, grapiest wine imaginable. Cortese is best past its first year or two. Arneis and favorito are also grown, and erbaluce, more rarely.

Barolo and Barbaresco

Nowhere does nebbiolo show its class as much as in the two zones of Barolo and Barbaresco. And nowhere else in Italy is there such a tight mesh of small vineyards, each vineyard firmly stamping its personality onto its wines, although nebbiolo and its

subvarieties (lampia, michet, and rosé) are the only grapes used. Barolo's western wines are marked by greater aroma and finesse and develop quicker, while those from the east have greater structure, body, power, and longevity. Barbaresco too shows marked variation in terrain and grapes. Differences in maceration and oaking mean there is no typical style. However, overall barolo is considered a little chunkier and fuller, more powerful and slower-aging than the more refined barbaresco.

Moscato wines

Moscato-based wines are grown in most of Italy, but the Piedmont area, Asti in particular, produces the best Asti spumante (spumante means "sparkling"). A fresh, light, sweet, frothy dessert wine, it is produced from moscato bianco grapes. Asti should be drunk as fresh as possible. An even lighter, more elegant, and more delicate version is the dessert wine moscato d'asti.

A Greco–Roman amphora from around 450BC, used to store and carry wine.

Producers		Barolo	
Carema		9	Elio Altare
1	Ferrando & C.	10	Ascheri
Gattinara		11	Michele Chiarlo
2	Antoniolo	12	Domenico Clerico
Barbera d'Asti		13	Giacomo Conterno
3	Braida	14	Poderi Aldo Conterno
Barbaresco		15	Fontanafredda
4	Produttori del	16	Bartolo Mascarello
	Barbaresco	17	Paolo Scavino
5	Gaja	18	Aldo Vajra
6	Bruno Giacosa	19	Vietti
7	Marchesi di Grésy	20	Robert Voerzio
8	Pelissero		**Gavi, Cortese di Gavi**
		21	La Scolca
			Oltrepò Pavese
		22	Albani

Producers

FERRANDO & C. *Established* 1900 *Owners* Ferrando family *Vineyard area* 17.5 acres (7 ha)

Luigi Ferrando, practically the only commercial producer of Carema, has three still versions of Erbaluce di Caluso; a brut sparkling wine from erbaluce; a late harvest, lightly sweet Erbaluce; and a Caluso Passito.

ANTONIOLO *Established* 1949 *Owners* Antoniolo family *Vineyard area* 37 acres (15 ha)

Coming from this Gattinara producer is Coste della Sesia Nebbiolo Juvenia, a wine from nebbiolo that does not require long aging. The estate's leading wine, the Gattinara *cru* Osso San Grato, has plentiful, soft, red-berried fruitiness to offset its natural austerity.

BRAIDA *Established* 1961 *Owners* Bologna family *Vineyard area* 70 acres (28 ha)

This pioneer of barbera in *barrique* makes Barbera d'Asti Bricco dell'Uccellone (a fat, deep, spicy wine) and the tighter-knit Bricco della Bigotta and late-harvested Ai Suma. Young lively Barbera La Monella and finely balanced Moscato d'Asti show the breadth of the range.

GAJA *Established* 1859 *Owner* Angelo Gaja *Vineyard area* 135 acres (55 ha)

Angelo Gaja's quest for quality has made him one of the most respected characters not only in Barbaresco, but in Italy. These wines are expensive but the combination of balance, complexity, and class is unparalleled.

BRUNO GIACOSA *Established* 1900 *Owner* Bruno Giacosa *Vineyard area* 37 acres (15 ha)

Giacosa's philosophy is generally to seek the best growers from the best sites and buy in grapes. The complex, floral, spicy, firm Barbaresco *cru* Santo Stefano di Neive is exemplary and stands out in a fairly large range.

MARCHESI DI GRÉSY *Established* 1973 *Owner* Alberto di Grésy *Vineyard area* 72 acres (29 ha)

Barbaresco's energetic Alberto di Grésy and his winemakers make highly individual, light, graceful wines from well-sited vineyards. *Crus* Gaiun, Camp Gros, and Martinenga are highly acclaimed and a good Moscato d'Asti, La Serra, is made but di Grésy is now investing extra effort in chardonnay, sauvignon, and cabernet sauvignon.

PAOLO SCAVINO *Established* 1921 *Owner* E. Scavino *Vineyard area* 22 acres (9 ha)

These are dense and elegantly perfumed wines with broad appeal. Scavino owns plots on some of Barolo's best sites: Cannubi, Bric del Fiasc, and Rocche dell'Annunziata.

Wine gives courage and makes men more apt for passion.
OVID (43 BC–AD 17)

FIIO ALTARE *Established* 1948 *Owner* Elio Altare *Vineyard area* 11 acres (4.5 ha)

Elio Altare is of the short-maceration school in Barolo. The wines are supple, complex, well-fruited, and refined. Top of the range is the *cru* Barolo Vigneto Arborina. Barbera d'Alba and Dolcetto d'Alba are also fruit-forward and attractively balanced.

The estate of Marchesi di Grésy, a winery in the Piedmont region.

LA SCOLCA *Established* 1919 *Owner* Giorgio Soldati *Vineyard area* 86 acres (35 ha)

Gavi's emergence as a wine of note derives from the efforts of this Cortese di Gavi estate. Scolca's best gavi is the black label Etichetta Nera. Like most gavis, it matures into a firm, fleshy, spicily fruity wine of good structure: a red-wine drinker's white. Also outstanding is a finely tuned brut sparkling wine.

PODERI ALDO CONTERNO *Established* 1969 *Owner* A. Conterno *Vineyard area* 55 acres (23 ha)

Aldo Conterno's wines are quite simply stunning, with a wealth of ripe fruit that balances the classic barolo astringency and acts as counterpoint to the classic barbera acidity. Wines from this Barolo concern are in very high demand.

FONTANAFREDDA *Established* 1878 *Owners* Amministrazione Immobiliare S.p.A. *Vineyard area* 170 acres (68 ha)

This winery is a landmark in Barolo. Wines are good value and an excellent introduction to the type (notably Barolo Serralunga d'Alba, a blend) especially for those wary of more austere versions. Barolo *crus* La Delizia, La Villa, Lazzarito, Gattinera, and La Rosa top a long list.

VIETTI *Established* 1905 *Owners* Corrado e Alfredo Vietti & C. *Vineyard area* 55 acres (22 ha)

Using the variety arneis, the wines produced here are beautifully balanced, well-typed and elegant. They are led by Barolo *crus* Rocche, Brunate, Lazzarito, Villero, and Castiglione. Well-structured barbera and dolcetto and finessed moscato d'Asti also feature.

Angelo Gaja

Without the vision and foresight of the Gaja family, barbaresco may never have achieved its rank as one of the world's finest reds. The Gajas opened a tavern in 1856, offering their own wines. The father, Angelo, accumulated some of the best vineyards in the area. Clotilda Rey, his wife, insisted on high quality. Their son, Angelo, has traveled the world to spread the word while also bringing innovations to his wines and to the region as a whole.

ALBANI *Established* 1992 *Owner* Riccardo Albani *Vineyard area* 37 acres (15 ha)

Riccardo Albani's carefully nurtured Oltrepò Pavese estate offers superbly refined wines of sheer class. There are just three: a slightly sparkling, off-dry bonarda; a stylish, slow-developing, varietally pure Rhine riesling; and Vigna della Casona, mainly from barbera, a wine that balances intensity and elegance with aplomb.

Also noteworthy in Piedmont and the Northwest are: Produttori del Barbaresco, Pelissero (both in Barbaresco), Ascheri, Michele Chiarlo, Domenico Clerico, Giacomo Conterno, Cantine Oddero, Bartolo Mascarello, Roberto Voerzio, and Aldo Vajra (all in Barolo).

The winery buildings at Cantine Oddero, in Piedmont.

North Central Italy   "VVV"

In the central part of northern Italy, Lake Garda, Italy's largest lake, warms the local vineyards and separates the more rural region of Veneto, with its major vineyard areas of Valpolicella and Soave, from Lombardy to the west. South of the lake is the white wine zone of Lugana, which grows lugana grapes. The wine is usually unoaked and enjoyed young and crisp, but can repay aging for a few years. Nudging the lake to the northwest of Lugana is the Bianco di Custoza zone where an intriguing mix of grapes gives zip to a gently fruited white. Nearby, the southern part of Bardolino offers a similar style, a little lighter, more linear, and more herbaceous. Bardolino also lends itself to vinification as a pale rosé called bardolino chiaretto, a sheer delight, yet poorly known.

In the Valpolicella heartland, the wine is from a three-plus grape blend, and corvina is the most important. Versatile in style, valpolicella can be made for drinking as a young, fresh, vibrant red or as a fuller, rounder, longer-aged wine. Amarone della valpolicella is a highly traditional wine; amarone retains the cherry-like characteristics

An easy way to remember the region of origin and the grape variety of Valpolicella is to think "V." Valpolicella wine is from the Veneto region. It is typically a light-bodied, unoaked, bitter cherry-imbued, refreshing dry red wine, ideal for lighter dishes with garlic. Innovative producers release a "souped up" valpolicella called ripasso, an impressive richer, more deeply flavored and rounder wine made by refermenting valpolicella on dried grape skins, giving higher alcohol and extract. Completing the trio is amarone, made from the ripest grapes that are then dried, or raisanated on straw mats giving a potent, warm, mouthfilling wine with a slightly bitter finish.

of valpolicella but is stronger and port-like. Sweet recioto is another variation. Soave, a little further east, uses predominantly garganega grapes to produce its dry whites. The popularity of soave and valpolicella has caused the regions' vineyards to spread beyond the heartland Classico areas out on to the surrounding plains—these non-Classico wines have less to offer.

Beyond Soave and Valpolicella, single-varietal wines are the norm. The most prominent region is Breganze, which produces a huge array of red and white varietal wines.

Colli Trevigiani, north of Venice, is the tiny realm of the prosecco grape. Prosecco wines are most frequently sparkling, the style a deliberately light, youthful fruitiness. The natural

Producers
Franciacorta
1 Bellavista
2 Ca' del Bosco
Lugana
3 Ca' dei Frati
Valpolicella Classico
4 Allegrini
5 Quintarelli
Soave Classico
6 Anselmi
7 Bolla
8 Inama
9 Pieropan
Breganze
10 Maculan
Prosecco di Valdobbiadene
11 Bisol

Winter vines are dusted with snow near the Veneto winery Monteforte Soave Classico.

aperitif throughout Italy, the wine can be anything from bone-dry to fairly sweet. Conegliano's wines are softer, Valdobbia-dene's tighter and more elegant, but the differences are not marked. Franciacorta's sparkling wine openly sought to emulate champagne—with remarkable success.

BELLAVISTA *Established* 1977 *Owner* Vittorio Moretti *Vineyard area* 290 acres (117 ha)

Using champagne for inspiration, the Bellavista sparkling wines are silky, graceful, supremely elegant, and very long. This Franciacorta estate also produces a top-rate range of still wines using cabernet sauvignon, chardonnay, and pinot nero.

CA' DEI FRATI *Established* 1956 *Owners* Pietro Dal Cero and Sons *Vineyard area* 90 acres (36 ha)

Here are elegant full wines of youthful charm but evident staying power, especially the Lugana Brolettino from late-picked grapes given *barrique* aging. This is complemented by the oak-free, beautifully crafted Lugana I Frati. Also gaining plaudits is Pratto.

PIEROPAN *Established* 1876 *Owner* Leonildo Pieropan *Vineyard area* 74 acres (30 ha)

Pieropan wines are beautifully crafted and well-knit, giving texture and depth to the Soave character. Pieropan helped save trebbiano di soave from extinction. Two wines from single vineyards, the *cru* Soaves—Vigneto Calvarino and Vigneto La Rocca—are slow-developing, concentrated, complex wines of great class. Recioto di Soave is archetypal.

MACULAN *Established* 1933 *Owner* Fausto Maculan *Vineyard area* 173 acres (70 ha)

A large range of characterful wines are found at Breganze's Maculan, once famed for the sweet Torcolato, the even sweeter Acini Nobili, and the delicate Dindarello. The best now are the Ferrata Cabernet Sauvignon and Ferrata Chardonnay.

BISOL *Established* 1875 *Owners* Bisol family *Vineyard area* 114 acres (46 ha)

One of Prosecco di Valdobbiandene's larger producers, Bisol offers a wide array of immaculate wines. Both tank-method and classic-method sparklers are produced, plus prosecco ranging from sweet to dry, from still to fully sparkling.

ALLEGRINI *Established* 1920 *Owners* Allegrini family *Vineyard area* 60 acres (24 ha)

Allegrini makes a warm, spicy, full but supple wine from one of Valpolicella's top sites. La Poja is an excellent single varietal corvina. Allegrini wines in general are marked by great vibrancy.

Other good regional producers in North Central Italy are Ca' del Bosco (in Franciacorta), Quintarelli (Valpolicello Classico), Anselmi, Bolla, and Inama (all Soave Classico).

Friuli–Venezia Giulia

Friuli (as this area is usually called) has its main growing area inland. The Grave wines are the most representative and are good, but exceptional wines come from the twin zones of Collio and Colli Orientali. They yield slow-maturing white wines of considerable depth and breadth. Isonzo wines, just a few notches below the quality of those of Collio and Colli Orientali, are far less expensive.

The coastal strip includes the zones of Latisana, Annia, Aquileia, and Carso. Aquileia is the best-known but Carso is the most intriguing. Producers in these zones make lean, somewhat astringent, but softly fruited wines.

There are almost thirty grape varieties grown in Friuli, including some internationals, a small group of Italian origin, and a fairly large group of local varieties. The area is best known for its white wines, although reds are also produced. The most important local white variety, tocai friulano, drunk young has a lively florality, but

In vino veritas.
(There is truth in wine.)
PLINY THE ELDER
(AD 23–79)

develops a nuttiness with hints of fennel. Ribolla gialla wines are almost buttery, with a lean, crisp edge, and lemony fruitiness. Verduzzo in Collio Orientali matures to a deep, honeyed fruitiness. For sweet wines, the picolot reigns supreme. Other local whites include vitovska and malvasia istriana. Pinot bianco and tocai friulano give wines that are balanced and attractive. The local red varieties include the chunky, herby refosco dal peduncolo rosso, the spicy, peppery schiopepettino, and tazzelenghe, pignolo, and franconia.

JERMANN *Established* 1881
Owner Silvio Jermann *Vineyard area* 110 acres (45 ha)

Jermann makes slow-developing, beautifully honed wines of perfume, depth, and varietal purity, including Rhine riesling and gewürztraminer. Also famed is Vintage Tunina, a white blend whose composition changes yearly, and an oaked chardonnay.

LE VIGNE DI ZAMÒ *Established* 1985/NA/1981
Owners Zamò family *Vineyard area* 25/NA/37 acres (10/NA/15 ha)

Each of the three estates in this grouping has a limited range of varieties chosen to maximize the potential of its site, although schioppettino shines at all three. At Vigne dal Leon, pinot bianco stands out; merlot marks out Zamò & Zamò (and the white blends here are most notable too). At Ronco del Gnemiz there is the glorious müller-thurgau.

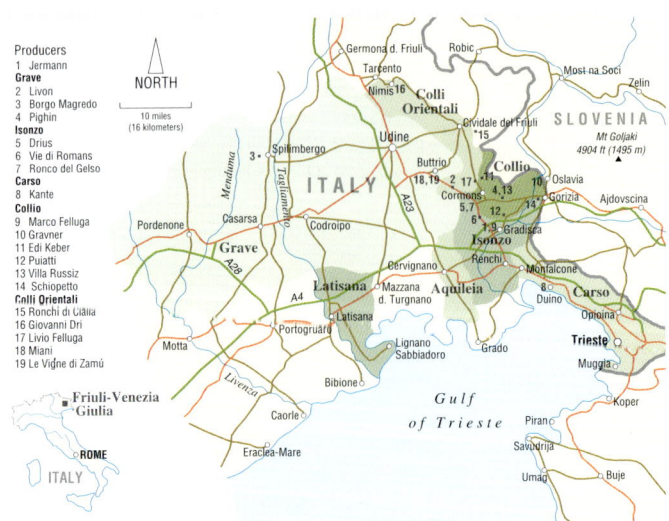

Producers
1 Jermann
Grave
2 Livon
3 Borgo Magredo
4 Pighin
Isonzo
5 Drius
6 Vie di Romans
7 Ronco del Gelso
Carso
8 Kante
Collio
9 Marco Felluga
10 Gravner
11 Edi Keber
12 Puiatti
13 Villa Russiz
14 Schiopetto
Colli Orientali
15 Ronchi di Cialla
16 Giovanni Dri
17 Livio Felluga
18 Miani
19 Le Vigne di Zamù

NORTH
10 miles
(16 kilometers)

A persimmon tree adorns the Colli Orientali del Friuli winery.

LIVON *Established* 1960
Owners Livon family *Vineyard area* 370 acres (150 ha)

This large company has holdings in Collio, Colli Orientali, and Grave, and cellars each zone. The wines are of reliably good quality throughout the large range, particularly the *crus*, but keep a watch for the non-*barriqued* whites destined for long aging.

KANTE *Established* 1980
Owner Edi Kante *Vineyard area* 18 acres (7 ha)

Carso estate Kante works primarily with the classic malvasia istriana and terrano, and the rare indigenous grape, vitovska. The estate also grows chardonnay and sauvignon.

VIE DI ROMANS *Established* 1976 *Owners* Gallo family *Vineyard area* 40 acres (16 ha)

An exquisitely crafted range is limited to varietal chardonnay, pinot grigio, sauvignon, and tocai, along with a white blend, Flores di Uis, and a red blend, Voos dai Ciamps. This is an Isonzo estate capable of reaching Collio quality.

EDI KEBER *Established* 1957 *Owner* Edi Keber *Vineyard area* 25 acres (10 ha)

One of Collio's rising stars, Keber concentrates on the varieties best suited to his terrain. He now produces a fabulously refined tocai and a richly fruited merlot. There is also a white blend and a red blend of similar quality.

SCHIOPETTO *Established* 1964 *Owner* Mario Schiopetto *Vineyard area* 57 acres (23 ha)

Mario Schiopetto brought *metodo friulano* to the area: cool-temperature, controlled fermentation.

Schiopetto wines are purely styled, long, and very classy, and certainly live up to the almost awe-inspiring reputation of this estate.

LIVIO FELLUGA *Established* 1956 *Owners* Livio Felluga & family *Vineyard area* 333 acres (135 ha)

Livio Felluga has plots of land in Colli Orientali, particularly around the Rosazzo subzone. Felluga's wines, which are greatly admired in many circles, are slim-styled and elegant.

MARCO FELLUGA/RUSSIZ SUPERIORE/ CASTELLO DI BUTTRIO *Established* 1905/ 1964/1994 *Owners* Felluga family *Vineyard area* 334/158/52 acres (135/64/21 ha)

Marco Felluga and Russiz Superiore (producing more intense wines) are both in Collio; Castello di Buttrio adds Colli Orientali to the portfolio. Early results here are distinctly promising.

Other good producers in Friuli are Borgo Magredo, Pighin (both in Graves), Drius, Ronco del Gelso (both in Isonzo), Villa Russiz, Gravner, Puiatti (all in Colli), Ronchi di Cialla, Colli Orientali del Friuli, Giovanni Dri, and Miani (all in Colli Orientali).

Trentino–Alto Adige

The region of Trentino–Alto Adige is Italy's northernmost. It links two provinces that once were part of Austria. The region is mountainous, and the vinelands follow the Adige river valley from the gorges of the north, broadening as the altitude drops, where vines become more prolific.

Nearly all wines here are single-varietals of three main groups: French origin (chardonnay, sauvignon, cabernet franc, cabernet sauvignon, pinot nero), German origin (müller-thurgau, Rhine riesling, sylvaner), and Italian or local origin (pinot bianco, malvasia, pinot grigio, moscato giallo, moscato rosa, rebo, schiava, lagrein, marzemino, nosiola, traminer aromatico, teroldego).

The local variety schiava is the most prolific and is particularly widely diffused in Alto Adige. It makes a lightish-colored, fresh, lightweight wine. Lagrein also finds its ideal growing conditions near Bolzano—lean and firm with plentiful fruit and good aging potential. On the Trentino side, marzemino makes a midweight red for simple quaffing but is better when grapes are grown in the Vallagarina, further south. Teroldego thrives on the Rotaliano Plain and makes a deep, firm, and rather well-structured wine of good acidity, richly berried with a herbal tang.

However, the region's image comes from its whites: pure-toned, with varietal character that can be piercingly fresh and with more penetrating perfume than most Italian whites. Chardonnay is now capturing the largest slice of the vineyard area. Trentino is also important for sparkling wine production, mostly from chardonnay, pinot bianco, pinot nero, and pinot meunier.

LAGEDER *Established* 1855 *Owner* Alois Lageder *Vineyard area* 42 acres (17 ha)

This large merchant house is moving steadily towards vineyard holdings and has several of note, the best known being Löwengang. There has also been investment in Casòn Hirschprunn, a separate estate. The estate wines have great individuality of character; the rest of the range, comprising over 20 wines, is well-typed and of good quality.

ABBAZIA DI NOVACELLA *Established* 1142 *Owner* Canonici Regolari Agostiniani di Novacella *Vineyard area* 45 acres (18 ha)

From its foundation in the middle of the twelfth century, the work of the Abbey of Novacella has included grape cultivation and winemaking. It is the prime exponent of the purity of aroma and freshness that Alto Adige wines can achieve. As well as being the focal point for research and development in Valle Isarco, this winery is the only commercial producer of any size north of the Isarco Valley.

Producers
Alto Adige
1 Hofstätter
2 Lageder
3 Abbazia di Novacella
4 Elena Walch
Trentino
5 Maso Cantanghel
6 Ferrari
7 Foradori
8 Tenuta San Leonardo
9 Pojer & Sandri
10 De Tarczal
11 Cantina La Vis

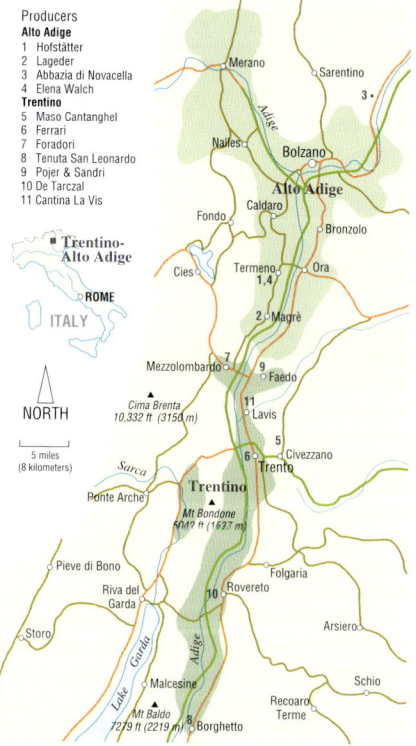

FERRARI *Established* 1902 *Owners* **Lunelli brothers** *Vineyard area* **190 acres (77 ha)**

This Trentino company, which passed from the Ferrari family to the Lunelli family in 1952, has always concentrated on sparkling wine at the top end of the market. The Ferrari sparklers now rival the best in Italy. A separate estate, Lunelli, has been set up recently, producing a range of still wines in line with the enterprise's reputation.

POJER & SANDRI *Established* 1975 *Owner* **Fiorentino Sandri & C.** *Vineyard area* **57 acres (23 ha)**

With high-sited vineyards at Faedo in northern Trentino, the steely, intensely perfumed delicacy of Pojer & Sandri's wines confound all those who claim there is a distinct difference between the styles of Alto Adige and Trentino.

DE TARCZAL *Established* 1700 *Owner* **Ruggeri dell'Adamo de Tarczal** *Vineyard area* **44 acres (18 ha)**

Though initially famous for Pragiara, a cabernet/merlot blend, De Tarczal's forte is marzemino, the most enjoyable, most dangerously drinkable wine of the

area. They also produce a somewhat more serious marzemino called Husar from selected grapes, and a small range of other varietals.

TENUTA SAN LEONARDO *Established* 1870 *Owners* **the Marquises Guerrieri Gonzaga** *Vineyard area* **44 acres (18 ha)**

Vines have been grown around this property in southern Trentino since at least the tenth century. The current owner, the Marquis Carlo Guerrieri Gonzaga, cultivates only merlot, cabernet sauvignon, and franc, and makes oaky, hugely powerful, slow-maturing wines that are unusual here.

Other significant producers in the Trentino–Alto Adige region are Hofstätter, Elena Walch (both in Alto Adige), Maso Cantanghel, Foradori, and Cantina La Vis (all in Trentino).

Right: *In Barolo, in the Piedmont region, the green vineyards contrast dramatically with the snow-covered mountain backdrop.* Below: *Buying grapes at the markets in Caprile, Castelli Romani, Lazio.*

Emilia–Romagna

Dappled shade beneath individually staked vines in the Emilio–Romagna region.

Whatever system one might use to classify Italy, the region of Emilia–Romagna doesn't fit. It is a long, straggly region, almost bisecting the country. Its topography and climate vary tremendously, but it does have highly fertile, perfectly flat, hazy countryside, famous for Parmesan cheese and Parma ham but not for vines. Vineyards are sparsely clustered on the poorer soils of the hilly outcrops.

In the far west lies the zone of Colli Piacentini, with similar grape varieties and wine styles to neighboring Oltrepò Pavese, except for guturnio, its own unique barbera/bonarda blend. In the center is the Colli Bolognesi—its core is the quality subzone of Zola Predosa. The wines, mainly single-varietals, come principally from the indigenous variety, pignoletto. A fair amount of barbera is grown, while the international varieties (cabernet sauvignon, merlot, chardonnay, sauvignon, and riesling) produce excellent, well-fruited wines here.

Growing across Romagna in the east are trebbiano di romagna, albana di romagna, sangiovese di Romagna, cagnina di romagna, and pagadebit di romagna. The strain of trebbiano grown here rarely produces wine worthy of much more than easy drinking. Albana is a middle-ranking white variety that requires considerable dedication and tenacity to produce wines of more than passing interest. Most of Romagna's sangiovese is a different strain from Tuscany's and can have a lively rusticity to it.

Lambrusco

Several strains of lambrusco are grown over a fair swathe of central–eastern and northeastern Italy but the area is largely concentrated near Modena. Its wine has become famous as something akin to sweetish, fizzy pop, a style that developed from cold weather halting natural fermentation. Not all lambrusco is like this; there are some dry versions around and some where the sweetness doesn't mask the wine's intrinsic fresh acidity and cherry-like natural character. There are three main strains: sorbara is often made dryer than most and has good perfume and good character; grasaparossa di Castelvetro is more fully flavored and often used for the sweeter wines; salamino di Santa Croce has both richness and acidity. White and pink are, in theory, still made from the red lambrusco grape but quite a bit of cheating goes on.

Producers
Colli Piacentini
1 Fugazza
2 La Stoppa
Lambrusco
3 Cavicchioli
4 Manicardi
5 Moro Rinaldo Rinaldi
Colli Bolognesi
6 Vigneto delle Terre Rosse
Romagna
7 Fattoria Paradiso
8 Fattoria Zerbina
9 Tre Monti

FUGAZZA *Established 1920 Owners Fugazza sisters Vineyard area 210 acres (85 ha)*

Maria Giulia and Giovannella Fugazza's land straddles the border between Emilia's Colli Piacentini and Lombardy's Oltrepò Pavese. Maria Giulia looks after the vineyards and Giovannella the cellars.

Their best wines are from bonarda and barbera, leading naturally to good gutturnio. They also work very well with malvasia and moscato.

MORO RINALDO RINALDINI *Established* 1972 *Owner* R. Rinaldini *Vineyard area* 37 acres (15 ha)

Rinaldini makes "serious" sparkling lambrusco (dry), with its second fermentation being in bottle rather than in tank. It also produces sparkling chardonnay, dry sparkling malvasia, and a lightly sparkling pinot, all with bottle fermentation.

FATTORIA PARADISO *Established* 1940 *Owner* Mario Pezzi *Vineyard area* 100 acres (40 ha)

The Pezzi family overturned public cynicism about the quality of Romagna wines. The *cru* Sangiovese di Romagna, Vigna delle Lepri, was well above all competition because it was made from the Tuscan strain of sangiovese. Pezzi wisely repropagated the disparaged pagadebit. He also discovered a deep, richly fruited variety he dubbed barbarossa, from what appeared to be a natural mutation of a single plant in his vineyards, and has propagated this to excellent effect.

VIGNETO DELLE TERRE ROSSE *Established* 1961 *Owners* Vallanias *Vineyard area* 49 acres (20 ha)

Vine cultivation as organic as possible, varieties suited to their terrain, and no use of oak in aging give rise to beautifully fruited, cleanly structured, and long-lived cabernet sauvignon, notably in the Cuvée Enrico Vallania, a refined chardonnay, a surprisingly complex malvasia, intriguing pinot grigio, and a wonderful, multilayered, minerally, balanced late-harvest riesling.

MANICARDI *Established* 1980 *Owners* Manicardi family *Vineyard area* 42 acres (17 ha)

This small estate is well-known for its balsamic vinegar. It has had a recent major upturn in the quality of its wines. All are from the Castelvetro sub-area and lambrusco di castelvetro strain. There is a dry version as well as the more common amabile, and a dry, lightly sparkling version.

Other excellent producers found in the Emilia–Romagne region include La Stoppa (in Colli Piacentini), Cavicchioli (in Lambrusco), Fattoria Zerbina, and Tre Monti (both in Romagna).

Tuscany

The heart of Tuscany is its central hills: Chianti's southerly massifs of Montalcino and Montepulciano. The soul is the sangiovese grape. Some liken its aromas to fresh tea with an overlay of prunes, sometimes plums or cherries. It is often notably spicy, with a good swathe of acidity that should be balanced by ripe tannins. Sangiovese makes lively wines but every extra ounce of quality requires greater care and skill, so a stunning sangiovese remains a challenge. Other traditional red grapes grown in the area include canaiolo, mammolo, ciliegiolo, and colorino.

The primary white variety is trebbiano toscano, fine as a neutral base in blends. Traditionally it was partnered with malvasia del chianti, which makes soft, round, gently perfumed wines. Malvasia and trebbiano are used to good effect in vin santo, a wine made from *passito* grapes; some are dry, traditional styles are sweet.

Chianti classico wine is the region's linchpin. Chianti is also made far beyond the Chianti Classico region; it is made from sangiovese with perhaps small quantities of canaiolo, trebbiano, and malvasia.

Brunello di montalcino is one of Italy's most distinguished wines. It is rich, ripe, mouth-filling, powerful, and intense. The "younger brother" rosso di montalcino is zippier, fruitier, and cheaper. Bolgheri is unusual because it is the only Tuscan area not dominated by sangiovese. Bolgheri's cabernet-based sassicaia, born in 1968, showed the way forward for this region. Carmignano, once notable for its finesse, is now moving toward greater attack and presence. In the Maremma, in Tuscany's south, morellino is grown, and morellino di scansano is comparatively soft, round, open, and cherry-like. The Parrina zone produces sangiovese-based reds of midweight and some good whites.

The most important area for white wine production is the zone of San Gimignano. Vernaccia di San Gimignano can be pale-hued, light, clean, and fresh or deep, ripe, round, and fat.

Because many Tuscan wines do not comply with the DOC(G) labelling constraints, some producers created a new informal category for their higher quality wines—the "Super-Tuscans."

Producers

MARCHESI DI FRESCOBALDI   *Established* 1300s
Owners Marchesi di Frescobaldi *Vineyard area*
2000 acres (800 ha)

The Frescobaldi family's main holdings are in
Chianti Rufina and Chianti Rufina *cru* Monte-
sodi is their leading wine, punchy, spicy, full,
and well-oaked. A joint venture led to Luce and
Lucente—both sangiovese and merlot blends.

TENUTA DI CAPEZZANA   *Established* c.800s
Owners Conti Contini Bonacossi *Vineyard area*
c.220 acres (90 ha)

Conte Ugo Contini Bonacossi is Carmignano's
principal producer and he has advanced the
area's style: supremely elegant wines, but with
good grip and fine aging potential. Their lively
Barco Reale di Carmignano and the drinkable
deep rosé, Vin Ruspo, stand out.

CASTELLO DI AMA   *Established* 1970s   *Owners*
Castello di Ama *Vineyard area* 235 acres (96 ha)

Ama wines differ from most chianti; stalkier,
leaner, and with a more restrained fruitiness that
can give them noticeable refinement. The estate
has three distinctive chianti classico *crus*, plus
merlot, pinot nero, sauvignon, and chardonnay.

ANTINORI   *Established* 1300s
Owners M. Antinori *Vineyard
area* c.850 acres (350 ha)

Antinori produces immensely
drinkable wines with broad
appeal. Santa Cristina and
Chianti Classico Peppoli are
popular; Solaia (cabernet/
sangiovese) and Tignanello
(sangiovese/cabernet) have
proved the estate's worth at
the higher end of the market.

*Rows of vines lead to a winery
building in Chianti, Tuscany.*

ISOLE E OLENA   *Established* 1971   *Owner* Paolo
de Marchi *Vineyard area* 110 acres (45 ha)

Paolo de Marchi has developed a particularly
lively, fruit-forward style, allied with great depth
and complexity. Super-Tuscan Cepparello (100
percent sangiovese) is extremely concentrated
and slow-developing; the rich Vin Santo is one of
the region's best. His syrah is one of the most
intriguing expressions of the grape in Italy.

CASTELLO DI VOLPAIA   *Established* NA   *Owner*
Giovannella Stianti *Vineyard area* 100 acres (40 ha)

Volpaia's vineyards are set particularly high on
a well-exposed site with a good sand content,
which gives a special elegance to the wines.
Sangiovese clones give the classy, assertive,
long-lived wines a further edge. Apart from
impeccable Chianti Classico there are two well-
honed Super-Tuscans, Coltassala and Balifico.

PONTE A RONDOLINO (ALSO TERUZZI E
PUTHOD)   *Established* 1974   *Owners* Enrico
Teruzzi and Carmen Puthod *Vineyard area*
94 acres leased (39 ha)

The round, rich style of Teruzzi's Vernaccia
brought the estate to prominence but now it is
the overtly oaked Terre di Tufi version that has
achieved the greater critical acclaim.

Tall cypresses line the road to the vineyard Castello di Volpaia, which is in Chianti, Tuscany.

AVIGNONESI   *Established* 1978   *Owners* Avignonesi S.p.A.–Falvo brothers   *Vineyard area* 250 acres (100 ha)

Avignonesi is of the big and powerful school of Vino Nobile di Montepulciano; their blockbuster wines are saved from unapproachability by a plentiful supple fruit. There are about a dozen other wines in the range, of which the Vin Santo Occhio di Pernice is legendary.

CASTELLO BANFI   *Established* 1978   *Owners* Banfi Vintners USA   *Vineyard area* 2,000 acres (800 ha)

About 370 acres (150 ha) are dedicated exclusively to brunello di montalcino. The cellar, one of Italy's largest, houses over 3,000 *barriques* and hundreds of larger barrels. Banfi spearheaded the revival of the moscadello di montalcino. The range of wines produced is large. All are well-made and unimpeachable in type.

BIONDI SANTI   *Established* 1700s   *Owners* Biondi Santi S.p.A.   *Vineyard area* 110 acres (45 ha)

As the "father" of Brunello di Montalcino, Biondi Santi is legendary for the longevity of his wines. The range (previously just Brunello and Rosso) has been enhanced by half-a-dozen other wines, especially Sassoalloro (sangiovese).

TENUTA DELL'ORNELLAIA   *Established* late 1970s   *Owner* Marchese Ludovico Antinori   *Vineyard area* 170 acres (70 ha)

The Marchese Ludovico Antinori's "California style" Ornellaia (85 percent cabernet sauvignon/merlot/cabernet franc) is fatter, riper, and punchier than sassicaia but less complex. The Bolgheri estate also stands out for Le Volte (cabernet sauvignon/merlot), the intense Masseto (merlot), and the racy Poggio alle Gazze (sauvignon).

IL POGGIONE   *Established* early 1900s   *Owners* NA   *Vineyard area* 155 acres (63 ha)

Il Poggione makes some of the most enthralling wines of Montalcino. The estate's former winemaker, Pierluigi Talenti, a stickler for quality, had an intuitive feel for viticulture. His detailed work in the vineyards brought Il Poggione to the fore. Talenti's place is now taken by Fabrizio Bindocci.

LE PUPILLE   *Established* 1972   *Owners* Gentili family   *Vineyard area* 40 acres (16 ha)

Le Pupille sets the tone in Scansano. Always refining its approach, the wines are big and punchy, with morellino made in three versions. There is also the highly regarded Saffredi (cabernet/merlot/alicante) and Solalto, a sweet wine (sauvignon/traminer/sémillon).

TENUTA DI VALGIANO   *Established* NA   *Owners* NA   *Vineyard area* 25 acres (10 ha)

Produced in Colline Lucchesi, the three Valgiano wines reach high levels of refinement and individuality. There is a racy, savory white, Giallo dei Muri; a vibrant and spicy red, Rosso di Palistorti; and the firmer, deeper Scasso dei Casari.

Other producers worth trying are Fattoria Selvapiana, Ruffino (both in Carmignano), Poliziano, Poderi Boscarelli (both Montepulciano), Casato Prime Donna, Costanti (both Montalcino), Fontodi, Agricola Querciabella, Castello di Brolio, Fattoria di Felsina, Montevertine (all Chianti Classico), and Tenuta San Guido (Bolgheri).

Central Italy

The central part of the Italian peninsula includes the regions of Marche, Umbria, and Lazio (sometimes called Latium). Widespread plantings of sangiovese and trebbiano form the base for much of the wine seen, but each region has at least one variety indigenous to one or more zones which put their stamp on the wines.

MARCHE

Marche is dominated by verdicchio, crisply acidic, softly fruited with flavors of various green and yellow fruits, and gently creamy but with good power behind. The main growing area is Verdicchio dei Castelli di Jesi but Verdicchio di Matelica makes a few superior wines: more muscular and intense.

An early stone carving held in the wine museum in Torgiano in Umbria.

Reds take second place here, yet there are two of note. Rosso conero is made almost exclusively from montepulciano, a grape producing a deeply colored, deeply flavored, richly fruited but well-structured, brambly red. Rosso piceno's best wines come from a small area called Rosso Piceno Superior.

BONCI *Established* 1962 *Owners* Bonci family *Vineyard area* 86 acres (35 ha)

One of Jesi's rising stars, the standard verdicchio is clean and well-styled but the estate's flair is shown by their verdicchio *crus*, Le Case and the perfumed, full, structured, warm, softly balanced

Producers
MARCHE
Verdicchio dei Castelli di Jesi
1   Fazi Battaglia
2   Bonci
3   Bucci
4   Colonnara
5   Umani Ronchi
6   Zaccagnini
Rosso Conero
7   Marchetti
8   Le Terrazze
Verdicchio di Matelica
9   La Monacesca
Rosso Piceno Superiore
10 Villa Pigna
11 Cocci Grifoni
UMBRIA
Torgiano
12 Lungarotti
Montefalco
13 Antonelli
14 Caprai
Orvieto
15 Bigi
16 Decugnano dei Barbi
17 Castello della Sala
18 Palazzone

LAZIO
Montefiascone
19 Falesco
Frascati
20 Colli di Catone
21 Fontana Candida
22 Castel de Paolis
23 Villa Simone
Marino
24 Colle Picchioni
Aprila
25 Casale del Giglio
Ciociaria
26 Colacicchi

San Michele. An attractive, sweet, *passito* verdicchio and a finely tuned brut sparkling verdicchio complete the range.

UMANI RONCHI   *Established* 1955 *Owners* Bernetti family *Vineyard area* 370 acres (150 ha)

This colossus of the Marche scene has quite a high reputation for its verdicchio and also for its rosso conero. Three verdicchio variants include the well-typed base version, the richer *cru* San Lorenzo, and the oaked Cumaro. *Cru* Casal di Serra stands out, but the entire range is really excellent value for money. Pèlago (a cabernet sauvignon/montepulciano/merlot blend) is achieving some acclaim.

Left: *Vegetable sellers in the markets in Lazio.* Below: *The fiery blaze of fall in the vineyards is a typical sight during October in Central Italy.*

ZACCAGNINI   *Established* 1974 *Owners* Zaccagnini brothers *Vineyard area* 70 acres (28 ha)

This estate produces single-vineyard, high-quality verdicchio wines. The oak-free *cru* Salmagina, intense, characterful, finely balanced, and of great depth, is still one of the best. In addition there are two finely honed sparkling verdicchios, Brut and Metodo Tradizionale.

MARCHETTI   *Established c.*1900 *Owners* Marchetti family *Vineyard area* 30 acres (12 ha)

Marchetti wines have set the standard for rosso conero. Once full, soft and deep, the style is now somewhat fresher and punchier while the intrinsic quality and longevity remain. The rosso conero selection, Villa Bonomi, is now the estate's leading wine.

LA MONACESCA   *Established* 1966 *Owner* Casimiro Cifola *Vineyard area* 55 acres (22 ha)

La Monacesca has long been the example par excellence of the Verdicchio di Matelica zone. Until recently the estate has concentrated almost exclusively on the verdicchio grape, but is now beginning to work with red grapes.

COCCI GRIFONI *Established* 1969 *Owner* Guido
Cocci Grifoni *Vineyard area* 100 acres (40 ha)

Cocci Grifoni is one of the longest standing
estates in the Piceno Superiore area. The wines
set the standards in the zone with their perfumed,
full-bodied, ripely fruited style. The estate also
works well with the white wines of the area.

UMBRIA

Much of Umbria is formed of tightly packed,
rounded hills, cut through by the upper reaches
of the River Tiber. Lake Trasimeno and the northern part of the river have adjacent vineyards, Colli
del Trasimeno and Colli Altotiberini respectively.
The wines include varietals from chardonnay,
pinot grigio, riesling italico, cabernet sauvignon,
and pinot nero, plus red torgiano made from a
sangiovese-based blend, and white torgiano from
trebbiano (mostly) and grechetto. Grechetto, a
native white variety, makes punchy but rounded
and rather nutty wines of good character. Its red
counterpart is sagrantino, a magnificent variety
that makes big, ripe, black-fruited wines of tremendous depth, length, and vigor. It is the power-
house behind the red wines of the Montefalco
zone. In the south, Colli Amerini is good value,
but most significant here is Orvieto, which turns
out well-made trebbiano-based wines.

*Umbria is typically a hilly region; here the small town of
Poggio Lavarino straddles a terraced hill.*

LUNGAROTTI *Established* 1950 *Owners*
Lungarotti family *Vineyard area* 750 acres (300 ha)

Lungarotti is quite simply synonymous with
Torgiano—the village and the wine. The wine
names, Torre di Giano (white) and Rubesco (red),
may even be better known than the denomination itself; the *riserva*-level wines, most notably
cru Vigna Monticchio, have starry reputations,
and the entire range is highly considered.

CAPRAI *Established* 1971 *Owners* Caprai family
Vineyard area 200 acres (80 ha)

Arnaldo Caprai concentrated on sagrantino to
become one of Montefalco's leading producers,
especially with Sagrantino di Montefalco Passito.

The Sagrantino di Montefalco is now *barriqued*,
tremendous in power and intensity, and made
for the long haul, especially the Sagrantino di
Montefalco 25 Anni.

DECUGNANO DEI BARBI *Established* 1973
Owners Barbi family *Vineyard area* 80 acres (32 ha)

The Barbi family cultivate organically and research clones of their varieties. The top of their
range of orvietos is the *barrique*-fermented IL,
although purists prefer the non-oaked Orvieto
Classico Decugnano dei Barbi. The simpler
Orvieto Classico Barbi, a botrytized orvieto, a
sparkling wine, and three reds complete the range.

CASTELLO DELLA SALA *Established* 1977 *Owner*
Marchese Antinori *Vineyard area* 350 acres (140 ha)

This medieval fortressed castle, built around
1350, was turned to wine production in 1977.
Piero Antinori's wines, perfectly constructed,
have won endless awards, especially Cervaro
della Sala, from chardonnay (with a little
grechetto). Muffato della Sala is from sauvignon,
grechetto, and others, and is botrytized. A pinot
nero has also gained renown.

Rows of vines flank the front of the old winery buildings at Torgiano in Umbria.

LAZIO

Lazio is near Italy's capital, Rome. Frascati is the main wine, made principally from trebbiano and the local malvasia di candia. In the reds, much use is made of sangiovese and montepulciano, and, increasingly, merlot, canaiolo, and ciliegiolo.

FALESCO   *Established* 1979 *Owner* Riccardo Cotarella *Vineyard area* All grapes bought in

Riccardo Cotarella's Est! Est!! Est!!! first brought this strangely named wine out of disrepute and there is now a *cru* version, Poggio dei Gelsi, nuanced and ripely fruity. Cotarella also produces a varietal Grechetto and Vitiano (merlot/ cabernet sauvignon/sangiovese) from grapes grown in Umbria, but the flagship is Montiano (100 percent merlot), which is a punchy giant of a wine.

FONTANA CANDIDA   *Established* 1958 *Owner* Gruppo Italiano Vini *Vineyard area* 225 acres (91 ha)

Almost half of all frascati is produced here. The *cru* Santa Teresa, with 30 percent malvasia del lazio, is one of the best frascatis on the market. The Frascati Terre dei Grifi, lighter and fresher, has a higher proportion of trebbiano; also from the Terre dei Grifi range is a broad but nuanced wine from 100 percent malvasia del lazio.

VILLA SIMONE   *Established* 1980 *Owners* Costantini family *Vineyard area* 50 acres (20 ha)

With the intent of making superior frascati, Piero Costantini replanted the vineyards with a goodly proportion of malvasia del lazio and modernized the cellar. The resultant wines are elegant, individually styled, and cleanly aromatic, especially the *crus* Vigneto Filonardi and Vigna dei Preti.

COLLE PICCHIONI   *Established* 1976 *Owners* P. & A. di Mauro *Vineyard area* 22 acres (9 ha)

Relying on the "minor" grapes of the Marino zone, Paola di Mauro's wines are intense, complex, long-lived and fascinating. Marino Etichetta Verde, the estate's base wine, is excellent. Marino Etichetta Oro is several notches richer as well as deeper; Le Vignole is slow-developing and exceptional. Its red partner, Vigna del Vassallo, is from merlot, cabernet sauvignon, and cabernet franc.

CASALE DEL GIGLIO   *Established* 1968 *Owners* Santarelli family *Vineyard area* 300 acres (120 ha)

In 1984 this estate embarked on a major research project to establish the varieties best suited to its lands near the coast in Aprilia, about 30 miles (50 km) southeast of Rome. Now working with a range of international varieties, its best known wine is Satrico (chardonnay/trebbiano).

COLACICCHI   *Established* 1950 *Owners* Trimani family *Vineyard area* 12 acres (5 ha)

The tiny but highly prestigious Colacicchi flagship is Torre Ercolana (cabernet sauvignon/merlot/cesanese). The wines are not released until ready for drinking; for Torre Ercolana, this means after about eight years. A younger red, Romagnano Rosso, is made from the same varieties, and there is a white, Romagnano Bianco.

Other good producers in Central Italy include Fazi Battaglia, Bucci, Colonnara, Le Terazze, Villa Pigna (all in Marche), Antonelli, Bigi, Colli di Catone, Palazzone, (all in Umbria), and Castel de Paolis (in Lazio).

Southern Italy

The southern realm is the sleeping giant of Italy. Despite an abundance of quality grape varieties, it has taken a very long time for a critical mass of good wine to be produced.

ABRUZZO, PUGLIA, AND MOLISE

Abruzzo is one of Italy's most beautiful regions, with sandy beaches and high peaks. Here montepulciano reigns. The wines are most structured and probably at their most typical around Pescara, while in L'Aquila they are lighter and more elegant. With white wine in Abruzzo, practically the only denomination is trebbiano d'abruzzo. Controguerra is produced only in Abruzzo's northeast corner: the red is from montepulciano blended with some cabernet sauvignon and/or merlot; the white is from trebbiano toscano with some of the indigenous variety, passerina.

Puglia is the south's go-ahead wine region, with a string of native grape varieties. Here, the center of attention is the narrow Salento Peninsula in the far south. The indigenous red variety, negroamaro, the "bitterblack," was renowned for deeply colored, impenetrably intense, bitter-finishing, and long-lived wines that needed a touch of the aromatic red malvasia to make them approachable. Negroamaro is now being shaped into a riper, fruitier, more drinkable wine.

The Salento's traditional wines made from primitivo are robust, mouth-filling, richly fruity, and strongly spicy red wines that are either dry (or off-dry) and strongly alcoholic, or sweet and fairly strongly alcoholic. Further north, uva di troia is the prime red grape, making a firm, stylish, minerally wine. Pampanuto is its white partner. They are at their best in Castel del Monte wines. Puglia also produces some of Italy's best rosés.

Molise is Italy's ugly-duckling region; there is just one producer of note, Di Majo Norante.

Producers
Abruzzo
1 Barone Cornacchia
2 Dino Illuminati
3 Masciarelli
4 Camillo Montori
5 Orlandi Contucci Ponno
6 Cantina Tollo
7 Valentini
Molise
8 Di Majo Norante
Puglia
9 Botromagno
10 Leone de Castris
11 Rivera
12 Rosa del Golfo
13 Pervini
14 Cosimo Taurino
15 Agricole Vallone
Campania
16 D'Ambra
17 Feudi di San Gregorio
18 Mastroberardino
19 Villa Matilde
20 Pietratorcia
21 Grotta del Sole
Calabria
22 Librandi
Basilicata
23 D'Angelo
24 Paternoster
Sardinia
25 Argiolas
26 Capichera
27 Cherchi
28 Contini
29 Santadi
30 Sella & Mosca

Many of the old buildings in Puglia feature exquisitely decorated facades, as shown in this intricate example from the town of Martina Franca.

In Puglia, wine bottles grace the walls of these stone trulli buildings, which house some local shops.

DI MAJO NORANTE

Established 1960s *Owner* Alessio di Majo *Vineyard area* 150 acres (60 ha)

Molise's sole quality producer cultivates organically, and concentrates on varietals from the south's most prized grapes: falanghina, fiano, greco, aglianico, and moscato. The wines have always been individual and characterful; quality varies.

MASCIARELLI *Established* 1981 *Owner* Gianni Masciarelli *Vineyard area* 122 acres (50 ha)

Masciarelli wines have great structure and complexity. The leading wine, Montepulciano d' Abruzzo Villa Gemma, is a remarkable mix of elegance and power. Marina Cvetic is a celebrated chardonnay. Wines are consistently well-made.

CAMILLO MONTORI *Established* 1879 *Owner* Camillo Montori *Vineyard area* 100 acres (40 ha)

Montori's attention to detail has ensured his wines have long been in Abruzzo's top rank, especially his leading Fonte Cupa line, although recently a more overtly oaky style has knocked them off-key. Montori makes a noteworthy Trebbiano d'Abruzzo.

COSIMO TAURINO *Established* late 1800s *Owners* Taurino family *Vineyard area* 270 acres (110 ha)

Cosimo Taurino has turned out some of Puglia's best wines. The estate's emblem is Patriglione, a big, overtly rich, chocolatey, spicy wine, while the leaner, firmer Notarpanaro is more typical of modern handling of negroamaro.

LEONE DE CASTRIS *Established* 1665 *Owner* Salvatore Leone de Castris *Vineyard area* 1,100 acres (450 ha)

This estate's Five Roses, a soft but fully flavored rosé, established Puglia's reputation for pink wines. Leone de Castris is also credited with shaping salice salentino. It is renowned for the *barrique*-aged red Donna Lisa Salice Salentino Riserva: intense, structured, spicy, and deep.

ROSA DEL GOLFO *Established* 1939 *Owners* Lina and Damiano Calò *Vineyard area* nil

Rosa del Golfo is one of Italy's top rosés. From negroamaro and malvasia nera, it is comparatively deeply colored, ripely perfumed, midweight, and pure-toned with abundant, strawberry-like fruit. Work is being done on negroamaro-based reds and a verdeca-based white.

VALENTINI *Established* 1650 *Owner* E. Valentini *Vineyard area* 155 acres (63 ha)

Valentini handcrafts his wines into some of the most exquisite bottles to be found anywhere. He handles only the peak of his grapes, and releases wines only when he considers them ready

A 1998 Rosso del Salento, from Puglia.

for drinking. The Montepulciano d'Abruzzo is legendary: slow-developing, with great longevity and outstanding complexity; while the Trebbiano d'Abruzzo is an astonishingly rich, structured, deeply perfumed, and multi-layered wine.

SARDINIA

For a long time Sardinia's wine fell into two categories: light, fresh, innocuous whites and heavy reds, usually from the cannonau variety, much appreciated by the locals. Cannonau is Sardinia's best known red grape, producing warm, broad, often alcoholic reds. Monica also makes lively drinkable red wines.

Among the white grapes, vermentino at its best expresses a lively, peach-like, almost buttery character. Torbato gives firm, creamy, lightly spicy wines. There is much demand for sweet and fortified wines, some of the most interesting being made from malvasia and moscato. Vernaccia di oristano is often compared with sherry.

CONTINI *Established* 1898 *Owners* Contini family *Vineyard area* NA

Contini has managed to keep the sherry-like Vernaccia di Oristano a living force. The wines, especially the Riservas, have an intense nuttiness with great individuality and complexity. The company has several other wines, mainly from vermentino, cannonau, and nièddera.

SELLA & MOSCA *Established* 1899 *Owners* Sella & Mosca S.p.A. *Vineyard area* 1,235 acres (500 ha)

Sella & Mosca has been Sardinia's leading estate for generations, and has an extensive and growing range of wines, all carefully made and of good style. This is practically the only producer to work consistently with torbato, most notably in the wine Terre Bianche. Anghelu Ruju is sweet, strong and port-like, from partially dried cannonau; the Marchese di Villamarina (cabernet sauvignon) is also gaining respect.

ARGIOLAS *Established* 1938 *Owners* Argiolas & C. SaS *Vineyard area* 540 acres (220 ha)

Argiolas's wines are made predominantly from vermentino, nuragus, monica, and cannonau and are of fine quality throughout, the top of the range being the *barrique*-aged red Turriga, from cannonau, carignano, and others, and the partially *barrique*-aged white Angialis, from nasco and malvasia.

CAMPANIA AND CALABRIA

Northern Campania was the home of Italy's most famous wine in Roman days—the revived falerno matches its ancient Roman forebear as closely as possible. White falerno del massico is floral, with elegant but pervasive fruit, notable depth, and good longevity. The red is refined and well-structured. Three of Campania's most important wines, taurasi (from aglianico), greco di tufo (greco), and fiano di avellino (fiano), come from the hill territory inland near Avellino. All three improve with age. Other important wine areas in Campania include the island of Ischia, home of two white varieties, biancolella and forastera, and Aversa, home of a lemony fresh asprinio.

Practically the only wine in Calabria with an international reputation is cirò, both red and white cirò being prime examples of Calabria's indigenous varieties, the red gaglioppo and white greco.

Detail of stone trulli storehouse rooftops in Puglia.

An old stone storehouse in Puglia.

are Critone (chardonnay/sauvignon), the softly attractive rosé Terre Lontane (gaglioppo/cabernet franc), and the classic white, rosé, and red Cirò. Le Pasulle is a finely honeyed, rich but not cloying sweet wine made from mantonico.

MASTROBERARDINO *Established* 1878 *Owners* **Antonio, Carlo, and Pietro Mastroberardino** *Vineyard area* 150 acres (60 ha)

Mastroberardino introduced Avellino's three leading wines: Taurasi, Fiano di Avellino, and Greco di Tufo. The wines are reliably good if not exceptional quality, although older vintages of Taurasi show great longevity.

FEUDI DI SAN GREGORIO *Established* 1986 *Owners* Capaldo and Ercolino families *Vineyard area* 200 acres (80 ha)

Now one of the best known Campanian names, the wines are reliable, carefully made, well typed and well priced. They are led by Campanaro and Pietracalda (both fiano di avellino), Serpico (aglianico/piedirosso/sangiovese), and Taurasi.

GROTTA DEL SOLE *Established* 1989 *Owners* Martusciello family *Vineyard area* 17 acres (7 ha)

Grotta del Sole produces a large range of wines but its interest lies in reinforcing the image of the area's traditional wines and restoring those fallen from favor. Thus it has been the force behind the revival of traditional, tree-trained asprinio (still and sparkling) and has also resurrected the much-maligned Lacryma Christi del Vesuvio. Quite unusually, a piedirosso *passito* is also produced.

LIBRANDI *Established* 1950 *Owners* Librandi family *Vineyard area* 160 acres (65 ha)

The top wines here are the half-modernist Gravello, from a blend of gaglioppo with 40 percent cabernet sauvignon, and the traditional Duca Sanfelice, exclusively from gaglioppo. Also good

BASILICATA

Basilicata is almost a one-grape (aglianico), one-wine (aglianico del vulture) region. The wines are initially tannic with firm balancing acidity, full and powerful, minerally and darkly fruity.

Eyes of the wolf

Campania, with Naples as its capital, is a wine region that was once known as the producer of some of the finest wines of the Mediterranean basin. Today the region is not quite as well known for quality wines, but still has plenty of legend and lore. Campania Felix, as the Romans called it, is the home of a dry white wine called "Lachryma Christi." The wine was said to be so good it would bring tears to the eyes of Christ. Interestingly, the grape variety used to make Lachryma Christi is "coda di volpe," or "eyes of the wolf."

PATERNOSTER *Established* 1925 *Owners* Paternoster family *Vineyard area* 16 acres (6.5 ha)

The Paternoster wines, when on form, excel for attack, structure, density, and deep, ripe fruitiness. Aglianico del Vulture Don Anselmo is produced only when the vintage warrants it but the standard Aglianico, made annually, is more classically styled. There is also a white wine, Bianco di Corte, from fiano, and a sparkling Moscato.

Other particularly good Southern Italy producers are shown on the location map on page 181.

Sicily

Sicily's master grape is nero d'avola. It yields deep color and intensely ripe, blackberry-like fruit with an undernote of brown sugar, and can give high alcohol. Other red grapes are frappato, the light-hued nerello mascalese, and perricone.

Sicily produces far more white wine than red, however, and the grape seen most widely is catarratto. While it can make wines lacking grace, it can also turn out well-structured, well-rounded wines with a good fruit core. More generally appreciated, particularly for its elegant, floral perfumes, is inzolia.

Grillo is easily the best grape for marsala production, yet restrictions mean most marsala houses primarily use catarratto. The sweet wines of the Aeolian archipelago to the northeast are made from malvasia and those of the island of Pantelleria from zibibbo, the local name for muscat d'alexandria.

Good wines are produced in a number of different locations on the island. The hills behind Palermo give wines full of character; Pachino (in the southeast) has rich, full nero d'avola; Cerasuola di Vittoria's blend of nero d'avola and frappato is developing; the zone of Contee di Scafini has many different wine types; and Etna's wines are improving all the time.

Marsala

Marsala's quality has returned and it comes in a broad array of styles. Although catarratto is the most widely used grape and grillo the ideal, up to seven varieties (three of them red) may be used. The classic wine is a light nut-brown, but the categories oro, ambra, and rubino exist for light

A stroll along the streets of northern Sicily reveals some delightful insights into the island's casual lifestyle.

golden, amber, and ruby-red respectively. The basic wine is fortified and often sweetened, then aged, usually in oak. The wines are classified according to alcohol, aging and sweetness, as marsala fine, marsala superiore, superiore riserva, and then, if the wine is dry, marsala vergine and marsala vergine/soleras riserva.

Producers

DUCA DI SALAPARUTA   *Established* 1824
Owners **Illva Saronno S.p.A.** *Vineyard area* **NA**

This company's brand, Corvo, was at one time synonymous with Sicilian wine. Mostly it offers enjoyable but unexceptional wines, however, two are superior: Duca d'Enrico, from nero d'avola, and Bianca di Valguarnera, from inzolia. Both are heavily oaked.

The satellite islands

Far off the southwest coast of Sicily, two-thirds of the way to Tunisia, lies the volcanic island of Pantelleria. The fierce winds, hot sun, and black soil, means little can grow except capers and vines low-planted in hollows. Here the zibibbo grape makes some of Italy's most delectable sweet wine. The classic style is *passito*, with the early-ripening, sugar-rich grapes quick-dried on mats in late summer. Moscato Passito di Pantelleria is redolent of dried fruits and cassata; it is mouth-filling and luscious, but never cloying. Moscato di Pantelleria Naturale, lighter and fresher, is made from non-*passito* grapes.

To the northeast of Sicily lie the Aeolian (Lipari) islands, an archipelago of volcanic outcrops. While theoretically it is possible to produce wines throughout the islands, in practice vines are cultivated only on the island of Salina. Trained low, the vines grow on narrow terraces. The styles produced are similar to those of Pantelleria: *passito* and *naturale*, both sweet and aromatic, but using the malvasia grape, which gives a peachier effect.

PLANETA   *Established* 1990s   *Owners* **Planeta family** *Vineyard area* **650 acres (260 ha)**

During recent years Planeta has become one of the country's most esteemed estates, with impeccable wines. Planeta's skills show best in the blends of (mainly) native with nonnative grapes: La Segreta Bianco (grecanico/cataratto/chardonnay), La Segreta Rosso (nero d'avola/merlot), Santa Cecilia (nero d'avola/syrah), and Alastro (grecanico/cataratto).

COS   *Established* 1980   *Owner* **Giusto Occhipinti** *Vineyard area* **50 acres (20 ha)**

Giusto Occhipinti aspired to make cerasuolo di vittoria the way he remembered it at his grandparents' table. He has gradually built Cos into the best Vittoria estate. Demand is now high and the range has broadened with varietal inzolia, chardonnay, and cabernet, and some stunning nero d'avola.

FLORIO   *Established* 1833   *Owners* **Illva Saronno S.p.A.** *Vineyard area* **NA**

On the Marsala seafront, the long-standing Florio makes distinguished wines. At the top of the range is Marsala Vergine Terre Arse, a concentrated dry marsala with good nuttiness, followed by the lighter-styled Marsala Vergine Baglio Florio.

A basket of freshly picked olives is a common sight in Sicily. The island's Mediterranean climate is ideal for growing olives just as it is for establishing vineyards. Olives are produced in other parts of Italy where vineyards are also cultivated, such as in Tuscany and Puglia.

Although the temperatures can soar in summer in Sicily, the hillsides are cooler so grapes can thrive on the slopes.

TASCA D'ALMERITA   *Established* 1830 *Owners* Tasca family *Vineyard area* 545 acres (220 ha)

Tasca d'Almerita, in Contea di Scafani, is best-known for its Regaleali. The wines produced here are excellent; the flagship Rosso del Conte (nero d'avola/perricone) is full, punchy, and spicy, while Nozze d'Oro from tasca (probably sauvignonasse) and inzolia, is rich, buttery, and herbal. The varietals cabernet sauvignon and chardonnay are both big, concentrated, and of impeccable varietal character.

MARCO DE BARTOLI–MARSALA/PANTELLERIA
Established 1978 *Owner* Marco de Bartoli *Vineyard area* 60 acres (25 ha)

Marsala has been restored to a wine of quality, thanks to Marco de Bartoli. With Vecchio Samperi, a marsala-type wine based on the grillo grape, de Bartoli put Marsala back on the world map. He did the same for Pantelleria. Vecchio Samperi 20 Anni (20 years old, from *solera*) is fine, as is the Moscato Passito di Pantelleria Bukkuram. There are other wines in the range.

BARONE DI VILLAGRANDE   *Established* 1727 *Owners* Nicolosi family *Vineyard area* 42 acres (17 ha)

Of all the Etna estates, this one produces the best wines. The firm, slow-developing white, Etna Bianco Superiore, is more successful than the red from nerello mascalese, a troublesome wine due to its light tone: good, deep color is of great importance in Italy. From a holding on Salina comes an elegant, balanced Malvasia delle Lipari.

CARAVAGLIO   *Established* NA *Owner* Antonino Caravaglio *Vineyard area* NA

A local hero on the island of Salina and an emerging winemaker of note in Sicily, Caravaglio is hardly known beyond. Yet he makes an archetypal Malvasia delle Lipari, both *naturale* and *passito*, and also a fairly respectable dry white, Salina Bianco.

Other noteworthy producers in Sicily include Fazio Wines, Firriato, Pellegrino, Cantina Valle dell'Acate, Donnafugata, Elorina, and Murana.

Spain

Avilés
La Coruña   Ferrol   Gijón   Santander   Getxo   Irún
       Oviedo   (Algorta)   San Sebastián
     Mieres   Sestao   Barakaldo   (Donostia)
Lugo   Basauri   Eibar
Santiago de Compostela   Vitoria (Gasteiz)   Pamplona
Cordillera Cantábrica   León   Miranda de Ebro   (Iruña)
Ponferrada   Ebro   Logroño   Navarra
Rías Baixas   Burgos   Rioja   Huesca
Pontevedra   Ourense   Soria   Zaragoza
Vigo   Ribeiro   Valdeorras   El Teleño   Somontano
Minho   7173 ft (2187 m)
Rías Baixas   Zamora   Valladolid   Embalse de
               Duero   Ribera del   Mequinenza
Embalse   Rueda   Duero
de Almendra
Palencia
Tierra de Campos
Segovia
Pico Peñalara
8095 ft (2468 m)
Guadalajara
Ávila   Alcobendas
MADRID   Alcalá de Henares
Sierra de Gata   Leganés   Torrejón de Ardoz
              Getafe
Embalse de   Talavera de   Vinos de Madrid   Cuenca   Ojos-Negros
Alcántara II   la Reina   Aranjuez   Vila-Real de los Infantes
Plasencia   Tajo   Toledo   Sagunt
Cáceres   S P A I N   Turia   Valencia   Burjass
Cañamero   La Mancha   Utiel-   Valenc
Montrranchez   Júcar   Requena   Torrent
Badajoz   Mérida   Tomelloso
Tierra de Barros   Ciudad Real   Albacete   Alamansa   Ga
               Puertollano   Valdepeñas   Valencia
Zafra   Jumilla   Alicante
       Azuaga   S I E R R A   M O R E N A   Elda   Alcoy
                 Andújar   Linares   Elx   Alicante
             Córdoba   Úbeda   Orihuela
Palma del Río   Jaén   Murcia
Lora del Río   Écija   Montilla-   Lorca   Cartagena
Huelva   Camas   Guadalquivir   Moriles   Mazarrón
      Seville   Dos Hermanas   Sistemas   Béticos
Huelva   Utrera   Granada   Gulf of
Gulf of Cádiz   Morón   Sierra Nevada   Mazarrón
       de la Frontera   Málaga   Mulhacén
Jeréz de la Frontera   11,421 ft (3482 m)   Almería
     Cádiz   Jeréz   Málaga   Motril
San Fernando   Chiclana de
        la Frontera
Cabo Trafalgar   Algeciras
          Gibraltar (U.K.)
Strait of Gibraltar

P Y R

NORTH

60 miles
(96 kilometers)

Spain

In Spain at the turn of the twentieth century, wine was an agri-cultural product, produced alongside potatoes, tomatoes, and peppers, and vines were grown to achieve quantity rather than quality. In those days, wine wasn't even regarded as an alcoholic drink—it was just another condiment in the gastro-nomic "mix" which included other essentials of the Spanish diet and formed the foundation of the *comida*—the midday meal that was the main food and drink event of the day. There were few famous names and only a couple of well-known regions—Jeréz and Rioja. Production often took place in local cooperative bodegas, and this is where the vast majority of the population went, usually on Sunday after church, to pick up their week's supply of wine.

A century on, there are still sleepy neighborhood cooperatives which sell in bulk, and rural areas where food and wine come together with happy anonymity, but these are now in the minority as Spanish wine regions have rediscovered and, in some cases, reinvented themselves to meet something which no one there even knew existed a century ago: the market.

Spanish wine is a microcosm of the whole vinous world, with frost-cool, fruit-up-front reds from mountain vineyards; classic dry whites with mouthwateringly ripe, citrus-fruit flavors; sparkling cava from Catalonia, and the old favorites too: gently oaky, rich, and cigar-box-scented rioja and magnificently ancient oloroso. Much of this success has been—and is still being—built on Spain's own native grape varieties. Although many of Spain's finest wines are made from such "international" varieties as cabernet sauvignon, merlot, and chardonnay, many winemakers have returned to their roots with delightful results. These include magnificent tempranillo, crisp verdejo in Rueda, peachy albariño and spicy godello in Galicia, the almost-forgotten graciano in Rioja, and the formerly disregarded monastrell in the Levant. Spain's mountainous terrain brings with it a wealth of microclimates and individual parcels of *terreño*, which all come together to create wines of particular individuality and history.

It was the Moors arriving from North Africa who introduced distilling to Spain and by the time they left Spain, the southwest's wines were reckoned the world's finest. While in the nineteenth century Spain had world-class wine in cava and rioja, sadly in the earlier part of the twentieth century the world lost interest in Spanish wines and most became regarded as cheap and cheerful plonk. However, the 1970s saw a "new wave" of Spanish winemaking, mainly in Catalonia, and there is a current wine renaissance in Galicia.

> *I love everything that's old: old friends, old times, old manners, old books, old wine.*
>
> **OLIVER GOLDSMITH**
> (1782–1874),
> *She Stoops to Conquer*

The countryside around Catalonia is not just a wine-producing area, it is also a major source of cork production.

Wines

SHERRY

Sherry has been through a hard time, thanks to changing fashions, but the *solera* system still makes it one of the world's best-value fine wines. Wines from the new vintage are introduced into a *criadera*, or "nursery" partly filled with wine from the previous vintage. The new wine takes on the characteristics of the old and this mixture is, in turn, passed to another, older *criadera* until eventually, the wine passes into the *solera*—the final row of barrels. The end result is a wine of impressive consistency and maturity.

There are several different styles of sherry. Fino is one of the palest and driest, lightly fortified. Amontillados are aged for ten or fifteen years, or more. Olorosos have a rich (not sweet), nutty character and can age for decades. Palo cortado, some of the finest wines of Jeréz, are rich, complex, and long-lived. Cream and Pale cream are blended wines for the mass market.

RIOJA

For rioja, the best grapes—mainly tempranillo and graciano—tend to come from the Alta and Alavesa areas; mazuelo and garnacha come from the warmer, drier Rioja Baja. Famous-name wines consist of a mixture of most or all of these varieties. The old *reservas*, at their best, have a wonderful mellow softness and age with grace. In the Alavesa region, however, they often make delicious red wines from pure tempranillo and drink them young. White and pink rioja are also made, of which the white, made usually from viura (macabeo) and malvasía riojana, is most prominent. Traditional whites are very rich, spicy, oaky, and aromatic. Modern styles may have just a touch of oak or none at all to maintain the natural freshness of the grape.

Barrels line the cellar at the Torres Winery in the Penedés zone of Catalonia.

Aging regulations

Joven means the wine has had less than six months in oak casks, or none at all. *Crianza* has at least six months in oak; white and pink must spend a year in the bodega, and red *crianza* two years. White and pink *reserva* must spend six months in oak and two years in the bodega; red *reserva* three years in the bodega (at least one in oak and at least one in bottle). *Gran reserva* wines spend an extra year in the bodega; red *gran reserva* at least two years in oak and three in bottle.

CAVA

Cava's birthplace was Catalonia, in the late 1800s; it mostly still comes from this area. Traditional cava continues to be made from any or all of the major three Catalan grape varieties: parellada, xarel-lo, and macabeo (viura). Chardonnay is also used by some producers. Cava must be made by the *método tradicional* and spend nine months on its lees before it can be released. Producers do particularly well making modestly priced wines that drink splendidly while young. There is a trend towards older, richer, more complex wines.

Galicia and the Basque Country

The north is known as "green Spain" because of its verdant pastures and woodlands. This is a cool, wet area, which favors grapes for white wines. Galicia is close to Portugal and separated from its nearest Spanish neighbor, Castilla-León, by mountains. Although in the past its wines have shared an affinity with *vinho verde*, new winemaking techniques and an enthusiasm for older native grape varieties have resulted in this region's own distinctive wine styles.

In Galicia there are five DO (*Denominación de Origen* or "denomination of origin") zones—Rías Baixas, Ribeiro, Ribeira Sacra, Monterrei, and Valdeorras—and all their best wines are the whites, made from albariño and godello. At the eastern end of the region, the northern Basque provinces of Vizcaya (Bizkaia in Basque) and Guetaria (Getaria) on the coast of the Bay of Biscay produce a very small amount of a rather unique wine called chacolí (txakoli). Here there are two DOs—Chacolí de Vizcaya and Chacolí de Guetaria.

Rías Baixas

The peachy, fresh, crisp albariño grape put Rías Baixas on the vinous map. The wines from here vie with those of Rueda for the title of the best whites of Spain.

MARTÍN CÓDAX   *Established* 1986 *Owners* Local shareholders *Vineyard area* 395 acres (160 ha)

Popular locally, this producer makes wines only from the albariño grape, and the wines are of excellent quality. The range includes the basic Martín Códax—a single-vineyard wine called Burgáns, Gallaecia (a late-harvest version), and Organistrum, a barrel-fermented wine with three months on the lees. Best wines: the entire range.

Also in Rías Baixas is Fillaboa, a small private estate vineyard, which produces a great albarino.

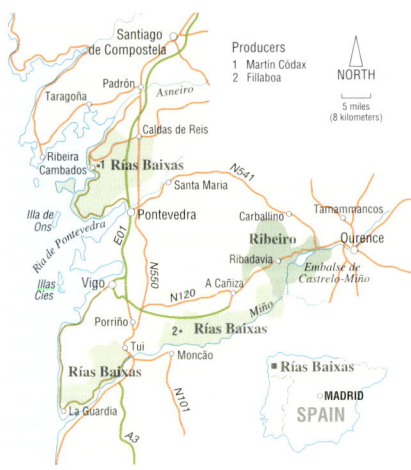

There are a number of specialized hand tools that are still used for a variety of tasks in the wine trade. Some tool designs date back many centuries.

Other Galician regions

The best wines from Ribeiro are whites made from godello—second only to the albariño in quality—and treixadura. Stunningly beautiful Ribeira Sacra sits on the gorge of the rivers Sil and Miño. It features incredibly steep slate-based vineyard slopes and historic monastic ruins. The best wines are very good but few, with great albariño whites and promising mencía reds. In Veldeorras, one or two bodegas are working hard to establish the region as a center for quality white wines made from godello and reds from mencía. Monterrei is a tiny area that makes mainly bland wines from palomino. However, there are a few quality white wines, made from doña blanca and verdello.

MOURE   *Established* 1980   *Owners* Private shareholders   *Vineyard area* 15 acres (6 ha)

Lovely Adegas Moure in the Ribeira Sacra region has immaculately terraced vineyards, high on the steep banks of the River Miño. In summer, José-Manuel Moure takes guests to the hilltop for lunch overlooking the river. He makes three wines under the Abadia da Cova label: the white albariño and two reds from the mencía, one *joven* and one *crianza*. All wines are excellent.

A. TAPADA   *Established* 1989   *Owners* Local shareholders   *Vineyard area* 25 acres (10 ha)

This is a very sharp, state-of-the-art winery surrounded by its own small estate of vineyards, in the Valdeorras region. There are two excellent wines, both called Guitian, one *joven* and one barrel-fermented with six months on the lees. This is expensive for Valdeorras wine but most probably the best.

GARGALO   *Established* 1998   *Owners* Private shareholders   *Vineyard area* 49 acres (20 ha)

This is a recent enterprise in the slowly emerging Monterrei region. Winemaker Mónica Carballo Coede makes a white wine from treixadura, godello, and doña blanca, and a red from tem-

Basque wining and dining

At ten in the morning a crowd is starting to form as locals tuck into a few tapas and rinse them down with thimbles full of tart, spritzy white wine. This is the scene in San Sebastion, Spain, as well as in numerous other Basque taverns in the northwest parts of Spain. The wine is called chacoli (Txacolina de Guetaria in Basque), an obscure white fiercely protected from oblivion by stubborn farmers along the Bay of Biscay. How surprised they might be to learn that their humble wine is highly sought after at its release each year by sommeliers in Paris and San Francisco, who scramble to lock up their allocations and brag among their colleagues about how many cases they got, and who go on to serve that simple wine in fine hand-blown Austrian crystal, no less.

The tempranillo grape is very widely grown in Spain. Its many regional nicknames include tinto fino, tinto del país, and cencibel.

pranillo, mencía, and a little bastardo. Although too soon to say what is achievable, early results are promising. Best wine: Terra de Gargalo white.

A. PORTELA   *Established* 1987   *Owners* Antonio González Pousa and Agustín Formigó Raña   *Vineyard area* 20 acres (8 ha)

The bulk of this Ribeiro bodega's production is a wine called Señorío de Beade, made from 40 percent jeréz grape and 60 percent made up of equal parts treixadura, torrontés, and godello, all of which (especially the last) have considerable claims to quality. There's also a red under the same label made from caiño, ferrón, and sousón. Best wines: Primacia de Beade (treixadura).

Castilla-León

Ribera del Duero

Only red and pink wines are made here; the main grape is the tinto fino. Wines have a soft, "summer-fruit" character and crisp, green tannins. They are splendid when made *joven* but some of the region's best are the *crianzas*. *Reservas* tend to be a little heavy on the oak except in good years, and only a few bodegas can make a really good *gran reserva*.

BODEGAS AALTO *Established* 1999 *Owners* Mariano García, Javier Zaccagnini & private investors *Vineyard area* 91 acres (37 ha)

With no permanent bodega, no wine will be made under the Aalto name until the vines are ten years old. In the meantime, the owners will buy grapes from old vines and establish themselves.

ALEJÁNDRO FERNÁNDEZ TINTO PESQUERA *Established* 1972 *Owners* Fernández family *Vineyard area* 494 acres (200 ha)

Pesquera only makes one wine—pesquera—which may be *crianza* or *reserva* according to the quality of the year, and is 100 percent tempranillo. In average years it's very good; in great years it's fantastic. Best wines are Pesquera, Condado de Haza, and Alenza.

HACIENDA MONASTERIO *Established* 1991 *Owner* Peter Sisseck *Vineyard area* 153 acres (62 ha)

This bodega looks like a giant pink flying saucer parked on a hillside above the town. The plantation is of tinto fino, cabernet sauvignon, merlot, and a little malbec, and one exceptional wine—Hacienda Monasterio. Dominio de Pingus is a very expensive wine of rare artifice and concentration sourced from 60-year-old vines.

VEGA SICILIA *Established* 1864 *Owners* Alvarez family *Vineyard area* 618 acres (250 ha)

Legendary wines—mainly tinto fino—are made here. There are plantations of merlot, malbec, cabernet sauvignon, and even a little albillo. Vega Sicilia Unico is the masterpiece here. There is a five-year-old *reserva* called Valbuena that is only released if the winemaker is happy with it, made only from wine produced in good to great years.

Rueda, Toro, Cigales, and Bierzo

Rueda is the land of the verdejo. The best rueda, one of Spain's best white wines, is made from verdejo grapes picked before sunrise, blanketed with nitrogen, and chilled before gentle pressing. Toro has reds made from the tinta de toro (the local version of tempranillo, with a thicker skin). Cabernet sauvignon and garnacha (mainly for pink wines) are also grown here, and cabernet/tempranillo blends can be excellent. Cigales is famous for its pink wines but its very best wines are reds made from the ubiquitous tinto del país (tempranillo) with, here and there, an admixture of garnacha and cabernet sauvignon. In the far northwest of the region, Bierzo produces fresh whites from godello and doña blanca, and, mainly, light reds made from mencía grapes.

Producers
1 Bodegas Aalto
2 Dehesa de los Canónigos
3 Alejándro Fernández Tinto Pesquera
4 Hacienda Monasterio
5 Pago de Carraovejas
6 Rodero
7 Vega Sicilia

Olive groves and vineyards grow side by side in Spain; both crops are among Europe's oldest forms of agriculture.

MARQUÉS DE RISCAL–VINOS BLANCOS DE CASTILLA

Established 1972 *Owners* Vinos de los Herederos del Marqués de Riscal *Vineyard area* 420 acres (170 ha)

Francisco "Paco" Hurtado de Amezaga, current head of the Riscal family, wanted to make a white wine worthy of his family name but he didn't like the traditional oaked or modern squeaky clean whites being made in Rioja. Attracted by the verdejo grape, which he felt showed great potential, he settled on Rueda. Now Riscal wines are among the region's best. They feature a sauvignon, a verdejo (with some viura, or macabeo), and an oak-aged Reserva Limousin Verdejo with eleven months in the cask. All are sold under the Marqués de Riscal label.

Alejándro Fernández

If it weren't for the vision of Alejándro Fernández, founder of Alejándro Fernández Tinto Pesquera, the wine-producing region Ribera del Duero would still look towards sugar beets instead of grapes as its mainstay. Always a dreamer, one day Fernández came up with the idea for a mechanical beet harvester that revolutionized the industry. With his newfound fortune, he decided to make wine. Pesquera is made from the grape variety known locally as tinto del pais, which is a synonym for tinto fino and tempranillo, the main grape of Rioja. Pesquera is usually deeply colored, firm in structure, and cellarworthy. Its hearty, rustic, intense style reflects the man who made it.

FARIÑA *Established* 1942 *Owners* Fariña family *Vineyard area* 988 acres (400 ha)

Manuel Farina was one of the first in Toro to espouse new technology. Colegiata is the name for *jovenes* in white, pink, and red, while Gran Colegiata is for *reservas* and *gran reservas* and a *"semi-crianza"* (a red wine which has had oak age but less than the regulation six months). There's also a premium *joven*, Primero.

ABADIA RETUERTA *Established* 1996 *Owner* Sandoz *Vineyard area* 504 acres (204 ha)

This old Bierzo vineyard estate in a twelfth-century abbey uses tempranillo, cabernet sauvignon, and a little merlot. Located just outside the relevant area and unfettered by DO Ribera del Duero regulations, winemaker Angel Anocibar Beloqui does as he pleases. The entire range is good, especially El Campanario, El Palomar, Pago Negralada, and Pago Valdebellón.

Other excellent producers to be found in the Castilla-León region include Dehesa de los Canónigos, Pago de Carraovejas, Rodero (all in Ribera del Duero DO), Belondrade y Lurton, Castilla la Vieja (both in Rueda), Perez Carames, and Mauro (both in Bierzo).

North–Central Spain

Rioja

Immediately south of the Cordillera Cantábrica on the Ebro is an area which has achieved most in the export market for Spain over the last century and more. The climate here is continental and the clay soil is rich in chalk. Rioja was classified under the new system in 1926 and is going through radical changes. Good producers are listed below; more are shown on the map.

CVNE (COMPAÑÍA VINÍCOLA DEL NORTE DE ESPAÑA) *Established* 1879 *Owners* Real de Asúa family *Vineyard area* 1,364 acres (552 ha)

This is one of Rioja's most respected companies. The wines are classic rioja, using the full mix of grapes, with the Viña Real range sourcing most of its tempranillo from the Rioja Alavesa and

Imperial from the Rioja Alta. Everything is first-class from this exceptional bodega, but some are more first-class than others. Best wines: *reservas* and *gran reservas* in the Imperial and Viña Real ranges; Real de Asúa Reserva; Contino.

MARTÍNEZ-BUJANDA *Established* 1889 *Owners* Martínez Bujanda family *Vineyard area* 988 acres (400 ha)

An old firm with the latest equipment, their wines range from a solid everyday range to some excellent new-wave stuff, including a barrel-fermented viura (macabeo), a varietal garnacha *reserva* with 20 months in oak, and a new *gran reserva* which is openly 50/50 tempranillo/cabernet sauvignon. Best wines: Vendimia Seleccionada Gran Reserva; Finca de Valpiedra; Valdemar.

MARQUÉS DE MURRIETA *Established* 1872 *Owner* Dominios Creixell *Vineyard area* 445 acres (180 ha)

This elegant bodega has been extended, new vineyards planted, and the wines revamped to appeal to the modern market without sacrificing quality. Its best wines are Reservas and Castillo Ygay Gran Reservas.

REMELLURI *Established* 1968 *Owner* J. Rodríguez Salis *Vineyard area* 260 acres (105 ha)

Remelluri's bodega makes only *reservas*. It supplies 80 percent of its own grapes, mostly tempranillo. The winemaking is a mix of traditional and modern, using refurbished oak vats and stainless steel; the wine typically spends around two years in *barricas*. The style and character of the wines are "textbook" classics for Basque Country rioja.

A little wind helps keep vines dry; too much can cause damage. Stone walls have been used in Spain for centuries to shield vines from wind.

Producers
1 Marqués de Cáceres - Union Vitivinícola
2 Campillo
3 CVNE
4 Martínez-Bujanda
5 Marqués de Murrieta
6 Remelluri
7 La Rioja Alta
8 Marqués de Riscal

■ Rioja
○ MADRID
SPAIN

NORTH

5 miles
(8 kilometers)

Labastida
Samaniego
Haro
San Vicente de la Sonsierra
Laguardia
Anguciana
N232
Rio
Bañares de Ebro
Viana
Bimileo
Briones
Elciego
Oyon
Casalarreina
Ollauri
Ebro
Cenicero
Fuenmayor
Logroño
A68
Navarrete

Rioja

124

A68

2
56 miles
(90 km)

The warm colors of fall grace the vineyards at Logroño, another wine producer in La Rioja.

Rioja in threes

Understanding Rioja is as easy as one, two, three. There are three wine-growing regions—Rioja Alta, Alavesa, and Rioja Baja; three types of wine—white or "blanco," rosé or "rosado," and red or "tinto." And there are three main grape varieties for the red Rioja—tempranillo, garnacha, and mazuelo. There are three quality levels for red rioja as well, based on minimum aging required by the Consejo Regulador. *Crianza*, which translates loosely to "cradle," refers to the youngest style and must be aged a minimum of one year in barrel and one in bottle. *Reserva* indicates a minimum of one year in barrel and two in bottle; while *gran reserva* indicates a minimum of two years in barrel plus three in bottle. Aging requirements are stricter in Rioja than any other region in Spain.

Navarra

Once under the shadow of neighboring Rioja, Navarra has reinvented itself as a source of some of Spain's most interesting new wines. An enological research station in Olite means the range of wines has never been more exciting.

JULIÁN CHIVITE   *Established* 1647 *Owners* Chivite family *Vineyard area* 865 acres (350 ha)
A barrel-fermented chardonnay and a tempranillo/merlot/cabernet *reserva* have been made in every good year since 1985. There's also a special *gran reserva* made from pure tempranillo with two years in oak and a splendid rich *vendímia tardía* (late vintage) moscatel with ten months in the barrel. The basic range, called Gran Feudo, features a particularly good pink wine made from 100 percent garnacha. Best wines: Colección 125 (the whole range—red, white, moscatel); Gran Feudo Rosado; moscatel.

Catalonia

The higher altitudes inland from the coast are beneficial for growing finer grapes, even this far south. Limestone-based soils provide the basic carbonate, which underpins the world's greatest vineyards, and the Catalonian highlands provide one of the best hot-climate bedrocks for vines—schistose comes to the surface in Priorato, Alella, and parts of the high Penedès—and its fragmented structure holds water, a refuge for the vine roots in the arid summers.

Penedès

Penedès has the lead in volume, reliability, innovation, and quality-control throughout Catalonia. Every Catalan grape, almost every Spanish grape, and many north European grapes are grown here, the myriad microclimates, soils, and altitudes providing ideal conditions for everything from the lightweight white wines to impressive cabernets and chardonnays.

MIGUEL TORRES   *Established* 1870 *Owners* Torres family *Vineyard area* 3,212 acres (1,300 ha)

Winemaker Miguel Torres was among the first to plant cabernet sauvignon and chardonnay in Catalonia but he also has a plantation of over 100 native Catalan varieties with which he experiments. The winery at Pacs del Penedès marries new technology with tradition, and Torres wines are regular international prizewinners. The best wines here are Fransola, Gran Viña Sol, Viña Esmeralda, Waltraud, Atrium, Mas la Plana, Gran Coronas, and Milmanda.

Two other excellent Penedès wine producers are Jané Ventura and Cavas Naveran.

Cava

The Cava DO is defined by grape type and production method rather than area, although since 1991, over 90 percent of all cava vineyards have been found in Catalonia. Most cava comes from the area around St. Sadurní d'Anoia in the province of Barcelona.

CODORNÍU   *Established* 1551 *Owners* Raventós family *Vineyard area* 2,965 acres (1,200 ha)

The biggest cava company, the idyllic estate in St. Sadurní possesses the biggest cellars in the world, totaling 15 miles (25 km) on five underground levels. It has a cutting-edge approach to wine, with constant experimenting and innovation. Codorníu introduced the first chardonnay to cava and is experimenting with pinot noir as well as selecting its own clones of the classic "big three" grapes (parellada, xarel-lo and macabeo). The best wines here are Cuvée Raventós, Non Plus Ultra, and Raïmat Gran Brut.

A leaf from the syrah vine, a grape that is widely grown in the Catalonia region.

Producers
1 Jané Ventura
2 Cavas Naveran
3 Miguel Torres

The best wines in the Empordá-Costa Brava region are the reds.

Workers weed the grounds of the vineyards of Miguel Torres, Spain's largest family-owned wine company.

FREIXENET
Established 1889 *Owners* Ferrer family *Vineyard area* 642 acres (260 ha)

Freixenet is also a "big name" cava house and the biggest sparkling wine producer in the world, with companies in the United States, Mexico, and France. This art deco bodega's most famous wine is Cordon Negro, in a very distinctive black frosted bottle. The Freixenet group includes Segura Viudas and Castellblanch which are run as separate operations. In general, Freixenet is against the use of chardonnay in cava, although its top-of-the-range Reserva Real contains about 20 percent of the grape. Best wines: Reserva Real; Cuvée DS; Segura Viudas Reserva Heredad.

JOSEP MARÍA RAVENTÓS I BLANC, *Established* 1986 *Owner* Manuel Raventós i Negra *Vineyard area* 217 acres (88 ha)

Josep-María Raventós's wines show great style and panache. He grows chardonnay as well as the native grapes, and established a name for the company very early on. The best wines here are Reserva, Gran Reserva, and Reserva Personal Manuel Raventós.

Alella
Alella wines are mainly white and made from pansá blanca (xarel-lo) and garnacha blanca grapes. There is also a substantial amount of chardonnay. The wines are fresh and light: new-wave examples may be barrel-fermented. There is some small amount of red, mainly made from ull de llebre (tempranillo).

Empordà-Costa Brava
On the border between Catalonia and France, Empordà-Costa Brava has reinvented itself as a dynamic and experimental zone. The local classic is a sweet red made from sun-dried garnacha grapes called garnatxa del empordà.

CAVAS DEL CASTILLO DE PERELADA
Established 1923 *Owners* Suqué-Matue family *Vineyard area* 247 acres (100 ha)

A magnificent castle in Perelada is the head office of the Perelada wine company, which has built a reputation for quality in all its wines. Cava is made in the cellars but most of the vinous work is carried out in a more prosaic winery with modern equipment. The vineyards grow tempranillo, garnacha, cariñena, and macabeo as well as cabernet sauvignon, merlot, chardonnay, and sauvignon blanc. Best wines: Castillo Perelada Reserva; cabernet sauvignon.

Conca de Barberà
This highland area in the province of Girona produces mainly *joven* wines in all three colors although there is the odd exception: Miguel Torres' barrel-fermented Milmanda Chardonnay comes from here, and there are many continuing

Freixenet winery at St. Sadurni has quite extensive old cellars. Within the art deco architectural style of this vast space sit numerous gleaming stainless steel vats, which are used to hold the wine before it is bottled.

experiments with oak-aged reds made from tempranillo and garnacha, often with an admixture of cabernet sauvignon and merlot.

CONCAVINS   *Established* 1988 *Owner* **Luis Carbonell Figueras** *Vineyard area* **NA**

Two separate ranges of wine are made here. First come the early-harvest supermarket blends of macabeo, parellada, and chardonnay, which are put through the system quickly. Then comes the main harvest, most likely cabernet sauvignon, merlot, and tempranillo. These are given the full malolactic treatment followed by extended cask-age, typically 12–18 months for *crianzas* and up to two years for *reservas*. The wines are very good and quality control is excellent. Best wines: Castillo de Montblanc Cabernet Merlot; Via Aurelia Masia les Comes.

Costers del Segre

Cynics have suggested that Costers del Segre was awarded DO status in 1988 simply because it was the home of the giant Raïmat estate, but some smaller firms are beginning to appear now. The area is fragmented into four subzones clustered around the city of Lleida (Lérida): Raïmat, Artesa (both in the province of Lleida), Vall du Riu Corb, and Las Garrigas (in Tarragona province). The best reds are generally made from tempranillo, cabernet sauvignon, and merlot, and the best whites from chardonnay and the "big three" Catalan grapes.

RAÏMAT   *Established* 1918 *Owners* **Codorníu family** *Vineyard area* 3,706 acres (1,500 ha)

This winery looks as if it might have come from another planet: mirrored walls, vines on the roof, neoclassical portals, and indoor water features. The wines here are Californian-style and aren't bad; arguably the best (Abadia) is a tempranillo/cabernet mix; also good is Mas Castell Reserva (cabernet sauvignon). They also make cava here.

Pla de Bages

This is a relatively small zone in the province of Barcelona with a reputation for making sound if unexceptional wines. However, excellent work has been done with the picapoll (the Spanish name for the French picpoul or piquepoul) grape for white wines and the cabernet sauvignon for reds.

MASIES DE AVINYÓ
Established 1983 *Owners* **Roqueta family** *Vineyard area* 99 acres (40 ha)

The Roqueta family has made wine for centuries at the Masia Roqueta (the family farmhouse) and opened a retail shop in Manresa in 1898. Wines today are sold under the company name and made from macabeo, picapoll (the French picpoul), and chardonnay for whites, garnacha, tempranillo, merlot, and cabernet sauvignon for reds. Masies best wines include a picapoll, and a cabernet sauvignon/tempranillo *crianza*.

The gentle grace of fall colors on the vines near Poboleda, in Catalonia.

Priorato

This is an ancient and particularly beautiful region with eight centuries of winemaking tradition which began with Carthusian monks. Situated in the hills of the province of Tarragona, this region is home to what is one of the toughest, blackest, and longest-lived wines of Spain.

Also located in the same region, in the hilltop town of Gratallops, are century-old garnacha vines, which sit side-by-side with a number of high-technology plantations of cabernet, merlot, and syrah. These are being used to produce some of the best of the new-wave wines presently coming out of Spain—not to mention some of the most expensive.

ALVARO PALACIOS *Established* 1989 *Owner* Alvaro Palacios *Vineyard area* 99 acres (40 ha)

Alvaro's wines are all magnificent. L'Ermita is now possibly the most expensive red wine in Spain, beating even the fabled Vega Sicilia. It is made from 100-year-old garnacha vines in a steep natural amphitheater on ancient schistose bedrock. The finished wine has 15 percent cabernet sauvignon for aroma and 5 percent cariñena (the Rioja name for mazuelo) for color, and spends 15 months in oak. Finca Dofi, his "estate" wine, is made with syrah and merlot as well as cabernet and cariñena. Las Terrasses is the mainstream wine, made from garnacha, cariñena, and cabernet sauvignon.

Tarragona

This region's fame rested on a single wine, now known as Tarragona Clásico. This is a fortified red wine made from garnacha grapes and stored in oak vats for a minimum of 12 years.

Elsewhere, the DO produces all types of wine in all three colors, though 70 percent of Tarragona's wine production is white. Grapes grown include tempranillo, garnacha, cariñena, and also cabernet and merlot. White wines tend to be made from the "big three" Catalan grapes (parellada, xarel-lo, and macabeo) and/or chardonnay. Sweet whites are made from moscatel.

CELLER CO-OPERATIU DEL MASROIG
Established 1917 *Owners* Co-op members
Vineyard area 1,235 acres (500 ha)

There's been a good deal of change in the co-ops in Tarragona and new thinking allows these once bureaucratic organizations to compete internationally. The grapes are the local specialties—garnacha blanca for whites, and tempranillo (here called ull de llebre) and cariñena for reds—but the wines speak for themselves. The best wine from this producer is Les Sorts.

These distinctively Spanish style wine vessels, cristal bota, are used to drink from, and also for storing the wine.

Terra Alta

This is a remote area of sleepy local co-ops but one or two "boutique" wineries are emerging. The wines are generally reds made from hefty local grapes—cariñena and garnacha—along with tempranillo and, in the more forward-looking wineries, cabernet and merlot. Most white wine is made from garnacha blanca and parellada, although there is some very good macabeo and some experimental chardonnay.

PIÑOL   *Established* 1940 *Owner* Josefina Piñol
Vineyard area 62 acres (25 ha)

Among many innovations here are an interesting light, sweet wine called Josefina Piñol, made from over-ripe garnacha blanca, and Viñ Orosina, a dry-fermented moscatel. The top red wines are named L'Avi Arrufi (Grandfather Arrufi). Best wines: L'Avi Arrufi Crianza; Nuestra Señora del Portal.

A few more recommended Catalonian producers are Gramona, Juvé Y Camps, Rovellats, Agusti Torello (all Cava), Castell del Remei (in Costers del Segre), and Mas Martinet Viticultores (in Priorato).

Vineyards in Terra Alta, one of the eight DOs in Catalonia.

Castilla-La Mancha and Valdepeñas

South of Madrid, La Mancha and Valdepeñas lie on the mostly flat plateau of central Spain, surrounded by a ring of mountain ranges, with a continental climate. In the 1980s, La Mancha was still regarded as little more than a bulk-wine producer for the cafés and bars of Madrid, but it reinvented itself in the 1990s and some of the best-value everyday wines in Spain are now being made here. Valdepeñas is famed for its warm, ripe, and modestly priced *reservas* and *gran reservas*, and has resisted the temptation to diversify, although some new ideas are on the way. Mentrida and Almansa are the other DOs in this region.

Windmills in Castilla-La Mancha, one of Spain's largest wine regions, attest to local windy conditions.

FELIX SOLIS   *Established* 1952 *Owners* Solis family *Vineyards* 1,730 acres (700 ha)

A mighty steel city rears up on the outskirts of Valdepeñas: Bodegas Felix Solis expanding again. Solis is the second-biggest wine company in Spain, after Bodegas y Bedbidas but B & B owns half a dozen wineries, whereas Solis has just the one … for now. There are many ranges of wines, including Peñasol (everyday-quality table wines),

Diego de Almagro, Los Molinos, and the most famous brand—and some of the best-value red wine to come out of Spain—Viña Albali. Best wines: Viña Albali Crianza; cabernet sauvignon; tempranillo *(joven)*; Diego de Almagro Crianza.

VINÍCOLA DE CASTILLA   *Established* 1976 *Owners* Private shareholders *Vineyard area* 494 acres (200 ha)

Buying in most of its grapes, this La Mancha DO company makes white wine from viura, airén, chardonnay, and sauvignon blanc; and red from garnacha, cencibel (tempranillo), cabernet, and merlot. Best wines: Señorío de Guadianeja Reserve, Gran Reserva; Castilla de Alhambra Rosado, Tinto.

PIQUERAS   *Established* 1915 *Owners* Piqueras family *Vineyard area* 248 acres (100 ha)

Almansa is often seen as a bit of "one-horse" DO as, year after year, the only bodega which makes itself felt in a wider market is this one. Piqueras

Parasol pines (Pinus pinea) *grace the very flat open fields in the southern part of La Mancha, which is due south of Madrid.*

DEHESA DEL CARRIZAL

Established 1987 *Owner* Marcial Gómez Sequeira *Vineyard area* 32 acres (13 ha)

The winemaker here, Ignacio de Miguel Poch, does only one thing, but he does it very well—that is, make a world-class cabernet sauvignon. Located some 30 miles (50 km) north-west of the city of Ciudad Real, in VdlT de Castilla, the reputation of Dehesa del Carrizal has advanced steadily to the point where it consistently challenges the finest wines of Spain in international tastings. The wine is 100 percent cabernet and spends, typically, 18 months in oak. All of the wines here are good.

showed wine can be made the traditional way using only local grapes. Winemaker Juan Pablo Bonete Piqueras grows (and buys) airén and macabeo for white wine and cencibel (the local word for tempranillo) and monastrell for red. The quality is excellent and there seems to be no good reason why other bodegas have not emerged to challenge for the leadership but, in the meantime, Piqueras reigns in this part of Spain. Best wines: Castillo de Almansa Crianza, Reserva.

MANUEL MANZANEQUE

Established 1992 *Owner* Manuel Manzaneque *Vineyard area* 84 acres (34 ha)

In VdlT (Vinho de la Tierra) Sierra de Alcaraz, these vineyards flourish at altitudes above 3,000 feet (900 m), with widely admired results: Manuel Manzaneque grows chardonnay as well as cabernet sauvignon, merlot, tempranillo, and syrah, and his wines are exemplary. Best wines: Chardonnay; Finca Elez Crianza (mainly cabernet); Gran Reserva.

An attractively decorated wine glass from the nineteenth century.

MARQUÉS DE GRIÑÓN

Established 1972 *Owners* Falcó family *Vineyard area* 104 acres (42 ha)

Feeling that the DO laws were far too constricting for his liking, Carlos Falcó makes VdM (Vino de Mesa) de Toledo wine the way he wants it to be, with outstanding results. The marqués grows cabernet, merlot, syrah, and petit verdot, and also makes varietals as well as a new wine made from cabernet, syrah, and petit verdot. In 2000 a new clone of graciano was planted, so the future for the wines of the Dominio de Valdepusa is entirely red. Anything carrying the Griñón name may be relied upon without question, but the very best wines are Dominio de Valdepusa Cabernet Sauvignon, Syrah, and Emeritus.

Andalusia

Andalusia is the most consistently hot of all Spanish regions, with a semiarid climate and rivers which habitually dry up in the summer. It includes Jeréz (sherry country) and thus some of the oldest vineyards in Europe. In the astonishingly chalk-rich soil of the province of Cádiz grows the palomino. Other grapes include the pedro ximénez (PX) and the moscatel, which are used alone or to sweeten wines. Typically, moscatel will have been fortified during fermentation to provide a naturally rich, sweet wine, and PX will have been dried in the sun before fermentation, providing a wine of intense color, richness, and sweetness. Elsewhere, traditional superripe grapes and high-strength wines denote the viticultural style.

Jeréz

In Jeréz/Xérès/Sherry y Manzanilla de Sanlúcar de Barrameda, about 20 companies now control the sherry business. The wines themselves are as good as, or better than, they have ever been.

PEDRO DOMECQ *Established* 1730 *Owner* **Allied-Domecq** *Vineyard area* 988 acres (400 ha) In spite of its membership of the multinational Allied-Domecq group, this bodega has managed to maintain its individuality, albeit with a reduced range of wines to accommodate the other members of the group (which includes the British company John Harvey, of Bristol Cream fame). In common with many other major companies the recent upturn in interest for "premium" sherry has encouraged Domecq to expand its quality range beyond the best-selling Fino La Ina. Best wines: Fino La Ina; Amontillado 51-1°; Sibarita Oloroso; Palo Cortado Capuchino; Venerable PX.

GONZÁLEZ-BYASS *Established* 1835 *Owners* **González family** *Vineyards* 2,523 acres (1,021 ha) This company, with its large-scale and beautiful bodega in the middle of Jeréz, went through a difficult financial patch in the 1980s when outside investors were involved. However, the stock is now all back in the hands of the family and sound leadership has restored the company to its former pre-eminence. González-Byass claims to

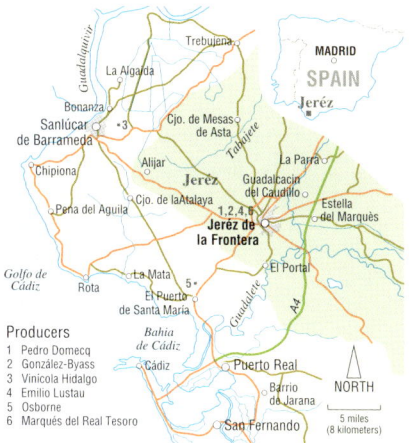

Producers
1 Pedro Domecq
2 González-Byass
3 Vinicola Hidalgo
4 Emilio Lustau
5 Osborne
6 Marqués del Real Tesoro

Vina el Caballo, a Jeréz winery. The 1980s and 1990s were a period of change for many sherry producers.

have produced the first fino in the modern style (Tio Pepe) in the 1850s, and has an impressive collection of ancient *soleras*. Their latest development is the Añadas collection of vintage sherries. The best wines: Tio Pepe; Amontillado del Duque; Apóstoles Dry Oloroso; Matúsalem Rich Old Oloroso.

EMILIO LUSTAU *Established* 1896 *Owners* Luís Caballero group *Vineyard area* 420 acres (170 ha)

This house has an excellent reputation for quality wines. Under the late Rafael Balao it established the Almacenista range of wines, bought from small producers and brokers and bottled in short runs for the "premium" sherry market, which has been a brilliant success. When the Caballero group bought Lustau in 1990, there were worries that it might be subsumed into the core business (which is "own label") but in the event this has not happened. The bodega remains a law unto itself and, with Caballero's backing, has gone from strength to strength. Best wines: all wines are among the best

Alonso of Aragon was wont to say in commendation of age, that age appears to be best in four things—old wood best to burn, old wine to drink, old friends to trust, and old authors to read.
FRANCIS BACON (1561–1626), *Apothegms*

in the Jeréz region, but especially good are Manzanilla Pasada Manuel Cuevas Jurado, Papirusa Manzanilla, Amontillado Escuadrilla, Moscatel Superior Emilín, and Pedro Ximénez San Emilio.

There are many other particularly good wine producers to be found around Jeréz, including Osborne, Vinícola Hidalgo, and Marqués del Real Tesoro, all of which are worth investigating.

Montilla-Moriles

Montilla is the mainstay wine of the Andalusian region—the wines are modestly priced and sold in dry, medium, and sweet styles. Unfortified, montilla achieves up to 15 percent alcohol by volume (abv) by natural fermentation. The grape here is the PX (pedro ximénez) and Montilla produces the ancient thick, black PX wines with exemplary grace. The best wines of Montilla are in the fortified styles—amontillado, oloroso, fino, and cream.

ALVEAR *Established* 1729 *Owners* Alvear family *Vineyard area* 618 acres (250 ha)

The approach here is quite meticulous, with the result that Alvear produces some of the region's finest wines. Producing montilla, Alvear is also a pioneer of the *joven afrutado* style. The best wines here are Capataz Fino; Solera Fundación Amontillado; Pelayo Oloroso.

Seville, a Spanish city in the heart of Andalusia, has a heritage of flamenco dancing. Nearby are Jeréz and Montilla–Moriles.

Local tavernas adorned with bullfighting posters advertise what is an integral part of Spanish culture.

Málaga

Peaking in the nineteenth century, the wines of this region have since been in decline. The grape is the pedro ximénez—but sunned and then fortified during fermentation, it produces a wine of almost toffee-like richness. The best wines are aged in a *solera* but are becoming harder to find.

LÓPEZ HERMANOS *Established* 1885 *Owners* López family *Vineyard area* 618 acres (250 ha)

Rekindling interest in the wonderful classic wines of Málaga, López Hermanos also produces a "pale cream" oloroso and a "dry" (more medium-dry) style as well. A new moscatel wine is being developed under the brand Pico Plata. Best wines: Trajinero Oloroso; Cartojal Pale Cream; Málaga Virgen.

Condado de Huelva

Producers here have turned to light, fruity *jovenes afrutados* and unfortified wines for the supermarket trade. However, the main business seems to be seasoning oak casks for the Scotch whisky industry: two years of oloroso wine in a new cask provides what a good malt needs.

VC Aljarafe

There are only a few independent bodegas working outside the mainstream wine-producing areas of Andalusia.

JOSÉ GALLEGO-GÓNGORA *Established* 1682 *Owners* Gallego-Góngora family *Vineyard area* 296 acres (120 ha)

Although the grape used here is the garrido fino, the wines are made very much in the Andaluz *generoso* style, and the wines are named "fino" and "amontillado," in the manner of sherry and montilla. In spite of its obscurity, the wines are astonishingly good: there are *jovenes afrutados* in the new fresh'n'crisp style, but the fortified wines are still the best: these are Amontillado Muy Viejo Selección Imperial and PX Dulce Añejo Selección Imperial.

Other Spanish Regions

VALENCIA

Valencia is an autonomous Mediterranean region, the wineries here are among the most technologically advanced in Europe. Alicante was once known for high-strength, sweet white wines, made from moscatel, and a legendary but expensive dessert red called fondillón, made from sun-dried monastrell grapes and aged for at least eight years. Modern Alicante also turns out fresh, crisp whites made from merseguera, airén, and macabeo. The best wines are probably reds made from monastrell, garnacha, bobal, and sometimes cabernet sauvignon. Utiel-Requena is famed for beefy reds made from the bobal. The Valencia DO is the supermarket wine capital of Spain, and tailor-made wines include a light, fresh, crisp, dry white made from the merseguera, a rich, sweet, fortified moscatel, a *crianza* red from tempranillo and cabernet, or anything in between.

MURCIA

Jumilla now makes good—even great—wine from the humble monastrell grape, showing reserves of spiciness and sheer rich fruit. Wines from garnacha and tempranillo are exemplary quality at silly prices. Yecla owes its current modest prominence to just one leading bodega. The monastrell here has been teased out to give softness, fruit, and a ripe, spicy fragrance as well as aging well in oak. There is some pleasant white, the best of which tends to be made

Barrels stacked outside a bodega in Calatayud DO, in Aragón.

from macabeo. The monastrell grape has done the trick in Bullas too, although there's also tempranillo and garnacha varieties, as well as some experimentation with cabernet, merlot, and syrah. White wines are predominantly made from macabeo.

MADRID AND EXTREMADURA

Bodegas in Vinos de Madrid now produce some stylish wines at moderate prices ideally suited to house-wine in the tapas bars of the city of Madrid. The better wines tend to be *joven* or occasionally *crianza* reds, made from tempranillo/tinto fino. However, the best wines come from Tierra de Barros.

Spanish islands

Spanish wine is made far from mainland Spain in the Canaries, 60 miles (100 km) off the coast of northwest Africa. There are seven islands in the archipelago, which has been under Spanish control since the fifteenth century. This was an important staging-post for ships travelling southeast to the expanding colonies of the East Indies and southwest to South America. One island, Lanzarote, has the most dramatic landscape of any vineyard area in the world. The soil is made up of black volcanic ash and the vines are planted in scooped-out hollows surrounded with low walls to protect the plants from the wind. Red and white wines are made here, including sweet malvasía and moscatel from sun-dried grapes in the old Canary-sack style. This was a lightly fortified sweet wine second only in popularity to "sherris" for much of the fifteenth and sixteenth centuries.

Closer to the mainland, on the Balearic Islands grows the mantonegro, a grape not found elsewhere in Spain. The wines it produces—with a little help from tempranillo and monastrell—are good to very good and, with judicious use of oak, age well.

ARAGÓN

The unique microclimates and rich soils of Somontano, located on the south side of the Pyrenees, make it possible to produce outstanding wine from almost any grape. Smart, modern wineries are making this an exciting new Spanish region. In the lowlands, Cariñena has achieved modest success for its red wines, made mainly from the garnacha. There's also tempranillo, a bit of cabernet sauvignon and a promising local called juan ibáñez. Campo de Borja has some decent reds, made mainly from garnacha. One or two bodegas in Calatayud are turning out good-quality wines at modest prices. The best wines in the region tend to be reds made from tempranillo and/or garnacha, and monastrell.

Right: *Situated among the hills of Aragón, the village of Maluenda is in the heart of wine country.*

Below: *Southwest Spain has vistas of lush plains and ancient villages, both of which are in abundance here.*

NORTH

30 miles
(48 kilometers)

MINHO

Chaves

TRÁS-OS-
MONTES

Braga

Valpaços

Vinho Verde

Planaltos-
Mirandes

Miño

Corgo

Matosinhos

Porto

Vila Nova de Gaia

Douro

Peso da
Regua

Pinhão

Porto/Douro

Castelo
Rodrigo

Varosa

Pinhel

Aveiro

Viseu

Dão

SERRA DA ESTRELA

Estrela
6537 ft (1993 m)

TRÁS-OS-
MONTES

Bairrada

Mealhada

Mondego

Cova
da Beira

Coimbra

Zêzere

BEIRA-BAIXA

Castelo Branco

Fátima

Tomar

Tagus

Peniche

Obidos

Santarem

Lourinha

Chamusca

Portalegre

Torres Vedras

Cartaxo

RIBATEJO

ESTREMADURA

Arruda

Almeirim

Bucelas

Coruche

Sorraia

Colares

Carcavelos

LISBON

Palmela

Estremoz

Borba

Almada

Barreiro

Sebútal

Évora

Redondo

Setúbal

Évora

Bay of
Setúbal

VR ALENTEJO

Reguengos

Barragem do
Alqueva

Sado

Grândola

Vidigueira

Granja-
Amareleja

Sineś

Moura

Beja

Guadiana

Panasqueira

Algarve

Lagos

Tavira

Faro

Porto Santo

Madeira Islands
(Portugal)

Pico Ruivo
6107 ft (1862 m)

Madeira

Madeira

Funchal

Deserta Granda

Bugio

Portugal

If a country can be said to have reinvented itself almost from scratch in the last quarter of the twentieth century, then Portugal is that country. In the 1960s Portuguese wine was represented in the outside world by one rather underwhelming rosé in a pretty bottle—Mateus—and an assortment of half-forgotten names from the 1930s such as bucelas and setúbal. Madeira was considered only suitable for cooking or for elderly tastes and even port was in a decline regarded by many industry commentators as terminal. Even in the 1970s—the decade when a new generation woke up to wine—Portugal lagged. Enthusiasts leapt upon Dão and Vinho Verde, a

few hardy souls rediscovered colares and the red wines of the Douro, but interest was minimal and the wines were, all too often, inconsistent. Then came the 1980s…and something started stirring in the *adegas* (wineries) and vineyards. Portuguese winemakers began to rediscover their native grape varieties and to use new technology to find out what they could really achieve. The consequences have been spectacular.

Maria Lopes shows off a basket of freshly picked olives from Tras Os Montes, in the north of Portugal, where hot dry summers are ideal for growing olives and grapes alike.

In 1910 only six wine regions were demarcated: Carcavelos, Colares, Dão, Moscatel de Setúbal, Port and Vinho Verde. By 1975 only two more regions (Bucelas and Madeira) had been added. However, since the country's entry into the European Union in 1986, Portuguese wine has changed beyond recognition, now offering a splendid mix of ancient and modern, rustic and high tech, new wave and traditional.

There are two leading wine producers in Portugal, with interests in more than one region. Sogrape was established in 1942 in Vila Real and is currently the biggest wine company in Portugal. The Symington group might be described as the "royal family" of fortified wines in Portugal and is currently the biggest producer of port in the country.

Landscape and climate

The country divides roughly in half, to the north and south of the Tagus River. The north is mountainous while the south is lower but climbs toward a central plain. The climate divides on similar lines: north of the Tagus there is more temperate influence, while in the south, the climate is more Mediterranean, with milder winters. In wine terms, Portugal can be split roughly into five mainland regions—the north, the area from the Douro to the Tagus Rivers; the center, Lisbon and the Tagus valley; Setúbal and the south; the Algarve; and the islands of Madeira and the Azores.

In the north, the land climbs from the west coast toward the Spanish border into granite mountains with outcrops of schist in the highlands of the port country. The great contrast here in winemaking is between the light, fresh, usually fizzy wines of Vinho Verde, where *vinho verde* ("green wine") is grown, and the heavyweights of the Douro, including port. Port country is some of the most beautiful and spectacular in the world. The River Corgo flows into the Douro near where the town of Régua splits the main production area of DOC Porto into two: Baixo Corgo, the area around the town and the confluence, is the westernmost area for port production and also the coolest and wettest. Cima Corgo, upstream from Régua, is the heartland of top-quality port production, centered around the town of Pinhão.

One of the oldest-established fine-wine areas lies between the points at which the rivers Douro and Tagus cross the Spanish border. Dão and Bairrada are prominent wine areas in this mountainous landscape.

In the country's center, the region of Estremadura stretches along the coast north of Lisbon. It is home to a vast array of grapes and a reputation for decent, if unexciting, everyday wines. Setúbal and the south covers almost a third of Portugal. This region is mainly undulating plain, fertile and heavily farmed. Setúbal has seen some of the most innovative and forward-thinking new ideas in recent years, creating some splendid wines and maintaining its reputation for the classic moscatel.

> *Say anything that you like about me except that I drink water.*
> W. C. FIELDS (1880–1946)

The quay at Vila Nova de Gaia, on the Douro River, which has served as a transport route for the wine trade for many centuries.

The Algarve is a very hot region of craggy inlets. Its winemaking tradition dates back to the days when fortified wines were shipped over to Spain. The biggest threat here to quality wine-making is the tourist market for which a large amount of unexciting wine is produced.

Madeira is a spectacularly beautiful volcanic island closer to Morocco than Portugal. Wine grapes are grown in terraced slopes, often in high and apparently inaccessible places. It's about the last place on Earth you'd expect to find one of the world's greatest wines. The climate here is temperate, though often humid.

The Azores is an archipelago in the Atlantic 870 miles (1,400 km) west of Portugal, and consists of nine main islands, volcanic in origin. The climate is subtropical with high humidity.

Two Wines: Port and Madeira

Port was born of seventeenth-century conflicts between the English and the French. Trade wars over French wine prompted English merchants to travel to Portugal. They began to export wine to which they added brandy to fortify it for the journey. One theory has it that port resulted from wine being doctored with alcohol to cover harsh, tannic flavors; another, that someone mixed brandy with the wine during fermentation, retaining the sweetness of the natural grape sugar.

Methods of making port today remain largely traditional, though there is fierce argument over whether the grapes are better pressed and fermented in steel tanks or pressed by foot in *lagares* (stone troughs) as they have been for centuries. Whichever method is used, the must is

The number of single-estate wineries in Portugal has increased with the relaxation of government bureacracy and entry to the European Union.

fermented to about 6–8 percent abv (alcohol by volume) and run off into holding tanks that are already a quarter full of a neutral grape spirit called *aguardiente*. This stops the fermentation without adding flavors or aromas to the wine. Then, after a suitable period of rest, the wine is passed to casks or tanks for maturation.

A bewildering variety of grapes may be used to make port, but only half a dozen are generally accepted to be in the front rank: touriga francesa, tinta roriz, mourisco, bastardo, tinta cão, and the favorite, touriga nacional. Vineyards are banded into Grades A to F, and growers paid on a sliding scale according to the level of quality of their produce.

Port is aged and classified according to its quality. Vintage port is a single-vintage wine from the very best years, and spends two years in cask and the rest in bottle. Single-quinta is made from the grapes of an individual quinta ("farm"). Colheita ports are single-vintage wines aged in wood until just before bottling. These may be very old, tawny-colored, and delicately nutty in flavor. Tawny, a lighter style of port, is blended from different vintages and aged in wood for six to seven years. Late-bottled vintage is a vintage port, typically from a second-string year and aged in wood for four to six years. Vintage character describes a port made "in the vintage style" but blended from a number of years. Ruby refers to a basic everyday port of any age but the very best rubies will have been aged for around four years.

The four noble varieties used to make madeira are malvasia (known by the English as malmsey), boal, verdelho, and sercial. As well, there have always been plantations of terrantez, bastardo, and moscatel on Madeira, as well as listrão on the neighboring island of Porto Santo. However, the most common grape grown in Madeira is tinta negra mole.

As with many fortified wines, the heating and cooling effects of the trip across the equator in the age of exploration seemed to improve the quality of the wine, and this led to the island's unique maturation methods. Grapes are bought in from small farmers and the noble varieties are fermented separately, often in oak casks or vats. The wines are fortified to 17–18 percent abv (alcohol by volume) during fermentation.

Estufa (stove) is the name of the unique method that madeira producers use to reproduce the gentle heating and cooling effects of an equatorial voyage. Carried out incorrectly, it can damage the wine, but the process can speed wine's development. Noble wines are usually aged by the *canteiro* system, in which casks of the wine are racked into heated warehouses and allowed to adjust to the changing ambient temperature.

Colheitas are single-vintage wines made from the noble varieties. Those from the very best years have been known to survive for up to 200 years. By law, they must be stored in cask for a minimum of 20 years and in bottle for a further two years before release.

Some solera wines result from a series of "scales," or rows, of increasingly older barrels blended with younger wines of the same type. In effect, new wine goes in at one end and old wine comes out of the other—after a period of many years. New wine takes on the characteristics of the old and matures much more quickly.

Malmsey, boal, verdelho, and sercial must be made from 85 percent of the named grape. They are usually sold as 5-year-old, 10-year-old, 15-year-old, and colheita. Sweet, medium-sweet, medium-dry, and dry madeiras are wines made from tinta negra mole and the four levels of sweetness are supposed to represent the styles of the four noble grapes.

Wine law

Several administrations over the past century have tried to organize the wine industry, with only limited success—until 1999, when all the anomalies were sorted out (for now). The new administrative body is the Instituto da Vinha e

Harvest time at Quinta do Noval, in the Douro Valley; the steep vineyards here require a great deal of stamina.

Have some madeira

Producers of madeira must be proud to know their product is found in almost every restaurant, hotel, and cruise ship on the planet. Unfortunately, this globally known wine is most likely a rather low-end, commercial grade product destined for the kitchen, not the dining room. Young Turks on the Ilha da Madeira, or Island of the Woods, are hacking through the jungle of government red tape to introduce the world at large to their world class wines, the single varietal sercials, verdelhos, buals, and malmseys, from the finest vineyards, heated gently by the tropical climate instead of furnaces or hot tanks. The finest madeiras are one of the wine world's remaining bargains. A well-aged sercial or verdelho, for example, is less than the price of an ordinary chardonnay, and will stay fresh for years after opening.

do Vinho (IVV) and the current terminology is as follows. The letters VQPRD stand for Vinho de Qualidade Produzidos em Regiões Determinadas (QWPSR in English—"Quality Wines Produced in Specific Regions"). This embraces two categories of quality wines: Denominação de Origem Controlada (DOC), the equivalent of Spain's DO or France's AOC, with a total of 36 DOC areas; and Indicação de Provenencia Regulamentada (IPR), a category created for emergent wine areas (there are currently nine regions in this classification.)

The table wine category divides into two. Vinho Regional (VR) covers country wines from fairly large areas, and allows for a vintage date, a regional name, and grape varieties on the label. Nine of them cover virtually the whole country, and they are administered directly by the IVV. Vinho de Mesa (VdM) is a simple table wine. It may be made in, and blended from grapes from, any part of Portugal. There are few controls on the way it is made.

The North

VR Minho is a country-wine area in the north-west. Its borders coincide roughly with those of the DOC Vinho Verde but regulation is far less stringent. The Vinho Verde area is best known for its slightly under-ripe ("green") wines with a bit of slightly sparkling spritzig character, though locally these are likely to be red and drunk young and fresh. Export wines are mainly white; the best made from the alvarinho grape in the sub-region of Monção.

In VR Trás-os-Montes, in the northeast of Portugal, the country wines are light whites in the *vinho verde* style as well as heavyweight whites and reds largely unseen outside this region. The southern part includes the Douro valley. The entire area includes Chaves, Valpaços, and Planalto-Mirandes IPRs. DOC Porto shares the same boundaries as DOC Douro and these two areas dominate wine production.

QUINTA DE ALDERIZ   *Established* NA *Owner* S. A. de Casa Pinheiro *Vineyard area* 25 acres (10 ha)
From Monção along the Minho to the west of Melgaço, this is where much of the best alvarinho grows. The Sociedade Agrícola da Casa Pinheiro, which is based at the quinta, makes a most excellent example of this wine, called Quinta de Alderiz Alvarinho.

SOGRAPE   *Established* 1947 *Owners* Sogrape *Vineyard area* 988 acres (400 ha)
Sogrape's *vinho verde* is Morgadio da Torre, made from 100 percent alvarinho at its winery in Barcelos. Aveleda is still made at the quinta in Penafiel and the company now sells both brands. Best wine: Morgadio da Torre.

A. A. FERREIRA S. A.   *Established* 1751 *Owners* Sogrape *Vineyard area* 370 acres (150 ha)
This Douro offshoot of the port house Ferreira makes what is perhaps Portugal's finest red wine—Barca Velha. It uses the finest grapes in only the finest years. The wine spends 18 months in French oak and a further seven or eight years in bottle. Other wines are Reserva Ferreirinha, Callabriga, and Vinha Grande.

NIEPOORT   *Established* 1842 *Owners* Niepoort family *Vineyard area* 62 acres (25 ha)
Niepoort makes a hefty red called Redoma at the Quinta do Carril. Unusually, he makes a white counterpart from gouveio and rabigato (rabo de ovelha) at the Quinta de Napolés. There's also a red made in the traditional manner (in *lagares*) from tinta roriz and touriga francesa grapes.

QUINTA DO CRASTO   *Established* 1615 *Owners* J. & L. Roquette *Vineyard area* 114 acres (46 ha)
This is a lovely old Douro estate with a beautifully restored country house and chapel. The wines and port are first-rate. The grapes are old-vine (up to 70 years)—touriga nacional, tinta roriz, touriga francesa, tinta cão—aged in oak. The best wine here is Quinta do Crasto Reserva.

Terraced vineyards contour the steep valleys of the Douro region.

RAMOS PINTO *Established*
1880 *Owner* Champagne Louis Roederer *Vineyard area* 494 acres (200 ha)

Wines are made here from a mixture of grapes drawn from Quinta da Ervamoira in the Côa valley (Douro superior) and Quinta de Bom Retiro in the Torto valley (cima corgo). The former provides grapes with freshness and acidity, the latter with weight, ripeness, and structure, and the result is called Duas Quintas. The best wine here is Duas Quintas Reserva.

Producers
1 Quinta do Crasto
2 A.A. Ferreira S.A.
3 Vinha do Fojo
4 Montez Champalimaud
5 Niepoort
6 Ramos Pinto
7 Quinta da Valado
8 Ferreira
9 Fonseca Guimaraens
10 Graham's
11 Quinta do Noval
12 Taylor, Fladgate & Yeatman
13 Warre's

FERREIRA *Established* 1751 *Owner* Sogrape *Vineyard area* NA

Antonia Adelaide Ferreira, the great-granddaughter of the founder, José Ferreira, consolidated the foundations of this company, which is now under the guidance of her great-great-grandson, Vito Olazebal, and his son, Francisco. Grapes for Ferreira port come from four quintas—do Porto (bought in 1863); do Seixo (1979); de Leida and do Caedo (1990). Best wines: LBV; Duque de Bragança 20-year-old tawny; vintages.

FONSECA GUIMARAENS *Established* 1822 *Owner* Taylor, Fladgate & Yeatman *Vineyard area* NA

Fonseca has its own house style and its own sources of grapes—most notably the Quinta do Cruzeiro and the Quinta do Santo Antônio in the Pinhão valley. Premium Ruby Bin 27 is its most famous name, but its aged tawnies are legendary, as is the late-bottled vintage, Fonseca-Guimaraens.

TAYLOR, FLADGATE & YEATMAN *Established* 1692 *Owner* Alistair Robertson *Vineyard area* NA

In the Douro, near Régua, Taylor's is generally recognized as the top port company. Major brands are LBV and some splendid old tawnies,

Historic Barca Velha

Portugal's Douro is most famous for the sweet, fortified port wine, but one firm, A. A. Ferreira, had staked its claim on a dry red, Barca Velha. This is Portugal's most expensive table wine and is made by Ferreira at Quinta do Vale de Meao. Just across the border are the vineyards for Spain's most expensive wine, Vega Sicilia. Barca Velha (the old barge) is made with the same grapes used in port, primarily touriga nacional and tinta roriz (which is also known as tempranillo or tinto fino across the border). The wine is ripe, spicy and has notes of mint, chocolate, and earth. Production is limited, so the wine is hard to find. Nonetheless, it has served as inspiration to the fledgling table wine industry of the Douro.

but the jewels are wines produced by the two quintas, Quinta da Terra Faita and Quinta de Vargellas. The latter turns out some of the finest wines in the region.

OTHER PRODUCERS
In the Douro, other good producers include António Esteves Ferreira, Vinha do Fojo, Montez Champalimaud, and Quinta do Valado; in Porto, Graham's, Quinta do Noval, and Warre's.

The Douro to the Tagus

The Beiras region covers the whole of the north-central part of Portugal, and wines made under the Vinho Regional epithet come in a huge array of styles, from sleepy local co-ops to some new wave, experimental wineries.

The VR Beiras area includes within it Lafões IPR and four DOCs. The most northerly of these is Távora/Varosa, which is best known for its Douro-style reds and whites, but is also emerging as a producer of some of Portugal's best sparkling wines. Next comes Beira Interior, offering some decent, full reds in the north. Further along there is long-serving Dão: its best wines are solid reds made from touriga nacional and other grapes, including bastardo, jaen, and tinta roriz; its best whites are made from cold-fermented encruzado, while the new wave wines have good fruit and a decent structure. Continuing even further south is Bairrada, which mostly produces red wines from the local baga grape. This area has some of Portugal's most forward-thinking winemakers. Lafões winemaking shows hints of nearby Dão and Vinho Verde styles.

QUINTA DOS ROQUES
Established 1989 *Owners* Oliveira and Lorenço families *Vineyard area* 99 acres (40 ha)

Manuel de Oliveira runs this vineyard at Dão. A new winery was built in 1990 and the wines show tremendous promise. Winemaking concentrates on quality reds made from touriga nacional, tinta roriz, tinta cão, and others, although there are good whites made from bical, malvasia, and sercial. Top wines from this producer are Touriga Nacional and Tinta Roriz.

CAVES DE MURGANHEIRA, VDME
Established 1974 *Owners* Partinvest, O. da Costa Lourenco *Vineyard area* 59 acres (24 ha)

This company, in the district of Varosa, made its name in new wave "classic method" sparkling wines (what used to be called *méthode champenoise*), none of which are entitled to any kind of official quality classification but must be labeled VdME. The company produces one of Portugal's best wines, made from malvasia, chardonnay, sercial, and pinto, with several months in oak after the first fermentation and a year on the lees after the second. Their very best wine here is Murganheira Varosa.

SOCIEDADE AGRICOLA DE SANTAR
Established 1790 *Owner* Soc. Agricola de Santar *Vineyard area* 247 acres (100 ha)

This is a single-estate winery that was completely redesigned back in the 1990s. Under the watchful eye of winemaker Pedro de Vasconcellos e Souza, it now concentrates on producing varietal wines. The best wines made here are Castas de Santar Alfrocheiro Preto and Touriga Nacional.

Producers
1 Quinta das Maias
2 Caves Messias
3 Quinta dos Roques
4 Quinta de Saes
5 Casa Agricola de Saima
6 Caves Aliança
7 Hotel Palace do Buçaco
8 Luis Pato
9 Caves Primavera
10 Caves São João

PORTUGAL
LISBON

Dão/Bairrada

Momenta da Beira
Barragem de Vilar
Antas
Vila Nova de Paiva
Benvende
Tamanhos
São Pedro do Sul
Célorico da Beira
Talhadas Cambra Viseu
Barra Aveiro
Ilhavo
Águeda Caramulo 3 Mangualde
Oliveira do Bairro 9
Praia de Mira 5,6 Sangalhos Tondela
Anadia 1 Gouveia
Bairrada Mealhada Carregal do Sal Seia
Cantanhede 2 7 Barragem Rojão Grande Dão 4
Buçaco da Aguieira Chamusca
Oliveira do Mondego
Carvalho Galizes
Tentúgal São Martinho Alva
Quiaios Mondego Coimbra
Vila Chã Barragem de Fronhas

NORTH
10 miles
(16 kilometers)

Vineyards in Dāo: this region is one of Portugal's longest-serving wine-producing areas.

CAVES ALIANÇA *Established* 1927 *Owners*
Neves family *Vineyard area* 25 acres (10 ha)

This is a family-run company making wine
here in Bairrada as well as in Dão and the
Alentejo. The winemaker is Francisco Antunes
and he makes crisp dry whites from bical and
chardonnay, as well as reds from baga and
(under the VR Beiras) cabernet sauvignon. Best
wines: Aliança Garrafeira (Bairrada); Galeria
Cabernet Sauvignon (Beiras).

HOTEL PALACE DO BUÇACO (VDM)
Established 1917 *Owners* Almeida group *Vineyard
area* 37 acres (15 ha)

This is a mind-boggling, postbaroque, forest-
antasy palace built deep in the woodlands of the
Serra de Buçaco as a country retreat for Carlos I.
It was leased to Alexandre d'Almeida in 1917
and he turned it into a hotel and vineyard. The
wines remain more or less as Almeida first
created them. The red is made from baga, tinta
pinheira, and bastardo, pressed and fermented
in stone *lagares* and aged for three years in enormous vats made from oak harvested from the
surrounding forest. The hotel lists vintages from

1945 onwards, and there are those who say that
to eat the roast suckling pig and to drink the red
wines of the Palace do Buçaco is to experience
the best gastronomy that Portugal has to offer.
Best wines: all of them.

CAVES SÃO JOÃO *Established* 1960 *Owners*
A. & L. Costa *Vineyard area* 86 acres (35 ha)

Much of the wine here is brought in, ready-made,
from local producers to supplement the production of the Quinta do Poço do Lobo. Red wines
tend to be the best, sold under the Frei João
label, with the *reserva* achieving the highest
quality. In addition, there's a non-DOC cabernet
sauvignon, and the company also makes wines
in the DOC Dão. Best wines: Quinta de Poço de
Lobo (baga, moreto, castelão nacional).

OTHER PRODUCERS
Other producers from the region that are highly
recommended include Quinta de Foz de Arouce
from the Beiras; Quinta das Maias, Caves
Messias, and Quinta de Saes from Dão; and
Casa Agrícola de Saima, Luís Pato, and Caves
Primavera from around Bairrada.

Lisbon and the Tagus Valley

VR ESTREMADURA

Estremadura is home to a huge range of grapes and decent, everyday wines. It has two IPR zones —Encostas d'Aire and Alcobaça—and eight DOC areas. Obidos has some decent reds; Lourinhã is considered Portugal's best brandy area; and Torres Vedras is a high-production area.

Alenquer has some promising wines made mainly from arinto, fernão pires, vital (white) and joão de santarém (red). Arruda makes red wines of youthful charm, while Bucelas produces dry white wines made mainly from the arinto grape. Colares's best is red—dark, hard and tannic when young, maturing after a decade or more. Carcavelos, on the edge of Lisbon, has all but disappeared and the wine is not easy to find.

Among the producers here, Quinta de Pancas produces outstanding wines: classic style, made

Above: Seacteurs for pruning vines and hand-picking grapes.
Below: The Tagus valley's soils provide the ideal growing conditions for vines.

from arinto and jampal (white), tinta roriz and touriga nacional (red); and "new wave," from chardonnay and cabernet sauvignon. Quinta da Murta makes serious white wines from arinto and a bit of esgana cão (sercial) and rabo de ovelha (rabigato). You may find one or two of the semi-fortified wines of the fabled Quinta da Barão still on sale. If you find it, drink it.

VR RIBATEJANO

The VR Ribatejano area includes within it Ribatejo/Tomar, site of a great convent–castle, an area once famous for its fairly hefty red wines but sadly no longer. Ribatejo/Almeirim has value-for-money everyday wines while Ribatejo/Chamusca is dominated by co-op wines. Almost half the DOC Ribatejo's wine comes from Ribatejo/Cartaxo, a source of good, everyday white and red wines. Ribatejo/Coruche has producers experimenting with a botrytized white made from fernão pires.

Producer Quinta da Lagoalva de Cima makes new wave style wines, with syrah, cabernet sauvignon, and pinot noir alongside the traditional joão de santarém and chardonnay beside the arinto and fernão pires. The best wine is Quinta da Logoalva de Cima (syrah). Other good producers in this region worth consideration are Casa Cadaval and Quinta Grande.

Setúbal and the South

Dusty cellared bottles of the 1912 vintage of boal, one of Madeira's four "noble" grape varieties.

VR TERRAS DO SADO

This region includes Palmela, in the north, which makes excellent reds from periquita and fresh, crisp whites from fernão pires. In the south, Setúbal still makes great classic sweet wine in the traditional way, fortified during fermentation (like port) and then allowed to macerate on its skins to give the classic muscat flavor.

Among the top producers is JP Vinhos, which makes Cova de Ursa, a barrel-fermented chardonnay, Má Partilha, a pure merlot, Quinta de Bacalhoa, a cabernet/merlot and a fortified JP Moscatel de Setúbal. João Pires Dry Muscat (a fully fermented moscatel wine) and JP Tinta Miúda are among their best.

Pegos Claros is owned by local shareholders. The best wine is Pegos Claros Periquita—100 percent periquita and aged for a year in oak.

José Maria da Fonseca's wines range from the everyday dry white Branco Seco Especial (BSE) to an impressive periquita red, including Primum (an interesting blend) and excellent garrafeira wines. This company is best known for saving the moscatel de setúbal from extinction. Its entire range is good, but the jewels in the crown are the old vintages of moscatel de setúbal.

In Palmela, also look out for Co-op Agrícola de Santo Isidro de Pegões.

VR ALENTEJANO

The wines made in this vast area of east-central Portugal may be humble country wines or declassified (or unclassifiable) wines from the eight DOC regions within it. Alentejo/Portalegre has some white wine made mainly from fernão pires. Alentejo/Borba offers red wines with fruit, freshness and a balanced acidity and decent whites. Alentejo/Redondo's reds have a pleasantly ripe, fruity freshness. Alentejo/Evora has good periquita and trincadeira reds and reasonable whites; watch Evora for quality wines in the near future. Other DOCs here include Alentejo/Reguengos, Alentejo/Granja-Amareleja, Alentejo/Vidigueira and Alentejo/Moura.

At Cortes de Cima, an innovative vineyard near Vidiguera, Hans Jørgensen has planted aragonês, trincadeira, periquita, syrah, and cabernet sauvignon, and early vintages show extremely well; the best wine here is Cortes de Cima Syrah Reserva.

The Society Agrícola da Herdade dos Coelheiros has a winery that relies on cabernet sauvignon as its "backbone." Tapada de Coelheiros is made from cabernet, trincadeira, and aragonês; Tapada de Coelheiros Garrafeira is cabernet and aragonês. The best wine here: Garrafeira.

Fundação Eugénio Almeida has its vineyard planted in trincadeira, periquita, moreto, aragonês, and alfrocheiro. Cartuxa and wines under the Monte de Pinheiros and Eugénio Almeida labels are made. The best wine is Pêra Manca. Other good producers in Alentejano are Quinta do Carmo and Esporão.

VR MADEIRA

VR Madeira covers the entire island. Barbeito has several venerable wines in its cellars, including one claimed to be from the 1795 vintage. More approachable (and affordable) is the splendid 1957. Best wines are colheitas and 100-year-old malmsey. Henriques & Henriques offers a panoply of ancient colheitas and its fabulous Reservas Velhissimas. Also good are Artur Barros & Sousa and the Madeira Wine Company.

England and Wales

The phrase "mad dogs and Englishmen" frequently comes to mind when discussing English wines. Being an island, England's weather is extremely fickle and even southern England is north of 50°N latitude. Considering that Britain imports a wide range of wines at all price levels from around the world, why would anyone contemplate planting a vineyard and making wine in such conditions? On the other hand, there is palatable wine produced from vineyards close to Alice Springs in the hot, arid, Australian interior; and down the road from Niagara Falls in bitterly cold Ontario, Canada; so why not? The mad dogs are at least supported by Her Majesty the Queen, who often serves English wine to visiting foreign dignitaries.

Cheviot Hills

Newcastle upon Tyne

Solway Firth

Scafell Pike
3204 ft (977 m)

Durham

DURHAM

Middlesborough

Isle of Man

Pennines

NORTH YORKSHIRE

Ouse

Aire

York

IRISH SEA

Kingston upon Hull

Huddersfield

St Helens

Liverpool

Birkenhead   Manchester   Sheffield

Holyhead

Snowdon
3558 ft (1085 m)

Trent

Grimsby

LINCOLN

ENGLAND

Nottingham

The Wash

Leicester

Norwich

Cardigan
Bay

Birmingham

NORFOLK

CAMBRIDGE

SUFFOLK

Northampton

Bury St Edmunds

WALES

HEREFORD &
WORCESTER

Severn

Cambridge

Ipswich

OXFORD-
SHIRE

ESSEX

Swansea

GWENT   GLOUCESTER

Newport

Thames

BUCKING-
HAMSHIRE

GLAMORGAN

Cardiff

Oxford

LONDON

Southend-on-Sea

Bristol Channel

Bristol

BERK-
SHIRE

Reading

WILTSHIRE

Basingstoke

SURREY   Maidstone   KENT

SOMERSET

HAMPSHIRE

Taunton

Southampton

WEST
SUSSEX

EAST
SUSSEX

Brighton

DEVON

DORSET

Portsmouth

Dartmoor
2027 ft (618 m)

Lyme
Bay

Bournemouth

Isle
of Wight

CORNWALL

ENGLISH CHANNEL

Plymouth

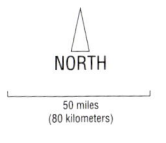

NORTH

50 miles
(80 kilometers)

Peter Hall among the vines at Breaky Bottom, Sussex. Viiticulture is a labor of love in less than ideal conditions.

British Wine is the legal term for "made wine," that is, made in Britain from imported grape concentrate. Still sold in the UK, it is a source of much confusion on labels. A wine labeled English Wine must be made from fresh grapes grown in English vineyards.

The vineyard area in England and Wales has grown from virtually zero 50 years ago, to about 2,170 acres (878 ha). There are about 400 active vineyards, and of these, just 14 are larger than 25 acres (10 ha), representing 38 percent of plantings. The vineyards are scattered across southern England and Wales.

Over the past 20 years or so, several wineries have proved that good-quality wine can be made from grapes grown in well-sited vineyards. Initially, all the efforts were with light, fresh, dry, and medium-dry fruity white wines, and this style remains definitive. However, specialties such as late-harvest or lightly oaked white wines, unusual reds, and traditional-method sparkling wines have enjoyed many accolades.

Climate

The climate is notoriously cool and damp and can be described as marginal for viticulture. To make the most of available heat and sunshine and to protect against the climatic hazards of wind, frost, and damp, vineyard siting is crucial. Only in areas with a maritime climate and warming effects of the Gulf Stream do grapes ripen at all this far north. However, the long growing season is ideal for flavor development in certain varieties. Production is erratic due to the variability of the weather.

Vines and wines

Most of the white grape varieties grown are of German origin, including müller-thurgau with 13 percent of total plantings, reichensteiner (12 percent), bacchus (10 percent), and schönburger (8 percent), with huxelrebe, ortega, ehrenfelser, faberrebe, and siegerrebe among the others planted. The main non-Germanic white grape is the hybrid seyval, the third-most important variety with 11 percent of plantings. Madeleine angevine, a table grape, has 7 percent of plantings, while the only classic variety with plantings of any size is chardonnay (4 percent), mainly for use in sparkling wines.

Most of the German crossings give floral or fruit flavors; some are quite leafy in character. White wines are light both in alcohol and flavor. Today, the delicate dry and off-dry whites do better than medium styles. High acidity enables these wines to age well, and they often develop a better balance with one to four years of bottle age.

A few wineries have achieved success with good dessert wines from botrytis-affected grapes. These dessert wines tend to be low in alcohol with vibrant honey and fruit flavors and high acidity balancing the sweetness.

Pinot noir is the most planted red grape, with tiny amounts of merlot and cabernet sauvignon the other classics.

A sheltered site is one of the key factors to growing grapes in England and Wales.

There are many dry and medium-dry rosés made, and the best are light and fresh with delicate strawberry fruit. Reds have been a struggle but there have been successes.

Good-quality traditional-method sparkling wines are made from base wine blends of German crossings, some also with seyval. Some producers have persevered with chardonnay and pinot noir and the resulting sparkling wines show tremendous quality. Other varieties are also proving good, such as auxerrois, pinot blanc, pinot meunier, and gamay.

My Friends should drink a dozen of claret on my Tomb.

JOHN KEATS (1795–1821),
letter to Benjamin Bailey,
August 14, 1819

Producers

Most producers sell only locally; a few have developed trade nationally and some export their product, but most UK retailers do not stock English wines. Significant producers, with wines available beyond the cellar door, include Chapel Down Wines (who use both their own and contract grapes), Valley Vineyards (with top quality wines) and those following.

DENBIES WINE ESTATE, SURREY   *Established 1986 Owner Denbies Wine Estate Vineyard area 265 acres (108 ha)*

Denbies Wine Estate's biggest successes have been with the large-production and good-value Surrey Gold (a medium-dry blend) and a Special Late-Harvested white from a blend of Germanic varieties, including the late ripening optima and ortega. Pinot noir also does well and has been produced on its own and as a blend with dornfelder. Denbies' wines are from estate-grown grapes only.

NYETIMBER VINEYARD, SUSSEX   *Established 1990 Owners Stuart and Sandy Moss Vineyard area 40 acres (16 ha)*

Nyetimber is England's largest dedicated sparkling wine producer. The wines have at least three years on yeast in bottle and more aging before release. The complex Première Cuvée Blanc de Blancs is creamy, spicy, and beautifully balanced. The Classic Cuvée is equally stylish, but richer.

Central Europe

CZECH REPUBLIC

Liberec
Most
Bohemia
Roudnice
Mělník
PRAGUE
Pilsen
Pradě́d
4893 ft (1492 m)
Ostrava
Morava
Olomouc
Ceske
Budejovice
Brno
Southern
Moravia

SLOVAKIA

Carpathian Mtns
Gerlachovský
8692 ft (2650 m)
Váh
Nitra
Eastern
Slovakia
Kosice
Central
Slovakia
Lesser
Carpathia
Nitra
Nitra
BRATISLAVA
Nové Zámky
Southern
Slovakia
Danube
Tokaj
Tokaj-
Hegyalja
Tokaj
Miskolc
Northeast
Hungary
Kékes
3312 ft (1010 m)
Gyöngyös
Nyíregyháza
Sopron
Győr
Tatabánya
Debrecen

HUNGARY

Northwest
Hungary
BUDAPEST
Székesfehérvár
Szolnok
Kecskemét
Körös
Lake Balaton
Lake
Balaton
Lake
Balaton
Central South
Hungary
Tolna
Szeged
Southwest
Hungary
Pécs
Subotica
Vojvodina

SLOVENIA

Drava
Maribor
Drava
Valley
Celje
Triglav
9380 ft (2860 m)
LJUBLJANA
Sava
Sava
Valley
Novo
Mesto
Littoral
Snežnik
5890 ft (1796 m)
ZAGREB
Rijeka
Karlovac
Pula

CROATIA

Osijek
Srem
Novi Sad
BELGRADE
Morava
River
Timok
Valley
Zadar
Banja Luka

BOSNIA-HERZEGOVINA

YUGOSLAVIA

Triglav
Troglav
8274 ft (1913 m)
SARAJEVO
Cacak
Drina
Cuprija
Split
Brac
Mostar
Morava
River
Morava
Nis
Neretva
Leskovac
Hvar
Durmitor
8272 ft (2522 m)
Dubrovnik
Pristina
Vranje
Podgorica
8432 ft
(2570 m)
Kosovo
Titov Vrh
9010 ft (2747 m)
Kumanovo
Lake
Skadar
Shkodër
Korab
9052 ft (2760 m)
SKOPJE
Veles

MACEDONIA

Shëngjin
Laç
TIRANA
Lushnja
Elbasan
Ohrid
Bitola
Vlorë
Lake
Ohrid
Lake Prespa
Devoll

ALBANIA

ADRIATIC
SEA

NORTH

50 miles
(80 kilometers)

Vltava

Central and Eastern Europe

This is a story of winemakers picking up the pieces after decades of communism had left them with collectivized vineyards, a dearth of up-to-date equipment, and neither the hard currency nor the know-how required for modern wine production. But, winemakers being the resourceful people they are, it is also a story of old identities being rediscovered and old traditions of quality being dusted off and re-examined.

None of these countries, with the exception of Hungary, has a great reputation for wine, although Slovenia deserves a better reputation than it has. Hungary's renown is based upon tokaji, one of the world's greatest dessert wines. Slovakia is in decline as a wine producer, and while in the Czech Republic the vineyard area has also fallen, this country should, in theory, have a brighter future.

In Eastern Europe the necessities of everyday life take priority over the making of fine wine and the local market has no particular regard for quality. Bulgaria has the longest history of producing export-friendly wines, and Moldova has at least as much potential. Romania's great problem is lack of consistency; the Ukraine and Russia focus on local markets but might—who knows?—yet prove to be sleeping giants.

Znovín Znojmo Vineyard, Moravia, in the Czech Republic.

Reds include regional favorites such as modrý portugal, frankovka, svatovavřinecké, and the crosses of the latter two cultivars (andré and zweigeltrebe), not to mention cabernet sauvignon, which is not at its best here. Pinot noir, however, expresses itself surprisingly well, especially in the Bohemian region, its ideal *terroir*.

CZECH REPUBLIC

During 40 years of communist control, wine was produced here at the lowest common denominator level. Despite a Wine Act, which came into force in 1995, and the privatization of most wineries, the rate of change has been sluggish.

Notwithstanding a preponderance of poor product, some things are improving in the Czech Republic. The development and cloning of several new varieties that are more resistant to frost, fungi and diseases is one example. Another positive sign is that foreign capital has recently found its way into the country.

Wines and producers

The main growing regions are in Southern Moravia and the much smaller Bohemian region.

Traditional white grape varieties are riesling, pinot gris, pinot blanc, gewürztraminer, sauvignon blanc, grüner veltliner, welschriesling, müller-thurgau, neuburger, sylvaner, and Moravian muscat, along with a number of local crossings, such as aurelius (riesling × neuburger) or palava (gewürztraminer × müller-thurgau). Chardonnay is also making deep inroads into the Czech wine industry.

An antique cork press, used when corks had to be inserted into each bottle manually.

SLOVAKIA

Slovakia has much in common with its former other half the Czech Republic: the same recent history, plantings of similar grape varieties, similar languages, and by and large the same economic conditions prevail.

Prior to the "velvet revolution" in 1989, Slovakia had 74,000 acres (30,000 ha) under vine, while today it has 24,380 acres (9,687 ha) of registered vineyard planting.

Wines and producers

The six growing regions of Slovakia are Lesser Carpathia, Southern Slovakia, Central Slovakia, Nitra, Eastern Slovakia, and Tokaj.

New wine laws, which came into force in 1996, classify wines into the following categories: table wines, quality varietal wines, quality brand wines, quality blends, wines with special attributes, sparkling wines, aromatized wines, and Tokaj wines.

Grape varieties planted are similar to those in the Czech Republic, with the addition of irsai oliver, leányka, lipovina (hárslevelű), furmint, bouviertraube, and locally developed crossings, such as devín, dunaj, and alibernet.

HUNGARY

Despite Hungary's checkered political history, viticulture thrived throughout the centuries and even under the communists—though quality suffered. However, between the mid-1980s and 1991 Hungary lost close to 75 percent of its wine exports, largely due to the collapse of the soviet system. Widespread bankruptcy followed; some estimates put total vineyard losses at up to 25 percent. But privatization laws and the sale of vineyards and wineries enabled a much slimmed-down industry to survive. The search for quality is now the driving force behind production.

The wine areas are evenly distributed throughout the country, except to the east of the Tisza River, and show considerable geological diversity.

Climate

Hungary has a broadly temperate climate that varies from wet temperate in the west to continental in the east and Mediterranean in the south. Spring comes early, summers tend to be long and winters short. In Tokaj-Hegyalja, autumnal sunshine and mists favor the formation of botrytis.

Vines and wines

The vineyard area is about 320,000 acres (130,000 ha), yielding a total annual production of 99 million gallons (375 million l), of which about 21 million gallons (80 million l) are exported. Hungary used to be mainly a producer of white wines, then red wine production began to increase in the 1960s, with new cabernet sauvignon and cabernet franc plantings, and in the late 1980s it increased rapidly. It is now over 30 percent of total production, and is soon expected to overtake white wine production. Rosé wine production has declined to a very small percentage of the total.

A winery in Badascony, an area which produces full-bodied, minerally wines described as "fiery."

Of the grape varieties recognized in Hungary, 35 are white and 15 red. They include the following (Hungarian names appear in brackets).

White: Rhine riesling (rajnairizling), Italian riesling (olaszrizling), sylvaner (zöld szilváni), müller-thurgau (rizlingszilváni), gewürztraminer (tramini), pinot gris (szürkebarát), pinot blanc (weissburgunder), chardonnay, sauvignon blanc, sémillon, chasselas, muscat ottonel (ottonel muskotály), yellow muscat (sárga muskotály), and grüner muscateller (zöld veltelini).

Red: cabernet sauvignon, cabernet franc, merlot (médoc noir), pinot noir (nágyburgundi or blau-burgunder), lemberger (kékfrankos), blauportugieser (kékoportó), and zweigelt.

The following are either native Hungarian varieties, or found almost exclusively in the region.

White: furmint, ezerjó, hárslevelű, juhfark, kéknyelű, oremus, irsai olivér, leányka, királyleányka, csaba gyöngye, cserszegi fűszeres, cirfadli, kövidinka, kunleány, and zefír.

Red: kadarka.

Apart from tokaji and bikavér, which are traditional blends, Hungarian wines are generally sold under their varietal names or, occasionally, as blends bearing a proprietary name.

Appellations and producers

There are currently 23 appellations in Hungary, the newest being Bortermohelyk, granted in mid-2000. State laws prescribe types and quality

categories, compositional standards, production methods, yields, labeling conventions and levels of quality control. A register of vineyards and wineries exists. Hungary's 23 appellations fall rather conveniently into six groups.

The Northeast includes Mátraalja, Bükkalja, and Eger; the Northwest: Sopron, Pannonhalma Sokoróalja, Aszá-Neszmély, Mór, Eytek-Buda, and Somló; Lake Balaton: Badacsony, Balatonfüred-Csopak, Balatonfeld-vidék, Dél-Balaton, and Balatonmelléke; the Southwest: Szekszárd, Tolna, Mecsekalja, and Villány-Siklós; Central South: Hajós-Baja, Csongrád, and Kiskunság; and Tokaj-Hegyalja.

> *They are not long, the days of wine and roses.*
> **ERNEST DOWSON**
> (1867–1900)

TOKAJ-HEGYALJA
This region produces Hungary's most famous wine, tokaji (or tokay, as it is known elsewhere). Today, Tokaj-Hegyalja includes 12,350 planted acres (5,000 planted ha), of which 83 percent is owned by independent grape-growers. Out of more than a score of producers, ten foreign-owned joint-venture companies share about 10 percent of the appellation area. Hungarian producers hold the last 5 percent of the vineyards.

Tokaji is made from hárslevelű, furmint, sarga muskotály, and, occasionally, oremus. The first two are the base for the sweet aszú, on which the reputation of tokaji rests. Traditionally, this was made by picking botrytized grapes which, under the pressure of their own weight, slowly provided small quantities of a barely alcoholic syrup called Eszencia. The grapes were then mashed to a paste and added in hodfuls (*puttonyos*) of approximately 55 pounds (25 kg) to 36-gallon (136-l) casks of the one-year-old base wine to macerate. After racking, the resulting wine was matured in cask for three years or longer, then stored, then as now, in rock-hewn galleried cellars up to 600 years old. The sweetness of the resulting aszú wines was measured by the number of *puttonyos* added, aszú eszencia being the highest quality, followed by tokaji aszú.

Some of the new producers have modified the traditional method, with excellent results.

Vineyards in the Tocaj-Hegyalja region, famous for tokaji, described as "the king of wines and the wine of kings."

SLOVENIA

With a vineyard area of around 58,000 acres (23,000 ha), the Slovenian wine industry is well managed and quality is assured: under Slovenian wine law only the best wines may be bottled in 75 cl (about 25½ fl. oz.) bottles. These generally bear the seal of the PSVVS (Business Association for Viticulture and Wine Production), an organization that polices itself quite effectively.

There are three wine areas in Slovenia: the Littoral, or Primorska, with four subregions; the Drava Valley, or Podravje, is the other major region, with six subregions; and the smallest region, the Sava Valley or Posavje, is divided into four subregions. Between them, the two major regions produce some 85 percent of Slovenia's wine.

With an amenable climate and landscape, plus the enthusiasm of its winemakers, the future for wine in this small country looks very healthy.

Hvar Island, pictured on the labels of local winery Plenkovic Wines Sv. Nedjela, in Croatia.

CROATIA

War interrupted this once significant producer of wine. However, since the cessation of hostilities there has been a rapid rise in the country's wine production.

Of the two distinct growing regions in Croatia, the main one is Kontinentalna Hrvatska (Inland Croatia), which covers much of the eastern half of the country and incorporates seven districts. The other, Primorska Hrvatska (Coastal Croatia), has four districts, extends along the entire seaboard and includes all the country's islands.

The cooler and more fertile inland area produces mainly white wine (95 percent), especially from the dull laski rizling, or welschriesling, whereas 70 percent of coastal production is red wine. The inland region also produces fruity, straw-colored kutjevacka graševina from Kutjevo, some respectable gewürztraminer, pinot blanc, sauvignon blanc, johannisberg or Rhine riesling, and even muscat ottonel.

Interesting reds from the coast include wines from the plavac mali vine. Both dingač and postup from the Peljesac Peninsula are highly regarded—the full international potential of these two wines, as well as wine from the Dalmatian sémillon grape, is yet to be fully explored.

BOSNIA AND HERZEGOVINA

Prior to the misery and upheaval of war, the vineyards in the south of the country covered 12,350 acres (5,000 ha). By 1997, declared production figures had halved to 1.4 million gallons (5.4 million l). Red wines were always less than persuasive, mainly due to the popularity of the unimpressive blatina grape, but white wines made from zilavka displayed its typical and welcome acidity. At the present time, it is impossible to predict future developments in Bosnia and Herzegovina's wine industry.

Almost all vineyard work is done by hand in investment-starved Macedonia.

SERBIA AND MONTENEGRO

In line with the area's cultural leanings, most of Serbia's wine was in the past flavor-designed to suit Russian tastes. Only the three northern regions of Serbia, influenced by neighboring Hungary and Romania, enjoyed wider acceptance.

The majority of vineyards follow the northerly course of the river Morava, from its source near Pristina in Kosovo to its confluence with the Danube, east of Belgrade. The southern regions concentrate on red wines, while the more northerly regions are planted primarily with white grapes. Viticultural practices are not modern, and are still mainly carried out through huge underfunded cooperatives.

Of Serbia's indigenous grapes, probably the finest is red prokupac, found everywhere south of the Danube valley. It is often used to lend a fruity taste to a blend with pinot noir or gamay. When used as a single variety, it is usually only lightly fermented to produce zupska ruzica rosé. A highly regarded white grape, smederevka, produces medium-sweet fruity wines and is grown in over 90 percent of the vineyards in the area around the town of Smederevo.

The Vojvodina region grows quite a number of mainly white grapes, and achieves some success with both traminers and merlots. The majority of the remainder of Serbia's vineyards are planted with "European" varieties, some of which display extremely unusual taste and bouquet signatures.

In Montenegro, wine production is small, though three regions are defined. The traditional crmnicko crno wine, from Lake Skadar, is of greatest significance. It is now called crnogorski vranac, and is made using the vranac grape.

MACEDONIA

"Close to ideal" would accurately describe Macedonia's grape-growing potential, in terms of landscape and climate, especially for red wines (80 percent of Macedonia's output). Whites also have potential. Unfortunately, the country's potential is likely to remain unrealized until there is sufficient political stability to make outside investment attractive.

The 75,000 acres (30,000 ha) of vineyards here are said to produce more than 27 million gallons (100 million l) of wine—few outside the country have ever tasted these. The vast majority (about 90 percent) of red wine is produced from indigenous vranac and kratosija varieties—the two, blended, produce kratosija, the country's most popular wine. Some cabernet sauvignon, merlot and grenache are also available.

The most common white varieties are laski riesling and local smederevka, often blended; small quantities of chardonnay and sauvignon blanc are also planted. Belan, from white grenache, is also popular—the zilavka variety, however, probably has greater potential.

BULGARIA

De-monopolization of the Bulgarian wine industry in the 1990s led to increased production, but not necessarily to better quality and variety. Investment in wineries has been immense, particularly by the biggest export company, Domaine Boyar. It received U.S. $30.5 million from the European Bank for Reconstruction and Development in 1999. Wine companies throughout Bulgaria now intend to invest in the vineyards, although issues of land ownership are still to be resolved.

Wine regions

NORTHERN REGION

Seven of the 28 Controliran regions are here. The area produces well-balanced, structured reds, particularly at the Russe winery. It produces elegant cabernet-based reds and clean chardonnays. Nearby Svishtov produces red wines only, from the excellent Gorchivka vineyard. Further south is Suhindol, which specializes in cabernet sauvignon and produces one of the best wines in Bulgaria—Czar Simeon.

EASTERN REGION

This is a major white wine area. The pick of the wineries is Pomorie, making floral, viscous chardonnays. Schumen has plain varietals that are much better than the branded Premium Oak wines, and Targovischte makes a promising sauvignon blanc.

SOUTHERN REGION

Perushtitza is excellent for local varieties such as the rich mulberry-like mavrud, and the lively, appley misket. At Iambol high-tech equipment produces fruity, clean cabernet sauvignons. Oriachovitza vineyards produce some of the best cabernet sauvignon and merlot in Bulgaria, for the Stara Zagora winery.

SUB-BALKAN REGION

Sliven is one of the biggest wineries in Bulgaria. It mostly turns out clean, well-made red wine (cabernet sauvignon and merlot). Slaviantzi produces some of Bulgaria's best chardonnays.

SOUTHWESTERN REGION

The tasty, spicy melnik grape is a local variety that has potential, particularly at Damianitza. This winery is deep in the south of the country.

The quality sometimes varies due to the heat, but some vineyards in the region are planted high, up to 3,300 feet (1,000 m), which gives them potential for greater longevity and improved concentration.

Right: *Replanting— vast areas of Bulgarian vineyards were uprooted during the Gorbachev era.* Below: *Vineyards on the outskirts of a town in Bulgaria.*

In the Dobrudja region, vineyards of the Murfatlar area produce rich, luscious white and late harvest wines. The Murfatlar winery majors in a range of floral versions of pinot gris and riesling italico.

Transylvania is a white wine area, with the best from the Tarnave Valley. Styles tend toward the Germanic, with a flinty acidity in the better examples. In the south, Apold de Sus produces a lively *méthode traditionelle* sparkling wine.

Northern Moldavia is predominantly white wine country, with the area producing the famous Cotnari wine. The Odobesti area makes a good grapefruity, spicy feteãscã albã variety. Cotesti produces a minty-flavored merlot.

The Drãgãsãni vineyards, in the Oltenia region, produce sauvignon blanc and some late harvest wines. Also in Oltenia, the Drincea area produces adequate examples of merlot and pinot noir.

Banat is a region that includes flat areas where table wines—Teremia and Recãs—are produced and hillier sites where white wines are made from the flourishing local creãtã grape.

ROMANIA

"The next Chile" or "the new Burgundy"? During the 1990s, these and other epithets were attached to the Romanian wine industry. However, storage and aging are low grade, and consistency is a problem—pinot noir can be full and savory and merlot can be grassy and herbaceous. Of the six main wine regions, only three export regularly and are of a quality that can be monitored.

Wine regions

In Muntenia, Dealul Mare is by far the major area, which is also large in terms of red wine production. At Tohani (linked to the excellent Ceptura winery), grapes are macerated below 82°F (28°C) to ensure clean fruit flavors. The Urlati winery specializes in well-extracted merlot and cabernet sauvignon. Petroade, a subdistrict, produces a golden, honeyed sweet wine from the tamîosa grape.

MOLDOVA

Many ex-communist countries around southeastern Europe and the Black Sea warrant the description "have potential," but none more so than Moldova. Its flat lands and temperatures coupled with annual rainfall provide almost ideal (by European standards) growing conditions.

Of all ex-USSR countries, Moldova is most similar to Hungary, Romania and Bulgaria, in that it has quantities of "European" varieties already established—cabernet sauvignon, merlot, and pinot noir for reds, and chardonnay, aligoté, sauvignon blanc, pinot gris, muscat ottonel, riesling, and gewürztraminer for whites.

Additionally, Moldova has probably the best selection of quality grapes indigenous to Black Sea countries—saperavi, black sereskia, and the teinturier variety gamay fréaux, plus the ubiquitous rkatsiteli and feteăscă. Six winemaking districts are delineated: Pucar, Balti, Ialoveni, Stauceni, Cricova, Romanesti and Hincesti.

UKRAINE

Like most countries around the Black Sea, wine production in this area actually stretches back into pre-history. However, it was not until modern times that wine and the vine became significant in the agricultural life of the region.

Vines and wines

The major growing areas of Crimea, Odessa, Kherson, Nikolayev, Transcarpathia, and Zaporozh'ye account for 90 percent of the vineyard area. Around 60 viticultural regions have been specified, and over 50 wine varieties approved.

Traditional varieties such as rkatsiteli and saperavi, and European varieties such as cabernet sauvignon, gewürztraminer, and aligoté are grown, as well as bastardo and sercial for fortified production, and a raft of indigenous and Magaratch-developed varieties. Products are often varietally named—cabernet kolchuginskoie, aligoté zolotaia blaka, rkatsiteli inkermanskoie, for example. One of the best blends is alushta, which uses cabernet sauvignon, morrastel, and saperavi. Sparkling wine production is still important. The most commonly used varieties are pinot noir, riesling, fetiaska, and aligoté. Around 50 million bottles a year of sparkling wine are produced, originating from Kiev, Odessa, Kharkov, Sevastopol, Artemovska, and Sudak.

Fill ev'ry glass,
for wine inspires us,
And fires us
With courage, love
and joy.
JOHN GAY (1685–1732),
The Beggar's Opera

RUSSIA

The five significant vineyard areas in Russia are, in order of importance: Dagestan, Krasnodar, Stavropol, the Don valley, and Chechnya-Ingushetia, where there are likely to be few remaining vineyards due to warfare. These regions represent around 95 percent of Russian production—the balance is split between Kabardino-Balkaria and Ossetia.

The most suitable growing regions are southern Dagestan and Krasnodar, and here, as elsewhere, winters are severe. Plantings of frost-resistant varieties now account for 25,000 acres (10,000 ha) of relatively successful production.

Vines and wines

In the Krasnodar region, the Abrau district is known for dry riesling, "cabernet" and sparkling wines. At Anapa (Krasnodar), riesling is the specialty, while at Gelendzhik, aligoté features. The Stavropol region offers both dry riesling and sylvaner alongside muscatel sweet wines. The Rostov (Don valley) region also offers sweet wines, the best known being Ruby of the Don, while the Caspian coast around Makhachkala (Dagestan) is almost entirely sweet wine country.

Muscat varieties are grown in much of Eastern Europe— Moldova, the Ukraine. and Russia.

Southern Europe

The country that towers head and shoulders above the others in this chapter is Greece. And yet it has only recently begun to show what it can do. For years its long and distinguished winemaking history seemed to be just that: history. But it has grape varieties found nowhere else in the world, and good ones, too: recent developments

BLACK SEA

Körklareli
Edirne ▲ Mahya 3378 ft (1030 m)
Epanomi-Thessalonika
Lüleburgaz
Zonguldak
Ereli
B

Gourmenissa
Serrai Drama Xanthi Komotini
Thrace-Marmara
Istanbul
Drama Kavala
Kesan Tekirdağ
Sea of Marmara Gebze
Izmit
Düzce
Amyndeo Naoussa Thessalonika
Alexandropolis
Thassos
Yalova Gölcük
Adapazarö

Veria
Agion Oros
Bandorma Bursa
Central Anatolia

Kozani
Katerini Thermaikos Kolpos
Lemnos
Çanakkale
Ulundaİ 8341 ft (2543 m) Inegol
Eskisehir
AN

Zitsa
GREECE Krania
Mt Olympus 9567 ft (2917 m)
Lemnos
Edremit
Balökesir
P

Corfu
Ioannina Trikala Larissa
AEGEAN
Kütahya

Arta
Karditsa Volos
SEA
Lesbos
Ayvalök

IONIAN
Preveza
Lamia Mt Parnassos 8058 ft (2457 m)
Sporades Skopelos Skiros
Mitilini
Bergama
Akhisar
Usak
Afyon Bolvadin

SEA
Agrinio
Attica
Chios
Manisa
Aegean Coast
Salihli
Aksehir

Cephalonia
Patras Levadia Halkida Euboea
Chios Çesme
Izmir
Bayöndir
Aegean Coast
Beysehir Gölü
Kon

Zakinthos
Pátras Acharnes Elefsina
ATHENS
Corinth Piraeus
Andros
Aydön
Denizli
Burdur Isparta

Amaliada Mantinia Nemea
Tinos Nikaria
Samos

Peloponnese Islands
Mykonos
Cyclades
Mediterranean Coast

Kalamata
Naxos
Kalimnos Bodrum
Muüla
Antalya
Alar

Milos
Amorgos
Astipalea
Rhodes

Cape Matapan
Kithira
Santorini
Santorini

Sea of Crete
Rhodes

MALTA
Dingli 820 ft (250 m) VALLETTA
Hania Crete Iraklion
Rethimnon Idi 8055 ft Crete (2456 m)
Stampalia
MEDITERRANEAN SEA
Troodos
Marathasa

Malta
Troodos
Troodos S

have shown that when good, modern winemaking is added to the Greek equation, the wines begin to look very attractive to consumers elsewhere. That might be true of Turkey as well; nobody knows, because only 3 percent of its grape production is turned into wine, and not very good wine at that. Wine counts for little in this country, and Turks prefer their alcohol in the form of brandy. Cyprus appears to be one big missed opportunity, as far as wine goes. It has a captive tourist market, and tourists would no doubt seek out Cypriot wines on their return home, if they were good enough. But they're not. Will Cypriot wines ever change? The omens are not good. And Malta? Wine production here is small scale, but there are signs that more interesting wines are being made.

GREECE

Wine has been an integral part of Greek culture for over 3,000 years, partly because Greece's geographic location has made it a natural crossroads for many different cultures. Throughout the ages, the fortunes of Greek wine have followed the country's tumultuous history, closely mirroring its rises and falls, its successes and failures.

Although Greece is mountainous, with a tremendous diversity of soil types and a generally maritime climate, much of the country is blessed with a near ideal climate for grape farming.

Vines and wines

An annual wine production of 10.6 million gallons (400 million l) makes Greece the sixth-largest wine producer in Europe. A wide spectrum of wine—encompassing all known classes and styles—is produced: it breaks down to roughly 70 percent white, 5 percent rosé, 3 percent sweet, and 22 percent red. Sparkling wines remain the most underdeveloped category.

Greece's native grapes provide the raw material for some fascinating wines. Approximately 200 indigenous *Vitis vinifera* varieties have been identified, but currently only about 30 of these are used commercially.

Important white grapes are assyrtiko, athiri, roditis, savatiano, vilana, robola, debina, and muscat. Saved from the brink of extinction are the elegant lagorthi and the semiaromatic malagousia, while the blanc de gris moscofilero, with its grapey fruit and natural high acidity, is exclusive to Mantinia. Recently, varieties such as chardonnay, sauvignon blanc, viognier, and sémillon have been introduced—they are used either as blends or for varietal wines.

The finest red grapes are aghiorghitiko and xynomavro, which are principally found in the two top red wine appellations, Neméa and Náoussa. Others include kotsifali and mandelaria. The first cabernet sauvignon plantings, at Averoff and Domaine Carras, date from 1963. More recently, cabernet franc and merlot were added; the most sighted new plantings now are syrah.

Greece used the French model for its appellation system. Thus it has 28 Appellations of Origin, two Appellations by Tradition, and more than 70 *vin de pays*.

Some winemaking and vineyard practices in Greece have changed little for hundreds of years.

MAINLAND GREECE

Drama

Drama was resurrected as a wine region in the 1980s, largely due to two leading estates: those of Nikos Lazaridis and brother, Kosta Lazaridis.

Nikos Lazaridis has a postmodernist winery that would not look out of place in Napa: it has a spacious cellar, a large art gallery, plus several tasting rooms and halls for lectures and seminars.

Ktima Kosta Lazaridis produces wines that are soft, with a fruit-driven style. The hugely successful fruity Amethystos white is the mainstay. The best red is Cava Amethystos.

Epanomi-Thessaloniki

Ktima Gerovassiliou produces an impressive range of fruit-driven whites. The cult-status wine named for the estate is a blend of steely assyrtiko and the white peach and mint taste of malagousia.

Goumenissa

J. Boutari Wineries S. A. has planted xynomavro and negoska varieties. They make a crisp, light- to medium-weight red wine; the best is Ktima Filiria.

Náoussa

The wines of Náoussa have a long history, although vintages vary enormously in quality. Vineyards here are home to the finest long-lasting xynomavro wines. Notable producers in Náoussa include Ktima Kyr-Yanni, J. Boutari & Son, Ktima Karydas, Dalamaras, and Melitzanis.

Amyndeo

This cool region produces wine high in malic acid. Aromatic whites are made from roditis, chardonnay, sauvignon blanc, gewürztraminer, and blanc de noir; excellent rosés and reds are produced from xynomavro. White wines are more consistent; rosés and reds are good only in the top vintages.

A private cellar storing the estate owners' selection.

Sparkling wines, both *cuve close* and *méthode classique*, are improving. Producers of note in this region include Amyndeo Co-Op and Grippa Wines.

Velvendos

This is xynomavro country for reds and rosés. Obscure local red varieties, such as moscomavro, are also grown. A significant producer here is Ktima Voyatzis.

Krania

Ktima Katsaros features organically farmed vineyards. A blend of cabernet sauvignon and merlot—a velvety smooth, cask-aged, smoky red—was their only wine until a 1999 *barrique* chardonnay appeared.

Zitsa

A fifth century BC black glaze kylix—drinking cup—from Attica.

This cool plateau is almost all given over to debina, producing still and fizzy light-bodied crisp wines, noted for their white pepper on the nose and green apple freshness on the palate. Zitsa Co-Op is a significant producer in the area.

Attica

Attica is home to large *négociants* and a few quality estates, and was, until the 1950s, the nation's single largest vineyard, planted solely with savatiano. With the growth of Athens, vine-planted land has shrunk to half its original 30,000 acres (12,000 ha). D. Kourtakis is a large merchant here.

THE PELOPONNESE

This region produces almost 29 percent of Greek wine, and is home to three quality appellations: Neméa, Pátras, and Mantinia.

Neméa

Neméa is the region of the largest quality red wine appellation. It is planted exclusively with the richly colored, smooth tannin aghiorghitiko. Neméa has a varied terrain, with two distinct vineyards: Neméa valley floor and high Neméa. Gaia Wines, in Koutsi, is notable for its affable Notios range, dark and smoky Gaia Estate, and hand-crafted Ritinitis Nobilis.

> *How simple and frugal a thing is happiness: a glass of wine, a roast chestnut, a wretched little brazier, the sound of the sea . . . All that is required to feel that here and now is happiness is a simple, frugal heart.*
> NIKOS KAZANTZAKIS (1885–1957), *Zorba the Greek*

Pátras

This major port is home to light, crisp, dry wines and to Mavrodaphne dessert wines. In Vassilikos, Antonopoulos is a quality producer making a range of delicate whites, including Adoli Ghis.

Mantinia

This 2,130 feet (650 m) plateau in the center of the Peloponnese is home to the grapey blanc de

Vineyard worker at Alagni Agricultural Enterprises Psarades, near Alagni, Crete.

gris variety moscofilero, whose aroma has the spice of a light gewürztraminer and a (dry) muscat. Natural acidity is high. The rose petal muscat aroma is more apparent in ripe vintages. Tselepos Vineyards & Winery is a fine estate, producing a more concentrated Mantinia than any other on the market, with a fruit-derived "smokyness" on the nose.

THE AEGEAN ISLANDS

Limnos

Limnos is a volcanic island producing sweet, sun-dried and fortified Muscat of Alexandria wines. It features two growers: the Co-Op, which specializes in the sweeter versions, and Honas-Kyathos, which concentrates on bone-dry wines. Samos is home to the finest Muscat from the muscat blanc, a petit grain. Top label Nectar, made with sun-dried grapes, is not fortified, and has peachy muscat flavors, followed by a very long finish.

Santorini

Santorini is an unusual volcanic island with top-quality vineyards planted with assyrtiko, the finest Greek white grape. Gaia Wines's Santorini winery produces the trendsetting, bone-dry Thalassitis. Sigalas, in Kampos, makes a cask-fermented Vareli Oia, one of the finest wooded Greek white wines. A good Mezzo is also produced by Sigalas.

Crete

There is a new momentum in Crete these days. Ktima Lyrarakis focuses on near-extinct white varieties such as daphne and plyto, and produces the wonderful Syrah-Kotsifali. Creta Olympias produces quality Vilana-sourced dry whites. At Ziros, organic producer Ekonomou makes perhaps the finest Vilana in Crete, plus the quirky, pale-colored Liatiko "red."

Vines in Marmara, Turkey—recorded by the epic writer, Homer, around 900 BC.

THE IONIAN SEA ISLANDS

Cephalonia

Cephalonia's best vineyards are found on limestone soils. Ungrafted high robola, with its trademark lemon and flint *terroir*, is unique in the Greek vineyard. Gentilini is a pioneer boutique winery producing the fruity and delicate Gentilini Classico and a new Syrah. Metaxa, in Mavrata, offers the rare white Zakynthino. The best wine here is Robola, with a modernist peachy aroma and a flinty aftertaste.

MALTA

The Maltese islands consist of Malta, the largest island, at 150 square miles (390 sq km), plus the much smaller islands of Gozo and Comino. This trio of tiny islands—62 miles (100 km) south of Sicily and 180 miles (290 km) north of Tripoli, in Libya—was host to one of the oldest civilizations in the Mediterranean, dating back to around 5,000 BC. Now it is a haven for winter-weary travelers and home to some world-class, high-quality, individual, unique wines.

Vines and wines

Locally grown white table grapes ghirghentina and gennarua and red gellewza were in the past blended with grapes imported from Italy, with no indication of this on the label. Local authorities are now cracking down on this, and there is an increased focus on new plantings of chardonnay, cabernet sauvignon, pinot bianco, trebbiano, and syrah.

Winemaking practices are improving, and local winemakers are gaining recognition on the international wine scene. For the local market, among the best-known wines are Emmanuel Delicata's Paradise Bay Red Wine and Gellewza Frizzante. Delicata and Marsovin together control about 90 percent of the local wine market.

Meridiana, an enterprise created by visionary Maltese wine expert Mark Miceli-Farrugia, is producing international-style wines, including barrel-fermented chardonnays, cabernet sauvignons, and merlots. Successful smaller producers include the Dacoutros Group, Farmers Wine Co-Op, Hal-Caprat, Master Wine, and Three Barrels.

TURKEY

If Noah did indeed plant a vineyard on the slopes of Mount Ararat, then Turkey could reasonably claim to be the cradle of viticulture. Today, Turkey has the fifth-largest area of vines in the world, but its predominantly Muslim lifestyle dictates that the majority of grapes are used for nonalcoholic products. Of the 3 percent fermented into wine, at least a quarter is distilled into local brandy or the aniseed-flavored spirit raki. White wines consumed domestically tend to be heavily oxidized and over-aged, while reds are relatively alcoholic and oversulfured. Export-quality wines are produced only fitfully and are seldom widely available.

Appellations and producers

Turkey's seven official wine districts are Thrace-Marmara, the Aegean Coast, the Mediterranean Coast, the Black Sea Coast, Ankara, Central Anatolia, and Eastern Anatolia. Thrace-Marmara produces 40 percent of Turkey's wines and, unusually, it focuses on clairette, sémillon, riesling, gamay, and pinot noir. The searingly hot Aegean Coast yields European varieties such as sémillon, grenache, and carignan. On the Mediterranean Coast, tourism is more important than winemaking. Both the Black Sea Coast and the Ankara region have considerable potential for grape growing. Vineyards in Central Anatolia are located at up to 4,000 feet (1,250 m), and suffer huge temperature extremes. Eastern Anatolia, bordering Georgia and Armenia, yields a lowly 374 gallons per acre (3500 l per ha).

The nationalized wine industry is administered by Tekel. Private producers are few, with the best known and most reputable being Kavaklidere, Doluca, and Diren in Anatolia. Charmingly named hosbag (Thrace gamay) and buzbag (local varieties from Eastern Anatolia) are valued domestically; the most consistent wines come from Doluca. A quality wine scheme has been introduced, but it seems to be limited to state-owned products.

CYPRUS

Cypriot winemakers have produced few outstanding wines, despite the fact that they have been making wine for around 4,000 years. The earliest archaeological evidence of viticulture here dates to the second millennium BC. The wine trade flourished, undeterred by repeated invasions, until the Turks invaded the island in 1571 and imposed restrictions on alcohol. When the British took control in 1878, the situation began to improve. However, by the interwar years, as Europe was resuming full-scale production, Cypriot winemaking had entered a decline that continues to this day, and the industry now faces a bleak future.

Rams head ryton dipping cup, late fourth century BC.

Vines and wines

The principal grape-growing areas lie on the southeastern plain and the lower slopes of the Troodos Mountains, up to 4,265 feet (1,300 m). The irrigated plains are superfertile and capable of awe-inspiring tonnages, although these are normally sold as table grapes. There is potential for quality wine production at higher altitudes.

Nearly three-quarters of Cypriot vineyards contain mavro (the Greek word for "black"), one of the world's least impressive grape varieties. White xinisteri is the next most widely planted variety—it is undistinguished and sensitive to overripeness, but can produce a lightly fragrant wine. Both palomino and the ancient malvasia are frequently used to improve xinisteri's performance.

Appellations and producers

Six viticultural regions have been created in Cyprus: Pitsilia (the highest), with its subregion Madhari; Troodos North; Marathasa; Commandaria; Troodos South, with its subregions Afames and Laona; and Troodos West, with its subregions Ambelitis, Vounitis Panayias, and Laona Kathhikas. Virtually all of the island's produce is vinified by one of the four large companies based in Limassol: KEO, ETKO, SODAP, or LOEL—all cooperatives or quasi-cooperatives. There are also a few boutique-style wineries.

Production methods are generally primitive, and transportation methods in particular leave a lot to be desired. Trade restrictions are yet another problem, as Cypriot agricultural authorities retain a legislative stranglehold on wine production, not least through extraordinary vine importation controls.

Island treasure

Commandaria, one of the world's oldest sun-dried or raisined wines, is a Cypriot specialty. The Greek poet Hesiod (circa 800 BC) recommended this procedure for drying the grapes: "Show them to the sun ten days and nights, then cover them over for five, and on the sixth day draw off into vessels the gifts of joyful Dionysus."

The word Commandaria derives from the Castle of Kolossi, built as the Grande Commanderie of the Knights of St. John of Jerusalem in the twelfth century. The lands surrounding the castle were the primary source of Nama, which gradually became known as Vin de la Commanderie, or Commandaria. Today, despite legislation defining the permitted growing area and production method, the quality and quantity of Commandaria has declined.

By law, Commandaria must spend a minimum of two years in wood; in practice it may undergo a three-tier *solera* aging procedure. Before bottling, it is examined and approved, whereupon it will be sold in wine shops for a pittance. Sadly, the products that today bear this distinguished name tarnish its remarkable heritage.

Right: *Irrigation is banned in Cyprus, largely as a result of overproduction.*
Below: *Production and transportation methods in Cyprus are often primitive.*

NORTH

50 miles
(80 kilometers)

Limpopo

▲ *Blouberg*
6711 ft (2046 m)

Pjetersburg

Krokodil

Marico

Mmabatho   Rustenburg   **PRETORIA** ◎   Mid

Mafikeng   **Roodepoort**   Witba

Lichtenburg   **Johannesburg** ◎ **Boksburg**
Carletonville ○   **Soweto**   **Springs**   Beth

Potchefstroom ○   Vanderbijlpark   **Vereeniging**   Star

Klerksdorp ○   *Vaal*

Vryburg ○   Orkney ○   Parys ○   *Vaal Dam*

Kroonstad ○

Sishen ○   Odendaalsrus ○
                              Welkom ○   Bethlehem   Harris

Upington ○   Virginia ○   Lad

*Orange River
Valley*   Kimberley ○

Orange   *Vaal*   Douglas
                                 Greenwater   Bloemfontein ○   *Champagne Cas
                                 Valley   11,073 ft (3376

                                                  Orange   **LESOTHO**

S O U T H   A F R I C A

De Aar ○

Carnarvon ○   Aliwal North ○

Olifantsrivier   Williston ○   Middelburg ○   **Umtata**
Vredenal ○

Saint Helena Bay   Beaufort West ○   Graaff Reinet ○   Cradock ○   ▲ *Groot-Winterberg*
Cape Columbine   *7777 ft (2371 m)*   Stutterheim

Picketberg   **King Williams Town**
                                                        Klipplaat ○   Fort Beaufort ○   **Mdantsane** **East London**
Swartland &
Tulbagh   *Roggeveld Mountains*   *Groot*

Malmesbury ○   *Nuweveldberge*   Grahamstown ○

Durbanville   **Franschhoek**   Ladismith ○ Calitzdorp ○
                       Worcester   Oudtshoorn ○
Cape Town ◎   **Paarl** Worcester ○ *Langeberg*   *Kougaberge*   Uitenhage ○   *Algoa Bay*
Constantia   ■ **Stellenbosch**   **Port Elizabeth**
  Simon's Town ○   Strand   **Klein Karoo**
Cape of Good Hope   **Swellendam**   Mossel Bay ○   *Cape Seal*   *Cape Saint Francis*
         Hermanus
Overberg   **Robertson &**
                    Bonnievale
         Cape Agulhas

False Bay

Nossop

Kuruman

Molopo

Orange

Olifants River

South Africa

The Cape wine industry originated with the start of formal white settlement in the middle of the seventeenth century. The Dutch East India Company identified Table Bay as a suitable site for the establishment of a colony to supply ships plying the long sea route between Europe and the East and appointed a former ship's doctor, Johan van Riebeeck, as its commander. In April 1652 his expedition anchored at the foot of Table Mountain.

It is possible that van Riebeeck brought grape seeds or even cuttings with him. Certainly, from the moment of his arrival he wrote with some enthusiasm about the agricultural potential of the Cape and urged the company's directors to procure young trees and vine cuttings for him. The motivation for this request was pragmatic, fitting in with the original purpose of the settlement. Wine was a common enough beverage in the maritime world: it improved the ship's drinking water; it had known antiseptic properties, and was useful in cases of gastro-intestinal illness; and it was held to be valuable in the treatment of scurvy.

wine quality had been established earlier. The wine-of-origin legislation, for example, dates from 1972. It defined and demarcated the major areas of origin. It distinguished between estate and branded wine and provided a policing and certification system to verify label claims relating to varietal, vintage, and appellation.

The first successful consignment of vine cuttings reached the Cape in July 1655. It was from these that Cape wine was first produced—on February 2, 1659. Van Riebeeck's logbook records both the quantity—4 gallons (15 l)—and the varietal (muscadel). Despite a resounding silence as to its quality, the Commander seems to have been sufficiently inspired to seek out additional land for vineyards. Thus began the wine industry in South Africa.

In the following centuries the industry's fortunes, especially in terms of quality, waxed and waned. Great estates gained international recognition, then succumbed to neglect—only to be revived at a later stage. In the twentieth century, political and economic isolation was a major factor in wine quality as was the stranglehold of the Cooperative Wine Growers' Association of South Africa, known by its Afrikaans initials as KWV.

While the real modernization of the Cape wine industry more or less coincided with the political transformation of South Africa in the 1990s, some of the regulations necessary to ensure a focus on

He makes grass grow for the cattle, and plants for man to cultivate— bringing forth food from the earth: wine that gladdens the heart of man.

Old Testament, the Book of Psalms

The legislation was launched at a time when producers were free to describe a wine without any regard to the contents.

Varietal consciousness and the beginnings of an understanding of *terroir* followed the wine-of-origin legislation. The next decade saw extensive plantings of a range of internationally accepted varietals. In 1973 the combined vineyard area of premium cultivars was less than 4 percent. By 1998 cabernet sauvignon, cabernet franc, merlot, pinot noir, shiraz, rhine riesling, sauvignon blanc, gewürztraminer, and chardonnay constituted some 20 percent of plantings.

However, it was only when political and trade isolation ended that the shortcomings of the wine-certification scheme were revealed. It became clear to grape growers that the tasting standards of the bureaucrats administering the scheme were not based on international benchmarks. The challenge of how to meet the quality and price expectations of an increasingly discerning international market has yet to be met.

Constantia

The Constantia region was until recently on the brink of extinction. By the 1970s there was just one surviving winery, Groot Constantia, and it depended on generous government handouts to survive. With a substantially cooler climate than Stellenbosch and Paarl, and a vineyard virus endemic to the Cape, grapes ripened unevenly and irregularly. Evidence of Groot Constantia's financial troubles discouraged the neighboring landowners from seeking redemption through grape growing. The turnaround in fortunes for the region, when it came, was swift, and the results have been so gratifying that it seems impossible to visualize the depressed conditions from which the Constantia phoenix arose.

In addition to those below, two other significant producers in the Constantia region include Constantia Uitsig and Steenberg Vineyards.

BUITENVERWACHTING *Established* 1796 *Owners* C. and R. Müller, Trustees, Buitenverwachting Farm Trust *Vineyard area* 250 acres (100 ha)

Buitenverwachting has played a key role in the restoration of the region and the renewed reputation of Cape wines as a whole. Some of its white

Sauvignon blanc grapes at the Steenberg winery, where an outstanding Sauvignon Blanc Reserve is produced.

wines are consistent front rankers, notably the rhine riesling, sauvignon blanc, and chardonnay. Several vintages of the proprietary red, a blend of cabernet franc and cabernet sauvignon sold under the brand name Christine, have come to enjoy almost cult status; an earlier merlot vintage won the Diners Club Winemaker of the Year Award for cellarmaster Jean Daneel.

KLEIN CONSTANTIA ESTATE *Established* 1823 *Owners* Duggie and Lowell Jooste *Vineyard area* 184 acres (74.5 ha)

Duggie Jooste purchased a run-down and derelict Klein Constantia and immediately began planting vineyards and planning a winery. The first vintage, the 1986, reminded the Cape of the extraordinary potential of Constantia: the sauvignon blanc won the trophy for the best white wine at the national young wine show; a year later the 1986 cabernet sauvignon carried off the trophy for the best wine on show.

Klein Constantia has subsequently acquired a special reputation for its Vin de Constance, a muscat de frontignan dessert wine—it is sweet, but not cloying, a beautifully structured botrytis-free late-harvested beverage. It has done more than any other wine to bring prominence to the Constantia area.

Producers
1 Buitenverwachting
2 Constantia Uitsig
3 Groot Constantia
4 Klein Constantia
5 Steenberg

Constantia

Diep

Plumstead

M38

Dieprivier
Princess
Vlei

M42

M3

Retreat

NORTH

Silvermine
Dam

1 mile
(1.6 kilometers)

Westlake

Sand
Vlei

M64

Lakeside

Silvermine

SOUTH
AFRICA

CAPE TOWN
Constantia

Muizenberg

False
Bay

Constantiaberg

Paarl

There has been long-standing rivalry between Paarl and Stellenbosch for supremacy in the South African wine industry, although Paarl is characterized by medium-size cellars producing good, rather than extraordinary, wine. Still, the appearance of Glen Carlou and Veenwouden, and the revolution wrought by Charles Back at Fairview—the most innovative of Paarl wineries—all suggest that an era of boutique wines of the highest quality is imminent.

Situated farther inland than Stellenbosch, Paarl is warmer and its wines are more robust. Bounded by Wellington (north), Franschhoek (east), and Stellenbosch (south), Paarl is too spread out to offer the same homogeneity of style that characterizes Constantia. The Agter-Paarl vineyards near Wellington, for example, are substantially warmer than the sites adjacent to Stellenbosch.

Some significant producers in Paarl, in addition to those below, include Glen Carlou Vineyards, Fairview, Veenwouden, KWV International, and Welgemeend Estate.

Chardonnay in a lab beaker, awaiting analysis.

BACKSBERG ESTATE   *Established* 1916 *Owner* Michael Back *Vineyard area* 408 acres (165 ha)

The late Sydney Back worked to establish the integrity of site-specific viticulture in South Africa. For more than two decades his wines were widely regarded as the best-value premium products on the market. He led the replanting revolution that followed the importation of quality chardonnay, sauvignon blanc, and merlot in the 1980s. Back established commercial volumes of wood maturation long before most of his competitors. He also set up social responsibility programs—long before they were fashionable—and Back's son Michael has maintained this policy. Backsberg's vineyard workers produce and manage their own separate brand, sold under the Freedom Road label.

NEDERBURG WINES   *Established* 1791 *Owner* Stellenbosch Farmers Winery *Vineyard area* 1,730 acres (700 ha)

Nederburg is South Africa's largest premium winery. The first of the modern high-volume deluxe brands, this commercial leviathan came to dominate the fine-wine industry in the 1960s and 1970s. The German-born cellarmaster of that era, Gunther Brözel, played a role in the South African wine industry in many ways similar to that of Max Schubert in Australia. For three decades he produced everything from German-style whites to cabernet and cabernet blends that rival even the best wines of modern, virus-free vineyards.

Among his many innovations was a wine called Edelkeur, a botrytized chenin blanc still traded only at the annual Nederburg Auction. Even the auction is a reflection of Brözel's drive and enthusiasm. Launched in 1975, it showcases the most complete array of South Africa's best wines. Nederburg's own selection of wines comprises a creditable range of premium reds, some fairly unremarkable dry whites, and several quality dessert wines.

PLAISIR DE MERLE, SIMONSBERG
Established 1964 *Owners* Stellenbosch Farmers Winery *Vineyard area* 988 acres (400 ha)

Three centuries of history belie this property's oenological modernity. It functions mainly as a supply farm to Nederburg. Successive replanting programs revealed

Rows of vines in a Paarl valley sheltered by a rugged mountain range.

specific vineyard blocks capable of producing super-premium wines. SFW accordingly established a small winery near the homestead to process this fruit. Paul Pontallier, Director of Château Margaux and consultant to the group, took a hands-on role for the first few vintages, and these reds show great concentration with a richness and texture typical of the best Paarl wines.

VILLIERA WINE   *Established* 1928 *Owners* Grier family *Vineyard area* 741 acres (300 ha)

This is one of the country's most popular good-value, high-quality operations. Jeff Grier won the Diners Club Winemaker of the Year Award and the Chenin Challenge in successive years. Despite successes, prices are modest. The *méthode champenoise* bubbly, often the country's top-rated Cap Classique, sells for little more than the big-brand charmat wines produced in industrial cellars.

Taste characteristics

Ripe yet crisp sauvignon aside, what characteristics tend to suggest South Africa in a blind tasting? Pinotage may be easiest. Being a cross between pinot noir and cinsault, the wines sometimes taste more like one parent than the other. The pinot-like versions are lighter in color and more berry flavored, and Rhône-like versions are more deeply colored with a smoked meat character. Both share the unique "pinotage" ester which is easier to taste than to describe. Other red wines such as cabernet sauvignon, merlot, and syrah tend to be more akin in structure to the "Old World" by virtue of fairly high acidities, astringent tannins, and a tendency toward smoky notes with age. The best can surely be world class, and all are good value.

Stellenbosch

Some 30 miles (50 km) northeast of Cape Town, Stellenbosch boasts several properties identified in land grants made in the last two decades of the seventeenth century. While few boast three centuries of viticulture, several have been associated with quality winemaking for much of this time.

The area is divided into several subregions, each of which experiences a distinctly different climate due to maritime influences or to the location of ridges, cliffs, or valleys. Stellenbosch soils also vary considerably, and within a very small area there can be several different soil types. Almost all are acidic and it is now standard vineyard practice to add a great deal of lime at the time of replanting. Uneven ripening of the grapes has its origins as much in geology as in canopy management and viticultural practices.

Stellenbosch cabernet sauvignon: Jordan 1993 and the boutique Grangehurst 1993.

There are now some 80 wineries in the Stellenbosch region. Ten years ago the number was roughly half. Given the flux and excitement, it is easy to understand why the area is regarded as the showcase of Cape wine. Some of the big brands of yesteryear, although falling behind, still produce creditable wine; the newcomers must work twice as hard simply to get noticed. Long-established contract growers suddenly decide to build their own cellars and make new wines from old plantings. Investors from other industries acquire run-down properties and breathe new life into them. In this sense Stellenbosch lies at the real heart of new-era South African wine.

Some producers of note in the region in addition to those below include Distillers Corporation (The Bergkelder), Grangehurst, Meerlust Estate, Rustenberg Wines, Spier Cellars, and Vergelegen.

DELHEIM WINES, SIMONSBERG

Established 1930 *Owners* H. O. Hoheisen and M. H. Sperling *Vineyard area* 371 acres (150 ha)

Spatz Sperling was as happy to win an award for the worst-taste wine label in the industry as he was to take home a gold medal at the national wine show. Recent improvements, mainly in red-wine production, have encouraged Sperling to draw a more marked distinction between the popular and prestige sides of his business. Using separate vineyards across the valley at Klapmutskop, he aims to establish the Vera Cruz estate for his premium wines, retaining the Delheim name for the tourist trade.

NEIL ELLIS WINES, JONKERSHOEK VALLEY

Established 1990 *Owners* Neil Ellis Trust, Oude Nektar, London Stone (Pty) Ltd *Vineyard area* 237 acres (96 ha), plus 74 acres (30 ha) elsewhere

A relative newcomer, Neil Ellis is a site-specific *négociant*-winemaker operation. Ellis ran an

Producers
1 Delheim
2 Distillers Corporation (The Bergkelder)
3 Neil Ellis
4 Grangehurst
5 Kanonkop
6 Meerlust
7 Rustenberg
8 Simonsig
9 Spier Cellars
10 Stellenbosch Farmers Winery
11 Thelema Mountain Vineyards
12 Vergelegen

A newly planted vineyard at Kanonkop Estate. The property lies along the northeastern slopes of the Simonsberg.

itinerant winemaking set-up until he met up with Hans Peter Schröder. The latter had recently acquired the Oude Nektar Estate, with its somewhat run-down vineyards and cellar. A partnership has been established that has changed the rankings of Cape producers.

Ellis's wines now dominate the awards. His Reserve reds (mostly from the Oude Nektar vineyards) represent pretty much the acme of current Stellenbosch achievement, while his regular range is almost as impressive. Most of the reds are made from Stellenbosch fruit, but there are white wines from Elgin and a sauvignon blanc from Groenekloof on the West Coast, near Darling.

KANONKOP ESTATE *Established* 1910 *Owners* J. and P. Krige *Vineyard area* 346 acres (140 ha)

Almost alone, Kanonkop estate established pinotage as a varietal worthy of international repute; it is also very much one of the country's putative "first growths." In the mid-twentieth century

bushvine vineyards were established with planting material from the original pinot noir–cinsault crossing. From its first commercial bottlings, the 1973 vintage, Kanonkop was clearly a leading red-wine site with a particular potential for dense, almost Rhône-like pinotage. However, it was only in the late 1980s that winemaker Beyers Truter invested the varietal with the kind of vinification and wood aging needed to bring out the fruit, concentration, and complexity of which the grape is clearly capable. Successive vintages of show-stopping quality—especially among the cuvées reserved for the Cape Winemakers Guild annual auction—have produced an international market for this wine and for the varietal.

Kanonkop's reputation does not rest solely on the quality of its Guild Pinotage. The regular cuvée is often as impressive and its other reds, notably the cabernet and the Paul Sauer Fleur (a cabernet blend), sell well in the superpremium segment of the market.

The Oom Samie General Store in Dorp Street, Stellenbosch, is famous for its charming wrought-iron detail.

Stellenbosch Farmers Winery. It pioneered many of the brands that comprised the unfortified wine market in South Africa until the 1970s. Names such as Grand Mousseux (still one of the largest-selling sparkling wines), Château Libertas (a popular dry red table wine first produced in the 1930s), Zonnebloem, Tassenberg, Lanzerac, and Lieberstein are all part of the more recent history of the Cape wine industry. Much of the bulk wine that went into these brands was sourced outside the Stellenbosch region.

SIMONSIG ESTATE   *Established* 1953 *Owners* Malan family *Vineyard area* 667 acres (270 ha)

Simonsig Estate was the first South African cellar to make a bottle-fermented sparkling wine, and it has been in the avant-garde of most of the country's vineyard and cellar developments. When times were tough they offered house brands and second labels. They elected to operate as a wine estate, using the certification system—with its promise of site-specific viticulture. They participated in every high-profile selling opportunity, from the annual Nederburg Auction to the Cape Winemakers Guild sale. The breadth of their current range (at one stage they offered about 20 different wines) has enabled them to fill every niche in the spectrum.

STELLENBOSCH FARMERS WINERY   *Established* 1925 *Owners* 30 percent each Rembrandt, KWV, SAB; 10 percent public domain *Vineyard area* 2,500 acres (1,000 ha), plus bought-in grapes

For much of the twentieth century the reputation of the region rested on the wholesale producing merchants, the most important undoubtedly the

THELEMA MOUNTAIN VINEYARDS   *Established* 1983 *Owners* McLean Family Trust and G. Webb *Vineyard area* 124 acres (50 ha)

A comparative newcomer on the wine scene, Thelema has swiftly eclipsed most of its competitors. Modern vineyard preparation, proper and consistent viticultural practices, and inspired winemaking have all combined to produce this cutting-edge brand. A decade after the release of its first vintage, Thelema had won every award of significance in the country.

Mist over the mountains as the morning sun warms rows of vines in Franschhoek.

Franschhoek

Settled by French Huguenots before the end of the 1600s, this region has only recently become a meaningful player on the Cape wine scene.

For most of the twentieth century, the industry was driven by the KWV's minimum wine price arrangements—based on a 10 percent alcohol content—and the climate of Franschhoek was not conducive to this type of wine production. The 1980s saw vast changes, however. The discovery that quality wine production was not dependent on the KWV's purchase criteria focused attention on cooler regions, and Franschhoek's relatively unspoilt charm attracted wealthy investors to the area. The growers banded together under the banner of the Vignerons of Franschhoek, and the village soon developed a more overt Huguenot/Cape Dutch/French feel.

The always enticing process of withdrawing the cork.

The success of the marketing efforts of small growers in this area led to an enormous increase in land prices and a proliferation of regional wines. Some of the producers who initially delivered their grapes to the cooperative for vinification have now built their own cellars, and today Franschhoek boasts some of South Africa's best-known wines.

BOSCHENDAL, GROOT DRAKENSTEIN
Established 1976 *Owner* Anglo American Corporation (Amfarms) *Vineyard area* 1,235 acres (500 ha)

Located near the boundaries of Paarl and Stellenbosch, Boschendal came to prominence in the early 1980s through the sale of South Africa's first blanc de noir. The cellar is now better known for its white wines, most of which are respectable examples of a standard range of varietal and blended wines.

LA MOTTE ESTATE
Established 1695 *Owner* Hanneli Koegelenberg (née Rupert) *Vineyard area* 257 acres (104 ha)

La Motte Estate makes some very good reds, of which the médoc blend (sold as Millennium) and the shiraz are consistently the best examples. Both of the old Rupert family properties have been beautifully restored, and both vinify and bottle their wines on the estate.

L'ORMARINS ESTATE
Established 1694 *Owner* Anthonij Rupert *Vineyard area* 494 acres (200 ha)

One of two Rupert family-owned properties, this producer offers a range of quality red and white wines in a reasonable volume. The other property is La Motte Estate.

Robertson–Bonnievale

The Robertson–Bonnievale region, less than two hours' drive from Cape Town, is an area in transition. The commercial success of the appellation's front-runners is encouraging many of the bulk-grape farmers to look to their own vinification and to take on their own marketing. Given the extensive replanting programs undertaken by the leading producers in recent years, it is fair to assume that both product profile and brand leaders will change dramatically.

The region was traditionally a brandy and fortified wine zone, a result both of its climate and the economics of the wine industry. The semi-desert inland areas lie beyond a cordon of mountains that shields them from much of the rainfall of the coastal region. Irrigation water from the Breede and Hex rivers has turned the region into a market garden: much of the country's best fruit is produced in these fertile valleys.

Some producers of note in the region include Graham Beck Wines, Springfield Estate, and Zandvliet Estate, together with those below.

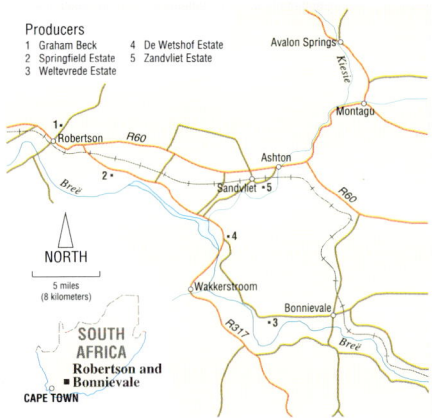

Producers
1 Graham Beck
2 Springfield Estate
3 Weltevrede Estate
4 De Wetshof Estate
5 Zandvliet Estate

WELTEVREDE ESTATE, ROBERTSON–BONNIEVALE
Established 1926 *Owner* Lourens Jonker *Vineyard area* 250 acres (100 ha)

Like most other properties in the region, this estate once focused solely on white and fortified wines. Recent plantings of cabernet sauvignon and merlot indicate a change in direction. Good chardonnay, concentrated rieslings, and an array of fortified muscats comprise the better wines in Weltevrede Estate's range.

DE WETSHOF ESTATE, ROBERTSON
Established 1947 *Owner* Danie De Wet *Vineyard area* 371 acres (150 ha)

In the early 1970s, most of the cellar's wines were sold in bulk. Today the cellar is the undisputed success story of the region. De Wetshof Estate's best wines are generally held to be chardonnays, which are offered in a range of styles from unoaked to wood-fermented and barrel-aged. Surprisingly, the estate also produces a couple of very fine rieslings. One is marketed as Mine d'Or, with mosel-like acidity masking the sugar, while the other is a botrytized noble late-harvest.

Left: *Many older wineries in the country have a treasure trove of artifacts, such as these carved barrels.*
Right: *The Red Hills area, near Calitzdorp in Klein Karoo, is home to several of the Cape's best port cellars.*

Other South African Regions

DURBANVILLE

Among the scattered appellations outside the established premium wine areas are several of the Cape's best producers. Durbanville used to be home to many growers before being overtaken by urban sprawl. There has been a resurgence of interest in wine production—on a boutique scale.

Meerendal has long been associated with one of the country's best-known shiraz wines, and as early as the 1970s produced good pinotage. Altydgedacht, a long-established estate, was for years the only cellar in the Cape to offer a barbera. Cabernet sauvignon and chardonnay have done well more recently.

DURBANVILLE HILLS   *Established* 1998
Owners Distillers Corp (seven farms) *Vineyard area* Grapes from the seven owner farms

Durbanville Hills's early releases show fine chardonnay and sauvignon blanc, with equally impressive reds waiting in the wings.

SWARTLAND AND TULBAGH

This traditional West Coast region is also seeing something of a boom. A few new wineries have sprung up, and replanting programs are replacing non-premium varietals with sauvignon blanc, merlot, and shiraz.

TWEE JONGE GEZELLEN ESTATE, TULBAGH
Established 1710 *Owners* Krone family *Vineyard area* 677 acres (274 ha)

Tulbagh is one of the country's most beautiful and least spoilt Cape Dutch villages. In the 1960s and 1970s the appellation was considered one of the best sources of white grapes in the country. This estate's premium brand, a 50/50 blend of chardonnay and pinot noir made without preservatives, sells under the Krone Borealis label.

KLEIN KAROO

The town of Calitzdorp has come to be known as the port capital of South Africa. Scene of the country's annual port festival, it is home to several of the Cape's best port cellars, including Axe Hill, Boplaas, and Die Krans.

HAMILTON RUSSELL VINEYARDS, HERMANUS
Established 1976 *Owner* Anthony Hamilton Russell *Vineyard area* 158 acres (64 ha)

Hamilton Russell was one of the first chardonnay and pinot producers in the Cape. Now, over two decades later, while other cellars are often seen outperforming Hamilton Russell wines, those who seek restraint still regard them as classics.

Australia

Australia

Wine has been made in Australia for almost 200 years, but the large-scale growth of wine production is a recent development because a widespread culture of table wine drinking has only developed over the last 40 years. This development is characterized in the industry structure in which most wine is made by a few large companies, in its willingness to ignore European tradition to produce interregional blends, and in the emphasis it places on technological development. The last 15 years have seen the emergence of very large companies, the largest of which, Southcorp, is responsible for almost 30 percent of wine production and incorporates such historic names as Penfolds, Lindemans, Wynns, and Seaview. Also important are BRL Hardy, Orlando Wyndham (itself owned by the French company Pernod Ricard), Mildara Blass, and Simeon Wines (most of whose production is sold in bulk). Between them, they control over 70 percent of all production.

A number of renowned middle-ranking producers, such as McWilliams and Rosemount, are still family owned. However, while there are now over 1,100 wine companies in Australia, 98 percent of them produce less than 5 percent of all of the country's wine.

Darwin
Palmerston
Arnhem Land

Joseph Bonaparte Gulf
Daly
Katherine
Roper
Gulf of Carpentaria

KIMBERLEY
Lake Argyle
Victoria
King Leopold Ranges
Ord
oome
35 m)
Fitzroy

Mitchell
Karumba
Cairns
Mt Bartle Frere
5299 ft (1616 m)

Townsville

Northern Territory
Barkly Tableland
Leichhardt
Flinders

Tanami Desert
Tennant Creek

SANDY
Mount Isa
Lake Dalrymple
Mackay
Mt Dalrymple
4190 ft (1277 m)

SERT
Lake Mackay
Georgina

Queensland

MacDonnell Ranges
Alice Springs
Longreach
Rockhampton
Gladstone

ointment
Gibson Desert
Lake Amadeus
Diamantina
Bundaberg

Katatjuta (Mt Olga)
3497 ft (1066 m)
Uluru (Ayers Rock)
2831 ft (863 m)
Mt Woodroffe
4708 ft (1435 m)
Musgrave Ranges
Finke
Simpson Desert
Cooper
Maryborough

South Burnett
Kingaroy
Gympie
Nambour

alia
GREAT VICTORIA
Alberga
Marla
Strzelecki Desert
Charleville
Warrego
Balonne
Caboolture
Toowoomba
Brisbane

urey
DESERT
Lake Eyre
Coober Pedy
Bullo
Paroo
Warrego
Warwick
Nerang

Rebecca
Lake Torrens
Lake Frome
Darling
Namoi
RANGE
Granite Belt
Ballina
Round Mtn
5203 ft
(1586 m)
Grafton
Sawtell

froy
Great Australian Bight
Eucla
Ceduna
Flinders Ranges
New South Wales
Tamworth
Armidale
Northern Rivers
Port Macquarie

ice
Nullarbor Plain
St Mary Peak
3832 ft (1168 m)
Broken Hill
Macquarie
Muswellbrook
Hunter Valley
Maitland

Port Augusta
Whyalla
Port Pirie
Dubbo
Mudgee
Orange
Cessnock
Newcastle

The Barossa
Riverland
Mildura
Northwest Victoria
Big Rivers
Griffith
Bathurst
Cowra
Katoomba
SYDNEY

Clare Valley
Gawler
Adelaide Hills
Murray Bridge
Wagga Wagga
Cootamundra
Goulburn
Wollongong

Port Lincoln
Adelaide
McLaren Vale
Langhorne Creek
Victoria
Rutherglen & NE Victoria
Albury
CANBERRA
Australian Capital Territory

Coonawarra & the Limestone Coast
Penola
Grampians & Pyrenees
Horsham
Central Victoria
Bendigo
Echuca
Wangaratta
Wodonga
Southern NSW

Mount Gambier
Portland
Ballarat
Geelong
Mt Hotham
6125 ft (1867 m)
Yarra Valley
Mt Kosciuszko
7313 ft (2228 m)
South Coast

Warrnambool
Port Phillip
Melbourne
Moe
Sale
Gippsland
Bairnsdale
Mornington Peninsula

Bass Strait

NORTH
200 miles
(320 kilometers)

Burnie
Devonport
Launceston
Mt Ossa
5305 ft (1617 m)
Tasmania

Hobart

The Charles Melton Wines vineyard located in the world-renowned Barossa Valley.

This concentration of production is also mirrored geographically. At one extreme, South Australia makes more than half of all Australian wine and is home to the largest producers. At the other, Tasmania, with 8 percent of the companies, makes less than 0.5 percent of the nation's wine.

Wine regions

Australia is a large country, so despite the distinctive national approach to wine, Australian wines are not all the same. Margaret River and Hunter Valley wines differ as much as sherry and tokay do. The three most important wine-producing states are South Australia, Victoria, and New South Wales. As well as bulk production, they each have specific premium wine regions.

In South Australia, the Clare Valley is renowned for its riesling, and the warmer Barossa Valley and McLaren Vale make big wines, chiefly from shiraz. In the cool Adelaide Hills, chardonnay and pinot noir show high quality. The cooler Coonawarra and surrounding Limestone Coast have an affinity with cabernet and cabernet blends. Riverland is the state's workhorse.

Leeuwin's Art Series reigns supreme among Australian chardonnays.

In Victoria, the Western Victoria zone includes the Grampians—well-known for its sparkling wines—and the Pyrenees. Fortified wines are the specialty in the hot region of Rutherglen. The state is best known for its disparate cool-climate wine regions, like the Yarra Valley and Mornington Peninsula. Also cool are the Gippsland, Macedon, and Geelong regions, which concentrate on pinot noir and chardonnay, while the warm Central Victoria region produces powerful and fruity reds.

Historically, the Hunter Valley was the only noted area in New South Wales—for its classic sémillons and shiraz. More recently, geographically diverse zones have been developed ranging from the subtropical Northern Rivers to the South Coast.

In Western Australia, the cooler southern regions are making high-quality table wine. The Margaret River region has gained much international recognition for its cabernet-based wines and chardonnay. The more recently developed Great Southern region is becoming known for its shiraz and riesling.

Queensland's most prominent wine-producing region, the Granite Belt, makes a range of cool-climate wines. Other regions rely on grape varieties that can thrive in hot, humid conditions.

In Tasmania, chardonnay and pinot noir are important. However, in the long term aromatic whites like riesling and sparkling wine may turn out to be its most important wines.

WESTERN AUSTRALIA

Margaret River

In a little over 30 years, Margaret River, which previously depended on dairying and forestry, has become a flourishing center for the wine industry, as well as a significant tourist destination. A key factor in this development has been the ability of the region's wineries to produce top-quality wines. Although the area is responsible for only about 1 percent of Australia's production, its wines account for 20 percent of the premium market. The cost of production is high, because yields are low and most wineries are small, and there is a consequent impact on economies of scale. Margaret River cabernet sauvignon and chardonnay are particularly highly regarded, with the region producing many of the country's best examples of these varietals. Its delicious sémillon/sauvignon blanc blends are popular on restaurant wine lists throughout Australia and overseas.

Margaret River's climate is the most maritime-influenced of any Australian wine region. It has a low mean annual temperature range and a long, dry period from October to April. Soils are mainly gravelly, or gritty sandy loam. Its major problems come with the strong salty winds in spring, which affect budburst and keep yields low. Chardonnay is especially affected by this.

A major development of the past few years has been the entry into the region of the major Australian wine companies. Southcorp has purchased the high-profile Devil's Lair, and BRL Hardy has bought 50 percent of Brookland Valley. McWilliams has entered into an agreement with Abbey Vale to become involved in the winemaking and release of some of their production under the Samphire label. All of these companies have vowed to maintain quality.

Some significant producers in the Margaret River region, in addition to those mentioned, include Amberley Estate, Hay Shed Hill Vineyard, Pierro, and Voyager Estate.

CAPE MENTELLE   *Established* 1970   *Owners* Veuve Clicquot and David Hohnen   *Vineyard area* 297 acres (120 ha)

Cape Mentelle's vineyard was one of the region's first. Its winery hit the national spotlight by winning Australia's prestigious Jimmy Watson Trophy in consecutive years, with its 1982 and 1983 Cabernet Sauvignon. David Hohnen and winemaker John Durham have steadily refined the reds and produced some impressive whites, especially its powerful and complex chardonnay and a classy sémillon sauvignon blanc.

CULLEN   *Established* 1971   *Owners* Cullen family   *Vineyard area* 70 acres (28 ha)

Cullen is one of Australia's finest boutique wineries. Their complex, classically structured, velvety cabernet merlot is the country's best, the

Producers
1 Amberley Estate
2 Brookland Valley Vineyard
3 Cape Mentelle
4 Chateau Xanadu
5 Cullen
6 Devil's Lair Wines
7 Hay Shed Hill
8 Leeuwin Estate
9 Moss Wood
10 Pierro
11 Vasse Felix
12 Voyager Estate

Gardens at Leeuwin Estate, a showcase winery attracting tourists from Australia and overseas.

MOSS WOOD *Established* 1969 *Owners* Keith and Clare Mugford *Vineyard area* 21 acres (8.5 ha)

Moss Wood is one of Australia's leading boutique wineries, and its vineyard is one of the country's most distinguished viticultural sites. The cabernet is recognized as one of the best produced in Australia, while the chardonnay and sémillon are highly sought after. Nearby Ribbon Vale has been purchased recently and will be marketed as a separate vineyard.

VASSE FELIX *Established* 1967 *Owners* Heytesbury Holdings *Vineyard area* 84 acres (34 ha)

Vasse Felix is a multiregional winery that owns the first vineyards established in both Margaret River and Great Southern. It has also been one of the state's outstanding wineries over the past decade or so. Both the shiraz and the noble riesling are the best produced in the west, and their sémillon and cabernet are among the Margaret River region's finest. Their top wines each year appear under the multiregional Heytesbury label, and the red blend is outstanding.

chardonnay is among Australia's most impressive, while the wood-aged sauvignon blanc sémillon has an enthusiastic following for its beautifully integrated oak and ripe, juicy flavors.

LEEUWIN ESTATE *Established* 1969 *Owners* Horgan family *Vineyard area* 230 acres (95 ha)

This showcase winery, venue for a biennial international wine tourism conference, acts as a magnet for tourists. Leeuwin Estate's reputation rests on the quality of its Art Series Chardonnay, regarded by most critics as the best in Australia. Since the first release in 1980, these opulent, full-flavored, and complex whites have aged more gracefully than any other Australian chardonnay. The Prelude Chardonnay and the Art Series Cabernet Sauvignon are also highly regarded.

CHATEAU XANADU *Established* 1977 *Owners* Chateau Xanadu Wines Ltd *Vineyard area* 334 acres (135 ha)

A cash injection has seen significant growth in the vineyard area and a major winery expansion. In the 1980s, Xanadu had a reputation for its whites, but improved vineyard management under Conor Lagan and winemaker Jürg Muggli dramatically improved the quality of the reds in the 1990s. The cabernets (especially the Reserve) are among the region's best, while the oak-matured sémillon, the chardonnay, and the sémillon sauvignon blanc are highly recommended.

Great Southern

Great Southern is Western Australia's coolest and Australia's largest viticultural region. It consists of five subregions centered around Mount Barker, with Denmark, Frankland, Albany, and the Porongurups all at least a half-hour drive away. While the climate of both Denmark and Albany are moderated by the sea, Frankland and Mount Barker experience more continental conditions. Soils are usually loams derived from granite and gneissic rocks, or lateritic gravelly sandy loams.

Given the size of the region, different sub-regions appear more suitable to some varieties than others. Mount Barker has been particularly successful with riesling, cabernet sauvignon, pinot noir, and shiraz; Denmark with chardonnay and pinot noir; Frankland with riesling, cabernets, and shiraz; Albany with chardonnay and pinot noir; and the Porongurups with riesling.

The last decade or so has seen significant change. Many of the growers have become more involved in the wine industry and are seeking greater control over wine production by having their own wineries. From mature vineyards such as Forest Hill at Mount Barker, Westfield (leased to Houghton) and Alkoomi at Frankland, Bouverie and Wyjup (Plantagenet), and Windy Hill (Goundrey), the quality of fruit is so impressive that there has been widespread development in recent years. The region is becoming an important producer of premium wines, and its best are stunningly good.

Vineyards at Goundrey Wines, in the relatively isolated Great Southern region.

GOUNDREY WINES   *Established* 1978   *Owner* Jack Bendat   *Vineyard area* 432 acres (175 ha)

Nowhere in Great Southern has there been expansion such as that at Goundrey. Capacity has increased threefold and vineyard plantings have proceeded apace. Wines are available at all prices, with the Reserve Shiraz being the standout red.

HOWARD PARK WINES   *Established* 1986   *Owners* Jeff and Amy Burch   *Vineyard area* 62 acres (25 ha)

This is one of the West's most significant producers. The riesling, one of Australia's best half dozen, has a tight, dry style, full of flavor; the cabernet merlot, also highly regarded, is a full-bodied, opulent, and powerful red that demands cellaring. The Madfish label is popular, with an unwooded and wooded chardonnay, pinot noir, and shiraz made for export only. White and red blends are well-made, fruity, medium-priced wines.

PLANTAGENET WINES   *Established* 1974   *Owners* Lionel Samson Pty Ltd   *Vineyard area* 200 acres (81 ha)

Plantagenet produces several very good to outstanding wines, notably its cabernet sauvignon, shiraz, and riesling. All its wines offer consistent high quality and good value.

Other Western Australian Regions

SWAN VALLEY

The Swan Valley is a flat alluvial plain, with deep, loamy, moisture-retentive soils. Its hot Mediterranean climate is best suited to verdelho, chenin blanc, and fortifieds, although chardonnay and shiraz can also be impressive.

For historical reasons and because of its proximity to Perth, two of the state's largest companies, Houghton (owned by BRL Hardy) and the independent Sandalford, have their headquarters in Swan Valley. Otherwise, the wineries of the area are quite small, family-owned businesses that offer modestly priced wines of very good to reasonable quality at the cellar door.

HOUGHTON WINE COMPANY *Established* 1836 *Owners* BRL Hardy *Vineyard area* 1,186 acres (480 ha)

Houghton is by far the largest and most influential wine company in the West, as it owns, leases, or buys fruit from vineyards in virtually all regions in the state, and it makes outstanding wines at every price. Houghton White Burgundy is still one of Australia's best selling white wines and represents remarkable value for money. The superpremium Jack Mann red blend is as good as it gets, while the Crofters and Moondah Brook ranges include many excellent wines.

SANDALFORD WINES *Established* 1840 *Owners* Peter and Debra Prendiville *Vineyard area* 358 acres (145 ha)

The quality of Sandalford wines, which are sourced from most of the state's viticultural regions, has risen dramatically under senior winemaker Bill Crapsley. His sound, well-made wines represent good value.

TALIJANCICH WINES *Established* 1932 *Owners* James and Hilda Talijancich *Vineyard area* 40 acres (16 ha)

The Talijancich fortifieds have long been among the best produced in the Swan Valley. Currently available are red and white liqueurs under the Julian James label and a special release of the thick, lush, and opulent 1969 Liqueur Tokay, with its deep, lingering treacle and molasses flavors. The most interesting table wines are sémillon and verdelho, which gain complexity from solids contact and bottle development.

GEOGRAPHE

Recently formed Geographe covers a wide and diverse region from Capel to the Ferguson Valley in the Bunbury hinterland, the farming lands of Donnybrook, and the dairy country around Harvey. Vineyards are being planted here at an astonishing rate.

The coastal strip from Capel to Harvey, with its fertile soils and warm temperatures moderated by sea breezes, is best suited to merlot, chardonnay, and verdelho.

In the Ferguson Valley and the hills behind Harvey, vineyards have been planted between 820 and 985 feet (250 and 300 m) above sea level. The most

Vines at Lamont Winery, Swan Valley, which produces chenin blanc, riesling, and vintage port.

suited grape varieties appear to be chardonnay, shiraz, sémillon, and sauvignon blanc. Willow Bridge is the largest winery in Ferguson Valley.

Donnybrook is a warm area for growing grapes. Orchards occupy the valley flats and vineyards the undulating slopes. David Hohnen of Cape Mentelle believes the area is suited to the production of medium-price dry reds and likes its shiraz, cabernet, zinfandel, and grenache.

CAPEL VALE *Established* 1974 *Owners* Dr. Peter and Elizabeth Pratten *Vineyard area* 400 acres (160 ha)

Capel Vale, one of the West's largest producers, now sources 85 percent of its production from its own vineyards in Geographe, Pemberton, Mount Barker, and Margaret River. The pick of their reserve range is the Whispering Hill Riesling, which is one of the best sourced from Great Southern. Wines represent good value, especially the tropical-fruited sauvignon blanc sémillon; the smooth, rich merlot; and the earthy, spicy shiraz.

PEMBERTON

The Pemberton region includes the Manjimup area, which is ideal for grape growing, having a comparable climate to Bordeaux. The Pemberton area, though, is cooler and wetter, with less sunshine. There is still debate about which grape varieties are most suitable for the region.

Above: *The low Darling Range in the background of the Talijancich Wines vineyard, Swan Valley.* Right: *Flat-topped wagon at Peel Estate, in the Geographe region. Peel is notable for a mellow, wood-aged chenin blanc.*

Recommendations include cabernet varieties, shiraz, and chardonnay for Manjimup, and pinot noir and cabernet varieties (especially franc and merlot) for Pemberton. Chardonnay and pinot noir have proved successful as a sparkling wine base, with Maiden Wood bubblies being impressive.

The stars of the region to date have been winemakers who established their reputations elsewhere. Moss Wood founder Bill Pannell and his son Dan have established Picardy. Their best wine so far is a stunning, velvety merlot cabernet. Both John Kosovich (Westfield) and John Brocksopp (Leeuwin Estate) have planted vineyards here. Kosovich's Bronzewing Chardonnay has been superb, while Brocksopp has made tiny quantities of a fruity roussane and a fine, medium-bodied shiraz with clear varietal definition. Keith Mugford produces a fine, taut chardonnay and a spicy, savory pinot from the Lefroy Brook vineyard, sold under the Moss Wood label.

SOUTH AUSTRALIA

Clare Valley

The Clare Valley is a pretty, winding, wooded region two hours's drive north of Adelaide, with a history of winemaking that dates back to the time of first European settlement. It is a curious region climatically and stylistically. Set in the middle of the dry mid-north wheat belt of South Australia, with hot summers and little ground water, Clare somehow manages to produce wines—such as its best-performing and best-known wine, riesling—that appear to come from a considerably cooler, wetter climate like that found in the famous Mosel region in Germany. This odd characteristic is attributed to cool afternoon breezes that blow through the Clare Valley in the warmer months, slowing and prolonging grape ripening.

Clare's main Australian competitor in the riesling stakes lies an hour away in the Eden Valley. Examples from both regions are regarded as Australian classics, but they differ somewhat in style: Eden Valley's are all restrained lime juice and steely in character, whereas Clare's add floral, perfumed, and spicy characters to the citrus aspects. Riesling is not the only star in Clare; it also produces big, firm, peppery shiraz and elegant, minty cabernets, both with plenty of backbone.

The Clare Valley is a mix of the large and small, as well as the old and new, but the most renowned producers have maintained their independence and remain small operations. Some significant producers, in addition to those described on the next page, include Crabtree, Stephen John Wines, Mitchell Winery, Mount Horrocks Wines, Paulett Wines, Sevenhill Cellars, and The Wilson Vineyard.

Above: *The tasting room at Knappstein is housed in an historic stone building.*

NORTH

1 miles
(1.6 kilometers)

Producers
1 Jim Barry Wines
2 Crabtree
3 Grosset Wines
4 Stephen John Wines
5 Knappstein
6 Mitchell Winery
7 Mount Horrocks Wines
8 Paulett Wines
9 Pikes Wines
10 Sevenhill Cellars
11 Taylors Wines
12 Wendouree Cellars
13 The Wilson Vineyard

AUSTRALIA
Clare Valley
CANBERRA

JIM BARRY WINES *Established* 1959 *Owners*
Barry family *Vineyard area* 494 acres (200 ha)

Originally gaining a reputation for its Watervale
Riesling, Jim Barry Wines is now best known for
its big, high-quality, full-bodied reds, the most
highly sought after of which is The Armagh.

GROSSET WINES *Established* 1981 *Owner*
Jeffrey Grosset *Vineyard area* 20 acres (8 ha)

When it comes to Australian riesling, Jeffrey
Grosset is the undisputed king. His superb wines
have brought him numerous awards, including
Riesling Winemaker of the Year at the 1998
Riesling Summit in the grape's German heartland.
He makes two styles, one from Watervale and
one from Polish Hill; both have the elegance and
complexity of great riesling. Grosset's other wines
include his highly acclaimed cabernet blend, Gaia,
and the fragrant Adelaide Hills Pinot Noir.

KNAPPSTEIN *Established* 1976 *Owners*
Petaluma Pty Ltd *Vineyard area* 220 acres
(89 ha)

Tim Knappstein began making an
excellent range of classic Clare wines
in 1976. Knappstein sold the business
to Petaluma in 1992, but little has
changed in terms of quality. Its riesling
is still the epitome of the region—fresh,
floral, and spicy—while cabernet sauvignon,
shiraz, and cabernet/merlot are
all big blockbuster examples
that need time to settle down.

An autumnal leaf from the shiraz vine.

PIKES WINES *Established* 1984
Owners Pike family *Vineyard area*
94 acres (38 ha)

Pikes Wines is located in one of the
cooler parts of Clare, resulting in a
longer ripening season for grapes
and a later harvest than most. This
produces intense flavors, complexity,

Pikes Wines's Polish Hill vineyard.

Shiraz

From workhorse to doghouse to superstar,
Australia's shiraz (syrah in France's Rhône Valley)
has seen it all. The backbone of Australian wine
for decades, even the classic cabernet region,
Coonawarra, built its reputation on shiraz. When
the trend turned to cool-climate wines in the
1980s, many old vines were pulled out. Then in
the 1990s, regions like Barossa and McLaren Vale
came into their own as the world woke up to the
joy of rich, opulent, full-flavored shiraz.

and fine acidity, resulting in elegant, long-lived
wines. Highlights are riesling and a good herb-
scented sangiovese.

TAYLORS WINES *Established* 1969 *Owners*
Taylor family *Vineyard area* 1,360 acres (550 ha)

Taylors Wines dominates both the local
industry and the southern end of
the Clare Valley. The first wine
released under the Taylors label,
the 1973 Cabernet, won gold
medals at every national Australian
wine show. Since then, the company's
reputation for producing high-quality
red wines has grown, though today the
emphasis is as much on white wines.
The St. Andrews premium range was
launched in 1999.

WENDOUREE CELLARS *Established* 1895
Owners Tony and Lita Brady *Vineyard area*
30 acres (12 ha)

Tony Brady makes small quantities of huge,
powerful red wines, which are regarded as among
Australia's best and sell out on release. The range
includes cabernet, malbec, mataro (mourvèdre),
and shiraz, plus varying blends of the four. There
is also a redoubtable vintage port style made with
muscat of alexandria. All wines age beautifully.

The Barossa

The Barossa—consisting of the Barossa and Eden Valleys—can justifiably claim to be Australia's best-known wine region, and is arguably its most important. Here, among the neat vineyards and rolling hills an hour northeast of Adelaide, are more than 50 wineries, including the home bases and headquarters of most of the country's leading wine companies. Australia's finest and most famous wines also come from here, including Penfolds Grange and Henschke Hill of Grace.

Fortified wines were the Barossa's mainstay for a long time, but from the 1950s, revolutionary winemakers started to produce the table wines that were to become the region's benchmarks—robust, full-bodied shiraz and steely, dry riesling. These two wine styles remain Barossa classics.

During the late 1970s and the early 1980s, demand for the Barossa's big sturdy reds declined. This resulted in substantial amounts of Barossa old shiraz, grenache, and mourvèdre vines—the backbone of the old fortified industry—being ripped out. Thankfully, not everyone followed suit. A number of winemakers and growers set up their own small independent wineries and started producing wines that highlighted their Barossa heritage. In doing so, they brought the region back to its roots and played a significant part in turning its fortunes around again.

The wines those producers made then, and continue to make now, exemplify the Barossa: big blockbuster reds packed full of spice, tannin, rich fruit, and depth—wines with tar and leather and chocolate. These opulent full-bodied beauties have made the Barossa into a thriving premium wine-making region of global importance. But a "riesling revival" is leading to wider distribution and acceptance, with the Australian charge being led by the Eden Valley and its northern neighbor, the Clare Valley wine region.

The Barossa Valley, with its Mediterranean climate, has brown fertile soils that will grow just about anything that is planted. Apart from shiraz, the grapes that do best, though, are Rhône varieties grenache and mourvèdre. Cabernet sauvignon can be ripe and full-bodied. The most prevalent white grape is sémillon, which traditionally has received a large dose of oak. These days, both oaked

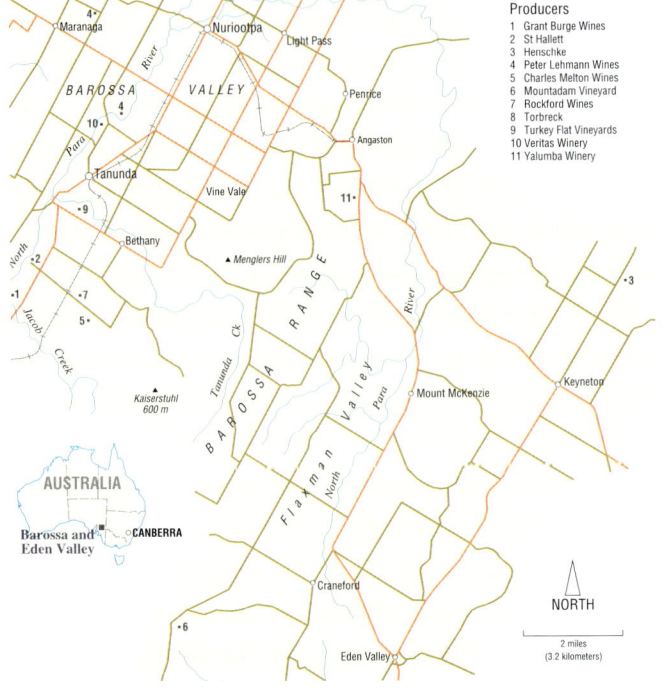

Producers
1 Grant Burge Wines
2 St Hallett
3 Henschke
4 Peter Lehmann Wines
5 Charles Melton Wines
6 Mountadam Vineyard
7 Rockford Wines
8 Torbreck
9 Turkey Flat Vineyards
10 Veritas Winery
11 Yalumba Winery

Settlement of the Barossa

At first glance, the Barossa seems dichotomous. There are two regions within it, each producing distinctive styles of wine. The Eden Valley is high-altitude hill country, producing elegant, structured wines, in particular rieslings. The Barossa Valley is on the valley floor, where classic, full-bodied old-vine shiraz and grenache are the order of the day. Each area was settled in the late 1830s by two very different groups of migrants, with their own particular cultures, lifestyles, and religions. Up in the hills it was English farmers and gentry, while down in the valley it was mainly German-speaking peasant farmers from Silesia (now part of Poland and eastern Germany) who established delightful European-style villages and settlements.

Henschke 1982 Hill of Grace.

But cultural differences didn't seem to stand in the way too much here. Mixed hamlets, villages, and townships sprang up, farms were established, and the settlers developed a strong sense of community. Equally importantly, they quickly realized that grapevines were one of the most suitable and flourishing crops, whether in the hills or the valley. For the English, bottles and casks from Bordeaux and Burgundy suffered badly on their passage through the tropics. And for the Silesians, viticulture and winemaking were as much a part of their tradition as making sausages or pickling vegetables. So, via this unexpectedly successful intertwining and establishment of lifestyle and cultures, the first Barossa wines were made in the

1840s, and many of the same vineyards planted then are still being worked today. Some of the oldest vines in the world can be found here, and many of the 500-plus growers producing grapes in the Barossa today are fifth- and sixth-generation descendants of the original settlers.

However, there was a time when the harmony of the Barossa faced its own unique pressures. The sense of community spirit that had been built up since settlement was severely tested by tensions between English descendants and those with German heritage during World War II. But the desire to maintain the community was strong, and organizations and events were started to rekindle a sense of unity, including the biennial Barossa Vintage Festival that still thrives today. The Silesian influence has given the area a unique food culture, and Australia's most distinctive regional cuisine. It has shaped the landscape with its mix of vineyards, historic cottages, and churches, and provided the force behind some of Australia's most successful wine companies.

The Barossa Valley's old-world charm attracts large numbers of tourists escaping the hustle and bustle of cities.

Peter Lehmann

Peter Lehmann, dubbed the Baron of the Barossa, is one of Australia's wine legends. These days it is hard to fathom that the Barossa ever needed saving, but many believe that without Lehmann's faith and efforts the Barossa was doomed. After years with both Yalumba and Saltram, whom he controversially left when its multinational owners refused to honor grape contracts, he formed his eponymous company. The team includes wife Margaret and son Doug as well as long-term winemaker Andrew Wigan. Peter Lehmann Wines is now a major producer in the region. His Stonewell Shiraz is one of the Barossa's great reds, while the Peter Lehmann Reserve Riesling has been awarded accolades around the globe. The entire Australian wine industry owes this man a debt of gratitude.

and unoaked are produced, and the best provide a luscious, lemony mouthful.

In the Eden Valley, cooler temperatures give a longer growing season, and, together with rocky, acidic soil and significant winter rainfall, create ideal conditions for top riesling. But it also suits shiraz, cabernet, and chardonnay, resulting in wines that are tighter and more elegant than their Barossa Valley brethren. A lesser-known Rhône classic, viognier, is also thriving in the Eden Valley.

Charles Melton Wines's outdoor processing center.

In 1996, in response to European pressure, Barossa winemakers and grape growers decided to define just what and where the Barossa is and where the Barossa and Eden Valleys start and end. The Geographic Indications provide security against misuse of the names by other regions or wineries, and the delineation of vineyard land guards against rampant growth.

Some significant producers in the Barossa and Eden Valleys, in addition to those below, include Peter Lehmann Wines, Mountadam Vineyard, St. Hallett, Torbreck, Turkey Flat Vineyards, and Veritas Winery.

GRANT BURGE WINES, BAROSSA VALLEY
Established 1985 *Owners* Grant Burge Wines Pty Ltd *Vineyard area* 815 acres (330 ha)

Grant and Helen Burge operate the largest privately owned vineyard network in the Barossa. Grant's winemaking history has come full circle. In 1972, he and Ian Wilson purchased the fledgling Krondorf winery. After 14 years, they had built it into a national brand and sold it to the Mildara Group. In 1988, Burge started his own premium wine business, Grant Burge Wines, which has been such a success that, in late 1999, he was able to buy back Krondorf.

HENSCHKE, EDEN VALLEY *Established* 1868 *Owners* C. A. Henschke & Co. *Vineyard area* 285 acres (115 ha)

Cyril Henschke was one of the Australian wine industry's true pioneers in the 1950s, developing and marketing, among others, quality single-vineyard table wines from two of his best sites—Mount Edelstone and Hill of Grace. A generation on, Stephen and Prue Henschke have built on those foundations in stellar fashion, and their wines are among the best anywhere.

Right: *Mountadam Vineyard offers spectacular views of the Eden Valley from the High Eden Ridge.*

CHARLES MELTON WINES, BAROSSA VALLEY
Established 1984 *Owners* Charles Melton Wines
Vineyard area 42 acres (17 ha)

The eponymous winemaker is not called Charles
at all, but Graeme. The reasons for this don't
matter, but the intense, spicy, refined wines produced at his compact winery do matter. In 1984,
after a ten-year apprenticeship under Peter Lehmann, Graeme Melton wanted
to take a new approach with
grapes and wine styles that were
being neglected elsewhere in
the Australian industry. Using
and cherishing old dry-grown
grenache and shiraz grapes, he's
become the Barossa's very own
Rhône Ranger, and his grenache/shiraz/mourvèdre
blend Nine Popes has reached cult status.

*A rusted old stencil, used for ident-
ifying the contents of barrels.*

ROCKFORD WINES, BAROSSA VALLEY
Established 1984 *Owners* Tanunda Vintners Pty Ltd
Vineyard area NA

Robert O'Callaghan has played a critical role in
preserving the old plantings of Barossa shiraz that
are vital to his full-bodied, richly flavored wines.
The winery itself is a superb collection of stone
and galvanized iron buildings containing restored
nineteenth-century equipment—from old station-
ary engine-driven crushers to slate open fermenters
and century-old wooden basket presses—used to
make Basket Press Shiraz, the dark and dangerous
sparkling Black Shiraz, Dry Country Grenache,
and other wines.

YALUMBA WINERY, BAROSSA
VALLEY *Established* 1849
Owners S. Smith & Son *Vineyard
area* 1,260 acres (510 ha)

Talented winemakers together
with marketing savvy have taken
Yalumba, Australia's oldest family-owned winery,
to a comfortable position. The company produces
successful wines at all levels, from reliable and
consistent basics like Angas Brut and Oxford
Landing, through the Antipodean, Growers,
Pewsey Vale, and Heggies ranges, to the big
benchmark reds, for example, The Menzies,
The Signature, and Octavius.

Adelaide Hills

The Adelaide Hills wine region lies less than a half-hour drive from the city of Adelaide up in the steep, wooded ranges that border the South Australian capital's eastern edge. It stretches from Mount Pleasant in the neighboring northerly wine region of Eden Valley, down to Mount Compass and the hills behind McLaren Vale in the south. Its restrained, lifted whites and elegant reds are attracting increasing international acclaim. Some of Australia's most respected winemakers have major interests in the area.

This is one of Australia's most picturesque wine regions. Oaks, green pastures, and a fair bit of mist and rain give a European feel to the area, and there are numerous microclimates and sub-regions. Any generalization about conditions and suitable varieties is hazardous, but the region's cool, moist climate provides excellent results from the most widely planted white grape, chardonnay, including two of Australia's most prestigious and expensive wines—

Petaluma Tiers and Penfolds Yattarna. Riesling is successful here also, showing lime-blossom characters when young and aging well, and nowhere else in Australia can match the Adelaide Hills for sauvignon blanc. It also produces fruit and base wine for the country's better sparkling wines.

The most widely planted red, indeed the most widely-planted grape, is cabernet franc, with pinot noir fast gaining a reputation for quality.

LENSWOOD VINEYARDS *Established* 1981
Owners **Tim and Annie Knappstein** *Vineyard area* **66 acres (26.7 ha)**

Tim Knappstein has been quietly making his presence felt in the Australian wine industry for nearly 40 years. In 1976, he set up his own winery in Clare and established his own eponymous label. In 1981, he expanded into the cooler climes of the Adelaide Hills, establishing the vineyards at Lenswood where he could indulge his passion for

NORTH

2 miles
(3.2 kilometers)

Producers
1 Ashton Wines
2 Chain of Ponds Wines
3 Hillstowe Wines
4 Lenswood Vineyards
5 Nepenthe Vineyards
6 Paracombe Wines
7 Petaluma Ltd
8 Shaw & Smith
9 Geoff Weaver

Houghton Millbrook
Reservoir

Paracombe
6

Torrens
River

Cudlee Creek

2
Gumeracha

Fox Peak
515 m

Kangaroo Creek
Reservoir

Mt Misery
468 m

4

9

Lobethal

Lenswood

Forest Range

AUSTRALIA

CANBERRA

Adelaide
Hills

To 1 (Ashton)
6 miles (10 km)

5

M O U N T   T O R R E N S   R A N G E S

River

8

Woodside

Onkaparinga

Inverbrackie

Oakbank

M1

Balhannah

Johnson Hill
458 m

Bridgewater

Aldgate

Verdun

3

making top-quality chardonnay and pinot noir. He sold his Clare base to Petaluma in 1992, and moved full-time to Lenswood. The resulting wines are consistently good and classic in style, particularly the chardonnay, riesling, cabernet sauvignon, and pinot noir.

PETALUMA LTD   *Established* 1976   *Owners* Petaluma Ltd   *Vineyard area* 309 acres (125 ha)

One of Australia's most respected producers, Brian Croser established Petaluma in 1976. Two years later, Petaluma became a joint venture with wine legend, Len Evans. In 1985, Bollinger became a major shareholder and the company went public in 1993. It has since acquired a number of well-known labels. Fruit is sourced from several regions, with the vineyards in the Adelaide Hills yielding premium grapes for stellar chardonnay (including the rare and expensive Tiers), riesling, and the Croser Pinot Noir/Chardonnay sparkler. There is also a second label, Petaluma's Bridgewater Mill.

SHAW & SMITH   *Established* 1989 *Owners* Martin Shaw and Michael Hill-Smith   *Vineyard area* 60 acres (24 ha)

These two Australian wine legends specialize in white wine production, and they make some of the finest examples in the region. Shaw and Hill-Smith started the business determined to concentrate on sauvignon blanc and chardonnay. They quickly gained a reputation for producing modern, clean classics of both. Their chardonnay is balanced, creamy, and smooth, with multiple layers of subtle flavors, while their sauvignon blanc is a match for some of New Zealand's finest.

A timber mill once stood on the site of Hillstowe Wines's Adelaide Hills vineyards.

Australian practice of blending wines/regions

Unburdened by any appellation system, Australia has developed its wine industry as desired. This freedom has allowed winemakers to blend wines in ways that their European counterparts would find unthinkable—and illegal. Not only can different grapes be blended in any manner the winemaker chooses, so too can grapes from different regions end up in the same wine. All that is required is that label integrity be respected. Hence, a wine may include cabernet from Western Australia, merlot from Tasmania, and shiraz from New South Wales. Freedom of choice has also led to such traditional Australian styles as cabernet/shiraz and sémillon/chardonnay blends.

Nepenthe Vineyards's fruit is used to produce wine that has gained cult status.

GEOFF WEAVER
Established 1982   *Owners* Geoff and Judith Weaver *Vineyard area* 27 acres (11 ha)

Geoff Weaver is a firm adherent to the maxim that good wine is made in the vineyard, and the quality of the fruit from his Stafford Ridge property certainly reinforces that belief. He aims to ensure that each grape variety is allowed to express its classic characteristics through fresh, complex wines. The theory works well, with chardonnay showing rich, buttery characters and white peach fruit; sauvignon blanc that's tight, green, peppery, and pungent; and riesling with balanced fruit and citrus flavors.

McLaren Vale

Most Australian wine regions take their influence from the migrants who settled there. In McLaren Vale it was a group of Englishmen who started the ball rolling. Two in particular laid the foundations for the region—John Reynell, who first planted vines in the area in 1838, and Thomas Hardy, whose influence has been integral to the region since he bought and developed the Tintara vineyards and winery in 1876.

Bordered to the east by the southern ranges of the Adelaide Hills and to the west by the Gulf of St. Vincent, the landscape of McLaren Vale is varied. The terrain is undulating and soil types vary widely. There is also significant climatic variation, due to differing degrees of exposure to or protection from the nearby sea and its cooling influence. Summer rainfall is low, so irrigation of the vineyards is generally necessary.

Because of this geographical and climatic diversity, nearly all grape varieties flourish here, and especially those suited to premium styles. The resulting wines tend to be intense, full-flavored reds and powerful, fruit-driven whites. Shiraz is a mainstay, producing deep-colored, richly flavored wines, with distinctive velvety characters. Cabernet sauvignon tends to be smooth, with a ripe richness and hints of chocolate, and merlot also does well. Among the whites, chardonnay excels, producing classic examples at many levels, from big, rich, buttery, toasty wines to elegant, peach-flavored, fruit-driven examples.

Right: Wine being tested at Chapel Hill Winery.

Producers
1 d'Arenberg Wines
2 Chapel Hill winery
3 Clarendon Hills
4 Coriole
5 Fox Creek Wines
6 Geoff Merrill
7 Tatachilla Winery
8 Wirra Wirra Vineyards
9 Woodstock Winery

Sauvignon blanc thrives here too, giving herby, asparagus-flavored wines with a prickly intensity. The region also produces some good fortifieds, and is home to a wide range of sparkling wines. As in so many regions worldwide, pinot noir struggles to graduate from being a sparkling wine component to a fully-fledged varietal red wine.

McLaren Vale's 50 wineries are a mixed bunch, with everything from one-man cellar door operations to corporate behemoths. But the biggest of all of them is BRL Hardy, the current incarnation of the company started by Thomas Hardy in the mid-1800s. In addition, Southcorp has a significant stake in the region as have Mildara Blass and Rosemount. But most of the wineries are considerably smaller, resulting in a range and variety of wines that reflects the diversity of the region and its producers.

Some significant producers in the region, in addition to those below, include Chapel Hill Winery, Clarendon Hills, Coriole, Fox Creek Wines, Geoff Merrill, and Woodstock Winery.

The tasting room at the award-winning Tatachilla Winery.

D'ARENBERG WINES *Established* 1912 *Owners* d'Arenberg Wines Pty Ltd *Vineyard area* 270 acres (110 ha)

Chester Osborn has held sway at d'Arenberg since the mid-1980s. He rejuvenated the old cellars and vineyards, brought in small stainless steel tanks, and gave the winemaking a bit of a revamp. Both the whites and reds have since attracted increasing acclaim.

TATACHILLA WINERY *Established* 1901 *Owners* Consortium headed by Vic Zerella and Keith Smith *Vineyard area* 37 acres (15 ha)

Tatachilla was bought in 1993 by a consortium, then revamped and reopened in 1995. Since then, with winemaker Michael Fragos at the helm, the wines have steadily improved and regularly do extremely well on the Australian wine show circuit. The cabernet sauvignon and merlot are particularly good.

WIRRA WIRRA VINEYARDS *Established* 1894 *Owners* Greg and Roger Trott *Vineyard area* 200 acres (80 ha)

Wirra Wirra was revived and restored by Greg and Roger Trott in 1969. They, with winemaker Ben Riggs, have been responsible for increasingly good wines, both white and red, including the popular Church Block Cabernet Blend and the rich and creamy Cousins Sparkling Pinot Noir/Chardonnay. Respected winemaker and consultant Tony Jordan took over as chief executive in the late 1990s.

Sparkling red—a very Australian wine

Known for decades as sparkling Burgundy, these rich, velvety wines are very Australian. Once highly popular, they became an endangered species in the 1970s as the market was repelled by a flood of poor quality, oversweet lookalikes. Seppelt, who had always led the way and whose wines from the 1940s and 1960s now bring huge prices at auction, maintained the faith. A few other believers joined them, and gradually other wineries dipped a toe in the water. Now, producers from all over the country offer a "spurgles." Although shiraz is the most popular grape, many other red varieties are used to make sparkling reds.

Coonawarra and the Limestone Coast

Coonawarra is known throughout Australia and the world for its elegant yet richly flavored cabernet sauvignon. Its fame rests on a narrow strip of paprika-colored soil: terra rossa. Loam overlays well-draining limestone and a high water table, and produces exceptional grape development and characters. It is only about 12.5 miles (20 km) long and 1 mile (1.5 km) wide, narrowing at each end, with the soil varying in depth from a few inches to 3 feet (a few centimeters to a meter).

John Riddoch discovered the region's viticultural potential, planting vines, largely shiraz and cabernet sauvignon, in 1890. He built the substantial limestone winery that remains at Wynns Coonawarra Estate today.

Although Coonawarra is more well known, the Padthaway region, 53 miles (85 km) north, now produces more grapes. Seppelt was the first to plant vines there, in 1963. The suitability of the soil and climate for grape growing was soon evident, though not for reds, but for white varieties, notably chardonnay. Hardy's and Lindemans have invested in Padthaway.

Less than 18.5 miles (30 km) from the coast, Mount Gambier is South Australia's southernmost viticultural region and awaits assessment of its full potential. There are five small producers, with chardonnay and cabernet sauvignon dominating plantings. The Mount Benson area, on the coast, is one of Australia's newest. Lindemans planted experimental vines in 1978, and Southcorp remains a significant investor, along with Cellarmaster Wines and, more recently, M. Chapoutier & Co, one of France's most notable Rhône Valley producers.

When shiraz became the dominant red grape in Australia and fortified the dominant wine style, Coonawarra retained small plantings of cabernet sauvignon, the variety which has

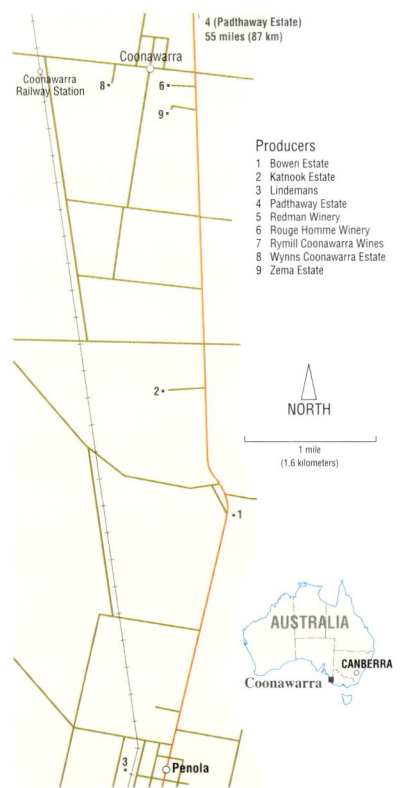

4 (Padthaway Estate)
55 miles (87 km)

Coonawarra

Coonawarra Railway Station

Producers
1 Bowen Estate
2 Katnook Estate
3 Lindemans
4 Padthaway Estate
5 Redman Winery
6 Rouge Homme Winery
7 Rymill Coonawarra Wines
8 Wynns Coonawarra Estate
9 Zema Estate

NORTH

1 mile
(1.6 kilometers)

AUSTRALIA

CANBERRA

Coonawarra

Penola

become its forte. The cool climate and terra rossa combine to give distinctive perfume and complexity to the wines. Coonawarra cabernet displays the blackcurrants, plums, cassis, and chocolatey richness of the variety, but is frequently tinged with hints of mint and eucalyptus.

Shiraz from the Limestone Coast has a fine history and remains a powerfully spicy form of the variety. Riesling from this area is surprisingly good, in a fruity and fragrant style made by only a few producers, most notably Wynns and Hollick. Rymill and Katnook Estate both envisage a great future for sauvignon blanc in the region. Chardonnay has seen mixed fortunes in Coonawarra but has become the forte of Padthaway, where it makes elegant but fruity still wines and complex sparkling wines. Mount Benson and Robe are still experimenting, but some recently released shiraz has been surprisingly lush, especially when treated with French oak.

Some significant producers in Coonawarra and the Limestone Coast, in addition to those below, include Padthaway Estate, Redman Winery, Rouge Homme Winery, Rymill Coonawarra Wines, and Zema Estate.

BOWEN ESTATE, COONAWARRA
Established 1972 *Owners* Doug and Joy Bowen *Vineyard area* 60 acres (25 ha)

Bowen Estate has a well-earned reputation for wines that reflect the premium nature of Coonawarra fruit when it is carefully tended, hand pruned, and sensitively handled. Its

Bowen Estate is family-owned and run, which is reflected in the care taken of the vineyard.

An unusual wine bottle containing original 1914 liqueur.

wines have layers of intense flavor, a lush mouthfeel, and remarkable length, and will further reward those wine lovers who have the patience to cellar them carefully.

KATNOOK ESTATE, COONAWARRA
Established 1890s *Owners* Wingara Wine Group *Vineyard area* 595 acres (240 ha)

This estate produces some of the Coonawarra's most intensely flavored and painstakingly crafted wines. A recent Jimmy Watson Trophy for the 1997 Shiraz highlights the calibre of the wines, even if unfinished. Odyssey, a wine of huge flavor and structure yet with fine balance and complexity, is made from the top 1 percent of hand-selected cabernet fruit.

LINDEMANS, COONAWARRA
Established 1908 *Owners* Southcorp Wines *Vineyard area* 250 acres (100 ha)

The Lindemans Coonawarra trio of Pyrus, Limestone Ridge, and St. George, the brand's flagship wines, are crafted from premium Coonawarra fruit and made only in great vintages. St. George is one of Australia's classic single-vineyard cabernets and shows rich plums, chocolate, and smoky wood on the palate.

WYNNS COONAWARRA ESTATE, COONAWARRA
Established 1891 *Owners* Southcorp Wines *Vineyard area* 1,975 acres (800 ha)

Samuel Wynn and his son David purchased this historic property in 1951. Their remarkable success in the following years was the impetus for investment in Coonawarra by many other companies, both small and large. Wynns Hermitage is regarded as *the* classic Coonawarra shiraz; it is beloved by many and remains a benchmark. The Black Label Cabernet Sauvignon is collected every year by aficionados. The premium John Riddoch Cabernet Sauvignon and Michael Shiraz are made only in exceptional years.

Other South Australian Regions

RIVERLAND

With so much emphasis placed on the fashionable regions producing premium wine, it would be easy to forget that the driving force in Australia's wine industry is the far less glamorous, vast open space of the Riverland. These endless acres of vines, watered by the Murray River, pump out more than half of South Australia's grapes and a third of the country's total crush. They provide the fruit for the Australian wine that people drink most of—the big name brands, the bags-in-boxes, the everyday quaffers. They are honest, enjoyable, good-value wines that are full of flavor.

It's hot and dry here, but the brown sandy loam soils are reasonably fertile. Rainfall is low and evaporation high, so there is little risk of disease. The main concern for the future of the Riverland is the health of the Murray River, where water levels are dropping and salinity levels are rising. It is hoped that new, more sensitive irrigation systems will help to alleviate the pressures on this invaluable resource.

Wine cheers the sad, revives the old, inspires the young, makes weariness forget his toil.
LORD BYRON
(1788–1824)

ANGOVE'S   *Established* 1886 *Owners* **Angove family** *Vineyard area* **1,185 acres (480 ha)**

This is one of Australia's largest privately owned wine companies, with a successful range of good-value varietals, fortified wines, and spirits, including Australia's best-known brandy, St. Agnes. Labels include the Classic Reserve, Stonegate, Sarnia Farm, Butterfly Ridge, and Misty Vineyards ranges.

BANROCK STATION   *Established* 1994 *Owners* **BRL Hardy Wine Ltd** *Vineyard area* **615 acres (250 ha)**

Banrock Station is a groundbreaking vineyard property, wetland reserve, and visitor center. Everything has been done with the environment and conservation in mind, from the solar-powered, recycled-water-using visitor center to vineyard irrigation controlled by computers. The wines themselves show what the region can achieve with the right handling; there is a delightful sparkling chardonnay, and fresh, modern examples of un-wooded chardonnay, shiraz, cabernet/merlot, and sémillon/chardonnay. These are good wines made with environmental common sense and marketing genius.

A tasting room with a colorful, geometric display of bottles.

VICTORIA

Grampians and Pyrenees

The landscape in this area varies from flat, golden pasture to rugged granite escarpment. The winters are cold and wet, the summers are cool and dry, and spring frosts are not uncommon. The average annual rainfall is low, and vines struggle without supplementary irrigation.

Flavors of the highly praised premium shiraz vary from region to region, but are always of juicy berry fruits. Cabernet sauvignon, demonstrating its chameleon-like nature, is frequently minty and tinged with eucalyptus. It is generally riddled with purple fruit flavors.

Sauvignon blanc from the Pyrenees is distinctive. A flinty dryness enriched by soft tropical fruit flavors suggests that this area may become a source of great varietal interest.

Ballarat frequently suffers the coldest temperatures in the state, but the winemakers are turning this to their advantage to produce pinot noirs of superb complexity. More recent plantings of sangiovese, pinot grigio, and viognier are adding interest and suggest that the area is yet to show its breadth. The remote far southwest of Victoria, with its maritime climate, is sparsely planted so far. The Seppelt vineyards at Drumborg are the most significant vineyard development.

Some significant producers in the Grampians and Pyrenees regions, in addition to those below, include Bests Wines, Blue Pyrenees Estate, Redbank Winery, and Seppelt Great Western.

DALWHINNIE WINERY, PYRENEES *Established 1976 Owners* David and Jenny Jones *Vineyard area* 44 acres (18 ha)

Winemaker David Jones produces outstanding cabernet sauvignon, chardonnay, and shiraz that show regional definition and intensity of fruit flavor, reflecting low-yield viticultural practices. Dalwhinnie's Eagle Series Shiraz is only released in exceptional years.

The Dalwhinnie Winery vineyard in the Pyrenees.

MOUNT LANGI GHIRAN WINERY, GRAMPIANS *Established* 1970 *Owners* Trevor Mast and Riquet Hess *Vineyard area* 173 acres (70 ha)

Winemaker Trevor Mast's premium shiraz is one of Australia's finest cool-climate reds, and it can be difficult to obtain. The cabernet merlot, riesling, and chardonnay are regional benchmarks. Recent releases of pinot grigio and sangiovese show a keen eye for development of the area's potential for these varieties.

Rutherglen and North East Victoria

The history of North East Victorian viticulture is littered with names that to this day evoke the region—Brown, Morris, Sutherland Smith, and Campbell. The first records of vines in the area are from 1851, and by 1870 Rutherglen was the largest vineyard area in the colony.

Rutherglen and Glenrowan are the epitome of a hot, continental climate; spring frosts can be a problem and rainfall is low. The Ovens Valley, overlooked by Mount Buffalo, has the high rainfall and cooler temperatures of an elevated region. The King Valley reflects its mountainous landscape, varying from sparse to abundant rainfall and from sterile to exceptionally fertile soils. Viticultural techniques vary throughout the region in response to these microclimates.

Brown Brothers plantings at Milawa serve as a mininursery for Italian grape varieties in Victoria.

They include nebbiolo, dolcetto, barbera, aleatico, and moscato, plus the Spanish variety graciano.

Rutherglen has also specialized in durif and shiraz to make its superb vintage ports, and transforms the brown muscat grape into rich, dark, barrel-aged liqueur muscats that are unique to North East Victoria. The local version of tokay, also a liqueur, is a product of the muscadelle grape; nowhere else in the world is it put to this use.

Some significant producers in Rutherglen and North East Victoria, in addition to those below, include All Saints Estate, Baileys of Glenrowan, R. L. Buller and Son, Campbells Wines, Chambers Rosewood Winery, and Pfieffer Wines.

BROWN BROTHERS MILAWA VINEYARD, KING VALLEY   *Established* 1889 *Owners* Brown family *Vineyard area* 717 acres (290 ha)

One of Australia's most successful family operations, Brown Brothers sources fruit from many of the surrounding regions, always acknowledging special vineyards on the labels. Consistency of quality and a kaleidoscope of varietals and styles have made them firm favorites.

GIACONDA VINEYARD, OVENS VALLEY
Established 1985 *Owner* Rick Kinzbrunner *Vineyard area* 5 acres (2 ha)

Giaconda Vineyard is a relatively new development in the region. The winery produces outstanding wines that are rationed out to restaurants and a mailing list of wine lovers. One of Australia's most opulently flavored, although elegantly structured, chardonnays is complemented by a surprisingly good Burgundian pinot noir.

MORRIS WINES, RUTHERGLEN   *Established* 1859
Owners Orlando Wyndham Group *Vineyard area* 250 acres (100 ha)

Veteran winemaker David Morris is an ebullient character who produces fortifieds that are benchmarks of North East Victoria. His table wines, especially the rich, full-bodied durif, boast a very loyal following.

Producers
1 All Saints Estate
2 Baileys of Glenrowan
3 Brown Brothers
   Milawa Vineyard
4 R.L. Buller & Son
5 Campbells Wines
6 Chambers Rosewood
   Winery
7 Giaconda Vineyard
8 Morris Wines
9 Pfieffer Wines

NORTH

5 miles
(8 kilometers)

AUSTRALIA

CANBERRA

NE Victoria ■

Lake Mulwala   NSW   Corowa   River
Murray   Wahgunyah
Bundalong   9   6   8   Gooramadda
      4   5   Rutherglen   Browns Plains
Norong Central   Lilliput
Norong   Chiltern
Peechelba   VICTORIA   Springhurst
Boorhaman
Yeerip   Killawarra   Mt Pilot
Mt Killawarra   Shannon Hill
Mt Bruno   Ovens River   M31   Wooragee
      Eldorado   Reids Creek
Lake Mokoan   ● Wangaratta   Everton   7 ●   Beechworth
Taminick   Tarrawingee
Mt   2   Laceby   Oxley   Milawa
Gledrowan   3 ●   Murmungee
Glenrowan   Markwood

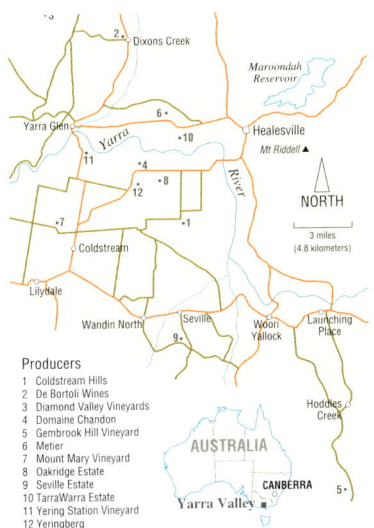

Producers
1 Coldstream Hills
2 De Bortoli Wines
3 Diamond Valley Vineyards
4 Domaine Chandon
5 Gembrook Hill Vineyard
6 Metier
7 Mount Mary Vineyard
8 Oakridge Estate
9 Seville Estate
10 TarraWarra Estate
11 Yering Station Vineyard
12 Yeringberg

The cellar door facilities at Domaine Chandon have sweeping views of manicured vineyards to the hills beyond.

Yarra Valley

In 1838 William Ryrie established Victoria's first commercial vineyard at the Yering cattle station in the Yarra Valley. Others followed—St. Huberts, Yeringberg—and the Yarra Valley went on to enjoy international success in the late 1800s, winning gold medals at European wine shows. However, a combination of economic depression, the threat of phylloxera, and the temperance movement brought an end to the valley's wine history.

In the 1970s, the Yarra Valley returned to wine, and today it is one of Australia's most successful and diverse wine-producing regions. Its undulating hills contain small boutique wineries and larger, more commercial enterprises. Close to Melbourne, it has become an attractive tourist destination, with the Yarra Valley Vignerons Association ensuring the success of festivals such as Grape Grazing (in early March).

The combination of good soil and a cool temperate climate makes the Yarra Valley ideal for growing grapes and making premium wine. The warmest vineyards can ripen cabernet sauvignon

and shiraz admirably, while cooler sites produce leaner wines and are better for pinot noir and chardonnay. Along with merlot, these are the predominant grape varieties grown in the valley. Sauvignon blanc, pinot gris, marsanne, and roussanne have been planted recently, but have not generally taken off yet.

The Yarra Valley is one of Australia's premium sites for sparkling wines and was selected by Champagne houses Devaux and Moët & Chandon as the site for their Australian sparkling wine ventures—Yarrabank and Domaine Chandon.

Some significant producers in the Yarra Valley, in addition to those below, include Coldstream Hills, Diamond Valley Vineyards, Gembrook Hill Vineyard, Metier, Oakridge Estate, Seville Estate, and Yeringberg.

DE BORTOLI WINES *Established* 1987 *Owners* de Bortoli family *Vineyard area* more than 320 acres (130 ha)

De Bortoli, one of the biggest players in the Valley, does not sacrifice quality for quantity and produces excellent wines across its range. Its cellar

Fruit-laden vines awaiting harvesting.

MOUNT MARY VINEYARD
Established 1971 *Owners* Dr. John and Marli Middleton *Vineyard area* 37 acres (15 ha)

Dr. John Middleton's wines are some of the greatest in Australia. His intense Cabernets Quintet (cabernet sauvignon/cabernet franc/merlot/malbec/petit verdot) always lives up to its reputation, as does his long-living pinot noir. The wines are available by mail order, at exclusive restaurants, or sometimes at auctions.

TARRAWARRA ESTATE *Established* 1983 *Owner* Marc Besen *Vineyard area* 72 acres (29 ha)

door facility carries five labels of varying style and price. The top of the range shows a lot of new oak, which falls into balance with age, and the cheaper Windy Peak range relies exclusively on fruit. Their Reserve Shiraz won the 1997 Jimmy Watson Trophy.

TarraWarra is regarded as one of the top producers of pinot noir in the Yarra Valley and in Australia. The TarraWarra Pinot Noir is powerful yet complex, with excellent structure supporting intense red and black berry fruit and brambly characters. The wines are made to last and are at their best with a little age.

DOMAINE CHANDON *Established* 1987 *Owners* Moët & Chandon *Vineyard area* 225 acres (90 ha)

Moët & Chandon purchased the Green Point vineyard in 1987 and planted 125 acres (50 ha) with the traditional champagne varieties—pinot noir, chardonnay, and pinot meunier. In 1994 they established another 100 acres (40 ha) in the Strathbogie Ranges. Chandon has always asserted they are not attempting to make a clone of champagne, but to produce the best Australian sparkling wines using traditional methods. Reserves of older wines are being built up, and the wines are becoming world class. The elegant 1993 Millenium Reserve, a very limited release, bears testimony to this.

The soft extractive note of an aged cork being withdrawn has the true sound of a man opening his heart.

WILLIAM SAMUEL BENWELL,
Journey to Wine in Victoria

YERING STATION VINEYARD
Established 1838, re-established 1987 *Owners* Rathbone family *Vineyard area* 290 acres (117 ha)

The historical site of Victoria's first winery, Yering Station is not resting on its laurels. Current winemaker Tom Carson produces a range of wines, some of which—the Yering Station Reserve Pinot Noir in particular—are superb. The pinot and chardonnay in the Reserve range are complex and lovely. Yering Station's new winery and restaurant facility rivals the grandeur of Domaine Chandon, a rivalry also manifested in Yering Station's joint venture with Devaux Champagne to produce the elegantly delicious Yarrabank Cuvée.

Mornington Peninsula

This is very much a boutique winery region that boasts more than 100 vineyards, with many producers crafting elegant and complex wines.

The Peninsula has a hilly landscape and the often marginal climate is cool to cold, with a maritime influence. A small region, it can be broken into at least five not as yet classified subregions: Moorooduc Downs, Red Hill, Dromana, Merricks, and Main Ridge. The subregions show diverse soil types and microclimates, and the wines reflect these differences.

A young region, it specializes in mediumbodied, dry table wines and is beginning to have success with sparkling wines. The predominant and most successful grape varieties are chardonnay and pinot noir. The latter already shows good complexity and structure, ranging in style from elegant and ethereal to huge, rich, and impressive. Chardonnay ranges from crisp, fruit-driven, unoaked wines with a fruit spectrum from citrus and melon through to tropical pineapple aromas and flavors. Shiraz and sauvignon blanc are enjoying recent success in the warmer sites, and pinot gris—which does well in the climate—is being touted as the "next big thing."

DROMANA ESTATE VINEYARDS *Established* 1982 *Owners* Gary and Margaret Crittenden *Vineyard area* 12 acres (4.9 ha)

Dromana Estate boasts the largest range of wines on sale on the Mornington Peninsula, from the lower-priced Schinus range through the Dromana Estate range to the Reserve wines. Made from estate-grown fruit and fermented by natural yeasts, the 1997 Reserve Chardonnay is particularly complex and rich. A range of wines made from Italian grape varieties grown in the King Valley is also produced. Although not strictly Mornington Peninsula wines, they are of outstanding quality—the "i" Sangiovese and Nebbiolo represent the most faithful Australian renditions of these Italian varieties.

T'GALLANT WINERY *Established* 1990 *Owners* Kevin McCarthy and Kathleen Quealy *Vineyard area* 25 acres (10 ha)

Kevin McCarthy and Kathleen Quealy produce fresh, fruit-driven, unoaked chardonnay and two versions of pinot gris—the Tribute Pinot Gris in homage to the Alsace wines made from this variety, and a pinot grigio in a crisper, more flinty Italian style. Their Lyncroft Pinot gets better each year, with rich, soft, dark berry fruit and velvety tannins. The image and style of wines are young, attractive, and original.

Right: *Grapes awaiting collection at Moorooduc Estate.*
Below: *Main Ridge Estate produces elegant, complex wines from a marginal site.*

Other Victorian Regions

GIPPSLAND

Gippsland, spreading over a large area of the state's southeastern corner, is Victoria's most recent viticultural area of rebirth, with current plantings beginning in the 1970s. The region's isolation and scattered nature of the wineries has kept it from achieving wider recognition.

Cool-climate classics chardonnay and pinot noir dominate production here. Spiciness and complexity characterize the fruit flavors. However, rainfall, soils, temperature, and terrain do vary considerably, reflecting the size of the zone and proximity to the coast. Likewise, styles vary with *terroir*, but production of sparkling wine in the region is negligible.

BASS PHILLIP WINES   *Established* 1979 *Owners* **Phillip and Sairung Jones** *Vineyard area* 44 acres (18 ha)

Some declare Bass Phillip Pinot Noir to be without equal in Australia. It is certainly a labor of love for winemaker Phillip Jones, whose closely planted vines require traditional hand-pruning and harvesting. His chardonnay is also made with distinction.

MACEDON

The elevation of the Macedon Ranges makes it one of Australia's coldest regions. Wind chill, autumn frosts, and unforgiving granite soils add to the challenge and lack appeal for larger companies.

The region's forte is sparkling wine made from the traditional

Nicholson River Winery, in the Gippsland region, produces an opulent chardonnay.

combination of chardonnay and pinot noir. Wines are crisp and intensely flavored. An acid backbone gives elegance to whites. Pinot noir can be earthy and complex. Shiraz from the region has developed a cult following, showing spice, surprising fruit weight, and soft tannins.

HANGING ROCK WINERY, MACEDON

Established 1982 *Owners* **John and Anne Ellis** *Vineyard area* 30 acres (12 ha)

The large production here reflects sourcing of fruit from other Victorian wine regions. Winemaker John Ellis's wines are of consistently good quality, and Macedon Cuvée, made from locally grown fruit, is a standout.

GEELONG

As one of Australia's most southerly regions, Geelong enjoys a long ripening period, allowing grapes to develop complexity and depth of flavor. Strongly maritime influenced, the *terroir* offers scant summer rainfall, chill winds, and poor clay soils. When Geelong wine is good, it is very good. Predictably, pinot noir and chardonnay are grown with distinction in the southerly climate.

Scotchmans Hill Vineyard & Winery, in the Geelong region, is notable for its tropical sauvignon blanc.

BANNOCKBURN VINEYARDS *Established 1974 Owners Hooper Family Vineyard area 62 acres (25 ha)*

The exceptional quality and complexity of winemaker Gary Farr's pinot noir, chardonnay, and shiraz demonstrate his skill in realizing the potential of grapes from Geelong. These are cult wines from a producer who avoids the trappings of the marketplace.

CENTRAL VICTORIA

The warm climate of Central Victoria's lower regions makes it highly suitable for red wines with powerful fruit flavors, particularly shiraz and cabernet—a fact recognized as early as 1873.

Since the 1960s, the Bendigo region, with its undulating hills and dense eucalyptus forest, has become home to many small wineries that produce limited quantities of high-quality wine.

Marsanne grown in commercial quantities is exclusive to the flat, fertile land of the Goulburn Valley. Chateau Tahbilk and Mitchelton produce

some of Victoria's best value and most interesting whites from this variety—aged marsanne is a rare treat for collectors.

The Central Victorian Mountain Country is influenced by altitude—1,000 to 6,000 feet (300 to 1,800 m)—throughout. Yields are lower, frosts are a concern, and most vineyards experience snow in winter. The Mountain Country specializes in cooler climate varieties—chardonnay is its forte for both still and sparkling wines. Riesling and gewürztraminer are developing a following for their crisp and fresh fruit flavors and balanced acid.

The red wines of Central Victoria often show distinctive minty, herbaceous characters. The wines tend to be strongly colored and have powerful fruit flavors.

Shiraz occupies the most acreage, closely followed by cabernet sauvignon. The warmer areas produce generous yields, but strong sunshine and low rainfall require canopy management.

CHATEAU TAHBILK WINES, GOULBURN VALLEY *Established 1860 Owners Purbrick Family Vineyard area 310 acres (125 ha)*

This is Victoria's oldest winery and it continues to occupy some of the original buildings. Some of the oldest vines in the country still produce an intensely flavored shiraz. The marsanne ages to honeyed richness, and is a favorite with collectors.

DELATITE WINERY, CENTRAL VICTORIAN MOUNTAIN COUNTRY *Established 1982 Owners Rosalind and David Ritchie Vineyard area 62 acres (25 ha)*

Picturesque vineyards produce superb cool-climate wines. The ethereal fragrance of winemaker Rosalind Ritchie's riesling and gewürztraminer demonstrates the potential for these varieties here.

JASPER HILL VINEYARD, BENDIGO *Established 1976 Owners Ron and Elva Laughton Vineyard area 57 acres (23 ha)*

Two separate shiraz vineyards named after the Laughtons's daughters produce the much lauded and deliciously different Emily's Paddock and Georgia's Paddock wines. The vines are not irrigated and so produce only small quantities of grapes, which are carefully pressed and softly oaked—they are benchmark reds of the region.

TASMANIA

Tasmania is a small island with a sublime landscape, situated off the southeast corner of Australia. Its cool-temperate climate and long growing season aids in the production of some very elegant wines. Although Geographic Indications denote it as one region, it can be divided into six subregions: the Northwest, Tamar Valley, Pipers Brook/River, East Coast, Derwent/Coal River Valleys, and the Huon Valley.

Experience and experimentation have pared down the grape selections in Tasmania's varied regions. Cabernet plantings are limited to the warmer slopes of the Tamar Valley, Coal River Valley, and East Coast. Pinot noir growers have found that a combination of microclimate and clonal selection is producing wines with layered bouquets and subtle, lingering flavors. Riesling is emerging as a star variety, with excellent examples from the Derwent/Coal River Valleys and Pipers Brook area.

A benchmark chardonnay style is yet to emerge; at present it is finding its expression alongside pinot noir in Tasmania's sparkling wine industry. Five of Australia's twenty best bubblies come from Tasmania; for a region that produces less than 1 percent of Australia's sparkling wines, this is an impressive achievement.

Significant producers in Tasmania, in addition to those below, include Stefano Lubiana, Moorilla Estate, and Stoney Vineyard.

Producers
1 Freycinet Vineyard
2 Stefano Lubiana
3 Moorilla Estate
4 Pipers Brook Vineyard
5 Stoney Vineyard

FREYCINET VINEYARD

Established 1980 *Owners* **Geoff and Sue Bull** *Vineyard area* **22 acres (9 ha)**

Consistently making one of the best pinot noirs in the country, Freycinet Vineyard's

A rainbow crowns a typical Tasmanian winter vineyard scene.

reputation is enhanced by its chardonnay, riesling, and the full-flavored sparkling Radenti. The East Coast region is warm and this, coupled with the vineyard's sun-embracing amphitheater, provides ample opportunity to work with ripe fruit—a luxury in Tasmania's mostly marginal climate.

PIPERS BROOK VINEYARD   *Established* 1974

Owner **Pipers Brook Vineyard Ltd** *Vineyard area* **435 acres (176 ha)**

Pipers Brook Vineyard boasts a range of wines from several labels, including Ninth Island, and seven vineyards scattered throughout Pipers Brook and the Tamar Valley. An ongoing search for great pinot noir is complemented by the refined package of pinot gris, gewürztraminer, and a well-pedigreed riesling, which are marketed as an Alsatian trio. Several tiers of quality are available, from the budget Wave Crest range to the single-vineyard Summit Chardonnay, the luxurious bubbly Pirie, and a superpremium pinot noir.

NEW SOUTH WALES

Hunter Valley

The Hunter Valley is one of Australia's best-known wine areas internationally, and its proximity to Sydney ensures its position as Australia's most visited wine region. Its unique sémillons have captured the hearts of wine lovers everywhere.

Until 1963, Hunter Valley wineries were large commercial enterprises. In that year, however, Dr. Max Lake launched Lake's Folly, Australia's first "boutique" winery, an event that would change the face of the country's winemaking.

Despite the Hunter Valley's extensive plantings, dozens of wineries, and a host of cellar door operations, many people think the Hunter is

unsuitable for viticulture. The reasons are many, including a high probability of rain during harvest. There is no doubt that site selection is critical and, notwithstanding the current proliferation of new plantings, the area under vine today is smaller than it was 30 years ago.

If there is one grape upon which the Lower Hunter has built its reputation, it is sémillon. Chardonnay is now more extensively planted, but aged Hunter sémillon is justifiably world famous. In time, these wines pick up toast, honey, butter, and lemon characters that are utterly entrancing. Over the years, Tyrrell's, McWilliams, Lindemans, Rothbury, Brokenwood, and others have excelled at the style. The district's chardonnay is popular, but its richness is not to the taste of every palate. Verdelho is likely to prove the pick of the other whites.

Hunter shiraz is as distinctive as the region's sémillon. Indeed, the Hunter's earthy, leathery flavors envelop all of its reds but work best with

Vineyard at Pokolbin, a sub-region in the Lower Hunter.

Producers

1 Allandale Winery
2 Bimbadgen Estate
3 Brokenwood Wines
4 Drayton's Family Wines
5 Glenguin Wine Company
6 Kulkunbulla
7 Lake's Folly
8 Margan Family Winegrowers
9 Brian McGuigan Wines
10 Pendarves Estate
11 Pepper Tree Wines
12 Petersons Wines
13 Reynolds Yarraman
14 Scarborough Wine Company
15 Tyrrell's Vineyards

Hunter Valley development

Although grape growing in New South Wales began soon after the arrival of the First Fleet in 1788, with vines planted near what is now Circular Quay on Sydney Harbour, the New South Wales wine industry first grew to prominence in the Hunter Valley. The Hunter was settled soon after it was named in 1797, but focus then was coal, not wine. It wasn't until the 1830s that James Busby, considered to be the father of Australian viticulture, and several others planted vines.

The Pokolbin and Rothbury subregions, now the center of the Lower Hunter vineyard area, weren't planted until the 1860s. The early vineyards proved encouraging, and the Hunter Valley Viticultural Association was formed in 1847. George Wyndham founded the Dalwood vineyards, which later belonged for a period to Penfolds, and Dan Tyrrell made his first vintage in 1883—at the age

This 1878 Scottish crystal decanter is decorated with the bust of Captain Cook.

of 14—beginning an amazing run of 76 consecutive vintages. At that time, the Hunter Valley was seen as ideal for grapes—it was hot, disease-free, and the rainfall is believed to have been more appropriate than that of today. The Lower Hunter has endured its ups and downs, but it has never suffered total failure like so many early Australian wine regions in Victoria and South Australia.

In 1921, one of Australia's greatest winemakers made his appearance. After studying in France, Maurice O'Shea returned to the Hunter to run the Mount Pleasant vineyards and winery his family had purchased. The vineyards had been established in 1880 by another legendary Hunter figure, Charles King. O'Shea joined with McWilliams in 1932, which was a difficult time in the Hunter as the market had changed considerably and 85 percent of production was devoted to fortifieds. The area under vines decreased from almost 2,600 acres (1,050 ha) in the mid-1920s to just over half that a decade later. Although consumers in the 1940s and 1950s were not seeking the wines O'Shea and others were producing, the wines he made at that time are eagerly sought after at auctions today, and many still drink superbly.

Left: *Drayton's have been making wine for over 150 years in the Lower Hunter Valley.* Below: *McWilliams's Mount Pleasant vineyards at Pokolbin.*

The entrance to the tourist stop at Brian McGuigan Wines, Lower Hunter.

shiraz. It seems improbable that pinot noir could work in the Hunter, and most agree that it doesn't and that it loses varietal character. But many wineries—notably Tyrrell's—persist in planting it. Many of the great O'Shea wines and some of Lindemans finest "Hunter River Burgundies" contain a small percentage of pinot.

Grapes were successfully grown in the Upper Hunter in the second half of the nineteenth century, but production had ceased by 1910, probably because of the slow transport of the day. The shift in tastes from table to fortified wine was also significant. Penfolds moved here from the Lower Hunter in 1960 but struggled. Their focus was on red wines but subsequent experience has shown that the region is best suited to whites. They also learned the hard way that irrigation is imperative. In 1996 Penfolds sold to Rosemount, and the other major winery of the district, Arrowfield, commenced operations. As with the Lower Hunter, there is a potential problem with rain during vintage in the Upper, but the overall rainfall is lower. The Upper Hunter has proved itself to be particularly well suited to both chardonnay and sémillon, but less so for reds.

Significant producers in the Hunter Valley, in addition to those below, include Allandale Winery, Bimbadgen Estate, Drayton's Family Wines, Glenguin Wine Company, Kulkunbulla, Margan Family Winegrowers, and Petersons Wines.

Hunter sémillon

Sémillon is the grape blended with sauvignon blanc to produce the white wines of Bordeaux and Sauternes. In Australia, it makes the finest botrytized styles but is better known as a dry table wine, reaching its pinnacle with the Hunter Valley's unique and long-lived wines. When young, Hunter sémillons, usually unwooded, can be crisp, pleasing, and have gentle citrus flavors. However, there is little to suggest that they will blossom into wonderful, toasty, complex wines after five or ten years of bottle aging. Lindemans and Rothbury made many of the great wines of the 1960s and 1970s. Today's classics come from Tyrrell's, McWilliams, and Brokenwood.

BROKENWOOD WINES, LOWER HUNTER
Established 1970 *Owners* private syndicate
Vineyard area 140 acres (57 ha)

A flagship winery for the Hunter Valley wine region, Brokenwood owns the highly regarded Yarra Valley winery, the Seville Estate, and also has significant interests in Cowra. Although Brokenwood has long sourced fruit from around the nation for its wines, the single-vineyard Graveyard Shiraz stands out. In extreme demand, this wine has established itself as the region's top shiraz. The Sémillon is also well received.

Tyrrell's Vineyards in the Lower Hunter.

LAKE'S FOLLY, LOWER HUNTER *Established*
1963 Owner Peter Fogarty *Vineyard area*
30 acres (12 ha)

Australia's first boutique winery, and the fore-
runner of so many more, changed the face of the
wine industry in Australia and quickly established
a cult following for its wines. The range here
consists of Cabernets, which is a blend of petit
verdot, cabernet sauvignon, shiraz, and merlot;
and a chardonnay. Both of these wines benefit
from extended cellaring.

BRIAN MCGUIGAN WINES, LOWER HUNTER
Established 1967 *Owners* Brian McGuigan Wines
Ltd *Vineyard area* 3,170 acres (1,280 ha)

Brian McGuigan is a significant producer of competent wines and has built a devoted following
over the years. One of the Australian wine industry's great marketers, he did much to pave the
way for Australian producers in the American
market during his time at Wyndham Estate. More
recently, he has turned the old Hungerford Hill
Wine Village into a tourist stop that includes a
cheese company, restaurant, cafe, and bakery,
in addition to the winery and tasting facilities.

PEPPER TREE WINES, LOWER HUNTER
Established 1983 *Owners* Pepper Tree Wines Pty
Ltd *Vineyard area* 150 acres (60 ha)

The Pepper Tree winery, part of an attractive
tourist complex, has a significant interest in
Coonawarra's Parker Estate, and multiregional
blends are a specialty here. Winemaker Chris
Cameron intends to create his biggest splash with
merlot, aiming to make Australia's best.

REYNOLDS YARRAMAN, UPPER HUNTER
Established 1968 *Owners* Jon and Jane Reynolds
Vineyard area 150 acres (60 ha)

Winemaker Jon Reynolds had a successful career
with Houghtons and Wyndham before taking
over the old Horderns Wybong Estate, which
dated back to 1837. Since taking over, he has
made some great wines, especially the sémillon.
Wines made from fruit sourced from the Orange
district are also highly recommended.

SCARBOROUGH WINE COMPANY, LOWER
HUNTER *Established* 1987 *Owners* Ian and
Merrelea Scarborough *Vineyard area* 30 acres (12 ha)

This winery, with a sensational view, is planted
on one of the few patches of terra rossa in the
Hunter Valley. Former contract winemaker Ian
Scarborough produces one of the region's very
best chardonnays, and also makes very small
amounts of pinot noir in some years. A second
chardonnay is produced for export markets.

TYRRELL'S VINEYARDS, LOWER HUNTER
Established 1858 *Owners* Murray and Bruce Tyrrell
Vineyard area 205 acres (510 ha)

Edward Tyrrell planted the first vines on this
estate in 1858. In 1883, at age 14, Dan Tyrrell
took over the winemaking and worked 76 consecutive vintages before nephew Murray took
over the reins. Shiraz and sémillon, especially
their Vat 1 Sémillon, are stars, but the pioneering
Vat 47 Chardonnay is one of Australia's finest.
Tyrrell's commercial lines, particularly the Long
Flat wines, are also very popular.

Other New South Wales Regions

NORTHERN RIVERS

Grape growing was revived at Hastings River by the Cassegrain family in the 1980s. Significant rainfall and high humidity can be a problem, which is one reason why the Cassegrains turned to chambourcin, a grape that is highly resistant to mildew and produces a wine of intense color and flavor. Both chardonnay and sémillon have been successful in some vintages.

CASSEGRAIN VINEYARDS, HASTINGS RIVER
Established 1980 *Owners* Cassegrain family *Vineyard area* 260 acres (105 ha)

While Cassegrain's early vintages were variable, winemaker David Barker's wines have been much more consistent in recent years. He makes a range of wines, including sparkling, rosé, and chardonnay; however, it is his chambourcin that has gained prominence.

CENTRAL RANGES

The Central Ranges regions all lie about 185 miles (300 km) inland in an area west to northwest of Sydney. One of them, Mudgee, is among Australia's oldest viticultural regions. The other two, Cowra and Orange, are relative newcomers.

Mudgee is noted for cabernet sauvignon; shiraz has also done well, and there are significant plantings of chardonnay. The winery most likely to bring Mudgee to the attention of the world is Rosemount Estate, with its superb Mountain Blue Shiraz Cabernet and the Hill of Gold range.

In Cowra, chardonnay is by far the predominant grape.

The region quickly made a name for itself with some exciting releases by Rothbury Estate in the Hunter Valley. Other notable outside producers also make wines from Cowra fruit.

The region of Orange is centered around Mount Canobolas. Much of the production of the district goes to large outside producers, such as Rosemount and Rothbury. Chardonnay plantings far exceed all others and have produced some memorable wines. Cabernet sauvignon is also now established, and shiraz looks promising.

HUNTINGTON ESTATE, MUDGEE *Established* 1969 *Owners* Bob and Wendy Roberts *Vineyard area* 106 acres (43 ha)

Several decades ago Bob Roberts revived quality winemaking in Mudgee. His wines, particularly his underpriced reds, have been very successful and age beautifully.

Right: *The vineyards and winery at Steins Wines, Mudgee area.*
Below: *Cassegrain Vineyards are in an unlikely location in the lush subtropics of northern New South Wales.*

BIG RIVERS

A lot of Big Rivers's wine ends up in ubiquitous casks, but it also produces much "sunshine in a bottle"—flavorful, great-value wines that sell well. Sémillon is the most widely planted grape, but chardonnay plantings are increasing. Shiraz is by far the dominant red variety.

Where Big Rivers has stunned critics has been with its botrytis sémillons—these luscious and concentrated dessert-style wines are world class.

DE BORTOLI *Established* 1928 *Owners* de Bortoli family *Vineyard area* 527 acres (213 ha)

If ever a wine company has made the leap from a producer of nondescript bulk wine to the top shelf, this is it. Much of de Bortoli's production is intended for the volume market, but its astonishing botrytis sémillons—Noble One and Black Noble—changed public perception of both de Bortoli and the Big Rivers wine region forever.

Left: *Entrance to Lark Hill in the Canberra District. Operating through the cellar door, the winery has a devoted following.*
Below: *Brindabella Hills Winery vineyard in the Canberra District.*

SOUTHERN NEW SOUTH WALES

The three regions that comprise Southern New South Wales—Hilltops, Canberra District, and Tumbarumba—each show distinctive characteristics and are grouped together for geographical rather than viticultural reasons.

In 1975, grape growing was reintroduced to Hilltops, and to date chardonnay, cabernet sauvignon, and especially shiraz have proved most successful. The McWilliams Barwang wines have established the potential of the region.

The Canberra District is the most established wine region in Southern New South Wales. Chardonnay, shiraz, cabernet sauvignon, and riesling have done well, and there is some support for pinot noir and sauvignon blanc.

High and remote, Tumbarumba is one of the cooler regions in Australia, and most of its grapes go into sparkling wines. Sauvignon blanc is the predominant table wine to date, but chardonnay could eventually become the most prominent white, and pinot noir has potential.

CLONAKILLA, CANBERRA DISTRICT *Established* 1971 *Owner* John Kirk *Vineyard area* 33 acres (13.5 ha)

Clonakilla makes a range of wines, but is most involved with the Rhône varieties. Tiny quantities of a straight viognier are made, and a very small amount of that grape is added to the shiraz in true Rhône fashion, resulting in a delicious, spicy, and very highly rated wine.

SOUTH COAST

A relative newcomer, the South Coast zone has climate problems—summer rainfall, humidity, rot, and mildew. Consequently the area's winemakers have been attracted to chambourcin, but chardonnay, shiraz, and cabernet sauvignon have all done well in good vintages. Some wineries, notably Coolangatta Estate and Cambewarra Estate, are producing quality wines.

QUEENSLAND

One of the many panoramic views in Queensland's Granite Belt wine region.

New plantings across Queensland will soon lead to its wine production exceeding that of Tasmania. Conditions in this huge state vary enormously. The Granite Belt is one of the highest wine regions in the country and cooler than coastal districts. In the Burnett, reduced fertility, rain during harvest, and the possibility of hail are potential problems. Western Queensland is hot and dry. Even in the established Granite Belt, it is too early to identify the most successful varieties. Cabernet sauvignon and shiraz dominate, and merlot is showing much potential. There is some interest in red Italian varieties, and chambourcin's ability to withstand rain and humidity has given it a following. Sémillon and chardonnay are by far the most successful whites.

GRANITE BELT PRODUCERS

BALLANDEAN ESTATE WINERY   *Established* 1968 *Owners* Angelo and Mary Puglisi *Vineyard area* 80 acres (32 ha)

Ballandean's best wines are its Black Label Cabernet and Chardonnay, while the idiosyncratic Late Harvest Sylvaner has its supporters.

KOMINOS WINES   *Established* 1976 *Owner* Tony Comino *Vineyard area* 35 acres (14 ha)

Red wines, particularly shiraz, impress more than white wines. Tony Comino has a serious interest in Greek varieties, and his Vin Doux is in the style of the dessert wine from the island of Samos.

PRESTON PEAK WINES   *Established* 1994 *Owners* Ashley Smith and Kym Thumpkin *Vineyard area* 24 acres (10 ha)

Preston Peak now has a winery in Toowoomba, in addition to its Wyerba facility. The white wines show a delicate touch, while the reds are among the state's most elegant. Preston Peak has had great success with its flagship chardonnay.

OTHER QUEENSLAND PRODUCERS

CLOVELY ESTATE, BURNETT   *Established* 1997 *Owner* Clovely Estate Ltd *Vineyard area* 450 acres (180 ha)

Clovely's three labels, in ascending order of quality, are Fifth Row, Left Field, and Clovely Estate. Much of the production will be exported.

MOUNT COTTON WINERY, BRISBANE   *Established* 2000 *Owner* Sirromet Wines Pty Ltd *Vineyard area* 12 acres (5 ha) at Mount Cotton; 200 acres (80 ha) at Ballandean

This state-of-the-art winery on the outskirts of Brisbane was developed as part of a tourist complex. Chambourcin has been planted in the hot, humid surrounding vineyards, and 20 different grape varieties have been planted at Ballandean.

ROMAVILLA WINERY, SOUTHEAST QUEENSLAND   *Established* 1863 *Owners* David and Joy Wall *Vineyard area* 20 acres (8 ha)

Romavilla's wide range encompasses some delicate whites (including one of Australia's better chenin blancs), midweight reds that are striving for elegance, and heavenly fortifieds.

New Zealand

North Cape

Kaitaia
Kerikeri

Whangarei

Auckland

Great Barrier
Island

Kaipara Harbour

*Hauraki
Gulf*
Takapuna
Waiheke Island
Waitakere
Auckland
Manukau
Papakura
Thames

**Waikato/
Bay of Plenty**

NORTH ISLAND

Tauranga
*Bay
of Plenty*
Hamilton
Matamata
Whakatane
*Lake
Rotorua*
Rotorua
Raukumara Range
Tokoroa

Gisborne
Gisborne

*North
Taranaki
Bight*
*Lake
Taupo*
Taupo

Turangi
Wairoa
New Plymouth
*Mahia
Peninsula*
Cape Egmont
▲ Mt Egmont (Mt Taranaki)
8259 ft (2518 m)
▲ Mt Ruapehu
9174 ft (2797 m)
*Hawke
Bay*

Hawkes Bay
Napier
*South
Taranaki Bight*
Hastings
Cape Kidnappers
Wanganui

NEW ZEALAND
Feilding
Palmerston North

TASMAN
Levin
Te Horo
Wairarapa/Wellington

SEA
Golden Bay
Takaka
*Tasman
Bay*
Masterton
Gladstone
Nelson
Porirua
Upper Hutt
Nelson
Martinborough
Blenheim
WELLINGTON
Wairau Valley
Wairau
Cook Strait
Marlborough
Cape Foulwind
Buller
Mt Travers
7668 ft (2338 m)

Greymouth
Kaikoura
*SOUTH
PACIFIC OCEAN*

SOUTH ISLAND
Waimak
**Canterbury/
Waipara**
Waipara
Pegasus Bay
Mt Cook (Mt Aoraki)
12,313 ft (3754 m)
Rakaia
Christchurch
Lyttelton
*Canterbury
Plains*
Banks Peninsula
Ashburton
*Lake
Pukaki*
*Canterbury
Bight*
*Lake
Wanaka*
Timaru
Mt Aspiring
9938 ft (3030 m)
Omarama
Wanaka
Waitaki
**Central
Otago**
Queenstown
*Lake
Wakatipu*
Oamaru
Lake Te Anau
Te Anau
Clutha
*Otago
Peninsula*
Dunedin
SOUTHERN ALPS
Mataura
Waiau
Invercargill
Foveaux Strait

Stewart Island

NORTH

75 miles
(120 kilometers)

New Zealand

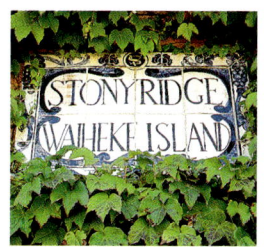

New Zealand's wine production pales in significance compared with its profile as a wine-producing nation. The country currently makes around 15.8 million gallons (60 million l) of wine annually, which is just 0.2 percent of the global total, yet all over the world its wines are both well known and highly sought-after. They first shot to fame in the mid-to late 1980s when the country's inimitable Marlborough Sauvignon Blanc attracted attention in Europe. Since then, New Zealand has shown similar potential for making small quantities of other high-quality wines, particularly Martinborough Pinot Noir and Gisborne Chardonnay. New Zealand is situ-

ated in the southern hemisphere, between the 32nd and 47th parallels. Both its isolation—the nearest sizeable landmass is Australia, 1,000 miles (1,600 km) away—and its maritime climate make the viticultural conditions, and the wines, unique. New Zealand's cool climate is its greatest asset for wine production, but the associated problems of high rainfall and humidity constitute a major challenge for the country's winemakers.

Grapes are grown all over New Zealand, with the exception of the west coasts of the North Island and South Island, and Stewart Island in the far south. There are nine official wine-producing regions: Auckland, Waikato/Bay of Plenty, Gisborne, Hawkes Bay, and Wairarapa/Wellington on the North Island; and Marlborough, Nelson, Canterbury/Waipara, and Central Otago located on the South Island.

Climatic variations

Generally, wine-producing regions in the North Island are warmer and wetter than those in the South. The exception to this is the Wairarapa/Wellington region. Marlborough, Martinborough in the Wairarapa, and Gisborne have the country's most consistent conditions for grape growing.

Canterbury and Central Otago in the southern half of the South Island have long been considered marginal for grape growing. But as growers succeed in matching grape varieties with specific sites, some consistency in grape quality and production is now starting to show. Central Otago is New Zealand's only wine-producing region with a continental climate. This means that frost is a threat around vintage time.

House of Nobilo's Huapai vineyard.

Vines and viticulture

New Zealand now has a total vineyard area of 20,163 acres (8,160 ha). Three-quarters of the vines are planted in the country's three largest and fastest-growing wine regions: Marlborough, Hawkes Bay, and Gisborne.

White-grape varieties account for around 70 percent of plantings, with chardonnay topping the list followed by sauvignon blanc and müller-thurgau. Over the next few years, plantings of müller-thurgau are expected to decrease while those of pinot gris, riesling, gewürztraminer, and sémillon are likely to increase significantly. Red-grape plantings are dominated by pinot noir, followed by cabernet sauvignon and merlot; however, plantings of merlot are soon likely to overtake those of cabernet sauvignon. Other grape varieties are grown in relatively small quantities.

Soils here are highly fertile, and many vines suffer from high vigor and overcropping. A number of growers use vine vigor to their advantage to produce high yields; some of the country's quality chardonnays now come from high-vigor sites.

The Integrated Wine Production (IWP) scheme provides growers with guidelines on sustainable vineyard practices. Pesticide and fungicide use threatens the environment—minimizing damage is a major challenge for the industry.

History

The first vines were planted in New Zealand by the Reverend Samuel Marsden in 1819, at Kerikeri in what is now the Northland area of the North Island. The first wine was made at nearby Waitangi in 1836 by James Busby. In the 1890s, Dalmatian immigrants began planting vines in Northland and near Auckland, where many of the wineries they founded still oper-

Mist behind Te Mata Estate Winery in Hawkes Bay.

ate today. Historically, the Hawkes Bay region is almost as significant as Northland and Auckland, being home to both New Zealand's oldest winery, Mission Estate, founded in 1851, and the country's oldest winery building that is still in operation, Te Mata Estate Winery, which was originally established in 1896.

The first viticulturist employed by the New Zealand government was Dalmatian-born Romeo Bragato, whose tenure ran from 1895 to 1909. His work included the identification of phylloxera and pinpointing suitable regions for grape growing. Bragato is remembered as a man of foresight; unfortunately, when he left the country, growers came up with the spectacularly unsuccessful idea of replacing diseased *Vitis vinifera* grapes with disease-resistant hybrid varieties. The quality of wine suffered as a result, and it was not until the second half of the twentieth century that *Vitis vinifera* varieties were taken seriously again.

Another setback in the development of the wine industry was the emergence of the New Zealand Temperance Society. Formed in 1836, it was

particularly influential between 1881 and 1918, when restrictive liquor legislation was in place. However, soldiers returning from World War I bolstered opposition to the society, and it began to lose power before a ban on all alcohol took effect; its influence finally dwindled during the 1920s and 1930s.

The wine industry was also inhibited by the country's conservative licensing laws. Until 1881, winery sales were illegal and the only outlets for alcohol were hotels. It was only in 1955 that permission was granted for specialist shops to sell wine; and in 1960 restaurants were finally granted licenses to do the same.

New Zealand's modern wine industry really began with the planting of vines in Marlborough in 1973 by Montana Wines. This was followed in the 1980s by small plantings in other areas such as Wairarapa/Wellington, Canterbury/Waipara, Central Otago, and Northland. Since then, the industry has grown quickly.

Auckland

Auckland is the name of New Zealand's largest city and its most diverse wine-producing region. The latter incorporates the subregions of Northland and Matakana in the north; the far-flung Great Barrier Island; and Greater Auckland, Kumeu/Huapai, Henderson, and Waiheke Island. Currently, Auckland has around 4 percent of the national vineyard area, and about 80 wineries.

Northland's wineries are generally small, and most concentrate on red wine production, mainly cabernet-sauvignon- and merlot-dominated blends plus a little pinotage and shiraz. Müller-thurgau, chardonnay, gewürztraminer, and sémillon are among the whites made in small quantities.

The country's most northerly winery, Okahu Estate, produces high-quality reds, including shiraz- and cabernet-sauvignon-dominated blends, as well as a range of others made from pinotage, merlot, and chambourcin. Farther south, there are several vineyards and wineries around Kerikeri and near Whangarei.

Matakana produces small amounts of top-quality red wine. Relatively new wineries here (mostly small) are concentrating on pinot gris, chardonnay, riesling, and cabernet-based reds.

Great Barrier Island is home to one operational vineyard, which yields only small quantities of cabernet sauvignon. However, several small vineyards are currently under development.

The subregions around the city of Auckland—Greater Auckland, Kumeu/Huapai, and Henderson—are not renowned for good viticultural conditions. The Greater Auckland subregion includes the recently developed Clevedon area, which is planted mainly with red grape varieties such as cabernet sauvignon, malbec, merlot, and a handful of Italian grape varieties, including sangiovese and nebbiolo.

Waiheke Island, situated in the Hauraki Gulf, concentrates on cabernet sauvignon, cabernet franc, malbec, merlot, and chardonnay. Some winemakers are trialing pinot noir, plus sangiovese and other Italian varieties. The quantities of wine made are tiny, but the cabernet sauvignon and merlot are among the country's best and most reliable in terms of consistent ripeness.

Producers of significance in the Auckland region, including those below, are Coopers Creek, Delegat's Wine Estate, Goldwater Estate, Harrier

Rise, Heron's Flight, Lincoln Vineyards, Obsidian, Okahu Estate, Peninsula Estate Wines, Twin Bays Vineyard, Vin Alto, and Waiheke Vineyards.

BABICH WINES   *Established* 1916 *Owners* Babich family *Vineyard area* 297 acres (120 ha)

Babich Wines's top-of-the-range Patriarch Chardonnay and Cabernet Sauvignon are big, powerful wines produced only in exceptional years. Irongate Chardonnay and Cabernet Merlot are consistently full flavored, but more elegantly styled and structured for bottle aging. The Mara Estate range produces some of the country's best value in subtle fruit, underplayed winemaking, and finesse, and has an outstanding syrah to its credit. A "Winemakers" series, pitched between Mara and Irongate, is stylish and well made. Babich's main-line Marlborough Sauvignon Blanc and Pinot Gris, Gisborne Unwooded Chardonnay, and Hawkes Bay Chenin Blanc provide some of New Zealand's best-value varietals.

CORBANS WINES   *Established* 1902 *Owners* Publicly listed shareholders *Vineyard area* 1,483 acres (600 ha)

Corbans Wines, New Zealand's second-largest winery, is a brand-driven company with a broad range of still and sparkling wines at virtually every price and quality level. Above the bulk level, Corbans produces inexpensive, competent White Label varietals, followed by a more regionally distinct Estate Range, and, when vintage quality merits, the premium Private Bin and ultrapremium Cottage Block ranges. Strengths in *méthode tradition-nelle* wines include the midpriced Verdi and the pricier Amadeus, both pinot noir and chardonnay based. Corbans is moving away from the cheap bulk wine market and toward greatly expanded exports driven by higher quality wines and a greater emphasis on single-vineyard and regional characteristics.

Vineyard workers prune the vines at Waiheke Vineyards on Auckland's Waiheke Island.

HOUSE OF NOBILO   *Established* 1943 *Owners* Nobilo family, BRL Hardy, and other shareholders *Vineyard area* 79 acres (32 ha)

Innovation and a willingness to take risks are the hallmark of this company. From its clever transformation of müller-thurgau-based White Cloud into an international brand, to the more recent midpriced Icon series, and the bargain-varietals Fernleaf series, Nobilo keeps the local competition on its toes. Its strongest suits include the Grand Reserve Chardonnay, a cross-regional blend of each vintage's best fruit (only when merited), and the Icon range's focused, fine-grained Gewürztraminer and Riesling. Wines in Nobilo's varietal range are always well made and often excellent value. In particular, their Pinotage is worth seeking out.

KUMEU RIVER WINES   *Established* 1944 *Owners* Melba Brajkovich and family *Vineyard area* 62 acres (25 ha)

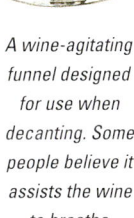

A wine-agitating funnel designed for use when decanting. Some people believe it assists the wine to breathe.

Kumeu River is one of New Zealand's finest small wineries. Winemaker Michael Brajkovich's Maté's Vineyard is a recent, state-of-the-art replant of the original estate. All Kumeu River chardonnays are 100 percent whole

Goldwater Estate, the first vineyard on Waiheke Island, proved this area could produce top-quality Bordeaux blends.

bunch pressed; wild yeast, barrel, and malolactic fermented; then lees and oak aged. Stylistically, these wines share seamless textures, fine balance, and buttery flavors. The basic "lightly wooded" Brajkovich signature series is aged in four-year-old French oak, whereas the creamy Kumeu River (mendoza clone) shows a stronger new-oak influence than the purposely subdued, subtly nutty, long-lived Dijon Clone 95 Maté's Vineyard. Merlot and cabernet franc, along with malbec, make up the winery's top red, Melba. Recent pinot noir and pinot gris releases suggest a promising future with these varietals.

MATUA VALLEY WINES   *Established* 1973
Owners **Ross and Bill Spence, Margan family, and Mark Robertson** *Vineyard area* **494 acres (200 ha)**

Ross and Bill Spence planted New Zealand's first sauvignon vineyard. By 1974, the seeds of a revolution had been bottled, and New Zealand sauvignon blanc was born. Other firsts to their credit include commercial quantities of pinot gris and unwooded chardonnay, with more recent forays into grenache and malbec. All are well made, varietally true, and good value.

Both the top-label Ararimu Chardonnay and Cabernet Merlot are produced only in exceptional years and are stylish, flavor-filled, concentrated, and smooth. The Judd Estate Chardonnay is a classic, big-fruited wine, and the Smith Dartmour red range can be excellent value in ripe years. The new Innovator series provides an outlet for ongoing experiments with small-batch production, and the new Settlers series covers the cheap, easy-drinking end of the market. Matua's Unwooded Chardonnay pioneered this style in New Zealand and remains one of the best, vibrantly pure, mid-priced examples available.

MONTANA WINES   *Established* 1944 *Owner* **Corporate Investments Limited** *Vineyard area* **3,460-plus acres (1,400-plus ha)**

This is New Zealand's largest winery and its most sophisticated international brand. Montana's branding strength lies above its bulk wines, starting with the Montana range, which is regionally and varietally typical, and moving up through the stylish Saints, Montana Reserve, and Church Road ranges, and the "letter-designated" single-vineyard Estate wines. All deliver focused fruit flavors, well-balanced and refined textures, and crisp acids, using each region's varietal strengths, for example, Marlborough's chardonnay, pinot noir, and sauvignon blanc; and Gisborne's sémillon.

Sparkling wines are made primarily from traditional champagne grapes, with the bargain-priced Lindauer (which includes chenin blanc) and the rich, biscuity, Lindauer Reserve (pinot noir and chardonnay) among the country's best-value bubblies. Farther up the scale, the Duetz Marlborough Cuvée and Blanc de Blancs are among New Zealand's most elegant sparklers.

STONYRIDGE VINEYARD *Established* 1982
Owner **Stephen White** *Vineyard area* **34 acres (13.6 ha)**

Stephen White's Waiheke flagship, Larose Cabernet, is New Zealand's most expensive wine and, arguably, its best Bordeaux-style red. A blend of cabernet sauvignon, merlot, cabernet franc, malbec, and petite syrah, it consistently sells out *en primeur*. Intense and savory, Larose is defined by condensed textures and multileveled flavors and is stacked full of fine-grained tannins; it ages superbly. The Airfield label is a more forward style and is usually very good in its own right. A limited-quantity syrah is also produced, and a malbec-dominated blend is in the works.

VILLA MARIA ESTATE *Established* 1961 *Owner* **George Fistonich** *Vineyard area* **185 acres (75 ha)**

Villa Maria is the country's third-largest wine producer, and it concentrates on premium wines. The

Honoring the vine in stained glass at the House of Nobilo.

solid Private Bin varietal ranges (strong in riesling and sauvignon blanc) increasingly have an uncluttered, elegant, nervier style. The midrange Cellar Selection Sauvignon Blanc, Chardonnay and Riesling are generally excellent, with very pure varietal expressions. The top-flight Reserve range, made only in good years, consistently produces two of New Zealand's best sauvignon blancs: the zesty, unwooded, leafy, passionfruit-laden Clifford Bay, and the deeper, darker, sweatier, more savory Wairau Valley, which is lightly kissed with oak. Both the riesling and gewürztraminer in this range combine power and intensity with elegant restraint; so too the blend of cabernet, merlot, malbec, and franc, with its savory, cigar-box overtones and fine-grained tannins. Finally, the Noble Riesling's varietal character is never overshadowed by botrytis, and shows a multilayered, well-structured palate.

Oak barrels stand by fermentation tanks, ready for filling, at Kumeu River Wines.

Waikato/
Bay of Plenty

Plantings in the De Redcliffe vineyards have shifted away from red varieties to whites.

Situated a short distance south of the city of Auckland, the neighboring districts of Waikato and Bay of Plenty make up New Zealand's smallest wine region. It includes 13 widely scattered wineries and 247 acres (100 ha) of vineyards—barely 1 percent of the national total. Most of the wineries are very small, although there are some larger establishments which source their grapes from farther afield. The region is divided into four subregions: Te Kauwhata, Hamilton, the Bay of Plenty, and the Mangatawhiri Valley.

Wine was first made in Waikato around the turn of the twentieth century at the Te Kauwhata Research Station. In the 1930s and 1940s, the station was used to make wine for American troops based in New Zealand, after which it was upgraded and used by the government. In the 1980s, it was bought by two of the station's officers who incorporated it in their winery, Rongopai.

The Te Kauwhata area has relatively high levels of sunshine and few frosts, but is very humid and wet. Many of the wineries use canopy management and vineyard spraying programs to counter the damp conditions; others turn the climate to their advantage to produce some of New Zealand's finest botrytized dessert wines. Te Kauwhata is renowned for its heavy clay loams, which appear to favor chardonnay.

There are only a few vineyards located around the city of Hamilton; all are small and situated on heavy clay-loam soils best suited to chardonnay and, some say, pinot noir. Although there is plenty of sunshine, rainfall levels are similar to those in Te Kauwhata and high humidity results in regular fogs.

The aptly named Bay of Plenty region has rich, fertile soils and experiences high levels of sunshine but also high levels of rainfall and humidity, particularly during the all-important ripening cycle. As a result of these less-than-ideal viticultural conditions, wine production has not been pursued vigorously here.

The most northerly subregion in the Bay of Plenty is the Mangatawhiri Valley, about an hour's drive from Auckland. This secluded, fertile valley is home to just one winery, De Redcliffe. It obtains most of its grapes from Hawkes Bay and Marlborough, but is growing increasing quantities of good-quality pinot noir.

The most planted grape variety in the Waikato/Bay of Plenty region is chardonnay (15 percent), followed by cabernet sauvignon (13 percent) and sauvignon blanc (11 percent). Other varieties include, in significantly smaller amounts, breidecker, chenin blanc, gewürztraminer, various muscats, palamino, riesling, sylvaner, blauberger, merlot, and pinot noir. Steady growth is expected over the next few years, most of which will be the result of increased plantings of cabernet sauvignon, chardonnay, sauvignon blanc, and malbec.

Some producers of significance in the region, in addition to those below, are Mills Reef Winery and Rongopai Wines.

> *...a new friend is as new wine; when it is old, thou shalt drink it with pleasure.*
> Old Testament

MORTON ESTATE WINES *Established* 1982 *Owner* **John Coney** *Vineyard area* **835 acres (338 ha)**

A medium-sized establishment, Morton Estate is renowned for consistent quality across a broad range of distinctive Marlborough and Hawkes Bay varietals, and has a solid reputation for sparkling wines. At the bottom of the three-tier output, the Mill Road range offers generally good quality and value; the unwooded chardonnay is the star. The mainstay White Label has a Marlborough range, including a crisply herbaceous sauvignon blanc, sharply priced pinot noir

Morton Estate has gained a reputation as an outstanding producer of sparkling wines.

(smooth, with hints of smoky bacon and red fruits), and a classy, tightly structured chardonnay. The Hawkes Bay range includes a syrah (all blackberries, vanilla, and pepper, with fine-grained tannins) and a rich, flowery, vanilla-and-oak-filled chardonnay. In the top-end Black Label range, a creamy, deeply viscous, meltaway chardonnay is consistently among the country's finest, and the merlot is the pick of the reds.

Morton Estate's fine *méthode champenoise* range consists of a chardonnay-dominated Recently Disgorged; a classy, complex Black Label (chardonnay and pinot noir dominated by meunier) released five years after vintage; as well as a good-value, finely balanced NV Brut.

DE REDCLIFFE WINERY *Established* 1976 *Owner* **Otaka Holdings** *Vineyard area* **62 acres (25 ha)**

De Redcliffe's strengths lie in white wines, particularly sémillon, although the home vineyard also produces the stylish, fruity Mangatawhiri Chardonnay. Both the Marlborough Riesling and Sauvignon Blanc are fruit focused, crisply structured, and relatively underpriced. The 20-year-old Millennium Reserve Tawny Port is New Zealand's best, and much more Australian in style than Portuguese.

Gisborne and Hawkes Bay

The east-coast wine regions of Gisborne and Hawkes Bay on New Zealand's North Island are close to each other geographically but distant relations when it comes to the wines they produce.

Gisborne is the country's third-largest grape-growing region, with 16 percent of the total New Zealand vineyard area. Traditionally a bulk grape-growing area where müller-thurgau and muscat ruled the viticultural roost, it is now known as the country's chardonnay capital.

Soils here are generally volcanic, but vary widely. The success of white-grape varieties reflects Gisborne's status as a cool-climate grape-growing area. Chardonnay is the most planted variety, with 41 percent of the vineyard area. This figure is expected to rise alongside increased plantings of pinot noir, sémillon, gewürztraminer, and merlot. Concurrently, chenin blanc, müller-thurgau, muscat, and sauvignon are expected to decrease. The gewürztraminer produced here vies with Marlborough's as New Zealand's best. Similarly, the chardonnay rivals the best offerings from Hawkes Bay and Marlborough, and, with its intense melon and tropical fruit flavors, is certainly the most distinctive of those made in New Zealand. Of the red wines, merlot has so far shown the most promise. Plantings of pinot noir are predicted to increase faster than merlot, but mainly to provide a base for sparkling wines.

Hawkes Bay currently accounts for 27 percent of the total New Zealand vineyard area; it also produces the country's most diverse range of wines, from tropical sauvignon blanc and elegant chardonnay to gutsy merlot and cabernet-based reds.

There are 41 wineries in the Hawkes Bay area. However, most of these wineries are relatively small, and recent short-term growth has been mainly the result of expansion undertaken by large industry players such as Montana and Corbans and small to medium-sized new wineries.

Hawkes Bay has traditionally been seen as the most promising region in New Zealand for cabernet- and merlot-based red wines, but the quality depends on where the grapes are grown. The soils here are all alluvial and vary vastly. A smattering of well-drained limestone soils provides some of the country's most

Combining vineyards and accommodation at Lombardi Wines in sunny Hawkes Bay.

impressive chardonnay, merlot, cabernet, and syrah. The stony soils of the Gimblett Gravels area are home to an increasing number of wineries whose focus is on the red varietals: cabernet franc, cabernet sauvignon, malbec, and merlot.

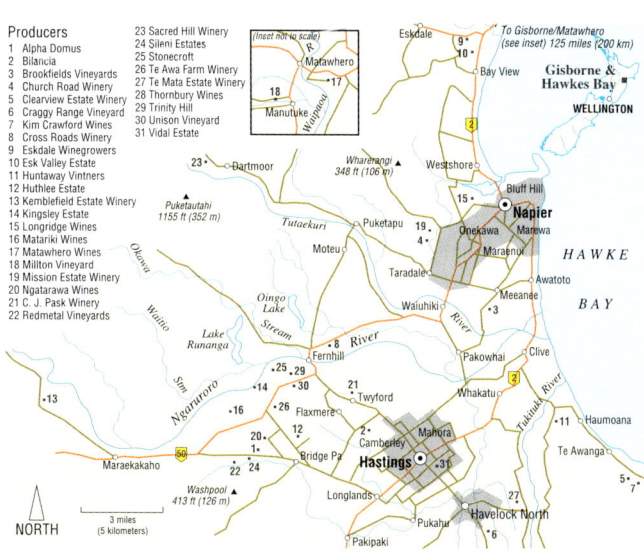

Generally, Hawkes Bay has a cool maritime climate and the highest average hours of sunshine in New Zealand. Chardonnay is the most widely planted grape variety, with 27 percent of the area's current vineyard plantings, and is predicted to increase. Cabernet sauvignon is the next most planted variety, but is likely to be overtaken by merlot. Currently level pegging with merlot is sauvignon blanc, which produces wines that are more tropical in flavor and softer in texture than the more intense Marlborough style. Proportions of cabernet sauvignon, cabernet franc, pinot noir, and syrah are also likely to increase in the near future. There are also small quantities of breidecker, chasselas, pinotage, gewürztraminer, malbec, pinot gris, sémillon, riesling, sylvaner, viognier, and a handful of Italian reds that are still in experimental phases.

Some significant producers located in the Gisborne and Hawkes Bay region, in addition to those below, are Alpha Domus, Bilancia, Brookfields Vineyards, Clearview Estate Winery, Cross Roads Winery, Eskdale Winegrowers, Esk Valley Estate, Huntaway Vintners, Huthlee Estate, Kembleﬁeld Estate Winery, Kingsley Estate, Longridge Wines, Matariki Wines, Redmetal Vineyards, Sacred Hill Winery, Te Awa Farm Winery, Thornbury Wines, Trinity Hill, Unison Vineyard, and Vidal Estate.

CHURCH ROAD WINERY (FORMERLY THE MCDONALD WINERY)   *Established* 1897
Owners Corporate Investments Ltd   *Vineyard area* 848 acres (343 ha)

Church Road's benchmark cabernet/merlot style displays ripe berry-fruit characters, a kiss of French oak, smooth-grained but firmly structured tannins, and a general air of restrained elegance. The barrel-fermented chardonnay and sauvignon blanc display a similar balance of fruit intensity and more subtle complexity. A slow-developing Reserve Chardonnay, Cabernet/Merlot, and occasional Merlot are produced from outstanding fruit in exceptional years and

Stained glass announcing Brookfields Vineyards in Hawkes Bay. Traditional strengths include the Gold Label Reserve Cabernet.

show greater intensity, complexity, and tighter structures. Two Grand-Cru-class limited releases were added to the range recently: an expensive, long-lived, Bordeaux blend named Tom, and the multilayered, plush-textured, botrytis-infected sémillon, Virtue.

Terroir

The concept of *terroir* is alive and well in New Zealand. A group of more than 30 wineries and growers banded together to promote themselves as a subregion of Hawkes Bay, known as Gimblett Gravels. Vineyards must be 95 percent within the defined region before their wines can display the GG logo. This 1,976 acre (800 ha) district differs from surrounding areas as it consists of gravelly soils which encourage thermal conductivity, resulting in temperatures three degrees warmer than the rest of the district. The subregion is now the site for some of New Zealand's best shiraz and Bordeaux blend wines.

CRAGGY RANGE VINEYARDS *Established* 1998
Owners **Terry Peabody and Steve Smith MW** *Vineyard area* 272 acres (110 ha)

This winery is intent on producing nothing but high-quality, single-vineyard wine. Marlborough-sourced first releases include the condensed, minerally Rapaura Road Riesling from 20-year-old fruit; a classic, pungent-with-sweat-and-passion-fruit sauvignon; and a well-focused, beautifully balanced Strugglers Flat Pinot Noir. The Hawkes Bay Chardonnay is beautifully integrated with underplayed oak.

KIM CRAWFORD WINES *Established* 1996
Owners **Kim and Erica Crawford** *Vineyard area* **None**

Kim Crawford's early successes included the vibrant Marlborough Sauvignon Blanc and a pure, well-focused, unoaked chardonnay. More recently, a higher-quality range (Hawkes Bay Reserve Chardonnay, Merlot, and Cabernet Franc) has shown sharply etched varietal characters, richness, and style. A super-reserve range, produced only in exceptional years, was recently released, including the Pia Chardonnay, Tane Merlot/Cabernet Franc, Reka Botrytized Riesling, as well as the Méthode Traditionnelle. All are excellent and distinctive.

MATAWHERO WINES *Established* 1975
Owner **Dennis Irwin** *Vineyard area* 79 acres (32 ha)

Matawhero made its name in the mid-1980s with a series of concentrated, edgy gewürztraminers. Subsequent vintages have been irregular. Other wines in the range are generally made in austere styles that need considerable bottle age to develop their full potential. Sometimes they also (perhaps intentionally) reflect volatile, oxidative, low-tech winemaking styles, with excellent results. This estate deserves bonus points for pushing the boundaries of winemaking.

Wine being transferred to oak barrels at Huntaway Vintners, one of New Zealand's largest wineries.

MILLTON VINEYARD *Established*
1984 Owners Millton family
Vineyard area 49 acres (20 ha)

One of the world's greatest organic wineries, Millton produces two of New Zealand's best whites: the barrel-fermented Te Arai Chenin Blanc, which is seamless, concentrated, and long lived; and the Opou Riesling, which is fleshy, seamless, and clear as a bell. Almost as good are the top-of-the-range, barrel-fermented, selected-fruit Clos Ste Anne Chardonnay and the second-level Barrel-Fermented Chardonnay. A recently introduced malbec is a fine-grained, flavor-filled, elegant red. A lively, sharply priced, off-dry, summer-quaffing Muskats@Dawn is clever marketing at its best, and the Late Harvested Chenin Blanc shows a feel for this varietal rarely seen outside of the Loire.

Mission Estate's vineyards; founded in 1851 by the Marist Brothers, this is New Zealand's oldest winery.

MISSION ESTATE WINERY *Established* 1851
Owner Society of Mary *Vineyard area*
87 acres (35 ha)

Recently, improved viticulture, a shift toward organic practices, careful deselection, and brand repositioning have led to improved quality across Mission Estate's three ranges: Estate, Reserve, and Jewelstone. At the lower level, the Estate's pinot gris, riesling, gewürztraminer, and merlot can offer outstanding value and personality. The strengths of the middle-level Reserve range are the chardonnay, sémillon, cabernet/merlot, and merlot. Jewelstone is only produced in the best years, and its leading wines are the pinot grigio, noble riesling, and chardonnay.

NGATARAWA WINES *Established* 1981 *Owners*
Alwyn and Brian Corban *Vineyard area*
49 acres (20 ha)

Output here is divided into the good-value Stables range and the top-line Glazebrook, both of which err on the understated, slightly austere side of fruit-forward, but are longer lived and more elegant for it. The Stables Noble Harvest Riesling and super-premium Alwyn are among Hawkes Bay's best. Both the Glazebrook Chardonnay, which displays underplayed oak, and the rich, supple Merlot/Cabernet Sauvignon improve with age and are complex, interesting wines. Ngatarawa Wines are now quietly experimenting with viognier.

C. J. PASK WINERY *Established* 1982 *Owners*
Pask family *Vineyard area* 148 acres (60 ha)

Pask's strength lies in standard-range and reserve-quality merlot and cabernet sauvignon and in a 70 percent cabernet/merlot blend. Remarkably consistent, the base range can closely match the reserve's quality level in hot years. All show vibrant varietal characters with generous, but not overpowering, well-integrated sweet oak, with the reserve range more concentrated and structured to age. Pask Chardonnay is a fruit-driven, very lightly oaked style, whereas the more powerful French-oak-fermented Reserve Chardonnay is buttery, and displays a deep, multilayered complexity. C. J. Pask Winery also produces an inexpensive but good-quality, age-worthy chenin blanc.

SILENI ESTATES *Established* 1997
Owners Avery, Cowper, and Edmonds families *Vineyard area* 247 acres (100 ha)

Sileni, one of Hawkes Bay's newest wineries, has extensive plantings waiting to come on line. The team of winemaking specialists has produced excellent early results, with notable offerings including the plummy, toasty merlot and long, impeccably balanced chardonnay.

STONECROFT *Established* 1982 *Owner* Alan Limmer *Vineyard area* 15 acres (6 ha)

Stonecroft's considerable reputation rests on two varietals, syrah and gewürztraminer—an odd couple that tends to overshadow a portfolio that is strong on all counts. The gewürztraminer is one of New Zealand's most thrilling: delicately spiced, earthy, minerally, creamy, and steely. Concealed in the shadows of the syrah and gewürztraminer are an outstanding, dense, atmospheric, smoky chardonnay, and the

This unusual corkscrew, made in England in 1870, was patented as the Lund King.

Crofter/Ruhanui blends of syrah, cabernet, and merlot. A zinfandel is currently being developed.

TE MATA ESTATE WINERY *Established* 1896
Owners Buck and Morris families *Vineyard area* 185 acres (75 ha)

From its first modern vintage in 1979, Te Mata's Cabernet/Merlot blend established a benchmark for all other New Zealand Bordeaux blends, and eventually became the country's most famous red.

A three-tiered red range begins with the bottom-end cabernet sauvignon/merlot, often excellent value as a result of catching intentional spillage from the upper-tier Coleraine and Awatea. Both of these wines are blended cabernet sauvignon, merlot, and cabernet franc, defined by seamless, smooth textures, complexity, and concentration. The Coleraine is the more so, and built for longer-term aging, while the cheaper Awatea drinks at about two years. Elston Chardonnay is fully French-oak and malolactic fermented, resulting in an earthy, buttery, mealy, minerally, long-lived wine. Declassified Elston often makes Te Mata Chardonnay excellent buying. The Bullnose Syrah is reaching the highest levels of style and quality, and a viognier style is now under development.

A host of tourism facilities and activities are offered by Sileni Estates, one of Hawkes Bay's most striking new wineries.

Wairarapa/ Wellington

The town of Martinborough is the "capital" of what is now known as the Wairarapa wine region.

Like New Zealand's own presence in the wine world, Wairarapa/Wellington has forged a reputation that far outweighs its level of production. Formerly known as Martinborough, after the tiny town of the same name that produced the area's first wines in the early 1980s, it is the country's sixth-largest winemaking region.

The 33 wine producers in the region constitute 12 percent of the country's winemakers, but only 3 percent of the country's vines. Moreover, the region's average vineyard size is less than half the national average. However, recently there has been a rapid increase in the area under production.

Wairarapa/Wellington is the North Island's coolest and driest winemaking region. Although some local winemakers believe in the potential of cabernet sauvignon and merlot, most have pinned their hopes on pinot noir and chardonnay. Within the next few years, pinot noir is expected to account for almost 50 percent of the vineyard. There are two particular pinot noir styles here: one tends to be more intensely fruit-driven and have higher alcohol, whereas the other is generally earthier and lighter.

The region's best chardonnays are stylistically complex, with flavors ranging beyond the realm of more fruit-driven styles. Sauvignon blanc also thrives here, producing wines that are intense in flavor. Many growers are also committed to high-quality, low-cropped riesling, which performs extremely well. Wairarapa/Wellington's pinot gris is among the best in the country. Also outstanding is the tiny quantity of gewürztraminer.

Some significant producers found in the region, in addition to those listed below, include Alana Estate, Alexander Vineyard, Benfield & Delamare, Hau Ariki, Lintz Estate, Margrain Vineyard, Murdoch James Estate, Palliser Estate, Stratford Wines, and Voss Estate.

ATA RANGI *Established* 1980 *Owners* Clive Paton, Phyll Pattie, Alison Paton, and Oliver Masters *Vineyard area* 25 acres (10 ha)

Ata Rangi's pinot noirs are among the best in the southern hemisphere. Their styles are consistently complex, multilayered, and richly textured. Ata Rangi also produces two barrel-fermented chardonnays: Craighall is designed for bottle maturation and marked by a savory complexity, while Petrie is for early drinking and has fruit to the fore. The savory Célèbre is cabernet/merlot based, untypically spiced with syrah, sangiovese, and nebbiolo, and contrasts with a charming rosé made from a similar blend. Recent additions to the range include a powerful pinot gris and a pure-fruit, young-vine pinot noir.

DRY RIVER WINES *Established* 1979 *Owners* Dawn and Neil McCallum *Vineyard area* 22 acres (9 ha)

Neil McCallum's stiffly spined, dark, and brooding pinot noir has achieved cult status. Low cropping from bunch-thinning and leaf-plucking ensure Dry River wines are deep in extract, concentrated, and complex, but never at the expense

of structure. All are crafted for long bottle maturation, err on the side of austerity, and on the whole require between five and ten years to open up. Recent results with syrah and viognier also suggest tremendous potential.

MARTINBOROUGH VINEYARD   *Established* 1980
Owners Derek and Duncan Milne, Claire Campbell, and Russel and Sue Schultz *Vineyard area* 67 acres (27 ha)

Both the Martinborough Vineyard Pinot Noir and the Reserve Pinot Noir are distinguished by a quest for greater complexity within the bounds of

The winery buildings at Palliser Estate are surrounded by gorgeous European-style gardens.

subtlety and multilayered textures. These wines are never as ripe and powerful as they could be, but always more interesting for it. Among the other varietals, the chardonnay is consistently rich and well structured for mature drinking, while the pinot gris, which is barrel-fermented in old oak, is one of New Zealand's finest. The Martinborough Vineyard Riesling and Late Harvest Riesling are also regularly among the best in their categories nationally.

TE KAIRANGA WINES   *Established* 1978 *Owners* 160 shareholders *Vineyard area* 86.5 acres (35 ha)

Te Kairanga's Reserve Chardonnay and Pinot Noir, formerly both hugely fruited, alcoholic, oaky, and a bit clumsy, have been transformed and now display greater complexity and tighter structures. Furthermore, the Castlepoint Cabernet/Merlot now ranks among the better buys in New Zealand reds.

The tasting room at renowned pinot noir producer, Martinborough Vineyard.

Marlborough

Located on the northeastern tip of the South Island and centered on the Wairau Valley and the town of Blenheim, Marlborough is New Zealand's largest wine region and home to its most famous viticultural product, Marlborough sauvignon blanc, which has wowed the wine world.

Marlborough is only the second-largest wine-producing area, but in terms of vineyard plantings it is by far the largest. Its subregions are Renwick/Rapaura, Fairhall, Brancott Valley, Omaka, the newish Waihopai, Awatere Valley, and the Kai-koura Ranges, a developing area that has yet to produce any wine.

One of Marlborough's greatest viticultural strengths is its free-draining alluvial soil, and variations in its makeup account for a stylistically diverse range of wines. It has a relatively cool maritime climate with abundant sunshine.

Sauvignon blanc is Marlborough's most widely planted grape variety, accounting for 42 percent of total vineyard area. The second most planted variety is chardonnay, followed by pinot noir, then riesling, cabernet sauvignon, and much smaller quantities of chenin blanc, breidecker, gewürztraminer, müller-thurgau, sémillon, pinot gris, cabernet franc, malbec, merlot, pinotage, and syrah.

With few exceptions, the sauvignon blanc from the Marlborough region tends to be more intense in flavor and have higher acid levels than sauvignon blanc produced in other parts of New Zealand. A new-style of sauvignon

blanc is slowly emerging that has more oak and malolactic fermentation influences, and can be aged. Marlborough's chardonnay can be of a very high quality, as can the riesling, which many winemakers believe has great, and as yet untapped, potential.

When it comes to red wines, winemakers have traditionally pinned their hopes on cabernet sauvignon. Merlot was long thought to hold promise for reds, but has failed to reach the planting levels of cabernet. Plantings of pinot noir have risen steadily, and have now claimed a place among the country's best.

Over the next few years, it is likely that sauvignon blanc wines will become even more dominant, occupying close to 50 percent of the total vineyard area. Plantings of chardonnay, pinot noir, and riesling are also likely to continue to increase; cabernet sauvignon is expected to continue a steady decline to around half its current plantings of 326 acres (132 ha).

Some significant producers in Marlborough, in addition to those below, are Brancott Estate,

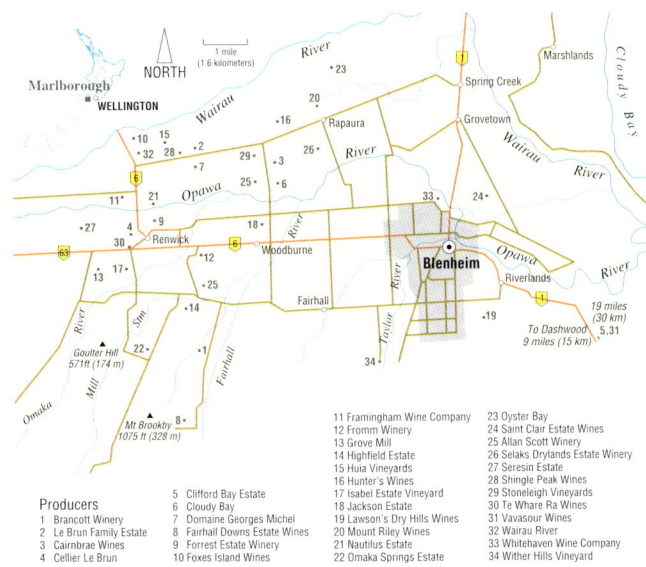

Producers
1 Brancott Winery
2 Le Brun Family Estate
3 Cairnbrae Wines
4 Cellier Le Brun
5 Clifford Bay Estate
6 Cloudy Bay
7 Domaine Georges Michel
8 Fairhall Downs Estate Wines
9 Forrest Estate Winery
10 Foxes Island Wines
11 Framingham Wine Company
12 Fromm Winery
13 Grove Mill
14 Highfield Estate
15 Huia Vineyards
16 Hunter's Wines
17 Isabel Estate Vineyard
18 Jackson Estate
19 Lawson's Dry Hills Wines
20 Mount Riley Wines
21 Nautilus Estate
22 Omaka Springs Estate
23 Oyster Bay
24 Saint Clair Estate Wines
25 Allan Scott Winery
26 Selaks Drylands Estate Winery
27 Seresin Estate
28 Shingle Peak Wines
29 Stoneleigh Vineyards
30 Te Whare Ra Wines
31 Vavasour Wines
32 Wairau River
33 Whitehaven Wine Company
34 Wither Hills Vineyard

Vines at Hunter's Wines, makers of benchmark sauvignon.

Le Brun Family Estate, Cairnbrae Wines, Clifford Bay Estate, Domaine Georges Michel, Fairhall Downs Estate Wines, Foxes Island Wines, Framingham Wine Company, Grove Mill, Jackson Estate, Lawson's Dry Hills Wines, Mount Riley Wines, Omaka Springs Estate, Oyster Bay, Saint Clair Estate Wines, Allan Scott Winery, Shingle Peak Wines, Te Whare Ra Wines, and Whitehaven Wine Company.

CELLIER LE BRUN *Established* 1980 *Owner* Recene Paint *Vineyard area* 79 acres (32 ha)

Style and quality are hallmarks here. The reasonably priced, well-made Terrace Road range includes a sauvignon blanc, chardonnay, *méthode traditionnelle*, and a pinot noir that is consistently among New Zealand's best buys. The sparkling range (which draws on chardonnay, pinot meunier, and/or pinot noir) includes a medium-bodied, yeasty Brut NV; the Brut Tache, a pinot-dominated rosé; and the crisp, elegant Blanc de Blancs.

CLOUDY BAY *Established* 1985 *Owners* Cape Mentelle and Veuve Clicquot Ponsardin *Vineyard area* 198 acres (80 ha)

All of Cloudy Bay's wines rank with the country's best. The sauvignon blanc is an explosion of mangoes, passionfruit, and pungent sweat, while the barrel-fermented Te Koko Sauvignon (pre-aged four years and on oak for 18 months) is quieter. The long-lived chardonnay is a flavor mix of low-yield fruit, French-oak fermentation, both wild and inoculated yeast, lees age, and partial malo. The Pelorus Méthode Traditionnelle, a barrel fermented pinot/chardonnay blend made with full malo, helped set a benchmark for top-end Kiwi bubblies. The Pinot Noir has steadily evolved a style that is multilayered, complex, and elegant. Made in small quantities, both the Late Harvest Riesling and relatively new Gewürztraminer are overlooked jewels.

FORREST ESTATE WINERY *Established* 1989 *Owner* John Forrest *Vineyard area* 173 acres (70 ha)

John Forrest has a preference for transparently fruited, nonoaked wine, and his portfolio has consistently shown savory complexities, suppleness, and structure. Strengths include a densely textured, lees-aged sauvignon blanc that carries a touch of barrel-fermented sémillon; a lees-influenced, lightly oaked, partially malo-fermented chardonnay; and, in ripe years, a plummy, richly textured merlot. Forrest is codeveloping a vineyard and label in Hawkes Bay, producing a Bordeaux blend branded Cornerstone.

Cloudy Bay is the iconic white of the South Pacific.

FROMM WINERY *Established* 1992 *Owners* Georg and Ruth Fromm *Vineyard area* 15 acres (6 ha)

Fromm's La Strada and, in good years, La Strada Reserve labels are marked by velvety textures, well-integrated fine tannins, rich flavors, and deep aromas. The consistency of La Strada Pinot Noir during the cool Marlborough 1995 and 1996 vintages had many local producers thinking they should pull out their cabernet and replace it with this grape. Fromm's radical approach has quietly begun a revolution that is only now yielding results.

HIGHFIELD ESTATE *Established* 1990 *Owners* Shin Yokoi and Thomas Tenuwera *Vineyard area* 10 acres (4 ha)

This modern winery has so far produced a commercial range of wines marked by safety rather than excitement. Its premium label, Elstree, has rarely commanded the quality or flair expected within its price bracket. The one exception is the Elstree Cuvée Méthode Traditionnelle, a light, elegant blend of equal parts chardonnay and pinot noir. The arrival of winemaker Alistair Soper may lead to improved wine quality.

HUIA VINEYARDS *Established* 1996 *Owners* Claire and Mike Allan *Vineyard area* 20.5 acres (8.3 ha)

This recently established winery should soon be among the very best of Marlborough's smaller

producers. The vineyards were chosen for their low vigor and planted with the newest French clones available. Winemaking here follows low-tech traditions, using natural yeast, minimal intervention, and no fining. First-release wines show great promise: the Dijon Clone 95/96 Chardonnay is subtle, minerally, long, and seamless with a fine viscosity; the gewürztraminer displays delicate rose-like aromas but is explosive and nervy on the palate; the spicy pinot gris has similar palate weight; and the fine-grained pinot noir has mushroom characters.

HUNTER'S WINES *Established* 1980 *Owner* Jane Hunter OBE *Vineyard area* 45 acres (18 ha)

Hunter's refreshingly herbaceous, passionfruit-filled, unoaked sauvignon blanc has a riper, fuller, barrel-influenced, fumé-styled cousin, which is a classic in its own right. The pure mendoza-clone chardonnay, incorporating purposely underplayed barrel fermentation, malo, and lees aging, was among the first New Zealand chardonnays to be recognized for its high quality. More recently, a steady refinement in the style of Hunter's pinot noir suggests a tremendous future. Two bargains

Cork or screw-caps?

Winemakers around the globe are seeking closure to one of the most contentious issues facing the wine industry—to use natural corks, synthetic corks, or screw-caps. Groups of winemakers in New Zealand and Australia, tired of seeing their efforts spoilt by cork taint, are leading the push for screw-caps. In Australia, it was riesling producers in the Clare Valley; in New Zealand, sauvignon blanc makers from Marlborough. In both countries the use of these superior but controversial closures has quickly spread.

of the Hunter's Wines range are an off-dry, spicy riesling and an intensely aromatic, creamy-textured gewürztraminer, both displaying deep extract and excellent acid support. A relationship with Domaine Chandon has ensured that Hunter's Brut consistently ranks in the country's top five sparkling wines.

ISABEL ESTATE VINEYARD   *Established* 1982
Owners Michael and Robyn Tiller *Vineyard area* 124 acres (50 ha)

Here, viticulture is paramount, intensive, and heading toward organic certification. Wine-making is *terroir*-oriented and noninterventionist, employing natural yeasts and soft handling. The three wines—Chardonnay, Sauvignon Blanc, and Pinot Noir—share a complex style, with transparent fruit underpinned by savory complexities, seamless textures, and great length. Isabel Estate Vineyard is a Marlborough winery that shows great deal of potential.

Frenchman Daniel le Brun showed wine industry sceptics that Marlborough could make great sparkling wine.

Lawson's Dry Hills estate is renowned for its intensely focused and stylish gewürztraminers.

NAUTILUS ESTATE   *Established* 1986 *Owner* Yalumba *Vineyard area* 54.3 acres (22 ha)

Generally, styles here show restraint and balance. The best wines include the complex, refined Cuvée Marlborough Méthode Traditionnelle; a classic, herbaceous sauvignon blanc; and a fine-grained, nutty chardonnay. The excellent-value second label, Twin Island, has successfully added the NV Pinot/Chardonnay Méthode Traditionnelle to a well-made, varietally defined chardonnay, sauvignon blanc, and riesling.

SELAKS DRYLANDS ESTATE WINERY
Established 1934 *Owner* Nobilo *Vineyard area* 45 acres (18 ha)

Since its takeover by Nobilo in 1998, the winery has produced Nobilo's multitiered Marlborough range, including its top-end Icon series. The Drylands' range quickly established itself in the mid-1990s with a run of bargain-priced, distinctive, single-vineyard wines including a herbaceous, passionfruit-laden, lees-aged sauvignon blanc and a barrel-fermented, lees-stirred chardonnay. Both are among Marlborough's best buys.

SERESIN ESTATE *Established* 1992 *Owner* Michael Seresin *Vineyard area* 136 acres (55 ha)

Intensive viticulture, clonal selection, and wild yeast ferments ensure complex, subtle, understated wines across Seresin's range. The low-cropped, varietally pure dry riesling is among Marlborough's top five, the sauvignon blanc (10 percent sémillon) is just as good, and the chardonnay, pinot gris, and pinot noir are distinguished by underplayed fruit, savoriness, finesse, and balance.

STONELEIGH VINEYARDS *Established* 1989 *Owner* Corbans *Vineyard area* 457 acres (185 ha)

Stoneleigh Vineyards is one of New Zealand's most internationally successful labels. Its strong reputation rests primarily on its zesty sauvignon blanc, which shows typical Marlborough "sweatiness," and the tightly knit, ripely fruited, honeysuckle-and-lime-scented riesling. The impressive range also includes a sharply priced, well-made, fruit-forward pinot noir and a more commercially driven, obviously oaked chardonnay.

VAVASOUR WINES *Established* 1986 *Owners* Tony Preston, Peter Vavasour, and 25 shareholders *Vineyard area* 72 acres (29 ha)

Vavasour's midpriced Dashwood wines are excellent value: rich and sharply etched in ripe years, and unexpectedly complex in difficult years when they incorporate declassified Vavasour. Both Vavasour's chardonnay and sauvignon blanc are barrel fermented, intense but supple, and finely balanced. Limited-quantity, single-vineyard versions are even more complex, concentrated, and refined. A pinot noir style is still evolving, but showing tremendous potential.

WAIRAU RIVER *Established* 1978 *Owners* Phil and Chris Rose *Vineyard area* 247 acres (100 ha)

Wairau's focus has been on a big, butter-and-oak chardonnay, and a zingy, full-bodied, herbs-and-passionfruit-scented sauvignon. Both are well made and reasonably priced.

WITHER HILLS VINEYARD *Established* 1987 *Owners* Brent and John Marris *Vineyard area* 230 acres (93 ha)

Since its establishment in 1987, Wither Hills has earned ten trophies, testament to the owners' original intention to make top-flight wine. From the first vintage, its chardonnay has been a Marlborough classic: huge, with mouthfilling tropical-fruit flavors, and butterscotch and toasted oak nuances. Wither Hills's sauvignon blanc has excelled for its opulent textures and intense tropical flavors, and the pinot noir has the potential to be one of the region's best.

Grove Mill draws mostly on Wairau Valley fruit for its wine.

Nelson is a small, isolated region with plenty of sunshine for ripening grapes.

GREENHOUGH VINEYARD & WINERY

Established 1980 *Owners* Andrew Greenhough and Jennifer Wheeler *Vineyard area* 12.4 acres (5 ha)

An existing vineyard was replanted with the clones and density determined to produce high-quality pinot noir, riesling, chardonnay, and sauvignon blanc. The wines of the reserve Hope Vineyard range are ripe, focused expressions of their respective varietals, with seamless textures, complexity, balance, and length. A star on the rise.

Nelson

Since the early 1970s, Nelson has attracted a small but dedicated band of winemakers. There are now 22 wineries in the region; however, most of them are small, covering just 2 percent of New Zealand's total vineyard area. Moreover, development is slow compared to other regions. Two long-established players, Seifried Estate and Neudorf Vineyards, dominate the region's production and profile.

Grapes are grown in two quite distinct areas around Nelson: the Waimea Plains and the Moutere Hills. Chardonnay is the most planted grape variety, followed by sauvignon blanc, pinot noir, and riesling. Other grape varieties include cabernet franc, cabernet sauvignon, malbec, gewürztraminer, merlot, pinot gris, and sémillon. White grapes have provided Nelson's most successful wines, with chardonnay and riesling being star performers, followed by sauvignon blanc.

Significant producers in Nelson, including those below, are Denton Winery, Glover's Vineyard, McCashins, Seifried Estate, Tohu Wines, and Waimea Estates.

NEUDORF VINEYARDS *Established* 1978 *Owners* Tim and Judy Finn *Vineyard area* 15 acres (6 ha)

Few would argue that Neudorf makes New Zealand's finest chardonnay. Both of Neudorf's chardonnays share similar seamless textures and a meltaway finish, but the Moutere is considerably more savory and slower to develop than the brighter-fruited, more forward Nelson. The Brightwater Riesling and the Sauvignon Blanc are often among the country's top examples of these varietals. The floral Brightwater is particularly dense and very long, whereas the sauvignon has a finely etched structure and strong aromas.

SPENCER HILL ESTATE *Established* 1990

Owners Philip and Sheryl Jones *Vineyard area* 57 acres (23 ha)

Tasman Bay Chardonnay is a big, fruit-driven, full-of-oak-and-butterscotch classic. The Tasman Bay Sauvignon Blanc and Pinot Noir consistently deliver a similar, fruit-forward message. The single-vineyard Spencer Hill range is nervier, concentrated, complex, savory, and seamless. Experiments with barrel-fermented pinot gris and pinotage are distinctive and promising.

Canterbury/ Waipara

The grape-growing areas of Canterbury and Waipara, on the east coast of New Zealand's South Island, are classified as a single entity, but in reality they are quite different. The soils, climates, and styles of wine produced in each area have little in common; indeed, all they share is an ability to produce excellent chardonnay, pinot noir, riesling, and, to a lesser extent, sauvignon blanc.

Together, Canterbury and Waipara form the country's fourth-largest wine-producing region, with just over 4 percent of the total national vineyard area. Currently, there are 39 wineries in Canterbury/Waipara. Canterbury has traditionally been the focus of grape growing and wine-making, but now Waipara is being recognized as a producer of top-quality, and perhaps even more consistent, wines.

There are two main grape-growing areas in Canterbury: Banks Peninsula and the Canterbury Plains, to the west of Christchurch. Generally, the soils are suited to chardonnay, pinot gris, pinot noir, and riesling, but it's too early in the region's viticultural life to say which locations best suit individual varieties.

The most planted varieties are chardonnay, pinot noir, and riesling, followed by pinot gris, sauvignon blanc, müller-thurgau, and small plantings of merlot, breidecker, sémillon, gewürztraminer, and syrah. Vintages tend to vary significantly from year to year due to climate variables.

Waipara has lower rainfall and fewer frost problems than Canterbury, and is sheltered from the cool, easterly breezes. Southerly winds are

Mountford Vineyard overlooks rolling countryside.

a double-edged sword, as they can interfere with fruit-set but can virtually eliminate overcropping, resulting in more intensely flavored wines.

The most planted grape variety in Waipara is sauvignon blanc, followed by riesling, chardonnay, and pinot noir. Cabernet sauvignon is the next most-planted variety, despite the fact that the resulting wines tend to be relatively herbaceous in flavor. It is followed at a long distance by cabernet franc, gewürztraminer, pinotage, and sémillon.

Significant producers in the region, in addition to those on the next two pages, are Chancellor, Fiddler's Green Wines, Floating Mountain, Melness Wines, Mountford Vineyard, Muddy Water Fine Wines, Torlesse Wines, and Waipara West.

Waipara's Mountford Vineyard specializes in only two varietals: chardonnay and pinot noir.

CANTERBURY HOUSE VINEYARDS *Established* 1997 *Owners* **Michael Reid and Kathleen Corsbie** *Vineyard area* **124 acres (50 ha)**

Plantings currently underway here will eventually produce chardonnay, merlot, pinot gris, pinot noir, sauvignon blanc, riesling, and viognier. Initial offerings have been impressive, and although the long-term plan is to focus on pinot noir, the sauvignon blanc was awarded a trophy for best of vintage in New Zealand. Canterbury's pinot gris and merlot are stylishly full-flavored.

GIESEN WINE ESTATE *Established* 1981 *Owners* **Theo, Alex, and Marcel Giesen** *Vineyard area* **124 acres (50 ha)**

Giesen Wine Estate is Canterbury's largest operation. Its wines have always demonstrated a remarkable European sense of balance, finesse, and restraint combined with clean, well-focused New Zealand fruit. The Marlborough Sauvignon Blanc is consistently one of New Zealand's best buys; so too is the low-yield, Pfalz-influenced, off-dry Riesling, which is floral and steely, and has mouthwatering acidity and high extract. The vineyard consistently produces the dry botrytis that drives one of the country's best late-harvested rieslings. During the mid-1990s, Giesen found repeated success with a complex pair of silky pinot noirs: one estate-grown, the second using fruit provided by

An English glass encased in colored cut crystal dates from the period 1900–1930.

Isabel Estate and other vineyards in Marlborough. Its restrained chardonnay is typical of the best Canterbury reserves, retaining a crisply acidic inner structure even after full malo and barrel fermentation. Most Giesen wines need a few years bottle aging.

KAITUNA VALLEY *Established* 1993 *Owners* **Grant and Helen Whelan** *Vineyard area* **25 acres (10 ha)**

The Whelans are pinot noir specialists, with vineyards in both South Canterbury and Marlborough's Awatere Valley. The former was replanted in 1999 with narrow rows of Burgundian clones of pinot noir and chardonnay. The owners' attention to intensive vineyard management is a reflection of their other business, a vine nursery. The pinot noir has won several trophies—testament to growing good fruit and letting it speak for itself.

ALAN MCCORKINDALE *Established* 1996 *Owner* **Alan McCorkindale** *Vineyard area* **5 acres (2 ha)**

Managing winemaker for many years at Corbans Marlborough, Alan McCorkindale has now established a small vineyard in Waipara to make *méthode traditionnelle* sparklers from selected clones of chardonnay, pinot noir, and pinot meunier. His first release, Millennium Brut, has an elegant style, savory flavors, and pronounced autolytic characters. McCorkindale also produces a riesling, chardonnay, pinot noir, and sauvignon blanc.

PEGASUS BAY *Established* 1992 *Owners* **Ivan and Chris Donaldson** *Vineyard area* **100 acres (40 ha)**

Pegasus Bay has established itself in a very short period as one of New Zealand's top

After years of service, decommissioned wine barrels are left to gather moss.

wineries. Generally, its wines are rich and ripe, but with added savory dimensions and multilayered complexities.

Pegasus rieslings have been outstanding: both the Arias, the off-dry and the late-harvest, are marked by silky, seamless textures; complex, varietally focused aromas; and rich, minerally flavors. The savory chardonnay employs Burgundian oxidative techniques, whole-bunch pressing, and extended lees aging to construct complexity and drive length. In sharp contrast, the whopping great sauvignon blanc/sémillon reeks of mango, guava, and other tropical fruits. The unfiltered, voluptuous pinot noir is headed in the right direction, although it has tended toward excessive alcohol and overripe fruit flavors in hot vintages. In these same hot years, however, the cabernet sauvignon/merlot shines splendidly, possessing classic cigar-box and cedar aromas, and dense textures. A second label, Main Divide, drawn from declassified Pegasus Bay and Marlborough fruit, can represent good value.

Pegasus Bay's landmark winery has been designed in a style that suggests a French château.

ST. HELENA WINE ESTATE *Established* 1978
Owner Robin Mundy *Vineyard area* 74 acres (30 ha)

Current winemaker Alan McCorkindale has lifted quality throughout St. Helena's good-value, but commercially styled, slightly pedestrian range. A recently introduced Reserve range (pinot noir, chardonnay, and pinot gris) has demonstrated sharper varietal definition as well as complexity, good length, and a dash of excitement. The future looks bright for St. Helena.

DANIEL SCHUSTER WINES *Established* 1984
Owners Daniel and Mari Schuster *Vineyard area* 42 acres (17 ha)

Daniel Schuster is an internationally respected "flying" viticulturist and coauthor of the classic work, *The Production of Grapes and Wine in Cool Climates*. As an early proponent of *terroir*-defined wine, and food-friendly styles, his views are often at odds with an industry known for its bold fruit. His Canterbury and pricey Selection range (chardonnay and pinot noir), made from Omihi Hills fruit, show restraint and subtlety.

Central Otago

Central Otago is the most southerly grape-growing region in the world. It is also one of New Zealand's smallest wine-producing regions, with just 2.5 percent of the total national vineyard area. Long-term this percentage is not expected to rise much. However, growth has been rapid in recent years with the success of pinot noir, which accounts for 73 percent of plantings. It is followed by chardonnay, riesling, pinot gris, and sauvignon blanc, and much smaller quantities of breidecker, gewürztraminer, sémillon, cabernet franc, cabernet sauvignon, merlot, and syrah. Future increases in vineyard area are expected to come mainly from increased plantings of pinot noir, pinot gris, and riesling.

Central Otago has four main subregions: Gibbston, Wanaka, Alexandra, and Cromwell, which is further divided into the three distinct areas of Bannockburn, Lowburn, and Bendigo. A fifth subregion, Lake Hayes, has few plantings, most of which are devoted to sparkling wine production. The area's most planted subregion is Cromwell, with 60 percent of the total vineyard, followed by Gibbston with 27 percent, Alexandra with 8 percent, and Wanaka with 4 percent.

Viticulture is marginal in Central Otago, the country's only inland wine region. Most vineyards here lie between 650 and 1,000 feet (200 and 300 m) above sea level and are planted on hillsides to take advantage of the region's high levels of sunshine and to avoid frost.

Differences in the style of wines arising from slight variations in climate and soil in each of the subregions are slowly being noticed. Gibbston and Wanaka, which are home to the oldest vines and have the coolest climates, tend to produce

Perrelle Lake Hayes aims to become the largest sparkling-wine producer in Central Otago, and the country's best.

more earthy, delicate styles of pinot noir compared to the more fruit-driven, lush styles emanating from other subregions. The warmest areas, Alexandra and Bannockburn, are already showing that they could yield outstanding chardonnay and gewürztraminer.

Both the chardonnay and sauvignon blanc grown in Central Otago tend to be higher in acid than elsewhere in New Zealand, although both produce classic fruit-driven styles. The region now has more than twice as many plantings of pinot noir as Wairarapa/Wellington. Central Otago also has the potential to produce top-quality pinot gris, plantings of which are increasing. As tends to occur with pinot gris, styles vary widely, from fresh and bracingly acidic to opulent and lush.

Some significant producers in the region, in addition to those below, are Black Ridge Wines, Mount Edward, Olssen's of Bannockburn, Peregrine, Perrelle Lake Hayes, Rippon Vineyard, and Two Paddocks.

CHARD FARM *Established* 1987 *Owners* Rob and Greg Hay *Vineyard area* 37 acres (15 ha)

Chard Farm's lees-stirred pinot gris, finely etched sauvignon blanc, and Judge and Jury Chardonnay are brilliant food wines, while the riesling and gewürztraminer often show great aromatic depth and a steely spine. The top pinot noirs (Finla Mor and Bragato) generally need time to marry textures and evolve savory characters. New secondary labels have been introduced, covering single-vineyard wines from emerging hot spots such as Bannockburn, Lowburn, and Lake Hayes.

FELTON ROAD WINES   *Established* 1991
Owners Stewart and Kate Elms   *Vineyard area* 30 acres (12 ha)

Felton Road arrived on the scene with a flourish of concentrated pinot noirs and a pair of richly textured, highly aromatic, steely rieslings (dry and semidry). Early success owes much to the winery's warm location, devotion to low-yield viticulture, and employment of traditional winemaking practices, including the use of wild yeasts to stamp *terroir* on the wines from inception.

GIBBSTON VALLEY WINES   *Established* 1981
Owner Ross McKay   *Vineyard area* 74 acres (30 ha)

This is one of Central Otago's largest wineries. When the local vintage is strong, the wines are site specific; in more difficult years, cross-blending helps fill in the gaps. Winemaker Grant Taylor's pinot noirs, which display the deep perfume, rich texture, and firm structure that typify cool-climate

Gibbston Valley Wines' cellar in Central Otago.

pinot, have won seven major international trophies. Other highlights from this winery include a finely balanced, complex riesling; a nervy, well-focused pinot gris from 20-year-old vines; and the excellent-value, unwooded Greenstone Chardonnay.

QUARTZ REEF   *Established* 1996   *Owner* Bendigo Estate Partnership   *Vineyard area* 7.4 acres (3 ha)

Quartz Reef Chauvet NV Méthode Traditionnelle (80 percent pinot noir and 20 percent chardonnay) is made from Marlborough fruit and aged two years on lees. Its strawberry characters and creamy palate are clearly shaped by French and Austrian concepts of elegance and restraint. Other projects include a pinot noir and a pinot gris, both of which display multilayered complexity.

Rippon Vineyard in Central Otago, which produces a pinot noir that is often among New Zealand's best.

Canada

Melville I.

Banks
Island

Prince
of Wales
Island

Admundsen
Gulf

Gulf of Boothia

Baffin Island

Victoria
Island

Fort McPherson

Mackenzie

Koidern

Mt Logan
19,550 ft (5959 m)

Yukon Territory

Haines Junction

Whitehorse

Great
Bear Lake

North West Territories

Mackenzie Mountains

Fort Simpson

Yellowknife

Great
Slave Lake

Watson Lake

Hay River

CANADA

Dubawnt
Lake

Nunavut

Baker Lake

Repulse Bay

Foxe
Basin

Southampton
Island

Cape Dorset

Salli

Yathkyed
Lake

Nueltin
Lake

HUDSON
BAY

ROCKY

British
Columbia

Alberta

Peace

Lake Athabasca

Wollaston
Lake

Athabasca

Cree Lake

Reindeer
Lake

Churchill

Churchill

Belcher
Islands

Peace River

Churchill
Lake

Nelson

Fort Severn

Queen
Charlotte
Islands

La Ronge

Manitoba

Severn

James
Bay

Mt Waddington
13,176 ft (4016 m)

MOUNTAINS

Edmonton

Saskatchewan

Cedar
Lake

Grand
Rapids

Lake
Winnipeg

Ontario

Moose
Factory

Albany

Vancouver
Island

Kamloops

Saskatoon

Lake
Winnipegosis

Fraser

Calgary

Fraser
Valley

Lake Okanagan
Kelowna

Vancouver

Okanagan
Valley

Medicine Hat

Regina

Lake
Manitoba

Lake
Seul

Kenora

Lake
Nipigon

Victoria

Vancouver Island

Winnipeg

Lake of
the Woods

Thunder Bay

Lake
Superior

Sud

Lake

Lake Michigan

Lake Erie
North Shore
Pelee Island

NORTH

200 miles
(320 kilometers)

Canada

Canada was hardly recognized as a wine-producing country until an Ontario dessert wine—the 1989 Inniskillin Vidal Icewine—won the Grand Prix d'Honneur at the 1991 Vinexpo in Bordeaux. This and subsequent prize-winning wines reflect the improvement in quality achieved since 1970 in the effort to counter Canada's legacy of inferior wines. Conscientious producers have worked together to develop an appellation system based on European models.

The Vintners' Quality Alliance (VQA) governs the use of geographic or varietal designations, grape types, and viticultural and winemaking practices. Now codified in the legislation of two producing provinces, Ontario and British Columbia, VQA requires passage into law at the federal level before international acceptance is complete.

The sale of alcoholic beverages in Canada is controlled by provincial monopolies (apart from Alberta, where it is privatized) and, consequently, wine prices carry heavy markups. These monopoly markup systems are so inflexible that many Canadian wines are sold only in the province of origin.

History

Experience has shown that wine from indigenous North American grapes comes up short on palatability. If it is true that Lief Ericsson's crew made wine from the grapes they found in 1001, they could be forgiven for a hearty endorsement of the wine's virtues after their harsh ocean crossing.

When Europeans arrived and settled in and around Québec and Montréal in the sixteenth century, wine was among their many deprivations. As in many areas of European settlement, the Catholic Church was instrumental in early wine production. In Canada, these early wines were based on local grapes and, according to the Jesuit missionaries, they were suitable only for mass. Since then, vineyardists have been searching for more desirable grape types that can survive the harsh climate, and experimentation has identified zones where *vinifera* vines can thrive.

Nineteenth-century cut-glass decanter.

Winemaking began in earnest in Ontario when Count Justin de Courtney purchased and expanded on some 1811 plantings near Toronto. He had some success in the 1860s producing wines from European varieties. Meanwhile, the regions that produce Ontario's wine today were being established on the Niagara Peninsula and Pelee Island. However, Ontario wine producers faced an uphill battle against the growing temperance movement. The ensuing struggle lasted more than 30 years, profoundly affecting the nature of the wines produced, and the results are still seen in the government monopoly on alcohol sales introduced in the early 1940s.

Riesling icewine grapes on the Niagara Peninsula, Ontario.

In British Columbia, winery development took a similar path if on a smaller scale. The first vineyard in BC's Okanagan Valley was planted in the nineteenth century by the Oblate fathers to make wine for sacramental purposes. Commercial ventures were established around Lake Okanagan, then other areas followed on Vancouver Island and on some smaller islands between Vancouver Island and the mainland. Much of the early wine industry centered on fruit other than grapes, and it wasn't until an oversupply of apples in the 1930s caused prices to drop that many farmers turned to grapes.

In the 1960s, light and sweet sparkling wines became the rage in North America. Fortunately it was a temporary fad and consumers gradually started to demand greater variety, which was fulfilled by an increase in imported European table wines. Many Canadian vineyards have now reached the levels of maturity that support the development of superpremium wines. The concomitant investment in technology has moved the Canadian wine industry into a position where it can compete with confidence at the international level.

Niagara Falls, on the Niagara Peninsula, with American Falls on the left and Horseshoe Falls on the right.

Wine is made in four distinct zones across Canada where microclimates provide respite from winter's icy blast. Ontario has the lion's share, with 80 percent of the country's wineries located on the Niagara Peninsula. The remaining three areas are in British Columbia, Québec, and Nova Scotia. Because of the marginal climate, both hybrid and *vinifera* grape varieties are used, but with emphasis on the latter. In the past the emphasis was on white grape varieties, although several reds—notably cabernet franc, pinot noir, and gamay—have now been found to produce well.

Landscape and climate

Winter is the most critical climatic factor influencing the production of wine in Canada. Even the most vine-conducive regions are susceptible to the occasional spell of –4°F (–20°C) weather. Where wine is most successfully produced, large bodies of water provide some degree of protection against extreme cold and spring frost.

The Niagara Peninsula is located on the same latitude as Tuscany, but lacks the benefit of a Mediterranean climate. Fortunately, the certainty of freezing temperatures assures consistent production of icewine. That vines can survive in Ontario at all is due to the mitigating influence of Lake Ontario and Lake Erie. In British Columbia, winemaking is dominated by tiny wineries. Most of the production occurs in the Okanagan Valley, where the altitude and semidesert environment give wines their lively flavors and high acidity.

The climates of Québec and Nova Scotia are less conducive to vine growing, particularly *vinifera* varieties. In Québec, the hybrids seyval, vidal, and maréchal foch exhibit the required characteristics. In the maritime province Nova Scotia, the industry survives by blending local wines with imported wines, but homegrown specialties are produced. Two hardy Russian varieties, michurinetz and severny from the genus *Amurensis*, are cultivated locally.

Vines and wines

Some very palatable wines are made with vidal, seyval blanc, maréchal foch, and baco noir (early

> *Wine is one of the most civilized things in the world and one of the most natural things of the world that has been brought to the greatest perfection, and it offers a greater range for enjoyment and appreciation than, possibly, any other purely sensory thing.*
> ERNEST HEMINGWAY (1899–1961),
> *Death in the Afternoon*

Parliament Hill in Ontario.

French vines that were cross-pollinated with indigenous varieties). Many single varietal wines are produced in all wine-growing regions in Canada, while blends of classic Bordeaux varieties, particularly reds, are increasing in Ontario and British Columbia. Proprietary blends are made for the lower price ranges, but are not entitled to a VQA designation. Preferred *vinifera* grapes are mostly French and German varietals. Hybrids are grown in all provinces and are the mainstay of the industry in Québec and Nova Scotia. A few specified, high-quality hybrids are permitted by the VQA designation in Ontario and BC.

Laws

To varying degrees, the governments in Canadian provinces control the sale of alcoholic beverages, however, winery owners have designed a set of standards regarding the production of wine. The Vintners' Quality Alliance (VQA) was established in Ontario in 1989 as a voluntary set of regulations. The VQA Act passed the Ontario provincial legislature in 1990, to become law in mid-2000. A similar system has been adopted in British Columbia, with some minor variance in criteria. Discussions aimed at harmonizing the Ontario and BC guidelines to form "VQA Canada" standards are progressing. Talks are also underway with Québec and Nova Scotia. The VQA rules cover a variety of quality issues.

Meanwhile, it is difficult to obtain Canadian wine outside the producing province—the liquor monopolies treat wine made in another province as an import, forcing prices up.

British Columbia

Although much of BC's early wine was made from fruit other than grapes, a handful of purists persisted in seeking the appropriate varietals and the most suitable locations. Those locations have been largely confined to the Okanagan Valley, with a few vineyards established in the Fraser Valley, and on Vancouver Island.

One of many significant events that changed BC's wine industry in the twentieth century was the Canada–U.S. Free Trade Agreement. The agreement caused a major crisis as it became apparent that continued dependence on hybrid varieties would not provide a competitive edge in the liberalized market. Eventually, growers tore up about 65 percent of their acreage and replanted with *vinifera* vines. Many of these new *vinifera* plantings leaned more to French varietals, such as chardonnay, pinot blanc, and pinot gris. Consequently, more wineries started to produce drier, French-style wines. Initial plantings of reds in the warmer, southern end of the Okanagan Valley are promising. Pinot noir, cabernet franc, merlot, and cabernet sauvignon are all in demand.

The 1993 International Wine and Spirits Competition confirmed that the BC wine industry had come of age when it conferred the Avery Trophy for Best Chardonnay in the World on the 1992 Mission Hill Grand Reserve Chardonnay.

Gewürztraminer grapes, a variety suited to BC's climate.

OKANAGAN VALLEY

The majority of British Columbia wineries are found in the Okanagan Valley, parts of which experience near-desert conditions. Etched out by a retreating glacier, this long, steep valley runs north–south, nearly equidistant from the Rocky Mountains to the east and the Pacific coast to the west. The southernmost tip of the valley reaches almost to the United States border. Lake Okanagan stretches for about 62 miles (100 km) and is a mitigating influence on climatic extremes. Consistent and predictable summers provide a favorable environment for vines.

In the warmest area, south of Lake Okanagan, rainfall is very low and irrigation is a necessity. At the southernmost point of the valley, Osoyoos Lake is a mitigating influence in winter. Just north of this, part of the west side of the valley is called the "Golden Mile" for its row of contiguous wine properties. Further to the north, the area around Okanagan Falls and Vaseaux Lake also enjoys reliably hot daytime temperatures. Continuing north, Naramata supports a wide range of grape types from hardy ehrenfelser to heat-loving syrah. Kelowna, in central Okanagan, is slightly cooler and from there north, crisp, flavorful German-style whites abound. Pinot noir and chardonnay are also cultivated successfully.

Significant producers in the Okanagan Valley, in addition those below, include Andrés Wines, Blue Mountain Vineyard & Cellars, Burrowing Owl Vineyards, Calona Wines, Cedar Creek Estate Winery, Domaine Combret, Gehringer Brothers Estate Winery,

Producers
1 Andrés Wines
2 Blue Mountain Vineyard & Cellars
3 Burrowing Owl Vineyards
4 Calona Wines
5 Cedar Creek Estate Winery
6 Domaine Combret
7 Gehringer Brothers Estate Winery
8 Gray Monk Cellars
9 Hainle Vineyards
10 Inniskillin Okanagan Vineyards
11 Kettle Valley Winery
12 Lang Vineyards
13 Mission Hill Winery
14 Nichol Vineyard & Farm Winery
15 Poplar Grove Farm Winery
16 Quails' Gate Estate Winery
17 St-Hubertus Estate Winery
18 St-Laszlo Vineyards
19 Sumac Ridge Estate Winery
20 Summerhill Estate Winery
21 Tinhorn Creek Vineyards
22 Vincor International
23 Wild Goose Vineyards

Vineyards at Naramata in the Okanagan Valley, BC.

Still at Mission Hill Winery, Okanagan Valley, BC.

acquired many accolades for their wines. Winery founder Bob Shaunessy was initially influenced by the success of the Napa Valley, and this influence is evident in the use of American oak and in the concentrated flavor of the wines.

VANCOUVER ISLAND

The Cowichan Valley on Vancouver Island and the few wineries on nearby smaller islands enjoy a milder climate more like that of Ontario's Niagara Peninsula than that of the Okanagan. The wines from this area show soft acids and rich fruit flavors. Wineries are a fairly new phenomenon for the island, but initial results indicate that this region has good potential.

Gray Monk Cellars, Hainle Vineyards, Inniskillin Okanagan Vineyards, Kettle Valley Winery, Lang Vineyards, Mission Hill Winery, Nichol Vineyard & Farm Winery, Poplar Grove Farm Winery, Quail's Gate Estate Winery, St. Hubertus Estate Winery, St. Laszlo Vineyards, Summerhill Estate Winery, and Wild Goose Vineyards.

VENTURI-SCHULZE VINEYARDS   *Established* 1993 *Owners* Giordano Venturi and Marilyn Schulze *Vineyard area* 20 acres (8 ha)

Initially, 25 different grape varieties were planted here. From those, the 11 best performers were chosen—pinot noir, auxerrois, pinot gris, schönberger, madeleine sylvaner, siegerrebe, ortega, kerner, chasselas, gewürztraminer, and madeleine angevin—to remain in this organically farmed vineyard. Only very small quantities of handcrafted wines are produced at Venturi-Schulze.

SUMAC RIDGE ESTATE WINERY   *Established* 1979 *Owner* Vincor International Inc. *Vineyard area* 131 acres (53 ha)

Sumac Ridge, the first medium-size winery in BC, was sold in early 2000 to Vincor International Inc., Canada's largest wine company. It was established by Harry McWatters, who, in 1991, went into partnership with Bob Wareham to develop Black Sage Vineyards—some of the best vineyard land in Canada and the major source of grapes for Sumac Ridge. Black Sage is planted with premium varietals, mostly red, including cabernet sauvignon, cabernet franc, merlot, pinot noir, and malbec. Its white varieties include chardonnay, pinot blanc, and sauvignon blanc. Oak is an important element in the Sumac Ridge style.

FRASER VALLEY

The Fraser Valley, with its temperate and humid climate, produces wines with a softer flavor profile than those from the Okanagan Valley.

DOMAINE DE CHABERTON   *Established* 1991 *Owner* Claude Violet *Vineyard area* 55 acres (22 ha)

Domaine de Chaberton is the only winery growing grapes in this BC designation just north of the United States border. The wines, from bacchus, madeleine angevine, madeleine sylvaner, ortega, chardonnay, and chasselas doré, are sold locally as well as being exported to various destinations.

TINHORN CREEK VINEYARDS   *Established* 1993 *Owners* Bob and Barbara Shaunessy, and Kenn and Sandra Oldfield *Vineyard area* 160 acres (65 ha)

Tinhorn Creek is a successful partnership between the Shaunessys and the Oldfields. Sandra Oldfield is the winemaker and Kenn Oldfield is the viticulturalist and general manager. The partners have

Ontario

The wine industry in Ontario looked extremely promising in 1867, when judges at the French exposition in Paris recorded that the Canadian wine submitted by Count Justin de Courtney "resembled more the great French table wines than any other foreign wines" they had tasted.

During the time de Courtney was seeking favor in Europe, a handful of vineyardists had discovered the potential of the Niagara Peninsula and, at the turn of the century, there were 35 commercial wineries operating there. The grape variety most commonly used then was the concord, an indigenous labrusca variety, which is virtually indestructible but it is better suited to making juice and jelly than making wine.

Coincident with the growth of wineries, however, came an increasingly strong temperance movement. The movement's influence culminated in the Ontario Temperance Act of 1916 prohibiting the sales of beverage alcohol. During the 1930s alcoholic beverages were legalized, but sales were restricted to government-run shops in a monopoly system. It has been liberalized over the years, but tight control remains over selection and pricing.

The wine-producing areas of Ontario benefit from the proximity of two of the Great Lakes, Ontario and Erie. In the summer, the lakes absorb and hold enough heat to cushion winter's frigid attack. The exchange of warm and cool air creates a constant flow that benefits most of the areas where vines are grown.

In the late 1970s, the provincial government's wine-industry assistance program included five-year interest-free loans to replant vineyards with *vinifera* and superior hybrid vines. Most growers planted white grapes known to be cold resistant, but some planted a broad range of white varietals and a number of reds. Now it has been shown that the vines can thrive, the percentage of red grapes has increased significantly. Favored reds are cabernet franc, pinot noir, merlot, cabernet sauvignon, gamay noir, baco noir, maréchal foch, and a few plantings of syrah. Favored whites are chardonnay, riesling, pinot blanc, pinot gris, gewürztraminer, chenin blanc, sémillon, and vidal.

Right: *Pinot noir grapes at Inniskillin vineyard, Ontario.*
Below: *The imposing entrance to the De Sousa winery in Ontario.*

NIAGARA PENINSULA

Lake Ontario's influence diminishes inland, on a level plain where cold air can settle. This means that spring frosts are often a problem here, and protective measures such as using fans to move the air are sometimes needed to prevent damage. In summer, however, temperatures rise quickly and fruit matures well—the heat contributes to ripeness, which translates into intense flavors. Chardonnay, for example, can show tropical nuances not found in the cooler Niagara Bench vineyards that are even further inland. There, the terrain slopes up the side of the Niagara Escarpment, and the area is characterized by good drainage and constant air circulation, which almost eliminates the risk of spring frost and humidity-related disease. The cooler environment of the bench encourages the acid needed for balance and elegance, while the warmer temperatures of the plain impart more intensity and richness.

Significant producers located on the Niagara Peninsula, in addition to those below, include Château des Charmes, Hernder Estate Wines, Hillebrand Estates, Kittling Ridge Estate Wines & Spirits, Konzelmann Winery, Lakeview Cellars Estate Winery, Magnotta Winery, Marynissen Estates, Peller Estates, Stonechurch Vineyards, Stoney Ridge Cellars, and Strewn Estate Winery.

Icewine

Half of Canada's wineries are clustered together in an agricultural region just minutes from Niagara Falls—the Niagara Peninsula. Known for decades as Canada's Banana Belt, the region is experiencing unprecedented growth. While garnering international attention as a producer of world-class icewine—the extreme climate facilitates production of this supersweet yet piercingly acidic wine—the jury is still out on its dry whites and reds. As with other developing regions, most local producers look to the superripe, highly extracted, and highly alcoholic styles popularized by the American wine press as their role models, rather than focusing on developing signature styles that are reflective of their origin.

CAVE SPRING CELLARS *Established* 1986
Owners Len Pennachetti and Angelo Pavan *Vineyard area* 155 acres (63 ha)

Cave Spring Cellars's ultrapremium wines exhibit concentrated fruit, reflecting their Beamsville Bench *terroir* and winemaker Angelo Pavan's signature elegance. This is one of the few medium-size wineries here to use only *vinifera* varieties. The beautiful stone winery building is a renovated 1870 apple warehouse.

HENRY OF PELHAM

Established 1983 *Owners* Speck family *Vineyard area* 225 acres (91 ha)

The Specks and winemaker Ron Giesbrecht concentrate on four varietals—riesling, chardonnay, cabernet sauvignon, and baco noir. They are the region's best producer of baco noir.

Producers
1 Cave Spring Cellars
2 Château des Charmes
3 Henry of Pelham
4 Hernder Estate Wines
5 Hillebrand Estates
6 Inniskillin Wines Inc.
7 Kittling Ridge Estate Wines & Spirits
8 Konzelmann Winery
9 Lakeview Cellars Estate Winery
10 Magnotta Winery
11 Malivoire Wine Company
12 Marynissen Estates
13 Peller Estates
14 Pillitteri Estates
15 Reif Estate Winery
16 Stonechurch Vineyards
17 Stoney Ridge Cellars
18 Strewn Estate Winery
19 Thirty Bench Vineyard & Winery
20 Vincor International Inc
21 Vineland Estate Wines
22 Willow Heights Winery

Temperatures are critical and must be between 18°F (–8°C) and 3°F (–16°C) when picking and crushing icewine grapes.

INNISKILLIN WINES INC. *Established* 1975
Owners Vincor International Inc. *Vineyard area* 120 acres (49 ha)

Inniskillin started the quality wine revolution in Canada when Donald Ziraldo and Karl Kaiser applied for a boutique winery license at a time when the industry was dominated by large companies selling wines of few redeeming features. They introduced well-made and representative varietal wines and, later, single-vineyard labels. When the 1989 Inniskillin Vidal Icewine won a gold medal at Vinexpo in 1991, Canada was finally recognized on the international stage as a cool-climate wine-producing country.

MALIVOIRE WINE COMPANY *Established* 1998
Owners Martin Malivoire and Moira Saganski *Vineyard area* 65 acres (26 ha)

Martin Malivoire erected a large Quonset hut on a slope of the escarpment, where he takes advantage of gravity to limit the need for pumps. The winery focuses on premium wines from gewürztraminer, chardonnay, pinot noir, and pinot gris. Under the direction of consultant winemaker Ann Sperling, the wines reflect elegance and balance. Ann has bottled several wines using both natural and synthetic corks and will compare them during their maturation.

PILLITTERI ESTATES WINERY *Established* 1993
Owner Gary Pillitteri *Vineyard area* 37 acres (15 ha)

Winery founder Gary Pillitteri came to Canada from Sicily after World War II and started growing grapes in the Niagara. Already a reputed amateur winemaker, Gary inaugurated his winery in 1993. A second generation of Pillitteris and their spouses now manage the vineyards, farm market, bakery, greenhouse, and tasting room. Winemaker Sue-Ann Staff produces a range of wines including barrel-aged chardonnay, riesling dry, pinot grigio, vidal sussreserve, gewürztraminer icewine, and cabernet sauvignon.

Wine education at Hillebrand Estates, Ontario.

REIF ESTATE WINERY   *Established* 1983 *Owner* Ewald Reif *Vineyard area* 135 acres (55 ha)

Ewald Reif's scenic vineyard, along the gorge of the Niagara River where it spills into Lake Ontario, benefits from the effects of the massive lake. In 1987, Ewald's nephew Klaus took up winemaking duties and immediately made a reputation for himself with a stunning vidal icewine that was subsequently included in Robert Parker's top ten of the year. Klaus now shares winemaking responsibilities with Roberto de Domenico.

THIRTY BENCH VINEYARD & WINERY   *Established* 1994 *Owners* Dr. Tom Muckle, Yorgos Papageorgiou, Frank Zeritsch, and Deborah Paskus *Vineyard area* 40 acres (16 ha)

This tiny winery boasts the "driest vineyard on the (Niagara) bench." Riesling is the emphasis here, and all styles are made. Increasing quantities of vidal, chardonnay, and a range of red *vinifera* are also made. The winery's philosophy emphasizes extensive cropping and long barrel aging.

VINELAND ESTATE WINES   *Established* 1988 *Owner* John Howard *Vineyard area* 300 acres (122 ha)

This winery is perched high on the side of the Niagara Escarpment. The constant flow of air from Lake Ontario protects the vineyards by minimizing the effects of extreme heat and cold. Riesling is the most planted grape on the estate, the legacy of previous owner, German grape-grower Herman Weis. It thrives on the well-drained slope of clay and loam. Winemaker Brian Schmidt is expanding the repertoire of red and white varieties with notable success.

WILLOW HEIGHTS WINERY   *Established* 1994 *Owners* Ron and Avis Speranzini *Vineyard area* 12 acres (5 ha)

Ron Speranzini's goal is to emulate the wines of Burgundy. He makes very limited quantities of handcrafted pinot. In 1998, the yield was thinned to 2 tons per acre (35 hl/ha), and the resulting wine showed delicate red berry fruit with a very elegant, balanced structure. Besides pinot noir, wines include chardonnay, riesling, vidal, gewürztraminer, merlot, and cabernet franc.

LAKE ERIE NORTH SHORE AND PELEE ISLAND

In the Lake Erie North Shore and Pelee Island regions, summer temperatures are warmer than in Niagara. However, Lake Erie is considerably shallower than Lake Ontario and cools more quickly in winter. In colder years, the lake freezes over and ice packs often surround Pelee Island.

COLIO WINES OF CANADA   *Established* 1978 *Owners* Enzo DeLuca and Joe Berardo *Vineyard area* 180 acres (73 ha)

The Colio vineyards are located within the North Shore Lake Erie VQA appellation, however, the winery buys grapes from all three of Ontario's delimited grape-growing areas. Many of Colio's wines are brand-named and sold within the lower price ranges, but they manage to escape the ordinary by reason of winemaker Carlo Negri's flair. A new line, which was established in 1999 under the Colio Estates Vineyard label, introduced premium and ultrapremium wines. It includes a line of red and white varietals and a vidal icewine.

Other Canadian Regions

QUÉBEC

Québec has a difficult climate for vine growing, particularly of *vinifera* varieties. Winter is vine-splittingly cold; summers are short and often humid. The region in which grapes are grown is situated on a vast glacial plain to the south and southeast of Montréal. The western sector of this plain—the Montérégie—is slightly warmer than neighboring Eastern Townships, where vineyards are clustered around Dunham. Experience shows that some varieties that grow well in the Monté-régie are not so successful in the Townships.

Vinifera varieties are in the minority here, although some growers have microclimates where auxerrois, chardonnay, and riesling can thrive. Preferred white hybrids are seyval blanc, vidal, cayuga, geisenheim, éona, and cliche-vandal; de chaunac, maréchal foch, st croix, seyval noir, baco noir, and chancellor are favored for reds. One advantage of the cold is that in some of the lesser varieties, the least attractive characteristics are minimized, in particular a peculiar musky odor termed "foxy."

Some significant producers in Québec include Vignoble Les Arpents de Neige, Vignoble Dietrich-Jooss, Vignoble Morou, Vignoble de L'Orpailleur, La Vitacée, and Domaine des Côtes D'Ardoise where riesling and gamay are grown as well as a number of successful hybrids.

NOVA SCOTIA

Although Nova Scotia's climate is only marginally suitable for growing grapes, the hardy Russian varieties michurinetz and severny do thrive here.

Also, trials have shown that certain resistant *vinifera* vines can grow in protected microclimates.

Wineries are located in the Annapolis Valley, bordering the Bay of Fundy, and on the northeast shore overlooking the Northumberland Strait. In both cases sheltered waters provide the necessary mitigating forces. A climatic advantage here is that the slow ripening of grapes over a cool summer benefits the flavor and structure of the wine.

Only about 200 acres (80 ha) of vines are growing in the province. Plantings of early-ripening *vinifera* vines are increasing. Grapes of choice are seyval blanc, new york muscat, l'acadie blanc, and geisenheim clone gm for whites. The most widely planted reds are michurinetz and maréchal foch. Significant producers here include Jost Vineyards, planted mostly with hybrids; and Sainte Famille Wines, with thriving plantings of chardon-nay, riesling, cabernet franc, and a selection of hybrids.

Right: *Riesling grapes.*
Below: *Château Frontenac, Québec City, Québec.*

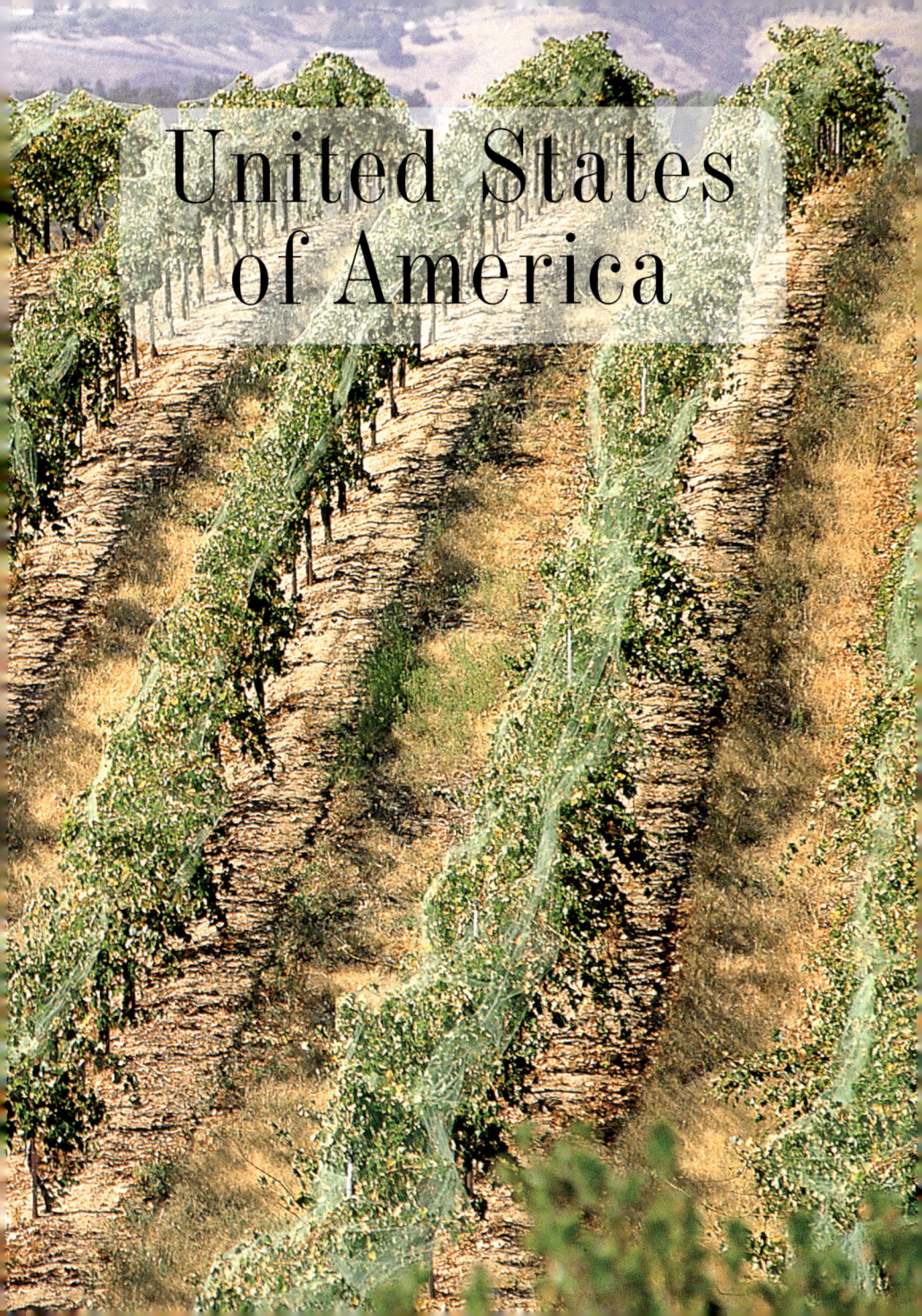

United States
of America

United States of America

Now the fourth-largest wine producer worldwide, America's impact upon the vine has loomed large. Phylloxera, Prohibition, the University of California at Davis, and scientific and economic clout have shaped the American and the international wine industries.

Grapevines were so abundant in the wilds of North America that explorer Leif Ericsson called it "Vineland." Early European settlers were dismayed that the native varieties produced wine with an unpleasant "foxy" characteristic. Grapevines traveled back and forth across the Atlantic. In the late 1800s the great regions of Europe were decimated by the root louse phylloxera—a native of North American soils, taken to Europe via cuttings.

Although native American vines are resistant to the louse, the pest infested European vineyards. Although the source of the devastation,

America was also the source of the cure, in the form of resistant rootstock for grafting. California dominates the American wine industry and the vine's ascendancy in the United States is directly linked to California's history. Early colonists soon turned from native varieties to imported grape varieties and winemaking expertise from Europe for their wine needs.

1 Hudson River Region
2 Western Connecticut Highlands
3 Southeastern New England
4 Central Delaware Valley
5 Lancaster Valley
6 Cumberland Valley
7 Catoctin
8 Shenandoah Valley
9 Northern Neck George
   Washington Birthplace
10 Monticello
11 North Fork of Roanoke
12 Rocky Knob

GULF OF MEXICO

NORTH

200 miles
(320 kilometers)

Christianity was significant in establishing viticulture in California, New Mexico, and Texas. In 1769, Father Juniperro Serra founded the first of 21 California missions (in San Diego). By 1823 these had reached Sonoma County at Solano. In 1833 the missions were secularized by the Mexican government and a small-scale wine industry evolved. By the early 1900s, Sonoma was the wine center of the United States. French, Swiss, and Italian winemakers greatly improved wine quality—California wine was winning awards in Europe.

Meanwhile, production in Ohio reached its peak in the 1850s. A challenging climate, industrial expansion, and the rise of California combined to stem production in the eastern states.

Prohibition (1919–1933) was a serious blow to the wine industry, and recovery was slow as the nation had developed a preference for spirits in the meantime.

The 1960s heralded the modern era of wine production with Joe Heitz and Robert Mondavi opening wineries in the Napa Valley. Mondavi embarked on vineyard and winery trials in a successful quest for quality. Château Ste. Michelle and Columbia Winery first put Washington State on the map. Gallo greatly impacted the industry by introducing chablis blanc and hearty burgundy in 1964. In 1973 Moët & Chandon began production of Chandon Sparkling Wine in Napa Valley and was the first champagne house in the United States. The 1973 vintage produced California wines that shook the wine world by winning the famed Paris tasting. This 1976 competition pitted California chardonnay and cabernet sauvignon against top wines from Burgundy and Bordeaux. The French judges ranked the 1973 Stag's Leap Cabernet Sauvignon the top red and the 1973 Château Montelena Chardonnay the top white—creating a marketing bonanza for the California wine industry.

The unstoppable David Lett and other pinot noir specialists established vineyards and wineries in Oregon during the early 1970s. Further California expansion took place in 1979 with Opus One, a joint venture between Mondavi and Baron Philippe de Rothschild. Producers from other parts of the world have followed with ventures in California, including Torres, Moueix, Perrin, Antinori, and Southcorp.

Prices stagnated in the late 1980s as supply exceeded demand. A new strain of phylloxera—biotype-B—appeared in Napa Valley and spread throughout California and into Oregon. As most of California's vines were planted on AXR-1 or *Vitis vinifera* stock, this created much damage. Luckily, the spread of phylloxera and the time to vine death takes years, allowing the existing vineyards to be ripped out and replanted with resistant rootstock.

A specially designed cup for sampling wine from tanks or vats.

Producers faced enormous debts that forced them into partnerships and restructured corporations. Nevertheless, replanting has afforded the opportunity to rethink—variety, clone, rootstock, spacing, trellising, aspect, and irrigation, so quality should improve markedly. Meanwhile, quality and quantity improved in Oregon, Washington, New York (Finger Lakes and Long Island), and Virginia, and impressive efforts have come from New Mexico and Texas.

Production in the early 1990s gained momentum

Pine Ridge Winery in California's Napa Valley.

when economic expansion brought increased demand. After a flurry of reports on the benefits of moderate wine consumption, red wines, such as cabernet sauvignon, pinot noir, zinfandel, and, particularly, merlot, became especially popular with health-conscious consumers. In spite of increased replanting costs and increased bordeaux prices (imported to help with production shortfalls), increased demand, record sales, and record prices led to record profits.

Currently another threat looms, Pierce's disease, particularly because of a new vector, the glassy-winged sharpshooter. Previous epidemics of Pierce's disease occurred from 1892 to 1906 and in the 1930s, wiping out thriving vineyards in Anaheim, California.

Despite some ideal climates for growing quality wine grapes, the American wine industry has had to grapple with many challenges. To date, the three "Ps," Prohibition, phylloxera, and Pierce's disease, have been the most overpowering. California—the state and its wine industry—continues to be an innovative, dominant, and resilient force. With a new wave of viticulture and a melding of the science and art of winemaking, the future of world-class wine from America appears to be a promising one.

Flying the flag in honor of a bountiful grape harvest.

WASHINGTON STATE

At the beginning of the millennium Washington State's phenomenal growth saw one new winery opening every 13 days. During the past 20-odd years a base of 19 wineries has grown to 145, with an increase in vineyard area from 5,000 to 25,000 acres (2,023 to 10,117 ha). Currently ranked second in premium varietal production within the United States, Washington State now exports its wine to more than 40 countries.

Washington's reputation for excellence in wines spread from its delicately perfumed rieslings in the 1970s to accolades in the 1980s for its elegant, well-focused merlots and chardonnays.

> *WINE, n. Fermented grape-juice known to the Women's Christian Union as "liquor" sometimes as "rum." Wine, madam, is God's next best gift to man.*
> AMBROSE BIERCE (1842–1914), *The Devil's Dictionary*

Landscape and climate

Washington's geology has been much influenced over time by volcanic activity and flood erosion on a monumental scale. Lava flows provided basalt foundations for both the gentle slopes and sharply etched east–west ridges now covered in vines. The generously irrigated, ever-sunny Columbia River Valley contains 99.9 percent of Washington's vineyards. The Columbia's growing season is marked by an intense early ripening period followed by a long, gentle "Indian summer" finish. Cool nights and consistent conditions create the deep perfumes, crystal-clear fruit flavors, and excellent natural acidity that define Washington's cool-climate wine styles.

Wines and vines

Eastern Washington's wine styles are defined by intense, vibrant fruit, and juicy natural acids. They are seen as relatively inexpensive alternatives to California wines. The state's most-planted grapes, merlot and chardonnay, generally show elegant style, varietal purity, fine structure, and balance. Both cabernet sauvignon and franc are bottled as straight varietals and/or combined with merlot in "Meritage" blends, among the most bordeaux-like in the country. Washington's sauvignon blanc, chenin blanc, and sémillon are among the finest examples in the United States.

Newcomers syrah, malbec, and viognier show great promise, but nebbiolo and sangiovese have been less consistent. Experimental plantings of carmenère, marsanne, rousssanne, and mourvèdre suggest that these have great potential. More serious treatment of grenache, lemberger (blaufränkisch), and cinsault has brought new life to these older, workhorse grapes. Relatively small quantities of other varieties are grown in western Washington's milder, wetter regions.

For premium wines, winemakers prefer that the grapes are picked by hand.

Yakima Valley

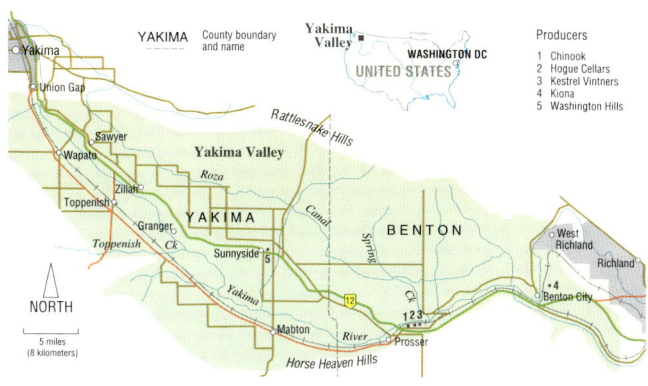

Washington's largest AVA (American Viticultural Area) is the Columbia Valley with 25,000 acres (10,125 ha) of vine plantings. It was conceived as a blanket appellation for virtually all of the state's vineyards. Within this large area are two smaller, more climatically distinctive AVAs: the semiarid Yakima Valley and Walla Walla River Valley. Relatively cooler than the surrounding Columbia AVA, the Yakima Valley produces about 40 percent of the state's wine. The region is bounded by the evocatively named Rattlesnake Hills and Horse Heaven Hills.

Some significant producers in the Yakima Valley, in addition to those below, include Chinook, Kestrel Vintners, and Washington Hills.

HOGUE CELLARS *Established* 1982 *Owners* Hogue family *Vineyard area* 1,800 acres (729 ha)

All of the wines here show crystal-clear varietal characters, understated elegance and are inexpensive for their quality. Highlights include riesling; a spicy, fleshy fumé blanc; leesy, creamy, crisp chardonnay; a more intense, nutty, complex Vineyard Selections Chardonnay; a blackberry and vanilla syrah with fine tannins; minty, juicy merlot; and a meaty, mocca, tobacco-tinged, soft, and deeply juicy Genesis Cabernet Franc.

KIONA *Established* 1979 *Owners* Holmes and Williams families *Vineyard area* 30 acres (12 ha)

Kiona is sited in chalky, high-pH soils on one of Yakima's driest, hottest sites, Red Mountain. Its lemberger vines are the oldest in the state and its cabernet grapes are considered among the best produced. The winery is also known for solid,

Itinerant pickers, here working at Hogue Cellars' vineyard, follow the grape harvest up the West Coast.

well-made, fruit-forward, excellent-value wines, with strengths especially in late-harvested riesling, chenin blanc, and lemberger wines.

OTHER WASHINGTON PRODUCERS

DELILLE CELLARS/CHALEUR ESTATE *Established* 1992 *Owners* Charles and Greg Lill, Jay Soloff, Christopher Upchurch *Vineyard area* NA

Sharply focused, site-specific, unfiltered wines have brought DeLille to the fore of Washington's more serious producers. Best wines include a superconcentrated, deeply integrated savory Chaleur (cabernet sauvignon/merlot/cabernet franc), a counterpoint to the plummy merlot-dominant D2. Chaleur Doyenne Syrah shows classic blackberry and white pepper aromas and a typically firm, dusty, tannic palate. A classy, beautifully balanced sauvignon/sémillon white is also produced.

Ivy grows over a long-disused wine press.

Columbia Valley syrah; and a fleshy, broadly perfumed Walla Walla syrah blend, which contains 5 percent viognier.

LEONETTI CELLAR *Established* 1977 *Owners* **Gary and Nancy Figgins** *Vineyard area* **NA**

Leonetti Cellar is Walla Walla's oldest winery and has its oldest merlot vines. The original vineyard, planted in 1974, is managed through intensive low-yield viticultural practices. More recent plantings have added cabernet franc, petit verdot, carmenère, and syrah. Stylistically, Leonetti's Cabernet Sauvignon, Cabernet Sauvignon Reserve, Merlot, and Sangiovese are big, powerful and oak-driven, with layers of opulent fruit. These are seriously sought-after wines.

ANDREW WILL *Established* 1989 *Owner* **Chris Camarda** *Vineyard area* **NA**

This Vashon Island winery makes tiny quantities of vineyard-designated wines from Ciel du Cheval, Boushey, Klipsun, and Pepper Bridge. Carmarda's supple, plummy, finely structured, age-worthy merlots, as well as Sorella (a cabernet sauvignon-dominated merlot/franc blend), and sangiovese, and chenin blanc are all highly sought after.

L'ECOLE NO 41 *Established* 1983 *Owners* **Clubb family** *Vineyard area* **NA**

Winemaker Marty Clubb makes Washington's best sémillons—ripe and rich-textured Fries Sémillon and barrel-fermented L'Ecole No 41 Sémillon, with green walnut and citrus characters. Another steal is the beeswax, melon, and citrusy chenin blanc. Reds show strength through a finely structured Seven Hills Merlot; expansive Apogee merlot/cabernet blend; and smooth, meaty, viscous Walla Walla Cabernet Sauvignon.

WOODWARD CANYON *Established* 1981 *Owner* **Richard Small** *Vineyard area* **NA**

Richard Small, one of Washington's great boutique winemakers, helped put Washington merlot, cabernet, and chardonnay on the premium map. Drawing low-yield fruit primarily from the lower Columbia and Walla Walla areas and a high-density planted home vineyard, wines are unfiltered, unfined, and not acidified. Woodward Celilo Chardonnay shows complex savory characters and is finely structured, counterpointing a fat, fleshy, peachy Walla Walla Chardonnay. Woodward Canyon reds include a juicy, chocolatey merlot with explosive midpalate; a dark, dense old-vine cabernet; and Charbonneau, which is a complex, silky, seamless merlot/cabernet sauvignon/franc blend.

GLEN FIONA *Established* 1995 *Owner* **Ronald White, Tony Weeks, Berle "Rusty" Figgins** *Vineyard area* **NA**

Rusty Figgins mainly produces variant blends of syrah, spiced by grenache, cinsault, or viognier. Vinification style takes its cue from the vintage, following an eclectic Franco-Australian mix of cold maceration, basket pressing, wild and Rhône yeast fermentation in neutral old oak, resulting in personality-filled wines: a peppery, concentrated

OREGON

Oregon has long held a reputation for progressivism and nonconformity in the United States, so it should come as no surprise that its wine industry grows the world's most difficult grape—pinot noir—in a hostile environment. As well as embracing harsh growing conditions, Oregonians imposed some of the world's toughest labeling laws on themselves in the 1970s, with varietal content and stated region of origin set at 100 percent. Although varietal content was eventually relaxed to 90 percent, with cabernet sauvignon given dispensation down to 75 percent, these parameters remain high by world standards.

Now ranked fourth in U.S. production with an output of one million cases annually, Oregon has 136 wineries, with 383 vineyards and 10,000 acres (4,050 ha) planted to *vinifera* varieties.

Landscape and climate

Oregon is climatically divided into dry eastern and wet western halves by the volcanic Cascade Mountains, which block clouds generated by the Pacific Ocean and cast a rain shadow over the great western valley. This maritime influence is somewhat mitigated by Oregon's northern position, which contributes lengthened days, indirect sunlight, and a broad diurnal temperature range within a long growing season.

Vines and wines

Winemaking in Oregon tends to follow traditional Burgundian practices, primarily using barrels of French or Oregon oak. The wineries are small, labor-intensive operations and hand-picking is the rule. Virtually all of the wineries produce pinot noirs in a style that echoes perfumes, structures, and textures found in Burgundy. These wines often require up to seven years to open up, with many capable of evolving for a decade or more. Chaptalization is allowed, but rarely applied.

Oregon's outstanding pinot gris is made in a style based on barrel and tank fermentation. Other Alsatian varieties—gewürztraminer, pinot blanc, and riesling—have thrived in the cool climate, and show consistently ripe, well-focused varietal characters in well-executed dry styles. Both riesling and gewürztraminer are often good value in semisweet, late-harvest, and icewine styles. Recently introduced Burgundian chardonnay clones have brought fuller, better balanced wines. Both white and red wines show subdued European fruit characters with nicely balanced acidity.

During ripening, grapes' sugar levels rise and acid levels drop.

Willamette Valley

Some 60 miles (96 km) wide and 100 miles (160 km) deep, the wet Willamette Valley AVA (with 40 inches/102 cm precipitation per annum) is home to 104 wineries. Almost all focus on pinot noir, followed by pinot gris, then riesling, chardonnay, pinot blanc, sauvignon blanc, and gewürztraminer fleshing out their portfolios. Vineyards are planted in relatively infertile soil on gentle slopes, primarily clustered around the Red Hills of Dundee, with the rest scattered throughout Washington County, Yamhill County, and the Eola Hills.

Some significant producers in the Willamette Valley, in addition to those below, include Amity Vineyard, Archery Summit Winery, Argyle Winery, Beaux Frères, Bethel Heights, Cameron, Elk Cove Vineyards, Evesham Wood, King Estate Winery, and Ponzi Vineyard.

DOMAINE DROUHIN *Established* 1987 *Owner* Joseph Drouhin *Vineyard area* 74 acres (30 ha)

Domaine Drouhin represents the greatest and most undisputed recognition by France of Oregon's potential. In 1987, Burgundian *négociant* house Joseph Drouhin planted a vineyard in Dundee with double the usual U.S. vine density. Drouhin's pinots, now Oregon benchmarks, show an elegantly underplayed, multilayered complexity that consistently ranks among the best produced outside Burgundy. Cuvée Laurene, a wine of excellent quality, is made only in top vintages.

EYRIE VINEYARDS *Established* 1966 *Owners* Lett family *Vineyard area* 50 acres (20 ha)

Visionary founding father of Oregon pinot noir, David Lett deserves equal credit for similarly establishing the

Multihued vinifera *foliage in the fall.*

Alsatian varietals pinot gris, muscat, and riesling. Lett follows traditional Burgundian winemaking practices, opting for a lighter, more delicately perfumed style of pinot noir. Tight and austere while young, these wines often begin to blossom only at 5 to 10 years of age. The pinot meunier ranks among the best anywhere and Lett's groundbreaking pinot gris is the area's benchmark. His chardonnays are elegant and seem to age forever.

POLK County boundary and name

Forest Grove · Hillsboro

WASHINGTON · Gaston

NORTH

10 miles (16 kilometers)

Yamhill · 4

Carlton · 17

7 · 2 · Newberg

McMinnville · 10

YAMHILL · 13 · 6

Sheridan · 1

Willamina

· 5

MARION

9 ·

Dallas

Salem · 15

POLK

Monmouth

· 16

Willamette Valley

Jefferson

BENTON

Corvallis

LINN

12

· 35 miles (56 km)

Columbia River

MULTNOMAH

● **Portland**

CLACKAMAS

West Linn

Oregon City

Canby

Willamette Valley

Woodburn

Producers
1 Amity Vineyard
2 Archery Summit Winery
3 Argyle Winery
4 Beaux Frères
5 Bethel Heights
6 Cameron
7 Domaine Drouhin
8 Elk Cove Vineyards
9 Evesham Wood
10 Eyrie Vineyards
11 Rex Hill Vineyards
12 King Estate Winery
13 Panther Creek Cellars
14 Ponzi Vineyard
15 St Innocent Winery
16 Willamette Valley Vineyards
17 Ken Wright Winery

Willamette Valley WASHINGTON DC

UNITED STATES

New vine plantings in Oregon to replace vines attacked by phylloxera biotype-B strain.

PANTHER CREEK CELLARS *Established* 1986 *Owners* Kaplan family *Vineyard area* Grapes are bought in

Panther Creek produces high-quality, un-filtered, low-production, low-yield (less than 180 cases), single-vineyard, age-worthy pinot noirs with generous fruit and balanced structures. Worth seeking out is *sur lie* Melón, produced from the melon de bourgogne grape.

REX HILL VINEYARDS *Established* 1982 *Owner* Paul Hart *Vineyard area* 400 acres (162 ha)

All Rex Hill wines show excellent fruit purity and fine balance. Pinot noirs show distinct *terroir* characters through a single-vineyard range, and multilayered complexity at Reserve level. Whites include a crisp unoaked sauvignon, varietally focused pinot gris and pinot blanc, and a fine-boned chardonnay. The bargain label Kings Ridge wines are well made, easy drinking, and sharply priced.

ST. INNOCENT WINERY *Established* 1988 *Owners* Mark Vlossak *Vineyard area* NA

Sharing winemaker Mark Vlossak with Panther Creek, the quality and styles of this winery are based on a different fruit source and made into a wide range of single-vineyard, concentrated, fine-grained pinot noirs, chardonnays, and pinot gris.

WILLAMETTE VALLEY VINEYARDS *Established* 1988 *Owners* Shareholders *Vineyard area* 50 acres (20 ha)

This winery goes from strength to strength. Fruit is drawn from two vineyards and is intensively managed. From its beginning, Willamette Valley Vineyards has shown steady improvement across a broad range of wines, with strengths in pinot noir, pinot gris, chardonnay, and riesling.

KEN WRIGHT WINERY *Established* 1994 *Owner* Ken Wright Cellars *Vineyard area* 28 acres (11.5 ha

Ken Wright draws grapes from a wide range of microclimates and soil types, producing single-vineyard pinot noirs that clearly delineate *terroir* differences within the Willamette Valley. The wines are complex and condensed and the melony chardonnay and pinot blanc are excellent.

OTHER OREGON PRODUCERS

The Umpqua Valley AVA mainly produces pinot noir, cabernet sauvignon, chardonnay, riesling and sauvignon blanc. Farther south, in the hotter, drier, and more elevated Rogue Valley, riesling, gewürztraminer, pinot gris, cabernet sauvignon, chardonnay, cabernet franc, merlot, and sémillon are favored. The state's eastern vineyards, near Colombia Gorge and the Walla Walla AVA, generally sell their grapes to Washington wineries.

BRIDGEVIEW VINEYARDS *Established* 1980 *Owners* Kerivan family and Ernie Brodie *Vineyard area* 74 acres (30 ha)

This southern Illinois Valley winery consistently produces some of Oregon's best-value varietals from a closely planted vineyard. The riesling, pinot noir and chardonnay are well-made, ripely flavored and sharply priced. They are among Oregon's best-value wines.

IDAHO

Idaho's wineries fall under the state classification of AO, or Appellation of Origin. Idaho is officially a subzone of tri-state Pacific Northwest with Oregon and Washington. Ste. Chapelle Winery along with the Idaho Grape Growers and Wine Producers Commission is currently determining boundaries in order to complete a multi-AVA application. Snake River Valley and two sub-AVAs of Sunny Slope and Arena Valley, a moon crater 20 minutes northwest of the Oregon border, are proposed.

The Pacific Northwest is the second-largest area in North America for *vinifera* grape production, with more than 45,000 acres (18,210 ha) under vine across the three states. Not unexpectedly, Idaho's contribution is the smallest—about 1,000 acres (405 ha). There are still fewer than 20 commercial wineries in Idaho. Although growth is slow, interest from larger, outside businesses is increasing. Also, with 57 percent of residents teetotal Mormons, producers must market their wines outside the state and internationally.

Varieties in production include cabernet franc, cabernet sauvignon, chardonnay, chenin blanc, lemberger (blaufrankisch), gewürztraminer, merlot, pinot gris, pinot noir, riesling, sauvignon blanc, sémillon, and syrah. Experimental plantings of tempranillo, valdespino, viognier, and zinfandel show great promise.

Landscape and climate

The wine industry is made up of two segments. In the southwest, the growers are clustered around Boise in a clockwise direction, starting with Gooding, to Twin Falls, Owyhee, Ada, and Canyon counties. The wineries, conversely, are set up in the central west near the Washington and Oregon borders, concentrated in an area appropriately named Sunny Slope.

Vines and wines

High-stress climatic conditions (high altitude and abundant sunshine) produce wines with high natural alcohol and high natural acidity. Fully ripe, high-acid, bone-dry, characterful riesling is a specialty, though not as popular as the chardonnays, which range from lean and tart to rich, viscous, oaky, and buttery. Bordeaux varietals are coming into their own, though many are bolstered with Washington fruit. Syrah is coming on strong, as it is elsewhere, though styles here are lighter, slightly less extracted, and less lavishly oaked.

Right: *A healthy bloom on ripening black grapes.*

Snake River Valley

Snake River Valley is currently the most important and certainly the most well-known of the wine-producing regions in Idaho, but it is worth noting that regions in the southwest are emerging and at present provide huge quantities of fruit for the Snake River Valley wineries.

Most of Idaho's wineries are located in the high mountain valleys of the Clearwater and Snake Rivers. The rivers, as they do in all of the world's premium wine-producing zones, provide a climate-tempering influence.

The most desirable vineyard sites are located in the south-facing hillsides along the Snake River, where convection currents pull freezing air off the hillsides during winter and cool the vines during summer. The average vineyard elevation is about 2,500–3,100 feet (760–940 m), although a handful can be found as high as 4,500 feet (1,370 m).

In addition to the Ste. Chapelle Winery, two other

Widely spaced vine rows provide room for mechanical harvesters.

significant producers in the Snake River Valley are Koenig Vineyards and Distillery, and Sawtooth Winery.

STE. CHAPELLE WINERY   *Established* 1976
Owner **Corus Brands, Inc.** *Vineyard area* **640 acres (259 ha) plus, 600 acres (242 ha) newly planted**

Ste. Chapelle Winery, named for La Sainte Chapelle in Paris, was Idaho's first and now its largest winery. It produces merlot and cabernet sauvignon labeled Idaho/Washington. Ste. Chapelle is directing the redevelopment or replanting of more than 1,000 acres (404 ha) of the original vineyard sites. Winemaker Chuck Devlin joined Ste. Chappelle Winery just before the harvest in 2000. He sees syrah and riesling as the varietals with the most potential for the area, and there are plans afoot to increase production to up to 300,000 cases a year.

OTHER IDAHO PRODUCERS

As well as Camas Winery, other Idaho producers of significance include Carmela Vineyards; Pend D'Oreille Winery; and South Hill/Hegy's Winery, which is one of Idaho's smallest wineries. Here, fruit is pressed with an antique Italian press, and all wine is bottled, labeled, and corked by hand.

CAMAS WINERY   *Established* 1983 *Owner* **Stuart L. Scott** *Vineyard area* **Grapes are bought in**

The Scotts purchase grapes from independent growers in the state of Washington and crush them in the field. They gather wild huckleberries, elderberries, and plums in the nearby Clearwater, St. Joe and Kaniksu National Forests. Their eclectic range of wines includes both *vinifera* varietals and fruit wines, handmade sparkling wines, honey meads, and an Ethiopian hopped honey wine. Camas is one of the oldest wineries in the state.

Producers
1 Koenig Vineyards and Distillery
2 Sawtooth Winery
3 Ste Chapelle Winery

ADA   County boundary and name

5 miles
(8 kilometers)

NORTH

PAYETTE

OREGON
IDAHO

CANYON   Caldwell

Snake River Valley

Snake

Clayton   Lake Lowell   Nampa

OWYHEE   Kuna

Bowmont

ADA

Snake River Valley   WASHINGTON DC
UNITED STATES   Walters Ferry

CALIFORNIA

The journey from the Californian mission vineyards of the eighteenth century to the present day of heady prices and record profits has been difficult. Cycles of boom and bust have been created by markets, disease, politics, war, folly, insight, and forward thinking. Long years of Prohibition had effects upon the U.S. wine industry which linger to this day. A modern wine industry arose during the 1950s and 1960s and grew in fits and starts, only to be hit with phylloxera biotype-B during the 1990s. Resilient as ever, Californians view this as an expensive lesson and an opportunity to improve upon past viticultural mistakes. Replanting and record profits have somewhat softened the phylloxera blow.

More than 554,000 acres (224,370 ha) of wine grapes are planted in California, and it is the fourth largest wine producer in the world after France, Italy, and Spain. Californian wine accounts for 91 percent of production and 72 percent of wine sales in the United States. Ninety-eight percent of U.S. wine exports hale from California and these have increased fivefold in value and three-fold in volume since 1990.

In 2000, 55 percent of the California crush was red grapes and 45 percent was white grapes.

Terroir in reverse

Site, soil, and climate have been extolled by the French, particularly in the promotion of wines demarcated by region. Better wines reflect a matching of variety with *terroir*. What about *terroir* that undervalues a variety? Petite sirah, known as the not-so-respected durif in France, proves the point. A moderate to warm climate, longer growing season, and California sunlight ripen the variety to produce a deeply colored, full and tannic red wine capable of impressive longevity. Not as complex as syrah, petite sirah can provide lush blueberry fruit and a blast of ripe tannin for the lover of big, bold wines. Thus, in the lesser *terroir* for the variety, durif floundered in France, while in more suitable Californian *terroir*, petite sirah has thrived.

Chardonnay was by far the leading white variety over colombard and chenin blanc. Cabernet sauvignon was the leading red, and was slightly ahead of zinfandel.

Landscape and climate

Understanding the Californian climate is not easy. Autumn is frequently warmer than summer, especially near the Pacific coast. Surface water temperatures are cold (50–60°F (10–16°C)) for most of the year along the California coast. This is due to a combination of interrelated factors resulting in warm surface water being pushed away from the shore and out to sea. Only in the south, and then only for a month or two during summer, does one venture into the Pacific Ocean without a wetsuit.

Two mountain ranges impact upon the state's viticulture—the

Schied Vineyards on Route 25, California

The remote Chalone Vineyards, located above the Salinas Valley floor in the Gavilan Mountains, has its own AVA.

westernmost is aptly named the Coastal Range and the range further inland is the Sierra Nevada Range. Between these two is the famed Central Valley, one of the great agricultural regions on earth. The Coastal Range runs along most of California's coastline, and can be a major obstacle to the cooling influence of the Pacific Ocean.

Although summer temperatures may indeed be lower in areas with significant coastal effects—Carneros, Arroyo Grande, and Santa Barbara—than such classic regions as Bordeaux and Burgundy, or even cool regions like Oregon, autumn climate patterns differ strongly. Whereas daily maximal temperatures decrease, sometimes markedly, during autumn in Europe and in the Pacific Northwest, the reverse tends to take place during the early fall period in coastal California. This allows for continued ripening, usually with cool evening temperatures. Under such conditions, and depending upon the length of "hang time," it is possible to obtain grapes with a ripe flavor

With good friends . . .
And good food on the board,
and good wine in the pitcher,
we may well ask: When shall we
live if not now?
M. F. K FISHER,
The Art of Living

profile suggestive of a warm climate, while retaining the acidity of a cooler climate.

Aspect too is very important and together with climate plays a greater role than soil type in influencing viticulture in California. Soils vary markedly and include shale, sandstone, limestone, sandy loams, clay loams, gravel, granite, sand, and volcanic. Short distances may yield much variation among soil types.

Vines and wines

Zinfandel, chardonnay, and cabernet sauvignon finished the twentieth century as dominant in the blush, white, and red table wine categories respectively.

Sweet and fortified wines, from the omnipresent mission grape, have gone out of fashion, though some very good examples remain.

Generalizations regarding style miss wines on the vanguard, which may be the standard bearers 20 years hence. There is increasing cross-pollination with producers in France, Italy, Australia, and South America and this has created some blurring of the boundaries both geographically and stylistically. As new plantings mature and

The vivid colors of fall at the Talley Vineyard, in California.

syrah producers are increasingly blending 10 to 15 percent viognier. Most varietal labeled chardonnay and pinot noir are not blended.

Meritage wines are blends of Bordeaux varieties, either red (merlot, cabernet sauvignon, cabernet franc, malbec, petite verdot) or white (sauvignon blanc, sémillon, muscadelle), which must meet legal criteria.

Wine laws

California's wine is subject to both state and federal laws. The Bureau of Alcohol, Tobacco and Firearms (BATF) has a powerful regulatory role in both designation and distribution. American viticultural areas (AVAs) are awarded by BATF, and are based on geography and history. AVAs were established in 1978. There are now 137 in total, 81 of them in California.

Unlike the system operating in France, there are no proscribed vineyard or winemaking techniques tied to an AVA. Neither are there limits on varieties grown.

Varietal and place of origin fall under state and federal laws, with the more stringent standard being that to which the industry is held.

new opinion makers appear (wine critics have immense power), these styles should evolve too.

Varietal wines—those with at least 75 percent of the variety on the label—have long been dominant in California. But changing styles means that a cabernet sauvignon wine is now more likely to contain merlot, sometimes all five red Bordeaux standards. In homage to Côte Rôtie,

Wine labeled as California must be entirely made from grapes grown within the state. The content standard for county of origin or varietal designation is 75 percent. However, there is no obligation to state which varieties comprise the remaining 25 percent. One with 70 percent cabernet sauvignon and 30 percent merlot may not carry a single varietal designation. Such a wine may be labeled with no varietal description or with the relevant percentages. An AVA origin-labeled wine carries an 85 percent or more content requirement. A designated vineyard is even more stringent, with a requirement that 95 percent of the grapes originate from the designated vineyard.

The three-tiered system—producer/importer, wholesaler, and retailer—was set up to increase competition and counter organized crime. Distribution of alcohol is controlled at federal, state, and local levels. This patchwork of laws is a throwback to the repeal of Prohibition. It is an unholy system of competing and confusing laws.

Viticulture

The greatest challenge to the industry both past and present has been phylloxera. Once thought resistant to phylloxera, AXR1 rootstock began failing in the mid-1980s falling prey to biotype-B, a new mutation. Extensive replanting of vineyards began and continues, putting an economic strain on the industry. But this offered growers an opportunity to regroup. Greater diversity of plant material is now available, including clones of the Dijon series from Burgundy, which may improve grape quality. More international varieties are being used as growers propagate their own vine and rootstock materials.

Training and pruning methods are also getting a facelift, resulting in improved quality with less vegetal flavors, less vine vigor, and greater ripeness.

California's generally warm and dry climate keeps disease pressure from becoming a major threat. In recent years, California viticulturalists have become more aware of the delicate balance of the ecosystem and, as a result, are more considerate in terms of vineyard practices.

The Sunstone Vineyard, California, tasting room is reminiscent of those around Provence in France.

Major vineyard problems still exist, but the two major players are still phylloxera and Pierce's disease. The latter is spread by a bacterium transported by the blue-green sharpshooter. Once it has taken hold there is no current treatment for it. Most prevalent in riparian areas, the bugs infect nearby vineyards and there is the fear that new vectors, like the glassy-winged sharpshooter, will travel up the highway system to ravage more vineyards.

Irrigation is used in most of California with the exception of a few dry-farmed sites. Without it, vine growing would be near impossible, and drip irrigation enables careful management of watering. Strict legislation controls water rights and sufficient water may not always be available for the vineyard and winery.

Although many innovations of agricultural techniques have been offered to California's viticulturalists, in recent years the movement has been towards a balance of tradition and technology.

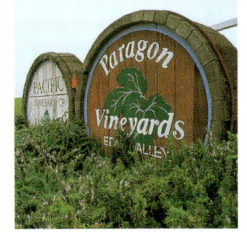

A barrel sign announcing the entrance to Paragon Vineyards in the Eden Valley, California.

Mendocino and Lake County

Forty-one wineries have their home in Mendocino, 90 miles (145 km) north of San Francisco. The region is quite possibly the most geographically diverse in California with mountain ranges, valleys, and lakes producing a wide variety of terrains and climates. Most vineyards are located on hillsides, with only 15 percent of producers growing grapes on the valley floor. There are 14,263 acres (5,776 ha) of vineyard plantings. No single producer in Mendocino farms more than 1,000 acres (405 ha). Varietal selection is diverse, with gewürztraminer, petite sirah, syrah, riesling, and zinfandel appearing as often as chardonnay, pinot noir, sauvignon blanc, and cabernet sauvignon.

Recent renewal of interest and investment in Mendocino wines are positive signs for the future.

The vineyard area of Lake County, to the east of Mendocino, covers about 5,500 acres (2,225 ha). It still has only five wineries, although investment in vineyard land by large companies is growing, as is the buying of fruit for labels such as Fetzer and Robert Mondavi.

Climate and landscape

Climate throughout the Mendocino region is diverse, ranging from cool to cold on the coast and at higher altitudes, to warmer temperatures on the valley floors. Cool nights retain acidity in the fruit, while warm days allow for ripeness. Rhône varieties such as viognier and grenache do well in warmer areas like the McDowell Valley, while cooler regions, such as the northwest section of the Anderson Valley, are planted with cool-climate varieties such as pinot noir. Soils are similar to those of Sonoma County, with light texture, sand, gravel, and powdery consistencies.

Lake County has cool nights and hot days during the growing season. From the west the county is shielded from fog and moisture by the Mayacamas Mountains while Clear Lake moderates the climatic influence on the vineyards.

Producers

Significant producers in Mendocino and Lake County, as well as those below, include Fetzer Vineyards, Handley Cellars, Lonetree Winery, Pacific Echo, Roederer Estate, and Steele/Shooting Star.

FIFE, MENDOCINO

Established 1996 *Owner* Dennis Fife *Vineyard area* 13 acres (5 ha)

Fife uses minimum handling and great fruit to make some fierce reds. The Redhead Zinfandel, named partly after the

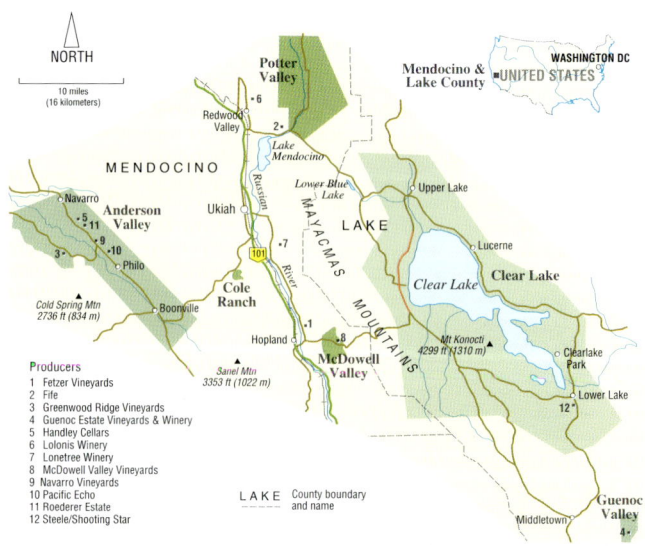

Vines at the Navarro Vineyards, Mendocino.

brick-red soil it grows in, is spicy and fiery without the coarseness of some zinfandels. MAX is a blend of syrah, petite sirah, charbono, and zinfandel.

GREENWOOD RIDGE VINEYARDS, MENDOCINO *Established* 1980
Owner Allan Green *Vineyard area* 16 acres (6 ha)

Allan Green is a great advocate of his region and every year since 1983 has held the California Wine Tasting Championships at his winery. He makes fantastic wines too, and Greenwood is well known for its pinot noir and zinfandel. It was the first winery to release wines under the new Mendocino Ridge appellation in 1998.

GUENOC ESTATE VINEYARDS & WINERY, LAKE COUNTY *Established* 1982 *Owner* Orville Magoon *Vineyard area* 340 acres (138 ha)

The Guenoc Estate, which covers the southern parts of Lake County, all of Guenoc Valley and the northwest portions of Napa Valley, includes some of the oldest vineyards in California. The region's warm days and cool nights are great for growing Bordeaux varieties and emphasis has been placed on carmenère. In 1981, Guenoc Valley was recognized as an AVA, the first in the United States owned by a single proprietorship.

LOLONIS WINERY, MENDOCINO
Established 1920 *Owner* Petros Lolonis *Vineyard area* 300 acres (121 ha)

Lolonis has been in the business of growing vines since before Prohibition. The winery itself was started in 1982. Lolonis is strongly opposed to using chemicals for most pest control, preferring to use natural methods such as ladybugs and praying mantis to control leafhoppers and spiders.

Red wine in a syrah glass.

McDOWELL VALLEY VINEYARDS, MENDOCINO
Established 1970 *Owners* Bill and Vicky Crawford *Vineyard area* 250 acres (101 ha)

This producer, which farms 90 of its acres (36 ha) organically, makes wines from traditional Rhône varieties like grenache, syrah, and viognier. Especially popular is its grenache rosé, a tasty dry alternative to white zinfandel.

NAVARRO VINEYARDS, MENDOCINO
Established 1974 *Owners* Deborah Cahn and Ted Bennett *Vineyard area* 60 acres (24 ha)

Navarro produces many styles from dry to *vendange tardive* (literally, late harvest), and even makes grape juice. Vineyard management includes natural methods of pest control so, when faced with the problem of a prolific insect, larvae of the pest's natural enemies are introduced. Pinot noir from Navarro is offered in both traditional and newer styles, and the gewürztraminer is excellent. All wines are of consistently high quality.

Sonoma County

Sonoma County is north of San Francisco and west of Napa Valley, adjacent to the Pacific coast. The region has 172 wineries on 43,314 acres (17,542 ha) and produces 104,162 tons (94,475 t) of grapes annually. Although on a grand scale geographically, Sonoma has more small wineries than Napa. And although it is quieter than Napa Valley in the middle of the summer tourist season, Sonoma is *the* hot spot for grape growing in California. Significant vineyard plantings are concentrating on producing prime grapes for the premium segment of the market.

Climate and landscape

Slightly cooler than Napa, cool sites in Sonoma County are ideal for growing more delicate varieties. The climate varies dramatically according to individual appellation—fog and offshore breezes keeping temperatures low by the ocean, near gaps in the coastal range, and to the south near Carneros.

Producers

Some significant producers in Sonoma County, in addition to those below, include Benziger Family Winery, David Bynum Winery, Carmenet Vineyards, Chalk Hill

Benziger Family Winery, Sonoma Valley, concentrates on affordable premium wines. Their merlot and chardonnay offer exceptional value.

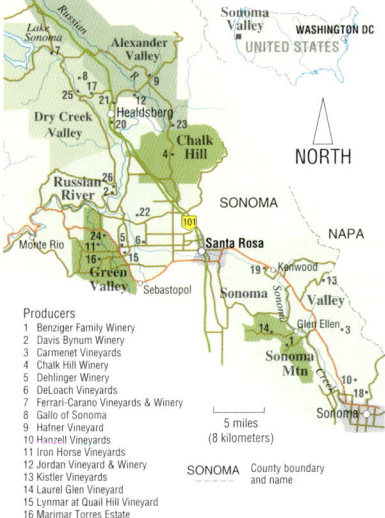

Producers
1 Benziger Family Winery
2 Davis Bynum Winery
3 Carmenet Vineyards
4 Chalk Hill Winery
5 Dehlinger Winery
6 DeLoach Vineyards
7 Ferrari-Carano Vineyards & Winery
8 Gallo of Sonoma
9 Hafner Vineyard
10 Hanzell Vineyards
11 Iron Horse Vineyards
12 Jordan Vineyard & Winery
13 Kistler Vineyards
14 Laurel Glen Vineyard
15 Lynmar at Quail Hill Vineyard
16 Marimar Torres Estate
17 Pezzi-King Vineyards
18 Ravenswood Winery
19 St Francis
20 Seghesio Family Vineyards
21 Simi Winery
22 Sonoma-Cutrer Vineyards
23 Stonestreet
24 Topolos at Russian River Vineyards
25 Unti Vineyards & Winery
26 Williams & Selyem Winery

Established in 1857, Buena Vista in Sonoma County is California's oldest premium winery.

Winery, DeLoach Vineyards, Gallo of Sonoma, Hafner Vineyard, Kistler Vineyards, Lynmar at Quail Hill Vineyard, Marimar Torres Estate, Pezzi-King Vineyards, Seghesio Family Vineyards, Stonestreet, and Williams & Selyem Winery.

DEHLINGER WINERY   *Established* 1975   *Owner* Tom Dehlinger   *Vineyard area* 50 acres (20 ha)

Taking full advantage of the cool and foggy weather of the Russian River Valley, the vines at Dehlinger produce outstanding pinot noir, syrah, and chardonnay. Winemaking techniques aim to extract as much flavor as possible from the grapes and on this prime site, there are tons to be had.

FERRARI-CARANO VINEYARDS & WINERY   *Established* 1981   *Owners* Don and Rhonda Carano   *Vineyard area* 1,200 acres (486 ha)

Don and Rhonda Carano have made their mark on the region by producing a number of great wines. Best known for its chardonnay, the winery also produces a Reserve Fumé Blanc with 100 percent barrel fermentation and extended lees aging. Winemaker

The tasting room at Ferrari-Carano Winery.

George Bursick has worked wonders with sangiovese for Siena, a proprietary wine. And almost impossible to find is their rare sweet dessert wine called El Dorado Gold.

HANZELL VINEYARDS   *Established* 1953   *Owners* Barbara and Alex deBrye   *Vineyard area* 26 acres (10 ha)

These vineyards were originally established by J. D. Zellerbach, whose passion for burgundy brought changes to Californian winemaking. He continues to be a force in the winemaking at Hanzell. Small French barrels and stainless steel equipment were just a few of his early innovations. Hanzell's pinot noir and chardonnay are recommended.

IRON HORSE VINEYARDS   *Established* 1979   *Owners* Sterling family and Forrest Tancer   *Vineyard area* 246 acres (100 ha)

Iron Horse was founded in Sonoma's Green Valley in 1979, with the goal of making unique high-quality wines. Only estate-grown grapes and those from Forrest Tancer's mother's ranch, T-bar-T, in Alexander Valley, are used, to ensure high-quality fruit. Iron Horse is particularly noted for its sparkling wine.

Zinfandel

Zinfandel, affectionately called "zin" by Americans had long been considered a native grape. When proven to be *Vitis vinifera*, and by definition, not native, theories on its importation abounded. Eventually, DNA analysis confirmed that Apuglia's primitivo and zinfandel were identical, though Italian records could only trace primitivo back some 150 years. Searches along the Dalmatian coast brought samples of the plavac mali vine back for analysis which demonstrated the variety to be an offspring of zinfandel. Finally, in 2001, further detective work proved zinfandel to be the Croatian variety crljenak. Top zinfandels come from vines up to 100 years old, from Sonoma, Amador County, and Paso Robles.

JORDAN VINEYARD & WINERY *Established* 1972 *Owner* Tom Jordan *Vineyard area* 275 acres (111 ha)

Located in the Alexander Valley, Jordan is a top producer of cabernet sauvignon and chardonnay and strives to produce wines that go well with food. The region has a long growing season with enough warmth for ripeness and fog to retain acidity. Plantings include merlot, cabernet franc, cabernet sauvignon, and chardonnay. Jordan's cabernet is very drinkable in its youth, but ages successfully as well. When the 1978 was made, sceptics believed it was too well integrated to age but a tasting of that vintage today proves that older wines don't need tannin and harshness to mature well.

LAUREL GLEN VINEYARD *Established* 1981 *Owner* Patrick Campbell *Vineyard area* 35 acres (14 ha)

One hundred percent estate-grown wines from 30-year-old vines are sold under the Laurel Glen and Counterpoint labels. As well, grapes from Chile and Argentina are used to make a red blend

Wineries in every direction in the Sonoma Valley.

called Terra Rosa, and REDS ("wine for the people"), a bistro-style wine, uses Californian grapes. Sangiovese and syrah are varieties currently being trialled to add aromatics.

PETER MICHAEL *Established* 1983 *Owner* Sir Peter Michael *Vineyard area* 76 acres (31 ha)

Peter Michael is one of those producers whose wines sell out in seconds. Wines are made using traditional methods on mountain vineyards. Production is limited, and thus demand exceeds supply without fail. Vines grow on 45° slopes for the most part and the elevation, 2,000 feet (610 m), allows for long slow ripening. Chardonnays include Mon Plaisir and Belle Côte, and if you see Point Rouge, buy it. A Bordeaux-style blend, Les Pavots, and L'Après Midi, a sauvignon blanc, are also winners.

RAVENSWOOD WINERY *Established* 1976 *Owners* Joel Peterson, Reed Foster and public shareholders *Vineyard area* 18 acres (7 ha)

Ravenswood purchases most of its fruit, often from dry-farmed sites with 70- to 100-year-old vines. The Ravenswood logo, "No wimpy wines," is borne out in its powerful zinfandels, ranging from complex vineyard-designates to a great-value zinfandel from Lodi. Although about three-quarters of the production is zinfandel, Ravenswood also does wonders with Bordeaux varieties, especially its Gregory Cabernet Sauvignon, which has a hint of mint, and its stalwart merlot from the famed Sangiacomo Vineyard in Carneros. The quality of wines produced by Ravenswood ranges from good to outstanding.

ST. FRANCIS *Established* 1979 *Owners* Joseph Martin, Lloyd Canton and Kobrand Corp. *Vineyard area* 800 acres (324 ha)

St. Francis was named after the patron saint of the last mission on the California trail. While St. Francis is noted for producing characteristically fruity yet firm red wines, it may be better known as the first premium winery to experiment with synthetic corks. It now uses them for its entire production. The estate's old-vine zinfandel is chocolatey and full in body.

SIMI WINERY *Established* 1876 *Owners* Canandaigua Brands *Vineyard area* 300 acres (121 ha)

Simi was established by two Tuscan brothers, Giuseppe and Pietro Simi. Cellars were built in 1890, but in the meantime, the first few vintages were made in San Francisco. Simi Winery's Sendal is a tasty white Bordeaux blend.

SONOMA-CUTRER VINEYARDS *Established* 1973 *Owners* Brown-Forman *Vineyard area* 400 acres (162 ha)

Sonoma-Cutrer has always been at the forefront of innovation, with cooling tunnels, sorting tables, membrane presses, and the like, making its wines state-of-the-art. One of California's first wineries to concentrate on only one variety, it was also the first to vineyard-designate chardonnay. The Russian River Ranches bottling is the standby, while the Cutrer Vineyard label has more intensity and needs more time to come around. Wines from Les Pierres Vineyard have a mineral note reminiscent of white burgundy. The last two wines took so long to evolve that a new cellar was built specifically for their barrel aging. The mission was to maintain a constant

48°F (9°C) temperature. To achieve this, leader of the pack once again, Sonoma-Cutrer devised a cooling system in the ceiling and floor that consists of tubes filled with chilled water and glycol.

TOPOLOS AT RUSSIAN RIVER VINEYARDS *Established* 1978 *Owner* Michael Topolos *Vineyard area* 27 acres (11 ha)

The Russian River Vineyards have existed since 1963. Owned by the Topolos family since 1978, they are now the source for environmentally friendly wines. Most of the production is organic with some biodynamic plantings. Dry-farmed old vines produce deep purple berries that pack a punch in the Piner Heights Zinfandel. Other wines in their range include sauvignon blanc, pinot noir, and charbono.

UNTI VINEYARDS & WINERY *Established* 1998 *Owners* Unti family *Vineyard area* 26 acres (10 ha)

Newcomer Unti is making a name for itself with a line of powerful reds including zinfandel and syrah from Dry Creek Valley. The family planted these grapes along with sangiovese for the very simple reason that it's what they enjoy drinking. Early reports suggest that consumers agree with them. Oak is restrained in order to keep the wines drinkable upon release.

Wine barrels, mostly made from French or American oak.

Napa Valley

Known around the world as the top premium wine-growing region in North America, the Napa Valley's diversity of appellations and wine styles defies definition. Some believe that with time, Napa Valley's diversity will be further made evident by appellations as detailed as those of Burgundy. A favorable climate and the talent of its winemakers contribute to its fame, though the scourge of phylloxera has forced Napa Valley's viticulturalists to review their choice of varieties and to concentrate on more strategic plantings.

History

Phylloxera and Prohibition reduced the valley's 1889 count of 140 wineries to a mere 25 by 1960. However, by 1990, over 200 were operating. Today, the number has swelled to over 240, with 37,486 acres (15,182 ha) under vine, yielding 102,354 tons (92,835 t) of fruit.

During Napa's evolution the Napa Valley Vintners Association, formed in 1943, and the Napa Valley Grape Growers Association, formed in 1975, were integral to marketing and improving the wines of the region. They remain a driving force. An ordinance in 1968, promoting agriculture as the prime use of land, protects 30,000 acres (12,150 ha) of land solely for growing grapes, and further regulations are in force to thwart erosion. Currently, the latest battle is in trying to prevent certain producers from using the

Lush Napa Valley vineyards surrounding winery buildings.

NAPA County boundary and name

Napa Valley ■ WASHINGTON DC
UNITED STATES

Producers
1 Anderson's Conn Valley Vineyards
2 Araujo Estate Wines/Eisele Vineyard
3 Beaulieu Vineyard
4 Benessere Vineyards
5 Cain Vineyard & Winery
6 Chappellet Winery
7 Clos du Val Wine Co.
8 Dalla Valle Vineyards
9 Diamond Creek Vineyards
10 Etude
11 Far Niente
12 Franciscan Oakville Estate
13 Frog's Leap
14 Grgich Hills Cellar
15 Heitz Wine Cellars
16 Hendry
17 Honig Cellars
18 Charles Krug Winery
19 Luna Vineyards
20 Louis Martini
21 Miner Family Vineyards
22 Robert Mondavi Winery
23 Chateau Montelena
24 Mount Veeder Winery
25 Niebaum-Coppola Estate Winery
26 Opus One
27 Pahlmeyer
28 Joseph Phelps Vineyards
29 Quintessa

30 Reverie on Diamond Mountain
31 Schramsberg Vineyards
32 Signorello Vineyards
33 Spottswoode
34 Staglin Family Vineyard
35 Stag's Leap Wine Cellars
36 Stag's Leap Winery
37 Stony Hill Vineyard
38 Trefethen Vineyards
39 T-Vine
40 Viader Vineyards
41 York Creek

NORTH

5 miles
(8 kilometers)

name "Napa" if their wines do not meet the requirements of the grape source.

Climate and landscape

Napa Valley includes part of the Carneros region at the mouth of the San Pablo Bay. It stretches about 30 miles (48 km) to the northwest and is a mere 5 miles (8 km) wide near the city of Napa, narrowing to 1 mile (1.6 km) near Calistoga. To the west, the valley is bounded by the green forests of the Mayacamas Mountains that separate it from Sonoma Valley and to the east, the much drier and rugged Vaca Range.

Climate is primarily Mediterranean—warm, dry summers; wet, cool winters. Rain is rare during the grape-growing season and most occurs from October through May. Fog, drawn up the valley as the air heats up inland during the day, is pulled in from the bay, and can be seen in the more southerly areas. Its effect is to keep the vines cool, which retains the natural acidity in the fruit. Nights tend to be cool and the days warm, allowing for slow ripening. Traveling north from Carneros to Calistoga in the summer, the temperature increases dramatically by as much as 1 degree per mile.

Soils are diverse—there were up to 32 different types at the last count—created from volcanic eruptions and earth movements. Sub-appellations of the valley include Atlas Peak, Howell Mountain, Los Carneros, Mount Veeder, Oakville, Rutherford, St. Helena, Spring Mountain District, Stags Leap District, and Wild Horse Valley. New appellations are constantly proposed.

> *During one of my treks through Afghanistan, we lost our corkscrew. We were compelled to live on food and water for several days.*
> CUTHBERT J. TWILLIE
> (W. C. Fields, 1880–1946)
> in *My Little Chickadee* (1940)

Producers

Some significant producers in Napa Valley, in addition to those below, include Anderson's Conn Valley Vineyards, Araujo Estate Wines/Eisele Vineyard, Chappellet Winery, Clos du Val Wine Co., Corison Wines, Etude, Far Niente, Franciscan Oakville Estate, Frog's Leap, Grgich Hills Cellar, Heitz Wine Cellars, Hendry, Honig Cellars, Charles Krug Winery, Luna Vineyards, Miner Family Vineyards, Niebaum-Coppola Estate Winery, Pahlmeyer, Quintessa, Reverie on Diamond Mountain, Signorello Vineyards, Spottswoode, Stag's Leap Winery, Stony Hill Vineyard, Trefethen Vineyards, T-Vine, Viader Vineyards, and York Creek.

BEAULIEU VINEYARD *Established* 1900 *Owners* United Distillers & Vintners *Vineyard area* 1,200 acres (486 ha)

Georges de Latour from Bordeaux established Beaulieu Vineyard in 1900, and was instrumental in importing grafted vines from France that were phylloxera-resistant. In 1938, André Tchelistcheff, an innovator who taught others techniques such as malolactic fermentation, cold fermentation, and filtration, joined Beaulieu. The founder's vision lives on in the winery's prestigious Georges de Latour Private Reserve Cabernet Sauvignon.

BENESSERE VINEYARDS *Established* 1995
Owners John and Ellen Benish *Vineyard area* 36 acres (15 ha)

Benessere is at the forefront of the Italian varietal craze. Winemaker Chris Dearden makes a killer sangiovese. In this, he has a little help from some friends. His two consultants are both on Italy's DOCG tasting board and help Benessere adapt Italian viticultural practices to California's microclimates. The result is a sangiovese with cherry aromas reminiscent of Italy's best.

CAIN VINEYARD & WINERY *Established* 1980
Owners Jim and Nancy Meadlock *Vineyard area* 84 acres (34 ha)

Cain Five—a meritage produced from the Spring Mountain District which is a blend of all five major Bordeaux varieties—is Cain Vineyard & Winery's most respected wine. Thin soils on the mountain slopes keep yields low and elevations of up to 2,100 feet (640 m) help to keep the vines cool, resulting in concentrated and complex fruit. Cain Cuvée, a lighter style, is a great alternative to Cain Five, and Cain Musqué is 100 percent sauvignon blanc from the floral musqué clone grown in Monterey.

DALLA VALLE VINEYARDS *Established* 1986
Owner Naoko Dalla Valle *Vineyard area* 25 acres (10 ha)

The winery specializes in cabernet sauvignon blended with some cabernet franc and merlot, but Dalla also makes Pietre Rosse, a spectacular sangiovese. Its cabernet sauvignon and a small proprietary bottling called Maya are collectors' items at auctions. Both wines are long-lived, lean, and tannic in their youth, but will develop exceptional grace with some age.

DIAMOND CREEK VINEYARDS *Established* 1968
Owners Al and Boots Brounstein *Vineyard area* 20 acres (8 ha)

Originally a pharmacist, Al Brounstein decided to pursue his passion for wine and waterfalls and has accomplished both in his vineyard oasis. He was one of the first to focus attention on *terroir* in California and his site contains three distinct soil types, after which he has named his wines—Gravelly Meadow, Volcanic Hill, and Red Rock Terrace. These wines are some of the first of California's vineyard-designated wines, and the winery is California's first cabernet-only estate.

LOUIS MARTINI *Established* 1922 *Owners* Martini family *Vineyard area* 600 acres (243 ha)

Louis P. Martini began clonal trials on pinot noir and chardonnay in 1948, resulting in the UC Davis Chardonnay Clone 108, which is now widespread in California. Martini is also believed to have been the first to plant pinot noir. The estate's line of classic varietals and reserve wines are excellent value, especially the Reserve Cabernet Sauvignon.

MIURA *Established* 1997 *Owner* Emmanuel Kemiji *Vineyard area* NA

Miura, named after the breeder of the most famous fighting bulls in Spain, is a reminder of Master Sommelier Emmanuel Kemiji's European heritage. Currently, he produces merlot from Carneros, pinot noir from Pisoni Ranch, and chardonnay fashioned after white

Experience the delights of the Napa Valley region by riding the historic wine train.

The elegant tasting room and vineyard of Domaine Carneros, Napa Valley.

burgundy. A Bordeaux-style blend is the only departure from the single-vineyard/single-variety theme.

ROBERT MONDAVI WINERY *Established* 1966 *Owners* Public shareholders *Vineyard area* 1,500 acres (607 ha)

Robert Mondavi is one of the most influential people in California's winemaking history. In 1943, he joined the Charles Krug Winery owned by his family and learned about California winemaking. A trip to Bordeaux in 1962 inspired him to pursue his own goals and in 1966 he opened his own winery. Robert Mondavi has never rested on his laurels and his experiments into almost every aspect of viticulture and vinification have contributed significant techno-logical advances to the region. In 1979, he went into partnership with Baron Philippe de Rothschild of Château Mouton-Rothschild to create Opus One. Recently Mondavi expanded to Chile and Italy and now covers all levels of the market, from value wines such as Woodbridge to prestige cuvées like Opus. Mondavi's projects include a winery that special-izes in Italian varieties and a collabora-tion with NASA to use aerial imagery to pinpoint phylloxera's spread through vineyards. Mondavi was the visionary behind the American Center for Food, Wine, and the Arts. Robert Mondavi Winery is currently the largest exporter of premium California wine, reaching more than 90 countries.

A 1996 cabernet sauvignon from the Mondavi estate.

CHATEAU MONTELENA *Established* 1882 *Owners* Barrett family *Vineyard area* 120 acres (49 ha)

Chateau Montelena may be most renowned for the famous Paris Tasting of 1976, when their second vintage of modern chardonnay, the 1973, won the award for top white wine. Although this helped to spur the growth of chardonnay as a premium California wine, Chateau Montelena is probably just as ac-claimed for its red wines. Its caber-net sauvignon has been proven to age extraordinarily well. As a result, Montelena is one of the first winer-ies in California to offer its cabernet *en primeur* (before bottling).

OPUS ONE *Established* 1979 *Owners* Baroness Philippine de Rothschild and Robert Mondavi *Vineyard area* 104 acres (42 ha)

The scale of this winery is awesome, considering it is solely devoted to the production of one wine—a meritage or cabernet blend. The wine is made with the utmost care, including careful vinification and 18-month aging in French oak, followed by 18-month aging in bottle before release. Even though luscious upon release, Opus One has

Trefethen Winery is noted for its Library Reserve wines.

SCHRAMSBERG VINEYARDS *Established* 1862
Owner Jamie Davies *Vineyard area* 54 acres (22 ha)

In 1965, when the late Jack Davies and his wife, Jamie, purchased the property they realized that not many wineries were making *méthode champenoise* wines in California. They decided to go for this corner of the market and to concentrate on exceptional fruit quality. By 1967, they released the first California sparkling wine produced with chardonnay that had a vintage date. In 1971, they were first to produce a California blanc de noirs. Schramsberg refuses to call its wines "sparkling," labeling them "champagne" in the domestic market. Their J. Schram bottling certainly rivals the best French champagne.

STAGLIN FAMILY VINEYARD *Established* 1985
Owners Shari and Garen Staglin *Vineyard area* 50 acres (20 ha)

Staglin makes limited quantities of some exquisite wines. Its cabernet sauvignon has lush fruit flavors yet sufficient power to enable it to age, and its chardonnay is well balanced in oak with focused fruit. The sangiovese, Stagliano, is a benchmark for the variety, but is only available in small quantities.

STAG'S LEAP WINE CELLARS
Established 1972 *Owners* Warren and Barbara Winiarski *Vineyard area* 180 acres (73 ha)

Warren Winiarski is famous, not only for the victory of his 1973 Cabernet Sauvignon at the Paris Tasting in 1976, but because he has always been ahead of the pack in producing wines of optimal quality in Napa Valley. While well known for the longevity of Stag's Leap Cask 23 Cabernet, SLV, and Fay Vineyard wines are also gaining ground. The latest venture is a new chardonnay from Arcadia Vineyard.

the capacity to age. The 1979 and 1980, the first releases, remain vibrant and alive today.

JOSEPH PHELPS VINEYARDS *Established* 1973
Owners Joseph Phelps family *Vineyard area* 395 acres (160 ha)

In 1974, Phelps produced Insignia, the first proprietary Bordeaux-style blend from California. In that same year, Phelps produced California's first syrah, and put Rhône-style wines on the map with his Vin du Mistral line. Le Mistral, a Rhône blend, is a great example, and the Phelps viognier shows exceptional richness and floral character. Joseph Phelps also makes high-quality cabernet sauvignon, sauvignon blanc, and many others, including a line of late-harvest dessert wines. Insignia and Backus cabernet sauvignons are the top-of-the-line reds, which are suitable for long cellaring.

The widely recognized Stag's Leap logo.

Carneros

Carneros straddles Napa and Sonoma Counties at their southernmost points and huddles closely around the San Pablo Bay, a northern part of the San Francisco Bay. It encompasses 36,900 acres (14,944 ha), of which 15,147 acres (6,138 ha) are suitable for viticulture. However, due to zoning limitations only 6,200 acres (2,511 ha) are currently planted. Of this, 48 percent is planted with chardonnay, 32 percent with pinot noir, 5 percent with cabernet sauvignon, and 6 percent, merlot.

Carneros was defined as an AVA in 1983, and after that investment in the area took off, with purchases of land by large companies such as Freixenet and Robert Mondavi. In 1985, the Carneros Quality Alliance, possibly California's most effective viticultural appellation marketing association, was born.

Climate and landscape
Unlike Napa Valley or Sonoma, the boundaries of Carneros were delineated by its

distinctive climate, due to the effects of the bay and differences in elevation. As a result, the character of Carneros wines is special and recognizable. The area's interesting microclimate is influenced by the San Pablo Bay, which has a moderating effect on temperature in spring and winter, helping to lengthen the growing season. However, wind off the bay stresses vines in some areas. In the summer, fog rolls off the bay to cool the vineyards in the mornings and afternoons.

The region's landscape is varied, from low-lying land at sea level near the bay to rolling hills reaching 1,000 feet (305 m) in the westerly hills. Soils are mostly clay-based and usually shallow. Carneros is designated Region I on the Winkler-Amerine heat summation scale, and is ideal for cooler climate grape varieties such as pinot noir and chardonnay, which are able to ripen while still maintaining good acidity. Winemakers are also exploring other varieties, notably merlot.

Growers note special features of the vines and attach these to the end of the rows.

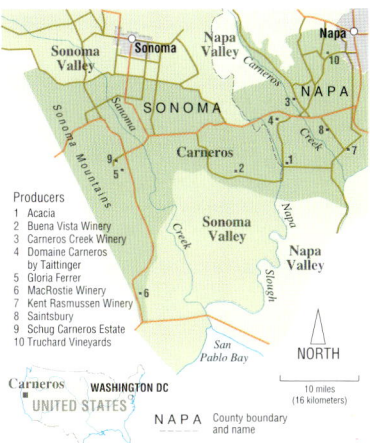

Producers

Significant producers in Carneros, in addition to those below, include Acacia, Buena Vista Winery, Carneros Creek Winery, Domaine Carneros by Taittinger, MacRostie Winery, Kent Rasmussen Winery, Saintsbury, and Schug Carneros Estate.

DOMAINE CHANDON *Established* 1973 *Owner* Louis Vuitton Moët-Hennessy *Vineyard area* 1,100 acres (445 ha)

Domaine Chandon is probably the most recognized sparkling wine producer in California. A leading innovator, and with the resources of Moët & Chandon at its disposal, it has been able to greatly enhance *méthode champenoise* production throughout California. Domaine's still pinot meunier, with its bright jammy fruit, is helping to create a following for that grape.

GLORIA FERRER *Established* 1982 *Owner* Freixenet, S.A. *Vineyard area* 335 acres (136 ha)

The Ferrer family from Spain, owners of Freixenet, S.A., are the largest producers of *méthode champenoise* wine in the world. The wines tend to rely heavily on pinot noir in the blend and are exceptional value for this quality of wine, not only in California, but internationally. The Royal Cuvée is a particularly good aperitif.

Skilled workers hand picking, which ensures only fruit of high-quality is used for production of premium wines.

The wines they are a-changin'

Wine styles continue to evolve in the golden state. Top white burgundy was used as a model by quality-seeking California winemakers from the 1960s onwards. Ripe, warm-climate fruit was subjected to the full set of winemaking techniques employed in Burgundy to flesh out cool-climate chardonnay; the resulting wines were often too rich, and alcoholic.

Phylloxera-induced replanting and changes in fashion have shifted top-quality chardonnay growing to much cooler regions such as Russian River Valley, Carneros, and Santa Barbara County. A more gentle hand by the winemaker, coupled with crisper, cooler climate fruit has led to more balanced yet distinctive wines which compete with the best chardonnay worldwide.

ROBERT SINSKEY VINEYARDS *Established* 1986 *Owners* Robert M. Sinskey and Robert M. Sinskey Jr. *Vineyard area* 150 acres (61 ha)

Robert Sinskey produces incredibly silky-textured pinot noir, as well as a merlot that has become a standard for the variety. Most wines come from Carneros plantings, which provides the wines with vivacious acidity. This winery's chardonnay is clean in flavor, one of the few from California to be made without malolactic fermentation.

TRUCHARD VINEYARDS *Established* 1989 *Owners* Tony and Jo Ann Truchard *Vineyard area* 250 acres (101 ha)

Truchard initially provided grapes to other well-known wineries, but by 1989 it was producing wine on its own. It is definitely on the right track, especially with pinot noir and spicy syrah. Truchard uses only estate fruit for its own wines and sells 80 percent of the grapes it produces.

Central Valley

The Central Valley AVA runs 400 miles (645 km) north to south, or nearly three-quarters of the length of the state of California. The spectacular Sierra Nevada range to the east protects this massive AVA from the desert climate of Nevada, and the coastal ranges to the west soften the effects from marine influences. The demarcation begins just north of Redding at Shasta Lake and runs to Bakersfield in the south. This AVA is divided into two subzones, to the north, the smaller, cool Sacramento River Valley; and south, the hot, multicounty San Joaquin Valley.

Three-quarters of California's grape tonnage (including raisin and table) is generated in the Central Valley. Colombard is the most widely planted varietal, followed by chenin blanc, sauvignon blanc, sémillon, muscat, chardonnay, zinfandel, grenache, barbera, carignane, carnelian, cabernet sauvignon, merlot, and mourvèdre; petite sirah and ruby cabernet are also widely planted. Plantings of pinot gris, sangiovese, viognier, and syrah are on the rise.

Canopy management is crucial to vines' health.

Landscape and climate

The Sacramento River Valley is a warm inland area, classified as Region IV. Temperatures climb to 100°F (38°C) in summer. However, the nearby Golden Gate Gap sends its fog and marine breezes as far inland as Lodi. In the summer months cool westerly "carquinez" breezes moderate the climate in Lodi. Clarksburg AVA also has a long, dry growing season, warm summer days, rich alluvial soils, and cooling delta breezes on summer evenings. January and February are foggy.

The San Joaquin Valley is classified as Region IV, warming to Region V in the deep southern plains. The valley floor flatlands of fertile sandy loam are marked with a network of irrigation canals and levees harnessing water from inland rivers and Sierra Nevada snow melts.

Gloves are an essential piece of equipment when picking grapes by hand.

Vines and wines

The Sacramento River Valley produces premium whites and reds. Regional style markers are balance, softer tannins in the reds, dry, restrained and rich fruit character and moderate oak usage. Clarksburg AVA produces good chenin blanc and the Clarksburg chardonnay is worth watching. Dunnigan Hills AVA is notable for the rhône-style and late-harvest wines of R. H. Phillips. Suisin Valley and Solano County–Green Valley AVAs each have one winery.

The zinfandel and carignane grown in Lodi is some of the finest anywhere in the state. Most Lodi reds have a distinct varietal character.

Upscale winemaking dominates in the north, with its emphasis on experimentation, artistry and premium winemaking techniques. Conversely, science and control are prevalent in the south, where continuous bulk production techniques yield consistent quality at low prices. California is far better at this large-scale production than any other region in the world.

Producers

Significant producers in Central Valley, in addition to those below, include Bogle Vineyards, Clayton Vineyards, Delicato Vineyards, Isom Ranch, Gallo, Lucas Winery and Vineyard, and Phillips Vineyards.

JESSIE'S GROVE
Established 1998 *Owner* Greg Burns *Vineyard area* 320 acres (130 ha)

A 32-acre (13 ha) live oak grove inspired this winery's name. The grove and vines that were planted in 1890 remain to this day. Part of one small patch of organically farmed estate zinfandel goes to Turley each year for their Spenker Vineyards Lodi Zinfandel—Greg Burns calls his wine from this same patch Royalty. Burns is crafting world-class zinfandel, and transforming the original 1830 barn into a winery and tasting room.

QUADY WINERY
Established 1977 *Owners* Quady family *Vineyard area* NA

Electra, Elysium, and Essensia are Quady's muscat line. Elysium is a fortified black muscat—rich, deep, and syrupy. Essensia is a paler, more delicate and floral fortified orange muscat. Electra is light, fizzy, and frothy, modeled after moscato d'asti. Quady Starboard port is made of tinta cao, tinta alvarelho, and tinta rouriz from Amador, as are the vintage and nonvintage bottlings.

ST. AMANT WINERY
Established 1980 *Owners* Richard and Barbara St. Amant Spencer *Vineyard area* 34 acres (13.8 ha)

This winery produces excellent old-vine zinfandel, smoky, deep, and low acid barbera, rich and decadent viognier, ripe and briny roussanne, and a port-style wine from five port varietals in open top fermenters à la Portugal. In fact, St. Amant uses these lagare-like low, wide vats to help integrate the tannins on all its reds. St. Amant also bottles a Mohr-Fry Ranch Zinfandel.

Sierra Foothills

The Sierra Foothills, with about 50 wineries, is small in comparison with other Californian regions. It spans the counties of Yuba, Nevada, El Dorado, Amador, Calaveras, Tuolumne, and Mariposa. Rustic country roads wind through pastoral scenes recalling a past era. Climate ranges from Region III to Region IV and varied exposures and elevations create significant fluctuations over the region. Nights are often cold even in summertime, with cold air coming from the peaks of the Sierra Nevada mountains directly into the vineyards.

Pressure from purchasers of fruit have pushed growers in the region to produce more zinfandel, barbera, sangiovese, syrah, and cabernet varieties. The region's wines tend to be less oaky than those from other Californian regions, with rich, dense fruit characters. Old-vine wines have outstanding concentration and Italian and Rhône styles are gaining popularity.

An old jug, used by winemakers for topping up wine barrels.

There are 4 AVAs in the region: North Yuba, El Dorado, California Shenandoah Valley, and Fiddletown. In 2001, the 250-acre (101 ha) Fair Play AVA was approved, in El Dorado County. Eleven wineries in the region focus on mountain-grown fruit. At elevations of 2,000 to 3,000 feet (610 to 915 m), Fair Play has the highest average elevation of any California appellation.

NORTH YUBA

North Yuba was established as an AVA in 1988. Annual rainfall is relatively high, and with well-drained soils, sauvignon blanc and riesling do very well. North Yuba is generally synonymous with the beautiful winery of Renaissance, which has terraced hillsides planted between 1,700 and 2,300 feet (520 to 755 m) with 27 distinct plots. Twelve plots are planted to cabernet sauvignon, which has become winemaker Ben Gideon's specialty. Late harvest sauvignon blanc and recently released viognier and syrah are less rustic and austere.

The Sierra Nevada mountains were initially settled by seekers of gold, many of whom later turned to grape growing.

*The luscious beauty of
the raw material.*

EL DORADO

El Dorado was granted an AVA in 1983. Most of its 16 wineries are east and southeast of Placerville. Currently around 416 acres (168 ha) are part of El Dorado County. Cool nights help the grapes retain high acidity, yet grapes have no problem ripening; soils are granitic, deep, and well drained. El Dorado is a prime site for Italian varieties.

EDMUNDS ST. JOHN VINEYARDS *Established* 1985 *Owners* Steve Edmunds and Cornelia St. John *Vineyard area* no estate acreage

The winery has a long-held reputation for rhône varietals, most notably a Sonoma Valley Durrell Vineyard syrah. El Dorado production includes a Wylie-Fenaughty syrah, a Matagrano Vineyard sangiovese, and a St. Johnson Vineyard pinot grigio. Another popular wine is Rocks and Gravel, a blend of syrah, grenache, and mourvèdre.

CALIFORNIA SHENANDOAH VALLEY

California Shenandoah Valley has 1,300 acres (526 ha) that overlap El Dorado and Amador counties. The AVA was founded in 1983. Snowy winters give way to warm springs which allow for growth, and cool night air flowing from the Sierra Nevadas preserves the vines' high acidity.

SHENANDOAH VINEYARDS/SOBON ESTATE *Established* 1977 *Owners* Leon and Shirley Sobon *Vineyard area* 167 acres (67.5 ha) plus 146 acres (59 ha) organically farmed

The Sobon Estate's Rocky Top, Cougar Hill, and Lubenko bottlings are each reflective of a particular old-vine zinfandel site. The intensely varietal Shenandoah sangiovese has leather and mint rounding out the luscious, dark cherry flavors.

AMADOR COUNTY

Amador County is home to Shenandoah Valley and Fiddletown AVAs and is a key source of old-vine zinfandel. High annual rainfall enables dry farming. Spring frost is common, but zinfandel fares well because it buds late.

MONTEVINA WINERY *Established* 1973 *Owners* Trinchero family *Vineyard area* 600 acres (243 ha)

Recent plantings here include sangiovese and syrah. Montevina is famous for its affordable zinfandel and barbera, and esoteric bottlings such as aglianico, freisa, refosco, and aleatico. The top Terra d'Oro line is well structured and dense.

CALAVERAS COUNTY

Just south of Amador, this region covers about 500 acres (1012 ha) and has seven wineries. Cooler temperatures make this a Region II on the Winkler-Amerine scale, which is particularly good for chardonnay and sauvignon blanc—both would thrive on the limestone and volcanic soils.

BLACK SHEEP WINERY *Established* 1986 *Owners* Dave and Jan Olson *Vineyard area* no estate acreage

Black Sheep is consistently producing small lots of very well-priced quality zinfandel. The Amador County zinfandel is aged in American oak while the Calaveras County line is aged half in American and half in French oak. True Frogs Lily Pad White (100 percent French colombard), is a snob-buster—a slightly sweet white quaffer.

TUOLUMNE COUNTY

SONORA WINERY AND PORT WORKS *Established* 1986 *Owners* Private Partnership *Vineyard area* 3 acres (1.2 ha)

Sonora produces vintage port with the same varietals and techniques as those in the Douro Valley, Portugal. They are also known for old-vine zinfandels. Newer projects include a vinho tinto, a dry red from three port varietals that has met with much critical acclaim, and a tawny port.

San Francisco Bay

San Francisco's magnificent attractions were not lost on those who petitioned for this AVA. Awarded in 1999, the BATF's approval of this AVA has met with much controversy from the industry. The area overlaps five counties which border the San Francisco Bay—San Francisco, San Mateo, Santa Clara, Alameda, Contra Costa, and parts of Santa Cruz and San Benito. There are 5,800 acres (2,349 ha) of vineyard plantings in the region and 39 wineries.

The export-minded Wente family of the Livermore Valley led the petition, convinced that buyers would recognize one of the world's favorite tourist attractions on labels, whereas the Livermore Valley appellation would mean little.

In addition to bringing more recognition to Livermore Valley itself, this new AVA is also home to several other appellation "orphans." Producers in the western Livermore Valley whose acreage falls outside of the current delineation previously deferred to the Central Coast AVA. Now they can use the San Francisco Bay appellation. The

Livermore Valley Winegrowers Association would like to see "San Francisco Bay—Livermore Valley" as the origin noted.

Other appellation orphans include those from Contra Costa County—a lone producer in Martinez, the Conrad Viano Winery—and all of the wines produced from Oakley fruit including those from Bonny Doon, Cline Cellars, Jade Mountain, and Rosenblum Cellars.

CONTRA COSTA COUNTY

Lumped into the larger Central Coast AVA until 1999, Contra Costa is now included in the slightly smaller San Francisco Bay AVA. Some 1,500 acres (607 ha) are planted to zinfandel, mourvèdre, carignane—"kerrigan" in local dialect—alicante bouchet, chardonnay, and palomino, but not a single winery remains.

Completed in 1937, the main span of San Francisco's Golden Gate Bridge is 4,200 feet (1,280 m).

5 miles
(8 kilometers)

To Los Angeles
85 miles (88 km)   Quail
Valley   Sun City

Lake Elsinore

Lake
Elsinore

215

15

RIVERSIDE

County boundary
and name   Murrieta

Producers
1 Callaway Vineyard & Winery
2 Cilurzo Vineyard & Winery
3 Hart Winery
4 Maurice Carrie Vineyard & Winery
5 Mount Palomar Winery
6 Temecula Crest Winery
7 Thornton Winery

Temecula   Temecula
Creek

To San Diego
50 miles (80 km)   SAN DIEGO

UNITED
STATES   WASHINGTON DC

Temecula
Valley

RIVERSIDE

NORTH

Lake
Skinner

Temecula
Valley

3 1   5   6
2   4

Vail Lake

Contra Costa County is an important source of old-vine zinfandel and rhône varietals. Rhône Rangers Bonny Doon, Cline Cellars, Jade Mountain, and zinfandel masters Rosenblum and Turley especially favor Oakley fruit. The Rhône Ranger movement started in Oakley—with old-vine mourvèdre—still a highly sought after old-vine fruit source.

Vineyards in Oakley are on flatlands at the confluence of the Sacramento and San Joaquin rivers and have deep sandy soil. A soft breeze comes through each afternoon and evenings are 10–35°F (2–12°C) cooler than afternoons. Fog sometimes comes up on the water, but it doesn't come out onto the vines.

Vines and wines

Mourvèdre is close to a century old here and finds particular success. It has to struggle to ripen and produces a small crop. Carignane, too, maintains acidity, allowing its particular varietal character to come through.

Old vines of all types are common and give dense, richly fruited wines. Lower end blends are reminiscent of days when wine was made of field blends mixed with water. The premium "zins" and mourvèdres represent the other extreme, fashioned into superextracted, lavishly oaked, and expensive wines. Cline's Small Berry Mourvèdre has a distinctive chocolate mint note, which, with its almost port-like alcohol, makes it a wonderful wine to enjoy after dinner. All but the low end wines have marked longevity.

Producers

Some significant producers in Contra Costa County, in addition to Rosenblum Cellars, include Cline Cellars and Conrad Viano Winery.

ROSENBLUM CELLARS *Established* 1973 *Owners* Kent and Kathy Rosenblum *Vineyard area* no estate vineyards

Two of the Rosenblum's four signature zinfandels come from vineyards in Oakley: Carla's and Continente. Henry's is from Napa Valley and Maggie's is from Sonoma. The wines have deliberately soft tannins and take full advantage of the 25 percent allowable blending, adding zinfandel, cabernet sauvignon, or carignane.

Rhône Rangers

Now a consumer-friendly organization with elaborate tastings, a newsletter, and a website, this term initially referred to a handful of California winemakers who dared to produce wine from such Rhône Valley varieties as marsanne, syrah, rousanne, viognier, grenache, and others.

Owing to the climate and the recent successes of Australian shiraz on world markets, Rhône varieties are booming in California. At the 2002 Rhône Ranger tasting in San Francisco, 130 producers poured hundreds of different offerings of Rhône-inspired wines. The Hospice du Rhône is an educational and charitable event, held in Paso Robles, that brings international Rhône-inspired producers and consumers together each June.

LIVERMORE VALLEY

The Livermore Valley AVA covers a 10 × 15 mile (16 × 24 km) transverse valley nestled into the base of San Francisco Bay's coastal ranges.

In a unique wine country model, developers here must contribute a percentage of land to permanent agriculture and make a donation to a land trust for each home that they want to build.

The current delineation of the AVA covers 96,000 acres (38,850 ha), of which 5,000 acres (2,023 ha) are planted to vines. Most of the Livermore Valley is classified as Region III, though locals quip that "we are Region II-and-a-half." With deep gravelly sedimentary soil, the area has been compared to the Graves region of Bordeaux.

Many vineyards are farmed organically, but few mention this on their labels. Growers constantly guard against the return of phylloxera.

Livermore Valley's ripened offerings.

Vines and wines

Varieties planted include the famous d'Yquem-cutting sauvignon blanc and sémillon, Wente clone chardonnay, cabernet sauvignon, and the first varietally labeled petite sirah. Secondary varietals include bianca, malvasia, merlot, and zinfandel. Cabernet sauvignon is the signature red wine, with petite sirah a close second. The Bordeaux white varietals of sémillon and sauvignon blanc represent the leading whites. In cooler, foggier areas growers plant chardonnay and merlot. Petite sirah has performed well here.

Chardonnay, with pear and melon characteristics, is richer and of higher alcohol than that from Sonoma, and less markedly oaked than that of Napa. The Wente clone gives characteristics of apples, peaches, and bananas. Cabernet sauvignon is beautifully round with classic dark berry fruit and balanced acidity. Lavishly oaked examples are few and far between, even at the super premium level. New plantings include sangiovese, syrah, and pinot gris—the latter two show early promise.

Producers

Significant producers in the Livermore Valley, in addition to those below, include Concannon Vineyards, Fenestra Winery, Ivan Tamas Winery, and Retzlaff Vineyards.

These colored, cut crystal glasses are from the period between 1900 and 1930.

CEDAR MOUNTAIN WINERY

Established 1990 *Owners* Earl and Linda Ault *Vineyard area* 17 acres (6.8 ha)

Cedar Mountain Winery's signature wine is cabernet sauvignon, which ages beautifully and has consistently been awarded gold medals. While cabernet sauvignon may have put Cedar Mountain on the map, they have also garnered accolades for port wines such as Cabernet Royale.

CHOUINARD VINEYARDS (CURRENTLY OUTSIDE THE LV AVA)

Established 1985 *Owners* George and Caroline Chouinard *Vineyard area* 6.5 acres (2.6 ha)

This isolated 100 acre (40.4 ha) estate perched at the top of the Walpert Ridge is far removed from "civilization." Picnics and hiking are encouraged, as is sampling the deeply flavored, elegant estate chardonnay and cabernet sauvignon.

WENTE VINEYARDS ESTATE WINERY

Established 1883 *Owners* Wente family *Vineyard area* 2,000 acres (809 ha)

The Wentes have an undying commitment to quality and to their area that started over 100 years ago. Today, over 80 percent of California's sauvignon blanc, sémillon, and chardonnay originates from the Wente (and former Cresta Blanca) clones. Concentrations are especially high in the North Coast. These wines are sold abroad to 150 countries. Recently the family purchased the famous Cresta Blanca Winery, a state historic landmark, and restored it and its original sandstone caves as a sparkling wine facility.

North Central Coast

California's North Central Coast begins at San Francisco Bay and ends north of Paso Robles in Monterey. The section covers the Santa Cruz Mountains and the adjacent Santa Clara Valley wine regions, the land between the Pacific Ocean and the Diablo Range just south of San Francisco which includes San Mateo, Santa Cruz, Santa Clara, and parts of San Benito counties.

Vineyards in the remote Santa Cruz Mountains are few and far between. Wineries, however, abound. Santa Cruz boasts 43 and Santa Clara 21. Winemakers use the abundant vineyards of Monterey as their primary source of fruit.

SANTA CLARA VALLEY

Santa Clara Valley is the Silicon Valley, there are few vineyards here, in only a few patches to the south. The Santa Clara AVA covers 332,800 acres (134,680 ha), including San Ysidro sub-AVA at 2,340 acres (947 ha) and part of Pacheco Pass

I made a mental note to watch which bottle became empty soonest, sometimes a more telling evaluation system than any other.
GERALD ASHER,
On Wine

AVA, a small valley that overlaps Santa Clara and San Benito counties. Vine area is small—an estimated 200 acres (81 ha), most of this in San Ysidro clustered in the southeast near Gilroy and inland and north of the mouth of Monterey Bay. The powerful marine influence, drawn in along the Pajaro River, cools the warm plains. This area is known as the Hecker Pass. Sarah's Vineyard, famous for chardonnays is here, and the grenache for Bonny Doon's Clos de Gilroy is farmed nearby.

The largest wineries in the valley are Mirassou and J. Lohr—showplaces housing offices rather than functioning wineries; grape growing and winemaking activities take place in Monterey or in the Livermore Valley.

Vines and wines

Santa Clara's fiercely independent winemakers have little production with which to make themselves known, thus commenting on their growing and winemaking is difficult. Only a handful of wines are distributed outside the borders but those tasted are a testament to their unique origin, and are truly reflective of distinct philosophies.

Producers

J. LOHR WINERY

Established 1974 *Owner* Jerry Lohr
Vineyard area 1,735 acres (702 ha)

Winemaker Jeff Meier crafts a Single Vineyard, Estates, and Cypress series, and a de-alcoholized line, Ariel. Bestsellers include a fairly dry Bay Mist riesling and a valdiguie, also known as gamay. Paso Robles syrah shows promise.

Vine leaves painted in autumnal beauty.

SANTA CRUZ MOUNTAINS

The Santa Cruz Mountains play host, albeit unwillingly, to the premier mountain vineyard area in the United States. In 1981, AVA status—the first based on geophysical and climatic factors—was granted. Elevation contour lines at 400 feet (122 m) in the west and 400–800 feet (122–244 m) along the eastern face mark the borders and surround the Santa Cruz Mountain range from Half Moon Bay in the north, to Mount Madonna near Watsonville in the south. Most of the AVA is classified Region I on the Winkler-Amerine scale.

The 350,000 acre (141,640 ha) AVA covers parts of three counties: San Mateo, Santa Cruz, and Santa Clara. Locals estimate that about 750 acres (304 ha) are under vine, mostly in terraces on the steep hillsides above the fog line at daybreak. Sub-AVA Ben Lomond, northwest of Santa Cruz, covers 38,400 acres (15,540 ha), 70 acres (28 ha) of which are planted to vines. Vineyard expansion is unlikely. Constant ocean breezes and maritime fog has facilitated the spread of Pierce's disease, which continues its devastation through the area, and the struggle for urban development continues.

Above: *The russet tones of these vine leaves herald the impending fall harvest.*
Right: *Late-harvest grapes sweetening on the vine.*

Vines and wines

One of U.S.'s cooler climate wine-growing regions, the area's reputation rests on its pinot noir and more recently its chardonnay. The long-lived, intense, brooding and tarry cabernet sauvignons of Kathryn Kennedy, Ridge Vineyards, and Mount Eden, however, are stealing the spotlight.

Randall Grahm resists what he calls the ever-monotonous and monochromatic chardonnay

Hand-picked grapes in California.

anyone else—his newsletters reach far-flung corners of the world. Luckily, production is vast enough to reach the legions of fans. His determination comes in the face of great challenges: Pierce's disease, which has devastated Bonny Doon; and an ill-fated winery plan for Pleasanton in the Livermore Valley. He jokes about his current "winery," a former granola factory in an outlying area of Santa Cruz on the "wrong" side of the tracks.

MT. EDEN VINEYARDS   *Established* 1972 *Owners* Jeffrey and Eleanor Patterson (major shareholders) *Vineyard area* 42 acres (17 ha)

and cabernet sauvignon. He first planted pinot noir here at the coastal vineyards of Bonny Doon. Results were not impressive so he switched to Rhône and Italian types, and some obscure varietals. His vineyards were among the first to fall victim to Pierce's disease and he now sources fruit from Monterey (as do most producers), Contra Costa, and Washington State, as well as from Spain, France, and Germany.

Jeffrey Patterson crafts two styles of chardonnay: a French-style estate version that fools most burgundy fans with its nutty, erotic notes, and the much fruitier, more forward California style MacGregor Vineyard bottling. The estate cabernet is deeply colored, lusciously fruited, and velvety. Mt. Eden wines are notable for their longevity. The Pattersons promote the concept of wine enjoyment at the table through photo and poetry exhibitions.

The average growing season is 300 days; some years, harvest continues well after Thanksgiving. The challenge is great in this cool, rugged terrain and individual styles vary greatly, but all agree that the fruit, not the winemaker, is responsible for greatness. In the 1960s the industry learned about the winery; in the 1990s the vineyard was the focus. Most vinification is typical of California approaches, but a few small producers still release rustic reds with untamed mountain tannins.

RIDGE VINEYARDS   *Established* 1959 *Owner* A. Otsuka *Vineyard area* 60 acres (24.3 ha)

Paul Draper, CEO and winemaker, was named *Decanter*'s Man of the Year 2000. His wines are very popular with the British trade, particularly his Montebello Cabernet Sauvignon with its estate-grown, old-vine fruit that is very restrained early in its life. Americans, according to Draper, prefer the showier, more opulent, corporal zinfandels. Draper is a perfectionist; wine from each plot in this fractured limestone ridge is identified and tasted before blending. Aside from the estate Montebello Cabernet Sauvignon and a series of North and Central Coast zinfandels, releases include an alicante, chardonnay, grenache, mataro, petite sirah, and syrah.

Producers

BONNY DOON VINEYARD   *Established* 1983 *Owners* Grahm family *Vineyard area* 70 acres (28.3 ha) bearing, 70 acres (28.3 ha) newly planted in Monterey

Iconoclast and self-proclaimed "tortured flower child" Randall Grahm has single-handedly brought more attention to the Santa Cruz Mountains than

Monterey County

The Monterey Peninsula coastline is cool, humid, and foggy most of the year, especially in the morning. The sun is shining brightly, however, about 10 miles (16 km) inland. This is the pot of gold at the end of the rainbow—Steinbeck country, where all you see for miles are rows of grape vines. This is Monterey's glorious wine country.

The full potential of the region was widely recognized in the 1950s and 1960s, after a 1944 UC Davis study conducted by A. J. Winkler and Maynard A. Amerine. They reported a climatic range here from low Region I near Monterey Bay to low Region III at King City—comparable with Napa, Sonoma, Burgundy, and Bordeaux. Wente, Mirassou, Paul Masson, and J. Lohr were among the first to seek out land for vineyards here.

Monterey and surrounding areas fall under the larger North Central Coast AVA. Monterey County ends just 30 miles (48 km) north of Paso Robles, the beginning of the South Central Coast.

The six AVAs of San Benito County are San Benito; Paicines; Cienega Valley and its subappellation, Lime Kiln Valley; Mt. Harlan; and Pacheco Pass, a small valley overlapping with Santa Clara County. Mt. Harlan is the county's most relevant AVA, home of Josh Jensens' world-famous Claera Winery, and Pietra Santa, Enz, De Rose, and Flint wineries. The seven AVAs of Monterey County are Monterey (which is geographically located in the Salinas Valley) and its

Well-tended vineyards in the Carmel Valley.

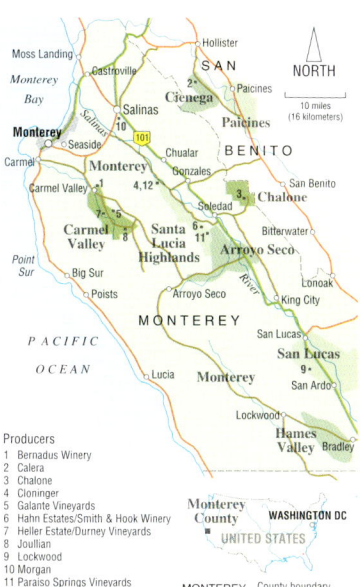

Producers
1 Bernadus Winery
2 Calera
3 Chalone
4 Cloninger
5 Galante Vineyards
6 Hahn Estates/Smith & Hook Winery
7 Heller Estate/Durney Vineyards
8 Joullian
9 Lockwood
10 Morgan
11 Paraiso Springs Vineyards
12 Robert Talbott Vineyards

four sub-AVAs of Arroyo Seco, Hames Valley, San Lucas, and the Santa Lucia Highlands, plus Chalone and Carmel Valley.

Monterey enjoys particular success with pinot blanc, chardonnay, riesling, cabernet sauvignon, pinot noir, and syrah. Chardonnay is the most widely planted, followed by cabernet sauvignon then merlot. Secondary varietals include gewürz-traminer, inzolia, muscat blanc/canelli, sémillon, viognier, white riesling, malvasia bianca, orange muscat, valdiguie (gamay), petite sirah, nebbiolo, and petit verdot.

This vast area is poised to become a significant contributor to the California wine industry.

Left: *Bust of author John Steinbeck, Cannery Row, in downtown Monterey.* The Grapes of Wrath *is his best-known work.* Below: The Big Sur *coast-line attracts numerous vis-itors but many are unaware that it is just a short jour-ney inland to Monterey's glorious wine country.*

Vines and wines

The long growing season with short daily bursts of heat gives intense varietal character if crops are restrained and the fruit reaches full maturity on the vine. Well-developed colors, excellent bal-ance of sugar and acid, fruit true to the natural flavor of the varietal, and the ability to age are becoming the descriptors for Monterey.

Bordeaux varietals thrive in the warmer Carmel and southern Salinas Valley locations. Burgundian varietals show restraint in the higher elevations, but give full throttle, showy, ripe, opulent expres-sions closer to the valley floor, where less day-to-night variation in temperature exists. Rhône and Italian varietals show early promise, especially syrah, which is vibrantly fruity, sometimes smoky, and not nearly as heavily oaked as it is in the North Coast. Potential is strong across the board as Monterey struggles into maturity.

Producers

Significant producers in Monterey County, in addition to those below, include Chalone, Cloninger, Hahn Estates/Smith & Hook Winery, Heller Estate/Durney Vineyards, Lockwood, and Robert Talbott Vineyards.

BERNARDUS WINERY *Established* 1990
Owner Bernardus Marinus Pon *Vineyard area* 52 acres (21 ha)

One of Bernardus Pon's dreams was to create a red wine of equal quality to the finest Bordeaux. He chose the Carmel Valley for its strong track record of producing intense, complex, and long-lived cabernet sauvignon and merlot. The newly released Marinus shows great promise.

CALERA *Established* 1975 *Owner* Josh Jensen
Vineyard area 47 acres (19 ha); 28 acres (11.3 ha) newly planted

Early viognier pioneer and burgundy fanatic Josh Jensen chose Mt. Harlan high in the Gavilan Mountains for the site of his vineyard. Jensen's early success with vineyard-designated pinot noir and chardonnay, as well as the country's first world-class viognier helped focus attention on San Benito County as a fine-wine producing region. Calera single-vineyard pinot noirs are some of the longest lived in America, certainly rivalling their peers in the Côte d'Or.

GALANTE VINEYARDS *Established* 1994 *Owners* Galante family *Vineyard area* 70 acres (28 ha)

Galante's estate wines include Blackjack Pasture, Red Rose Hill, and Rancho Galante cabernet sauvignons. The Rancho Galante is drinkable right out of the gate; the others would benefit from a few years in the cellar, especially the more tannic Red Rose bottling. All three are intense, deeply fruited, rich, balanced wines that represent a benchmark for the region.

JOULLIAN *Established* 1982 *Owners* Ed Joullian and Dick Sias *Vineyard area* 40 acres (16.2 ha)

This 655-acre (265 ha) estate in the heart of the Carmel Valley is a partnership of the Joullian and Sias families. After extensive and expensive contouring and terracing, they planted 40 acres (16.2 ha) to primarily Bordeaux varietals, with a small area going to chardonnay, zinfandel, and petite sirah. Winemaker Ridge Watson is turning

Winery sign and "château" buildings in Carmel Valley.

out truly world-class sauvignon blanc and cabernet sauvignon. He is tinkering with petite sirah because he likes what another "Ridge"—Paul Draper's Ridge Vineyards—does with it.

MORGAN *Established* 1982 *Owners* Dan and Donna Lee *Vineyard area* 65 acres (26.3 ha)

Winemaker Dean De Korth, a burgundy fanatic, is best known for his reserve pinot noir and chardonnay. His newly released syrah and pinot gris are sure to keep the press humming and the consumers lining up at the door. The vineyards are in the Santa Lucia Highlands.

PARAISO SPRINGS VINEYARDS *Established* 1987 *Owners* Rich and Claudia Smith *Vineyard area* 400 acres (162 ha)

The family is very active in the wine grape growing community locally, nationally, and internationally. Their estate vineyard is in the Santa Lucia Highlands. It is no surprise that winemaker Zorn, trained in enology at Bad Kreuznach, makes the benchmark riesling of the county. In fact, the bone-dry, rich, petrolly riesling caught the attention of connoisseurs around the globe. Answering to consumer demand, however, the winery recently reverted to an off-dry style. Paraiso Springs is renowned for its elegant, deeply flavored pinot noir, syrah, chardonnay, and pinot blanc. Zorn makes Cobblestone Chardonnay, a joint venture with the Levine family, owners of the Arroyo Seco vineyard, as well as own-label Tria with fellow winemaker Bill Knuttel of Chalk Hill.

South Central Coast

California's central coast runs from Santa Barbara in the south to Santa Cruz in the north. The south central coast comprises two counties: San Luis Obispo (SLO) in the north and Santa Barbara (SB) in the south. Proximity to the cooling effect of coastal waters and breezes is particularly marked in these regions. The transverse orientation of the coastal mountain range allows the channeling of cool marine-influenced air inland, resulting in cool climates in the westerly reaches of the Santa Ynez, Santa Maria, Los Alamos, and Edna Valleys. Long growing seasons, sunshine, and relative warmth in the fall ensure ripe grapes with good retained natural acidities.

San Luis Obispo County has four AVAs: Edna Valley, Arroyo Grande, Paso Robles, and York Mountain. Santa Barbara County's AVAs are the Santa Ynez, Santa Maria, and Los Alamos Valleys.

A traditional wine decanter resting on its stand.

EDNA VALLEY AND ARROYO GRANDE

Edna Valley and Arroyo Grande are adjacent and have many shared characteristics, including a joint vintners' and grape growers' association. Located next to the charming university town of San Luis Obispo, Edna Valley was granted AVA status in 1982. Arroyo Grande is located just to its south. Together they cover 2,000 acres (810 ha). Edna Valley's development as a wine-producing region really began in the late 1960s, with the Niven family being particularly prominent. They are owners of the Paragon Vineyard and have formed two strategic alliances, the first being a partnership with the Chalone Wine Group in the formation of

Laetitia vineyards in Arroyo Grande.

Edna Valley Winery in 1980. The most recent partnership occurred when Australia's giant Southcorp bought into the Seven Peaks Winery.

Arroyo Grande has also been the scene of international partnerships. Maison Deutz was a 1982 Franco-American joint venture involving the Deutz Champagne house. Currently owned by other Frenchmen and renamed Laetitia, this one-time sparkling-wine-only specialist now also produces table wines.

Edna Valley is a designated Region I–II. The east-to-west valley opens up to the cooling effects of the Pacific Ocean at Morro Bay. Arroyo Grande's climate varies significantly as one moves inland.

Vines and wines

Edna Valley and Arroyo Grande represent a continuum of viticulture from the 1970s to the present. Saucelito Canyon is an exception with its 100-year-old zinfandel vines. More recent plantings have included newer clones and altered spacing as in the rest of the state. Modern techniques mirror much of California with some notable exceptions. Maison Deutz brought classic champagne-production techniques to the region. These, along with traditional techniques from Burgundy, continue to be practiced at Laetitia by the French winemaker there. Seven Peaks has an Australian winemaker producing wines in the Roseworthy tradition.

Producers

ALBAN VINEYARDS

Established 1986
Owner John Alban
Vineyard area 60 acres
(24.3 ha)

Alban's winery was the
first all-Rhône variety
winery in California.
Grenache, syrah, viognier,
and roussanne are pro-
duced. Wines are well
made and good value.

EDNA VALLEY VINEYARD

Established 1979 *Owners*
Chalone Wine Group and
the Niven family *Vineyard
area* 1,000 acres (405 ha)

The wines at Edna Valley are well made, well
priced, and reliable for chardonnay and pinot
noir. A traditional-method sparkling wine available at the winery is also good.

Above: *Extensive vine-
yards near Paso Robles.*
Right: *A picnic at
Meridian Vineyards,
Paso Robles.*

PASO ROBLES

Paso Robles, the largest of the San Luis Obispo
County AVAs, consists of 20,000 acres (8,100 ha)
of plantings. In 1999, 2 million cases were produced by 45 wineries. This represents remarkable
growth, up from 6,500 acres (2,633 ha) and
25 wineries in 1994.

In 1989 phylloxera biotype-A struck Paso
Robles. Planting and replanting occurred throughout the 1990s. The region did well as the nation
turned to red wine (Paso Robles has a history
of producing better red wines, particularly full-
throttle zinfandels, than whites.) Zinfandel,
cabernet, and merlot plantings all increased.
New rootstocks, new clones, new varieties, and
higher-density plantings were all the rage.

Paso Robles is the warmest of California's
coastal valleys—Region III–IV, but diurnal variation is marked, usually 40–50°F (4–10°C). Cool
air makes its way
through the Templeton
Gap in the late after-
noon to early evening.
Early mornings are very cool and it takes a while
for the land and the vines to heat up.

The west side of the valley is hilly and somewhat cooler than the flat east side. Soils are well-
drained and of low-to-moderate vigor. Rainfall
occurs mostly during the winter. Western vineyards average 30 inches (76 cm), while the east
side receives a paltry 9 inches (23 cm) annually.

Vines and wines

Planted varieties include zinfandel, chardonnay
and the classic varieties from Bordeaux, the
Rhône Valley and central–northern Italy. Older,
phylloxera-resistant plantings are on Rupestris St.
George rootstock. Own-rooted vines are either

New plantings in Paso Robles.

and mourvèdre are fairly recent, and successful, additions. Both Rhône-inspired wines are well structured with true varietal character and good intensity of ripe fruit.

YORK MOUNTAIN WINERY

Established 1882 *Owner* **Max Goldman** *Vineyard area* 5 acres (2 ha)

York Mountain Winery was established by Andrew York as the Ascension Winery, and is the region's oldest winery in continuous operation. It was also the first commercial winery in the region. Owing to its location in far western and cooler Paso Robles, and its long history, York Mountain Winery was awarded its own AVA in 1983.

scheduled for replanting or doomed to repeat history. A host of resistant rootstocks is being utilized, including 110R, 140R, 1103P, and 3309C. Nematodes can cause problems in this area and this may influence the choice of rootstock.

Since the climate is warm and dry, there is little disease pressure and many growers are opting for an organic approach. Cover crops and decreased spraying are popular measures. Also, smaller producers are making their wines with an eye to minimizing such interventions as fining and filtering; others try to keep sulfur dioxide at a minimum.

Producers

EBERLE WINERY
Established 1983 *Owner* **Gary Eberle** *Vineyard area* 42 acres (17 ha)

Gary Eberle was involved in the planting at the Estrella River Winery and was one of the first to introduce syrah to the region. His wines are good across the board and very reliable, and his ripe-styled cabernet ages very well. The syrah and viognier are regional standards.

WILD HORSE WINERY
Established 1983 *Owners* **Ken and Tricia Volks** *Vineyard area* 50 acres (20 ha)

Wild Horse is a reliable source of well-made and well-priced merlot and cabernet sauvignon. Syrah

SANTA BARBARA COUNTY (SBC)

The Santa Ynez, Santa Maria, and Los Alamos Valleys comprise 4,000, 12,000, and 8,000 acres (1,620, 4,860, and 3,240 ha) respectively. This expanding region currently has 46 wineries, and local wine volume increased 230 percent between 1992 and 1998.

Santa Barbara is at the demarcation between central and southern California. The natural expectation is that vineyards here would be warmer than those north of San Francisco, but they are not. The opening of the Santa Maria Valley is much larger than the Santa Ynez Valley, which accounts for cooler conditions at similar distances from the coast. Thus as one moves farther inland, conditions change from untenable for grape growing to Region I to Region II. As the coastal influence ultimately falls off inland, temperatures rise rapidly, yielding Regions III and IV.

Santa Barbara County is dry, receiving some 8–10 inches (20–25 cm) of rain a year, mostly from November to March. Soils are variable, tending toward sandy loams; and the growing season is long.

More so than places in northern California, Santa Barbara is prone to some very warm temperatures during the fall. Maximum temperatures may be 85–90°F (29–32°C), cooling off to 50°F (10°C) at night. This gives an extended growing season that allows chardonnay, pinot noir, and syrah time to ripen.

Vines and wines

Chardonnay and pinot noir are the primary varieties here. Chardonnay combines ripeness with good-to-very-good retained natural acidity. Most are barrel fermented, with the better wines having a balance between apple or pear or tropical fruit notes and oak. Many other white varieties are treated like chardonnay with the better efforts letting the fruit show through the influence of new oak. Pinot noir has had a spiced-tea note added to very good underlying berry fruit.

The Screw Pull. A popular and efficient corkscrew, resting in its stand.

This seems to have been a function of the planting material. New clones do not have the herbal notes and are nicely perfumed. Overall, the style is fairly robust and occasionally somewhat rustic.

Merlot, cabernet franc, and cabernet sauvignon are certainly less ripe than their Napa counterparts. Herbaceousness has been problematic in the past but planting on warmer sites and better canopy management is yielding riper fruit. Syrah shows promise here. Warmer vintages add smoked-meat aromas to clean-berry fruit. Cooler vintages tend toward peppery notes. The better wines have good acidity and balanced tannins.

Vineyards planted during the 1970s through to the early 1990s were not planted on rootstock. Phylloxera was discovered in 1994 but has spread slowly on the sandy soils. New plantings were at higher densities, and involved a variety of rootstocks, new varieties, and different clonal selections of such standards as pinot noir and chardonnay.

Overhead-trained sauvignon blanc vines in the Santa Ynez Valley, California.

Chardonnay, pinot noir, and syrah are the main grapes grown on Cambria Winery's sweeping slopes.

Producers

AU BON CLIMAT (ABC) *Established* 1982
Owners **Morgan and Jim Clendenen** *Vineyard area*
43 acres (17 ha)

Jim Clendenen produces some of California's best pinot noir and chardonnay from a number of vineyard sites. His pinot noir brims with berry fruit and shows intense yet delicate flavors, balance, and length. His chardonnay demonstrates power and finesse, while retaining good acidity and balance. Additionally, Jim is part of the brains trust that combines the talents of ABC, Qupé, Makor, Il Podere de Olivos, Vita Nova, and the Hitching Post. Other ventures include Vita Nova and Ici La Bas. Vita Nova is successful with Italian varieties and Bordeaux blends. Its Acceomicus, a blend of petite verdot and cabernet sauvignon, shows nice cassis fruit.

FOXEN *Established* 1987 *Owners* **Bill Wathen and Richard Dore** *Vineyard area* **15 acres (6 ha)**

Foxen produces bold, well-crafted wines. Chardonnay is uniformly excellent; pinot noir is muscular and ages well. Foxen's Bordeaux blends prove that given the right site, these varieties can do well here. The barrel-fermented chenin blanc is one of the best examples in the state.

LONGORIA *Established* 1982 *Owners* **Rick and Diana Longoria** *Vineyard area* **8 acres (3.2 ha)**

This family-operated business handcrafts their wines. Rick Longoria's pinot noir is one of the region's best, as are his merlot and cabernet franc. The 1997 Pinot Noir Reserve from the Bien Nacido vineyard combines expansive notes of smoky game, berry fruit, and oak on the palate with good balance and length of finish.

QUPÉ *Established* 1982 *Owner* **Bob Lindquist** *Vineyard area* **12 acres (4.9 ha)**

Qupé means golden poppy in the local Chumash Indian language. Bob Lindquist, the rock-solid counterpoint to Jim Clendenen's flamboyance, produces very good chardonnay, and is one of California's leading Rhône Rangers. He also makes fine viognier, marsanne, and red Rhône blends. A pioneer of syrah in the region, his syrah is the local benchmark, with berry aromatics and smoked-meat flavors framed in oak, and is recognized as among the state's best.

Southern California

Temecula and Cucamonga are Southern California's AVAs of significance. Ever-growing metropolitan Los Angeles chips away at Cucamonga's old vines, offering them an uncertain future. Pierce's disease has ravaged Temecula and places this improving region in peril. Yet, both regions are important from historical and current viticultural perspectives.

Vines and wines

The Cucamonga Valley still contains 1,000 acres (405 ha) of vines, with old, dry-farmed vines maintaining such Rhône varieties as mourvèdre, syrah, grenache, and cinsault. Old-vine mission grapes are still found and provide a vital link to the past. Deep sandy soils have protected the vines from phylloxera. The absence of citrus and other hosts for the leafhopper have also kept Pierce's disease away, though not from Temecula.

Viticulture in Temecula has seen quality improvement over the past decade or so, particularly with new varieties. Although chardonnay has been successful—65 percent of plantings—the shift to Rhône and Italian varieties better suited to the warm climate

has yielded the best wines to date. Viognier here has been high quality, clean and fruity with variable amounts of oak. Chenin blanc produces a clean, floral, fruity wine with good retained acidity. Cabernet sauvignon and merlot from Temecula—though not as successful as petite sirah or zinfandel—have improved and produce rich, alcoholic, and tannic wines.

Old-vine palomino and several Portuguese varieties provide excellent material for fortified wines from Cucamonga. Sherry- and port-style wines have richness and length of finish. They are some of the state's best.

Sparkling, sweet, and fortified wines are all represented in the two regions, with table wines having the greatest economic impact. Both areas are too warm to produce high-quality chardonnay, though Temecula chardonnay has had good marketing and commercial success.

The real excitement comes from other varieties. Cucamonga produces alcoholic, full-throttle Rhône-style wines from old-vine grenache, syrah,

Pierce's disease is a threat to vines in Temecula.

5 miles
(8 kilometers)

UNITED
STATES
WASHINGTON DC

Temecula
Valley

To Los Angeles
55 miles (88 km)   Quail
Valley   Sun City

Lake Elsinore

RIVERSIDE

Lake
Elsinore   215

NORTH

Lake
Skinner

RIVERSIDE

County boundary
and name   Murrieta

Temecula
Valley

5 · 6
3 · 7 · · 2
1

Vail Lake

Producers
1 Callaway Vineyard & Winery
2 Cilurzo Vineyard & Winery
3 Hart Winery
4 Maurice Carrie Vineyard & Winery
5 Mount Palomar Winery
6 Temecula Crest Winery
7 Thornton Winery

Temecula

Creek

To San Diego
50 miles (80 km)   SAN DIEGO

cinsault, carignane, and mourvèdre. Temecula has also produced good wines from the same Rhône varieties, as well as barbera, sangiovese, and cortese.

CUCAMONGA VALLEY

The Cucamonga Valley has vines scattered amid freeways, the Ontario airport, industrial developments, and new housing. Though in decline as a viticultural region, it remains an important source of old-vine grenache, mourvèdre, syrah, mission, and zinfandel for California.

GALLEANO WINERY *Established* 1927 *Owner* Don Galleano *Vineyard area* 100 acres (40.1 ha) owned; 500 acres (202 ha) leased

Galleano is a producer of note—it is a resource for dry-farmed, old-vine Rhône varieties and zinfandel. The grenache rosé has attracted many medals; it is dry, clean, and packed with peppery, berry grenache. Zinfandel, grenache, carignane, and mourvèdre—barrel and vat—demonstrate purity of varietal fruit and great character.

TEMECULA VALLEY

Cool air from the Pacific moderates temperatures from late afternoon via the Rainbow and Santa Margarita gaps in the coastal ranges. Well-drained granitic soils and low rainfall necessitate irrigation. Pierce's disease is the primary challenge to the more than 3,000 acres (1,214 ha) of vines. In excess of 200 acres (80 ha) were lost in 1999 with about 30 percent of the vines affected. Phylloxera is not a problem.

Mechanical harvesting is quick but less selective than harvesting by hand.

Significant producers in the Temecula Valley, in addition to those below, include Callaway Vineyard & Winery, Cilurzo Vineyard & Winery, Maurice Carrie Vineyard & Winery, Temecula Crest Winery, and Thornton Winery.

HART WINERY *Established* 1974 (vineyard), 1980 (winery) *Owners* Hart family *Vineyard area* 11 acres (4.5 ha)

Hart has a reputation for the best quality production in Temecula. Every wine has balance and delightful fruit that is allowed to take center stage, with judicious use of oak. The grenache rosé is one of California's best blush wines. Viognier demonstrates wonderful apricot aromatics with refreshing acidity and balance. Red Rhône varieties are all well made, as is barbera. With rare exceptions, cellar-door prices represent very good value.

MOUNT PALOMAR WINERY *Established* 1975 *Owners* Poole Properties Inc. *Vineyard area* 75 acres (30.4 ha)

Mount Palomar makes quality wines and also supplies grapes to other growers. Most remarkable is an unoaked, cleanly made cortese with good intensity of fruit, lively acidity, good balance, and a long finish. Varietal and blended white Rhône varieties under the Rey Sol label have also been successful.

SAN PASQUAL VALLEY

Located 15 miles (24 km) from the Pacific Ocean, the San Pasqual Valley AVA is cooler than either Temecula or Cucamonga. This is also the newest area, and one that is up-and-coming.

ORFILA VINEYARDS & WINERY *Established* 1994 *Owner* Alejandro Orfila *Vineyard area* 40 areas (16 ha)

Orfila's wines have been turning heads over the past two years. Its syrah and viognier have received rave reviews and won handfuls of medals. The merlot and sangiovese are also well done.

EASTERN UNITED STATES

In the early 1990s the wine industry in the eastern United States was restricted to isolated vintners producing regional curiosities with a modest local following. Aggressively flavored and usually sweet, wines were almost always made from native American grapes (principally *Vitis labrusca*) and/or French–American hybrids. Today, the European *Vitis vinifera* dominates the east and its wines are attracting critical acclaim, both internationally and in upscale restaurants.

Whites showed early promise, especially riesling, chardonnay, and hybrids seyval and vidal. More recently red wines have improved, including cabernet sauvignon, franc, and merlot.

History

Wine has been made in the United States since Europeans arrived. The colonists found grapes in the new land—there are more grape varieties in the region between the Atlantic coast and the Rocky Mountains than anywhere else on earth. European cuttings were brought to Virginia in 1619, and for 350 years America struggled to establish a viable commercial wine industry. Climate took its toll, but the worst enemy was disease. While native grapes were resistant to Pierce's disease, black rot, phylloxera, mildews, and other indigenous fungal problems, European imports were not.

Once phylloxera was brought under control in the late 1800s, the Californian wine industry soared. In the cooler, damper, eastern states, *vinifera* vines remained an impossible dream and viticulturists turned to hybrids. With improved vineyard practices, the industry began to flourish, particularly

New York City is only about 40 miles (65 km) south of the Hudson River AVA.

around Lake Erie and the Finger Lakes. Yet before the boom had begun, Prohibition brought it to a halt.

It was almost 30 years before various states in the east began to cultivate vines in earnest. Only in the past decade has growth surged: in 1976, for example, Virginia had six wineries; by 1999 it had 60. Ninety percent of all U.S. wine is produced in California, with the remaining 10 percent divided among the other 47 wine-producing states. Yet production continues at an astonishing rate. Other states may soon be producing wine commercially. Vermont, with a climate once

> *I know never to take a wine for granted. Drawing a cork is like attendance at a concert or at a play that one knows well, when there is all the uncertainty of no two performances ever being quite the same. That is why the French say, "There are no good wines, only good bottles."*
>
> GERALD ASHER,
> *On Wine*, 1982.

growing season. Viticultural Uplands include northern New Jersey, the Delaware River Valley, much of Pennsylvania, Maryland, northern and central Virginia, Connecticut, and the Hudson River Valley and Finger Lakes regions of New York.

The Mountains' high altitudes and harsh climate make grapegrowing difficult, but in certain isolated microclimates in the mountains of Virginia and central Pennsylvania the right combination of soil and sunlight provides a hospitable environment for vines.

Above: *Green vistas and fertile farmland in Pennsylvania, part of the Atlantic Uplands.*
Left: *Riesling grapes, among the earliest varieties grown in the eastern United States.*

considered unsuitable for viticulture, has seen successful plantings of *vinifera*.

Landscape and climate
There are three distinct viticultural areas: Benchlands, Atlantic Uplands, and Mountains. The Benchlands are benches of sand, sediment, and stone formed from debris left by drifting glaciers thousands of years ago. The Benchlands include southeastern Massachusetts and the coastal sections of Rhode Island, Connecticut, Long Island, New Jersey, and Virginia. Weather here is usually temperate. Farther inland, the viticultural region around Lake Erie resembles the Benchlands.

The Atlantic Uplands is a vast plateau between the coastal zones of the Atlantic Ocean and the eastern mountain ranges. The Uplands has mineral-rich, well-drained soils and a relatively long

Vines and wines
The best white grapes in the east include chardonnay, with a wide stylistic range, although wines lack the fruitiness of California wine. Riesling (dry, semidry, or sweet) is well-suited to the cooler regions around Lake Erie and the Finger Lakes. Gewürztraminer, especially from New England and the Finger Lakes areas, can yield fragrant and delicate wines. Seyval blanc can resemble a fragrant blend of chardonnay and pinot blanc. But vidal blanc promises most—especially grapes from the Finger Lakes or the mountains of Virginia—as a late-harvest or icewine with intense honeyed flavors and bracing acidity. Vignoles also makes outstanding late-harvest and icewine.

The best red grapes include merlot, the dominant red in Virginia and on Long Island, where it can produce full-bodied lively single-varietal wines and is important in red blends. Cabernet franc is often thin and herbaceous, but is improving. Sometimes good as a single varietal, cabernet sauvignon is at its best in Bordeaux-style blends. Pinot noir is starting to show but is very dependent on a good weather, full ripeness and low yields—as well as superior winemaking.

New York State

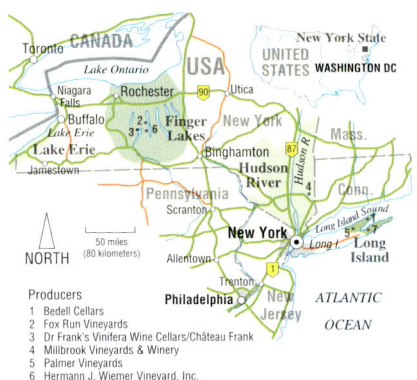

New York State is arguably the most promising wine-producing state in the east. Along with Virginia, it has led the eastern states in wine production since the repeal of Prohibition. Although wine production goes back 170 years, two-thirds of the state's 139 wineries have been established since 1985. The industry is a work in progress; certain varietals—for example, riesling from the Finger Lakes—may be better suited to the east than to more temperate West Coast climes.

Significant producers in Eastern United States, in addition to those below, include Bedell Cellars, Fox Run Vineyards, Millbrook Vineyards & Winery, Palmer Vineyards, and Herman J. Wiemer Vineyard, Inc. (all in New York), and Sakonnet Vineyards (New England).

DR. FRANK'S VINIFERA WINE CELLARS/CHÂTEAU FRANK *Established* 1963 *Owners* Frank family *Vineyard area* 76 acres (31 ha)

The riesling and gewürztraminer from here are among the region's best. Recent chardonnays have been crisp and flavorful. Sister winery, Château Frank, makes sprightly sparklers.

WOLFFER ESTATE *Established* 1992 *Owner* Christian Wolffer *Vineyard area* 50 acres (20 ha)

This is the most important winery on Long Island's South Fork. Production here is restricted to a few varietals, a flinty and refreshing char-

donnay, and a merlot with juicy, cherry flavors. The sparkling wine has elegance and structure.

OTHER EASTERN PRODUCERS

BARBOURSVILLE VINEYARDS, VIRGINIA *Established* 1976 *Owners* Zonin family *Vineyard area* 120 acres (48.6 ha)

This was the first producer to succeed with *vinifera* varieties in Virginia. Italian classics—pinot grigio, sangiovese, and barbera, as well as pinot noir, chardonnay, merlot, cabernet franc, and cabernet sauvignon are produced. There are good vintages of lush dessert wines—philéo (muscat, riesling, and malvasia), and malvasia reserve.

HORTON VINEYARDS, VIRGINIA *Established* 1993 *Owners* Dennis and Sharon Horton *Vineyard area* 100 acres (40.5 ha)

This winery is one of Virginia's success stories. Dennis Horton concentrates on viognier, syrah, marsanne, mourvèdre, grenache, and malbec. Another hot-climate success is touriga nacional. Horton's norton, a native grape that produces inky purple wine redolent of plums and cherries, is a favorite.

Tending the vines at Brimstone Hill Winery, on the Shawangunk Wine Trail, New York.

Other U.S. Regions

THE SOUTHWEST

The Southwest is the oldest wine-producing region in the United States. Spanish missionaries planted grapes in New Mexico in the 1500s, and in Texas in the 1600s. Scores of vineyards and wineries thrived until 1920 and Prohibition. Replanting did not begin in earnest until the 1970s. Today Texas is the fifth-largest wine-producing state in the United States, with more than 3,000 acres (1,214 ha) of mostly *vinifera* plantings and around 40 wineries. New Mexico has 22 wineries and foreign investment has been strong. Colorado has 26 wineries, with virtually all its vineyards on the western slopes of the state.

The Southwest, where the sun shines intensely, has the warmest summer weather of any grape-growing region, yet winters can be bitterly cold. Lack of water in parched areas is a problem. Best growing sites combine high altitude, dry air, and relatively cool temperatures in the growing season.

As in most other states, restrictive laws make selling wine a challenge, although this is changing. In Arizona, for example, recent changes in state law will make it easier for vintners to sell their wine direct within the state itself.

Chardonnay, cabernet sauvignon, and merlot all do well in most of the southwestern viticultural regions. Sauvignon blanc, chenin blanc, and riesling are also favored. Zinfandel is gaining a foothold, particularly in western Texas, and syrah, sangiovese, and tempranillo all show promise. Good dessert wines, especially fortified port-style wines, are quite successful in areas where the hot summers and cold winters resemble the climate of the Douro Valley in Portugal.

FALL CREEK VINEYARDS, TEXAS *Established* 1975 **Owners** Ed and Susan Auler *Vineyard area* 65 acres (26 ha)

Fall Creek produces chardonnay, chenin blanc, riesling, cabernet sauvignon, and merlot. Of particular note is the high-end and very limited Meritus, a blend of merlot, cabernet sauvignon, and malbec.

TWO RIVERS WINERY, COLORADO *Established* 1999 **Owners** Bob and Billie Witham *Vineyard area* 17 acres (7 ha)

Colorado's youngest winery, Two Rivers has already been getting good press for its merlot and chardonnay, and especially for its earthy cabernet sauvignon. Production is expected to double over the next few years.

THE MIDWEST

The weather is a challenge in the Midwestern states, but recent viticultural research, advances in cool-climate production technology, and a string of good vintages have all contributed to some outstanding progress.

The Midwest's strongest wine-producing states are

Dry-stone walls, built without mortar, are used as protective windbreaks and to define borders.

Ohio, Michigan, and Missouri. By the 1850s, Ohio was the leading wine-producing state, but 75 years later, Prohibition and disease had destroyed most of the region's wine industry. Serious rebuilding did not begin until the 1970s, but Ohio is now booming—it boasts 70 wineries.

Michigan had few wineries before Prohibition, but boutique wineries are now thriving, particularly in the southwestern corner of Lake Michigan's shoreline.

In Missouri, the first wines were made in 1823 by French Jesuits. Stone Hill—the state's leading wine estate—was founded in 1847. It became a mushroom farm during Prohibition.

The stable temperatures of the Great Lakes' deep waters warm the air blowing across the lakes and over surrounding areas, reducing the threat of late spring and early fall frosts and prolonging the growing season. In winter, heavy snow packs insulate the dormant vines.

Because of the severe Midwest winters, cool-climate grapes do best. Hybrids dominate, but *vinifera* types are gaining a following. White wines are riesling, chardonnay, gewürztraminer, seyval, and vignoles. Pinot noir (for sparkling wine) and cabernet franc lead red *vinifera* plantings.

The Midwest's prospects are bright, as Ohio has introduced initiatives and incentives that have effectively promoted viticulture and winemaking. Neighboring states are beginning to follow suit.

Above: *Expanses of well-spaced, trained vines—typical of a United States vineyard.*
Right: *Freshly harvested gewürztraminer grapes.*

CHÂTEAU GRAND TRAVERSE, MICHIGAN
Established 1974 *Owners* O'Keefe family *Vineyard area* 112 acres (45.5 ha)

This winery established Michigan's *vinifera* industry. The johannisberg, riesling, pinot gris, chardonnay, pinot blanc, icewine, and cabernet franc are all noteworthy.

L. MAWBY VINEYARDS, MICHIGAN *Established* 1978 *Owner* Larry Mawby *Vineyard area* 12 acres (5 ha)

Mawby's sparkling brut wines include chardonnay/pinot noir/pinot meunier cuvée, blanc de noirs, *blanc de blancs*, rosé, and vignoles.

ST. JULIAN WINE COMPANY, MICHIGAN
Established 1936 *Owner* David Braganini *Vineyard area* 200 acres (81 ha)

St. Julian Wine Company is Michigan's oldest and largest winery. It makes a vast assortment of wines from hybrid and *vinifera* grapes.

STONEHILL WINERY, MISSOURI *Established* 1847 *Owners* Held family *Vineyard area* 92 acres (37 ha)

Stonehill produces hybrid and a few labrusca wines. Especially noteworthy are a bold red norton, a deliciously dry seyval, and a good sparkler.

Mexico and South America

It is well known that Chile and Argentina (see pages 402–416) have the potential to unsettle the best traditional winemakers; but neighboring Mexico, Perú, Brazil, and Uruguay each have a significant industry and great history behind them. Mexico and Perú were the most important centers of Spain's colonial empire, and each had a viceregal court. As a conse-

quence, they were influenced by many of Spain's habits, including the cultivation of vines and winemaking. Both Mexico and Perú are a touch hot for the best viticulture, yet important winemaking industries survive in each. Brazil was the jewel in Portugal's empire and has inherited an interest in wine. Its economy is currently the most important in Latin America and

its domestic wine market is huge. The core of Brazil's wine industry nestles on the cooler southern border with Uruguay, which has a most successful wine industry. Tannat is a grape variety that is as adaptable as any, and in Uruguay's several wine regions it has achieved an expressive quality found nowhere else in the world.

NORTH

250 miles
(400 kilometers)

MEXICO

Mexico benefits from its long links with Europe as well as having nearby California as an influential winemaking example. This gives it a certain charm combined with some of the scientific approach so typical of its northern neighbor. Taken as a whole, these elements make for some interesting viticultural potential within a setting that, in truth, is not ideally suited to *Vitis vinifera*.

Nevertheless, major producers such as Domecq, Hennessy, and Martell have significant investments in Mexico. Sparkling wine interests have also entered the market.

Wine regions

Baja California in the northwest and the high-altitude valleys of the Sierra Madre offer the best potential for winemaking in Mexico.

More than 10,000 acres (4,000 ha) are planted here, mainly near Ensenada. Bodegas Santo Tomás makes commendable chardonnay and some passable cabernet sauvignon. Bodegas Santo Tomás and Monte Zenic give Mexican winemaking a diversity that is evident in the varieties used, and includes chardonnay, viognier, barbera, cabernet sauvignon, and pinot noir. L. A. Cetto makes Mexico's most recommendable range of wines. Their nebbiolo and petit syrah have met with some critical success.

Vineyards in the Guadalupe Valley, Mexico.

Laguna, Torreón, has seen recent investment at Bodega Vergel. New equipment struggles admirably to coax aromatic life out of grapes.

Parras Valley's altitude, 1,500 feet (458 m), comes to the rescue here—still, brandy remains king. Viñedos San Marcos produces reasonable sparkling wine and modest cabernet sauvignon.

San Juan del Río takes viticulture to 6,000 feet (1,830 m), allowing for somewhat more aromatic potential. Cavas de San Juan makes some interesting cabernet sauvignon and tentative pinot noir; its Carte Blanche sparkling wine is definitely worthy of note.

Zacatecas and Aguascalientes plateaus grow grapes at up to 7,000 feet (2,135 m). Bodegas Altiplano has some reasonable wines. A fairly new region, Querétaro, may yet provide further potential for aromatic properties in varietals.

PERÚ

Perú was the first country on the continent of South America to benefit from viticulture. The first vineyards were planted in the 1540s, however, climatic conditions did not favor the production of quality wine. But with the advent of distillation into grape brandy, the prospects for viticulture changed considerably.

The Pisco Valley, 100 miles (160 km) south of the capital, Lima, proved a suitable spot for cultivating moscatel, torontel, albillo, and a host of lesser-known grape varieties, all destined to be distilled into a spirit also called Pisco.

Landscape and climate

Perú is divided into three main geographical areas: coastal, central mountain, and the Amazon

Above: *A wineskin popularized in peasant societies but little more than a curiosity in most cultures these days.*
Left: *Sampling the wares at a wine seller's in Parras, Baja California, Mexico.*

Basin. All viticulture of note takes place on the coastal area, reaching up into the foothills of the Andes mountain range. Winter temperatures remain too high for vines to go into full dormancy, which makes it difficult to restrain vigor, although careful monitoring of anhydrous stress can yield reasonable results. Most producers of Pisco can obtain two harvests per year.

Vines and wines

Quality wine production is concentrated mainly around the city of Ica. The main force in Peruvian winemaking today is Tacama, based a short distance outside Ica. Varietal malbec and blends such as Gran Vino Tinto Reserva Especial form the backbone of Tacama's quality production. Other producers include Viña Ocucaje, also based in Ica; Canepa in Tacna; and Fábrica Nacional de Licores in Surco.

BRAZIL

Brazil was settled by the Portuguese, who soon introduced *Vitis vinifera* into their new territory. Now it is South America's third-largest wine producer after Argentina and Chile.

If big is beautiful, Brazil has it all. Commercially, demographically, and geographically, it is a giant. The eighth-largest economy in the world is certainly a place to sell wine. Although Brazilian interest in wine is still nascent, with annual consumption at less than half a gallon (2 l) per capita, the potential is plain to see.

Landscape and climate

Brazil is not ideal for viticulture—the climate is far too moist and hot, and it is difficult to find varietal character in grapes grown in such conditions—so viticulture is concentrated in the cooler southernmost regions. There are two main clusters: Rio Grande do Sul, which includes the hilly Serra Gaucha region, and Frontera. Even here humidity, rainfall, and heat can cause problems, particularly near harvest. While Serra Gaucha developed as a result of immigrant settlement, Frontera was chosen for its viticultural potential on slightly more scientific grounds and so holds most promise. There have also been some attempts at tropical viticulture near Recife, but these have yet to attract serious attention.

Vines and wines

Only the bravest or those with the most to gain pit themselves against the elements to make wine in Brazil. Market leaders such as Remy Martin and Moët & Chandon are all found here. Sparkling wine is made to reasonably high standards and Serra Gaucha may be better suited to this type of production than to still wine. The Aurora cooperative is based in Bento Gonçalves and makes a commendable effort to market still wines.

Vineyards and buildings at Establecimineto Juanicó, in the Canelones region near Montevideo, Uruguay.

The *parrera*, or traditional overhead vine-training, is being discarded in favor of more advanced styles in an effort to improve fruit quality. Fruit is certainly the key to the future here, where there is so often a need to chaptalize.

URUGUAY

When wine buyers first started to trace wines from interesting places around the world, few would have considered this small cosmopolitan country. Despite this, Uruguayan wines have been a presence at international wine fairs for longer than those of Argentina. Its winemakers have succeeded in penetrating even the most demanding markets with products that are imaginative and well made. With an annual domestic wine consumption of some 8 gallons (30 l) per head, international wine lovers are lucky to see any of it. The future holds great promise for this tiny producer nation.

History

Uruguay was first settled in 1726 by 25 families from the Canary Isles. With them came the

knowledge of how to make wine in difficult conditions. It is presumed that the earliest varieties grown were all related to the moscatel.

In the early 1880s, Francisco Vidiella succeeded in producing substantial fruit from the folle noire variety that went on to take his name in Uruguay. Pascual Harriague also had a profound effect on Uruguayan viticulture. He set about making wine in the style of the Médoc, and the grape he chose was tannat. By 1883 he had 300 *barricas* maturing in his bodega.

Vines and wines

Uruguay has eight wine regions encompassing 15 smaller subregions. The most important of these are Canelones, Montevideo, Colonia, and Artigas. There are over 24,700 acres (10,000 ha) of vineyards planted, divided among 370 bodegas. Total annual production is about 24 million gallons (91 million l) per year.

While Uruguay may not have ideal natural conditions for winemaking, careful vineyard techniques allow for more than adequate viticultural conditions. Rainfall, especially toward the Brazilian border, causes some problems. One solution adopted in 1984 was to train vines on the Lyre system, known here as the *Lira*. This system optimizes photosynthetic effect and foliage aeration. To date, about 865 acres (350 ha) have been planted and are growing under this system, the most significant area anywhere in the world. Another important fact is that the tannat planted by Harriague has adapted very well to its local environment and has gone on to make exceptionally smooth and velvety wine with depth and complexity. Today there is more tannat planted here than anywhere else.

Producers

IRURTIA, COLONIA *Established* 1913 *Owners* Irurtia family *Vineyard area* 865 acres (350 ha)

This bodega harnesses cabernet franc (probably

Uruguay's best white wine is produced from Castillo Viejo's grapes.

Uruguay's second-best grape) and tannat to good effect. Try the Posada del Virrey Tannat.

LOS CERROS DE SAN JUAN, COLONIA
Established 1854
Owners Terra family *Vineyard area* 198 acres (80 ha)

This historic winery is near the beautiful town of Colonia. It has one of the world's most remarkable temperature-controlled fermentation systems, designed in the early 1900s. Today, its winemaker produces deep and chewy tannat wines from grapes grown in what are among the most interesting and picturesque vineyards in Uruguay.

> *From wine what sudden friendships springs.*
> JOHN GAY (1685–1732)
> *Fables*

ESTABLECIMINETO JUANICÓ, CANELONES *Established* 1979
Owners Deicas family *Vineyard area* 544 acres (220 ha), plus 988 acres (400 ha) managed

With its impressive vineyards, this winery exudes an air of efficiency and enthusiasm. Wines such as the exquisite Preludio demonstrate clear vision and attention to detail, down to using the tiniest percentage of petit verdot to complement a tannat, cabernet franc, and cabernet sauvignon blend.

CASTEL PUJOL, MONTEVIDEO *Established* 1976
Owners Carrau brothers *Vineyard area* 222 acres (90 ha)

In an old colonial-style winery near Montevideo the Carrau brothers ferment and oak-age a wide range of well-made wines. The jewel in this bodega's crown is a new, purpose-built winery located near the Brazilian border. Wines made here are just beginning to appear on the market.

Chile and Argentina

Despite a winemaking heritage that goes back to the arrival of the Spanish conquistadores in the sixteen century, it is only since the early 1980s that Chile has been regarded as a "viticultural paradise." Chile's geographic isolation has meant that it is one of only a few wine regions in the world to remain phylloxera-free, and the wines produced here—including blockbuster merlots, splendid carmenères, and great-value sauvignon blancs—have become powerful commercial products around the world.

When Argentine wine began to appear in the international market, few consumers realized the magnitude of the phenomenon involved. In wine terms, this was the last great undiscovered land. Its size and isolation are subjects that merit special attention, but even more intriguing for the wine lover is the potential within such a vast viticultural landscape.

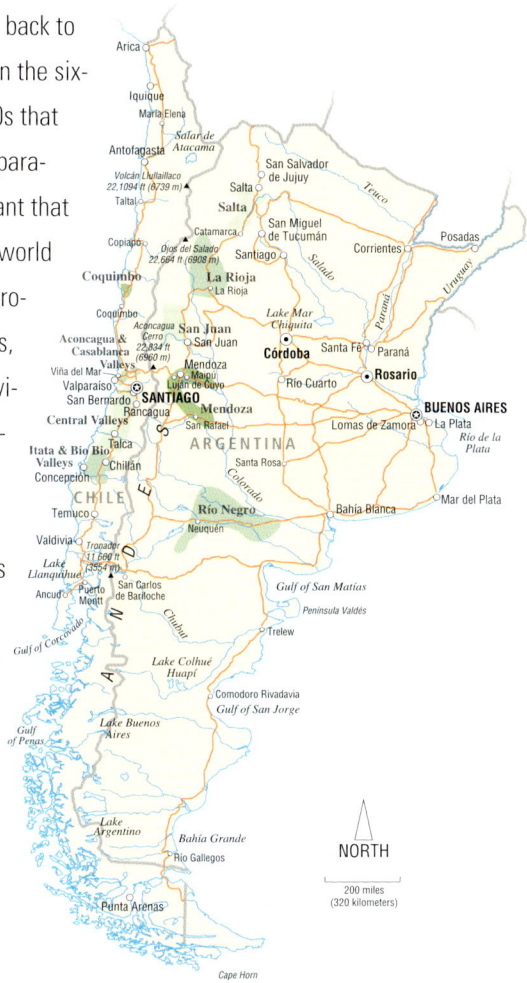

Vineyards at Cousiño Macul, in the Maipo Valley near Santiago.

canals, dams, and storage tanks; they even devised a legal framework that ensured its equitable distribution to all.

This development also transformed the underlying ecology of the valley, with silt from the rivers improving the fertility of the land. When the Spanish conquistadores arrived in about 1536, they found a wealth of food items they had never before seen, including tomatoes, maize, chilies, and a vast array of tubers such as potatoes.

CHILE

Chile's location on the southwestern extremity of Latin America lends it an air of isolation, reinforced by the Andes mountain range in the east. A smaller ridge rises to 3,000 feet (900 m) above sea level on the forward edge of the landmass, and between this ridge and the Andes lies a longitudinal depression called a "valley." This valley extends southward from latitude 32° to 42°, where it begins to submerge and form fjord-like inlets.

The protected environment created between the two ranges provides a shelter for flora and fauna. The only problem is that low rainfall levels limit life to a semi-arid existence on newly exposed and poor soil in most of the valley. The violence of the geological forces that created the Andes means that much of the surface is not so much soil as the chaotic remnants of smashed and tortured rock.

Agriculture

The limited agriculture in existence in Chile prior to the arrival of the Incas was dramatically transformed by these talented agriculturists. The Incas harnessed the available water with an array of

Advanced viticulture

In the early 1830s, a forward-thinking Frenchman, Claude Gay, obtained the backing of the Chilean government to establish a nursery for botanical species from around the world. Called the Quinta Normal, it was to play a decisive role in viticulture. A wide range of botanical specimens was brought in, including a fairly complete compendium of grape varieties. This collection of plants, isolated from the infections that later ravaged vineyards across the world, proved invaluable in restocking nursery vineyards in Europe.

Looking back, it is difficult to imagine the disaster for European agriculture that was the phylloxera infestation of little more than a century ago. In the catastrophe's aftermath, Europe turned to Chile for virus-free vine cuttings.

Landscape and climate

Chile's vineyards are located at between 32°30' and 38° south latitude, and they are a similar distance from the equator as some of their northern hemisphere equivalents. The effect of the Pacific currents and the significant barrier to continental heating supplied by the Andes ensure a cooler environment than seems possible. The Humboldt Current in particular brings the cooling influence of the Antarctic to Chile's coastal regions.

The great altitude of the Andes inevitably traps and precipitates clouds and atmospheric humidity as high-altitude rain and snow. As temperatures fluctuate, melting snow runs down the slopes and makes its way to the sea. The consequences flowing from this are in several ways important to life in the valley. The water creates oases, and the erosion at higher altitudes fills the rivers with silt which they disgorge in the valley, providing a more attractive *milieu* for plant life. Significantly, the rivers breach the second ridge on their way to the sea, opening the ecosystem of the valley

to maritime influences, which helps to temper the natural tendency toward desertification. Once daylight temperatures rise in the valley, rising hot air draws in cooling, humid air from the coast; at night the effect is reversed. Annual rainfall averages are generally below 32 inches (800 mm) in the wettest areas. The rainy season comes in winter and its effects are felt mostly in the south and to a lesser extent in the west, in the shadow of the coastal ridge.

Spanish influence

Chile's population grew rapidly throughout the eighteenth and nineteenth centuries principally through European migration. The eighteenth-century migration came chiefly from Spain and was composed to a great extent of Basque families. Nineteenth-century immigrants tended to

Carmenère

The vigorous carmenère is the grape variety behind many of Chile's finest red wines. It produces deeply flavored, smooth, carmine-colored wines. For many years carmenère was mislabeled as merlot, but is now coming into its own. Agustin Hunees, President of Veramonte Winery, says "It's a great grape, but it's one dimensional. It has the best mouthfeel of any red; low in acidity but with lots of flavor. We have three choices: eliminate it, promote it as our national grape or use it as a unique component in blends. I think the future lies in our last option."

Sauvignon blanc grapes ready for crushing—this variety has been enormously successful for the Chilean wine trade.

originate more from Germany, England, and Italy. Fortunes made by exploiting Chile's vast natural wealth gave rise to a status-conscious, land-owning class that felt it was appropriate to include winemaking estates in its portfolios. Eventually, about ten powerful families (principally Basque) controlled fruit and wine production in Chile.

Over time, per capita consumption of wine in Chile increased to the point where it became attractive to the exchequer from a taxation point of view. Slowly, as taxes increased, the incentive to be bold and invest receded from the Chilean wine industry.

Toward the end of the 1960s, investment in the industry was very slow and quality was generally patchy. Still, Chile's reputation was already beginning to take shape, and it was

Above: *A mold-blown green goblet.*
Below: *Female vineyard workers prune the vines at an estate near Chile's capital city, Santiago.*

possible to find some respectable wine at good prices. Chile eventually descended into a disastrous period of political and economic turmoil that led to little wine being exported and even less money being directed to vineyards and wineries.

Modernization

Nothing remains the same for long in regions as promising as Chile. Fresh blood, a commitment to improving quality and expanding markets, and new investment have all been rewarded.

Playing its strongest hand, Chile began by improving and marketing its red wines. It was cabernet sauvignon that appeared first. Initially, cabernet was harvested slightly early, leading to capsicum and tomato bush aromas. These were formerly considered faults in the wine but are now, to some extent thanks to Chilean cabernets, quite enjoyed by wine lovers around the world.

The arrival of the vine

The spot chosen by the conquering Spaniards for the new capital city, Santiago de Chile, was strategically placed at the northern edge of the valley, from then on to be known as el Valle Central, the central valley. Each of the smaller valleys crisscrossing the Valle Central retained the name of its river, some reflecting the pre-Columbian cultures that had once flourished there.

To begin with, viticulture was not an imperative in Chile. Although vines were imported into Mexico early on, the first Spaniards to arrive in South America were much more interested in the glint of gold. The political reality they faced was also pretty snarled. Some vines were inevitably imported with other foodstuffs and would have entered South America via Perú. It is generally assumed that vines arrived near Santiago de Chile in the mid-sixteenth century. To complicate matters even further, by the seventeenth century Spain dictated that no wine should be produced in the new lands of *las indias*, the Indies, in an effort to protect and even boost domestic wine production in the Iberian Peninsula. It is difficult to imagine how the instigators of this law ever imagined it could be enforced.

The first varieties grown appear to have been grapes for eating. What is certain is that it was always going to be difficult to enforce the letter

Cabernet sauvignon grapes.

of the law in such a vast expanse of land. Research suggests that small vineyards, producing wine for personal consumption, were soon in full swing around the early settlements. Another factor in the early spread of viticulture involves the Church. As an integral part of the holy sacrament, wine simply had to be available for the communion service. Early missions would have ensured a supply of wine by one means or another. In fact, the grape variety that proliferated in the Viceroyalty of New Spain (which later became Mexico) and its northernmost province of La California is to this day known as *mission*. This same variety is known as *país* in Chile and *criolla chica* in Argentina.

As more settlers arrived from Europe, mainly migrants from the harsh, southwestern provinces of Spain, grape-growing became quite a well-established adjunct to farming. We can imagine that winemaking was equally prevalent. Evidence of this can be found in a recommendation sent by the Governor of Chile in 1678, exhorting Spain to lift the ban on vineyards so as to encourage the establishment of more homesteads or *estancias*. By this stage it must have been obvious that grapes were well-suited to the environment. A lack of humidity during the vegetative and fruit cycles led to healthy bunches come harvest time, the dry conditions reducing the risk of fungal infections to an absolute minimum. The absence of downy and powdery mildew would have meant bigger yields and much healthier crops than were possible in Europe.

A display in the tasting room at Concha y Toro in Chile's Maipo Valley.

Above: *The foreman oversees the harvest in the vineyards at Viña Los Vascos, Santiago.* Left: *Barrel room at Cousiño Macul, a traditional bodega in the old sense of the word. There was a time when it was considered the greatest.*

States, Chilean sauvignon blanc became a hit in the wine-bar and health-club circuits—this was a major breakthrough.

Not content with conquering middle markets, Chile joined with some of the greatest stars in the firmament of enology to tackle the top end of the market. So a new generation of Chilean super-wines was born. Names like Château Lafite-Rothschild, Château Mouton-Rothschild, Lurton, Robert Mondavi, Marnier Lapostolle, and others were folded into the fabric of Chilean wine. As these wines emerged—towering wines aimed at capturing exclusive markets—the price of Chilean wines generally began to rise.

Great names have been added to the nomenclature of serious winemaking. Caballo Loco, Montes Alpha "M," Almaviva, Domus Aurea, Finis Terrae, and Seña all stand as testaments to the unimpeachable quality of Chilean wine.

Argentina might have its malbec, South Africa its pinotage and Uruguay its tannat, but Chile has great-value sauvignon blanc and very accessible merlot and carmenère. All of these wines come together under the umbrella of top wines of increasing sophistication.

Next, Chile turned to white wines. By this time new money was being invested, including in new areas such as Casablanca. Research had shown that cooler areas would help produce aromatically charged white wines. Although Casablanca was farther north and nearer the equator, it was cooled by the maritime influences that had proved so successful in New Zealand. The gamble paid off.

Sauvignon blanc was the variety of choice in many of the new plantations. The results were more than encouraging. In Britain and the United

Central Valleys and Other Regions

MAIPO VALLEY

This is perhaps the best-known name in Chilean wine, mainly because the valley is nearest to the capital, Santiago. As many of the original bodegas were built within a day's drive of the city, most are dotted around Maipo and its subregions, including Llano de Maipo and Buin. Today, those regions which are offering higher-quality fruit deserve greater recognition.

CONCHA Y TORO *Established* 1883 *Owners* Public company *Vineyard area* 8,154 acres (3,300 ha)

Concha y Toro's Puente Alto vineyard provides grapes for the Marqués de Casa Concha cabernet sauvignon, for Don Melchor, and Casillero del Diablo. These are wines that seldom disappoint. Cabernet sauvignon (and an excellent barrel-fermented sauvignon blanc) form the basis of these quality wines. A less-expensive line, Trio, offers great value for money. When it comes to high-quality wine, Concha y Toro has linked up with none other than Château Mouton-Rothschild to produce Almaviva. As a consequence, some very high prices are paid for Almaviva wines. Every vintage has seen notable improvement.

This is just one of the Maipo Valley's high-profile, high-quality wines.

COUSIÑO MACUL *Established* 1856 *Owners* Cousiño family *Vineyard area* 1,359 acres (550 ha)

Domus Aurea is produced from a single vineyard on the Quebrada de Macul slope—it is a wine full of promise. This wine is the result of a venture to make a single-vineyard wine that expresses the unique *terroir* of the Maipo valley. Cousiño Macul has also joined forces with the Lurton brothers to produce Finis Terrae, an expensive

super-premium wine following the Bordeaux blend, which has engendered good reviews.

RAPEL VALLEY

Farther south and slightly cooler than Maipo is Rapel. This vine-growing area is subdivided further, with Cachapoal to the north and Colchagua to the south. Important wineries have major vineyard holdings here, including Santa Rita, Santa Emiliana, and Undurraga. There is no doubt of the depth and concentration that wines from this valley can achieve. Cono Sur succeed in making interesting pinot noir at 13 percent by volume. Smaller, boutique wineries, such as Luis Felipe Edwards based in Colchagua, make a good-value cabernet sauvignon called Pupilla, while topping the list is the cabernet sauvignon Reserva. Luis Felipe Edwards' spectrum is broadened by carmenère and chardonnay.

CASA LAPOSTOLLE *Established* 1994 *Owners* Marnier-Lapostolle (Grand Marnier), France and Rabat family, Chile *Vineyard area* 741 acres (300 ha)

This winery set off something of a chain reaction with the launching of its superb Cuvée Alexandre Merlot. So seductive is this wine that some wine experts consider it an alternative to Pétrus. Casa Lapostolle's more recent Clos Apalta takes its carmenère/merlot to an unfiltered and highly concentrated level of quality; the first vintage was 1997.

MAULE VALLEY

With the arrival of dynamic and revolutionary winemaker Miguel Torres in this region, history began to change for Chilean winemaking. Miguel Torres chose Curicó, situated directly south of Colchagua, although his vineyards are slightly to the east and near the cooling influence of the Andes. Maule contains other regions that are equally interesting, such as Cauquenes, Linares, Lontue, Parral, and Talca—over 61,775 acres (25,000 ha) make up this viticultural region.

AURELIO MONTES, CURICÓ   *Established* 1988   *Owners* Douglas Murray, Alfredo Vidaurre, Aurelio Montes, and Pedro Grand   *Vineyard area* 544 acres (220 ha)

The quality of Aurelio's wines is beyond doubt. His Montes Alpha Cabernet Sauvignon is vivid and concentrated. His super premium Montes Alpha "M" seems to be made to age for . . . well, no-one has tasted one nearing maturity. The whole range is closed tight. There will be some stunning wines when they open up. While waiting for this happy event, you might like to try his refined sauvignon blanc or malbec.

COQUIMBO

This is the most northerly region in Chile. Too hot to make viable quality wine, the grapes grown here are used to make another famous drink, Pisco. Basically, Pisco is an *aguardiente*, literally a "firewater." It is distilled from muscat and pedro ximénez grapes. The process takes place in pot stills to give four categories of Pisco: Gran Pisco (43 percent by volume), Reservado (40 percent), Especial (35 percent), and Selección (30 percent). As an aperitif, Pisco is second to none.

An early corkscrew designed to fit easily and surreptitiously into a lady's handbag.

Farther south, and straddling the Aconcagua River, the Aconcagua Valley is the most northerly of Chile's quality wine regions. Inland from the coast, at Viña Panquehue, lies the Don Maximiano vineyards of Errazuriz.

ERRAZURIZ PANQUEHUE, VIÑA PANQUEHUE   *Established* 1870   *Owners* Chadwick family   *Vineyard area* 927 acres (375 ha)

The real class of this Coquimbo bodega can be seen in the uniform quality of its array of wines, from delicate and quite special Wild Ferment Chardonnay (made with natural yeasts), to characterful sauvignon blanc and chardonnay. The high spots are in the reds. These now include pinot noir, syrah, a Curicó Merlot that would please anyone, Aconcagua Merlot Reserva to blow the cobwebs away, and some gloriously aromatic cabernet blends, culminating in the Seña that combines cabernet with 10 percent carmenère and a touch of merlot.

CASABLANCA VALLEY

Planting began in the Casablanca Valley in the early 1980s, concentrating on white grapes. Initially, chardonnay was the grape of choice, but since then considerable plantations of sauvignon blanc have gone in as a result of its relative success in export markets. Some cabernet sauvignon and merlot complement the white varieties grown here.

VIÑA CASABLANCA
Established 1992   *Owners* Viña Santa Carolina S. A. *Vineyard area* 148 acres (60 ha), plus 544 acres (220 ha) under a long-term lease

Viña Casablanca was set up to exploit the success the region has had with white varieties. Winemaker Ignacio Recabarren has guided this bodega to international acclaim, using fruit from the Santa Isabel Estate, but red grapes are bought in from other areas to enhance local bodegas' *tinto* vinification.

BÍO-BÍO VALLEY

This is the southernmost viticultural region of Chile. Once dedicated to the more humble varieties of grapes, such as moscatel de alejandria and país, recent times have witnessed a much keener interest in quality plantations. There are currently test plantings of 20 different varieties in the Bío-Bío Valley, mourvèdre and viognier among them.

VIÑA GRACIA
Owners Córpora Wineries

Córpora established Viña Gracia, an exceptionally stylish winery, to vinify fruit from vineyards in Aconcagua, Maipo, Cachapoal, and, notably, Bío-Bío. The winery is run by Jacques Antoine Toublanc, a Frenchman. The bodega has a total

capacity of 1.25 million gallons (4.7 million l). Experimentation with yeasts has achieved some interesting results. One is a *barrique*-fermented chardonnay from Tatiwe made using yeast 1080, a culture native to Portugal's Vinho Verde.

Right: *Fermentation vessel containing 1986 cabernet.*
Below: *Cabernet sauvignon vines growing at Viña Los Vascos near Santiago.*

ARGENTINA

Argentina is of great importance to the wine world because of the amount of land dedicated to the vine, the quantity of wine produced, the diversity of *terroir* involved, the specific varietals grown, and, as a consequence, the styles of wine possible. It ranks with the United States as the world's fourth-largest wine producer, after Italy, France, and Spain, so it is rather surprising to find that until very recently it exported almost no wine.

> *What though youth gave love and roses, Age still leaves us friends and wine.*
>
> THOMAS MOORE (1779–1852),
> *National Airs*, Spring and Autumn

Things are changing fast. No one can be in any doubt that, despite a stumbling start, Argentine wine will soon form an important part in the broad spectrum of international wines available to consumers around the world. How far it will choose to go and how great it will become are questions to exercise the mind and stir the imagination.

The arrival of the vine

Vines were well-established in the Mendoza region by the sixteenth century. Although these early wines were intended mainly for local consumption, word began to spread that they were much better than some made elsewhere.

Things progressed slowly until 1880 when French botanist Aimé Pouget introduced the first French varieties. He chose Mendoza as the site for new plantations and discovered that top-quality vines thrived. One variety that did particularly well in the western and northwestern areas of Mendoza was *la uva francesa*, the French grape, or malbec. Such was the perceived quality of this adapted variety that much of the red-grape plantations were dedicated to it, especially around Mendoza city and in neighboring Luján de Cuyo. Grown at around 2,623 feet (800 m) above sea level, it produced

Vineyards lining the road at Chandon, Mendoza.

a lusty red wine, full of color and vibrancy that survived well in barrel, bottle, and the leather pouch.

Following the completion of a rail link to Buenos Aires, a great explosion in wine-related activity began in Mendoza with a rapid proliferation of vineyards and bodegas. Quality was not initially sacrificed to profit. However, by the early twentieth century, wine consumption in Argentina had peaked at nearly 26.4 gallons (100 l) per capita, and with little regard for quality the industry went head-on into mass production. Good-quality vineyards, including prize malbec plots, were grubbed up and replaced with whatever yielded the most grapes.

The collapse began in 1980, with the national economy struggling and Argentina's foreign policy taking several turns for the worse. The huge Grupo Greco collapsed, bankrupting Bodega Arizu; other collapses followed. By 1988, the wine industry sank into the doldrums. There are still vast, untended, overgrown vineyards and abandoned workers' houses dotted around San Rafael in Mendoza.

From this low point Argentina has risen once again to merit inclusion in international markets, though it is still dogged by political and economic strife.

Landscape and climate

Argentina is sometimes referred to as six continents crammed into one immense country, so diverse and extensive is its geography. Argentina sweeps from north

Grape harvest, Proviar Vineyards, Argentina.

of the Tropic of Capricorn (21° 46') to Tierra del Fuego at latitude 55° 03' south. From sea level to 22,816 feet (6,959 m) higher (Mount Aconcagua), the variety within this nation includes the widest imaginable spread of climatic conditions.

Argentine vineyards have been spared the devastation of phylloxera, although it certainly exists—you can occasionally see the mites clinging onto *vinifera* roots when you pull them up, but they seem to be kept well in check by several factors. Perhaps most crucial is the flood irrigation used to water the vineyards. Being aerobic, phylloxera probably detests being flooded. Global warming is a worry, though, as water runoff from the Andes appears to be diminishing with warmer weather, an effect that is quite noticeable in Argentina. This has led to many growers opting for drip irrigation. In these cases most growers have taken the precaution of grafting vines onto resistant American rootstock.

Wine regions

Within Argentina are five main wine-producing regions spread over 15 geographically very different provinces.

Mendoza is responsible for about 95 percent of all exports because its 1,038 bodegas produce 75 percent of Argentina's wines, and it was the first region to adapt to higher-quality production.

By and large Mendoza vineyard care is natural and well-attuned to modern health and ecological considerations. In some regions conditions are conducive to developing wine styles of character.

San Juan, to the north of Mendoza, has yet to provide wine lovers with a winery of note. This situation may change soon, as massive investment has gone into planting international varietals in new, irrigated vineyards. When El Niño brought bad weather to Mendoza, San Juan came to the rescue with fruit of reasonable quality.

La Rioja is famous for its torrontés grape, locally called torrontés riojano. Originally this area supplied cheap wines for mass consumption on the domestic market but has now begun to move upmarket. The Cooperativa La Riojana is the largest in America. With a sizeable research budget, it is now a major presence on export markets, providing good-value wines at modest prices. Their Santa Florentina Torrontés has tamed the wildest excesses of the variety and offers a charming aperitif wine. Red wines are benefiting from antipodean techniques.

Salta is composed of many valleys, including Valles Calchaquíes, surely one of the most beautiful wine-producing valleys on earth. Bodegas Etchart (also found in Mendoza) has its principal

Susana Balbo

In a country dominated by male winemakers, Susana Balbo stands out for her incredible skill and experience. For 20 years, Susana produced wines for Argentina's top bodegas, and planned and built the most innovative winery in the nation, Bodegas Catena. Susana was the first Argentine winemaker to be hired as a consultant to make wine outside of Argentina. Currently she is concentrating on her own label, Bodegas Susana Balbo. Her current releases are Malbec, Cabernet Sauvignon, and Brioso, which means "tenacity or strength of spirit."

winery here. Outstanding among its fine wines is the older, more mature style Arnaldo B. Etchart. This wine blends malbec with varying quantities of cabernet sauvignon and other French varietals to give quite an active nose and a well-rounded palate. Etchart has made an art of torrontés wines and this variety is at its most subtle here. Varietal cabernet sauvignon has won positive comment and will continue to improve.

Río Negro, in the south of Patagonia, contains a wine region of great promise. A deep rift valley protects the region around the General Roca, providing a macroclimate that appears to suit viticulture and soft fruits exceptionally well. The main producer here is Humberto Canale. From quality fruit come wines with some delicacy and a great deal of promise. With greater investment in the winery who knows what may be possible. Another venture worthy of note is the French-owned Fabre-Montmayou, maker of the well-received Infinitus wines.

Pickers with boxes filled to the brim wait for the truck at Proviar Vineyards.

Mendoza

Mendoza's wine-producing regions can be divided roughly into three areas, the main cluster in the north surrounding the city of Mendoza, one higher up and nearer the Andes to the west, and one to the south, toward the middle of the province.

The cluster around the city includes two of Mendoza's three DOs *(Denominación de Origen)*, Luján de Cuyo and Maipú. This area is itself subdivided into three regions.

There is a bewildering array of grape varieties grown in Mendoza's wine-producing regions. The Zona Alta imparts special characteristics to many of the varieties grown there. Those varieties that reach world-class standards include bonarda, malbec, chardonnay, and tempranillo. Local torrontés grapes are somewhat more delicate than some found in other provinces.

The Región del Norte produces lively chenin blanc, ugni blanc, and sangiovese; there is also a great deal of pedro ximénez. The Región del Este specializes in cabernet sauvignon, syrah, sangiovese, chenin blanc, chardonnay, and some less-than-typical sauvignon blanc. The cooler Valle de Uco yields chardonnay, merlot, and malbec. The Región del Sur can claim some chardonnay, cabernet sauvignon, and bonarda.

Producers

BODEGA BALBI, SAN RAFAEL   *Established* 1930
Owner **Allied Domecq**

Balbi is singularly successful with a range of bright, well-made white wines. They also make a rosé that sells well in most markets. Their reds are approachable, clean, and well-focused.

BODEGA CATENA   *Established* 1999   *Owner* **Nicolás Catena**

This is the newest and without a doubt most innovative winery in Argentina. Unquestionably, the wines emerging from here are bound to provide another quantum leap in terms of quality.

Winemaker Raoul de la Mota in the cellars at Bodegas & Cavas de Weinert, Mendoza.

BODEGAS & CAVAS DE WEINERT, CARRODILLA, LUJÁN DE CUYO   *Established* 1976   *Owner* **Bernardo Weinert**   *Vineyard area* **NA**

Fortunes here have waxed and waned. Some wines are deep and well extracted, but quality has been variable mainly because, though the fruit is of good quality, the winery has yet to modernize. Old wood is still used to store wine, at times to very good effect; at other times this method is less than convincing. Carrascal is a traditional line, and some premium malbec is also sold.

extraordinary complexity for the price. Alamos Ridge wines fill the next medium-price bracket with some aplomb, and below these the bodega produces an interesting range of wines called Argento, which should not be missed.

BODEGAS ETCHART, PERDRIEL, LUJÁN DE CUYO
Established 1938 (Salta), 1992 (Mendoza) *Owner* Pernord Ricard *Vineyard area* 138 acres (56 ha)

This firm has two bodegas, one in Mendoza, the other in northern Salta. The firm's best work is done in Salta.

BODEGA NORTON, LUJÁN DE CUYO
Established c.1890 *Owners* Swarowski family *Vineyard area* 74 acres (30 ha) Agrelo, plus 395+ acres (160+ ha) Luján de Cuyo

Heavy investment in new and replanted vineyards, and a new vinification plant, promises a bright future for this bodega. Norton Privada is a Bordeaux-style wine that ages very well in bottle, and the chardonnay has also come a long way, with improvement showing in recent vintages. Lighter and less exalted wines, such as the vivacious torrontés, provide depth to a line that also includes a very acceptable sparkling wine.

NAVARRO CORREAS, MAIPÚ
Established c.1798 *Owners* CINBA *Vineyard area* Small holdings in Luján de Cuyo, Maipú, and Tupungato

This bodega's current vineyards include the land that was once Tiburcio Benegas's famous bodega El Trapiche. The drinks company CINBA has invested heavily to return this company to the limelight. Its bottle-fermented 100 percent pinot noir is Argentina's best bubbly. Though successful on the domestic market, the reds and whites have still to overcome their fusty image.

BODEGA ESMERALDA
Established 1970s *Owner* Nicolás Catena

In Bodega Esmeralda's Catena Alta range, the chardonnay is world class, the malbec definitive, and the cabernet sauvignon sets new standards. Below this category are Catena wines, providing

TRAPICHE, MENDOZA (MAIPÚ)
Established c.1900 *Owners* Luis Alfredo Pulenta and others *Vineyard area* 1,235 acres (500 ha)

Peñaflor is the largest bodega in Mendoza and Trapiche is an appendage to it. An array of wines is produced here, from mass-produced tetra bricks called Thermidor to fine products under the Trapiche label. The bodega appears to be in two minds about whether to leave Trapiche as its premium line or to upgrade Peñaflor to a similar level.

Wine Reference Table

While every effort has been made to provide an interesting selection of wines across many countries, tastes, and price ranges, this list is by no means exhaustive. The table below is intended to be a guide only. The asterisks represent the approximate price of each wine in its country of origin. One asterisk represents easily affordable wines, two asterisks denote a moderate expense, and three asterisks, a more costly wine. Foods listed under compatible foods are intended only to be suggestions. Of course it is possible to drink any wine with any food; these suggestions are simply a guide.

Wine name	Style	Flavor/ Bouquet	Compatible Foods	Price Range
FRANCE				
Alsace				
A. Zimmermann Fils Gewürztraminer Cuvée Alphonse	White	Citrus, spicy	Asian	**
Cave Kientzheim-Kaysersberg Muscat Réserve	White	Grapey, citrus	Chicken	**
Cave Vincole de Pfaffenyheim et Gueberschwihr Gewürztraminer Grand Cru oldert	White	Spicy, chalky	Asian	**
Cave Vincole de Pfaffenheim et Gueberschwihr Gewüzrtraminer Grand Cru Zinnkoepfle Westhalten	White	Spicy, floral	Asian	**
Cave Vinicole de Pfaffenheim et Gueberschwihr Gewürztraminer Cuvée Bacchus	White	Spicy, complex, smoky	Fish	**
Cave Vinicole de Turckheim Gewürztraminer Vieilles Vignes	White	Spicy, floral	Chicken	**
Domaine Albert Boxler Tokay Pinot Gris Grand Cru Brand	White	Spicy, minerally	Pork	**
Domaine Albert Mann Muscat	White	Citrus, floral	Fruit	**
Domaine Allimant-Laugner Muscat	White	Citrus, grapey	Cold meats, stew, offal	*
Domaine André Ehrhart et Fils Tokay Pinot Gris Cuvée Elise	White	Floral, citrus	Veal	**
Domaine André Kientzler Muscat Grand Cru Kirchberg	White	Floral, citrus	Fruit	**
Domaine André Kientzler Riesling Grand Cru Osterberg	White	Zingy, floral	Veal	**
Domaine Bruno Sorg Gewürztraminer Pfersigberg	White	Floral, spicy	Pasta	**
Domaine Bruno Sorg Muscat Grand Cru Pfersigberg	White	Grapey, spicy	Sausages	**
Domaine des Marroniers Gewürztraminer	White	Minerally, spicy	Fruit	**
Domaine des Marroniers Riesling Kastelberg	White	Citrus, spicy	Veal	**
Domaine Eric Rominger Gewürztraminer Grand Cru Zinnkoepfle Les Sinneles	White	Spicy, floral	Asian	**
Domaine Ernest Burn Tokay Pinot Gris Vendanges Tardives	White	Sweet, complex, floral	Fruit	**
Domaine Fritsch Pinot Noir Rouge de Marlenheim Barriques	Red	Berry, gamey	Sausages	**
Domaine Gérard Neumeyer Tokay Pinot Gris Grand Cru Bruderthal	White	Floral, oily	Cheese	**
Domaine Gérard Schueller et Fils Gewürztraminer Bildstoeckle	White	Spicy, chalky	Chicken	**
Domaine Hering Pinot Noir Cuvée du Chat Noir	Red	Berry, plums	Cold meats, stew, offal	**
Domaine Jean Sipp Riesling Grand Cru Kirchberg	White	Floral, citrus	Chicken	**
Domaine Jean-Pierre Dirler Gewürztraminer Grand Cru Saering	White	Floral, spicy	Antipasto	**
Domaine Jean-Pierre Dirler Muscat Grand Cru Spiegel	White	Citrus, grapey, floral	Fish, pork	**
Domaine Kehren Muscat Cuvée Patricia	White	Floral, citrus	Shellfish	**
Domaine Kirmann Sylvaner	White	Citrus, floral	Pasta	*
Domaine Léon Boesch Gewürztraminer Grand Cru Zinnkoepfle	White	Floral, minerally	Cold meats, stew, offal	**

Wine name	Style	Flavor/ Bouquet	Compatible Foods	Price Range
Domaine Lucien Albrecht Gewürztraminer Réserve	White	Spicy, chalky	Fish	**
Domaine Lucien Albrecht Tokay Pinot Gris Grand Cru Pfingstberg Vendanges Tardives	White	Sweet, floral	Fruit	***
Domaine Marcel Deiss Riesling Burg de Bergheim	White	Floral, citrus, complex	Fish	**
Domaine Marcel Deiss Riesling Grand Cru Altenberg de Bergheim	White	Complex, floral, minerally	Chicken	**
Domaine Martin Schaetzel Gewürztraminer Grand Cru Kaefferkopf Cuvée Catherine	White	Chalky, spicy	Veal	**
Domaine Martin Schaetzel Riesling Grand Cru Kaefferkopf Cuvée Nicolas	White	Minerally, citrus	Pork	**
Domaine Meyer-Fonné Riesling Grand Cru Kaefferkopf	White	Floral, citrus	Antipasto	**
Domaine Mittnacht Klack Tokay Pinot Gris Vendanges Tardives	White	Sweet, oily, floral	Cheese	**
Domaine Ostertag Gewürztraminer Fronholz Vendanges Tardives	White	Powerful, sweet, floral	Fruit	***
Domaine Ostertag Sylvaner Vieilles Vignes	White	Floral, citrus	Cheese	**
Domaine Ostertag Tokay Pinot Gris Fronhoz	White	Citrus, oily	Veal	**
Domaine Paul Blanck Riesling Furstentum Vieilles Vignes	White	Floral, citrus	Chicken	**
Domaine René Muré Gewürztraminer Schultzengass	White	Minerally, chalky	Asian	**
Domaine René Muré Pinot Noir Clos Saint-Landelin	Red	Berry, gamey	Cold meats	**
Domaine René Muré Riesling Grand Cru Vorbourg Clos Saint-Landelin	White	Spicy, minerally	Asian	**
Domaine René Muré Sylvaner Clos Saint-Landelin Cuvée Oscar	White	Floral, minerally	Fish	**
Domaine René Muré Tokay Pinot Gris Lutzeltal	White	Floral, citrus	Fish	**
Domaine Rolly Gassmann Muscat Moenchreben de Rorschwihr	White	Floral, grapey	Fruit	**
Domaine Rolly Gassmann Pinot Noir de Rodern	Red	Smoky, berry	Duck	**
Domaine Rolly Gassmann Riesling Kappelweg de Rorschwihr	White	Floral, spicy	Pork	**
Domaine Schlumberger Gewürztraminer Cuvée Christine	White	Smoky, spicy	Asian	***
Domaine Schlumberger Riesling Grand Cru Kessler	White	Floral, minerally	Pasta	**
Domaine Schlumberger Tokay Pinot Gris Grand Cru Kitterle	White	Spicy, oily	Fish	**
Domaine Schoffit Gewürztraminer Grand Cru Rangen Clos Saint-Théobald Vendanges Tardives	White	Sweet, powerful, chalky	Fish	**
Domaine Schoffit Tokay Pinot Gris Cuvée Alexandre	White	Oily, spicy	Chicken	**
Domaine Schoffit Tokay Pinot Gris Grand Cru Rangen de Thann Clos Saint-Théobald	White	Citrus, floral, oily	Fish	**
Domaine Seppi Landmann Gewürztraminer Zinnkoepfle	White	Citrus, floral, spicy	Veal	**
Domaine Seppi Landmann Sylvaner Vallée Noble	White	Floral, honey	Fruit	**
Domaine Seppi Landmann Tokay Pinot Gris Grand Cru Zinnkoepfle	White	Spicy, citrus, floral	Fish	**
Domaine Weinbach Riesling Grand Cru Schlossberg	White	Complex, floral, minerally	Chicken	***
Domaine Weinbach Tokay Pinot Gris Quintessence de Grains Nobles	Sweet	Sweet, complex, spicy	Dessert	***
Domaine Zind Humbrecht Gewürztraminer Hengst	White	Complex, powerful, spicy	Veal	***
Domaine Zind-Humbrecht Gewürztraminer Grand Cru Goldert	White	Powerful, complex, spicy	Cheese	***
Domaine Zind-Humbrecht Riesling Rangen de Thann Clos Saint-Urbain	White	Powerful, minerally, floral	Fish	***
Domaine Zind-Humbrecht Tokay Pinot Gris Clos Jebsal Sélection de Grains Nobles	Sweet	Sweet, complex, citrus, floral	Dessert	***
Domaine Zind-Humbrecht Tokay Pinot Gris Grand Cru Rangen de Thann Clos Saint-Urbain	White	Spicy, oily, powerful	Chicken	***
Domaine Zind-Humbrecht Tokay Pinot Gris Windsbuhl	White	Spicy, oily, complex	Chicken	***

Wine name	Style	Flavor/ Bouquet	Compatible Foods	Price Range
Dopff au Moulin Gewürztraminer Riquewihr Vendanges Tardives	White	Sweet, floral	Fruit	***
Dopff au Moulin Riesling Riquewihr Proprieté	White	Citrus, spicy	Fish	**
Dopff et Irion Tokay Pinot Gris Les Maquisards	White	Spicy, citrus	Mediterranean	**
Gewürztraminer Grand Cru Scholnenbourg (Marc Tempé)	White	Spicy, minerally	Asian	**
Gewürztraminer Sigillé Confrérie de Saint-Etienne (Jean-Baptiste Adam)	White	Spicy, citrus	Fish	**
Hugel et Fils Gewürztraminer Sélection de Grains Nobles	Sweet	Sweet, complex, citrus, spicy	Dessert	***
Hugel et Fils Riesling Sélection de Grains Nobles	Sweet	Sweet, complex, powerful, floral	Dessert	***
Hugel et Fils Tokay Pinot Gris Hommage (Jean Hugel)	White	Oily, floral	Cheese	***
Josmeyer Gewürztraminer Les Archenets	White	Floral, minerally	Fish	**
Josmeyer Riesling Grand Cru Hengst	White	Floral, citrus	Veal	**
Kuentz Bas Gewürztraminer Eichberg	White	Spicy, minerally, floral	Veal	**
Kuentz Bas Riesling Grand Cru Pfersigberg	White	Citrus, floral	Chicken	**
Maison Trimbach Riesling Clos Saint-Hune	White	Citrus, floral, complex	Fish	***
Maison Trimbach Riesling Cuvée Frédéric-Emile	White	Floral, minerally, complex	Veal	***
Maison Trimbach Tokay Pinot Gris Réserve Personelle	White	Smoky, citrus	Chicken	**
Muscat Vendanges Tardives (Roger Jung et Fils)	White	Sweet, floral	Fish	**
Pierre Sparr et ses Fils Riesling Grand Cru Schoenenbourg	White	Minerally, floral	Shellfish	**
Pinot Noir Cuvée Frédéric (Pierre Becht)	Red	Berry, floral	Game	**
Pinot Noir Rouge d'Alsace (Louis Hauller)	Red	Berry, gamey	Pasta	**
Riesling Comtes d'Eguisheim (Léon Beyer)	White	Citrus, apples	Shellfish	**
Riesling Grand Cru Schoenenbourg (François Lehmann)	White	Citrus, minerally	Fish	**
Riesling Stein (Pierre et Jean Rietsch)	White	Citrus, floral	Shellfish	**
Tokay Pinot Gris (André Thomas et Fils)	White	Spicy, floral	Fish	**
Tokay Pinot Gris Comtes d'Eguisheim (Léon Beyer)	White	Floral, spicy	Mediterranean	**
Beaujolais				
Domaine Yvon Metras Fleurie	Red	Berry, floral, jam, earthy	Chicken, pork, veal, beef	**
Georges Du Boeuf Morgon	Red	Jam, berry, intense	Chicken, veal, pork	**
Georges Du Boeuf Moulin-à-Vent	Red	Berry, earthy, minerally	Chicken, veal, pork	**
Guy Breton Morgon Vieilles Vignes	Red	Jam, spicy, earthy	Chicken, veal, pork	**
Jean Foillard Morgon	Red	Berry, floral, intense	Chicken, veal, pork	**
Jean-Paul Thévenet Morgon Cuvée Cielles Vignes	Red	Berry, spicy, intense	Chicken, fish, pork, pizza	**
Louis Jadot Château des Jacques Moulin-à-Vent	Red	Berry, vanillin, complex	Pork, veal, beef	**
Louis Jadot Domaine du Monnet Brouilly	Red	Berry, spicy, earthy	Pork, veal, beef	**
Louis Latour Morgon Les Charmes	Red	Jam, floral, berry, complex	Chicken, veal, pork	**
Marcel LaPierre Morgon	Red	Berry, rich, minerally	Chicken, veal, pork	**
Paul Janin et Fils Moulin-a-Vent	Red	Berry, powerful, citrus, minerally	Pork, veal, beef	**
Sylvan Fessy Beaujolais-Villages	Red	Berry, spicy	Fish, pork, pizza	*
Bordeaux				
Château Angélus	Red	Minerally, plums	Lamb	**
Château Ausone	Red	Minerally, earthy, plums, herbaceous	Beef	***

Wine name	Style	Flavor/ Bouquet	Compatible Foods	Price Range
Château Balestard-la-Tonnelle	Red	Herbaceous, minerally, spicy	Game	**
Château Barrabaque	Red	Berry, earthy	Cold meats	**
Château Barreyre	Red	Herbaceous, fruity	Stew	**
Château Bastor-Lamontagne	Sweet	Sweet, floral, mandarin	Dessert	***
Château Batailley	Red	Berry, spicy, herbaceous	Stew	**
Château Beaumont	Red	Berry, smoky	Cold meats, stew, offal	**
Château Beauregard	Red	Spicy, minerally, plums	Lamb	**
Château Beauséjour	Red	Minerally, berry	Lamb	**
Château Beau-Séjour Bécot	Red	Minerally, tannic, herbaceous	Beef	**
Château Bel Air	Red	Herbaceous, berry	Stew	**
Château Belair	Red	Berry, plums	Stew	***
Château Bel-Air La Royère	Red	Berry, fruity	Stew	**
Château Bel-Air Marquis d'Aligre	Red	Smoky, berry	Lamb	**
Château Belgrave	Red	Berry, plums	Lamb	**
Château Beychevelle	Red	Berry, herbaceous, tannic	Stew	**
Château Biston-Brillette	Red	Spicy, berry	Pasta	**
Château Bonnet (also Bordeaux)	Red	Herbaceous, berry	Stew	**
Château Branaire	Red	Berry, floral	Cheese	**
Château Brane-Cantenac	Red	Berry, herbaceous	Cold meats	**
Château Brillette	Red	Herbaceous, berry	Pork	**
Château Brondelle	White	Citrus, herbaceous, vanillin	Fish, chicken	**
Château Brulesécaille	Red	Berry, spicy	Cold meats, stew, offal	**
Château Calon (Montagne)	Red	Herbaceous, plums	Lamb	**
Château Calon-Ségur	Red	Berry, tannic	Lamb	**
Château Camensac	Red	Minerally, berry	Cheese	**
Château Canon	Red	Herbaceous, tannic	Cold meats	**
Château Canon	Red	Smoky, berry	Cold meats	***
Château Canon de Brem	Red	Spicy, berry	Pork	**
Château Canon-La Gaffelière	Red	Berry, herbaceous	Cold meats, stew, offal	**
Château Cantemerle	Red	Berry, spicy	Cold meats, stew, offal	**
Château Cantenac Brown	Red	Herbaceous, spicy, smoky	Lamb	**
Château Cap de Faugères	Red	Berry, licorice	Pork	**
Château Carbonnieux	Red	Minerally, berry	Beef	**
Château Carsin (also Cadillac)	Red	Berry, minerally	Cold meats	**
Château Cassagne Haut-Canon	Red	Minerally, herbaceous	Pasta	**
Château Castelneau	Red	Berry, herbaceous	Pizza	*
Château Castenet-Greffier	Red	Spicy, earthy	Stew	**
Château Cayla	Red	Earthy, berry	Pizza	*
Château Certan de May	Red	Berry, floral, complex	Game	***
Château Charmail	Red	Berry, herbaceous	Stew	**
Château Chasse-Spleen	Red	Berry, tannic	Stew	**
Château Cheval Blanc	Red	Minerally, berry, powerful, complex, herbaceous	Lamb	***

Wine name	Style	Flavor/ Bouquet	Compatible Foods	Price Range
Château Cissac	Red	Berry, tannic	Sausages	**
Château Citran	Red	Spicy, minerally	Cheese	**
Château Clarke	Red	Herbaceous, berry	Pasta	**
Château Clerc Milon	Red	Berry, herbaceous	Lamb	**
Château Climens	Sweet	Sweet, complex, honey	Dessert	***
Château Clinet	Red	Berry, tannic, minerally	Beef	***
Château Clos Haut-Peyraguey	Sweet	Sweet, honey, mandarin	Cheese	***
Château Cos d'Estournel	Red	Minerally, tannic, herbaceous, berry	Beef	***
Château Cos Labory	Red	Berry, tannic	Lamb	**
Château Côte Montpezat	Red	Minerally, earthy	Cheese	**
Château Coufran	Red	Smoky, herbaceous	Lamb	**
Château Couhins-Lurton	Red	Berry, minerally	Pasta	**
Château Coutet	Sweet	Sweet, honey, mandarin	Dessert	***
Château d'Angludet	Red	Earthy, berry	Cheese	**
Château d'Archambeau	White	Stone fruit, waxy, vanillin	Fish, chicken	**
Château d'Armailhac	Red	Berry, tannic	Lamb	**
Château d'Issan	Red	Tannic, berry	Cold meats, stew, offal	**
Château d'Yquem	Sweet	Sweet, complex, honey, mandarin, citrus	Foie gras	***
Château Dalem	Red	Elegant, spicy	Pork	**
Château Dauzac	Red	Plums, floral	Stew	**
Château de Cérons	Red	Spicy, herbaceous	Sausages	**
Château de Chantegrive (also Cérons)	White	Citrus, minerally	Fish	**
Château de Chelivette	Red	Minerally, herbaceous	Pork	**
Château de Cugat	Red	Berry, spicy	Cold meats, stew, offal	**
Château de Fargues	Sweet	Sweet, citrus, mandarin	Dessert	***
Château de Fieuzal	Red	Minerally, tannic, herbaceous	Beef	***
Château de Fontenille	Red	Herbaceous, plums	Cold meats, stew, offal	*
Château de Francs	Red	Smoky, herbaceous	Sausages	**
Château de l'Abbaye de St-Ferme	Red	Herbaceous, berry	Cold meats	**
Château de Malle	Sweet	Sweet, citrus	Dessert	***
Château de Myrat	Sweet	Sweet, fruity	Fruit	**
Château de Parenchère	Red	Berry, plums	Stew	**
Château de Reignac	Red	Minerally, berry	Lamb	**
Château de Sales	Red	Earthy, plums	Lamb	**
Château de Valandraud	Red	Herbaceous, minerally, berry	Cold meats	***
Château des Tourtes	Red	Spicy, berry	Cold meats, stew, offal	**
Château Doisy-Daëne	Sweet	Sweet, mandarin, minerally	Dessert	***
Château Doisy-Védrines	Sweet	Sweet, citrus, mandarin	Dessert	***
Château du Cros	Sweet	Sweet, mandarin	Dessert	**
Château du Mont	Sweet	Sweet, honey	Dessert	**
Château du Tertre	Red	Berry, earthy	Cold meats	**

Wine name	Style	Flavor/ Bouquet	Compatible Foods	Price Range
Château Ducluzeau	Red	Berry, smoky	Stew	**
Château Ducru-Beaucaillou	Red	Berry, minerally, herbaceous, tannic	Beef	***
Château Duhart-Milon	Red	Berry, tannic	Beef	**
Château Durfort-Vivens	Red	Berry, herbaceous, tannic	Cold meats, stew, offal	**
Château Falfas	Red	Herbaceous, plums	Pasta	*
Château Ferrière	Red	Berry, plums	Stew	**
Château Figeac	Red	Herbaceous, berry, minerally, tannic	Cheese	***
Château Fleur Cardinale	Red	Berry, spicy	Lamb	**
Château Fonbadet	Red	Berry, herbaceous, tannic	Pork	**
Château Fontenil	Red	Minerally, floral	Cheese	**
Château Fougas	Red	Smoky, herbaceous	Stew	**
Château Fourcas-Dupré	Red	Plums, smoky	Cold meats, stew, offal	**
Château Garraud	Red	Berry, herbaceous	Lamb	**
Château Gazin	Red	Berry, tannic, minerally	Stew	**
Château Gilette	Sweet	Sweet, complex, honey, mandarin	Cheese	***
Château Giscours	Red	Plums, spicy	Lamb	**
Château Gloria	Red	Plums, herbaceous, tannic	Lamb	**
Château Grand Mayne	Red	Berry, tannic	Stew	**
Château Grand Ormeau	Red	Spicy, earthy	Pork	**
Château Grand Renouil	Red	Berry, plums	Stew	**
Château Grand-Mouëys	Red	Minerally, plums	Cheese	**
Château Grand-Puy-Ducasse	Red	Berry, smoky	Beef	**
Château Grand-Puy-Lacoste	Red	Plums, herbaceous, spicy	Lamb	**
Château Gressier-Grand-Poujeaux	Red	Spicy, herbaceous, berry	Sausages	**
Château Greysac	Red	Herbaceous, floral	Pork	**
Château Gruaud-Larose	Red	Minerally, earthy, herbaceous, complex, tannic	Beef	***
Château Guerry	Red	Plums, herbaceous	Lamb	**
Château Guiraud	Sweet	Sweet, complex, citrus	Dessert	***
Château Haut Bertinerie	Red	Plums, herbaceous	Sausages	**
Château Haut Carles	Red	Plums, spicy	Stew	**
Château Haut-Bages-Libéral	Red	Herbaceous, berry	Cold meats, stew, offal	**
Château Haut-Bailly	Red	Herbaceous, spicy, tannic	Cheese	**
Château Haut-Batailley	Red	Berry, tannic	Cold meats, stew, offal	**
Château Haut-Beauséjour	Red	Berry, spicy, herbaceous	Stew	**
Château Haut-Brion	Red	Complex, tannic, minerally, berry	Lamb	***
Château Haut-Chaigneau	Red	Earthy, herbaceous	Stew	**
Château Haut-Grelot	Red	Plums, herbaceous	Cheese	**
Château Haut-Marbuzet	Red	Berry, tannic	Beef	**
Château Jonqueyres	Red	Berry, floral	Pork	*

Wine name	Style	Flavor/ Bouquet	Compatible Foods	Price Range
Château Kirwan	Red	Tannic, herbaceous, berry	Lamb	**
Château l'Arrosée	Red	Berry, spicy, tannic	Cold meats, stew, offal	**
Château L'Eglise-Clinet	Red	Spicy, berry, minerally	Cold meats, stew, offal	***
Château L'Evangile	Red	Minerally, berry, tannic	Cheese	***
Château La Cardonne	Red	Berry, herbaceous	Lamb	**
Château La Conseillante	Red	Plums, floral, spicy	Lamb	***
Château La Dominique	Red	Berry, spicy, complex	Lamb	***
Château La Fleur Cailleau	Red	Earthy, herbaceous	Cold meats, stew, offal	**
Château La Fleur Milon	Red	Berry, herbaceous	Stew	**
Château La Fleur Pétrus	Red	Complex, berry, plums, herbaceous	Stew	***
Château La Gaffelière	Red	Minerally, berry, herbaceous	Lamb	**
Château La Lagune	Red	Berry, herbaceous, tannic	Game	**
Château La Louvière	Red	Spicy, minerally, tannic	Pasta	**
Château La Mission Haut-Brion	Red	Complex, tannic, herbaceous, minerally	Lamb	***
Château La Mondotte	Red	Herbaceous, berry, smoky, tannic	Beef	***
Château La Rame	Sweet	Sweet, honey	Dessert	**
Château La Raz Caman	Red	Berry, spicy	Pasta	**
Château La Rivière	Red	Berry, tannic	Game	**
Château La Tour Blanche	Sweet	Sweet, honey, citrus	Dessert	***
Château La Tour Carnet	Red	Smoky, berry	Cold meats, stew, offal	**
Château La Tour de By	Red	Berry, plums	Stew	**
Château La Tour Figeac	Red	Minerally, herbaceous, berry	Stew	***
Château La Tour Haut-Brion	Red	Minerally, herbaceous, tannic	Lamb	**
Château La Vieille Cure	Red	Herbaceous, spicy	Pork	**
Château Labégorce-Zédé	Red	Berry, smoky	Lamb	**
Château Lacombe-Noaillac	Red	Spicy, herbaceous, earthy	Pasta	**
Château Lafaurie-Peyraguey	Sweet	Sweet, mandarin, citrus	Cheese	***
Château Lafite-Rothschild	Red	Complex, berry, smoky, tannic	Lamb	***
Château Lafleur	Red	Minerally, plums, spicy	Lamb	***
Château Lafon	Red	Berry, plums	Pasta	**
Château Lafon-Rochet	Red	Berry, spicy, herbaceous	Lamb	**
Château Lagrange	Red	Berry, herbaceous, tannic	Lamb	**
Château Lamotte de Haux	Red	Herbaceous, minerally	Beef	**
Château Lanessan	Red	Berry, tannic	Lamb	**
Château Langoa Barton	Red	Berry, smoky	Beef	**
Château Lapeyronie	Red	Herbaceous, minerally	Sausages	***
Château Larcis Ducasse	Red	Berry, smoky	Cheese	**
Château Larmande	Red	Plums, herbaceous, spicy	Cheese	**
Château Lascombes	Red	Herbaceous, smoky, spicy	Beef	**
Château Latour	Red	Complex, berry, powerful, tannic	Lamb	***

Wine name	Style	Flavor/ Bouquet	Compatible Foods	Price Range
Château Latour à Pomerol	Red	Complex, spicy, herbaceous, minerally	Beef	***
Château Latour-Martillac	Red	Berry, tannic	Beef	**
Château Laville	Red	Spicy, berry	Pasta	**
Château Laville Haut-Brion	Red	Minerally, berry, herbaceous	Game	***
Château Le Bon Pasteur	Red	Tannic, spicy, berry	Beef	**
Château Le Bonnat	White	Apples, melon, waxy, herbaceous	Fish, chicken	**
Château Le Crock	Red	Spicy, herbaceous, tannic	Stew	**
Château Le Pin	Red	Complex, powerful, tannic, spicy, herbaceous	Cold meats, stew, offal	***
Château Le Sens	Red	Berry, fruity	Lamb	**
Château Le Tertre Roteboeuf	Red	Earthy, plums, minerally, tannic	Lamb	***
Château Léhoul	Red	Spicy, plums	Pizza	**
Château Léoville Barton	Red	Berry, complex, herbaceous, smoky	Lamb	**
Château Léoville Las Cases	Red	Complex, minerally, herbaceous, berry	Lamb	***
Château Léoville Poyferré	Red	Berry, herbaceous, minerally	Cold meats, stew, offal	**
Château Les Arromans	Red	Herbaceous, earthy	Cold meats, stew, offal	**
Château Les Carmes Haut-Brion	Red	Spicy, herbaceous, earthy	Cold meats, stew, offal	**
Château Les Grands Chênes	Red	Herbaceous, berry	Stew	**
Château Les Jonqueyres	Red	Plums, smoky	Pasta	**
Château Les Justices	Sweet	Sweet, citrus	Fruit	**
Château Les Ormes-de-Pez	Red	Minerally, tannic	Beef	**
Château Les Ormes-Sorbet	Red	Smoky, herbaceous	Game	**
Château Les Trois Croix	Red	Earthy, berry	Cheese	**
Château Lestage Simon	Red	Berry, spicy	Cheese	**
Château Lilian-Ladouys	Red	Tannic, floral, herbaceous	Game	**
Château Loubens	Sweet	Sweet, minerally, honey	Dessert	**
Château Loudenne	Red	Tannic, berry	Cold meats, stew, offal	**
Château Loumède	Red	Herbaceous, smoky	Stew	**
Château Lynch-Bages	Red	Berry, tannic, herbaceous	Lamb	***
Château Magdelaine	Red	Minerally, earthy, herbaceous	Lamb	***
Château Magneau	Red	Herbaceous, plums	Stew	**
Château Malartic-Lagravière	Red	Minerally, herbaceous, tannic	Cold meats, stew, offal	**
Château Malescasse	Red	Spicy, plums	Lamb	**
Château Malescot-St-Exupery	Red	Berry, spicy	Stew	**
Château Manos	Red	Berry, fruity	Pasta	**
Château Marbuzet	Red	Berry, herbaceous, tannic	Cold meats, stew, offal	**
Château Margaux	Red	Complex, minerally, berry, tannic, spicy	Lamb	***
Château Marquis de Terme	Red	Berry, floral	Stew	**
Château Maucaillou	Red	Berry, plums	Sausages	**
Château Maucamps	Red	Plums, herbaceous	Stew	**

Wine name	Style	Flavor/ Bouquet	Compatible Foods	Price Range
Château Mayne Lalande	Red	Herbaceous, smoky	Game	**
Château Mémoires (also Cadillac)	Sweet	Sweet, honey	Dessert	**
Château Mercier	Red	Herbaceous, smoky	Pizza	*
Château Meyney	Red	Minerally, herbaceous, tannic	Cheese	**
Château Monbousquet	Red	Berry, herbaceous, tannic	Stew	**
Château Monbrison	Red	Berry, herbaceous	Cold meats, stew, offal	**
Château Mondésir-Gazin	Red	Herbaceous, berry	Game	**
Château Montrose	Red	Minerally, complex, powerful, berry	Beef	***
Château Moulin Haut-Laroque	Red	Herbaceous, berry	Beef	**
Château Moulin St-Georges	Red	Berry, plums	Beef	**
Château Moulin-de-Launay	Red	Plums, herbaceous	Pizza	*
Château Mouton-Rothschild	Red	Complex, berry, herbaceous, tannic, spicy	Lamb	***
Château Nairac	Sweet	Sweet, floral, citrus	Dessert	**
Château Nardique-la-Gravière	Red	Berry, herbaceous	Pasta	**
Château Nodoz	Red	Herbaceous, smoky	Pizza	*
Château Palmer	Red	Complex, tannic, herbaceous, berry	Cheese	***
Château Pape Clément	Red	Berry, minerally	Stew	**
Château Patache d'Aux	Red	Herbaceous, berry	Stew	**
Château Pavie	Red	Minerally, plums, herbaceous	Lamb	***
Château Pavie-Decesse	Red	Herbaceous, smoky	Stew	**
Château Pavie-Macquin	Red	Plums, berry	Pasta	**
Château Penin	Red	Berry, herbaceous	Pizza	*
Château Petit-Village	Red	Berry, spicy	Sausages	**
Château Pétrus	Red	Complex, spicy, herbaceous, berry, tannic	Game	***
Château Phélan-Ségur	Red	Spicy, earthy, herbaceous	Lamb	**
Château Pibran	Red	Berry, spicy	Stew	**
Château Pichon-Longueville	Red	Berry, smoky, tannic, herbaceous	Beef	***
Château Pichon-Longueville (Comtesse de Lalande)	Red	Berry, plums, complex, tannic	Lamb	***
Château Pipeau	Red	Minerally, spicy, tannic	Cold meats, stew, offal	**
Château Plaisance	Red	Berry, spicy	Sausages	**
Château Pontet-Canet	Red	Herbaceous, spicy	Cold meats	**
Château Potensac	Red	Tannic, berry	Lamb	**
Château Poujeaux	Red	Berry, herbaceous	Cheese	**
Château Poupille	Red	Berry, spicy	Cheese	*
Château Prieuré-Lichine	Red	Berry, tannic	Lamb	**
Château Puy-Bardens	Red	Berry, minerally	Sausages	**
Château Puygueraud	Red	Plums, berry	Pasta	**
Château Rabaud-Promis	Sweet	Sweet, citrus, mandarin	Dessert	**
Château Rahoul	Red	Berry, herbaceous	Sausages	**

Wine name	Style	Flavor/ Bouquet	Compatible Foods	Price Range
Château Ramage-la-Batisse	Red	Plums, berry	Pasta	**
Château Rauzan-Ségla	Red	Smoky, tannic	Cold meats	***
Château Raymond-Lafon	Sweet	Sweet, complex, honey	Foie gras	***
Château Rayne Vigneau	Sweet	Sweet, mandarin, honey	Dessert	***
Château Renon	Red	Herbaceous, fruity	Stew	**
Château Respide Médeville	Red	Smoky, plums	Pasta	**
Château Reynon	Red	Berry, herbaceous	Stew	**
Château Rieussec	Sweet	Sweet, complex, honey, mandarin	Dessert	***
Château Robin	Red	Spicy, minerally	Pasta	**
Château Roc de Cambes	Red	Fruity, berry	Cold meats, stew, offal	**
Château Rolande-la-Garde	Red	Earthy, plums	Cheese	**
Château Rollan de By	Red	Spicy, herbaceous, earthy	Beef	**
Château Roquefort	Red	Spicy, earthy	Beef	**
Château Saint-Pierre	Red	Plums, spicy, berry	Beef	**
Château Sigalas-Rabaud	Sweet	Sweet, citrus, floral	Dessert	**
Château Siran	Red	Berry, plums	Cold meats, stew, offal	**
Château Smith-Haut-Lafitte	Red	Minerally, herbaceous, tannic	Beef	**
Château Sociando-Mallet	Red	Plums, tannic	Cold meats, stew, offal	**
Château Soutard	Red	Plums, berry	Lamb	**
Château Ste-Catherine	Red	Berry, herbaceous	Game	**
Château Ste-Marie	Red	Spicy, earthy	Stew	*
Château St-Robert	White	Citrus, waxy, herbaceous, vanillin	Fish, chicken	**
Château Suau	Red	Herbaceous, minerally	Pasta	**
Château Suduiraut	Sweet	Sweet, complex, citrus	Dessert	***
Château Talbot	Red	Berry, herbaceous, minerally	Sausages	**
Château Tayac	Red	Plums, berry	Cold meats	*
Château Thieuley	Red	Berry, herbaceous	Game	**
Château Tour du Haut-Moulin	Red	Berry, spicy	Beef	**
Château Tour Haut-Caussan	Red	Berry, herbaceous	Stew	**
Château Tour-de-Mirambeau (also Bordeaux)	Red	Earthy, spicy	Stew	**
Château Trocard	Red	Plum, herbaceous	Cold meats, stew, offal	**
Château Troplong-Mondot	Red	Spicy, minerally, berry	Lamb	**
Château Trotanoy	Red	Complex, spicy, minerally, tannic	Game	***
Château Trottevieille	Red	Plums, minerally	Lamb	**
Château Turcaud	Red	Herbaceous, plums	Cold meats, stew, offal	"
Château Vieux Robin	Red	Spicy, berry	Lamb	**
Château Villars	Red	Plums, berry	Stew	**
Clos de l'Oratoire	Red	Berry, spicy	Stew	**
Clos Floridène	White	Spicy, minerally	Shellfish	**
Clos Fourtet	Red	Plums, spicy	Pork	**
Clos Jean	Sweet	Sweet, mandarin	Dessert	**

Wine name	Style	Flavor/ Bouquet	Compatible Foods	Price Range
Clos l'Eglise	Red	Berry, minerally, herbaceous, tannic	Beef	***
Cru Barréjats	Sweet	Sweet, citrus	Dessert	*
Domaine de Bouillerot	Red	Spicy, earthy	Pizza	**
Domaine de Chevalier	Red	Berry, herbaceous, tannic, minerally	Beef	***
Domaine de Courteillac	Red	Herbaceous, berry	Cheese	**
Domaine du Noble	Sweet	Sweet, honey	Dessert	**
Grand Enclos du Château de Cérons	Red	Berry, spicy	Sausages	**
Lussac Château de la Grenière	Red	Herbaceous, minerally	Stew	**
Lussac Château Lyonnat	Red	Berry, fruity	Cold meats, stew, offal	**
Montagne Château Faizeau	Red	Plums, smoky	Beef	**
Puisseguin Château Durand-Laplagne	Red	Berry, smoky	Stew	**
Pusseguin Château Guibeau-La-Fourvieille	Red	Berry, herbaceous	Stew	**
St-Georges Château St-André Corbin	Red	Berry, plums	Cold meats	**
St-Georges Château St-Georges	Red	Spicy, herbaceous, plums	Cold meats	**
Vieux Château Certan	Red	Herbaceous, berry, spicy, minerally, tannic	Beef	***
Vieux Château Champs de Mars	Red	Spicy, plums	Pasta	**
Vieux Château Gaubert	White	Citrus, minerally	Fish	**
Villa Bel Air	White	Citrus, herbaceous, vanillin	Fish, chicken	**
Bugey				
Domaine Monin Bugey Brut Méthode Traditionnelle	Sparkling	Crisp, fruity, citrus	Aperitif	**
Domaine Monin Vin du Bugey Chardonnay	White	Tropical fruit, citrus	Chicken	**
Burgundy				
Amiot-Bonfils Puligny Montrachet Les Demoiselles	White	Mandarin, nutty	Fish	**
Ampeau Meursault Perrières	White	Citrus, spicy, nutty	Cheese	**
Bachelet Charmes Chambertin Vieilles Vignes	Red	Gamey, leathery	Duck	***
Barthod Chambolle Musigny	Red	Berry, spicy	Pasta	**
Bize Savigny-Les-Beaune Les Vergelesses	Red	Minerally, spicy	Cold meats, stew, offal	**
Blain-Gagnard Chassagne Morey	White	Minerally, citrus	Fish	**
Blain-Gagnard Criots-Bâtard-Montrachet	White	Minerally, complex, rich	Fish	***
Bonhomme Macon Viré	White	Citrus, spicy	Pasta	**
Bonneau du Martray Corton Charlemagne	White	Complex, nutty, smoky, spicy	Fish	***
Bouchard Père et Fils Beaune Vigne de l'Enfant Jésus	Red	Berry, earthy	Lamb	**
Boyer Martenot Meursault	White	Tropical fruit, citrus	Chicken	**
Burguet Gevrey Chambertin Vieilles Vignes	Red	Berry, spicy, earthy	Lamb	**
Carillon Bienvenues Bâtard Montrachet	White	Citrus, spicy	Fish	***
Carillon Puligny Montrachet Les Perrières	White	Smoky, citrus	Chicken	**
Chablis (A. Boudin)	White	Minerally, spicy	Shellfish	**
Chablis (L. Michel)	White	Citrus, minerally	Shellfish	**
Chablis Les Clos (V. Dauvissat)	White	Minerally, complex, citrus	Veal	***
Chablis Les Preuses (V. Dauvissat)	White	Citrus, floral, minerally	Fish	***
Chambolle Musigny (P. Rion)	Red	Elegant, berry	Duck	**

Wine name	Style	Flavor/ Bouquet	Compatible Foods	Price Range
Chandon de Briailles Corton Bressandes	Red	Berry, earthy, complex	Duck	***
Chandon de Briailles Pernand Vergelesses Ile de Vergelesses	Red	Minerally, floral	Veal	**
Charmes Chambertin (C. Dugat)	Red	Spicy, earthy, gamey	Lamb	***
Chassagne Montrachet Girardin	White	Spicy, citrus, smoky	Fish	**
Chassagne Montrachet Les Embrazées (Bernard Morey)	White	Citrus, complex, spicy	Cheese	**
Château de Chamirey Mercurey	Red	Berry, earthy	Cheese	**
Château de Fuissé Pouilly Fuissé	White	Minerally, citrus	Fish	**
Château de Meursault Meursault	White	Citrus, spicy	Chicken	**
Clair Chambertin Clos de Bèze	Red	Spicy, minerally, berry	Duck	***
Clair Morey St-Denis en la Rue de Vergy	Red	Berry, leathery	Cold meats, stew, offal	**
Clair Savigny-Les-Beaune La Dominode	Red	Spicy, berry	Cold meats	**
Clos de la Roche (H. Lignier)	Red	Spicy, gamey, complex	Cold meats	***
Clos de Vougeot (A. Gros)	Red	Gamey, leathery, spicy	Game	***
Coche Dury Corton Charlemagne	White	Spicy, complex, minerally	Chicken	***
Coche Dury Meursault	White	Citrus, nutty	Fish	**
Coche Dury Meursault Perrières	White	Complex, citrus, spicy	Fish	**
Coche Dury Volnay Premier cru	Red	Spicy, gamey	Duck	**
Colin-Deleger Chassagne Montrachet	White	Citrus, complex, spicy	Veal	**
Colin-Deleger Puligny Montrachet Les Demoiselles	White	Spicy, citrus, nutty	Veal	**
Corton Charlemagne (Louis Jadot)	White	Citrus, floral, tropical fruit	Chicken	***
Corton Charlemagne (Louis Latour)	White	Nutty, citrus, oaky	Veal	***
Corton Charlemagne (Michel Juillot)	White	Oaky, spicy, nutty	Chicken	***
Corton Perrières (Michel Juillot)	Red	Smoky, berry	Cold meats, stew, offal	***
Darviot-Perrin Chassagne Montrachet Blanchots	White	Citrus, oaky, spicy	Chicken	**
de Courcel Pommard Rugiens	Red	Spicy, gamey, earthy	Beef	***
de Montille Pommard Pézerolles	Red	Berry, spicy	Game	**
de Montille Pommard Rugiens	Red	Berry, spicy	Cheese	**
de Montille Puligny Montrachet Les Caillerets	White	Spicy, citrus, minerally	Fish	**
de Montille Volnay Taillepieds	Red	Spicy, gamey	Cold meats, stew, offal	**
de Suremain Monthelie	Red	Berry, plums	Pasta	**
de Villaine Bourgogne Aligoté de Bouzeron	White	Spicy, citrus	Pasta	**
de Villaine Bourgogne Blanc	White	Tropical fruit, citrus	Fish	**
de Vogüé Bonnes Mares	Red	Rich, complex, gamey, berry	Duck	***
de Vogüé Chambolle Musigny Les Amoureuses	Red	Gamey, silky, berry	Cheese	***
de Vogüé Le Musigny	Red	Complex, berry, silky, gamey	Duck	***
Domaine de l'Arlot Nuits St-Georges Clos des Forêts St-Georges	Red	Spicy, gamey, berry	Duck	**
Domaine de la Romanée Conti Echézeaux	Red	Complex, floral, spicy, earthy	Duck	***
Domaine de la Romanée Conti Grands Echézeaux	Red	Spicy, complex, minerally, berry	Lamb	***
Domaine de la Romanée Conti La Tâche	Red	Spicy, earthy, silky, complex	Duck	***
Domaine de la Romanée Conti Le Montrachet	White	Minerally, complex, spicy,	Fish	***
Domaine de la Romanée Conti Richebourg	Red	Gamey, spicy, complex	Game	***
Domaine de la Romanée Conti Romanée Conti	Red	Complex, spicy, earthy	Duck	***

Wine name	Style	Flavor/ Bouquet	Compatible Foods	Price Range
Domaine de la Romanée Conti Romanée St. Vivant	Red	Complex, minerally, smoky, earthy	Game	***
Domaine des Lambrays Clos des Lambrays	Red	Earthy, plums, spicy	Lamb	***
Domaine Leflaive Bâtard Montrachet	White	Complex, spicy, smoky	Fish	***
Domaine Leflaive Bienvenues Bâtard Montrachet	White	Complex, citrus, nutty	Veal	***
Domaine Leflaive Chevalier Montrachet	White	Complex, nutty, spicy, citrus	Fish	***
Domaine Leflaive Puligny Montrachet Les Combettes	White	Complex, spicy, citrus	Veal	***
Domaine Leflaive Puligny Montrachet Les Pucelles	White	Complex, smoky, spicy, citrus	Chicken	***
Drouhin Beaune Clos des Mouches	White	Minerally, citrus	Fish	**
Drouhin Puligny Montrachet	White	Citrus, minerally	Pork	**
Drouhin Vosne Romanée Petits Monts	Red	Floral, minerally, gamey	Cold meats, stew, offal	**
Dujac Clos de la Roche	Red	Complex, gamey, earthy	Duck	***
Dujac Clos St. Denis	Red	Earthy, minerally, berry	Beef	***
Engel Clos de Vougeot	Red	Spicy, earthy, berry	Beef	***
Engel Grands Echézeaux	Red	Berry, minerally, spicy	Duck	***
Ente Meursault	White	Smoky, citrus	Pork	**
Faiveley Corton Charlemagne	White	Citrus, minerally, spicy	Veal	***
Faiveley Corton Clos des Cortons	Red	Berry, gamey	Lamb	***
Faiveley Mazis Chambertin	Red	Earthy, minerally, berry	Beef	***
Faiveley Mercurey	Red	Berry, earthy	Pasta	**
Faiveley Nuits St. Georges Clos de la Maréchale	Red	Minerally, earthy, berry	Beef	***
Fichet Meursault	White	Citrus, spicy	Veal	**
Fontaine-Gagnard Chassagne Morey	White	Citrus, spicy	Pasta	**
Forest Pouilly Fuissé	White	Minerally, spicy	Fish	**
Gagnard-Delagrange Bâtard Montrachet	White	Complex, nutty, minerally	Fish	***
Gagnard-Delagrange Chassagne Morey	White	Nutty, spicy	Veal	**
Garaudet Monthelie	Red	Spicy, earthy	Sausages	**
Gevrey Chambertin (C. Dugat)	Red	Berry, spicy	Beef	**
Gevrey Chambertin (D. Mortet)	Red	Berry, licorice	Stew	**
Givry (F. Lumpp)	Red	Floral, berry	Pasta	**
Gouges Nuits St. Georges Les St. Georges	Red	Earthy, berry	Game	**
Gouges Nuits St. Georges Les St. Porrets	Red	Plums, berry	Cheese	**
Gouges Nuits St. Georges Vaucrains	Red	Smoky, spicy	Cheese	**
Grivot Clos de Vougeot	Red	Complex, earthy, berry	Lamb	***
Grivot Nuits St. Georges Boudots	Red	Spicy, gamey	Duck	***
Grivot Vosne Romanée	Red	Complex, berry	Lamb	**
Groffier Bonnes Mares	Red	Berry, gamey, spicy	Lamb	***
Groffier Chambolle Musigny Les Amoureuses	Red	Berry, spicy	Duck	***
Grossot Chablis	White	Minerally, apples	Fish	**
Guffens-Heynen Pouilly Fuissé	White	Minerally, floral	Shellfish	**
Jadot Beaune Boucherottes	Red	Berry, earthy	Cheese	**
Jadot Beaune Clos des Ursules	Red	Berry, earthy	Stew	**
Jadot Chevalier Montrachet Les Demoiselles	White	Spicy, smoky	Chicken	***

Wine name	Style	Flavor/ Bouquet	Compatible Foods	Price Range
Jadot Corton Pougets	Red	Berry, leathery	Duck	***
Jadot Puligny Montrachet	White	Minerally, spicy	Veal	**
Javillier Meursault	White	Nutty, citrus	Chicken	**
Jean-Noel Gagnard Chassagne Montrachet Les Caillerets	White	Nutty, complex, spicy	Fish	**
Joblot Givry	Red	Spicy, floral	Sausages	**
Lafarge Beaune Grèves	Red	Plums, berry	Duck	**
Lafarge Volnay Clos des Chênes	Red	Spicy, earthy	Stew	**
Lafarge Volnay Clos du Château des Ducs	Red	Smoky, berry	Pasta	**
Latour Puligny Montrachet	White	Citrus, smoky	Chicken	**
Le Montrachet (Baron Thenard)	White	Complex, citrus, tropical fruit, spicy	Chicken	***
Le Montrachet (Comte Lafon)	White	Complex, smoky, minerally	Fish	***
Le Montrachet (Marquis de Laguiche)	White	Complex, nutty, smoky, spicy	Fish	***
Leroy Auxey Duresses	Red	Earthy, berry	Pasta	**
Leroy Clos de Vougeot	Red	Earthy, minerally, complex, spicy	Duck	***
Leroy Richebourg	Red	Complex, spicy, earthy	Beef	***
Leroy Romanée St. Vivant	Red	Complex, spicy, minerally	Lamb	***
Leroy Savigny-Les-Beaune Narbantons	Red	Minerally, floral	Stew	**
Leroy Volnay Santenots	Red	Floral, smoky	Cold meats, stew, offal	**
Leroy Vosne Romanée Les Beaux Monts	Red	Spicy, earthy, minerally	Duck	***
Méo-Camuzet Clos de Vougeot	Red	Minerally, berry, spicy, earthy	Duck	***
Méo-Camuzet Nuits St. Georges aux Murgers	Red	Berry, earthy	Lamb	***
Méo-Camuzet Vosne Romanée Chaumes	Red	Gamey, spicy, earthy	Cold meats, stew, offal	***
Méo-Camuzet Vosne Romanée Les Brulées	Red	Spicy, berry, gamey	Stew	***
Mercurey (M. Juillot)	Red	Spicy, berry	Sausages	**
Merlin Macon La Roche Vineuse Vieilles Vignes	White	Minerally, tropical fruit	Mediterranean	**
Meursault (Michel Bouzereau)	White	Spicy, smoky	Veal	**
Meursault Charmes (Comte Lafon)	White	Nutty, spicy, complex	Veal	***
Meursault Charmes (François Jobard)	White	Nutty, smoky	Chicken	**
Meursault Charmes (Rémi Jobard)	White	Spicy, smoky	Fish	***
Meursault Clos de la Barre (Comte Lafon)	White	Complex, minerally, nutty	Fish	***
Meursault Genevrières (Comte Lafon)	White	Complex, minerally, spicy	Fish	***
Meursault Perrières (Comte Lafon)	White	Citrus, spicy, minerally	Fish	***
Monthelie Duresses (Comte Lafon)	Red	Berry, earthy	Cold meats, stew, offal	**
Morot Beaune Teurons	Red	Minerally, berry	Cold meats, stew, offal	**
Mugnier Chambolle Musigny Les Amoureuses	Red	Spicy, gamey	Game	***
Mugnier Le Musigny	Red	Berry, spicy, complex	Game	***
Niellon Chevalier Montrachet	White	Citrus, smoky	Cold meats, stew, offal	***
Nuits St. Georges Hauts Pruliers (D. Rion)	Red	Elegant, spicy	Cold meats	**
Nuits St. Georges Les Cailles (R. Chevillon)	Red	Gamey, spicy	Cold meats, stew, offal	**
Nuits St. Georges Les St. Georges (R. Chevillon)	Red	Spicy, leathery	Pasta	**
Nuits St. Georges Vaucrains (R. Chevillon)	Red	Berry, spicy	Game	**

Wine name	Style	Flavor/ Bouquet	Compatible Foods	Price Range
Pernot Bâtard Montrachet	White	Smoky, citrus	Chicken	***
Pommard Clos des Epeneaux (Comte Armand)	Red	Earthy, berry, smoky	Duck	***
Pommard Saussilles (Jean-Marc Boillot)	Red	Spicy, gamey, berry	Game	**
Ponsot Clos de la Roche Vieilles Vignes	Red	Spicy, gamey, berry	Game	***
Ponsot Clos St-Denis	Red	Berry, spicy	Game	***
Ponsot Griotte Chambertin	Red	Berry, gamey	Duck	***
Pouilly Fuissé (Madame Ferret)	White	Minerally, citrus	Shellfish	**
Pousse d'Or Santenay Clos des Tavannes	Red	Floral, minerally	Pasta	**
Pousse d'Or Volnay Clos de la Pousse d'Or	Red	Berry, spicy	Game	***
Pousse d'Or Volnay Clos des 60 Ouvrées	Red	Complex, elegant, spicy	Cheese	***
Prince de Mérode Corton Bressandes	Red	Spicy, berry, gamey	Game	***
Puligny Montrachet La Truffière (Jean-Marc Boillot)	White	Spicy, citrus, minerally	Fish	**
Ramonet Bâtard Montrachet	White	Complex, tropical fruit, smoky	Fish	***
Ramonet Chassagne Montrachet Cailleret	White	Spicy, citrus	Pork	**
Ramonet Chassagne Montrachet Ruchottes	White	Spicy, floral, minerally	Chicken	**
Ramonet Le Montrachet	White	Citrus, smoky, minerally	Chicken	***
Raveneau Chablis Les Clos	White	Complex, nutty, minerally	Chicken	***
Raveneau Chablis Montée de Tonnerre	White	Minerally, nutty, complex	Fish	***
Richebourg (A. Gros)	Red	Minerally, berry, gamey	Game	***
Roty Charmes Chambertin Très Vieilles Vignes	Red	Berry, earthy	Cold meats, stew, offal	***
Rouget Echézeaux (formerly H. Jayer)	Red	Gamey, berry, earthy	Beef	***
Rouget Vosne Romanée Cros Parantoux	Red	Earthy, spicy, minerally	Stew	***
Roulot Meursault Perrières	White	Smoky, complex	Fish	**
Roulot Meursault Tesson Le Clos de Mon Plaisir	White	Citrus, nutty	Veal	**
Roumier Bonnes Mares	Red	Complex, berry, silky	Game	***
Roumier Chambolle Musigny	Red	Berry, spicy	Cold meats, stew, offal	**
Roumier Chambolle Musigny Les Amoureuses	Red	Silky, gamey, berry	Game	***
Roumier Morey St. Denis Clos de la Bussière	Red	Complex, elegant, spicy	Cold meats	***
Roumier Ruchottes Chambertin	Red	Elegant, spicy, gamey	Game	***
Rousseau Chambertin	Red	Complex, silky, berry, gamey	Game	***
Rousseau Chambertin Clos de Bèze	Red	Elegant, spicy, minerally	Duck	***
Rousseau Clos de la Roche	Red	Complex, silky, gamey, spicy	Cold meats, stew, offal	***
Rousseau Gevrey Chambertin Clos St. Jacques	Red	Complex, elegant, berry, spicy	Duck	***
Saint Aubin (Marc Colin)	White	Tropical fruit, nutty	Pasta	**
Saint Aubin Les Murgers Dents de Chien (Hubert Lamy)	White	Citrus, spicy	Fish	**
Saint Aubin Premier Cru (G. Thomas)	White	Minerally, citrus	Cheese	**
Saint Romain (Alain Gras)	Red	Berry, spicy	Pasta	**
Santenay Clos des Tavannes (L. Muzard)	Red	Spicy, minerally	Pizza	**
Santenay Gravières (Vincent Girardin)	Red	Minerally, spicy	Sausages	**
Sauzet Bâtard Montrachet	White	Complex, nutty, smoky	Chicken	***
Sauzet Puligny Montrachet Les Combettes	White	Smoky, citrus	Chicken	***
Serafin Gevrey Chambertin Vieilles Vignes	Red	Berry, spicy	Game	**
Thevenet Macon Clessé Cuvée Levroutée	White	Minerally, mandarin	Pasta	**

Wine name	Style	Flavor/ Bouquet	Compatible Foods	Price Range
Thevenet Macon Clessé Domaine de Bon Gran	White	Citrus, minerally	Chicken	**
Tollot-Beaut Chorey-lès-Beaune	Red	Berry, minerally	Pizza	**
Volnay Champans (Comte Lafon)	Red	Earthy, gamey	Game	***
Volnay Clos des Chênes (Comte Lafon)	Red	Earthy, minerally, spicy	Lamb	***
Volnay Clos des Ducs (Marquis d'Angerville)	Red	Berry, plums	Beef	**
Volnay Santenots-du-Milieu (Comte Lafon)	Red	Berry, spicy	Cold meats	**
Volnay Taillepieds (Marquis d'Angerville)	Red	Gamey, spicy, earthy	Cold meats	**
Champagne				
Alfred Gratien Brut NV	Sparkling	Toasty, berry, austere	Chicken	**
Alfred Gratien Cuveé Paridis	Sparkling	Berry, toasty, yeasty	Veal	**
Alfred Gratien Vintage	Sparkling	Berry, complex, nutty	Fish	**
Ayala Vintage	Sparkling	Berry, citrus	Shellfish	**
Billecart-Salmon Blanc de Blancs	Sparkling	Citrus, elegant	Aperitif	**
Billecart-Salmon Brut	Sparkling	Citrus, floral, berry	Shellfish	**
Billecart-Salmon Cuvée N.F. Billecart	Sparkling	Complex, citrus, berry, elegant	Fish	***
Billecart-Salmon Rosé	Sparkling	Berry, floral	Lamb	**
Billecart-Salmon Rosé Cuvée Elizabeth	Sparkling	Berry, complex, floral	Pork	**
Bollinger R.D.	Sparkling	Complex, powerful, berry, yeasty	Chicken	***
Bollinger Special Cuvée	Sparkling	Powerful, berry, apples, complex	Antipasto	**
Bollinger Vieilles Vignes Françaises	Sparkling	Complex, berry, rich	Game	***
Bollinger Vintage	Sparkling	Berry, complex, toasty, powerful	Fish	**
Bruno Paillard Vintage	Sparkling	Crisp, citrus, berry	Shellfish	**
C. H. Blanc des Millenaires	Sparkling	Complex, citrus, berry	Veal	***
Canard-Duchéne Vintage	Sparkling	Berry, floral, yeasty	Fish	**
Cattier Brut	Sparkling	Yeasty, berry, floral	Shellfish	**
Cattier Clos du Moulin	Sparkling	Berry, complex, powerful	Chicken	***
Charbaut Certificate	Sparkling	Berry, citrus	Cheese	**
Charles Heidsieck Brut Mis en Cave NV	Sparkling	Berry, floral, yeasty	Shellfish	**
Charles Heidsieck Champagne Charlie	Sparkling	Berry, complex, powerful, rich	Chicken	***
Charles Heidsieck Vintage	Sparkling	Berry, complex, toasty	Veal	**
De Castellane Vintage	Sparkling	Yeasty, citrus, berry	Antipasto	**
De Cazenove Stradivarius	Sparkling	Yeasty, citrus, berry, complex	Fish	**
De Venoge Des Princes	Sparkling	Complex, floral, berry	Aperitif	**
De Venoge Vintage	Sparkling	Berry, crisp	Fish	**
Delamotte Vintage	Sparkling	Berry, citrus, crisp	Shellfish	**
Deutz Blanc de Blancs	Sparkling	Citrus, elegant, crisp	Aperitif	**
Deutz Brut	Sparkling	Berry, citrus, floral	Fish	**
Deutz Cuveé (William Deutz)	Sparkling	Berry, complex, citrus	Veal	***
Deutz Vintage	Sparkling	Berry, citrus	Fish	**
Diebolt Vintage (100% Chardonnay)	Sparkling	Citrus, crisp	Aperitif	**
Drappier Grande Sendrée	Sparkling	Berry, complex, powerful	Pork	***

Wine name	Style	Flavor/ Bouquet	Compatible Foods	Price Range
Drappier Vintage	Sparkling	Crisp, fruity	Fish	**
Gardet Vintage	Sparkling	Berry, citrus, crisp	Shellfish	**
Gosset—special bottlings such as Quatramine Centenaire/Célibris	Sparkling	Complex, berry, yeasty, powerful	Duck	***
Gosset Brut Excellence	Sparkling	Berry, minerally, crisp	Chicken	**
Gosset Grand Millésime	Sparkling	Complex, berry, rich	Veal	**
Heidsieck & Monopole Diamant Bleu	Sparkling	Crisp, citrus, berry	Antipasto	***
Heidsieck & Monopole Vintage	Sparkling	Crisp, toasty, berry	Cheese	**
Henriot Cuveé Baccarat	Sparkling	Complex, elegant, citrus, berry	Fish	***
Henriot Vintage	Sparkling	Elegant, berry, yeasty	Chicken	**
J. Lassalle Blanc de Blancs	Sparkling	Crisp, citrus, elegant	Aperitif	**
Jacquart Vintage	Sparkling	Austere, berry, citrus	Fish	**
Jacques Selosse Extra Brut	Sparkling	Berry, complex	Shellfish	**
Jacques Selosse Vintage	Sparkling	Complex, berry, powerful	Game	**
Jacquesson Dégorgement Tardif	Sparkling	Austere, berry	Shellfish	**
Jacquesson Perfection	Sparkling	Complex, citrus, berry, dry	Cheese	***
Jacquesson Signature	Sparkling	Complex, berry, powerful	Chicken	**
Jacquesson Signature Non Dosé	Sparkling	Dry, austere, crisp, citrus	Shellfish	**
José Michel Vintage	Sparkling	Citrus, crisp	Fish	**
Joseph Perrier Cuvée Royale	Sparkling	Berry, citrus, floral	Aperitif	**
Joseph Perrier Josephine	Sparkling	Complex, berry, citrus	Chicken	**
Krug Clos du Mesnil	Sparkling	Complex, citrus, yeasty, powerful	Shellfish	***
Krug Grande Cuvée	Sparkling	Berry, complex, powerful	Fish	***
Krug Rosé	Sparkling	Berry, complex, floral	Lamb	***
Krug Vintage	Sparkling	Powerful, complex, berry	Game	***
Lanson Black Label	Sparkling	Austere, crisp, berry	Shellfish	**
Lanson Noble Cuvée	Sparkling	Citrus, berry, complex, toasty	Chicken	***
Lanson Vintage	Sparkling	Austere, berry, zingy	Veal	**
Launois Vintage	Sparkling	Crisp, citrus, berry	Pork	**
Laurent-Perrier Brut	Sparkling	Crisp, citrus	Aperitif	**
Laurent-Perrier Grand Siècle	Sparkling	Complex, berry, floral	Fish	***
Laurent-Perrier Grand Siècle Alexandra Rosé	Sparkling	Berry, floral, melon, complex	Lamb	***
Laurent-Perrier Grand Siècle Vintage	Sparkling	Berry, complex, yeasty	Fish	***
Laurent-Perrier Ultra Brut	Sparkling	Austere, dry, crisp, citrus	Shellfish	**
Laurent-Perrier Vintage	Sparkling	Dry, citrus, berry	Antipasto	**
Legras Cuveé St. Vincent	Sparkling	Citrus, crisp, berry	Chicken	**
Legras Présidence	Sparkling	Berry, complex, floral	Fish	**
Lilbert Vintage	Sparkling	Crisp, berry	Cheese	**
Louis Roederer Brut Premier NV	Sparkling	Berry, citrus, minerally	Antipasto	**
Louis Roederer Cristal	Sparkling	Complex, citrus, floral, crisp, elegant	Fish	***
Louis Roederer Cristal Rosé	Sparkling	Berry, floral, complex	Lamb	***
Louis Roederer Rosé	Sparkling	Floral, berry	Cheese	**

Wine name	Style	Flavor/ Bouquet	Compatible Foods	Price Range
Louis Roederer Vintage	Sparkling	Berry, citrus, complex	Fish	**
Mercier Vintage	Sparkling	Berry, fruity	Cheese	**
Moet & Chandon Brut NV	Sparkling	Berry, earthy, yeasty	Fish	**
Moet & Chandon Dom Perignon	Sparkling	Complex, citrus, berry, elegant, powerful	Fish	***
Moet & Chandon Dom Perignon Rosé	Sparkling	Floral, berry, powerful, complex	Game	***
Moet & Chandon Rosé	Sparkling	Floral, berry	Lamb	**
Moet & Chandon Vintage	Sparkling	Berry, toasty, minerally	Chicken	**
Mumm Cordon Rouge	Sparkling	Fruity, sweet, berry	Cheese	**
Mumm de Crémant	Sparkling	Citrus, yeasty, honey	Antipasto	**
Mumm Grand Cordon	Sparkling	Berry, toasty, complex	Chicken	***
Mumm René Lalou	Sparkling	Berry, yeasty, floral	Cheese	***
Mumm Vintage	Sparkling	Berry, yeasty	Fish	**
Nicholas Feuillatte Palmés d'Or	Sparkling	Berry, fruity, citrus	Chicken	**
Palmer Amazone	Sparkling	Berry, citrus, complex	Game	***
Paul Bara Vintage	Sparkling	Crisp, berry	Cheese	**
Perrier-Jouet Belle-Epoque	Sparkling	Berry, citrus, complex, toasty	Fish	***
Perrier-Jouet Belle-Epoque Rosé	Sparkling	Floral, berry, complex	Game	***
Perrier-Jouet Blason de France	Sparkling	Berry, complex, toasty	Fish	**
Perrier-Jouet Brut NV	Sparkling	Crisp, citrus, berry	Antipasto	**
Perrier-Jouet Vintage	Sparkling	Berry, minerally, complex	Fish	**
Philipponnat Clos des Goisses	Sparkling	Berry, complex, powerful, toasty	Duck	***
Philipponnat Vintage	Sparkling	Berry, yeasty	Chicken	**
Pierre Peters Vintage	Sparkling	Crisp, berry	Antipasto	**
Piper-Heidsieck Brut	Sparkling	Crisp, zingy, apples	Shellfish	*
Piper-Heidsieck Florens-Louis	Sparkling	Berry, minerally, citrus	Fish	***
Piper-Heidsieck Rare	Sparkling	Austere, berry, complex	Fish	***
Piper-Heidsieck Vintage	Sparkling	Berry, toasty	Chicken	**
Pol Roger Blanc de Chardonnay	Sparkling	Citrus, elegant, complex	Aperitif	**
Pol Roger Brut NV (White Foil)	Sparkling	Berry, floral, yeasty	Shellfish	**
Pol Roger Cuvée Sir Winston Churchill	Sparkling	Powerful, complex, berry, rich	Duck	***
Pol Roger PR	Sparkling	Complex, berry, yeasty	Cheese	**
Pol Roger Rosé	Sparkling	Berry, floral	Game	**
Pol Roger Vintage	Sparkling	Berry, complex, toasty	Fish	**
Pommory Brut	Sparkling	Crisp, citrus	Aperitif	**
Pommery Cuvée Louise	Sparkling	Complex, citrus, berry, elegant	Fish	***
Pommery Cuvée Louise Rosé	Sparkling	Floral, berry, complex	Lamb	***
Pommery Flaçon	Sparkling	Complex, berry, rich, powerful	Game	***
Pommery Summertime	Sparkling	Floral, citrus	Aperitif	**
Pommery Vintage	Sparkling	Citrus, berry, yeasty	Fish	**
R. H. Coutier Vintage	Sparkling	Crisp, berry	Cheese	**
Ruinart Brut	Sparkling	Berry, yeasty	Veal	**

Wine name	Style	Flavor/ Bouquet	Compatible Foods	Price Range
Ruinart Dom Ruinart	Sparkling	Berry, citrus, elegant	Fish	***
Ruinart Dom Ruinart Rosé	Sparkling	Floral, berry, complex	Lamb	***
Ruinart Vintage	Sparkling	Berry, complex, toasty	Fish	**
Salon	Sparkling	Complex, citrus, powerful, toasty	Fish	***
Taittinger Brut NV	Sparkling	Citrus, floral, sweet	Aperitif	**
Taittinger Comtes de Champagne	Sparkling	Citrus, floral, complex, powerful	Shellfish	***
Taittinger Comtes de Champagne Rosé	Sparkling	Berry, complex, powerful	Duck	***
Taittinger Vintage	Sparkling	Citrus, elegant, floral	Fish	**
Veuve Clicquot Brut	Sparkling	Berry, yeasty	Shellfish	**
Veuve Clicquot La Grande Dame	Sparkling	Berry, complex, minerally	Game	***
Veuve Clicquot La Grande Dame Rosé	Sparkling	Berry, powerful, floral, rich	Lamb	***
Veuve Clicquot Vintage	Sparkling	Berry, toasty, complex	Fish	**
Cognac				
AE Dor Cognac	Brandy	Spirity, fiery	After dinner	***
Bisquit Cognac	Brandy	Spirity, fiery, earthy	After dinner	***
Camus Cognac	Brandy	Spirity, complex, minerally	After dinner	***
Chainier Cognac	Brandy	Spirity, earthy	After dinner	***
Château Paulet Cognac	Brandy	Spirity, fiery	After dinner	***
Couprié Cognac	Brandy	Spirity, minerally	After dinner	***
Courvoisier Cognac	Brandy	Spirity, complex, minerally	After dinner	***
Croizet Cognac	Brandy	Spirity, minerally	After dinner	***
Daniel Bouju Cognac	Brandy	Spirity, fiery, earthy	After dinner	***
Delamain Cognac	Brandy	Spirity, rich, complex	After dinner	***
Denis Charpentier Cognac	Brandy	Spirity, earthy, fiery	After dinner	***
Dupuy Cognac	Brandy	Spirity, minerally, earthy	After dinner	***
François Peyrot Cognac	Brandy	Spirity, minerally, complex	After dinner	***
Frapin Cognac	Brandy	Spirity, fiery, earthy	After dinner	***
Gautier Cognac	Brandy	Spirity, complex	After dinner	***
Godet Cognac	Brandy	Spirity, fiery	After dinner	***
Gousseland Cognac	Brandy	Spirity, nutty, earthy	After dinner	***
Hennessy Cognac	Brandy	Spirity, fiery, minerally	After dinner	***
Hine Cognac	Brandy	Spirity, minerally	After dinner	***
Louis Royer Cognac	Brandy	Spirity, fiery, complex	After dinner	***
Martell Cognac	Brandy	Spirity, berry, complex	After dinner	***
Ménard Cognac	Brandy	Spirity, fiery, earthy	After dinner	***
Otard Cognac	Brandy	Spirity, complex, fiery	After dinner	***
Paul Giraud Cognac	Brandy	Spirity, complex	After dinner	***
Prince Hubert de Polignac Cognac	Brandy	Spirity, fiery, complex, minerally	After dinner	***
Prunier Cognac	Brandy	Spirity, complex, minerally	After dinner	***
Rémy Martin Cognac	Brandy	Spirity, fiery, earthy	After dinner	***
Renaud Delile Cognac	Brandy	Spirity, earthy	After dinner	***

Wine name	Style	Flavor/ Bouquet	Compatible Foods	Price Range
Renault Cognac	Brandy	Spirity, fiery	After dinner	***
Roullet Cognac	Brandy	Spirity, complex	After dinner	***
Vallade Fils Cognac	Brandy	Spirity, fiery, minerally	After dinner	***
Corsica				
Clos Capitoro Rouge	Red	Spicy, earthy	Chicken, veal, pork	**
Clos Landry Rouge	Red	Fruity, spicy	Chicken, veal, pork	**
Clos Nicrosi Blanc	White	Citrus, minerally, zingy	Shellfish, fish	**
Clos Nicrosi Muscat du Cap Corse	White	Fruity, floral	Asian, fruits, fish	**
Domaine Arena Grotti di Sole	Red	Fruity, rich, complex	Beef, lamb	**
Domaine Arena Grotti di Sole	White	Stone fruit, crisp	Shellfish, fish	**
Domaine Comte Peraldi Blanc	White	Citrus, minerally, zingy	Shellfish, fish	**
Domaine Comte Peraldi Rouge	Red	Spicy, earthy	Chicken, veal, pork	**
Domaine de Tanelle Cuvée Alexandra	Red	Powerful, complex	Beef, lamb	***
Domaine de Torraccia Cuvée Oriu	Red	Rich, smoky	Beef, lamb	***
Domaine Fuimicicoli Rouge	Red	Spicy, elegant	Chicken, veal, pork	**
Domaine Leccia Blanc	White	Stone fruit, crisp	Shellfish, fish	**
Domaine Leccia E Crose Blanc	White	Rich, elegant	Shellfish, fish, cheese	**
Domaine Leccia Petra Bianca	Red	Powerful, earthy	Beef, lamb	**
Domaine Leccia Rouge	Red	Spicy, herbaceous	Chicken, veal, pork	**
Drenga de Gaffery Cuvée des Gouverneurs	Red	Spicy, oaky	Beef, lamb	***
Jura				
Arbois Savagnin (Frédéric Lornet)	White	Zingy, citrus	Shellfish	**
Arbois Trousseau Vieilles Vignes (Jacques Puffeney)	Red	Berry, earthy	Lamb	**
Arbois Vin Jaune (André et Mireille Tissot)	White	Nutty, complex	Chicken	**
Baud Père et Fils Côtes du Jura Chardonnay	White	Melon, spicy	Fish	**
Baud Père et Fils Côtes du Jura Tradition Blanc	White	Melon, fruity	Fish	**
Château d'Arlay Côtes du Jura Vin Jaune	White	Nutty, complex	Chicken	***
Château de l'Etoile Crémant du Jura	Sparkling	Fruity, citrus	Aperitif	**
Château de l'Etoile L'Etoile Vin Jaune	White	Nutty, spicy	Chicken	**
Château-Chalon (Baud Père et Fils)	White	Complex, minerally, nutty	Chicken	**
Château-Chalon (Jean Macle)	White	Nutty, floral	Veal	**
Crémant du Jura (André et Mireille Tissot)	Sparkling	Fruity, creamy	Aperitif	**
Désiré Petit et Fils Arbois-Pupillin Vin de Paille	Sweet	Raisiny, complex, sweet	Nuts	***
Domaine Berthed-Bonet Château-Chalon	White	Nutty, spicy	Chicken	**
Domaine Berthed-Bonet Côtes du Jura Vin de Paille	Sweet	Raisiny, sweet	Nuts	***
Domaine de Montbourgeau L'Etoile Blanc	White	Minerally, fruity	Fish	**
Fruitière Vinicole d'Arbois Arbois Savagnin	White	Citrus, spicy, zingy	Salad	**
Fruitière Vinicole d'Arbois Arbois Vin Jaune	White	Nutty, minerally, complex	Chicken	**
Fruitière Vinicole de Voiteur Côtes du Jura Vin Jaune	White	Complex, spicy, nutty	Chicken	**
Rolet Père et Fils Arbois Rouge Tradition	Red	Berry, spicy	Stew	**
Rolet Père et Fils Arbois Trousseau Memorial	Red	Berry, spicy	Veal	**
Rolet Père et Fils Arbois Vin Jaune	White	Complex, nutty	Veal	**

Wine name	Style	Flavor/ Bouquet	Compatible Foods	Price Range
Languedoc				
Aimery Sieur d'Arques Limoux Toques et Clochers Terroir Haute Vallée	Sparkling	Citrus, smoky, minerally	Aperitif	**
Banyuls Dom La Tour Vieille Vin de Méditation (Vincent Cantie et Christine)	Fortified	Chocolatey, powerful, rich	Nuts	**
Cabardès Château Salitis (Alice Depaule-Marandon)	Red	Berry, spicy	Game	*
Cabardès Château Ventenac Cuvée les Pujols (Alain Maurel)	Red	Earthy, berry	Stew	**
Cave Co-op de la Lavinière Minervois La Cave des Coteaux du Haut-Minervois	Red	Spicy, berry	Sausages	*
Chamayrac Coteaux du Languedoc La Clape Château Mire l'Etang Cuvée Tradition	Red	Peppery, berry	Pizza	*
Corbières Château Cascadais (Philippe Courrian)	Red	Spicy, gamey	Pizza	*
Corbières Château Gleon Montanié Selection Combe de Berre (Jean-Pierre and Philippe Montanié)	Red	Berry, minerally	Stew	**
Corbières Château La Baronne Vieilles Vignes (Blanc) (Suzette Lignères)	White	Spicy, citrus, minerally	Lamb	**
Corbières Château La Voulte-Gasparets Cuvée Réservée (Patrick Reverdy)	Red	Berry, gamey	Cold meats, stew, offal	**
Corbières Château La Voulte-Gasparets Cuvée Romain Puic (Patrick Reverdy)	Red	Spicy, berry	Sausages	**
Corbières Dom Serres-Mazard (Annie and Jean-Pierre Mazard)	Red	Earthy, spicy	Game	*
Coteaux du Languedoc Abbaye de Valmagne (Philippe d'Allaines)	Red	Herbaceous, spicy, earthy	Stew	**
Coteaux du Languedoc Château Saint-Martin de la Garrigue	Red	Berry, spicy	Pork	**
Coteaux du Languedoc Dom Clavel La Méjanelle (Pierre Clavel)	Red	Spicy, minerally	Stew	**
Coteaux du Languedoc Dom d'Auphilac (Sylvain Fadat)	Red	Earthy, berry	Sausages	*
Coteaux du Languedoc Dom de la Coste Saint-Christol (Luc and Elizabeth Moynier)	Red	Smoky, berry	Pasta	**
Coteaux du Languedoc Dom Peyre-Rose Clos des Cistes (Marlène Soria)	Red	Berry, spicy	Veal	**
Coteaux du Languedoc La Clape Château Pech Redon Selection (Christophe Bousquet)	Red	Spicy, earthy	Pasta	**
Coteaux du Languedoc La Clape Château Pech-Céleyran (Jacques de St. Exupéry)	Red	Berry, earthy	Stew	*
Coteaux du Languedoc Mas Jullien Les Depierre (Olivier Jullien)	Red	Spicy, gamey	Lamb	**
Coteaux du Languedoc Mas Jullien Les Vignes Oubliées (Olivier Jullien)	Red	Smoky, spicy	Stew	*
Coteaux du Languedoc Pic St. Loup Château Lascaux Noble Pierre	Red	Berry, spicy	Sausages	**
Coteaux du Languedoc Pic St. Loup Domaine de l'Hortus (Jean Orliac)	Red	Gamey, earthy	Cold meats, stew, offal	**
Coteaux du Languedoc Pic St. Loup Mas Bruguière	Red	Berry, herbaceous	Cold meats	*
Crémant de Limoux Sieur d'Arques Grande Cuvée Renaissance	Sparkling	Citrus, minerally, spicy	Aperitif	**
de Volontat Corbieres Château les Palais Randolin	Red	Earthy, gamey	Beef	**
Fardel-Lubac Faugères Château Grezan Cuvée (Arnaud Lubac)	Red	Spicy, earthy	Stew	*
Faugères Château de la Liquière Cistus (Bernard Vidal)	Red	Berry, minerally	Mediterranean	*
Faugères Château des Estanilles (Michel Louison)	Red	Minerally, floral	Stew	**
Faugères Dom Ollier Taillefer (Alain Ollier)	Red	Spicy, berry	Lamb	*
Faugères Domaine Gilbert Alquier Les Bastides	Red	Gamey, berry	Cold meats, stew, offal	**
Faugères Domaine Raymond Roc	Red	Smoky, berry	Pizza	*

Wine name	Style	Flavor/ Bouquet	Compatible Foods	Price Range
Fitou Terroir de Tuchan Les Producteurs du Mont Tauch	Red	Berry, plums	Game	**
Les Coteaux du Rieu Berlou St. Chinian Berloup Schisteil	Red	Berry, smoky	Sausages	*
Limoux Dom de l'Aigle Classique (Jean-Louis Denois)	Sparkling	Crisp, citrus, minerally	Aperitif	**
Minervois Château Sainte-Eulalie (Isabelle Coustal)	Red	Berry, spicy	Pasta	*
Minervois Château Villerambert Julien (Michel Julien)	Red	Berry, spicy	Pizza	*
Minervois Clos Centeilles (Patricia Boyer and Daniel Domergue)	Red	Gamey, earthy	Pizza	*
Minervois Dom Piccinini Clos l'Angely (Jean-Christophe Piccinini)	Red	Gamey, berry	Cold meats, stew, offal	**
Minervois La Tour Boisée Cuvée Marie-Claude (Jean-Louis Poudou)	Red	Gamey, smoky	Cold meats, stew, offal	**
St. Chinian Château Cazal-Viel Cuvée des Fées (Henri Miguel)	Red	Berry, earthy	Pork	*
St. Chinian Château Maurel Fonsalade Cuvée Frédéric (Philippe and Thérèse Maurel)	Red	Berry, spicy	Pasta	*
St. Chinian Château Milhau-Lacugue Cuvée des Chevaliers	Red	Smoky, earthy	Mediterranean	*
St. Chinian Dom des Jougla Cuvée Signé (Alain Jougla)	Red	Spicy, gamey	Pizza	*
Loire				
Bonnezeaux Cuvée Prestige (Philippe Gilardeau)	Sweet	Sweet, mandarin	Dessert	***
Bouvet-Ladubay Saumur Brut Trésor	Sparkling	Crisp, fruity, citrus	Aperitif	**
Bouvet-Ladubay Saumur-Champigny Les Non Pareils	Red	Berry, spicy	Cold meats, stew, offal	**
Cave des Vignerons de Saumur Saumur Blanc les Pouches	White	Zingy, citrus, minerally	Fish	**
Château Bellerive Quarts de Chaume Quintessence	Sweet	Sweet, mandarin	Fruit	**
Château d'Epiré Savennières	White	Minerally, spicy	Shellfish	**
Château de Chasseloir Muscadet de Sèvre et Maine	White	Minerally, citrus, zingy	Shellfish	**
Château de Fesles Bonnezeaux Château de Fesles	Sweet	Sweet, apples, honey	Dessert	***
Château de Goulaine Muscadet de Sèvre et Maine Cuvée des Millénaires	White	Minerally, citrus, floral	Fish	**
Château de la Grille Chinon	Red	Earthy, berry	Cold meats, stew, offal	*
Château de la Ragotière Muscadet de Sèvre et Maine	White	Citrus, minerally	Shellfish	**
Château de Plaisance Coteaux du Layon Confidence	Sweet	Sweet, mandarin, honey	Dessert	**
Château de Targé Saumur-Champigny	Red	Berry, plums	Stew	**
Château de Tracy Pouilly-Fumé	White	Zingy, herbaceous	Pork	**
Château de Villeneuve Saumur-Champigny Vieilles Vignes	Red	Berry, gamey	Game	**
Château des Noyers Coteaux du Layon Réserve Vieilles Vignes	Sweet	Sweet, mandarin, citrus	Dessert	***
Château du Breuil Coteaux du Layon Orantium	Sweet	Sweet, honey	Dessert	**
Château du Cléray Muscadet de Sèvre et Maine (Sauvion et Fils)	White	Minerally, melon, citrus	Shellfish	**
Château du Hureau Coteaux du Saumur	White	Medium-sweet, mandarin, minerally	Fruit	**
Château du Hureau Saumur-Champigny Cuvée Lisagathe	Red	Berry, fruity	Cold meats, stew, offal	**
Château du Nozet Pouilly-Fumé	White	Complex, spicy, grassy	Fish	***
Château Gaudrelle Vouvray Réserve Personelle Moelleux	Sweet	Sweet, citrus, honey	Dessert	***
Château la Varière Bonnezeaux les Melleresses	Sweet	Sweet, citrus, honey	Dessert	***
Château Meslière Muscadet des Coteaux de la Loire	White	Minerally, citrus, zingy	Shellfish	**
Château Pierre Bise Quarts de Chaume	Sweet	Sweet, honey	Dessert	**
Clos de l'Abbaye Bourgueil	Red	Berry, spicy	Cold meats, stew, offal	**
Clos Roche Blanche Touraine Sauvignon Blanc	White	Zingy, citrus, grassy	Shellfish	**
Clos Rougeard Saumur-Champigny Les Poyeux	Red	Minerally, earthy	Pasta	**

Wine name	Style	Flavor/ Bouquet	Compatible Foods	Price Range
Coteaux de l'Aubance Les Fontenelles (Christian et Agnès Papin)	Sweet	Minerally, sweet, apples	Cheese	**
Coulée de Serrant Savennières Becherelle	White	Minerally, citrus	Fish	**
Coulée de Serrant Savennières Coulée de Serrant	White	Minerally, spicy, citrus, complex	Chicken	***
Domaine Alphonse Mellot Sancerre Génération XIX	White	Grassy, citrus	Fish	***
Domaine Bernard Baudry Chinon les Grèzeaux	Red	Berry, earthy, gamey	Stew	**
Domaine Breton Bourgueil les Galichets	Red	Earthy, spicy	Cold meats	**
Domaine Cady Coteaux du Layon Saint-Aubin Cuvée Volupté	Sweet	Sweet, citrus, honey	Dessert	***
Domaine Charles Joguet Chinon les Varennes du Grand Clos	Red	Herbaceous, berry, spicy, complex, earthy	Lamb	**
Domaine Couly-Dutheil Chinon Clos de l'Echo	Red	Spicy, herbaceous, berry	Veal	**
Domaine d'Ambinos Coteaux du Layon Beaulieu Séléction des Grains Nobles	Sweet	Sweet, honey	Dessert	***
Domaine de Beauregard Muscadet de Sèvre et Maine Fief du Clairay	White	Floral, fruity, zingy	Shellfish	**
Domaine de la Bigotière Muscadet de Sèvre et Maine	White	Minerally, zingy, floral	Fish	*
Domaine de la Gallière Touraine Mesland Cuvée (François Premier)	Red	Berry, herbaceous, spicy	Cheese	**
Domaine de la Louvetrie Muscadet de Sèvre et Maine Clos du Château de la Carizière	White	Zingy, citrus	Fish	**
Domaine de la Motte Coteaux du Layon Rochefort	Sweet	Sweet, minerally, honey	Fruit	**
Domaine de la Perrière Chinon Blanc Confidentiel	White	Berry, minerally, herbaceous	Veal	**
Domaine de la Sansonnière Anjou Gamay	Red	Berry, crisp	Cold meats, stew, offal	**
Domaine de la Taille aux Loups Montlouis Liquoreux Cuvée Romulus	Sweet	Honey, sweet	Dessert	***
Domaine de Ladoucette Sancerre (Comte Lafond)	White	Zingy, grassy	Cheese	**
Domaine de Saint-Just Saumur-Champigny Clos Moleton	Red	Fruity, earthy	Stew	**
Domaine des Aubuisières Vouvray sec Le Marigny	White	Apples, citrus, minerally	Fish	**
Domaine des Baumard Anjou Blanc Clos de la Folie	White	Apples, citrus, minerally	Shellfish	**
Domaine des Baumard Coteaux du Layon Clos de Sainte Catherine	Sweet	Sweet, minerally, honey	Fruit	***
Domaine des Baumard Quarts de Chaume	Sweet	Sweet, honey, mandarin	Dessert	***
Domaine des Baumard Savennières Clos du Papillon	White	Minerally, citrus, complex	Veal	***
Domaine des Corbillères Touraine Angeline	White	Herbaceous, earthy	Fish	**
Domaine des Epinaudières Coteaux du Layon Saint-Lambert Cuvée Clément	Sweet	Sweet, honey, mandarin	Dessert	**
Domaine des Petits Quarts Bonnezeaux	Sweet	Sweet, honey	Nuts	**
Domaine des Roches Neuves Saumur Insolite	Red	Berry, spicy	Cold meats	**
Domaine des Roches Neuves Saumur-Champigny Marginale	Red	Gamey, berry	Pizza	**
Domaine des Sablonettes Coteaux du Layon Rablay Les Erables	Sweet	Sweet, citrus, honey	Cheese	**
Domaine Didier Dagueneau Pouilly-Fumé Astérôde	White	Zingy, citrus, herbaceous	Mediterranean	***
Domaine Didier Dagueneau Pouilly-Fumé Pur Sang	White	Minerally, citrus, spicy	Fish	***
Domaine Dominique et Vincent Richard Muscadet de Sèvre et Maine Domaine de la Haie Trois Sols	White	Minerally, citrus	Shellfish	**
Domaine Druet Bourgueil Grand Mont	Red	Berry, gamey	Stew	**
Domaine du Clos Naudin Vouvray Moelleux Réserve	Sweet	Sweet, honey, minerally	Cheese	***
Domaine du Closel Savennières Clos du Papillon	White	Complex, minerally	Chicken	**
Domaine Eric Nicolas Jasnières Discours de Tuf	White	Minerally, citrus	Cheese	**
Domaine Filiatreau Saumur-Champigny Cuvée Vieilles Vignes	Red	Minerally, plums	Game	**

Wine name	Style	Flavor/ Bouquet	Compatible Foods	Price Range
Domaine Gérard Millet Sancerre Fut de Chîne	White	Citrus, minerally, herbaceous	Salad	**
Domaine Gitton Père et Fils Sancerre Galinot	White	Herbaceous, grassy	Shellfish	**
Domaine Henri Bourgeois Sanerre le M.D. de Bourgeois	White	Minerally, floral	Veal	**
Domaine Henry Marionnet Touraine Gamay Les Cépages Oubliés	Red	Berry, spicy	Game	**
Domaine Henry Pellé Menetou-Salon Clos des Banchais	White	Rich, minerally, zingy	Salad	**
Domaine Huet-L'Echansonne Vouvray Clos du Bourg	White	Minerally, citrus, apples	Fish	**
Domaine Huet-L'Echansonne Vouvray Le Haut-Lieu	White	Minerally, citrus, zingy	Fish	***
Domaine Jacky Marteau Touraine Gamay	Red	Spicy, gamey	Stew	**
Domaine Jean-Max Roger Sancerre Le Grand Chemarin	White	Citrus, cold tea	Fish	**
Domaine Jean-Paul Balland Sancerre Grande Cuvée	White	Zingy, citrus	Shellfish	**
Domaine Jo Pithon Coteaux du Layon Saint-Lambert	Sweet	Sweet, honey, citrus	Cheese	***
Domaine Joel Taluau et Foltzenlogel Saint-Nicolas de Bourgueil	Red	Berry, spicy	Cold meats	**
Domaine Laffourcade Anjou-Villages Château Perray Jouannet	Red	Spicy, gamey	Sausages	**
Domaine les Grands Vignes Anjou Gamay	Red	Berry, spicy	Mediterranean	**
Domaine Lucien Crochet Sancerre Le Chîne	White	Herbaceous, minerally, citrus	Cheese	**
Domaine Lucien Crochet Sancerre Rouge Prestige	Red	Herbaceous, spicy, berry	Cold meats	**
Domaine Masson-Blondelet Pouilly-Fumé Tradition Cullus	White	Grassy, minerally	Salad	**
Domaine Ogereau Anjou Villages Prestige	Red	Berry, spicy, earthy	Stew	**
Domaine Ogereau Coteaux du Layon Saint-Lambert	Sweet	Sweet, citrus, minerally	Dessert	**
Domaine Philippe Tessier Cour-Cheverny	White	Cold tea, minerally, apples	Shellfish	**
Domaine Pichot Vouvray le Peu de la Moriette	White	Minerally, spicy	Veal	**
Domaine Pierre Aguilas Coteaux du Layon Saint-Aubin	Sweet	Sweet, citrus, minerally	Dessert	**
Domaine Pierre Soulez Savennières Roches-aux-Moines Chamboureau Cuvée d'Avant	White	Spicy, citrus, minerally	Fish	**
Domaine René-Noël Legrand Saumur-Champigny Les Rogelins	Red	Berry, spicy	Stew	**
Domaine Retiveau-Retif Coteaux du Saumur	White	Medium-sweet, citrus	Fruit	**
Domaine Richou Coteaux de l'Aubance Les Trois Demoiselles	Sweet	Sweet, citrus, apples	Dessert	**
Domaine Thierry Boucard Bourgueil Cuvée Marion	Red	Spicy, berry	Game	**
Domaine Vacheron Sancerre Rouge	Red	Berry, herbaceous	Cold meats, stew, offal	**
Domaine Vincent Pinard Sancerre Harmonie	White	Zingy, herbaceous	Shellfish	**
Domaine Yannick Amirault Bourgueil Vieilles Vignes Petite Cave	Red	Berry, earthy	Sausages	**
Domaines Chéreau Carré Muscadet de Sèvre et Maine Comte Saint-Hubert	White	Crisp, minerally, citrus	Shellfish	**
Gadais Père et Fils Muscadet de Sèvre et Maine Grande Réserve du Moulin	White	Minerally, citrus, zingy	Fish	**
Henri Beurdin et Fils Reuilly Blanc	White	Zingy, spicy	Cheese	**
Langlois-Château Crémant de Loire Quadrille	Sparkling	Fruity, crisp, citrus	Aperitif	**
Maison Guy Saget Pouilly-Fumé Les Logères	White	Zingy, citrus	Chicken	**
Montlouis les Lys (François Chidaine)	Sweet	Sweet, mandarin, citrus	Dessert	***
Muscadet de Sèvre et Maine (Guy Bossard)	White	Minerally, floral, citrus	Shellfish	**
Muscadet de Sèvre et Maine Cuvée Expression de Granit (Guy Bossard)	White	Minerally, herbaceous, citrus	Shellfish	**
Muscadet de Sèvre et Maine Cuvée Orthogenesis (Guy Bossard)	White	Minerally, floral, citrus	Shellfish	**
Pouilly-Fumé Cuvée Majorum (Michel Redde et Fils)	White	Herbaceous, grassy, citrus	Cheese	**

Wine name	Style	Flavor/ Bouquet	Compatible Foods	Price Range
Pouilly-Fumé Domaine des Riaux (Jeannot Père et Fils)	White	Citrus, grassy	Fish	**
Pouilly-Fumé Les Griottines (Michel Bailly)	White	Zingy, grassy	Shellfish	**
Reuilly Blanc (Jean-Michel Sorbe)	White	Citrus, grassy	Shellfish	**
Saint-Nicolas de Bourgueil Cuvée les Graviers (Yannick Amirault)	Red	Herbaceous, berry, spicy	Pasta	**
Sancerre (Joseph Verdier)	White	Zingy, citrus	Salads	**
Sancerre Le Chïne Marchand (Pascal Jolivet)	White	Zingy, grassy	Shellfish	**
Saumur-Champigny Le Petit Saint-Vincent (Dominique Joseph)	Red	Spicy, berry	Lamb	**
Serge Dagueneau et Filles Pouilly-Fumé	White	Citrus, herbaceous, minerally	Fish	**
Vouvray Cuvée Tries de Vendange (Didier Champalou)	White	Citrus, crispy, minerally	Chicken	**
Vouvray La Cabane Noire (Thierry Cosme)	White	Minerally, apples, citrus	Fish	**
Provence				
Cave Coopérative de Taradeau Oppidum	Red	Berry, gamey	Stew	**
Château Calissanne (Jean Bonnet)	Red	Berry, spicy	Cold meats, stew, offal	**
Château Coussin (Jean-Pierre Sumeire)	Red	Earthy, gamey	Cold meats	**
Château de Berne (Bruno Guillermier)	Red	Minerally, herbaceous, spicy	Cold meats	**
Château de l'Escarelle (M. Lobier)	Red	Spicy, earthy, herbaceous	Cold meats	**
Château de Pibarnon (Eric de St. Victor)	Red	Earthy, berry	Stew	***
Château de Pourcieux (Michel d'Espagnet)	Red	Spicy, berry	Veal	**
Château de Roquefort (Raimond de Villeneuve Flayosc)	Red	Herbaceous, berry	Lamb	**
Château du Seuil (Philippe Carreau-Gaschereau)	Red	Berry, earthy	Stew	**
Château Ferry Lacombe (Frédérique Chossenot)	Red	Minerally, spicy	Pasta	**
Château Galoupet (Jean-Pierre Marty)	Red	Berry, spicy	Stew	**
Château l'Arnaude (H. & A. Knapp)	Red	Berry, herbaceous, spicy	Pasta	**
Château Maïme (Jean-Louis Sirban)	Red	Berry, gamey	Pizza	*
Château Maravenne (Jean-Louis Gourjon)	Red	Berry, spicy	Cheese	**
Château Marouine (Mary-Odile Marty)	Red	Spicy, herbaceous, gamey	Game	**
Château Miraval (Emmanuel Gaujal)	Red	Berry, gamey	Lamb	**
Château Réal d'Or (Elphège Bailly)	Red	Berry, spicy	Pizza	*
Château Réal Martin (Gilles Meimoun)	Red	Berry, gamey	Stew	*
Château Reillanne (Comte G. de Chevron-Villette)	Red	Berry, spicy	Cold meats, stew, offal	**
Château Romanin (Jean-André Charial)	Red	Herbaceous, spicy, gamey	Lamb	**
Château Roubine (Philippe Riboud)	Red	Berry, earthy	Sausages	**
Château Simone (René Rougier)	Red	Spicy, gamey	Cold meats, stew, offal	*
Château Ste. Marguéritte (Jean-Pierre Fayard)	Red	Berry, spicy	Stew	**
Château Ste. Roseline (Christophe Bernard)	Red	Minerally, spicy	Cheese	**
Château Testavin (Aya Kerfridin)	Red	Earthy, minerally	Pizza	*
Château Thuerry (M. Parmentier)	Red	Berry, herbaceous, spicy	Beef	**
Château Vignelaure (David O'Brien/Hugh Ryman)	Red	Berry, spicy, earthy	Pork	**
Clos d'Iére/Domaine Rabiéga (Lars Torstenson)	Red	Minerally, spicy, herbaceous	Game	**
Clos la Neuve (Fabienne Joly)	Red	Spicy, gamey	Lamb	**
Clos Val Bruyère (Sophie Cerciello)	White	Herbaceous, zingy	Salad	**
Domaine Couronne de Charlemagne (Bernard Piche)	White	Herbaceous, spicy, zingy	Fish	**
Domaine de l'Estello (Roger Tordjman)	Red	Berry, spicy	Stew	**

Wine name	Style	Flavor/ Bouquet	Compatible Foods	Price Range
Domaine de la Bastide Neuve (Jérome Paquette)	Red	Berry, earthy	Stew	**
Domaine de la Lauzade (Aline Bouvier)	Red	Earthy, gamey	Pasta	**
Domaine de la Vallongue (Philippe Paul-Cavallier)	Red	Spicy, fruity	Cold meats, stew, offal	**
Domaine de Marchandise (Pierre Chauvier)	Red	Spicy, earthy	Cold meats, stew, offal	**
Domaine de Mauvan (Gaëlle Maclou)	Red	Spicy, berry	Sausages	**
Domaine de Mont Redon (Françoise Torné)	Red	Berry, spicy	Cheese	**
Domaine de Souviou (M. Cagnolari)	Red	Spicy, minerally, berry	Game	**
Domaine de Trévallon (Eloi Durrbach)	Red	Berry, earthy	Pasta	**
Domaine des Chaberts (Betty Cundall)	Red	Spicy, gamey	Stew	**
Domaine des Thermes (M. Robert)	Red	Gamey, spicy	Pork	**
Domaine la Suffrene (Cédric Gravier)	Red	Spicy, berry	Cold meats, stew, offal	**
Domaine Lafran-Veyrolles (Jouve Férec)	Red	Earthy, spicy	Cold meats	**
Domaine les Toulons (Denis Alibert)	Red	Berry, spicy	Sausages	*
Domaine St. André de Figuière (Alain Combard)	Red	Berry, earthy	Pasta	**
Domaine Tempier (Jean-Marie & François Peyraud)	Red	Complex, tannic, berry, spicy	Beef	***
Domaine Turenne (Philippe Benezet)	Red	Earthy, berry	Cheese	**
Mas de Cadenet (Guy Négrel)	Red	Berry, spicy	Pizza	*
Mas de la Dame (Marc Caysson)	Red	Berry, earthy	Sausages	**
Sack Zafiropulo Clos Ste. Magdalene	White	Zingy, cold tea, minerally	Fish	**
Rhône				
Alain Graillot Crozes Hermitage	Red	Berry, spicy, earthy, minerally	Pork, beef	**
Auguste Clape Comas	Red	Berry, earthy, minerally, complex	Beef, lamb	**
Auguste Clape St. Peray	White	Floral, fruity	Shellfish, fish	**
Cave de Cairanne Côtes du Rhône Villages Cuvée Temptation	Red	Berry, peppery, powerful	Beef, lamb	**
Chapoutier Châteauneuf-du-Pape La Bernadine	Red	Jam, peppery, rich	Beef, lamb	**
Chapoutier Côtes du Rhône	White	Stone fruit, minerally	Fish, chicken	**
Chapoutier Côtes du Rhône Belleruche	Red	Berry, spicy, juicy	Pizza, chicken	*
Château Beaucastel Châteauneuf-du-Pape	Red	Powerful, tannic	Beef, lamb	**
Château Beaucastel Châteauneuf-du-Pape	White	Floral, citrus, intense	Fish, veal	**
Château Beaucastel Châteauneuf-du-Pape Hommage à Jacques Perrin	Red	Berry, jam, complex	Beef, lamb	***
Château Beaucastel Châteauneuf-du-Pape Roussanne Vieilles Vignes	White	Floral, citrus, stone fruit, rich	Fish, veal	**
Château Beaucastel Côtes du Rhône Coudoulet	Red	Berry, earthy, minerally, rich	Chicken, veal, pork	**
Château Beaucastel Côtes du Rhône Coudoulet	White	Stone fruit, floral, rich	Fish, veal	**
Château Beaucastel Côtes du Rhône Perrin Reserve	Red	Berry, herbaceous, spicy	Chicken, veal, pork	**
Château Beaucastel Côtes du Rhône Perrin Reserve	White	Stone fruit, floral, powerful	Fish, chicken, veal	**
Château Cabrieres Châteauneuf-du-Pape	Red	Jam, spicy, leathery	Beef, lamb	**
Château de la Gardine Châteauneuf-du-Pape Cuvée des Generations	Red	Berry, jam, vanillin, intense	Beef, lamb	**
Château de la Nerthe Châteauneuf-du-Pape Cuvée des Cadettes	Red	Berry, vanillin, powerful	Beef, lamb	**
Château de Saint Cosme Gigondas	Red	Berry, spicy, peppery	Chicken, veal, pork	***
Château des Roques Vacqueyras	Red	Jam, peppery, rich	Pork, veal, beef	**
Château du Trignon Gigondas	Red	Berry, jam, tannic, complex	Pork, beef	**

Wine name	Style	Flavor/ Bouquet	Compatible Foods	Price Range
Château Grillet Condrieu	White	Floral, fruity, minerally, elegant	Fish, fruits	***
Château la Canorgue Côtes du Lubéron	Red	Berry, earthy, spicy	Pizza, chicken	**
Château Rayas Châteauneuf-du-Pape	Red	Powerful, complex, berry, jam	Beef, lamb	***
Château Rayas Fonsolette Côtes du Rhône	Red	Berry, spicy, earthy, rich	Chicken, veal, pork	**
Château Rayas Pignan Châteauneuf-du-Pape	Red	Berry, jam, rich, intense	Beef, lamb	**
Château St. Estève Viognier "Jeune Vignes"	White	Floral, stone fruit, elegant	Fish, fruits	**
Château Val-Joanis Cotes du Luberon	Red	Berry, spicy	Pizza, chicken	*
Clairette de Die Méthode Dioise Ancestrale (Jean Claude Raspail)	Sparkling	Stone fruit, minerally, crisp	Shellfish, Asian	**
Delas Frères Condrieu Clos Boucher	White	Stone fruit, floral, rich	Fish, fruits	**
Delas Frères Condrieu La Galopine	White	Stone fruit, minerally, elegant	Fish, fruits	**
Domaine Brusset Gigondas Le Grand Montmirail	Red	Berry, vanillin, rich	Beef, lamb	**
Domaine d'Andezon Côtes du Rhône Syrah Veilles Vignes	Red	Berry, jam, intense	Beef, lamb	**
Domaine de Beaurenard Châteauneuf-du-Pape Cuvée Boisrenard	Red	Jam, powerful, vanillin	Beef, lamb	**
Domaine de Durban Muscat de Beaumes-de-Venise	Sweet	Floral, tropical fruit, rich	Dessert	*
Domaine de l'Oratoire St. Martin Côtes du Rhône Cairanne	Red	Berry, earthy, spicy	Pizza, chicken	**
Domaine de la Charbonnière Vacqueyras	Red	Berry, herbaceous, leathery, intense	Pork, beef, lamb	**
Domaine de la Grangeneuve Rasteau	Sweet	Fruity, tangy	Cheese	**
Domaine de la Janasse Châteauneuf-du-Pape	Red	Berry, peppery, earthy, spicy	Beef, lamb	**
Domaine de la Janasse Côtes-du-Rhône	Red	Berry, spicy	Pizza, chicken	*
Domaine de la Mordorée Châteauneuf-du-Pape Cuvée de la Reine des Bois	Red	Berry, licorice, spicy, earthy	Pork, beef	**
Domaine de la Mordorée Lirac Cuvée de la Reine des Bois	Red	Berry, licorice, herbaceous	Veal, pork, beef	**
Domaine de la Mordorée Tavel	Rosé	Berry, rich, fruity	Asian, fish	**
Domaine de la Renjarde Côtes du Rhône-Villages	Red	Berry, fruity, intense	Pizza, chicken	*
Domaine du Caillou Châteauneuf-du-Pape	Red	Berry, floral, elegant	Beef, lamb	**
Domaine du Cayron Gigondas	Red	Berry, herbaceous, elegant	Pork, beef	**
Domaine du Pegau Châteauneuf-du-Pape Cuvée Reservée	Red	Berry, licorice, herbaceous, rich	Beef, lamb	**
Domaine François Villard Condrieu "Poncins"	White	Minerally, earthy, stone fruit, floral	Fish, fruits	**
Domaine François Villard St. Joseph	Red	Berry, earthy, peppery, rich	Pork, beef	**
Domaine Max Aubert Châteauneuf-du-Pape Le Nonce	Red	Berry, peppery, jam	Beef, lamb	**
Domaine Max Aubert Châteuneuf-du-Pape Domaine de la Présidente	Red	Spicy, peppery, tannic	Beef, lamb	**
Domaine Paul Antard Châteauneuf-du-Pape Cuvée Classique	Red	Powerful, jam, licorice	Beef, lamb	**
Domaine Paul Antard Châteauneuf-du-Pape La Côte Ronde	Red	Berry, oaky, rich	Beef, lamb	**
Georges Vernay Condrieu Coteaux du Vernon	White	Stone fruit, minerally, powerful	Fish, fruits	**
Guigal Châteauneuf-du-Pape	Red	Berry, earthy, leathery, intense	Beef, lamb	**
Guigal Condrieu	White	Stone fruit, minerally, floral, complex	Fish, fruits	**
Guigal Condrieu la Doriane	White	Stone fruit, minerally, oaky	Fish, chicken	***
Guigal Côte-Rôtie Blonde et Brune	Red	Berry, smoky, rich, elegant	Beef, lamb	**
Guigal Côte-Rôtie La Landonne	Red	Berry, peppery, licorice, complex	Beef, lamb	***
Guigal Côte-Rôtie La Mouline	Red	Floral, berry, nutty, complex	Beef, lamb	***

Wine name	Style	Flavor/ Bouquet	Compatible Foods	Price Range
Guigal Côte-Rôtie La Turque	Red	Berry, peppery, licorice, intense	Beef, lamb	***
Guigal Côtes du Rhône	Red	Fruity, berry, spicy	Pizza, chicken	*
Guigal Côtes du Rhône	White	Floral, stone fruit, crisp	Fish, chicken	*
Guigal Gigondas	Red	Berry, earthy, austere	Veal, pork, beef	**
Guigal Hermitage	Red	Berry, licorice, mushroom, rich	Beef, lamb	**
J. L. Chave Hermitage	Red	Complex, rich, earthy	Beef, lamb	***
J. L. Chave Hermitage	White	Powerful, floral, minerally	Fish, veal	***
J. L. Chave St. Joseph	Red	Berry, minerally, complex	Pork, beef	**
Jamet Côte-Rôtie	Red	Jam, berry, earthy, complex	Beef, lamb	**
Jasmin Côte-Rôtie	Red	Rich, complex, floral, berry, earthy	Beef, lamb	**
Jean-Luc Colombo Cornas Le Terre Brûlée	Red	Berry, spicy, minerally, complex	Beef, lamb	**
Jean-Luc Colombo Côtes du Rhône les Figuieres	White	Floral, stone fruit, rich	Fish, chicken	**
Jean-Luc Colombo Muscat de Rivesettes les Saintes	Sweet	Citrus, floral, intense, zingy	Dessert	*
La Vieille Ferme Côtes du Lubéron	Red	Berry, spicy	Pizza, chicken	*
Marc Sorrel Hermitage	Red	Berry, rich, oaky	Beef, lamb	**
Michel Chapoutier Condrieu	White	Floral, stone fruit, complex	Fish, fruits	**
Michel Chapoutier Côte-Rôtie	Red	Berry, herbaceous, spicy	Pork, beef	**
Michel Chapoutier Crozes Hermitage les Meysonniers	Red	Berry, spicy, earthy	Chicken, veal, pork	**
Michel Chapoutier Hermitage Chante Alouette	White	Floral, minerally, nutty, intense	Fish, chicken	**
Michel Chapoutier Hermitage La Sizeranne	Red	Berry, floral, intense, complex	Beef, lamb	**
Michel Chapoutier Hermitage Vin de Paille	Sweet	Floral, exotic, complex, rich	Dessert	***
Noël Veirset Cornas	Red	Berry, licorice, minerally	Beef, lamb	**
Paul Jaboulet Aîné Côtes du Rhône Parallel Y5	Red	Berry, peppery	Pizza, chicken	*
Paul Jaboulet Aîné Crozes-Hermitage Thalabert	Red	Spicy, herbaceous, berry, complex	Veal, pork	**
Paul Jaboulet Aîné Gigondas	Red	Berry, earthy, minerally	Beef, lamb	**
Paul Jaboulet Aîné Hermitage La Chapelle	Red	Berry, earthy, rich, complex	Beef, lamb	**
Paul Jaboulet Aîné Muscat Beaumes-de-Venise	Sweet	Powerful, mandarin, floral	Dessert	*
Pierre Gaillard Côte-Rôtie "Rose Poupre"	Red	Complex, elegant, earthy	Beef, lamb	**
René Rostaing Condrieu	White	Stone fruit, minerally, floral	Fish, fruits	**
René Rostaing Côte-Rôtie Côte Blonde	Red	Floral, berry, elegant, intense	Beef, lamb	***
Tardieu Laurent Comes Vieilles Vignes	Red	Floral, berry, mushroom, rich	Beef, lamb	**
Vieux Télégraphe Châteauneuf-du-Pape	Red	Berry, herbaceous, spicy, rich	Beef, lamb	**
Yves and Matilde Gangloff Côte-Rôtie Vieilles Vignes	Red	Berry, peppery, earthy, complex	Beef, lamb	**
Yves Cuilleron Condrieu les Ayguets	White	Stone fruit, minerally, rich	Fish, fruits	**
Yves Cuilleron Condrieu les Chaillets Vieilles Vignes	White	Stone fruit, rich, floral, complex	Fish, fruits	**
Yves Guilleron Côte-Rôtie "Bassenon"	Red	Intense, earthy, minerally	Beef, lamb	**
Roussillon				
Campadieu Banyuls Blanc Vial-Magnères (Monique Sapéras)	Fortified	Rich, sweet, spirity	Chocolate	**
Campadieu Banyuls Dom de la Rectorie Hors d'Age Cuvée du Docteur Camou (Marc and Thierry Parcé)	Fortified	Chocolatey, spirity, sweet	Dessert	**

Wine name	Style	Flavor/ Bouquet	Compatible Foods	Price Range
Campadieu Banyuls Grand Cru Cellier des Templiers Cuvée Amiral (François Vilarem)	Fortified	Chocolatey, rich, powerful, sweet	Fruit	**
Campadieu Banyuls Grand Cru Cellier des Templiers Cuvée Amiral (Henry Vidal)	Fortified	Sweet, chocolatey	Chocolate	**
Campadieu Banyuls L'Etoile Grande Réserve	Fortified	Chocolatey, sweet, spirity	Dessert	**
Campadieu Collioure Dom de la Rectorie Cuvée Coume Pascole (Marc and Thierry Parcé)	Red	Earthy, gamey	Cold meats, stew, offal	*
Campadieu Collioure Dom La Tour Vieille (Vincent Cantie et Christine)	Red	Spicy, earthy	Lamb	**
Campadieu Côtes de Roussillon Cazenove	Red	Berry, spicy	Stew	*
Campadieu Côtes de Roussillon Dom Ferrer-Ribère Empreinte des Temps (Denis Ferrer et Bruno Ribière)	Red	Gamey, spicy	Cold meats, stew, offal	**
Campadieu Côtes de Roussillon Dom Joliette Cuvée (André Mercier)	Red	Gamey, berry	Pasta	*
Campadieu Côtes de Roussillon Domaine du Mas Cremat (Jeanin-Mongeard)	Red	Berry, spicy	Stew	**
Campadieu Côtes du Roussillon Villages Dom des Chenes Les Alzines Razungles	Red	Berry, smoky	Pork	**
Campadieu Côtes du Roussillon Villages Dom Força Real Les Hauts de Força Real (J-P Henriqués)	Red	Spicy, earthy	Pasta	**
Campadieu Côtes du Roussillon Villages Dom Gauby Vieilles Vignes (Gérard Gauby)	Red	Berry, earthy	Game	**
Campadieu Maury Dom la Pleidade Vintage	Fortified	Chocolatey, rich	Dessert	**
Campadieu Maury Mas Amiel Vintage Réserve (Charles Dupuy)	Fortified	Spirity, smoky, chocolatey	Nuts	**
Campadieu Muscat de St. Jean de Minervois Dom de Barroubio (Marie-Thérèse Miquel)	Fortified	Chocolatey, spirity	Chocolate	**
Campadieu Rivesaltes Domaine Cazes Cuvée (Aimé Cazes)	Fortified	Spirity, powerful, chocolatey	Fruit	**
Savoie				
Cave de Chautagne Vin de Savoie Chautagne Gamay	Red	Berry, spicy	Cold meats, stew, offal	**
Château de la Violette Vin de Savoie Abymes	White	Citrus, apples	Salad	**
Château de Ripaille Vin de Savoie Ripaille	White	Slight sparkle, crisp, citrus	Aperitif	**
Domaine de l'Idylle Vin de Savoie Cruet Vieilles Vignes	White	Minerally, citrus	Fish	**
Domaine de Rocailles Vin de Savoie Apremont (Pierre Boniface)	White	Citrus, zingy	Fish	**
Domaine du Prieuré St. Christophe Roussette de Savoie Altesse (Michel Grisard)	White	Zingy, citrus	Fish	**
Domaine du Prieuré St. Christophe Vin de Savoie Mondeuse (Michel Grisard)	Red	Peppery, berry	Sausages	**
Eugène Carrel et Fils Vin de Savoie Jongieux	White	Zingy, citrus	Fish	**
Eugène Carrel et Fils Vin de Savoie Jongieux Gamay Vieilles Vignes	Red	Spicy, berry	Pizza	**
Maison Mollex Roussette de Savoie Seyssel La Taconnière	White	Citrus, spicy	Shellfish	**
Roussette de Savoie Marestel (Edmond Jacquin et Fils)	White	Citrus, zingy	Mediterranean	**
Roussette de Savoie Marestel (Noël Dupasquier)	White	Zingy, citrus	Fish	**
Vin de Savoie Mondeuse Cru Arbin Vieilles Vignes (Louis Magnin)	Red	Peppery, spicy	Cold meats, stew, offal	**
Vin de Savoie Mondeuse d'Arbin (Charles Trosset)	Red	Peppery, fruity	Game	**
Vin de Savoie Mondeuse Vieilles Vignes (André et Michel Quénard)	Red	Peppery, spicy	Cold meats	**
Southwest France				
Baldes Cahors Château Triguedina	Red	Spicy, herbaceous, tannic	Lamb	**
Bergerac Château Tour des Gendres (Luc de Conti)	Red	Berry, spicy	Cold meats	**

Wine name	Style	Flavor/ Bouquet	Compatible Foods	Price Range
Bergerac Château Tour des Gendres Cuvée la Gloire de Mon Père (Luc de Conti)	Red	Berry, minerally	Stew	**
Bergerac Sec Moulin des Dames Anthologia (Luc de Conti)	White	Herbaceous, zingy, citrus	Fish	**
Bernède et Fils Cahors Clos la Coutale	Red	Herbaceous, spicy, earthy	Sausages	**
Biesbrouck Cahors Dom des Savarines	Red	Berry, tannic	Lamb	**
Burc et Fils Cahors Château Pineraie	Red	Spicy, herbaceous, berry	Sausages	**
Cahors Château Haute-Serre (Georges Vigouroux)	Red	Earthy, minerally	Lamb	**
Cahors Château Lamartine (Alain Gayraud)	Red	Berry, herbaceous, tannic	Cold meats, stew, offal	**
Cahors Château Triguedina Prince Probus	Red	Berry, earthy	Cheese	**
Cave-Coop des Vins d'Irouléguy Irouléguy Dom de Mignaberry	Red	Earthy, berry	Cold meats	*
Château de Bachen Tursan Baron de Bachen (Michel Guérard)	White	Melon, oaky, spicy	Fish	**
Côtes d'Olt Cahors Château Les Bouysses	Red	Berry, earthy	Pasta	**
Côtes de Bergerac Château Court-les-Muts	Red	Berry, spicy	Veal	**
Côtes de Duras Dom du Grand Mayne Rosé (Andrew Gordon)	Red	Berry, earthy	Antipasto	*
Côtes de Duras Dom du Grand Mayne Rouge (Andrew Gordon)	Red	Spicy, berry	Pasta	**
Côtes du Marmandais Cave de Cocument Tersac	Red	Minerally, spicy	Mediterranean	**
Entraygues et du Fel Jean-Marc Viguier	Red	Berry, spicy	Cold meats	**
Fronton Château Baudare (Claude Vigouroux)	Red	Spicy, herbaceous, berry	Cold meats, stew, offal	**
Fronton Château Montauriol	Red	Berry, spicy	Mediterranean	**
Gaillac Cave de Tecou Passion	Red	Berry, minerally	Cold meats, stew, offal	**
Gaillac Domaine de Causse-Marines Delires D'Automme Doux (Patrice Lescarret)	Red	Spicy, berry	Sausages	**
Gaillac Domaine de Causse-Marines Les Greilles (Patrice Lescarret)	Red	Earthy, minerally	Pasta	**
Gaillac Vin D'Autan de Robert Plageoles et Fils Doux	White	Apples, zingy	Sausages	**
Gaillac Vin de Voile de Robert Plageoles (Robert Plageoles)	White	Nutty, rich	Chicken	**
Irouléguy Dom Brana (Jean et Adrienne Brana)	Red	Berry, spicy	Cold meats, stew, offal	**
Jouffreau Cahors Clos de Gamot	Red	Berry, earthy	Sausages	**
Jurançon Bru-Baché L'Eminence (Claude Loustalot)	Sweet	Sweet, citrus	Dessert	**
Jurançon Clos Uroulat (Charles Hours)	Sweet	Sweet, honey	Fruit	**
Jurançon Dom Bellgarde Cuvée Thibault (Pascal Labasse)	White	Citrus, minerally, zingy	Aperitif	**
Jurançon Dom Cauhapé Noblesse du Temps (Henri Ramonteau)	Sweet	Sweet, honey	Fruit	**
Jurançon Dom Cauhapé Quintessence du Petit Manseng (Henri Ramonteau)	Sweet	Sweet, citrus	Cheese	**
Jurançon Sec Clos Lapeyre (Jean-Bernard Larrieu)	White	Zingy, citrus	Shellfish	**
Jurançon Sec Cuvée Marie (Charles Hours)	White	Citrus, minerally, zingy	Aperitif	**
Jurançon Sec Dom Bellegarde (Pascal Labasse)	White	Citrus, zingy	Aperitif	**
Jurançon Sec Dom Cauhapé Chant des Vignes (Henri Ramonteau)	White	Minerally, spicy, citrus	Fish	**
Madiran Chapelle Lenclos (Patrick Ducorneau)	Red	Berry, earthy	Cold meats, stew, offal	**
Madiran Château d'Aydie (Pierre Laplace)	Red	Earthy, tannic	Sausages	**
Madiran Château d'Aydie Ode d'Aydie (Pierre Laplace)	Red	Berry, tannic	Mediterranean	**
Madiran Château Laffitte-Teston (Jean-Marc Laffitte)	Red	Berry, earthy	Mediterranean	**
Madiran Château Montus Cuvée Prestige (Alain Brumont)	Red	Tannic, earthy	Stew	**
Madiran Dom de Bouscassé Vieilles Vignes (Alain Brumont)	Red	Berry, tannic	Cold meats	**
Madiran Domaine Meinjarre (Alain Brumont)	Red	Spicy, tannic	Antipasto	**

Wine name	Style	Flavor/ Bouquet	Compatible Foods	Price Range
Marcillac Jean-Luc Matha Cuvée Spéciale	Red	Spicy, peppery, berry	Game	**
Monbazillac Château Tirecul la Gravière (Claudie and Bruno Bilancini)	Sweet	Sweet, honey	Dessert	**
Pacherenc du Vic-Bilh Château Montus Sec (Alain Brumont)	White	Zingy, citrus	Fish	**
Pacherenc du Vic-Bilh Domaine Bouscassé Vendange Décembre (Alain Brumont)	White	Citrus, minerally, zingy	Shellfish	**
Producteurs Plaimont Côtes de Saint-Mont (VDQS) Château de Sabazan	Red	Berry, earthy	Mediterranean	**
Producteurs Plaimont Côtes de Saint-Mont (VDQS) Monastère de Saint-Mont	Red	Berry, minerally	Mediterranean	**
Resses et Fils Cahors Château la Caminade La Commandery	Red	Minerally, tannic	Stew	**
Ribes Fronton Château le Roc Cuvée Don Quichotte	Red	Herbaceous, berry	Cold meats	**
Rigal Cahors Château Saint-Didier Parnac	Red	Berry, tannic	Pasta	**
Saussignac Clos d'Yvigne (Patricia Atkinson)	Sweet	Sweet, citrus	Dessert	**
Verhaeghe Cahors Château de Cedre Le Prestige	Red	Berry, spicy, earthy	Pizza	**
Vignerons de Buzet Buzet Château de Gueyze	Red	Earthy, berry	Sausages	*
Vin de Pays				
Caves des Hauts de Seyr VDP Coteaux de Charitois Chardonnay Le Montaillant	White	Tropical fruit, citrus	Veal	**
Ducelliers VDP Côtes de Thongue Les Chemins de Bassac Vignelongue	Red	Berry, smoky	Stew	*
Frères Couillaud VDP Jardin de la France Dom Couillaud Chardonnay	White	Tropical fruit, spicy	Chicken	*
Grassa VDP Côtes de Gascogne Domaine du Tariquet Gros Manseng Premières Grives	White	Zingy, citrus	Shellfish	**
Laroche VDP d'Oc Chardonnay Laroche Grand Cuvée 'L'	White	Tropical fruit, citrus	Fish	**
Les Coteaux du Rieu Berlou VDP d'Oc Berloup Collection	Red	Berry, herbaceous, spicy	Pasta	**
Les Vignerons de Thézac-Perricard VDP Thézac-Perricard Vin du Czar	Red	Berry, earthy	Mediterranean	*
Southcorp VDP d'Oc James Herrick Chardonnay	White	Citrus, tropical fruit	Fish	**
Southcorp VDP d'Oc James Herrick Cuvée Simone	White	Tropical fruit, citrus	Veal	**
VDP Comte Tolosan Dom de Ribonnet Chardonnay	White	Melon, fruity	Fish	*
VDP Coteaux de l'Ardèche Syrah Les Vignerons Ardechois Cuvée Prestige	Red	Earthy, berry	Stew	*
VDP Coteaux des Baronnies Dom du Rieu Frais Cabernet Sauvignon (Jean-Yves Liotaud)	Red	Herbaceous, berry	Lamb	*
VDP Coteaux des Baronnies Dom du Rieu Frais Syrah (Jean-Yves Liotaud)	Red	Berry, earthy	Pizza	*
VDP Côtes Catalanes Domaine Cazes le Canon de Maréchal	Red	Plum, spicy	Sausages	**
VDP Côtes Catalanes Domaine Cazes Le Credo	Red	Smoky, spicy	Cold meats	*
VDP Côtes de Gascogne Dom de St. Lannes (Michel Duffour)	Red	Berry, spicy	Cheese	*
VDP Côtes de Thongue Dom de Limbardie (Henri Boukandoura)	Red	Berry, spicy	Pizza	*
VDP Côtes de Thongue Domaine Teisserenc Cabernet de l'Arjolle	Red	Berry, earthy	Cold meats, stew, offal	*
VDP d'Oc Clos Centeilles Carignanissime (Patricia Boyer and Daniel Domergue)	Red	Herbaceous, berry	Stew	**
VDP d'Oc Domaine de Coussergues Cabernet Sauvignon	Red	Berry, herbaceous	Lamb	**
VDP d'Oc Domaine de la Baume Syrah Tête de Cuvée (B. R. L. Hardy)	Red	Earthy, spicy	Pasta	**
VDP d'Oc Domaine St. Hilaire Old Vine Merlot (A. Hardy)	Red	Plum, spicy	Cold meats, stew, offal	**
VDP d'Oc Fat Bastard Chardonnay (Gabriel Meffre)	White	Tropical fruit, melon	Chicken	**

Wine name	Style	Flavor/ Bouquet	Compatible Foods	Price Range
VDP d'Oc Ptomaine des Blagueurs Grenache Bonny Doon	Red	Berry, spicy	Stew	**
VDP d'Oc Utter Bastard Chardonnay (Gabriel Meffre)	White	Tropical fruit, oaky	Chicken	**
VDP de la Nièvre Dom des Granges Sauvignon (Myriam de Lessps-Dorise)	White	Zingy, citrus	Shellfish	*
VDP des Bouches-du-Rhône Dom de Trevallon (Eloi Dürrbach)	Red	Spicy, earthy	Mediterranean	**
VDP du Gers Cave Cooperative de Plaimont Blanc	White	Citrus, minerally	Salads	*
VDP Haute Vallée de l'Aude Pinot Noir Domaine de l'Aigle (Jean-Louis Denois)	Red	Spicy, berry	Pizza	**
VDP Herault Domaine Capion Syrah (Adrian Buhrer)	Red	Spicy, earthy	Pasta	*
VDP Herault Domaine Grange des Pères	Red	Berry, spicy	Stew	**
VDP Herault Mas de Daumas Gassac (red) (Aimé Guibert)	Red	Berry, spicy, complex, tannic	Beef	***
VDP Herault Mas de Daumas Gassac (white)	White	Zingy, citrus, minerally	Fish	***
VDP Jardin de la France Dom de Bablut Chardonnay (Christophe Daviau)	White	Tropical fruit, melon	Fish	*
VDP Jardin de la France Michel Robineau Sauvignon	White	Berry, herbaceous	Shellfish	*
VDP Jardin de la France Rémy Pannier Chenin Blanc	White	Melon, apples	Aperitif	*
VDP Pyrénées-Orientales Mas Chichet Merlot	Red	Plum, spicy	Stew	*
VDP Val de Montferrand Domaine de l'Hortus Grand Cuvée (Jean Orliac)	Red	Berry, spicy	Cold meats, stew, offal	**

GERMANY

Baden

Blankenhorn Schliengener Sonnenstück Riesling Eiswein	Sweet	Mandarin, sweet, complex	Dessert	***
Dr. Heger Ihringer Winklerberg Muskateller TBA	Sweet	Mandarin, sweet, honey	Dessert	***
Dr. Heger Ihringer Winklerberg Riesling Beerenauslese	Sweet	Complex, sweet, mandarin	Dessert	***
Durbacher Winzergenossenschaft Durbacher Plauelrain Riesling Auslese	White	Honey, sweet, citrus	Dessert	**
Laible Durbacher Plauelrain Riesling Eiswein	Sweet	Mandarin, honey, sweet	Dessert	***
Schloss Ortenberg Riesling Eiswein	Sweet	Honey, sweet, minerally	Dessert	***
Stigler Ihringer Winklerberg Riesling TBA	Sweet	Complex, citrus, sweet	Dessert	***
Winzergenossenschaft Achkarren Achkarrer Schlossberg Ruländer TBA	Sweet	Sweet, honey	Dessert	***
Winzergenossenschaft Königschaffhausen Königschaffhauser Hasenberg Ruländer TBA	Sweet	Sweet	Dessert	***
Winzergenossenschaft Pfaffenweiler Oberdürrenberg Ruländer Eiswein	Sweet	Mandarin, sweet	Dessert	***
Wolff Metternich Durbacher Schloss Grohl Riesling Auslese	White	Minerally, smoky, sweet	Dessert	**

Franken

Am Lump Erschendorfer Lump Riesling Eiswein	Sweet	Sweet, minerally, mandarin	Dessert	***
Bürgerspital Randersackerer Pfülben Rieslaner Beerenauslese	Sweet	Floral, sweet, minerally	Dessert	***
Bürgerspital Würzburger Stein Riesling Spätlese	White	Sweet, citrus	Asian	**
Bürgerspital Würzburger Stein Riesling TBA	Sweet	Complex, honey, sweet	Dessert	***
Castell Casteller Kugelspiel Rieslaner Beerenauslese	Sweet	Sweet, honey	Dessert	***
Castell Casteller Kugelspiel Silvaner Eiswein	Sweet	Sweet, mandarin	Dessert	***
Fürst Bürgstadter Centgrafenberg Rieslaner Beerenauslese	Sweet	Mandarin, sweet, honey	Dessert	***
Juliusspital Randersackerer Pfülben Rieslaner Auslese	White	Sweet, minerally	Dessert	**

Wine name	Style	Flavor/ Bouquet	Compatible Foods	Price Range
Juliusspital Würzburger Stein Riesling Beerenauslese	Sweet	Sweet, mandarin	Dessert	***
Sauer Erschendorfer Lump Riesling Beerenauslese	Sweet	Sweet, honey	Dessert	***
Schloss Sommerhausen Sommerhäuser Reifenstein Scheurebe Eiswein	Sweet	Sweet, mandarin	Dessert	***
Schloss Sommerhausen Sommerhäuser Steinbach Rieslaner TBA	Sweet	Complex, sweet, minerally	Dessert	***
Schmitt's Kinder Randersackerer Pfülben Riesling Auslese	Sweet	Honey, mandarin, sweet	Dessert	**
Schmitt's Kinder Randersackerer Sonnenstuhl Rieslaner Beerenauslese	Sweet	Sweet, honey	Dessert	***
Staatlicher Hofkeller Würzburger Stein Riesling Auslese	White	Honey, sweet	Dessert	**
Staatlicher HofkellerWürzburger Stein Riesling TBA	Sweet	Complex, mandarin, sweet	Dessert	***
Wirsching Iphofer Julius-Echter-Berg Silvaner Spätlese Trocken	White	Floral, citrus	Veal	**
Wirsching Iphöfer Kronsberg Riesling Spätlese	White	Citrus, sweet	Fish	**
Hessische Bergstrasse				
Staatsweingut Bergstrasse Heppenheimer Centgericht Riesling Auslese	White	Sweet, honey	Dessert	***
Staatsweingut Bergstrasse Heppenheimer Centgericht Riesling Eiswein	White	Sweet	Dessert	***
Weingut der Stadt Bensheim Bensheimer Kirchberg Riesling Beerenauslese	Sweet	Sweet, complex	Dessert	***
Mittelrhein				
Albert Lambrich Oberweseler Römerkrug Riesling Auslese	White	Sweet, minerally	Dessert	**
Bopparder Hamm Feuerlay Riesling Auslese (H. Müller)	Sweet	Mandarin, sweet	Dessert	**
Goswin Lambrich Oberweseler Römerkrug Riesling Eiswein	Sweet	Sweet, mandarin	Dessert	***
Jost Bacharacher Hahn Riesling Auslese	White	Sweet, minerally	Dessert	**
Jost Bacharacher Hahn Riesling TBA	Sweet	Minerally, sweet, complex	Dessert	***
Lanius-Knab Engehöller Bernstein Riesling Beerenauslese	Sweet	Honey, sweet, complex	Dessert	***
Lorenz Bopparder Hamm Mandelstein Riesling Auslese	White	Sweet, honey, citrus	Dessert	**
Mades Bacharacher Wolfshöhle Riesling Spätlese	White	Sweet, minerally, zingy	Fish	**
Ratzenberger Bacharacher Kloster Fürstental Riesling TBA	Sweet	Complex, sweet, honey	Dessert	***
Ratzenberger Steeger Sankt Jost Riesling Auslese	White	Sweet, mandarin, minerally	Dessert	**
Weingart Bopparder Hamm Feuerlay Riesling Auslese	White	Sweet, floral	Dessert	**
Mosel-Saar-Ruwer				
Bernkasteler Doctor Riesling Auslese (J. Wegeler Erben)	White	Sweet, minerally, floral	Dessert	**
Bischöfliche Weingüter Kaseler Nies'chen Riesling Eiswein	Sweet	Mandarin, sweet, complex	Dessert	***
Brauneberger Juffer-Sonnenuhr Riesling Auslese (Willi Haag)	White	Sweet, complex, minerally	Dessert	**
Brauneberger Juffer-Sonnenuhr Riesling Beerenauslese (Fritz Haag)	Sweet	Complex, honey, sweet	Dessert	***
Brauneberger Juffer-Sonnenuhr Riesling Kabinett (Fritz Haag)	White	Floral, zingy	Fish	**
Dr. Loosen Erdener Prälat Riesling Auslese	White	Sweet, minerally, citrus	Dessert	**
Dr. Loosen Erdener Treppchen Riesling Spätlese	White	Sweet, zingy, smoky	Fruit	**
Dr. Loosen Urziger Würzgarten Riesling TBA	Sweet	Minerally, complex, sweet	Dessert	***
Dr. Loosen Wehlener Sonnenuhr Riesling Kabinett	White	Apples, minerally, citrus	Chicken	**
Egon Müller Scharzhofberger Riesling Auslese	White	Sweet, apples, minerally	Dessert	***
Egon Müller Scharzhofberger Riesling Eiswein	Sweet	Complex, honey, sweet, minerally	Dessert	***
Egon Müller Scharzhofberger Riesling TBA	Sweet	Complex, mandarin, sweet	Dessert	***

Wine name	Style	Flavor/ Bouquet	Compatible Foods	Price Range
Graacher Domprobst Riesling Beerenauslese (Max. Ferd. Richter)	Sweet	Mandarin, sweet, complex	Dessert	***
Graacher Domprobst Riesling Beerenauslese (Willi Schaeffer)	Sweet	Mandarin, sweet, honey	Dessert	***
Graacher Himmelreich Riesling Kabinett (Willi Schaeffer)	White	Crisp, minerally, apples	Fish	**
Graacher Himmelreich Riesling Spätlese (J. J. Prüm)	White	Floral, minerally, sweet	Cheese	**
Grans-Fassian Trittenheimer Apotheke Riesling Beerenauslese	Sweet	Apples, honey, sweet	Dessert	***
Heinz Wagner Saarburger Rausch Riesling Auslese	White	Sweet, citrus, floral	Dessert	**
Heribert Kerpen Wehlener Sonnenuhr Riesling Auslese	White	Sweet, minerally, floral	Dessert	**
Heymann-Löwenstein Winninger Uhlen Riesling TBA	Sweet	Complex, sweet, mandarin	Dessert	***
Karp-Schreiber Brauneberger Juffer-Sonnenuhr Riesling TBA	Sweet	Complex, sweet, mandarin	Dessert	***
Karthäuserhof Eitelsbacher Karthäuserhofberg Auslese	White	Sweet, floral, citrus	Dessert	**
Kesselstatt Scharzhofberger Riesling Beerenauslese	Sweet	Sweet, minerally, complex	Dessert	***
Le Gallais Wiltinger Braune Kupp Riesling Auslese	White	Sweet, minerally, apples	Dessert	**
Maximin Grünhäuser Abtsberg Riesling Eiswein (Maximin Grünhaus)	Sweet	Sweet, mandarin	Dessert	***
Maximin Grünhäuser Abtsberg Riesling Kabinett (Maximin Grünhaus)	White	Minerally, apples, floral	Fish	**
Maximin Grünhäuser Herrenberg Riesling Spätlese (Maximin Grünhaus)	White	Sweet, floral, citrus	Cheese	**
Meulenhof Erdener Treppchen Riesling Auslese	White	Sweet, floral, citrus	Dessert	**
Mülheimer Helenenkloster Riesling Eiswein (Max. Ferd. Richter)	Sweet	Sweet, honey	Dessert	***
Ockfener Bockstein Riesling Spätlese (Heinz Wagner)	White	Sweet, floral	Fish	**
Pauly-Bergweiler Bernkasteler Alte Badstube am Doctorberg Riesling TBA	Sweet	Honey, sweet, complex	Dessert	***
Pauly-Bergweiler Urziger Würzgarten Riesling TBA	Sweet	Complex, honey, sweet	Dessert	***
Piesporter Goldtröpfchen Riesling Spätlese (Kurt Hain)	White	Floral, minerally, citrus	Fish	**
Reinhold Haart Wintricher Ohligsberg Riesling Spätlese	White	Sweet, floral	Asian	**
Reverchon Filzener Herrenberg Riesling Spätlese	White	Sweet, minerally, apples	Cheese	**
Sankt Urbans-Hof Ockfener Bockstein Riesling Auslese	Sweet	Citrus, minerally, sweet	Dessert	***
Schloss Lieser Lieser Niederberg Riesling Auslese	White	Sweet, floral, honey	Dessert	**
Schloss Saarstein Serriger Schloss Saarstein Riesling Beerenauslese	Sweet	Sweet, complex, mandarin	Dessert	***
Selbach-Oster Bernkasteler Badstube Riesling Eiswein	Sweet	Sweet, minerally	Dessert	**
Selbach-Oster Zeltinger Sonnenuhr Riesling TBA	Sweet	Complex, sweet, honey	Dessert	***
Studert-Prüm Wehlener Sonnenuhr Riesling Auslese	White	Sweet, citrus, minerally	Dessert	**
Urziger Würzgarten Riesling Auslese (J. J. Christoffel Erben)	White	Sweet, citrus, floral	Dessert	**
Urziger Würzgarten Riesling Auslese (Robert Eymael)	White	Minerally, citrus, sweet	Dessert	**
von Hövel Oberemmeler Hütte Riesling Auslese	White	Sweet, floral, citrus	Dessert	**
Wehlener Sonnenuhr Riesling Auslese (J. J. Prüm)	White	Sweet, minerally, apples	Dessert	***
Wehlener Sonnenuhr Riesling Auslese (S. A. Prüm)	White	Sweet, citrus, minerally	Dessert	**
Wehlener Sonnenuhr Riesling Kabinett (S. A. Prüm)	White	Minerally, apples	Veal	**
Weins-Prüm Erdener Prälat Riesling Auslese	White	Minerally, floral, sweet	Dessert	**
Weins-Prüm Wehlener Sonnenuhr Riesling Kabinett	White	Citrus, minerally	Fish	**
Wwe. H. Thanisch–Erben Thanisch Bernkasteler Badstube Riesling Kabinett	White	Zingy, austere, minerally	Fish	**
Wwe. H. Thanisch–Erben Thanisch Bernkasteler Doctor Riesling Auslese	Sweet	Honey, minerally, sweet,	Dessert	***
Zeltinger Sonnenuhr Riesling Auslese (J. J. Prüm)	White	Sweet, minerally, citrus	Dessert	***

Wine name	Style	Flavor/ Bouquet	Compatible Foods	Price Range
Zilliken Saarburger Rausch Riesling Eiswein	Sweet	Mandarin, sweet, complex	Dessert	***
Nahe				
Diel Dorsheimer Pittermännchen Riesling Auslese	Sweet	Sweet, mandarin	Dessert	**
Dönnhoff Oberhäuser Brücke Riesling Eiswein	Sweet	Honey, sweet, complex	Dessert	***
Emrich-Schönleber Monzinger Frühlingsplätzchen Riesling Auslese	White	Sweet, floral	Dessert	**
Finkenauer Kreuznacher Kahlenberg Riesling Auslese	White	Sweet, citrus, minerally	Dessert	**
Göttelmann Münsterer Rheinberg Riesling Spätlese	White	Sweet, citrus	Fruit	**
Gutsverwaltung Niederhausen-Schlossböckelheim Niederhäuser Hermannsberg Riesling Eiswein	Sweet	Sweet, mandarin	Dessert	***
Gutsverwaltung Niederhäuser Hermannshöhle Riesling Beerenauslese	Sweet	Sweet, honey	Dessert	***
Königswingert Guldentaler Hipperich Riesling Auslese	White	Sweet, mandarin, floral	Dessert	**
Korrell Kreuznacher St. Martin Riesling Auslese	White	Sweet, citrus	Dessert	**
Kreuznacher Brückes Riesling Auslese (Paul Anheuser)	White	Sweet, floral, minerally	Dessert	**
Kruger-Rumpf Münster Dautenpflänzer Riesling Auslese	White	Citrus, sweet	Dessert	**
Kruger-Rumpf Münsterer Pittersberg Riesling Eiswein	Sweet	Mandarin, sweet, complex	Dessert	***
Lötzbeyer Feilbingerter Künigsgarten Riesling Eiswein	Sweet	Complex, mandarin, sweet, minerally	Dessert	***
Lötzbeyer Norheimer Dellchen Riesling Auslese	White	Minerally, sweet, elegant	Dessert	**
Mathern Niederhäuser Rosenberg Riesling Auslese	White	Sweet, floral	Dessert	**
Prinz zu Salm-Dalberg Wallhäuser Felseneck Riesling Auslese	White	Sweet, citrus	Dessert	**
Prinz zu Salm-Dalberg Wallhäuser Johannisberg Riesling Spätlese	White	Sweet, floral	Fruit	**
Schmidt Obermoscheler Schlossberg Riesling Kabinett	White	Minerally, apples	Shellfish	**
Sitzius Langenlonsheimer Löhrerberg Riesling Spätlese	White	Sweet, citrus, minerally	Cheese	**
Tesch Laubenheimer Karthäuser Riesling Eiswein	Sweet	Sweet, complex	Dessert	***
Pfalz				
Bassermann-Jordan Forster Jesuitengarten Riesling Spätlese	White	Sweet, floral	Asian	**
Bassermann-Jordan Forster Ungeheuer Riesling Eiswein	Sweet	Mandarin, honey, sweet	Dessert	***
Bassermann-Jordan Ruppertsberger Reiterpfad Riesling TBA	Sweet	Complex, sweet, mandarin	Dessert	***
Biffar Deidesheimer Kieselberg Riesling Auslese	White	Sweet, citrus, floral	Dessert	**
Biffar Deidesheimer Mäushöhle Riesling Eiswein	Sweet	Complex, sweet, mandarin	Dessert	***
Bürklin-Wolf Forster Ungeheuer Riesling Spätlese Trocken	White	Spicy, minerally	Veal	**
Bürklin-Wolf Wachenheimer Gerümpel Riesling Eiswein	Sweet	Minerally, honey, sweet	Dessert	***
Christmann Deidesheimer Hohenmorgen Riesling Beerenauslese	Sweet	Mandarin, sweet, complex	Dessert	***
Christmann Ruppertsberger Reiterpfad Riesling TBA	Sweet	Mandarin, sweet, citrus	Dessert	***
Darting Dürkheimer Fronhof Scheurebe TBA	Sweet	Sweet, mandarin	Dessert	***
Darting Ungsteiner Herrenberg Riesling Auslese	White	Sweet, citrus	Dessert	**
Deinhard Deidesheimer Grainhübel Riesling Auslese	White	Sweet, floral	Dessert	**
Deinhard Ruppertsberger Reiterpfad Riesling Eiswein	Sweet	Sweet, mandarin	Dessert	***
F. Becker Schweigener Sonnenberg Riesling Spätlese	White	Sweet, citrus	Cheese	**
Forster Kirchenstück Riesling Auslese Trocken (Eugen Müller)	White	Citrus, spicy, floral	Fish	**
Forster Stift Riesling Eiswein (Eugen Müller)	Sweet	Sweet, mandarin	Dessert	***
Forster Ungeheuer Riesling Auslese Trocken (J. L. Wolf)	White	Citrus, spicy	Chicken	**
Koehler-Ruprecht Kallstadter Saumagen Riesling Beerenauslese	Sweet	Honey, sweet, complex	Dessert	***

Wine name	Style	Flavor/ Bouquet	Compatible Foods	Price Range
Koehler-Ruprecht Kallstadter Saumagen Riesling Spätlese	White	Sweet, apples, citrus	Fish	**
Lucashof Forster Stift Riesling Eiswein	Sweet	Complex, mandarin, sweet	Dessert	***
Mosbacher Forster Freundstück Riesling Eiswein	Sweet	Smoky, sweet, mandarin	Dessert	***
Mosbacher Forster Pechstein Riesling Auslese	White	Sweet, minerally	Dessert	**
Müller-Catoir Haardter Bürgergarten Muskateller Kabinett Trocken	White	Minerally, apples	Chicken	**
Müller-Catoir Haardter Bürgergarten Riesling Eiswein	Sweet	Minerally, sweet, floral	Dessert	***
Müller-Catoir Haardter Mandelring Scheurebe Eiswein	Sweet	Mandarin, sweet	Dessert	***
Müller-Catoir Mussbacher Eselshaut Rieslaner Auslese	White	Sweet, apples, honey	Dessert	**
Pfeffingen Ungsteiner Herrenberg Riesling Spätlese	White	Sweet, floral	Asian	**
Pfeffingen Ungsteiner Herrenberg Scheurebe Beerenauslese	Sweet	Mandarin, sweet	Dessert	***
Siben Deidesheimer Leinhöhle Riesling Spätlese	White	Citrus, sweet	Cheese	**
von Buhl Forster Jesuitengarten Riesling Eiswein	Sweet	Complex, sweet, minerally	Dessert	***
von Buhl Forster Ungeheuer Riesling Auslese	White	Sweet, minerally, floral	Dessert	**
von Buhl Forster Ungeheuer Riesling TBA	Sweet	Mandarin, sweet, honey	Dessert	***
Wachenheimer Gerümpel Riesling Spätlese (J. L. Wolf)	White	Sweet, minerally, apples	Fruit	**
Weegmüller Haardter Bürgergarten Riesling Eiswein	Sweet	Minerally, sweet, honey	Dessert	***
Rheingau				
Breuer Rüdesheimer Bischofsberg Riesling TBA	Sweet	Sweet, honey	Dessert	***
Hattenheimer Schützenhaus Riesling Auslese (Hans Lang)	White	Minerally, sweet, citrus	Dessert	**
Hessische Staatsweingüter Kloster Eberbach Steinberger Eiswein	Sweet	Mandarin, complex, sweet	Dessert	***
J. Wegeler Erben Oestricher Lenchen Riesling TBA	Sweet	Complex, sweet, mandarin	Dessert	***
Johannishof Johannisberger Goldatzel Riesling Kabinett	White	Minerally, smoky, citrus	Veal	**
Johannishof Rüdesheimer Berg Rottland Riesling Auslese	White	Sweet, citrus, floral	Dessert	**
Kesseler Rüdesheimer Bischofsberg Riesling TBA	Sweet	Complex, sweet, honey	Dessert	***
Knyphausen Erbacher Siegelsberg Riesling Eiswein	Sweet	Mandarin, citrus, sweet	Dessert	***
Künstler Hochheimer Hölle Riesling Beerenauslese	Sweet	Honey, sweet, complex	Dessert	***
Leitz Rüdesheimer Berg Rottland Riesling Auslese	White	Floral, sweet	Dessert	**
Oestricher Lenchen Riesling Auslese (J. Wegeler Erben)	White	Sweet, citrus, floral	Dessert	**
Oestricher Lenchen Riesling Eiswein (August Eser)	Sweet	Complex, mandarin, sweet	Dessert	***
P. J. Kuhn Riesling Eiswein	Sweet	Minerally, sweet, honey	Dessert	***
Prinz Hallgartener Jungfer Riesling Auslese	White	Sweet, minerally, apples	Dessert	**
Prinz von Hessen Johannisberger Klaus Riesling Spätlese	White	Sweet, citrus	Cheese	**
Ress Hattenheimer Nussbrunnen Riesling Spätlese	White	Sweet, citrus, smoky	Cheese	**
Ress Oestricher Doosberg Riesling Beerenauslese	Sweet	Smoky, citrus, sweet	Dessert	***
Ress Oestricher Doosberger TBA	Sweet	Complex, sweet, honey	Dessert	***
Riesling TBA (P. J. Kuhn)	Sweet	Complex, mandarin, sweet	Dessert	***
Schloss Johannisberger Riesling Auslese	White	Minerally, sweet, citrus, floral	Dessert	**
Schloss Johannisberger Riesling Beerenauslese	Sweet	Complex, honey, sweet	Dessert	***
Schloss Reinhartshausen Erbacher Schlossberg Riesling Auslese	White	Sweet, minerally, apples, citrus	Dessert	**
Schloss Reinhartshausen Erbacher Siegelsberg Riesling Beerenauslese	Sweet	Mandarin, sweet, complex	Dessert	***
Schloss Schönborn Erbacher Marcobrunn Riesling Erstes Gewächs	White	Citrus, floral	Fish	**
Schloss Schönborn Erbacher Marcobrunn Riesling TBA	Sweet	Honey, minerally, sweet	Dessert	***

Wine name	Style	Flavor/ Bouquet	Compatible Foods	Price Range
Schloss Schönborn Rüdesheimer Berg Schlossberg Riesling Beerenauslese	Sweet	Complex, sweet, honey	Dessert	***
von Kanitz Lorcher Kapellenberg Riesling Beerenauslese	Sweet	Complex, sweet, minerally	Dessert	***
Weil Kiedricher Gräfenberg Riesling Auslese	White	Citrus, floral, sweet	Dessert	**
Weil Kiedricher Gräfenberg Riesling Eiswein	Sweet	Honey, sweet	Dessert	***
Weil Kiedricher Gräfenberg Riesling TBA	Sweet	Complex, sweet, mandarin	Dessert	***
Weisser Burgunder Spätlese Trocken (Hans Lang)	White	Citrus, minerally	Pizza	**
Rheinhessen				
Balbach Niersteiner Hipping Riesling Auslese	Sweet	Sweet, citrus	Dessert	**
Göhring Nieder-Flörsheimer Frauenberg Riesling Spätlese	White	Sweet, floral	Fruit	**
Gunderloch Nackenheimer Rothenberg Riesling Auslese	White	Sweet, citrus	Dessert	**
Guntrum Oppenheimer Herrenberg Silvaner Eiswein	Sweet	Mandarin, sweet	Dessert	***
Heyl zu Herrnsheim Niersteiner Pettental Riesling Auslese	Sweet	Minerally, sweet, citrus	Dessert	**
Keller Dalsheimer Hubacker Riesling Eiswein	Sweet	Mandarin, sweet, citrus	Dessert	***
Keller Dalsheimer Hubacker Riesling TBA	Sweet	Complex, sweet, mandarin	Dessert	***
Kühling-Gillot Oppenheimer Sackträger Riesling Auslese	White	Sweet, mandarin	Dessert	**
Kühling-Gillot Oppenheimer Sackträger Riesling TBA	Sweet	Complex, sweet, mandarin	Dessert	***
Michel-Pfannebecker Westhofener Steingrube Riesling Auslese	White	Sweet, floral, citrus	Dessert	**
Niersteiner Pettental Riesling Auslese (Franz Karl Schmitt)	White	Sweet, floral	Dessert	**
Posthof Gau-Bischofsheimer Glockenberg Riesling Spätlese	White	Sweet, citrus, floral	Asian	**
Sankt Antony Niersteiner Auglangen Riesling Spätlese	White	Sweet, citrus	Fruit	**
Sankt Antony Niersteiner Oelberg Riesling Beerenauslese	Sweet	Mandarin, sweet	Dessert	***
Schales Rieslaner Auslese	White	Sweet, citrus	Dessert	**
Schales Riesling Eiswein	Sweet	Minerally, sweet, mandarin	Dessert	***
Schneider Niersteiner Orbel Riesling Spätlese	White	Sweet, citrus	Asian	**
Seebrich Niersteiner Orbel Riesling Spätlese	White	Sweet, citrus, smoky	Fruit	**
Staatliche Weinbaudomäne Niersteiner Glück Scheurebe Beerenauslese	Sweet	Smoky, sweet, mandarin	Dessert	***
Strub Niersteiner Oelberg Riesling Spätlese	White	Spicy, sweet, minerally	Asian	**
Villa Sachsen Binger Scharlachberg Riesling Beerenenauslese	Sweet	Sweet, mandarin	Dessert	***
Villa Sachsen Binger Scharlachberg Riesling Spätlese	White	Sweet, floral	Cheese	**
Wittmann Westhofener Morstein Riesling Spätlese	White	Sweet, minerally, citrus	Dessert	**

AUSTRIA

Donauland

Fritsch Perfektion Grüner Veltliner	White	Crisp, citrus	Veal	**

Kamptal

Retzl Bergjuwel Riesling	White	Floral, minerally	Salads	**
Schloss Gobelsburg Ried Grub Grüner Veltliner	White	Citrus, minerally	Fish	**
Willi Bründlmayer Grüner Veltliner: Ried Lamm	White	Citrus, melon	Veal	**
Willi Bründlmayer Riesling: Zöbinger Heiligenstein	White	Floral, minerally	Shellfish	**
Salomon Riesling: Kögl	White	Floral, minerally	Fish	**

Neusiedlersee

Lang Scheurebe Trockenbeerenauslese und Eiswein	Sweet	Sweet, honey	Dessert	***

Wine name	Style	Flavor/ Bouquet	Compatible Foods	Price Range
Neusiedlersee-Hügelland				
Schandl Ausbruch	Sweet	Sweet, citrus, rich	Dessert	***
Wenzel Ausbruch	Sweet	Rich, citrus, sweet	Dessert	***
Wachau				
Emmerich Knoll Kellerberg Riesling	White	Floral, minerally	Shellfish	**
Emmerich Knoll Schütt Grüner Veltliner	White	Floral, citrus	Chicken	**
F. X. Pichler Kellerberg Grüner Veltliner	White	Floral, citrus	Fish	**
F. X. Pichler Kellerberg Riesling	White	Minerally, citrus	Fish	**
F. X. Pichler Loibner Berg Grüner Veltliner	White	Citrus, spicy, floral	Chicken	**
F. X. Pichler Steinertal Riesling	White	Floral, citrus	Fish	**
Hirtzberger Honivogl Grüner Veltliner	White	Minerally, fruity	Fish	**
Hirtzberger Schön Grüner Veltliner	White	Fruity, minerally	Asian	**
Hirtzberger Singerriedl Riesling	White	Floral, citrus	Shellfish	**
Lagler Vordersieber Grüner Veltliner	White	Spicy, complex, floral	Chicken	**
Saahs Im Weingebirge Riesling	White	Floral, minerally	Aperitif	**
Saahs Steiner Hund Riesling	White	Citrus, minerally	Salads	**
Schmidl Kuss den Pfennig Riesling	White	Floral, spicy	Veal	**
SWITZERLAND				
Eastern Switzerland				
Weinbau Nussbaumer Baselbieter Kluser Pinot Gris Barrique (Basel)	White	Melon, citrus, oaky	Fish	**
Geneva				
Domaine Les Hutins Dardagny Le Bertholier Rouge	Red	Berry, spicy	Stew	**
Domaine Les Hutins Dardagny Pinot Noir	Red	Gamey, smoky	Duck	**
Neuchâtel				
Caves Châtenay-Bouvier Oeil-de-Perdrix	Red	Berry, floral	Pasta	**
Ticino				
I Vini di Guido Brivio Merlot del Ticino Riflessi d'Epoca	Red	Plums, berry	Beef	**
Tamborini Merlot del Ticino Vigna Vecchia	Red	Spicy, plums	Beef	**
Valsangiacomo Merlot del Ticino Vigneto Roncobello di Morbio	Red	Plums, oaky	Pasta	**
Valais				
Bon Père Germanier Syrah Cayas	Red	Earthy, spicy	Stew	**
Bon Père Germanier Vétroz Fendant Les Terrasses	White	Fruity, minerally	Fish	**
Caveau de Salquenen Salquenen Pinot Noir	Red	Gamey, smoky	Cold meats, stew, offal	**
Domaine du Mont d'Or Johannisberg Moelleux	Sweet	Sweet, minerally, citrus	Dessert	***
Provins Brindamour Malvoisie de Sierre	White	Minerally, citrus	Fish	**
Provins Vieilles Vignes Blanc	White	Melon, fruity	Chicken	**
Vaud				
Henri Badoux et Fils Aigle Pinot Noir	Red	Gamey, berry	Duck	**
Les Frères Dubois Dézaley-Marsens De La Tour	White	Citrus, spicy	Chicken	**
Luc Massy L'Epesses Clos du Boux	White	Floral, minerally	Chicken	**
St-Saphorin Roche Ronde (Jean et Pierre Testuz)	White	Floral, citrus	Pork	**

Wine name	Style	Flavor/ Bouquet	Compatible Foods	Price Range
ITALY				
Central Italy				
Cantine Lungarotti Torgiano Rosso Riserva DOC Vigna Monticchio	Red	Berry, earthy, leathery	Beef, lamb	**
Castel de Paolis Frascati Superiore DOC Vigna Adriana	White	Citrus, crisp	Shellfish, fish	**
Castello della Sala Cervara della Sala IGT	White	Apples, minerally	Fish, chicken	**
Colli di Catone Frascati Superiore DOC	White	Citrus, crisp	Shellfish, fish	**
La Monacesca Verdicchio di Matelica DOC	White	Stone fruit, melon	Shellfish, fish	**
Palazzone Orvieto Classico DOC Campo del Guardiano	White	Citrus, stone fruit, crisp	Shellfish, fish	**
Sagrantino di Montefalco DOC (Arnaldo Caprai)	Red	Intense, berry, earthy, complex	Beef, lamb	**
Verdicchio dei Castelli di Jesi Classico DOC (F. lli Bucci)	White	Citrus, crisp	Shellfish, fish	**
Verdicchio dei Castelli di Jesi Classico Superiore DOC Casal di Serra, Umani Ronchi	White	Citrus, honey, crisp	Shellfish, fish	**
Emilia-Romagna				
Cavicchioli Lambrusco di Sorbara DOC Vigna del Cristo	Red	Berry, fruity, crisp	Veal, pork, beef	**
Fattoria Zerbina Albana di Romagna Passito DOCG Scacco Matto	Sweet	Sweet, honey, waxy, floral	Dessert	***
Fattoria Zerbina Marzieno Ravenna Rosso IGT	Red	Berry, spicy	Veal, pork, beef	**
Tenuta Bonzara Colli Bolognesi Merlot DOC	Red	Plums, spicy	Chicken, veal, pork	**
Tenuta La Palazza Il Tornese Chardonnay IGT, Drei Dona	White	Apples, minerally	Fish, chicken	**
Tre Monti Colli d'Imola Cabernet DOC Turico	Red	Berry, spicy	Pork, beef	**
Friuli-Venezia Giulia				
Friuli Isonzo Pinot Bianco DOC (Mauro Drius)	White	Apples, melon, crisp	Fish, chicken	**
Girolamo Dorigo Colli Orientali del Friuli Chardonnay DOC Vigneto Ronc di Juri	White	Apples, butter, vanillin	Fish, chicken	**
Kante Carso Malvasia DOC	White	Floral, fruity	Asian, shellfish	**
Le Due Terre Colli Orientali del Friuli Rosso Sacrisassi IGT	Red	Berry, spicy	Pizza, pasta	**
Livio Felluga Colli Orientali del Friuli Rosazzo IGT Bianco Terre Alte	White	Citrus, crisp, stone fruit	Shellfish, fish	**
Miani Colli Orientali del Friuli Sauvignon DOC	White	Grassy, zingy	Shellfish, cheese	**
Pierpaolo Pecorari Colli Orientali del Friuli Merlot IGT Baolar	Red	Plums, spicy	Veal, pork, beef	**
Puiatti Collio Pinot Grigio DOC	White	Stone fruit, nutty, crisp	Fish, chicken	**
Vie di Romans Friuli Isonzo Sauvignon DOC Vieris	White	Grassy, zingy	Shellfish, cheese	**
Villa Russiz Collio Tocai Friulano DOC	White	Citrus, elegant	Shellfish, fish	**
Vinnaioli Jermann Vintage Tunina IGT	White	Rich, fruity, complex	Fish, chicken	***
Piedmont/Northwest Italy				
Almondo Roero Arneis DOC Bricco delle Ciligie	White	Citrus, nutty, floral	Fish, chicken	**
Barbera d'Asti Superiore DOC Montruc (Franco M. Martinetti)	Red	Berry, spicy, crisp	Chicken, veal	**
Barolo DOCG Vigneto Arborina (Elio Altare)	Red	Berry, licorice, vanillin	Beef, lamb	***
Bartolo Mascarello Barolo DOCG	Red	Powerful, berry, spicy	Beef, lamb	***
Braida Brachetto d'Acqui DOC	Red	Berry, crisp, floral	Pizza, chicken	**
Ca' Viola Dolcetto d'Alba DOC Barturot	Red	Berry, peppery, crisp	Pasta, chicken, pork	**
Conterno Fantino Langhe Rosso IGT Monpra	Red	Berry, licorice, elegant	Veal, pork, beef	**
Gaja Barbaresco DOCG Sori San Lorenzo	Red	Berry, licorice, earthy, rich	Beef, lamb	***
Gianfranco Alessandria Barbera d'Alba DOC Vittoria	Red	Jam, crisp, rich	Pizza, chicken	**
La Scolca Gavi dei Gavi DOC Etichetta Nera	White	Stone fruit, nutty, rich	Fish, chicken	**

Wine name	Style	Flavor/ Bouquet	Compatible Foods	Price Range
Poderi Aldo Conterno Barolo Riserva DOCG Gran Bussia	Red	Complex, berry, spicy, earthy,	Beef, lamb	***
Produttori del Barbaresco Barbaresco DOCG Vigneti in Rio Sordo	Red	Berry, licorice, leathery, intense	Beef, lamb	***
Sicily				
COS Cerasuolo di Vittoria DOC	Red	Berry, spicy, earthy	Veal, pork, beef	**
D'Ancona Passito de Pantelleria DOC Solidea	Sweet	Sweet, floral, waxy, rich	Dessert, nuts	**
Fazio Wines Torre dei Venti Rosso IGT	Red	Berry, spicy	Veal, pork, beef	**
Firriato Santagostino Rosso IGT	Red	Berry, spicy	Veal, pork, beef	**
Marco de Bartoli Moscato Passito di Pantelleria DOC Bukkuram	White	Sweet, floral, fruity, elegant	Dessert	**
Planeta Chardonnay IGT	White	Apples, minerally	Fish, chicken	**
Settesoli Nero d'Avola IGT	Red	Plums, spicy, earthy	Beef, lamb	**
Vinicola Italiana Florio Marsala Superiore Riserva DOC Vecchioflora	Sweet	Sweet, intense, licorice, tangy	Cheese, dessert	**
Soave Classico, Valpolicella Classico/North Central Italy				
Allegrini La Poja IGT	Red	Berry, licorice, spicy	Pork, lamb	***
Anselmi Recioto di Soave DOC I Capitelli	Sweet	Sweet, honey, nutty, minerally, rich	Dessert	**
Bellavista Franciacorta DOCG Gran Cuvée Brut	Sparkling	Stone fruit, yeasty, minerally	Shellfish, nuts	***
Bisol Prosecco di Valdobbiadene DOC Extra Dry Vigneti del Fol	Sparkling	Citrus, minerally, crisp	Shellfish	**
Ca' dei Frati Lugana DOC I Frati	White	Citrus, nutty, crisp	Fish, chicken	**
Ca' del Bosco Maurizio Zanella IGT	White	Stone fruit, rich, minerally	Fish, chicken	**
Maculan Breganze Cabernet Sauvignon DOC Ferrata	Red	Berry, herbaceous, toasty	Beef, lamb	**
Pieropan Soave Classico Superiore DOC La Rocca	White	Citrus, crisp, stone fruit	Shellfish, fish	**
Quintarelli Amarone della Valpolicella DOCG	Red	Powerful, spicy, earthy	Pork, lamb, cheese	***
Tommaso Bussola Recioto della Valpolicella Classico DOC	Red	Berry, licorice, leathery, intense	Beef, pork, lamb	**
Valpolicella Classico Superiore DOC Sant'Urbano (F. lli Speri)	Red	Berry, spicy	Pizza, chicken	**
Southern Italy				
Amano Primitivo IGT (Mark Shannon)	Red	Berry, earthy	Chicken, veal, pork	**
Camillo Montori Montepulciano d'Abruzzo DOC Fonte Cupa	Red	Fruity, spicy	Pizza, chicken	**
Cantina Sociale di Santadi Carignano del Sulcis DOC Tre Torri	Red	Rich, plums, earthy	Veal, pork, beef	**
D'Angelo Aglianico del Vulture DOC	Red	Berry, earthy, minerally	Veal, pork, beef	**
Feudi di San Gregorio Taurasi DOC	Red	Rich, fruity, earthy	Beef, lamb	**
Leone de Castris Salice Salentino Rosso Riserva DOC Donna Lisa	Red	Powerful, earthy	Beef, lamb	**
Mastroberadino Greco del Tufo DOC	White	Floral, nutty, minerally	Shellfish, fish	**
Montepulciano d'Abruzzo DOC Riparossa (Dino Illuminati)	Red	Fruity, spicy	Pizza, chicken	**
Pervini Primitivo di Manduria DOC Archidamo	Red	Berry, earthy	Chicken, veal, pork	**
Tenute Capichera Vermentino di Gallura DOC	White	Crisp, fruity	Shellfish, Asian	**
Trebbiano d'Abruzzo DOC (Edoardo Valentini)	White	Crisp, citrus, minerally	Shellfish, fish	**
Trebbiano d'Abruzzo DOC Marina Cvetic (Gianni Masciarelli)	White	Crisp, fruity	Shellfish, fish	**
Turriga IGT (Antonio Argiolas)	White	Fruity, nutty, elegant	Fish, chicken	**
Trentino-Alto Adige				
Alto Adige Lagrein Scuro Riserva DOC Untermoserhof (Georg Ramoser)	Red	Plums, spicy	Pizza, chicken	**

Wine name	Style	Flavor/ Bouquet	Compatible Foods	Price Range
Cantina Produttori San Michele Appiano Alto Adige Chardonnay DOC St. Valentin	White	Apples, citrus, minerally	Fish, chicken	**
Cesconi Trentino Pinot Grigio DOC	White	Stone fruit, nutty	Shellfish, fish	**
Foradori Teroldego Rotaliano DOC Sgarzon	Red	Plums, jam	Chicken, veal, pork	**
Hofstatter Gewürztraminer DOC Kolbenhof	White	Floral, tropical fruit, spicy	Fish, pasta, Asian	**
Maso Cantanghel Trentino Pinot Nero DOC	Red	Berry, spicy	Fish, chicken	**
Tuscany				
Antinori Tignanello IGT	Red	Elegant, spicy, toasty	Beef, lamb	***
Boscarelli Vino Nobile di Montepulciano DOCG Vigna del Nocio	Red	Rich, earthy, leathery	Beef, lamb	***
Costanti Brunello di Montalcino DOCG	Red	Intense, berry, leathery, earthy	Beef, lamb	***
Fattoria di Felsina Chianti Classico Riserva DOCG Rancia	Red	Rich, berry, spicy, complex	Beef, lamb	***
Frescobaldi Nipozzano Chianti Rufina Riserva DOCG	Red	Berry, spicy, elegant	Beef, lamb	***
Isole e Olena Vin Santo DOC	Sweet	Sweet, honey, waxy, nutty	Dessert	**
Le Pupille Morellino di Scansano DOC	Red	Plums, spicy	Pizza, chicken	**
Mazzei Chianti Classico Riserva DOCG Castello di Fonterutoli	Red	Complex, licorice, earthy, spicy	Beef, lamb	***
Ornellaia Poggio alla Gazze DOC	Red	Berry, spicy, earthy, toasty	Beef, lamb	***
Tenuta San Guido Sassicaia DOC	Red	Berry, spicy, earthy, toasty	Beef, lamb	***
Teruzzi e Puthod Vernaccia di San Gimignano DOCG	White	Citrus, crisp	Shellfish, fish	**

SPAIN

Alicante/Valencia

Gutiérrez de la Vega Casta Diva Cosecha Miel	Fortified	Fruity, rich	Dessert	*

Andalucía

Alvear Asunción	Fortified	Minerally, nutty	Cold meats, nuts	**
Alvear Carlos VII	Fortified	Minerally, nutty	Cold meats, nuts	**
Alvear CB	Fortified	Minerally, nutty	Cold meats, nuts	**
Alvear Pedro Ximénez 1830	Fortified	Sweet, caramelly	Dessert	**
Alvear Pedro Ximénez 1927	Fortified	Sweet, caramelly	Dessert	**
Antonio Barbadillo Jerez Dry Cuco	Fortified	Minerally, nutty	Nuts, cold meats	**
Antonio Barbadillo Jerez Dulce Pedro Ximénez	Fortified	Sweet, caramelly	Dessert	**
Antonio Barbadillo Obispo Gascon	Fortified	Minerally, nutty	Nuts, cold meats	**
Antonio Barbadillo Principe	Fortified	Minerally, zingy	Cold meats, shellfish	**
Antonio Barbadillo Solear	Fortified	Minerally, nutty	Cold meats, nuts	**
Aragón y Cía Araceli	Fortified	Minerally, nutty	Cheese, nuts	**
Blázquez (Domecq) Carta Blanca	Fortified	Minerally, nutty	Cold meats, nuts	**
Bobadilla Romántico	Fortified	Minerally, nutty	Cold meats, nuts	**
El Maestro Sierra Oloroso Viejo 1/4	Fortified	Yeasty, tangy	Cold meats, shellfish	**
Emilio Hidalgo Gobernador	Fortified	Minerally, nutty	Cold meats, nuts	**
Emilio Lustau Amontillado Escuadrilla	Fortified	Tangy, nutty	Cold meats, nuts	**
Emilio Lustau Moscatel Superior Emilín	Fortified	Sweet, rich	Fruits, dessert	**
Emilio Lustau Papirusa	Fortified	Tangy, yeasty	Nuts, cheese	**
Emilio Lustau Pedro Ximénez San Emilio	Fortified	Sweet, caramelly	Dessert	**
Emilio Lustau Península	Fortified	Minerally, nutty	Cold meats, nuts	**

Wine name	Style	Flavor/ Bouquet	Compatible Foods	Price Range
Emilio Lustau Puerto Fino	Fortified	Tangy, nutty	Cold meats, nuts	**
Garvey Pedro Ximénez Gran Orden	Fortified	Sweet, caramelly	Dessert	**
González Byass Amontillado del Duque	Fortified	Tangy, nutty	Cold meats, nuts	**
González Byass Apóstoles	Fortified	Minerally, nutty	Cold meats, nuts	**
González Byass Matusalem	Fortified	Minerally, nutty	Cold meats, nuts	**
González Byass Noë	Fortified	Minerally, nutty	Cold meats, nuts	**
González Byass Solera 1847	Fortified	Complex, nutty	Cold meats, nuts	***
Gracia Hermanos Montearruit	Fortified	Minerally, nutty	Cheese, nuts	**
Gutiérrez Colosa Sangre y Trabajadero	Fortified	Fruity, rich	Cheese, nuts	**
Hijos de Rainera Pérez Marín La Guita Manzanilla	Fortified	Crisp, tangy	Cold meats, shellfish	**
Infantes de Orleans-Borbón Atlantida	Fortified	Minerally, nutty	Cold meats, nuts	**
Infantes de Orleans-Borbón Fenicio	Fortified	Minerally, complex	Cold meats, nuts	**
John Harvey Bristol Cream	Fortified	Sweet, nutty	Dessert, cheese	**
José Gallego Góngora Amontillado muy Viejo Selección Imperial	Fortified	Fruity, rich	Dessert, nuts	*
José Gallego Góngora PX Dulce Añejo Selección Imperial	Fortified	Sweet, rich	Dessert	*
López Hermanos Trajinero	Fortified	Sweet, caramelly	Dessert, cheese	**
M. Gil Luque Amontillado de Bandera	Fortified	Nutty, yeasty	Cold meats, nuts	**
M. Gil Luque Moscatel de Bandera	Fortified	Sweet, rich	Fruits, dessert	**
M. Gil Luque Oloroso de Bandera	Fortified	Yeasty, tangy	Cold meats, shellfish	**
M. Gil Luque Palo Cortado de Bandera	Fortified	Nutty, tangy	Cold meats, nuts	**
M. Gil Luque Pedro Ximénez de Bandera	Fortified	Sweet, caramelly	Dessert	**
Manuel de Argüeso Pedro Ximénez en Candado	Fortified	Sweet, caramelly	Dessert	**
Marqués del Real Tesoro Del Principe	Fortified	Minerally, nutty	Cheese, nuts	**
Osborne y Cía Alonso el Sabio	Fortified	Minerally, nutty	Cold meats, nuts	**
Osborne y Cía Bailen	Fortified	Minerally, nutty	Cold meats, nuts	**
Osborne y Cía Coquinero Dry	Fortified	Minerally, nutty	Cold meats, nuts	**
Osborne y Cía Fino Quinta	Fortified	Minerally, zingy	Cold meats, shellfish	**
Osborne y Cía Moscatel Fruta	Fortified	Sweet, rich	Fruits, dessert	**
Osborne y Cía Pedro Ximénez 1827	Fortified	Sweet, caramelly	Dessert	**
Osborne y Cía Solera India	Fortified	Rich, nutty	Cheese, nuts	**
Osborne y Cía Very Old Dry Oloroso	Fortified	Tangy, complex	Cheese, nuts	**
Pedro Domecq Amontillado 51-1ª	Fortified	Tangy, nutty	Cold meats, nuts	**
Pedro Domecq Botaina	Fortified	Minerally, nutty	Cold meats, nuts	**
Pedro Domecq Capuchino	Fortified	Minerally, nutty	Cold meats, nuts	**
Pedro Domecq La Ina	Fortified	Minerally, zingy	Cold meats, nuts	**
Pedro Domecq Rio Viejo	Fortified	Minerally, nutty	Cold meats, nuts	**
Pedro Domecq Venerable	Fortified	Complex, rich	Cheese, nuts	**
Pérez Barquero Gran Barquero Amontillado	Fortified	Tangy, nutty	Cold meats, nuts	**
Pérez Barquero Gran Barquero Pedro Ximénez	Fortified	Sweet, caramelly	Dessert	**
Pilar Aranda Amontillado 1730	Fortified	Tangy, nutty	Cold meats, nuts	**
Pilar Aranda Oloroso 1730	Fortified	Tangy, yeasty	Cheese, nuts	**
Pilar Aranda Palo Cortado 1730	Fortified	Tangy, minerally	Cold meats, nuts	**
Sandeman-Coprimar Armada	Fortified	Minerally, sweet	Cheese, nuts	**

Wine name	Style	Flavor/ Bouquet	Compatible Foods	Price Range
Sandeman-Coprimar Royal Ambrosante	Fortified	Minerally, nutty	Cheese, nuts	**
Sandeman-Coprimar Royal Esmerelda	Fortified	Minerally, nutty	Cheese, nuts	**
Toro Albalá Don PX Gran Reserva 1972	Fortified	Complex, caramelly	Dessert	***
Toro Albalá Viejísimo Solera 1922	Fortified	Minerally, nutty	Cold meats, nuts	***
Valdespino PX Solera Superior	Fortified	Nutty, rich	Cheese, nuts	**
Valdespino Solera 1842	Fortified	Nutty, complex	Cheese, nuts	**
Vinícola Hidalgo y Cía Napoleon Pedro Ximénez	Fortified	Sweet, caramelly	Dessert	**
Aragón				
Alto Aragón Enate Chardonnay-234	White	Apples, oaky	Chicken, fish	**
Alto Aragón Enate Reserva Especial	Red	Earthy, oaky	Beef, lamb, pork	**
Bodega Pirineos Merlot/Cabernet-Sauvignon	Red	Plums, toasty, earthy	Beef, lamb, pork	**
Solar de Urbezo Viña Urbezo	Red	Berry, plums	Pork, lamb	**
Venta D'Aubert Domus	Red	Jam, spicy	Pork, beef, lamb	**
Viñas del Vero Clarión	White	Fruity, floral	Chicken, fish	**
Viñas del Vero Gran Vos	Red	Berry, spicy	Veal, chicken, pork	**
Binissalem/Balearic Islands				
Macia Batle	White	Fruity, floral	Fish, chicken, veal	**
Castilla-La Mancha				
Ayuso Estola	Red	Berry, earthy	Pork, veal, lamb	**
Casa de la Viña	Red	Plums, earthy	Beef, lamb, pork	**
La Invincible Valdeazor	Red	Plums, spicy	Beef, lamb, pork	**
Piqueras Castillo de Almansa	Red	Plums, berry	Veal, pork, beef	**
Vinícola de Castilla Castillo de Alhambra	Red	Plums, jam	Pork, lamb, beef	**
Castilla-León				
Abadia Retuerta	Red	Berry, licorice	Pizza, pork, cheese	*
Abadia Retuerta Abado Retuerta Cuvée el Campanario	Red	Berry, oaky	Pork, beef, cheese	***
Abadia Retuerta Abado Retuerta Pago Negralada	Red	Berry, oaky	Pork, beef, cheese	***
Alejandro Fernández Pesquera	Red	Plums, leathery, earthy	Lamb, beef, pork	**
Alión	Red	Plums, earthy, oaky	Lamb, beef, cheese	***
Alvárez y Díaz Mantel Blanco Sauvignon Blanc	White	Herbaceous, zingy	Shellfish, salads	**
Angel Lorenzo Chachazo Carmín	Rosé	Fruity, floral	Antipasto, salads, shellfish	**
Antaño Viña Mocen Rueda Superior	White	Spicy, fruity	Shellfish, fish	**
Arroyo Tinto Arroyo	Red	Berry, spicy	Veal, pork, lamb	**
Balbas Ardal	Red	Berry, spicy	Pork, lamb, beef	**
Blancos de Castilla Marqués de Riscal Sauvignon	White	Herbaceous, zingy	Shellfish, salads	**
Briego Albe Briego	Red	Berry, earthy	Lamb, beef, pork	**
Cerrosol Doña Beatriz	White	Spicy, fruity	Shellfish, fish	**
Condada de Haza Alenza	Red	Plums, earthy, oaky	Lamb, beef, cheese	***
Condado de Haza	Red	Plums, leathery, spicy	Lamb, beef, pork	***
Dehesa de los Canónigos	Red	Plums, spicy	Lamb, beef, pork	**
Emilio Moro	Red	Berry, spicy	Veal, beef, pork	**
Félix Callejo Callejo	Red	Plums, spicy	Lamb, beef, pork	**

Wine name	Style	Flavor/ Bouquet	Compatible Foods	Price Range
Félix Sanz Viña Cimbron Rueda Superior	White	Spicy, fruity	Shellfish, fish	**
Fuentespina	Red	Plums, spicy	Lamb, beef, pork	**
Gormaz Doce Linajes Roble	Red	Plums, spicy	Lamb, beef, cheese	**
Grandes Bodegas Marqués de Velilla	Red	Plums, spicy	Lamb, beef, pork	**
Hacienda Monasterio Dominio de Pingus	Red	Plums, oaky	Lamb, beef, pork	**
Herederos de Doroteo San Juan Blasón de Costajan	Red	Plums, spicy	Lamb, beef, pork	**
Javier Sanz Villa Narcisa Rueda Superior	White	Spicy, fruity	Shellfish, fish	**
López Cristobal	Red	Plums, spicy	Lamb, beef, pork	**
Los Curros Yllera	Red	Plums, berry	Chicken, beef, pork	**
Mauro San Roman	Red	Berry, spicy	Pizza, pork, beef	**
Perez Caramés Casar de Santa Inés	Red	Berry, spicy	Pizza, pasta, pork	**
Real Sitio de Ventosilla Pradorey	Red	Berry, vanillin	Lamb, beef, pork	**
Reyes Teófilo Reyes	Red	Plums, leathery, earthy, complex	Lamb, beef, pork	***
Santa Eulalia Riberal	Red	Plums, leathery	Lamb, beef, pork	**
Valpincia	Red	Plums, spicy	Lamb, beef, pork	**
Vega Sicilia Único	Red	Rich, complex, plums, earthy	Lamb, beef, cheese	***
Catalonia				
Agustí Torelló Mata	Sparkling	Crisp, minerally	Cold meats, shellfish	**
Albet i Noya Tempranillo D'Anyada	Red	Berry, vanillin	Pork, beef, lamb	**
Antonio Mascaró Mascaró Brut Monarch	Sparkling	Crisp, minerally	Cold meats, shellfish	**
Can Rafols dels Caus Gran Caus	Sparkling	Crisp, minerally	Cold meats, shellfish	**
Canals & Munné Brut Nature	Sparkling	Crisp, minerally	Shellfish, Asian	**
Castell del Remei 1780	Red	Plums, spicy	Pork, veal, beef	**
Cavas Recaredo Recaredo Brut Nature	Sparkling	Austere, stone fruit	Shellfish, Asian	**
Caves Catasús Casanovas Mas Xarot Gran Reserva	Sparkling	Crisp, powerful	Cold meats, cheese, fish	**
Clos Mogador	Red	Berry, vanillin	Pork, lamb, beef	**
Codorníu Gran Codorníu	Sparkling	Yeasty, rich	Cold meats, shellfish, nuts	**
Codorníu Jaume de Codorníu	Sparkling	Crisp, nutty	Cold meats, cheese, fish, pasta	**
Costers del Siurana Dolç de L'Obac	Sweet	Berry, toasty	Pork, lamb, beef	**
Ferret Ezequiel Ferret	Sparkling	Crisp, minerally	Cold meats, shellfish	**
Jean León Merlot	Red	Plums, spicy	Lamb, beef	**
Joan Raventós Rosell Heretat Vall-Ventos Chenin	White	Fruity, floral	Salads, pasta, fish	**
Josep María Raventós i Blanc Reserva Personal Manuel Raventós	Sparkling	Nutty, yeasty	Asian, nuts	**
Juve y Camps Gran Juve Camps	Sparkling	Crisp, minerally	Cold meats, shellfish	**
Mas Martinet Vinicultors Clos Martinet	Red	Berry, spicy	Pork, lamb, beef	**
Masroig Les Sorts	Red	Plums, spicy	Beef, lamb, pork	**
Miguel Torres Gran Coronas	Red	Plums, earthy	Lamb, beef, pork	**
Miguel Torres Gran Viña Sol	White	Rich, fruity	Pasta, chicken	**
Miguel Torres Mas la Plana Gran Coronas	Red	Plums, toasty	Lamb, beef, pork	***
Miguel Torres Viña Esmerelda	White	Spicy, fruity	Shellfish, salads	**
Nadal Cava Nadal Especial	Sparkling	Crisp, minerally	Cold meats, shellfish	**

Wine name	Style	Flavor/ Bouquet	Compatible Foods	Price Range
Parxet Marqués de Alella Chardonnay	White	Apples, fruity	Fish, chicken	**
Parxet Marqués de Alella Clásico	White	Stone fruit, floral	Shellfish, fish, chicken	**
Reserva Mont-Ferrant Mont-Ferrant Brut Reserva	Sparkling	Nutty, stone fruit	Fish, Asian	**
Rimarts	Red	Berry, spicy	Chicken, veal, beef	**
Segura Viudas Reserva Heredad	Sparkling	Powerful, minerally	Fish, pasta, Asian	**
Signat	Sparkling	Crisp, minerally	Cold meats, shellfish	**
Vilella de la Cartoixa Fra Fulco Selecció	Red	Berry, spicy	Pork, lamb, beef	**
Vinícola del Priorat L'Arc	Red	Berry, spicy	Pork, lamb, beef	**
Murcia				
Agapito Rico Carchelo	Red	Plums, jam	Pasta, pork	**
Agapito Rico Carchelo Syrah	Red	Berry, spicy	Pork, lamb	**
Castaño Monastrell	Red	Plums, earthy	Beef, lamb, pork	**
Finca Luzón Castillo de Luzón	Red	Plums, jam	Pasta, pork, veal	**
Julia Roch e Hijos Casa Castillo Monastrell	Red	Plums, earthy	Pork, veal, beef	**
Navarra				
Castillo de Monjardín	White	Fruity, floral	Fish, chicken, pasta	**
Guelbenzu Lautus	Red	Berry, vanillin	Pork, beef, lamb	**
Irache Castillo Irache	Red	Plums, earthy	Lamb, beef, cheese	**
Julian Chivite Chivite Colección 125	White	Stone fruit, minerally	Fish, chicken, pasta	**
Julian Chivite Gran Feudo	Rosé	Fruity, floral	Salads, Asian, fish	**
Marco Real Homenaje	Red	Berry, spicy	Pizza, pork, beef	**
Rías Baixas/Galacia				
Adegas Galegas Don Pedro de Soutomaior Carballo	White	Stone fruit, minerally	Shellfish, fish	**
Adegas Galegas Veigadares	White	Floral, minerally	Shellfish, fish	**
Agro de Bazán Granbazan Ambar	White	Crisp, minerally	Shellfish, fish	**
La Val Viña Ludy	White	Minerally, floral	Shellfish, fish	**
Martín Códax	White	Minerally, floral	Shellfish, fish	**
Palacio de Fefiñanes Albariño	White	Minerally, floral	Shellfish, Asian	**
Rioja				
Bretón y Cía Dominio de Conte	Red	Berry, licorice, oaky	Veal, pork, beef	**
Campillo Reserva Especial	Red	Earthy, spicy	Lamb, cheese	**
Compañía Vinícola del Norte de España Real de Asúa	Red	Earthy, leathery	Lamb, beef, cheese	**
Contino Graciano	Red	Earthy, mushrooms	Lamb, beef, cheese	**
Cosecheros Alaveses Artadi Pagos Viejos	Red	Plums, earthy	Lamb, pork, beef	**
Escudero Solar de Becquer	Red	Berry, spicy	Lamb, pork, beef	**
Faustino Crianza	Red	Gamey, leathery	Cheese, lamb	*
Finace Allende Aurus	Red	Plums, spicy	Beef, lamb, pork	**
Granja Ntra. Sra. de Remelluri Remelluri	Red	Plums, vanillin	Lamb, beef, cheese	***
Herminia Viña Herminia	Red	Plums, spicy	Beef, lamb, pork	**
La Rioja Alta Gran Reserva 904	Red	Earthy, spicy	Beef, lamb, pork	***
La Rioja Alta Viña Ardanza	Red	Plums, earthy	Beef, lamb, pork	**
Lan Viña Lanciano	Red	Plums, earthy	Beef, lamb, pork	**
Lopez Heredia Viña Tondonia	Red	Plums, spicy	Beef, lamb, pork	**

Wine name	Style	Flavor/ Bouquet	Compatible Foods	Price Range
Luís Cañas	Red	Plums, spicy	Beef, lamb, pork	**
Luís Cañas Recian	Red	Plums, spicy	Beef, lamb, pork	**
Marqués de Murrieta Castillo Ygay	Red	Rich, plums, earthy, toasty	Beef, lamb, pork	**
Marqués de Murrieta Dalmau	Red	Plums, spicy	Beef, lamb, pork	**
Marqués de Riscal	Red	Earthy, leathery	Beef, lamb, pork	**
Marqués de Riscal Baron de Chirel	Red	Plums, spicy	Beef, lamb, pork	**
Martínez Bujanda Finca Valpiedra	Red	Berry, licorice, oaky	Veal, pork, beef	***
Martínez Bujanda Valdemar	Red	Plums, earthy, spicy, oaky	Beef, lamb, pork	**
Martínez Bujanda Vendímia Selecciónada	Red	Complex, earthy	Beef, lamb, pork	***
Montecillo	Red	Earthy, gamey	Lamb, cheese	**
Muga Prado Enea	Red	Rich, oaky	Beef, lamb, pork	***
Palacio Reserva Especial	Red	Plums, spicy	Beef, lamb, pork	**
Primicia Viña Carravalseca	Red	Plums, earthy	Beef, lamb, pork	**
Primicia Viña Diezmo	Red	Plums, spicy	Beef, lamb, pork	**
Remirez de Ganuza	Red	Plums, spicy	Beef, lamb, pork	**
Riojanas Monte Real	Red	Plums, earthy	Beef, lamb, pork	**
Riojanas Viña Albina	Red	Plums, spicy	Beef, lamb, pork	**
Roda I	Red	Rich, oaky	Beef, lamb, pork	***
Sierra Cantabria Collección Privada	Red	Plums, spicy	Beef, lamb, pork	**
Torre de Oña Baron de Oña	Red	Berry, oaky	Beef, lamb, pork	**
Union de Cosecheros de Labastida Manuel Quintano	Red	Plums, spicy	Beef, lamb, pork	**
Union Viti-Vinícola Gaudium	Red	Earthy, spicy	Beef, lamb, pork	**
Valdelana	Red	Plums, spicy	Beef, lamb, pork	**
Viña Herminia Duque de Huescar	Red	Plums, spicy	Beef, lamb, pork	**

PORTUGAL

Alentejano

Finagra Esporão Touriga Nacional	Red	Gamey, berry	Cold meats, stew, offal	**
Hans Kristian Jørgensen Cortes de Cima Reserva	Red	Earthy, plums	Veal	**
João Portugal Ramos Antão Vaz	White	Crisp, citrus	Salads	**
João Portugal Ramos Marquês de Borba	White	Citrus, minerally, crisp	Fish	**
João Portugal Ramos Trincadeira	Red	Berry, earthy	Cold meats, stew, offal	**
José Maria da Fonseca José de Sousa Mayor	Red	Berry, gamey	Veal	**
Quinta do Mouro	Red	Earthy, gamey	Pork	**
Soc. Agrícola Quinta do Carma Quinta do Carmo	Red	Smoky, berry	Pizza	*

Alentejo

Finagra Esporão Reguengos Reserva	White	Fruity, citrus	Chicken	**
Fundação Eugénio de Almeida Cartuxa Reserva	Red	Smoky, berry	Stew	**
João Portugal Ramos Marquês de Borba Reserva	Red	Smoky, spicy	Lamb	**

Algarve

Adega Co-op. de Lagoa Afonso XIII	Fortified	Spirity, powerful, complex	Nuts	**

Bairrada

Caves Aliança Garrafeira	Red	Berry, tannic	Stew	**

Wine name	Style	Flavor/ Bouquet	Compatible Foods	Price Range
Luis Pato Vinha Barrosa	Red	Spicy, berry	Pasta	**
Beiras				
Castas de Santar Touriga Nacional	Red	Gamey, berry	Cold meats	**
Caves Primavera Lda. Primavera Baga/Cabernet Sauvignon	Red	Berry, herbaceous	Game	**
Caves São João Poço do Lobo Cabernet Sauvignon	Red	Herbaceous, spicy, berry	Lamb	**
Quinta de Foz de Arouce	Red	Spicy, berry	Stew	*
Soc. Agrícola das Beiras Entre Serras Colheita Seleccionada	Red	Spicy, berry	Pizza	*
Sociedade Agrícola da Beira Entra Serras Chardonnay	White	Citrus, fruity	Chicken	**
Bucelas				
Alcântara Agrícola Morgado de Sta. Catherina	White	Floral, citrus	Fish	**
Quinta de Murta	White	Crisp, floral	Salads	**
Carcavelos				
Quinta da Barão Carcavelos range, Old wines	Fortified	Spirity, berry, nutty	Nuts	**
Quinta dos Pesos Carcavelos range, Old wines	Fortified	Spirity, powerful, rich	Cheese	**
Dão				
Caves Messias Messias Reserva Touriga Nacional	Red	Berry, tannic	Beef	**
Caves São João Porta dos Cavaleiros Reserva Seleccionada	White	Citrus, minerally	Fish	**
Maria de Lourdes Osório Quinta da Ponte Pedrinha	Red	Smoky, berry	Mediterranean	**
Pedro Borges da Gama Quinta da Alameda Touriga Nacional	Red	Smoky, tannic	Sausages	**
Quinta de Saes Quinta da Pellada 100% Touriga Nacional	Red	Berry, tannic	Cold meats, stew, offal	**
Quinta de Saes Quinta da Pellada Jaen/Touriga Nacional	Red	Berry, smoky	Cold meats	**
Quinta dos Roques Alfrocheiro Preto	Red	Berry, gamey	Pasta	**
Quinta dos Roques Reserva	Red	Berry, tannic	Cold meats, stew, offal	**
Quinta dos Roques Tinta Roriz	Red	Berry, plums	Cold meats	**
Quinta dos Roques Touriga Nacional	Red	Berry, tannic	Pasta	**
Douro				
Casa Burmester	Red	Berry, plums	Veal	**
Casa Ferreirinha Barca Velha	Red	Powerful, berry, spicy	Beef	***
Casa Ferreirinha Quinta da Leda Touriga Nacional	Red	Berry, tannic	Sausages	**
Casa Ferreirinha Reserva Especial	Red	Berry, tannic	Cold meats, stew, offal	**
Domingos Alves de Sousa Quinta da Gaivosa	Red	Tannic, earthy	Game	**
Domingos Alves de Sousa Quinta do Vale da Raposa Tinta Cão	Red	Tannic, spicy	Stew	**
José Arnaldo Coutinho Quinta de Mosteirô	Red	Spicy, berry	Sausages	**
Lemos & van Zeller Quinta do Vale D. Maria	Red	Spicy, berry	Cold meats, stew, offal	**
Maria Antónia Ferreirinha Vallado	Red	Berry, tannic	Stew	**
Niepoort Passadouro	Red	Spicy, earthy, tannic	Sausages	**
Niepoort Redoma	Red	Spicy, earthy	Cheese	**
Quinta do Noval Vinhos Quinta de Roriz	Red	Berry, tannic	Pasta	**
Ramos Pinto Duas Quintas	Red	Berry, tannic	Sausages	**
Ramos Pinto Duas Quintas Reserva	Red	Plums, tannic	Stew	**
Real Companhia Velha Evel Grande Escolha	Red	Berry, plums	Sausages	**
Sandeman Confradeiro	Red	Berry, spicy	Cold meats, stew, offal	**
Soc. Agrícola da Quinta do Crasto Quinta do Crasto Reserva	Red	Berry, spicy	Cheese	**

Wine name	Style	Flavor/ Bouquet	Compatible Foods	Price Range
Soc. Quinta do Portal Quinta do Portal Reserva	Red	Gamey, berry	Lamb	**
Soc. Quinta do Portal Tinta Roriz	Red	Earthy, spicy	Cold meats, stew, offal	**
Sogrape Reserva	White	Minerally, citrus	Salads	**
Madeira				
Artur Barros & Sousa Madeira range, esp. Boal & Terrantez	Madeira	Nutty, complex	Cheese	**
Barbeito Madeira range	Madeira	Nutty, spirity, complex	Aperitif	**
Borges Madeira range	Madeira	Complex, rich	Cheese	**
Henriques & Henriques Madeira range	Madeira	Rich, nutty, complex	Nuts	**
Justino Henriques Madeira range	Madeira	Complex, nutty	Aperitif	**
Leacock, Rutherford & Miles Cossart Gordon Madeira range	Madeira	Nutty, complex	Nuts	**
Oliveira Madeira range	Madeira	Rich, complex	Nuts	**
Silva Vinhos Madeira range	Madeira	Complex, nutty	Nuts	**
Minho				
Quinta da Covela Covela Branco Colheita Seleccionada	White	Crisp, floral	Fish	**
Palmela				
José Maria da Fonseca Garrafeira CO	Red	Berry, gamey	Pizza	**
Soc. Agrícola de Pegos Claros Lda. Pegos Claros	Red	Berry, spicy	Stew	**
JP Vinhos JP Tinta Miúda	Red	Minerally, berry	Cold meats, stew, offal	**
Porto				
Barros Almeida Port range, esp. Colheitas	Port	Sweet, nutty	Chese	**
Borges & Irmã Port range	Port	Sweet, spirity	Cheese	**
Burmester Port range, esp. Colheitas, Vintage	Port	Spirity, sweet	Cheese	**
Cálem Port range, esp. Quinta de Foz	Port	Spirity, sweet	Cheese	**
Churchill Graham Port range, esp. Quinta da Gricha	Port	Complex, berry, sweet	Cheese	**
Churchill Port range, esp. Vintage	Port	Spirity, sweet, complex	Cheese	**
Cockburn Smithes Port range, including Quinta dos Canais	Port	Complex, sweet, spirity	Cheese	**
Croft Port range, including Delaforce	Port	Spirity, sweet	Nuts	**
Da Silva Port range, esp. Colheitas	Port	Sweet, spirity	Nuts	**
Dow Port range, esp. Vintage	Port	Rich, sweet, complex, spirity	Nuts	***
Ferreira Port range, esp. Vintage	Port	Spirity, sweet	Cheese	**
Fonseca Guimaraens Port range, esp. Vintage	Port	Complex, powerful, rich, sweet	Cheese	***
Gassiot Port range, esp. Quinta da Eira Velha	Port	Sweet, spirity	Cheese	**
Graham Port range, esp. Quinta dos Malvedos, Quinta del Vesúvio	Port	Rich, complex, sweet, spirity	Cheese	***
Kopke Port range, esp. Quinta de São Luiz	Port	Sweet, berry, spirity	Nuts	**
Messias Port range	Port	Sweet, rich	Nuts	**
Niepoort Port range, esp. old tawnies, Quinta do Passadouro	Port	Spirity, sweet	Cheese	**
Niepoort Port range, esp. Vintage	Port	Sweet, spirity	Nuts	**
Noval Port range, esp. Vintage, Nacional	Port	Sweet, complex, rich	Cheese	***
Osborne Port range, esp. Vintage	Port	Spirity, sweet	Cheese	**
Poças Port range	Port	Rich, spirity	Cheese	**
Quarles Harris Port range, esp. old tawnies	Port	Rich, nutty, spirity	Nuts	**
Quinta do Crasto	Port	Sweet, spirity	Cheese	**
Ramos–Pinto Port range, esp. Colheitas	Port	Rich, nutty, spirity	Nuts	**

Wine name	Style	Flavor/ Bouquet	Compatible Foods	Price Range
Rosa Port range	Port	Sweet, rich	Cheese	**
Royal Oporto Port range, esp. old tawnies	Port	Sweet, rich	Cheese	**
Rozés Port range	Port	Spirity, sweet	Cheese	**
Sandeman Port range, esp. Quinta do Vau	Port	Rich, sweet	Cheese	**
Smith-Woodhouse Port range, esp. Vintage	Port	Rich, sweet, spirity	Nuts	**
Taylor's Port range, esp. Vintage, Quinta de Vargellas, Quinta da Terra Feita	Port	Rich, complex, powerful, sweet	Cheese	***
Warre's Port range, esp. Quinta da Cavadinha	Port	Sweet, rich, berry, complex	Cheese	***
Ribatejano				
Soc. Agrícola Faldas da Quinta da Logoalva de Cima Quinta da Logoalva	Red	Berry, tannic	Stew	**
Falua Tercius	Red	Floral, zingy	Sausages	**
Setúbal				
JP Vinhos Moscatel de Setúbal Range, Vintage	Fortified	Spirity, sweet	Nuts	**
José Maria da Fonseca Moscatel de Setúbal Range, Vintage	Fortified	Sweet, spirity	Cheese	**
Trás-os-Montes				
Casal de Valle Pradinhos Valle Pradinhos	Red	Berry, gamey	Game	*
Ramos Pinto Quinta dos Bons Ares	Red	Berry, spicy	Game	**
Vinho Verde				
Aleixo Brito Caldas Quinta da Baguinha Alvarinho	White	Citrus, minerally	Fish	**
António Esteves Ferreirinha Soalheiro Alvarinho	White	Crisp, minerally	Shellfish	**
Coop. Regional de Monção Alvarinho Deu la Deu	White	Crisp, citrus	Mediterranean	**
Dona Paterna	White	Zingy, floral	Shellfish	**
Encostas de Paderne Alvarinho	White	Fruity, crisp	Asian	**

ENGLAND AND WALES

Hampshire/Wessex				
Wooldings Vintage Brut	Sparkling	Citrus, minerally, crisp	Shellfish, fish	**
Southwest and Wales				
Beenleigh Red (Sharpham Partnership)	Red	Berry, plums, herbaceous	Veal, pork, beef	**
Three Choirs Vineyards Phoenix/Seyval	White	Grassy, tangy	Shellfish, Asian	**
Three Choirs Vineyards Siegerrebe	White	Citrus, spicy, tangy	Shellfish, Asian	**
Thames and Chiltern				
Chiltern Valley Dry	White	Fruity, floral	Asian, fish	**
Old Luxters Dessert Wine (Chiltern Valley)	Sweet	Honey, waxy, floral	Dessert	**
Thames Valley Vineyards Clocktower Pinot Noir	Red	Berry, spicy	Fish, chicken, pork	**
Thames Valley Vineyards Heritage Brut	Sparkling	Citrus, crisp	Shellfish, fish	**
Thames Valley Vineyards Heritage Fumé	White	Fruity, oaky	Fish, chicken	**
Weald and Downland				
Biddenden Ortega	White	Floral, herbaceous	Shellfish, salads	**
Breaky Bottom Seyval Brut	Sparkling	Citrus, crisp	Shellfish, fish	**
Breaky Bottom Seyval Dry	White	Grassy, tangy	Shellfish, Asian	**
Chapel Down Bacchus	White	Floral, fruity, herbaceous	Shellfish, fish, Asian	**
Chapel Down Epoch I	Red	Berry, plums, spicy	Veal, pork, beef	**

Wine name	Style	Flavor/ Bouquet	Compatible Foods	Price Range
Chapel Down Epoch Vintage Brut	Sparkling	Citrus, minerally	Shellfish, nuts	**
Chapel Down Schönburger	White	Stone fruit, spicy	Asian, fish	**
Denbies Wine Estate Dornfelder/Pinot Noir	Red	Fruity, spicy	Chicken, fish	**
Denbies Wine Estate Special Late Harvested	Sweet	Fruity, honey, floral	Dessert	**
Denbies Wine Estate Surrey Gold	White	Fruity, floral	Asian, fish	**
Denbines Wine Estate Pinot Blanc	White	Stone fruit, nutty, minerally	Fish, chicken	**
Hidden Spring Dark Fields Red	Red	Berry, spicy	Pizza, chicken	**
Nutborne Sussex Reserve	White	Fruity, floral	Asian, fish	**
Nyetimber Classic Cuvée Vintage Brut	Sparkling	Citrus, minerally, yeasty	Shellfish, fish	***
Nyetimber Première Cuvée Blanc de Blancs Vintage Brut	Sparkling	Apples, citrus, minerally, yeasty	Shellfish, nuts	***
Ridge View Estate Cuvée Merret Brut	Sparkling	Citrus, crisp	Shellfish, fish	**

CENTRAL EUROPE

CZECH REPUBLIC/Moravia

Mikros-vin Gruener Veltliner	White	Spicy, crisp	Fish	**
Novy Saldorf Znojmo Spalkovy	Red	Berry, earthy	Pasta	**
Velke Pavlovice Radomil Aloun Neuburger Spaetlese	White	Citrus, medium-sweet	Veal	**
Velke Pavlovice Vinium a. s. Pinot Blanc Kabinet	White	Melon, minerally	Fish	**
Znovin Znojmo Riesling Praedikat (spaetlese equivalent)	White	Sweet, floral	Fish	**

CZECH REPUBLIC/Velke Zernoseky/Bohemia

Vendule Zernosecke Vinarstvi s.r.o Riesling Kabinet	White	Floral, minerally, spicy	Salads	**

SLOVAK REPUBLIC

Pezinok Dornfelder	Red	Plums, smoky	Cold meats	**
Vino Nitra Barrique Cabernet Sauvignon	Red	Berry, herbaceous	Lamb	**

HUNGARY/Lake Balaton

Fine Wine Borászati Vállalkozás Pécselyi Sémillon	White	Honey, nutty	Fish, chicken, veal	**
Ôdon Pince Olaszrizling	White	Floral, rich	Asian, fish	**
Szent Donatus Pincészct Kft Balatonlellei Cabernet	Red	Plums, earthy	Beef, lamb	**
Szent Orbán Pince Irsai Olivér	White	Floral, fruity	Fruit, Asian	*
Szent Orbán Pince Olaszrizling Late Harvest	White	Floral, fruity	Asian, dessert	**

HUNGARY/Eger/The Northeast

GIA Kft Egri Barrique Chardonnay	White	Apples, vanillin	Fish, chicken	**
GIA Kft Egri Bikavér	Red	Berry, spicy	Chicken, veal, pork	**
Lauder-Láng Pinceszét Egri Bikavér	Red	Berry, spicy	Chicken, veal, pork	**
Thummerer Pince Egri Bikavér	Red	Berry, spicy	Chicken, veal, pork	**
Vincze Béla Magánpincézete Egri Cabernet Sauvignon	Red	Plums, earthy	Beef, lamb	**
Zwack Kft Egri Bikavér	Red	Berry, spicy	Chicken, veal, pork	**

HUNGARY/The Northwest

Franz Weninger Soproni Kékfrankos Barrique	Red	Fruity, peppery, oaky	Pork, beef	**
Györgykovács Pince Furmint	White	Spicy, zingy	Fish, chicken, pasta	**
Györgykovács Pince Hárslevel"o	White	Floral, spicy	Fish, chicken	**
Hilltop Neszmély Rt Riverview Kékfrankos	Red	Plums, peppery	Pizza, pork, beef	**

Wine name	Style	Flavor/ Bouquet	Compatible Foods	Price Range
HUNGARY/The Southwest				
Aliscavin Borászati Rt Cabernet Franc	Red	Plums, berry	Pork, beef, lamb	**
Bajor Pince Siklósi Rajnai Rizling	White	Floral, fruity	Asian, shellfish	**
Bock Pince Villányi Cabernet Sauvignon	Red	Plums, spicy	Pork, beef, lamb	**
Európai Bortermel˝ok Kft Bátáapati Estate Barrique Chardonnay	White	Apples, vanillin	Fish, chicken	**
Európai Bortermel˝ok Kft Mocsényi Sauvignon Blanc	White	Citrus, herbaceous	Shellfish, cheese	**
Heimann Ferenc Szekszárdi Bikavér	Red	Berry, spicy	Chicken, veal, pork	**
Takler Pince Szekszárdi Bikavér	Red	Berry, spicy	Chicken, veal, pork	**
Takler Pince Szekszárdi Merlot	Red	Plums, jam	Veal, pork, beef	**
Tiffán's Bt Cabernet Sauvignon/Kékfrankos	Red	Berry, spicy	Veal, pork, beef	**
Tiffán's Bt Kékoportó Vylyan Rt Villányi Kékoportó Barrique	Red	Powerful, oaky	Beef, lamb	**
Vida Pince Szekszárdi Cabernet Franc/Merlot	Red	Berry, jam, earthy	Pork, beef, lamb	**
Vida Pince Szekszárdi Merlot	Red	Plums, jam	Veal, pork, beef	**
Vylyan Rt Villányi Cabernet Sauvignon	Red	Plums, leathery	Pork, beef, lamb	**
HUNGARY/Tokaj-Hegyalja				
Ch Pajzos és Ch Megyer Rt Aszús under the Pajzos label Disznók˝o Rt Aszús	Sweet	Honey, waxy, floral, nutty	Dessert	***
Márta Wille-Baumkauff Pince Kft Aszús	Sweet	Honey, waxy, floral, nutty	Dessert	***
Royal Tokaji Wine Company Kft Aszús	Sweet	Honey, waxy, floral, nutty	Dessert	***
Tokaj Oremus Kft Aszús	Sweet	Honey, waxy, floral, nutty	Dessert	***
SLOVENIA/Podravje				
Jeruzalem Ormoz VVS d.d. Renski Rizling	White	Floral, minerally	Fish	**
Kemetijski Kombinat Ptuj Chardonnay	White	Melon, citrus	Chicken	**
Kmecka Zadruga Krsko Cvicek	Red	Berry, spicy	Game	*
Kmetijska Zadruga Metliska Crnina	Red	Berry, earthy	Game	*
Ljutomercan d.d. Ranina	White	Crisp, fruity	Fish	**
Radgonske Gorice d.d. Zlata Radgonska Penina Demi-sec	Sparkling	Crisp, medium-sweet, fruity	Aperitif	**
Slovenske Konjice Zlati Gric Renski Rizling–Jagodni Izbor	Sweet	Sweet, citrus	Fruit	**
Valter Zorin Poljcane Laski Rizling–Suhi Jagodni Izbor	Sweet	Sweet, citrus	Cheese	**
Vinag d.d. Maribor Sauvignon–Pozna Trgatev	Sweet	Sweet, zingy	Shellfish	**
Vino Brezice d.d. Chardonnay–Jagodni Izbor	Sweet	Sweet, melon	Fruit	**
Vino Brezice d.d. Laski Rizling–Jagodni Izbor	Sweet	Sweet, floral	Cheese	**
SLOVENIA/Primorska				
Agroind Vipava 1894 d.d. Cabernet Sauvignon	Red	Berry, herbaceous	Lamb	**
Agroind Vipava 1894 d.d. Laski Rizling	White	Floral, citrus	Shellfish	*
Agroind Vipava 1894 d.d. Theodosius Extra Dry	Sparkling	Crisp, minerally	Aperitif	**
Kmetijska Zadruga Kraski Teran	Red	Berry, spicy	Pasta	**
Kmetijska Zadruga Sivi Pinot	White	Zingy, citrus	Salads	*
Vinakoper Cabernet Sauvignon	Red	Berry, herbaceous	Lamb	**
Vinakoper Chardonnay Prestige	White	Tropical fruit, oaky	Chicken	**
Vinakoper Malvazija	White	Minerally, citrus	Fish	**
MONTENEGRO/Plantaze Agrokombinat Podg				
Monte Cheval Vranac	Red	Berry, plums	Sausages	**

Wine name	Style	Flavor/ Bouquet	Compatible Foods	Price Range
EASTERN EUROPE				
BULGARIA/Eastern Region				
Domaine Boyar Schumen Premium Cuveé Cabernet Sauvignon	Red	Berry, herbaceous	Lamb	**
Domaine Boyar Schumen Premium Oak Chardonnay	White	Tropical fruit, oaky	Veal	**
Preslav Khan Krum Chardonnay Reserve	White	Tropical fruit, oaky	Chicken	**
BULGARIA/Northern Region				
Controliran Yantra Valley Cabernet Sauvignon	Red	Berry, herbaceous	Cold meats	**
Russe Chardonnay Reserve	White	Tropical fruit, oaky	Chicken	**
Suhindol Cabernet Sauvignon Estate Selection	Red	Berry, herbaceous, tannic	Beef	**
BULGARIA/Southern Region				
Domaine Boyar Iambol Premium Reserve Merlot Gamza	Red	Plums, spicy	Cheese	**
Sakar Azbuka Merlot	Red	Plums, spicy	Cheese	**
Stambolovo Merlot Reserve	Red	Fruit cake, berry	Lamb	**
BULGARIA/Sub-Balkan Region				
Azbuka Sliven Cabernet Sauvignon	Red	Berry, herbaceous	Pasta	**
Sliven Cabernet Sauvignon Reserve	Red	Berry, tannic, herbaceous	Lamb	**
ROMANIA				
Carl Reh Winery River Route Pinot Grigio	White	Crisp, minerally	Fish	**
Dealul-Mare Premiat Merlot	Red	Berry, spicy	Chicken, veal, pork	*
Dealul-Mare Valley of the Monks Merlot	Red	Berry, herbaceous	Chicken, veal, pork	*
Murfatlar Pinot Gris	White	Floral, apples	Shellfish, fish	*
St. Ursula Lupu Negru Cabernet Sauvignon Merlot	Red	Berry, herbaceous	Lamb	**
GEORGIA				
Georgian Wines & Spirits Co Matrasa	Red	Berry, earthy	Sausages	**
SOUTHERN EUROPE				
GREECE/Aegean Islands				
Samos Co-op Samos Nectar	Sweet	Honey, floral, tropical fruit	Dessert	*
Greece/Macedonia				
Domaine Carras Cimnio Cotes de Meliton	Red	Berry, spicy	Pork, beef	**
Domaine Carras Melisanthi Cotes de Meliton	White	Honey, floral	Fish, chicken	**
GREECE/Mainland Greece				
Babatzim Portogo Thessaloniki	Red	Earthy, peppery	Beef, lamb	**
Semeli Chateau Semeli	Red	Rich, plums, earthy, oaky	Beef, lamb	**
Greece/Peloponnese				
Ambelones Tselepos Mantinia	White	Crisp, citrus, zingy	Shellfish, salads	**
Ktima Papaioannou Palea Klimata	Red	Berry, spicy	Veal, pork, beef	**
MALTA				
Delicata Grand Vin de Hauteville–Cabernet Sauvignon	Red	Berry, spicy	Sausages	**
Delicata Green Label Dry	White	Zingy, citrus	Fish	*
Delicata Paradise Bay Red	Red	Earthy, berry	Pasta	**
Delicata Red Label Gellewza	Red	Berry, spicy	Pizza	**
Delicata St. Paul's Bay White	White	Fruity, melon	Fish	*

Wine name	Style	Flavor/ Bouquet	Compatible Foods	Price Range
Marsovin Antonin Red	Red	Earthy, spicy	Pasta	*
Marsovin Cassar de Malte, Méthode Traditionelle	Sparkling	Crisp, fruity	Aperitif	**
CYPRUS				
ETKO Olympus	Red	Smoky, berry	Cold meats	**
ETKO Salera Red	Red	Berry, gamey	Pasta	*
KEO Alkion	White	Crisp, citrus	Shellfish	*
KEO Commanderie St. John	Sweet	Sweet, honey, raisiny	Nuts	**
KEO Heritage	Red	Earthy, berry	Sausages	**

AFRICA

ALGERIA/Alger

ONCV Miliana Coteaux du Zaccar	Red	Berry, plums	Stew	**

ALGERIA/Oran

ONCV Algerian Red	Red	Earthy, spicy	Cold meats, stew, offal	*
ONCV El Bordj Domaine El Bordj	Red	Berry, spicy	Stew	**
ONCV Tlemcem Impressions	Red	Berry, spicy	Sausages	**
ONCV Tlemcem Sand Ripples	Red	Plums, spicy	Pasta	*

SOUTH AFRICA

Coastal

Graham Beck Pinotage	Red	Earthy, berry	Sausages	**
KWV Cathedral Cellars Cabernet Sauvignon	Red	Berry, herbaceous	Lamb	**
KWV Cathedral Cellars Pinotage	Red	Berry, earthy	Cold meats, stew, offal	**

Constantia

Buitenverwachting Chardonnay	White	Melon, citrus	Chicken	**
Buitenverwachting Christine Red Blend	Red	Berry, smoky	Cold meats, stew, offal	**
Constantia Uitsig Reserve Chardonnay	White	Melon, oaky	Chicken	**
Groot Constantia Chardonnay Reserve	White	Citrus, apples	Chicken	**
Groot Constantia Shiraz	Red	Earthy, berry	Beef	**
Klein Constantia Shiraz	Red	Earthy, plums	Beef	**
Steenberg Oaked Semillon	White	Grassy, oaky	Veal	**

Durbanville

Diemersdal Pinotage	Red	Berry, plums	Cold meats, stew, offal	**

Franschhoek

Boekenhoutskloof Shiraz	Red	Berry, tannic	Sausages	**
Boschendal Chardonnay Reserve	White	Tropical fruit, oaky, spicy	Veal	**
Plaisir de Merle Cabernet Sauvignon	Red	Herbaceous, tannic	Lamb	**

Klein Karoo

Boplaas Port	Fortified	Sweet, raisiny	Cheese	**
Boplaas Vintage Reserve Port	Fortified	Sweet, spirity, fruity	Cheese	**
Karoo Die Krans Vintage Reserve Port	Fortified	Sweet, spirity, powerful	Nuts	**

Paarl

Backsberg Cabernet Sauvignon	Red	Berry, tannic, herbaceous	Lamb	**

Wine name	Style	Flavor/ Bouquet	Compatible Foods	Price Range
Backsberg Shiraz	Red	Earthy, tannic	Beef	**
Cape Levant Pinotage	Red	Berry, earthy	Stew	**
Fairview Cabernet Sauvignon	Red	Berry, herbaceous	Lamb	**
Fairview Shiraz	Red	Berry, gamey	Stew	**
Glen Carlou (Reserve) Chardonnay	White	Tropical fruit, oaky	Fish	**
Glen Carlou Peter Devereux Chenin Blanc	White	Apples, tropical fruit	Fish	**
Nederburg Auction Cabernet Sauvignon	Red	Berry, herbaceous	Lamb	**
Nederburg Bin R115 Red Blend	Red	Spicy, berry	Beef	**
Nederburg Bin S316 Noble Late Harvest	Sweet	Sweet, citrus	Dessert	**
Nederburg Edelkeur Dessert Wine	Sweet	Sweet, mandarin	Dessert	***
Nederburg Eminence Dessert Wine	Sweet	Sweet, complex, mandarin	Dessert	***
Nederburg Noble Late Harvest Dessert Wine	Sweet	Sweet, citrus	Dessert	**
Simonsvlei Hercules Paragon Shiraz	Red	Berry, earthy	Cold meats, stew, offal	**
Veenwouden Merlot	Red	Plums, fruit cake	Lamb	**
Robertson				
De Wetshof Finesse Chardonnay	White	Tropical fruit, melon	Fish	**
De Wetshof Noble Late Harvest	Sweet	Sweet, mandarin	Dessert	**
Graham Beck The Ridge Shiraz	Red	Berry, tannic, earthy	Cheese	**
Zandvliet Chardonnay	White	Melon, minerally	Fish	**
Stellenbosch				
Alto Cabernet Sauvignon	Red	Tannic, herbaceous	Lamb	**
Beryerskloof Pinotage	Red	Berry, leathery	Pizza	**
Bouwland Cabernet Merlot	Red	Herbaceous, plums	Lamb	**
Bouwland Pinotage	Red	Leathery, plums	Stew	**
Cordoba Shiraz	Red	Earthy, tannic, berry	Beef	**
De Trafford Shiraz	Red	Berry, earthy	Cold meats, stew, offal	**
Delheim Cabernet Sauvignon	Red	Berry, herbaceous	Lamb	**
Delheim Shiraz	Red	Earthy, tannic, berry	Beef	**
Genesis Cabernet Sauvignon	Red	Herbaceous, tannic	Lamb	**
Grangehurst CIWG Cabernet Sauvignon	Red	Berry, minerally, complex	Lamb	***
Grangehurst CIWG Pinotage	Red	Berry, earthy	Stew	**
Grangehurst Merlot	Red	Fruit cake, complex	Game	***
Grangehurst Red Blend	Red	Complex, tannic, berry	Beef	***
Hartenberg Chardonnay	White	Melon, tropical fruit	Fish	**
Hartenberg Shiraz	Red	Earthy, berry	Beef	**
Hidden Valley Pinotage	Red	Earthy, leathery	Stew	**
Jacobsdal Pinotage	Red	Leathery, plums	Cold meats, stew, offal	**
Jordan Chardonnay	White	Melon, tropical fruit	Fish	**
Kaapzicht Pinotage	Red	Berry, plums	Stew	**
Kaapzicht Reserve Pinotage	Red	Berry, earthy, complex	Stew	**
Kanonkop CIWG Pinotage	Red	Earthy, berry	Stew	**
Kanonkop Paul Sauer Red Blend	Red	Berry, complex, tannic	Lamb	**
Kanonkop Pinotage	Red	Earthy, leathery	Stew	**

Wine name	Style	Flavor/ Bouquet	Compatible Foods	Price Range
L'Avenir Cabernet Sauvignon	Red	Berry, herbaceous	Lamb	**
L'Avenir CIWG Pinotage	Red	Berry, earthy	Stew	**
L'Avenir Vin de Meurveur Dessert Wine	Sweet	Sweet, citrus	Dessert	**
Laibach Cabernet Sauvignon	Red	Berry, herbaceous	Lamb	**
Le Riche Reserve Cabernet Sauvignon	Red	Herbaceous, berry	Lamb	**
Lievland Noble Late Harvest Reserve Dessert Wine	Sweet	Honey, sweet	Dessert	**
Longridge Merlot	Red	Plum, berry	Lamb	**
Meerlust Rubicon Red Blend	Red	Spicy, earthy, oaky	Beef	**
Morgenhof Premier Selection Red Blend	Red	Earthy, berry	Cheese	**
Neethlinghsof Semillon Noble Late Harvest Dessert Wine	Sweet	Sweet, mandarin	Dessert	**
Neil Ellis Cabernet Sauvignon	Red	Herbaceous, berry	Lamb	**
Neil Ellis Reserve Shiraz	Red	Berry, earthy	Cold meats, stew, offal	**
Overgaauw Cape Vintage Port	Fortified	Sweet, rich	Nuts	**
Overgaauw Touirga Nacional Port	Fortified	Sweet, raisiny	Cheese	**
Rust en Vrede Estate Red Blend	Red	Earthy, spicy	Pasta	**
Rusterberg Peter Barlow Red Blend	Red	Earthy, smoky	Cheese	**
Saxenburg Private Collection Pinotage	Red	Earthy, spicy	Cold meats, stew, offal	**
Saxenburg Reserve Shiraz	Red	Berry, spicy	Cold meats	***
Simonsig Frans Malan Reserve Red Blend	Red	Earthy, berry, oaky	Lamb	**
Simonsig Pinotage	Red	Earthy, spicy	Cold meats, stew, offal	**
Simonsig Reserve Shiraz	Red	Earthy, spicy, oaky	Beef	**
Simonsig Tiara Red Blend	Red	Fruity, berry	Cold meats	**
Slaley Shiraz	Red	Earthy, spicy	Pizza	**
Stellenzicht Chardonnay	White	Melon, oaky	Fish	**
Stellenzicht Reserve Semillon	White	Tropical fruit, citrus	Veal	**
Stellenzicht Syrah Shiraz	Red	Earthy, berry	Beef	**
Thelema Cabernet Sauvignon	Red	Herbaceous, berry	Cheese	***
Thelema Eds Reserve Chardonnay	White	Citrus, oaky	Veal	**
Thelema Merlot	Red	Plums, berry	Lamb	**
Uiterwyk Estate Blend Red Blend	Red	Earthy, berry	Beef	**
Uiterwyk Top of the Hill Pinotage	Red	Earthy, spicy	Cold meats, stew, offal	**
Vergelegen Reserve Chardonnay	White	Melon, tropical fruit	Fish	**
Vergenoegd Cabernet Sauvignon	Red	Herbaceous, berry	Lamb	**
Vergenoegd Port	Fortified	Sweet, raisiny	Cheese	**
Warwick Chardonnay	White	Melon, tropical fruit	Fish	**
Warwick Trilogy Red Blend	Red	Earthy, smoky	Cold meats	**
Zevenwacht Chardonnay	White	Tropical fruit, citrus	Fish	**
Zevenwacht Reserve Merlot	Red	Plums, spicy	Beef	**
Zonnebloem Pinotage	Red	Earthy, spicy	Cold meats, stew, offal	**
Swartland				
Darling Cellars Cabernet Sauvignon	Red	Herbaceous, berry	Lamb	**
Darling Cellars Groenkloof Pinotage	Red	Spicy, earthy	Cold meats	**
Spice Route Reserve Pinotage	Red	Earthy, spicy	Pasta	**

Wine name	Style	Flavor/ Bouquet	Compatible Foods	Price Range
Walker Bay				
Beaumont Natural Sweet Dessert Wine	Sweet	Honey, sweet	Dessert	**
Hamilton Russell Chardonnay	White	Melon, tropical fruit	Fish	**
Hamilton Russell Pinot Noir	Red	Berry, spicy	Duck	***
Southern Right Pinotage	Red	Earthy, spicy	Cold meats, stew, offal	**
Worcester				
Nuy Wit Muskadel Fortified Dessert Wine	Sweet	Complex, raisiny	Nuts	**

MIDDLE EAST

ISRAEL/Galilee

Wine name	Style	Flavor/ Bouquet	Compatible Foods	Price Range
Barkan Cellars Cabernet Sauvignon Superieur	Red	Berry, herbaceous	Lamb	**
Barkan Cellars Emerald Riesling Reserved	White	Floral, crisp	Salads	**
Binyamina Wine Cellars Special Reserve Merlot	Red	Fruit cake, earthy	Sausages	**
Dalton Chardonnay	White	Tropical fruit, citrus	Chicken	**
Golan Heights Winery Gamla Cabernet Sauvignon	Red	Berry, herbaceous	Lamb	**
Golan Heights Winery Yarden Brut NV	Sparkling	Crisp, fruity	Aperitif	**
Golan Heights Winery Yarden Chardonnay	White	Tropical fruit, citrus	Fish	**
Golan Heights Winery Yarden Katzrin Cabernet Sauvignon	Red	Herbaceous, spicy, berry	Lamb	**
Golan Heights Winery Yarden Katzrin Chardonnay	White	Tropical fruit, citrus	Fish	**
Golan Heights Winery Yarden Mount Hermon Red	Red	Berry, spicy	Game	**
Margalit Cabernet Sauvignon	Red	Herbaceous, berry	Stew	**
Margalit Merlot	Red	Plums, spicy	Sausages	**
ISRAEL/Judean Hills				
Carmel Merlot Private Collection	Red	Plums, spicy	Stew	**
Israel/Samson				
Baron Cellars Tishbi Estate Merlot	Red	Spicy, plums	Sausages	**
ISRAEL/Shomron				
Baron Cellars Jonathan Tishbi Chardonnay	White	Tropical fruit, minerally	Chicken	**
Carmel 1998 Carmel Selected Emerald Riesling	White	Floral, zingy, minerally	Fish	**

AUSTRALIA

Adelaide Hills/South Australia

Wine name	Style	Flavor/ Bouquet	Compatible Foods	Price Range
Ashton Hills Chardonnay	White	Nutty, complex	Chicken	**
Ashton Hills Reserve Pinot Noir	Red	Spicy, berry	Duck	**
Ashton Hills Riesling	White	Citrus, floral	Shellfish	**
Blass Adelaide Hills Cabernet Merlot	Red	Berry, spicy, oaky	Beef	**
Chain of Ponds Amadeus Cabernet Sauvignon	Red	Herbaceous, berry	Lamb	**
Chain of Ponds Ledge Shiraz	Red	Spicy, berry	Beef	**
Chain of Ponds Riesling	White	Citrus, floral, zingy	Cheese	**
Geoff Weaver Chardonnay	White	Complex, tropical flavor	Fish	**
Geoff Weaver Sauvignon Blanc	White	Zingy, grassy	Shellfish	**
Glenara Cabernet Sauvignon Merlot	Red	Herbaceous, berry	Lamb	**
Hamilton The Hills Chardonnay	White	Melon, complex	Chicken	**

Wine name	Style	Flavor/ Bouquet	Compatible Foods	Price Range
Henschke Abbot's Prayer	Red	Berry, spicy	Lamb	**
Henschke Green's Hill Riesling	White	Citrus, floral	Asian	**
Hillstowe Buxton Sauvignon Blanc	White	Grassy	Shellfish	**
Hillstowe Udys Mill Pinot Noir	Red	Berry, spicy	Game	**
Lenswood Vineyards Chardonnay	White	Complex, melon, nutty	Fish	**
Lenswood Vineyards Pinot Noir	Red	Spicy, berry, complex	Duck	**
Lenswood Vineyards Sauvignon Blanc	White	Zingy, grassy	Salads	**
Malcolm Creek Cabernet Sauvignon	Red	Herbaceous, berry	Lamb	**
Malcolm Creek Chardonnay	White	Nutty, tropical	Chicken	**
Nepenthe Lenswood Pinot Noir	Red	Berry, spicy, gamey, complex	Duck	**
Nepenthe Lenswood Semillon	White	Tropical fruit, citrus	Antipasto	**
Nepenthe The Fugue Cabernet Sauvignon Merlot	Red	Herbaceous, berry	Lamb	**
Paracombe Cabernet Franc	Red	Herbaceous	Sausages	**
Penfolds Adelaide Hills Chardonnay	White	Nutty, tropical fruit	Chicken	**
Penfolds Yattarna Chardonnay	White	Complex, nutty, citrus	Fish	***
Petaluma Chardonnay	White	Complex, nutty, melon	Fish	**
Petaluma Croser	Sparkling	Crisp, yeasty, citrus, austere	Aperitif	**
Petaluma Tiers Chardonnay	White	Complex, nutty, tropical fruit, melon	Fish	***
Ravenswood Lane Sauvignon Blanc	White	Zingy, herbaceous	Salads	**
Shaw and Smith Sauvignon Blanc	White	Zingy, tropical fruit, herbaceous	Shellfish	**
Starvedog Lane Shiraz	Red	Berry, spicy	Beef	**
Whisson Lake Carey Gully Pinot Noir	Red	Berry, spicy	Cold meats	**
Barossa/South Australia				
Barossa Valley Estate E Black Pepper Shiraz	Red	Berry, oaky, earthy	Beef	***
Barossa Valley Estate E Sparkling Shiraz	Sparkling	Oaky, plums, berry	Cold meats	**
Barossa Valley Estate Ebenezer Cabernet Merlot	Red	Berry, tannic	Lamb	**
Barossa Valley Estate Ebenezer Shiraz	Red	Berry, oaky, tannic	Beef	**
Basedow Shiraz	Red	Berry, plum, oaky	Pasta	**
Bethany GR Shiraz	Red	Earthy, berry	Stew	**
Bethany Grenache Pressings	Red	Earthy, berry, tannic, powerful	Stew	**
Blass Barossa Valley Shiraz	Red	Berry, spicy, tannic	Beef	**
Blass Vineyard Selection Cabernet Sauvignon	Red	Berry, herbaceous, oaky	Sausages	**
Charles Cimicky Merlot	Red	Fruit cake, berry, plum	Lamb	**
Charles Cimicky Shiraz	Red	Berry, plum	Stew	**
Charles Melton Nine Popes	Red	Berry, complex, earthy	Cold meats, stew, offal	**
Charles Melton Rose of Virginia	Rosé	Berry, floral	Cheese	**
Charles Melton Sparkling Red	Sparkling	Berry, smoky, powerful	Cold meats	**
David Wynn Patriarch Shiraz	Red	Berry, earthy	Beef	**
Elderton Command Shiraz	Red	Berry, powerful, oaky, tannic	Beef	***
Elderton Golden Semillon	Sweet	Sweet, mandarin, citrus	Dessert	**
Glaetzer Wines Bishop Shiraz	Red	Earthy, berry, tannic	Beef	**

Wine name	Style	Flavor/ Bouquet	Compatible Foods	Price Range
Grant Burge Filsell Shiraz	Red	Berry, tannic	Stew	**
Grant Burge Meshach Shiraz	Red	Berry, tannic, oaky	Beef	***
Grant Burge The Holy Trinity Grenache Shiraz Mourvedre	Red	Earthy, berry, oaky	Cold meats, stew, offal	**
Grant Burge Zerk Semillon	White	Tropical fruit, oaky	Veal	**
Greenock Creek Creek Block Shiraz	Red	Berry, earthy, tannic	Beef	**
Haan Prestige Merlot	Red	Berry, fruit cake	Pork	**
Heggies Riesling	White	Citrus, floral	Shellfish	**
Heggies Viognier	White	Tropical fruit, floral	Fish	**
Henschke Cyril Henschke Cabernet Sauvignon Merlot Cabernet Franc	Red	Berry, spicy	Lamb	**
Henschke Hill of Grace	Red	Complex, berry, oaky, minerally	Beef	***
Henschke Joseph Hill Gewürztraminer	White	Spicy, floral	Asian	**
Henschke Julius Eden Valley Riesling	White	Citrus, floral	Shellfish	**
Henschke Mount Edelstone	Red	Complex, berry	Beef	***
Heritage Estate Shiraz	Red	Berry, earthy	Stew	**
Irvine Grand Merlot	Red	Berry, oaky, fruit cake	Lamb	***
Irvine Petit Meslier	Sparkling	Crisp, floral, fruity	Antipasto	**
Karl Seppelt Springton Cabernet Sauvignon	Red	Berry, herbaceous	Lamb	**
Leo Buring Leonay Eden Valley Riesling	White	Citrus, floral, zingy	Fish	**
Magpie Estate The Malcolm	Red	Powerful, tannic, berry	Pizza	***
Mountadam Chardonnay	White	Nutty, complex, tropical fruit	Fish	**
Mountadam Pinot Noir	Red	Gamey, berry, spicy	Duck	**
Orlando Centenary Hill Shiraz	Red	Berry, oaky, powerful, tannic	Beef	**
Orlando St. Helga Riesling	White	Citrus, floral	Fish	**
Orlando Steingarten Riesling	White	Citrus, minerally, floral	Fish	**
Penfolds Bin 707	Red	Berry, minerally, tannic, oaky	Lamb	***
Penfolds Eden Valley Riesling	White	Citrus, floral	Chicken	**
Penfolds Grandfather Port	Fortified	Raisins, sweet, complex	Nuts	***
Penfolds Grange	Red	Complex, powerful, tannic, oaky, berry, earthy	Beef	***
Penfolds Kalimna Block 42	Red	Complex, powerful, berry, tannic	Beef	***
Penfolds Old Vine Grenache Mourvedre Shiraz	Red	Berry, spicy, plum	Cold meats, stew, offal	**
Peter Lehmann Eden Valley Riesling	White	Citrus, floral, zingy	Shellfish	*
Peter Lehmann Reserve Riesling	White	Citrus, floral, complex	Chicken	**
Peter Lehmann Semillon	White	Tropical fruit, oaky	Veal	*
Peter Lehmann Stonewell Shiraz	Red	Berry, oaky, complex, tannic	Beef	**
Peter Lehmann The Mentor	Red	Berry, oaky, plum	Stew	**
Pewsey Vale Riesling	White	Citrus, floral, minerally	Salads	**
Richmond Grove Eden Valley Riesling	White	Citrus, floral	Antipasto	**
Rockford Basket Press Shiraz	Red	Complex, berry, earthy	Beef	**
Rockford Black Shiraz	Sparkling	Powerful, plum, berry, earthy, complex	Cold meats	***
Rockford Dry Country Grenache	Red	Plum, berry, earthy	Cold meats, stew, offal	**

Wine name	Style	Flavor/ Bouquet	Compatible Foods	Price Range
Saltram Mamre Brook Cabernet Sauvignon	Red	Berry	Stew	**
Saltram Mamre Brook Shiraz	Red	Berry, earthy	Stew	**
Seppelt DP117 Show Fino	Fortified	Dry, yeasty	Aperitif	**
Seppelt DP90 Show Tawny	Fortified	Complex, nutty, sweet	Nuts	**
Seppelt Para Liqueur Vintage Tawny Port	Fortified	Sweet, raisiny	Cheese	**
St. Hallett Eden Valley Riesling	White	Citrus, floral	Shellfish	**
St. Hallett Old Block Shiraz	Red	Berry, earthy, tannic, powerful	Beef	**
The Willows Semillon	White	Tropical fruit, nutty	Pork	**
The Willows The Doctor Sparkling Red	Sparkling	Berry, plum	Cold meats	**
Tollana Botrytis Riesling	Sweet	Sweet, citrus	Dessert	**
Tollana Eden Valley Riesling	White	Citrus, floral	Asian	*
Torbreck Runrig	Red	Berry, earthy, tannic	Beef	**
Torbreck The Steading	Red	Berry, earthy, tannic, oaky, powerful	Beef	***
Turkey Flat Butcher's Block	Red	Berry, earthy	Beef	**
Turkey Flat Shiraz	Red	Berry, tannic, powerful	Beef	**
Veritas Bull's Blood Shiraz Mourvedre Pressings	Red	Tannic, powerful, berry	Stew	**
Wolf Blass Black Label Cabernet Shiraz Merlot	Red	Berry, oaky	Lamb	***
Wolf Blass Gold Label Riesling	White	Crisp, citrus, floral	Fish	*
Yalumba Signature Cabernet Sauvignon Shiraz	Red	Berry, plum	Cold meats, stew, offal	**
Yalumba The Octavius	Red	Oaky, tannic, berry, powerful	Stew	***
Central Victoria				
Balgownie Cabernet Sauvignon	Red	Herbaceous, berry	Lamb	**
Balgownie Shiraz	Red	Berry, spicy	Beef	**
Blackjack Shiraz	Red	Berry, earthy	Cold meats, stew, offal	**
Chateau Leamon Shiraz	Red	Spicy, berry	Beef	**
Chateau Tahbilk Cabernet Sauvignon	Red	Earthy, berry	Cold meats, stew, offal	**
Chateau Tahbilk Marsanne	White	Citrus, tropical fruit	Antipasto	*
David Traeger Verdelho	White	Tropical fruit	Veal	**
Delatite Dead Man's Hill Gewürztraminer	White	Spicy, floral	Asian	**
Delatite Riesling	White	Floral	Shellfish	**
Jasper Hill Emily's Paddock Shiraz	Red	Berry, complex, spicy	Beef	***
Jasper Hill Georgia's Paddock Riesling	White	Citrus, floral	Shellfish	**
Jasper Hill Georgia's Paddock Shiraz	Red	Berry, complex, spicy	Beef	***
Mitchelton Blackwood Park Botrytis Riesling	Sweet	Sweet, citrus	Fruit	**
Mitchelton Blackwood Park Riesling	White	Citrus, floral	Fish	*
Mitchelton Marsanne	White	Tropical fruit, oaky	Chicken	**
Mitchelton Print Label Cabernet Sauvignon	Red	Oaky, berry	Lamb	**
Mitchelton Print Label Shiraz	Red	Oaky, berry, earthy	Beef	**
Passing Clouds Angel Blend Red	Red	Berry	Pasta	**
Passing Clouds Graeme's Blend Red	Red	Berry	Stew	**
Plunkett's Gewurztraminer	White	Spicy, fruity	Asian	**
Plunkett's Shiraz	Red	Spicy, peppery	Beef	**

Wine name	Style	Flavor/ Bouquet	Compatible Foods	Price Range
Punkett's Unwooded Chardonnay	White	Citrus, melon	Salads	**
Water Wheel Cabernet	Red	Berry, herbaceous	Lamb	**
Water Wheel Chardonnay	White	Melon, tropical fruit	Fish	**
Water Wheel Shiraz	Red	Spicy, berry	Cold meats, stew, offal	**
Wild Duck Creek Estate Alan's Cabernet	Red	Berry, herbaceous	Stew	**
Wild Duck Creek Estate Black Label Reserve Cabernet	Red	Herbaceous, berry	Lamb	**
Wild Duck Creek Estate Black Label Reserve Shiraz	Red	Spicy, powerful	Beef	**
Wild Duck Creek Estate Duckmuck	Red	Powerful, spicy, berry	Beef	***
Wild Duck Creek Estate The Blend Red	Red	Berry, earthy	Stew	**
Clare Valley/South Australia				
Annie's Lane Contour Shiraz	Red	Berry, tannic, spicy	Beef	**
Annie's Lane Riesling	White	Citrus, floral	Shellfish	**
Annie's Lane Semillon	White	Tropical fruit, nutty	Antipasto	**
Brian Barry Juds Hill Cabernet Sauvignon	Red	Berry, herbaceous	Lamb	**
Crabtree Watervale Cabernet Sauvignon	Red	Berry, herbaceous	Veal	**
Crabtree Watervale Riesling	White	Citrus, floral	Shellfish	**
Crabtree Watervale Shiraz Cabernet Sauvignon	Red	Berry, spicy	Stew	**
Galah Wines Cabernet Sauvignon	Red	Berry	Lamb	**
Galah Wines Shiraz	Red	Berry, earthy	Pasta	**
Grosset Gaia (Cabernet blend)	Red	Berry, herbaceous, minerally	Lamb	**
Grosset Pinot Noir	Red	Berry, spicy, gamey	Duck	**
Grosset Polish Hill Riesling	White	Citrus, floral, complex, minerally	Shellfish	**
Grosset Watervale Riesling	White	Citrus, floral, minerally	Fish	**
Jim Barry The Armagh	Red	Berry, spicy, complex, oaky, powerful, tannic	Beef	***
Jim Barry Watervale Riesling	White	Citrus, floral	Antipasto	**
Knappstein Enterprise Cabernet Sauvignon	Red	Berry, herbaceous	Lamb	**
Knappstein Enterprise Shiraz	Red	Berry, spicy	Beef	**
Leasingham Classic Clare Riesling	White	Citrus, floral, honey	Veal	**
Leo Buring Clare Valley Riesling	White	Floral	Asian	*
Leo Buring Clare Valley Shiraz	Red	Berry	Beef	**
Mitchell Peppertree Vineyard Shiraz	Red	Berry, spicy	Beef	**
Mitchell Watervale Riesling	White	Citrus, floral	Shellfish	**
Mount Horrocks Cordon Cut Riesling	Sweet	Sweet, citrus	Dessert	**
Pauletts Andreas Shiraz	Red	Berry, spicy, oaky	Beef	**
Pauletts Cabernet Merlot	Red	Berry, herbaceous	Lamb	**
Pauletts Riesling	White	Citrus, floral	Fish	*
Pike's Premio Sangiovese	Red	Berry, earthy, savory	Mediterranean	**
Pike's Reserve Riesling	White	Citrus, floral, austere	Chicken	**
Richmond Grove Watervale Riesling	White	Citrus, floral	Shellfish	*
Sevenhill Cellars Shiraz	Red	Berry, spicy, earthy	Stew	**
Skillogalee Riesling	White	Citrus, floral	Fish	**

Wine name	Style	Flavor/ Bouquet	Compatible Foods	Price Range
Skillogalee Shiraz	Red	Berry, spicy	Beef	**
Skillogalee The Cabernets	Red	Berry, herbaceous	Lamb	**
Stephen John Watervale Pedro Ximenez	White	Crisp, apple	Shellfish	**
Tapestry Cabernet Sauvignon	Red	Berry, herbaceous	Pizza	*
Taylors Cabernet Sauvignon	Red	Berry	Pasta	*
The Clare Essentials Carlsfield Riesling	White	Citrus, floral	Fish	**
Tim Adams Aberfeldy Shiraz	Red	Spicy, berry, powerful	Beef	**
Tim Adams The Fergus Grenache	Red	Earthy, berry, plum	Cold meats, stew, offal	**
Tyrell's Rufus Stone McLaren Vale Shiraz	Red	Berry, spicy	Beef	**
Wendouree Cellars Cabernet Sauvignon	Red	Berry, powerful, tannic	Lamb	**
Wendouree Cellars Malbec	Red	Berry, spicy, tannic	Cold meats, stew, offal	**
Wendouree Cellars Shiraz	Red	Berry, complex, spicy, tannic, powerful	Beef	**
Will Taylor Clare Valley Riesling	White	Citrus, floral	Chicken	**
Coonawarra/South Australia				
Balnaves of Coonawarra Cabernet Merlot	Red	Herbaceous, berry	Lamb	**
Balnaves of Coonawarra Chardonnay	White	Melon	Veal	**
Bowen Estate Cabernet Sauvignon	Red	Berry, herbaceous, tannic, minerally	Lamb	**
Bowen Estate Chardonnay	White	Tropical fruit, nutty	Fish	**
Bowen Estate Shiraz	Red	Berry, spicy, tannic	Beef	**
Hollick Cabernet Merlot	Red	Berry, herbaceous	Sausages	**
Hollick Chardonnay	White	Nutty, tropical fruit	Chicken	**
Hollick Ravenswood Cabernet Sauvignon	Red	Complex, berry, tannic, herbaceous	Lamb	***
Hollick Sparkling Merlot	Sparkling	Berry, fruit cake	Cold meats	**
Katnook Estate Cabernet Sauvignon	Red	Berry, oaky, herbaceous	Lamb	**
Katnook Estate Chardonnay	White	Nutty, tropical fruit, melon, complex	Chicken	**
Katnook Estate Chardonnay Brut	Sparkling	Crisp, citrus, fruity	Shellfish	**
Katnook Estate Merlot	Red	Berry, fruit cake, tannic	Game	**
Katnook Estate Odyssey Cabernet Sauvignon	Red	Berry, complex, tannic, oaky, herbaceous	Lamb	***
Katnook Estate Riesling	White	Citrus, floral	Antipasto	**
Katnook Estate Sauvignon Blanc	White	Tropical fruit, zingy	Salads	**
Leconfield Cabernets	Red	Berry, tannic, herbaceous, complex	Lamb	**
Leconfield Merlot	Red	Berry, fruit cake	Cold meats	**
Leconfield Noble Riesling	Sweet	Sweet, citrus, melon,	Dessert	**
Leconfield Shiraz	Red	Berry, spicy, tannic	Cold meats, stew, offal	**
Lindemans Limestone Ridge Shiraz Cabernet	Red	Spicy, berry, herbaceous	Beef	**
Lindemans St. George Cabernet Sauvignon	Red	Herbaceous, berry, oaky	Lamb	**
Lindemens Pyrus Cabernet blend	Red	Berry, spicy, tannic	Stew	**
Majella Cabernet Sauvignon	Red	Berry, herbaceous, tannic	Lamb	**
Majella Mallea Cabernet Shiraz	Red	Spicy, berry, tannic, complex	Beef	**

Wine name	Style	Flavor/ Bouquet	Compatible Foods	Price Range
Majella Shiraz	Red	Spicy, berry, tannic	Cold meats, stew, offal	**
Majella Sparkling Shiraz	Sparkling	Plum, berry, earthy	Cold meats	**
Mildara Cabernet Sauvignon	Red	Berry, tannic	Pasta	*
Mildara Jamiesons Run Reserve Red Blend	Red	Berry, oaky, tannic	Beef	**
Mildara Robertson's Well Cabernet Sauvignon	Red	Tannic, berry, herbaceous	Lamb	**
Mildara Robertson's Well Shiraz	Red	Berry, spicy, plum	Cold meats	**
Mildara Shiraz	Red	Berry	Pizza	*
Parker First Growth Cabernet Sauvignon	Red	Berry, herbaceous, complex, tannic, oaky	Lamb	***
Parker Terra Rossa Cabernet Sauvignon	Red	Herbaceous, berry, spicy, tannic	Lamb	**
Penley Estate Cabernet Sauvignon	Red	Berry, complex, herbaceous, tannic	Lamb	***
Penley Estate Hyland Shiraz	Red	Spicy, berry, tannic	Beef	**
Penley Estate Phoenix Cabernet Sauvignon	Red	Berry, herbaceous, tannic	Pork	**
Punters Corner Cabernet Sauvignon	Red	Herbaceous, berry, tannic	Lamb	**
Punters Corner Chardonnay	White	Nutty, tropical fruit	Chicken	**
Redman Cabernet Merlot	Red	Berry, herbaceous, tannic	Stew	**
Redman Cabernet Sauvignon	Red	Berry, herbaceous	Lamb	**
Redman Shiraz	Red	Berry, tannic, spicy	Pasta	*
Rouge Homme Cabernet Sauvignon	Red	Berry, tannic, herbaceous	Lamb	**
Rouge Homme Richardsons Block Red Blend	Red	Berry, spicy, tannic	Stew	**
Rymill Cabernet Sauvignon	Red	Berry, herbaceous, complex, minerally, tannic	Lamb	**
Rymill Merlot Cabernets	Red	Berry, spicy	Cold meats, stew, offal	**
Rymill Pinot Noir Chardonnay Sparkling	Sparkling	Crisp, yeasty, citrus	Aperitif	**
Rymill Sauvignon Blanc	White	Grassy	Cheese	**
Rymill Shiraz	Red	Berry, spicy, earthy	Sausages	**
S. Kidman Sauvignon Blanc	White	Zingy, tropical fruit	Salads	**
S. Kidman Shiraz	Red	Berry, spicy, tannic	Beef	**
Wynns Cabernet Sauvignon	Red	Berry, minerally, herbaceous, complex	Lamb	**
Wynns John Riddoch Cabernet Sauvignon	Red	Complex, berry, herbaceous, tannic, powerful	Lamb	***
Wynns Michael Shiraz	Red	Oaky, berry, tannic	Stew	***
Wynns Riesling	White	Floral, citrus	Shellfish	**
Wynns Shiraz	Red	Berry, spicy, tannic	Cold meats, stew, offal	*
Zema Estate Cabernet Sauvignon	Red	Berry, herbaceous	Cold meats	**
Zema Estate Cluny Red Blend	Red	Berry, spicy, tannic	Beef	**
Zema Estate Family Selection Cabernet Sauvignon	Red	Tannic, berry, herbaceous	Lamb	**
Zema Estate Shiraz	Red	Berry, tannic, spicy	Sausages	**
Geelong/Victoria				
Bannockburn Cabernet Sauvignon	Red	Minerally, berry, herbaceous	Lamb	**
Bannockburn Chardonnay	White	Nutty, complex, melon	Fish	**
Bannockburn Pinot Noir	Red	Gamey, earthy, complex	Duck	**

Wine name	Style	Flavor/ Bouquet	Compatible Foods	Price Range
Bannockburn Shiraz	Red	Complex, spicy, berry	Beef	**
Idyll Vineyard Gewurtztraminer	White	Spicy, floral	Salads	**
Idyll Vineyard Shiraz	Red	Berry, peppery	Stew	**
Innisfail Vineyards Chardonnay	White	Tropical fruit	Fish	**
Prince Albert Vineyard Pinot Noir	Red	Earthy, berry	Game	**
Scotchmans Hill Cabernet	Red	Herbaceous, berry	Cold meats	**
Scotchmans Hill Chardonnay	White	Tropical fruit, melon	Fish	**
Scotchmans Hill Pinot Noir	Red	Spicy, berry	Duck	**
Scotchmans Hill Sauvignon Blanc	White	Tropical fruit, citrus	Cheese	**
Gippsland/Victoria				
Bass Phillip Chardonnay	White	Melon, nutty	Fish	***
Bass Phillip Pinot Noir	Red	Complex, berry, gamey	Duck	***
Lyre Bird Hill Pinot Noir	Red	Berry, spicy	Duck	**
Narkoojee Vineyard Chardonnay	White	Melon	Fish	**
Nicholson River Chardonnay	White	Complex, minerally	Chicken	***
Nicholson River Semillon	White	Complex	Veal	**
Paradise Enough Pinot Noir	Red	Spicy, berry	Game	**
Phillip Island Winery Chardonnay	White	Melon, tropical fruit	Chicken	**
Wa-de-lock Vineyards Chardonnay	White	Melon, tropical fruit	Chicken	**
Wild Dog Winery Barrel-fermented Chardonnay	White	Complex, nutty, melon	Chicken	**
Wild Dog Winery Shiraz	Red	Berry, spicy	Stew	**
Grampians & Pyrenees/Victoria				
Best's Bin 0 Shiraz	Red	Complex, earthy, berry	Beef	**
Best's Pinot Meunier	Red	Berry, earthy	Pizza	**
Best's Pinot Noir	Red	Spicy, berry	Game	**
Best's Thomson Family Shiraz	Red	Berry, earthy	Beef	**
Blue Pyrenees Estate Chardonnay	White	Tropical fruit, melon	Veal	**
Blue Pyrenees Estate NV Reserve	Sparkling	Crisp, citrus	Aperitif	**
Blue Pyrenees Estate Red Blend	Red	Herbaceous, minerally, berry	Lamb	**
Cathcart Ridge Cabernet Merlot	Red	Berry	Cold meats	**
Cathcart Ridge Shiraz	Red	Spicy, berry	Beef	**
Dalwhinnie Pinot Noir	Red	Spicy, earthy, berry	Duck	**
Dalwhinnie Chardonnay	White	Complex, melon, nutty	Fish	**
Dalwhinnie Eagle Series Shiraz	Red	Complex, spicy, berry	Beef	***
Dalwhinnie Moonambeel Cabernet	Red	Berry, minerally, herbaceous	Lamb	**
Garden Gully Sparkling Pinot Noir	Sparkling	Crisp, berry	Antipasto	**
Garden Gully Sparkling Red	Sparkling	Berry, spicy	Cold meats	**
Kara Kara Sauvignon Blanc	White	Grassy	Salads	**
Mount Avoca Cabernets	Red	Herbaceous, berry	Lamb	**
Mount Avoca Sauvignon Blanc	White	Zingy, tropical fruit	Cheese	**
Mount Avoca Shiraz	Red	Spicy, berry	Beef	**
Mount Langi Ghiran Billi Billi Red Blend	Red	Berry, earthy	Pasta	**
Mount Langi Ghiran Cabernet Merlot	Red	Berry, minerally, herbaceous	Stew	**

Wine name	Style	Flavor/ Bouquet	Compatible Foods	Price Range
Mount Langi Ghiran Pinot Grigio	White	Tropical fruit, citrus	Antipasto	**
Mount Langi Ghiran Riesling	White	Citrus, floral	Shellfish	**
Mount Langi Ghiran Shiraz	Red	Complex, spicy, berry	Beef	***
Redbank Sally's Paddock Red Blend	Red	Complex, berry	Stew	**
Seppelt Chalambar Shiraz	Red	Berry, earthy, fruity	Pasta	*
Seppelt Great Western Shiraz	Red	Earthy, complex, spicy	Stew	**
Seppelt Original Sparkling Shiraz	Sparkling	Fruity, berry	Nuts	**
Seppelt Rhymney Sauvignon Blanc	White	Zingy	Shellfish	**
Seppelt Sheoak Riesling	White	Floral, citrus	Shellfish	**
Seppelt Show Reserve Sparkling Shiraz	Sparkling	Complex, spicy, berry, earthy	Cold meats	***
Seppelt Sunday Creek Pinot Noir	Red	Berry, spicy	Cold meats	**
Summerfield Cabernet Sauvignon	Red	Herbaceous, berry	Stew	**
Summerfield Shiraz	Red	Berry, spicy	Cold meats, stew, offal	**
Taltarni Brut Tache	Sparkling	Crisp, berry	Cheese	**
Taltarni Merlot	Red	Berry, fruit cake	Lamb	**
Taltarni Reserve Cabernet Sauvignon	Red	Berry, herbaceous, powerful, tannic	Lamb	**
Warrenmang Vineyard Grand Pyrenees (Red Blend)	Red	Spicy, berry	Lamb	**
Warrenmang Vineyard Late Harvest Traminer	Sweet	Sweet, floral	Fruit	**
Yellowglen Cuvee Victoria	Sparkling	Crisp, yeasty	Antipasto	**
Macedon/Victoria				
Cleveland Winery Macedon Brut	Sparkling	Complex, citrus	Aperitif	**
Cleveland Winery Pinot Noir	Red	Spicy, berry	Game	**
Cobaw Ridge Chardonnay	White	Melon, tropical fruit	Fish	**
Cobaw Ridge Lagrein	Red	Berry, fruity	Antipasto	**
Cobaw Ridge Shiraz	Red	Earthy, berry	Beef	**
Cope-Williams R.O.M.S.E.Y. Brut	Sparkling	Crisp, complex, berry	Shellfish	**
Cope-Williams Willow (fortified white)	Fortified	Sweet, complex	Nuts	**
Hanging Rock Winery Macedon Cuvee	Fortified	Complex, yeasty, berry, powerful	Fish	***
Hanging Rock Winery Victoria Chardonnay	White	Melon, tropical fruit	Fish	**
Knights Granite Hills Riesling	White	Floral, citrus	Shellfish	**
Knights Granite Hills Shiraz	Red	Spicy, peppery, berry	Beef	**
Knights Granite Hills Sparkling Pinot Noir Chardonnay	Sparkling	Crisp, yeasty	Aperitif	**
Rochford Chardonnay	White	Tropical fruit, complex	Fish	**
Rochford Pinot Noir	Red	Spicy, berry	Game	**
Virgin Hills Red Blend	Red	Herbaceous, minerally, berry	Lamb	**
McLaren Vale/South Australia				
Chapel Hill Cabernet Sauvignon	Red	Berry, herbaceous, complex	Lamb	**
Chapel Hill Shiraz	Red	Berry, spicy	Beef	**
Chapel Hill The Vicar Cabernet Sauvignon Shiraz	Red	Berry, spicy, tannic, oaky	Lamb	**
Chapel Hill Verdelho	White	Tropical fruit	Salads	**
Clarendon Hills Cabernet Sauvignon	Red	Berry, tannic, powerful	Lamb	**

Wine name	Style	Flavor/ Bouquet	Compatible Foods	Price Range
Clarendon Hills Kangarilla Vineyard Old Vines Grenache	Red	Berry, plum, powerful	Cold meats, stew, offal	***
Clarendon Hills Piggott Range Vineyard Shiraz	Red	Spicy, berry, earthy, tannic, oaky	Sausages	***
Coriole Diva Sangiovese Cabernet Sauvignon	Red	Berry, herbaceous	Cold meats, stew, offal	**
Coriole Lalla Rookh Semillon	White	Tropical fruit	Veal	**
Coriole Redstone Shiraz Cabernet Sauvignon Grenache Merlot	Red	Berry, tannic	Stew	**
D'Arenberg D'Arry's Original Shiraz Grenache	Red	Berry, earthy	Sausages	*
D'Arenberg Peppermint Park Sparkling Chambourcin	Sparkling	Fruit cake, berry	Cold meats	**
D'Arenberg The Footbolt Shiraz	Red	Berry	Cold meats, stew, offal	**
D'Arenberg Twenty Eight Road Mourvedre	Red	Berry, spicy, oaky, tannic	Stew	**
Dowie Doole Chenin Blanc	White	Tropical fruit, nutty	Chicken	**
Dowie Doole Merlot	Red	Berry, fruit cake, oaky	Lamb	**
Fox Creek JSM Shiraz Cabernets	Red	Berry, plum	Sausages	**
Fox Creek Reserve Shiraz	Red	Complex, berry, oaky, tannic, powerful	Beef	***
Fox Creek Vixen Sparkling Cabernet Sauvignon/Shiraz	Sparkling	Plum, berry	Cold meats	**
Geoff Merrill Cabernet Merlot	Red	Berry, herbaceous	Lamb	**
Hamilton Hut Block Cabernet	Red	Berry, tannic, complex	Lamb	**
Hardys Eileen Hardy Shiraz	Red	Berry, tannic, complex, oaky	Beef	***
Hardys Tintara Shiraz	Red	Powerful, tannic, earthy, berry	Beef	**
Haselgrove H Botrytis Sauvignon Semillon	Sweet	Sweet, mandarin	Dessert	**
Haselgrove H Futures Shiraz	Red	Berry, oaky, powerful	Beef	**
Hillstowe Mary's Hundred Shiraz	Red	Berry, tannic, powerful	Beef	**
Ingoldby Cabernet Sauvignon	Red	Berry, tannic	Cold meats, stew, offal	*
Kangarilla Road Shiraz	Red	Berry, spicy	Beef	**
Kangarilla Road Zinfandel	Red	Berry, plum	Stew	**
Kay's Amery Cabernet Sauvignon	Red	Berry, tannic	Lamb	**
Maglieri Steve Maglieri Shiraz	Red	Berry, tannic, complex	Beef	***
Maxwell Reserve Merlot	Red	Fruit cake, berry, tannic	Lamb	**
Normans Chais Clarendon Cabernet Sauvignon	Red	Herbaceous, berry, tannic	Lamb	**
Normans Chais Clarendon Shiraz	Red	Spicy, berry, earthy	Beef	**
Normans Chardonnay	White	Tropical fruit, melon	Veal	**
Rosemount Balmoral Syrah	Red	Powerful, berry, spicy, oaky, complex	Beef	***
Rosemount GSM Grenache Shiraz Mourvedre	Red	Berry, tannic, spicy	Cold meats, stew, offal	**
Scarpantoni Block 3 Shiraz	Red	Berry, spicy	Sausages	**
Seaview Edwards & Chaffey Shiraz	Red	Berry, oaky, tannic	Beef	**
Tatachilla Clarendon Vineyard Merlot	Red	Berry, fruit cake, spicy	Stew	**
Wirra Wirra Chardonnay	White	Nutty, tropical fruit, melon	Fish	**
Wirra Wirra RSW Shiraz	Red	Berry, complex, spicy	Beef	**
Woodstock The Stocks Shiraz	Red	Berry, earthy, tannic	Sausages	**
New South Wales				
Allandale Chardonnay	White	Nutty, tropical fruit	Fish	**
Andrew Harris Reserve Shiraz	Red	Complex, berry, spicy	Beef	*

Wine name	Style	Flavor/ Bouquet	Compatible Foods	Price Range
Andrew Harris The Vision	Red	Oaky, complex, berry	Beef	***
Arrowfield Show Reserve Shiraz	Red	Berry, earthy	Stew	**
Ballingal Estate Botrytis Semillon	Sweet	Sweet, mandarin	Dessert	**
Barwang Shiraz	Red	Berry, spicy	Cold meats	**
Bimbadgen Semillon	White	Citrus	Veal	**
Bloodwood Chardonnay	White	Tropical fruit, melon	Chicken	**
Bloodwood Ice Riesling	Sweet	Sweet, citrus	Dessert	**
Botobolar Shiraz	Red	Berry, earthy	Cold meats, stew, offal	**
Brangayne of Orange Reserve Chardonnay	White	Tropical fruit, complex	Fish	**
Briar Ridge Stockhausen Semillon	White	Citrus, toasty, complex	Chicken	**
Briar Ridge Stockhausen Shiraz	Red	Berry, earthy, leathery	Beef	**
Brokenwood Graveyard Shiraz	Red	Berry, complex, tannic	Beef	***
Brokenwood ILR Semillon	White	Complex, toasty, citrus	Pork	***
Brokenwood Semillon	White	Citrus	Fish	**
Canobolas-Smith Chardonnay	Red	Tropical fruit, nutty	Fish	**
Capercaillie Chardonnay	White	Tropical fruit	Shellfish	**
Cassegrain Reserve Chambourcin	Red	Berry, plum	Cold meats	**
Cassegrain Reserve Chardonnay	White	Tropical fruit, melon	Fish	**
Charles Sturt University Cabernet Sauvignon	Red	Berry, herbaceous	Sausages	**
Chateau Francois Semillon	White	Citrus, fruity	Chicken	**
Clonakilla Riesling	White	Citrus, floral	Asian	**
Clonakilla Shiraz/Viognier	Red	Berry, minerally, complex	Veal	**
Coolangatta Estate Chardonnay	White	Tropical fruit, melon	Chicken	**
Cowra Estate Cabernet Franc Rosé	Rosé	Berry, fruity	Antipasto	**
Cranswick Autumn Gold	Sweet	Citrus, mandarin, sweet	Fruit	**
De Bortoli Black Noble	Fortified	Sweet, raisiny, fruit cake	Nuts	**
De Bortoli Noble One	Sweet	Sweet, citrus, mandarin	Dessert	**
Doonkuna Estate Chardonnay	White	Melon, nutty	Fish	**
Doonkuna Estate Riesling	White	Citrus, floral	Salads	**
Drayton's William Shiraz	Red	Berry, leathery	Stew	**
Evans Family Hunter Valley Chardonnay	White	Tropical fruit, melon	Fish	**
Glenguin Merlot	Red	Berry, fruit cake	Cold meats	**
Glenguin Semillon	White	Citrus, toasty	Shellfish	**
Hungerford Hill Tumbarumba Chardonnay	White	Melon, nutty	Fish	**
Huntington Estate Cabernet Sauvignon	Red	Berry, minerally, tannic	Lamb	**
Huntington Estate Reserve Shiraz	Red	Berry, tannic, powerful, spicy	Beef	**
Huntington Estate Shiraz	Red	Berry, tannic, spicy	Stew	**
Kulkunbulla Brokenback Chardonnay	White	Tropical fruit, melon	Fish	**
Kulkunbulla The Glandore Semillon	White	Citrus, tropical fruit	Chicken	**
Kyeema Estate Shiraz	Red	Peppery, spicy, berry	Pork	**
Lake's Folly Cabernet	Red	Berry, leathery, herbaceous	Lamb	***
Lake's Folly Chardonnay	White	Tropical fruit, complex	Fish	***
Lark Hill Chardonnay	White	Melon, citrus	Chicken	**

Wine name	Style	Flavor/ Bouquet	Compatible Foods	Price Range
Lark Hill Riesling	White	Citrus, zingy	Antipasto	**
Lindemans Hunter River Reserve Porphyry	Sweet	Sweet, floral, citrus	Fruit	**
Lindemans Hunter River Semillon	White	Citrus, toasty, complex	Fish	*
Lindemans Hunter River Shiraz	Red	Leathery, berry	Stew	**
Lindemans Steven Vineyard Shiraz	Red	Leathery, berry, spicy	Beef	**
Lowe Family Chardonnay	White	Melon, tropical fruit	Pork	**
Lowe Family Merlot	Red	Berry, earthy, fruit cake	Cold meats	**
Madew Riesling	White	Floral, citrus	Fruit	**
Margan Family Semillon	White	Citrus, zingy	Shellfish	**
Margan Family Shiraz	Red	Berry, earthy	Cold meats, stew, offal	**
Meerea Park Chardonnay	White	Tropical fruit	Fish	**
Miranda Golden Botrytis Semillon	Sweet	Mandarin, sweet	Dessert	**
Montrose Barbera	Red	Berry, earthy	Mediterranean	**
Montrose Black Shiraz	Red	Berry, earthy	Pasta	**
Mount Pleasant Elizabeth Semillon	White	Citrus, complex, toasty	Fish	*
Mount Pleasant Lovedale Semillon	White	Complex, toasty, honey	Chicken	**
Mount Pleasant Maurice O'Shea Shiraz	Red	Berry, leathery	Beef	**
Mount Pleasant Rosehill Shiraz	Red	Berry, leathery	Stew	**
Pendarves Verdelho	White	Tropical fruit	Fish	**
Pepper Tree Reserve Semillon	White	Citrus, toasty	Pork	**
Pepper Tree Shiraz	Red	Leathery, tannic, berry	Stew	**
Petersons Chardonnay	White	Tropical fruit	Chicken	**
Poole's Rock Chardonnay	White	Tropical fruit, melon	Chicken	**
Reynolds Yarraman Orange Chardonnay	White	Nutty, tropical fruit, complex	Fish	**
Reynolds Yarraman Semillon	White	Citrus, toasty	Shellfish	**
Reynolds Yarraman Shiraz	Red	Spicy, berry, earthy	Beef	**
Richmond Grove Cowra Chardonnay	White	Tropical fruit	Fish	**
Rosemount Giant's Creek Chardonnay	White	Tropical fruit, citrus, melon	Chicken	**
Rosemount Hill of Gold Chardonnay	White	Tropical fruit, melon	Fish	**
Rosemount Hill of Gold Shiraz	Red	Berry, spicy, tannic	Beef	**
Rosemount Mountain Blue Shiraz Cabernet	Red	Complex, tannic, berry, spicy	Beef	***
Rosemount Orange Chardonnay	White	Tropical fruit, melon, complex	Fish	**
Rosemount Roxburgh Chardonnay	White	Melon, complex, nutty, toasty	Chicken	***
Rosemount Show Reserve Chardonnay	White	Melon, tropical fruit	Veal	**
Rosemount Show Reserve Semillon	White	Tropical fruit, citrus	Fish	**
Rothbury Estate Brokenback Chardonnay	White	Tropical fruit	Pork	**
Rothbury Estate Brokenback Semillon	White	Citrus, minerally	Fish	**
Rothbury Estate Brokenback Shiraz	Red	Leathery, berry	Stew	**
Saddlers Creek Marrowbone Chardonnay	White	Tropical fruit, melon	Fish	**
Scarborough Chardonnay	White	Complex, melon, nutty	Fish	**
Sutherland Semillon	White	Citrus, toasty	Shellfish	**
Tamburlaine The Chapel Reserve Red	Red	Berry, leathery	Beef	**
Thistle Hill Cabernet Sauvignon	Red	Berry, herbaceous	Lamb	**

Wine name	Style	Flavor/ Bouquet	Compatible Foods	Price Range
Tower Estate Semillon	White	Citrus, zingy	Fish	**
Tulloch Hector of Glen Elgin Red	Red	Berry, earthy	Beef	**
Tyrell's Brokenback Shiraz	Red	Berry, leathery	Cold meats	**
Tyrell's Lost Block Semillon	White	Citrus, tropical fruit	Chicken	**
Tyrell's Moon Mountain Chardonnay	White	Tropical fruit, nutty	Fish	**
Tyrell's Vat 1 Semillon	White	Citrus, toasty, complex	Shellfish	**
Tyrell's Vat 47 Chardonnay	White	Complex, tropical fruit, melon	Chicken	**
Tyrell's Vat 5 Dry Red	Red	Berry, complex, leathery	Beef	**
Tyrell's Vat 9 Dry Red	Red	Berry, leathery, tannic	Stew	**
Westend 3 Bridges Cabernet	Red	Berry	Pasta	**
Westend Golden Mist Botrytis Semillon	Sweet	Citrus, sweet	Dessert	**
Wilton Estate Botrytis Semillon	Sweet	Sweet, citrus	Dessert	**
North East Victoria/Victoria				
All Saints Aleatico	Red	Fruity	Asian	**
All Saints Show Reserve Tokay	Fortified	Sweet, complex	Nuts	**
Auldstone Cellars Late-picked Riesling	Sweet	Sweet, floral	Fruit	**
Auldstone Cellars Shiraz	Red	Berry, earthy	Stew	**
Baileys of Glenrowan 1920s Block Shiraz	Red	Powerful, berry, tannic	Stew	**
Baileys of Glenrowan Founders Muscat	Fortified	Sweet, complex, raisiny	Nuts	**
Baileys of Glenrowan Founders Tokay	Fortified	Complex, sweet, cold tea	Cheese	**
Brown Brothers Barbera	Red	Savory, earthy	Mediterranean	**
Brown Brothers Classic Release Cabernet Sauvignon	Red	Berry, herbaceous	Lamb	**
Brown Brothers Late Harvested Noble Riesling	Sweet	Sweet, complex, citrus	Dessert	**
Brown Brothers Late Harvested Orange Muscat and Flora	Sweet	Sweet, citrus	Fruit	**
Brown Brothers Nebbiolo	Red	Earthy, berry, tannic	Pasta	**
Brown Brothers Shiraz	Red	Earthy, berry	Beef	**
Brown Brothers Very Old Liqueur Muscat	Fortified	Sweet, complex, raisiny	Nuts	**
Brown Brothers Vintage Port	Fortified	Sweet, licorice	Cheese	**
Bullers Museum Release Muscat	Fortified	Sweet, complex, raisiny	Nuts	***
Campbells Isabella Tokay	Fortified	Sweet, cold tea	Cheese	***
Campbells Merchant Prince Muscat	Fortified	Sweet, complex, raisiny	Nuts	***
Campbells The Barkly Durif	Red	Powerful, earthy, tannic	Stew	**
Chambers Rosewood Rare Muscat	Fortified	Raisiny, complex, sweet	Nuts	**
Chambers Rosewood Rare Tokay	Fortified	Complex, sweet, cold tea	Nuts	**
Cofield Chenin Blanc	White	Tropical fruit	Pasta	**
Cofield Late Harvest Tokay	White	Sweet, floral	Fruit	**
Cofield Sparkling Shiraz	Sparkling	Berry, plum	Cold meats	**
Giaconda Chardonnay	White	Complex, nutty, minerally, tropical fruit	Fish	***
Giaconda Pinot Noir	Red	Earthy, gamey, spicy, complex, berry	Duck	***
Jones Winery Shiraz	Red	Berry, tannic	Stew	**
Morris Durif	Red	Earthy, tannic	Beef	**

Wine name	Style	Flavor/ Bouquet	Compatible Foods	Price Range
Morris Old Premium Muscat	Fortified	Complex, sweet, raisiny	Nuts	**
Morris Old Premium Tokay	Fortified	Complex, sweet, raisiny, cold tea	Cheese	**
Morris Sparkling Durif Shiraz	Sparkling	Earthy, berry, plum	Cold meats	**
Mount Prior Vineyard Chardonnay	White	Melon, nutty	Chicken	**
Mount Prior Vineyard Durif	Red	Berry, earthy, tannic	Stew	**
Pfieffer Chardonnay	White	Melon, fruity	Veal	**
Pfieffer Christopher's Vintage Port	Fortified	Sweet, licorice	Cheese	**
Pfieffer Gamay	Red	Berry	Cheese	**
Sorrenberg Chardonnay	White	Nutty, tropical fruit, complex	Chicken	**
Stanton & Killeen Premium Liqueur Gold Tokay	Fortified	Complex, sweet, cold tea	Nuts	***
Stanton & Killeen Special Old Liqueur Muscat	Fortified	Raisiny, complex, sweet	Nuts	***
Stanton & Killeen Vintage Port	Fortified	Sweet, licorice, berry	Cheese	**
Queensland				
Bald Mountain Chardonnay	White	Tropical fruit	Fish	**
Bald Mountain Late Harvest Sauvignon Blanc	Sweet	Sweet, citrus	Fruit	**
Ballandean Black Label Cabernet Sauvignon	Red	Berry, herbaceous	Lamb	**
Ballandean Black Label Chardonnay	White	Melon, tropical fruit	Fish	**
Ballandean Black Label Merlot	Red	Fruit cake, berry	Game	**
Ballandean Late Harvest Sylvaner	Sweet	Sweet, citrus	Fruit	**
Barambah Ridge Chardonnay	White	Tropical fruit	Mediterranean	**
Clovelly Estate Left Field Chardonnay	White	Fruity	Chicken	**
Crane Sparkling Chambourcin	Sparkling	Berry, plum	Cold meats	**
Golden Grove Chardonnay	White	Fruity	Fish	**
Granite Ridge Cabernet Sauvignon	Red	Berry, minerally, herbaceous	Lamb	**
Hidden Creek Nebbiolo	Red	Berry, tannic, savory	Pasta	**
Hidden Creek Shiraz	Red	Berry	Pizza	**
Ironbark Ridge Chardonnay	White	Nutty, tropical fruit	Fish	**
Kominos Shiraz	Red	Berry, earthy	Sausages	**
Mountview Shiraz	Red	Berry, earthy	Pasta	**
Mountview Sparkling Shiraz	Sparkling	Berry, plums	Cold meats	**
Mt. Tamborine Cedar Creek Chardonnay	White	Fruity, tropical fruit	Fish	**
Mt. Tamborine Tehembrin Merlot	Red	Berry, fruit cake	Stew	**
Preston Peak Chardonnay	White	Tropical fruit, nutty	Chicken	**
Preston Peak Shiraz	Red	Berry, spicy	Veal	**
Rimfire Shiraz	Red	Berry, spicy	Beef	**
Robinsons Family Cabernet Sauvignon	Red	Herbaceous, earthy, berry	Sausages	**
Robinsons Family Sparkling	Sparkling	Crisp, citrus	Aperitif	**
Romavilla Very Old Tawny Port	Fortified	Sweet, raisiny, complex	Nuts	**
Rumbalara Semillon	White	Citrus, apples	Shellfish	**
Severn Brae Shiraz	Red	Berry, spicy	Stew	**
Stone Ridge Chardonnay	White	Tropical fruit, nutty	Fish	**
Stone Ridge Shiraz	Red	Berry, earthy, spicy, tannic	Beef	**

Wine name	Style	Flavor/ Bouquet	Compatible Foods	Price Range
Stuart Range Estate Goodger Chardonnay	White	Melon, fruity	Fish	**
Violet Cane Sparkling Shiraz	Sparkling	Berry, earthy, plum	Cold meats	***
Violet Cane Vineyard Merlot	Red	Fruit cake, berry	Duck	**
Windermere Sangiovese Cabernet	Red	Berry, spicy, savory	Pasta	**
Windermere Shiraz	Red	Berry, spicy, tannic	Beef	**
Winewood Shiraz Marsanne	Red	Berry, spicy	Stew	**
Riverland/South Australia				
Angove's Classic Reserve Cabernet Sauvignon	Red	Berry, plum	Stew	**
Angove's Classic Reserve Chardonnay	White	Tropical fruit	Pork	**
Angove's Classic Reserve Shiraz	Red	Berry, earthy	Pasta	**
Banrock Station Shiraz	Red	Berry	Pizza	*
Banrock Station Shiraz Cabernet	Red	Berry	Pizza	*
Banrock Station Sparkling Chardonnay	Sparkling	Citrus, melon	Salads	*
Bonneyview Cabernet Petit Verdot	Red	Berry, herbaceous	Stew	**
Bonneyview Chardonnay	White	Tropical fruit	Chicken	**
Bonneyview Petit Verdot Merlot	Red	Berry	Pasta	**
Kingston Estate Cabernet Sauvignon	Red	Berry, plum	Pasta	*
Kingston Estate Chardonnay	White	Tropical fruit, melon	Chicken	*
Kingston Estate Merlot	Red	Berry, plum	Stew	*
Normans Chandlers Hill Chardonnay Semillon	White	Fruity	Asian	**
Normans Chandlers Hill Shiraz	Red	Berry	Pizza	**
Normans Lone Gum Vineyard Cabernet Merlot	Red	Berry, plum	Stew	*
Normans Lone Gum Vineyard Shiraz Cabernet	Red	Berry, earthy	Mediterranean	*
Normans Lone Gum Vineyard Unwooded Chardonnay	White	Melon, fruity	Salads	*
Renmano Chairman's Selection Reserve Chardonnay	White	Tropical fruit	Fish	*
Yalumba Oxford Landing Limited Release Merlot	Red	Berry, earthy	Pasta	*
Yalumba Oxford Landing Limited Release Semillon	White	Tropical fruit	Fish	*
Yalumba Oxford Landing Sauvignon Blanc	White	Fruity	Pizza	**
Western Australia				
Abbey Vale Verdelho	White	Citrus, tropical fruit	Chicken	**
Alkoomi Blackbutt Cabernet Sauvignon	Red	Berry, oaky, tannic	Lamb	***
Alkoomi Riesling	White	Floral	Shellfish	**
Alkoomi Sauvignon Blanc	White	Tropical fruit	Salads	**
Amberley Cabernet Merlot	Red	Berry	Lamb	**
Amberley Semillon Sauvignon Blanc	White	Tropical fruit	Shellfish	**
Amberley Shiraz	Red	Berry, earthy	Beef	**
Ashbrook Semillon	White	Grassy, floral	Salads	**
Brookland Valley Chardonnay	White	Melon, tropical fruit	Fish	**
Brookland Valley Sauvignon Blanc	White	Grassy, zingy	Shellfish	**
Cape Mentelle Cabernet Sauvignon	Red	Berry, complex, minerally	Lamb	***
Cape Mentelle Chardonnay	White	Nutty, tropical fruit	Fish	**
Cape Mentelle Semillon Sauvignon Blanc	White	Grassy, tropical fruit	Salads	**
Cape Mentelle Shiraz	Red	Earthy, berry	Stew	**

Wine name	Style	Flavor/ Bouquet	Compatible Foods	Price Range
Cape Mentelle Zinfandel	Red	Earthy, berry	Beef	**
Capel Vale Riesling	White	Floral	Salads	**
Chateau Xanadu Cabernet Reserve	Red	Berry, minerally, complex	Lamb	***
Chateau Xanadu Semillon	White	Grassy	Antipasto	**
Chatsfield Shiraz	Red	Berry	Stew	**
Chestnut Grove Verdelho	White	Tropical fruit	Veal	**
Cullen Cabernet Merlot	Red	Complex, minerally, berry	Lamb	***
Cullen Chardonnay	White	Nutty, complex, melon	Fish	**
Cullen Sauvignon Blanc Semillon	White	Grassy, zingy	Salads	**
Devils Lair Cabernet Sauvignon	Red	Minerally, herbaceous, earthy	Lamb	**
Devils Lair Chardonnay	White	Melon, nutty	Fish	**
Evans & Tate Redbrook Semillon	White	Fruity, tropical fruit	Shellfish	**
Evans & Tate Shiraz	Red	Earthy, minerally	Beef	**
Frankland Estate Isolation Ridge Shiraz	Red	Earthy, berry	Stew	**
Frankland Estate Olmo's Reward Bordeaux Blend	Red	Complex, herbaceous, berry	Lamb	**
Frankland Estate Riesling	White	Citrus, floral	Asian	**
Gilberts Riesling	White	Floral	Salads	**
Goundrey Reserve Chardonnay	White	Melon, nutty	Chicken	**
Goundrey Reserve Shiraz	Red	Minerally, oaky, berry	Beef	**
Gralyn Cabernet Sauvignon	Red	Herbaceous, minerally	Stew	**
Gralyn Old Vine Shiraz	Red	Earthy, berry	Cold meats, stew, offal	**
Hay Shed Hill Cabernet Sauvignon	Red	Berry	Pasta	**
Houghton Jack Mann Cabernet Sauvignon Malbec Shiraz	Red	Complex, berry, minerally, earthy	Lamb	***
Howard Park Cabernet Sauvignon Merlot	Red	Complex, herbaceous, minerally	Lamb	***
Howard Park Chardonnay	White	Nutty, complex, melon	Chicken	***
Howard Park Riesling	White	Citrus, floral, zingy	Shellfish	**
Jane Brook Wood Aged Chenin Blanc	White	Nutty, fruity, oaky	Pork	**
Karriview Pinot Noir	Red	Earthy, berry	Game	**
Lamont Barrel-Fermented Chardonnay	White	Melon, oaky	Fish	**
Lamont Chenin Blanc	White	Fruity, tropical fruit	Pasta	**
Lamont Family Reserve Premium Red Blend	Red	Berry	Stew	**
Lamont Verdelho	White	Tropical fruit	Fish	**
Lamont Vintage Port	Fortified	Sweet, earthy	Cheese	**
Leeuwin Estate Art Series Cabernet Sauvignon	Red	Herbaceous, minerally	Lamb	***
Leeuwin Estate Art Series Chardonnay	White	Complex, nutty, tropical fruit, melon	Fish	***
Lenton Brae Semillon Sauvignon Blanc	White	Grassy, zingy	Salads	**
Moondah Brook Cabernet Sauvignon	Red	Herbaceous, berry	Cold meats	**
Moondah Brook Shiraz	Red	Earthy, berry	Stew	**
Moss Wood Cabernet Sauvignon	Red	Complex, minerally, berry	Lamb	***
Moss Wood Chardonnay	White	Nutty, tropical fruit	Fish	**
Moss Wood Semillon	White	Grassy, fruity	Asian	**

Wine name	Style	Flavor/ Bouquet	Compatible Foods	Price Range
Pattersons Pinot Noir	Red	Earthy, berry	Duck	**
Paul Conti Chardonnay	White	Melon, tropical fruit	Fish	**
Peel Estate Chenin Blanc	White	Tropical fruit	Chicken	**
Peel Estate Shiraz	Red	Oaky, earthy	Stew	**
Picardy Pinot Noir	Red	Berry, complex	Duck	**
Picardy Shiraz	Red	Complex, berry	Beef	**
Pierro Chardonnay	White	Complex, nutty, melon	Chicken	***
Pierro Semillon Sauvignon Blanc	White	Zingy, grassy	Shellfish	**
Plantagenet Cabernet Sauvignon	Red	Herbaceous, berry	Lamb	**
Plantagenet Omrah Chardonnay	White	Fruity, citrus	Salads	**
Plantagenet Riesling	White	Citrus, zingy	Shellfish	**
Plantagenet Shiraz	Red	Earthy, berry	Beef	**
Salitage Pinot Noir	Red	Gamey, earthy	Duck	**
Sandalford Verdelho	White	Tropical fruit	Veal	**
Talijancich Julian James Red Liqueur	Fortified	Sweet, berry	Cheese	**
Vasse Felix Cabernet Sauvignon	Red	Herbaceous, oaky, berry	Lamb	**
Vasse Felix Heytesbury Chardonnay	White	Complex, tropical fruit, nutty	Chicken	**
Vasse Felix Heytesbury Red	Red	Complex, herbaceous, minerally	Beef	***
Vasse Felix Noble Riesling	Sweet	Sweet, citrus	Dessert	**
Vasse Felix Semillon	White	Grassy	Salads	**
Vasse Felix Shiraz	Red	Earthy, berry	Beef	**
Voyager Cabernet Sauvignon Merlot	Red	Herbaceous, minerally, berry	Lamb	**
Voyager Chardonnay	White	Tropical fruit	Chicken	**
Westfield Chardonnay	White	Melon, fruity	Chicken	**
Westfield Liqueur Muscat	Fortified	Sweet	Nuts	**
Wignalls Pinot Noir	Red	Gamey, earthy	Game	**

NEW ZEALAND

Auckland

Kumeau Brajkovich Cabernet Franc	Red	Herbaceous, berry	Cold meats	**
Kumeau Brajkovich Chardonnay	White	Austere, citrus	Fish	**
Kumeau River Chardonnay	White	Austere, citrus	Shellfish	**
Kumeau River Mates Chardonnay	White	Austere, citrus, toasty	Chicken	***
Okahu Kaz Syrah	Red	Earthy, berry	Beef	**
Okahu Pinotage	Red	Berry, earthy	Pasta	**
Vina Alta Retico Amarone-style Cabernet Franc/Merlot	Red	Berry, plums, rich	Cheese	**

Canterbury/Waipara

Danniel Schuster Selection Pinot Noir	Red	Cherry, plums, oaky	Duck	***
Giesen Reserve Chardonnay	White	Melon, tropical fruit	Chicken	**
Giesen Reserve Pinot Noir	Red	Berry, earthy, gamey	Fish, veal, pork	***
Giesen Reserve Riesling	White	Citrus, floral	Fish	**
Kaituna Valley Pinot Noir	Red	Berry, plum	Sausages	**

Wine name	Style	Flavor/ Bouquet	Compatible Foods	Price Range
Mountford Pinot Noir	Red	Berry, spicy	Duck	**
Muddy Water Pinot Noir	Red	Earthy, berry	Pasta	**
Pegasus Bay Aria Late Picked Riesling	Sweet	Sweet, mandarin	Dessert	**
Pegasus Bay Chardonnay	White	Tropical fruit, melon	Fish	**
Pegasus Bay Pinot Noir	Red	Gamey, earthy, berry	Game	**
Pegasus Bay Prima Donna Pinot Noir	Red	Berry, smoky, complex	Duck	***
Pegasus Bay Riesling	White	Citrus, zingy	Cheese	**
Rossendale Reserve Pinot Noir	Red	Berry, spicy	Pasta	**
Sandihurst Reserve Pinot Noir	Red	Gamey, spicy	Duck	**
St. Helena Reserve Pinot Gris	White	Tropical fruit, spicy	Salads	**
Torlese Gewürztraminer	White	Spicy, floral	Asian	**
Waipara Springs Riesling	White	Floral, citrus	Fish	**
Waipara West Chardonnay	White	Tropical fruit, melon	Chicken	**
Waipara West Pinot Noir	Red	Earthy, berry	Game	**
Waipara West Riesling	White	Citrus, floral	Fish	**
Central Otago				
Black Ridge Pinot Noir	Red	Earthy, gamey	Duck	**
Chard Farm Bragato Pinot Noir	Red	Berry, spicy	Game	**
Chard Farm Finla Mor Pinot Noir	Red	Berry, tannic	Game	**
Chard Farm Judge and Jury Chardonnay	White	Austere, melon, toasty	Chicken	***
Chard Farm Pinot Gris	White	Apples, melon	Chicken	**
Chard Farm Riesling	White	Citrus, floral	Fish	**
Felton Road Block Three Pinot Noir	Red	Complex, berry, gamey	Duck	***
Felton Road Chardonnay	White	Oaky, tropical fruit	Veal	**
Felton Road Dry Riesling	White	Citrus, dry	Fish	**
Felton Road Riesling	White	Floral, sweet	Cheese	**
Gibbston Valley Pinot Gris	White	Citrus, tropical fruit	Shellfish	**
Gibbston Valley Reserve Pinot Noir	Red	Complex, berry, earthy	Duck	***
Gibbston Valley Sauvignon Blanc	White	Zingy, grassy	Antipasto	**
Kawarau Estate Reserve Pinot Noir	Red	Oaky, spicy	Cold meats, stew, offal	**
Nevis Bluff Pinot Gris	White	Zingy, rich	Salads	**
Olssen's of Bannockburn Pinot Noir	Red	Fungal, berry	Pasta	**
Peregrine Pinot Noir	Red	Spicy, berry	Sausages	**
Peregrine Riesling	White	Zingy, citrus	Fish	**
Quartz Reef Chauvet Méthode Traditionnelle	Sparkling	Citrus, crisp	Cheese	**
Quartz Reef Pinot Gris	White	Spicy, melon	Fish	**
Quartz Reef Pinot Noir	Red	Berry, spicy	Duck	**
Rippon Gewürztraminer	White	Spicy, floral	Asian	**
Rippon Pinot Noir	Red	Berry, spicy	Duck	***
Rippon Sauvignon Blanc	White	Zingy, citrus	Cheese	**
Two Paddocks Pinot Noir	Red	Spicy, gamey, earthy	Game	**
Valli Pinot Noir	Red	Berry, acid, earthy	Pizza	**
William Hill Gewürztraminer	White	Floral, spicy	Cold meats, stew, offal	**

Wine name	Style	Flavor/ Bouquet	Compatible Foods	Price Range
William Hill Pinot Noir	Red	Earthy, berry, spicy	Pasta	**
William Hill Riesling	White	Floral, zingy	Fish	**
Hawkes Bay				
Alpha Domus AD Cabernet Sauvignon Merlot Malbec	Red	Berry, oaky	Lamb	**
Alpha Domus The Navigator (merlot/malbec/cabernet franc)	Red	Earthy, oaky, berry	Beef	**
Babich Irongate Cabernet Sauvignon Merlot	Red	Herbaceous, berry	Lamb	**
Babich Irongate Chardonnay	White	Melon, spicy	Fish	**
Bilancia Reserve Pinot Gris	White	Minerally, tropical fruit	Fish	**
Brookfields Pinot Gris	White	Tropical fruit, melon	Chicken	**
Brookfields Riesling	White	Floral, citrus	Cheese	**
C. J. Pask Chardonnay	White	Spicy, melon	Salads	**
C. J. Pask Reserve Chardonnay	White	Toasty, ripe, citrus	Shellfish	***
Church Road Reserve Cabernet Sauvignon Merlot	Red	Tannic, berry, smoky	Beef	***
Church Road Reserve Chardonnay	White	Oaky, melon	Fish	***
Clearview Old Olive Block Cabernet Sauvignon Cabernet Franc	Red	Ripe, berry, tannic	Cold meats, stew, offal	**
Clearview Reserve Cabernet Sauvignon	Red	Berry, minerally	Lamb	**
Coopers Creek Reserve Hawkes Bay Merlot Cabernet Franc	Red	Plums, berry	Lamb	**
Coopers Creek Swamp Reserve Chardonnay	White	Melon, spicy	Veal	**
Craggy Range Chardonnay	White	Complex, minerally, spicy	Fish	***
Cross Roads Talisman (up to 6 varieties)	Red	Oaky, berry, rich	Beef	***
Delegates Reserve Merlot	Red	Herbaceous, earthy	Venison	**
Esk Valley Chardonnay	White	Tropical fruit, melon	Fish	**
Esk Valley Merlot	Red	Spicy, herbaceous	Venison	**
Esk Valley The Terraces Malbec Merlot Cabernet franc	Red	Berry, tannic, ripe	Beef	***
Forrest Estate Cornerstone Cabernet Sauvignon Merlot Cabernet Franc Malbec	Red	Herbaceous, spicy	Pasta	**
Huntaway Pinot Gris	White	Melon, tropical fruit	Antipasto	**
Huthlee Merlot	Red	Fruit cake, berry	Cold meats, stew, offal	**
Matawhero Gewürztraminer	White	Floral, citrus	Sausages	**
Matua Valley Judd Chardonnay	White	Melon, berry	Chicken	**
Mills Reef Reserve Cabernet Sauvignon Merlot	Red	Berry, smoky	Veal	**
Mills Reef Reserve Chardonnay	White	Nutty, melon	Fish	**
Mills Reef Traditional Method	Sparkling	Crisp, fruity	Aperitif	***
Millton Barrel Fermented Chardonnay	White	Nutty, spicy	Veal	**
Millton Viognier	White	Tropical fruit, floral	Fish	**
Mission Jewelstone Pinot Gris	White	Citrus, spicy	Fish	**
Mission Reserve Cabernet Sauvignon	Red	Berry, spicy	Mediterranean	**
Morton Estate Black Label Cabernet Sauvignon	Red	Berry, complex	Beef	***
Morton Estate Black Label Merlot	Red	Oaky, tannic, tobacco	Pasta	***
Ngatarawa Glazebrook Cabernet Sauvignon	Red	Berry, tannic	Pasta	**
Ngatarawa Glazebrook Noble Harvest Riesling	Sweet	Sweet, mandarin	Dessert	**
Nobilos Icon Chardonnay	White	Melon, tropical fruit	Shellfish	**
Phoenix Gewürztraminer	White	Spicy, floral	Asian	**

Wine name	Style	Flavor/ Bouquet	Compatible Foods	Price Range
Redmetal Vineyards Basket Press Merlot Cabernet Franc	Red	Berry, chocolate, tannic	Beef	***
Revington Chardonnay	White	Tropical fruit, zingy	Fish	**
Sacred Hill Barrel Fermented Sauvignon Blanc	White	Tropical fruit, nutty	Chicken	**
Sacred Hill Basket Press Cabernet Sauvignon	Red	Berry, earthy	Pasta	**
Sacred Hill Basket Press Merlot	Red	Berry, plums	Venison	**
Sacred Hill Brokenstone Merlot	Red	Berry, plums	Venison	**
Saints Chardonnay	White	Citrus, spicy	Veal	**
Saints Gewürztraminer	White	Floral, spicy, citrus	Asian	**
Sileni Chardonnay	White	Fruity, tropical fruit	Fish	**
Sileni Merlot Cabernet Sauvignon Cabernet Franc	Red	Leathery, berry	Beef	***
Stonecroft Gewürztraminer	White	Floral, spicy	Asian	**
Stonecroft Syrah	Red	Spicy, berry	Duck	***
Te Awa Farm Boundary (cabernet sauvignon/merlot/cabernet franc/malbec)	Red	Herbaceous, berry	Beef	**
Te Awa Farm Merlot	Red	Berry, spicy, herbaceous	Lamb	**
Te Awa Frontier Chardonnay	White	Melon, nutty	Fish	**
Te Awa Longlands Chardonnay	White	Tropical fruit, spicy	Shellfish	**
Te Mata Awatea Cabernet Sauvignon Merlot	Red	Berry, herbaceous	Beef	***
Te Mata Bullnose Syrah	Red	Smoky, berry	Cold meats, stew, offal	***
Te Mata Cape Crest Sauvignon Blanc	White	Zingy, grassy	Salads	**
Te Mata Coleraine Cabernet Sauvignon Merlot	Red	Herbaceous, berry, complex	Beef	***
Te Mata Elston Chardonnay	White	Tropical fruit, nutty, toasty	Fish	***
Thornbury Merlot	Red	Herbaceous, plums	Venison	**
Trinity Hill Cabernet Sauvignon	Red	Berry, tannic	Pasta	***
Trinity Hill Gimbless Road Cabernet Sauvignon Merlot	Red	Smoky, tannic	Venison	***
Trinity Hill Merlot	Red	Berry, leathery	Lamb	***
Trinity Hill Syrah	Red	Spicy, berry, powerful	Beef	***
Trinity Hills Shepherds Croft Merlot Cabernet Franc Syrah	Red	Berry, oaky	Beef	**
Trinity Hill Chardonnay	White	Fruity, citrus	Cheese	**
Unison Merlot Cabernet Sauvignon Syrah	Red	Spicy, berry, oaky	Beef	**
Vidal Estate Cabernet Sauvignon	Red	Tannic, berry	Stew	**
Vidal Estate Reserve Cabernet Sauvignon Merlot	Red	Smoky, berry, tannic	Cold meats, stew, offal	***
Vidal Reserve Chardonnay	White	Melon, toasty	Shellfish	***
Vidal Reseve Noble Semillon	Sweet	Sweet, mandarin	Dessert	**
Villa Maria Reserve Gewürztraminer	White	Spicy, citrus	Asian	**
Villa Maria Reserve Hawkes Bay Cabernet Sauvignon Merlot	Red	Berry, tannic	Beef	***
Villa Maria Reserve Hawkes Bay Chardonnay	White	Nutty, citrus, tropical fruit	Fish	**
Villa Maria Reserve Merlot	Red	Berry, minerally, herbaceous	Venison	**
Virtu Noble Semillon	Sweet	Sweet, floral	Dessert	**
Marlborough				
Allan Scott Riesling	White	Floral, spicy	Cheese	**
Babich Marlborough Sauvignon Blanc	White	Zingy, citrus	Salads	**
Cairnbrae Chardonnay	White	Tropical fruit, melon	Fish	**

Wine name	Style	Flavor/ Bouquet	Compatible Foods	Price Range
Cairnbrae Reserve Riesling	White	Citrus, minerally	Cheese	**
Cloudy Bay Chardonnay	White	Melon, toasty	Fish	***
Cloudy Bay Pinot Noir	Red	Gamey, leathery	Duck	***
Cloudy Bay Sauvignon Blanc	White	Tropical fruit, zingy	Shellfish	***
Corbans Amadeus Classic Reserve Méthode Traditionnelle	Sparkling	Toasty, crisp	Aperitif	**
Corbans Private Bin Marlborough Chardonnay	White	Melon, tropical fruit	Fish	**
Corbans Private Bin Marlborough Sauvignon Blanc	White	Grassy, zingy	Shellfish	**
Craggy Range Riesling	White	Citrus, floral, zingy, complex	Shellfish	***
Craggy Range Sauvignon Blanc	White	Tropical fruit, zingy	Aperitif	***
Daniel Le Brun Vintage Brut Méthode Traditionnelle	Sparkling	Toasty, complex	Aperitif	***
De Redcliffe Marlborough Riesling	White	Floral, citrus	Fish	**
Deutz Blanc de Blancs Méthode Traditionnelle	Sparkling	Citrus, crisp	Cheese	***
Domaine Chandon Marlborough Brut Méthode Traditionnelle	Sparkling	Toasty, crisp, minerally	Aperitif	**
Domaine Georges Michel Chardonnay	White	Nutty, tropical fruit	Fish	**
Duetz Marlborough Cuvée Blanc de Blancs Méthode Traditionnelle Chardonnay	Sparkling	Crisp, citrus, toasty	Aperitif	**
Duetz Marlborough Cuvée Méthode Traditionnelle	Sparkling	Austere, citrus	Fruit	**
Forrest Estate Sauvignon Blanc	White	Zingy, citrus, minerally	Shellfish	**
Framingham Dry Riesling	White	Citrus, zingy	Fish	**
Fromm La Strada Chardonnay	White	Complex, nutty, tropical fruit	Veal	**
Fromm La Strada Merlot	Red	Berry, complex, spicy	Lamb	***
Fromm La Strada Pinot Noir	Red	Berry, oaky, complex	Chicken	***
Fromm La Strada Riesling	White	Floral, citrus	Fish	**
Fromm La Strada Riesling Auslese	Sweet	Sweet, citrus, floral	Dessert	**
Giesen Marlborough Sauvignon Blanc	White	Zingy, tropical fruit	Shellfish	**
Goldwater Roseland Marlborough Chardonnay	White	Toasty, melon	Chicken	**
Grove Mill Chardonnay	White	Melon, tropical fruit	Fish	**
Grove Mill Sauvignon Blanc	White	Citrus, zingy	Shellfish	**
Highfield Elstree Méthode Traditionnelle	Sparkling	Crisp, toasty	Aperitif	**
Huia Gewürztraminer	White	Floral, spicy, complex	Sausages	**
Huia Méthode Traditionnelle	Sparkling	Toasty, complex	Fish	***
Huia Sauvignon Blanc	White	Tropical fruit, spicy, zingy	Shellfish	**
Hunters Riesling	White	Citrus, floral	Pasta	**
Hunters Sauvignon Blanc	White	Zingy, citrus	Shellfish	**
Isabel Estate Chardonnay	White	Tropical fruit, citrus	Fish	**
Isabel Estate Pinot Noir	Red	Spicy, oaky, berry	Cold meats	***
Isabel Estate Sauvignon Blanc	White	Zingy, spicy	Shellfish	**
Kim Crawford Marlborough Sauvignon Blanc	White	Tropical fruit, zingy	Shellfish	**
Lawson's Dry Hills Chardonnay	White	Melon, citrus	Pork	**
Lawson's Dry Hills Riesling	White	Floral, citrus	Veal	**
Le Brun Family No. 1 Méthode Traditionnelle	Sparkling	Toasty, berry, spicy	Shellfish	***
Matua Shingle Peak Riesling	White	Floral, citrus	Fish	**
Montana Reserve Chardonnay	White	Nutty, minerally, citrus	Chicken	**

Wine name	Style	Flavor/ Bouquet	Compatible Foods	Price Range
Montana Reserve Merlot	Red	Berry, tannic, herbaceous	Lamb	**
Montana Reserve Pinot Noir	Red	Berry, spicy, earthy	Game	**
Nautilus Chardonnay	White	Melon, tropical fruit	Fish	**
Nobilos Icon Riesling	White	Citrus, floral	Chicken	**
Omaka Springs Chardonnay	White	Melon, fruity	Salads	*
Oyster Bay Sauvignon Blanc	White	Zingy, citrus, fruity	Shellfish	**
Pegasus Bay Main Divide Sauvignon Blanc	White	Tropical fruit, zingy	Aperitif	**
Pelorus Méthode Traditionnelle	Sparkling	Complex, toasty	Shellfish	***
Ponder Riesling	White	Floral, minerally	Shellfish	**
Saint Clair Rapaura Reserve Merlot	Red	Tannic, berry	Lamb	**
Saint Clair Riesling	White	Citrus, spicy, floral	Fish	**
Saints Noble Riesling	Sweet	Mandarin, sweet	Dessert	**
Selaks Drylands Chardonnay	White	Melon, nutty	Fish	**
Selaks Drylands Riesling	White	Floral, citrus	Veal	**
Selaks Drylands Sauvignon Blanc	White	Tropical fruit, zingy	Salads	**
Selaks Premium Riesling	White	Citrus, zingy	Chicken	**
Seresin Chardonnay	White	Nutty, melon, complex	Chicken	**
Seresin Noble Riesling	Sweet	Sweet, honey, citrus	Dessert	**
Seresin Pinot Gris	White	Tropical fruit, citrus	Fish	**
Seresin Pinot Noir	Red	Fungal, earthy, gamey	Duck	**
Seresin Riesling	White	Floral, citrus, spicy	Fish	**
Stoneleigh Sauvignon Blanc	White	Zingy, minerally	Shellfish	**
Te Whare Ra Duke of Marlborough Chardonnay	White	Melon, oaky	Chicken	**
Thornbury Sauvignon Blanc	White	Grassy, tropical fruit	Cheese	**
Tohu Sauvignon Blanc	White	Zingy, tropical fruit	Shellfish	**
Vavasour Chardonnay	White	Nutty, melon, minerally	Fish	**
Vavasour Dashwood Sauvignon Blanc	White	Zingy, tropical fruit	Fish	**
Vavasour Pinot Noir	Red	Gamey, berry	Duck	**
Vavasour Riesling	White	Citrus, floral	Veal	**
Vavasour Sauvignon Blanc	White	Zingy, tropical fruit	Shellfish	**
Vavasour Single Vineyard Sauvignon Blanc	White	Zingy, tropical fruit, citrus	Fish	**
Vidal Sauvignon Blanc	White	Grassy, zingy	Cheese	**
Villa Maria Clifford Bay Reserve Sauvignon Blanc	White	Zingy, tropical fruit	Shellfish	**
Villa Maria Reserve Barrique Fermented Chardonnay	White	Melon, nutty, toasty	Chicken	***
Villa Maria Reserve Marlborough Chardonnay	White	Melon, citrus	Pork	**
Villa Maria Reserve Marlborough Riesling	White	Floral, minerally	Veal	**
Villa Maria Reserve Noble Riesling	Sweet	Sweet, mandarin	Dessert	***
Villa Maria Wairau Valley Reserve Sauvignon Blanc	White	Zingy, minerally	Shellfish	**
West Brook Riesling	White	Floral, citrus	Chicken	**
Whitehaven Single Vineyard Reserve Sauvignon Blanc	White	Zingy, grassy	Shellfish	**
Wither Hills Chardonnay	White	Melon, nutty	Fish	**
Wither Hills Pinot Noir	Red	Earthy, fungal	Game	**
Wither Hills Sauvignon Blanc	White	Zingy, minerally	Cheese	**

Wine name	Style	Flavor/ Bouquet	Compatible Foods	Price Range
Martinborough				
Alana Pinot Noir	Red	Spicy, berry, smoky	Mediterranean	***
Alexander Vineyard Pinot Noir	Red	Spicy, berry, earthy	Veal	**
Ata Rangi Celebre Cabernet Sauvignon Merlot Syrah	Red	Berry, oaky, spicy	Lamb	**
Ata Rangi Craighall Chardonnay	White	Citrus, melon, oaky	Chicken	***
Ata Rangi Pinot Gris	White	Tropical fruit, complex	Pork	**
Ata Rangi Pinot Noir	Red	Spicy, gamey, berry	Cold meats, stew, offal	***
Dry River Chardonnay	White	Melon, stone fruit, spicy	Shellfish	**
Dry River Craighall Botrytis Riesling	Sweet	Sweet, honey	Dessert	**
Dry River Craighall Riesling	White	Floral, citrus	Fish	**
Dry River Gewürztraminer	White	Spicy, floral, minerally	Chicken	**
Dry River Pinot Gris	White	Melon, spicy	Fish	**
Dry River Pinot Noir	Red	Powerful, earthy, smoky, berry	Duck	***
Dry River Syrah	Red	Plums, berry, earthy	Beef	***
Lintz Pinot Noir	Red	Spicy, berry	Pizza	**
Lintz Syrah	Red	Earthy, berry, herbaceous	Beef	**
Margrain Pinot Gris	White	Citrus, tropical fruit	Pork	**
Margrain Pinot Noir	Red	Spicy, berry	Game	**
Martinborough Pinot Gris	White	Zingy, apples	Fish	**
Martinborough Vineyard Chardonnay	White	Melon, nutty, complex	Chicken	**
Martinborough Vineyards Late Harvest Riesling	Sweet	Honey, mandarin, sweet	Dessert	**
Martinborough Vineyards Pinot Noir	Red	Spicy, earthy, berry	Game	***
Martinborough Vineyards Reserve Pinot Noir	Red	Oaky, berry, gamey	Duck	***
Murdoch James Syrah	Red	Spicy, berry, earthy	Beef	**
Nga Waka Riesling	White	Floral, citrus	Mediterranean	**
Palliser Chardonnay	White	Melon, nutty	Chicken	**
Palliser Estate Pinot Noir	Red	Gamey, berry	Game	***
Palliser Estate Sauvignon Blanc	White	Zingy, grassy	Shellfish	**
Pencarrow Pinot Noir	Red	Earthy, berry	Game	**
Pencarrow Sauvignon Blanc	White	Zingy, grassy	Salads	**
Stratford Pinot Noir	Red	Berry, smoky	Cold meats	**
Te Kairanga Reserve Chardonnay	White	Citrus, toasty, melon	Veal	**
Te Kairanga Reserve Pinot Noir	Red	Complex, berry, spicy	Duck	***
Nelson				
Greenhough Chardonnay	White	Citrus, melon	Fish	**
Neudorf Brightwater Riesling	White	Floral, citrus	Fish	**
Neudorf Moutere Chardonnay	White	Tropical fruit, toasty, nutty	Shellfish	***
Neudorf Moutere Reserve Pinot Noir	Red	Earthy, gamey, berry	Game	***
Neudorf Nelson Chardonnay	White	Citrus, zingy	Chicken	**
Seifried Barrel Fermented Chardonnay	White	Melon, nutty	Veal	**
Seifried Winemaker's Collection Riesling Ice Wine	Sweet	Sweet, citrus, floral	Dessert	**
Waiheke Island				
Goldwater Estate Cabernet Sauvignon Merlot	Red	Berry, complex	Lamb	***

Wine name	Style	Flavor/ Bouquet	Compatible Foods	Price Range
Goldwater Zell Chardonnay	White	Nutty, melon	Fish	**
Obsidian Cabernet Sauvignon Merlot	Red	Tannic, berry, herbaceous	Lamb	**
Stoneyridge Larose Cabernets (cabernet sauvignon/ malbec/merlot/cabernet franc/petite verdot)	Red	Berry, complex, tannic, oaky	Lamb	***
Twin Bays Fenton Merlot Cabernet Franc	Red	Berry, herbaceous	Lamb	**
Waiheke Vineyards Te Motu Cabernet Sauvignon Merlot	Red	Berry, tannic	Lamb	***
Waikato/Bay of Plenty				
Goldwater Esslin Merlot	Red	Leathery, spicy, tannic	Beef	***
Rongopai Winemakers Reserve Botrytised Riesling	Sweet	Sweet, citrus	Dessert	***
Wairarapa/Wellington				
Voss Estate Pinot Noir	Red	Earthy, gamey, berry	Game	**
Voss Estate Waihenga Cabernet Sauvignon Merlot	Red	Herbaceous, berry	Lamb	**
Walnut Ridge Pinot Noir	Red	Oaky, berry, plums	Game	**
Winslow Turakrae Reserve Cabernet Sauvignon Cabernet Franc	Red	Earthy, berry, tannic	Lamb	***

CANADA

British Columbia

Wine name	Style	Flavor/ Bouquet	Compatible Foods	Price Range
Blue Mountain Vineyard and Cellars Reserve Pinot Blanc	White	Stone fruit, oaky	Cheese, fish	**
Blue Mountain Vineyard and Cellars Reserve Pinot Gris	White	Fruity, minerally	Cheese, shellfish	**
Blue Mountain Vineyard and Cellars Reserve Pinot Noir	Red	Jam, vanillin	Veal, pork, beef	**
Calona Vineyards Artist Series Chardonnay	White	Butter, oaky	Fish, pasta, chicken	***
Calona Vineyards Artist Series Pinot Blanc	White	Stone fruit, complex	Pasta, fish, chicken	***
Calona Vineyards Private Reserve Cabernet Sauvignon	Red	Berry, oaky, earthy	Lamb, beef	**
Calona Vineyards Private Reserve Fumé Blanc	White	Stone fruit, citrus	Salads, shellfish, fish, cheese	**
Calona Vineyards Private Reserve Late Harvest Ehrenfelser	White	Fruity, floral	Dessert, cheese	**
Calona Vineyards Private Reserve Merlot	Red	Berry, oaky	Lamb, beef	**
Calona Vineyards Sandhill Pinot Blanc	White	Stone fruit, minerally	Shellfish, fish, chicken	**
Cedar Creek Estate Winery Cabernet Franc	Red	Berry, spicy	Veal, pork, chicken	**
Cedar Creek Estate Winery Chardonnay	White	Fruity, oaky	Fish, chicken, veal	**
Cedar Creek Estate Winery Reserve Chardonnay Icewine	White	Fruity, nutty	Dessert	**
Cedar Creek Estate Winery Riesling	White	Tropical fruit, floral	Asian, pasta	*
Domaine Combret Cabernet Franc	Red	Berry, oaky	Beef, chicken, veal	**
Domaine Combret Chardonnay	White	Fruity, butter	Fish, chicken	**
Domaine Combret Riesling	White	Fruity	Cheese, pizza, fish	*
Domaine de Chaberton Estates Bacchus	White	Fruity	Pizza, pasta, Asian, cheese	**
Gehringer Bros. Estate Winery Auxerrois	White	Fruity, floral	Pizza, pasta, salads, chicken	*
Gehringer Bros. Estate Winery Minus 9 Ehrenfelser Icewine	White	Tropical fruit, spicy	Dessert	**
Gray Monk Estate Winery Riesling	White	Tropical fruit, floral	Asian, pasta	*
Gray Monk Estate Winery Select Late Harvest Ehrenfelser	White	Fruity, spicy	Dessert, cheese	**
Gray Monk Estate Winery Unwooded Chardonnay	White	Stone fruit, minerally	Shellfish, fish, chicken, veal	**
Hawthorne Mountain Vineyards Chardonnay	White	Butter, oaky	Fish, chicken, veal	**

Wine name	Style	Flavor/ Bouquet	Compatible Foods	Price Range
Hawthorne Mountain Vineyards Chardonnay/Semillon	White	Tropical fruit, waxy	Pasta, fish, chicken	**
Hawthorne Mountain Vineyards Ehrenfelser Icewine	White	Tropical fruit, floral	Dessert	***
Hawthorne Mountain Vineyards Gamay Noir	Red	Fruity, jam	Pasta, pizza, Asian, pork	*
Hawthorne Mountain Vineyards Gewürztraminer	White	Tropical fruit, floral	Asian, fish	*
Hawthorne Mountain Vineyards Lemberger	Red	Fruity, spicy	Pizza, pasta, chicken	*
Hawthorne Mountain Vineyards Merlot	Red	Berry, earthy	Pork, beef	**
Hawthorne Mountain Vineyards Riesling	White	Tropical fruit, floral	Asian, pasta	*
Hester Creek Estate Winery Blanc de Noirs	Rosé	Berry, fruity	Pizza, pasta, Asian	**
Hester Creek Estate Winery Estate Pinot Blanc	White	Stone fruit, nutty	Shellfish, fish	**
Hester Creek Estate Winery Late Harvest Trebbiano	White	Fruity, citrus	Asian, fruits, dessert	**
Hester Creek Estate Winery Reserve Pinot Blanc Icewine	White	Floral, nutty	Dessert	***
Hillside Estate Winery Late Harvest Vidal	White	Nutty, stone fruit	Dessert	**
Inniskillin Okanagan Ehrenfelser Icewine	White	Tropical fruit, floral	Dessert	***
Inniskillin Okanagan Riesling Icewine	White	Stone fruit, complex	Dessert	***
Inniskillin Okanagan Vidal Icewine	White	Nutty, fruity, complex	Dessert	***
Jackson-Triggs Vintners Proprietors' Grand Reserve Chardonnay	White	Butter, oaky	Fish, chicken, veal	**
Jackson-Triggs Vintners Proprietors' Grand Reserve Merlot	Red	Berry, oaky, complex	Lamb, pork, beef	**
Jackson-Triggs Vintners Proprietors' Grand Reserve Riesling Icewine	White	Tropical fruit, floral	Dessert	***
Jackson-Triggs Vintners Proprietors' Reserve Cabernet Sauvignon	Red	Berry, earthy, oaky	Lamb, beef	**
Jackson-Triggs Vintners Proprietors' Reserve Chardonnay	White	Butter, oaky	Fish, veal	**
Jackson-Triggs Vintners Proprietors' Reserve Chenin Blanc Icewine	White	Tropical fruit, floral	Dessert	**
Jackson-Triggs Vintners Proprietors' Reserve Merlot	Red	Berry, earthy	Lamb, beef	**
Jackson-Triggs Vintners Proprietors' Reserve Pinot Blanc	Red	Stone fruit, oaky	Fish, chicken, veal	**
Jackson-Triggs Vintners Proprietors' Reserve Riesling Icewine	White	Floral, tropical fruit	Dessert	***
Lake Breeze Vineyards Pinot Blanc	White	Stone fruit, minerally	Shellfish, fish, chicken, veal	**
Mission Hill Winery Grand Reserve Cabernet Sauvignon	Red	Berry, leather, earthy	Lamb, beef	**
Mission Hill Winery Grand Reserve Chardonnay	White	Butter, oaky	Fish, chicken, veal	**
Mission Hill Winery Grand Reserve Pinot Gris	White	Nutty, floral	Pasta, fish, veal	**
Mission Hill Winery Grand Reserve Pinot Noir	Red	Berry, oaky	Veal, chicken, pork	**
Mission Hill Winery Private Reserve Merlot	Red	Berry, oaky	Lamb, beef	**
Peller Estates Wines Limited Edition Pinot Gris	White	Nutty, floral	Shellfish, fish, veal	**
Peller Estates Wines Trinity Icewine	White	Floral, fruity	Dessert	***
Pinot Reach Cellars Riesling Brut	Sparkling	Citrus, complex	Antipasto, pizza, Asian	*
Poplar Grove Cabernet Franc	Red	Berry, oaky	Beef, chicken, veal	**
Poplar Grove Chardonnay	White	Fruity, butter	Fish, chicken	**
Poplar Grove Merlot	Red	Berry, oaky	Veal, pork, lamb, beef	**
Quails' Gate Estate Winery Family Reserve Pinot Noir	Red	Berry, oaky	Pork, veal	**
Quails' Gate Estate Winery Late Harvest Botrytis Affected Optima	White	Fruity, nutty	Dessert, cheese	***
Quails' Gate Estate Winery Limited Release Chenin Blanc	White	Fruity, floral	Pasta, salads, fish	**
Quails' Gate Estate Winery Limited Release Dry Riesling	White	Floral, tropical fruit	Shellfish, Asian	**
Quails' Gate Estate Winery Limited Release Meritage	Red	Oaky, berry, complex	Lamb, beef	**
Quails' Gate Estate Winery Limited Release Old Vines Foch	Red	Berry, spicy	Pizza, pasta, chicken	**

Wine name	Style	Flavor/ Bouquet	Compatible Foods	Price Range
St. Hubertus Estate Winery Gamay Rosé	Rosé	Fruity, floral	Antipasto, pizza, shellfish	*
St. Hubertus Estate Winery Oak Bay Chardonnay/Pinot Blanc	White	Fruity, minerally	Pasta, fish, chicken, veal	**
St. Hubertus Estate Winery Oak Bay Pinot Meunier	Red	Fruity, berry	Pizza, pasta, chicken	**
St. Hubertus Estate Winery Pinot Blanc Icewine	White	Nutty, complex	Dessert	***
St. Hubertus Estate Winery Pinot Blanc/Riesling Icewine	White	Floral, complex	Dessert	***
Sumac Ridge Estate Cabernet Sauvignon	Red	Berry, earthy, oaky	Lamb, beef	**
Sumac Ridge Estate Meritage White	White	Oaky, waxy, stone fruit	Shellfish, fish, veal	**
Sumac Ridge Estate Merlot	Red	Berry, spicy	Pork, beef	**
Sumac Ridge Estate Okanagan Blush	Rosé	Berry, floral	Salads, pizza, pasta	*
Sumac Ridge Estate Pinot Blanc Icewine	White	Nutty, complex	Dessert	***
Sumac Ridge Estate Private Reserve Gewürztraminer	White	Floral, spicy	Asian, fish, cheese	**
Sumac Ridge Estate Private Reserve Pinot Blanc	White	Stone fruit, oaky	Fish, chicken, veal	**
Summerhill Estate Winery Cipes Aurora Blanc de Blancs	White	Fruity, floral	Shellfish, veal	**
Summerhill Estate Winery Gewürztraminer Reserve	White	Tropical fruit, floral	Asian, fish, cheese	**
Summerhill Estate Winery Late Harvest Riesling Icewine	White	Floral, tropical fruit	Dessert	**
Summerhill Estate Winery Pinot Blanc	White	Stone fruit, minerally	Shellfish, fish, chicken, veal	**
Summerhill Estate Winery Platinum Series Cabernet Sauvignon	Red	Berry, leather, oaky	Lamb, beef	**
Summerhill Estate Winery Platinum Series Pinot Noir	Red	Berry, spicy	Pork, veal	**
Summerhill Estate Winery Riesling Icewine	White	Floral, tropical fruit	Dessert	**
Tinhorn Creek Vineyards Cabernet Franc	Red	Berry, spicy	Veal, pork, chicken	**
Tinhorn Creek Vineyards Chardonnay	White	Butter, oaky	Fish, chicken, veal	**
Tinhorn Creek Vineyards Kerner Icewine	White	Spicy, fruity	Dessert	***
Tinhorn Creek Vineyards Merlot	Red	Berry, oaky	Pork, beef	**
Wild Goose Vineyards and Winery Autumn Gold	White	Fruity, floral	Cheese, Asian	*
Wild Goose Vineyards and Winery Pinot Blanc	White	Fruity, minerally	Shellfish, fish, chicken, veal	**
Lake Erie North Shore				
Colio Cabernet Franc	Red	Berry, spicy	Pizza, beef, chicken	**
D'Angelo Estate Cabernet Franc	Red	Berry, spicy	Pizza, beef, chicken	**
D'Angelo Estate Vidal Icewine	White	Citrus, tropical, fruit, minerally	Dessert	***
LeBlanc Estate Winery Oaked Cabernet Franc	Red	Berry, vanillin	Beef, chicken, veal	**
LeBlanc Estate Winery Vidal Icewine	White	Citrus, tropical fruit, minerally	Dessert	***
Ontario				
Cave Spring Cellars Cabernet/Merlot	Red	Earthy, berry	Beef, lamb	**
Cave Spring Cellars Chardonnay Reserve	White	Fruity, oaky	Fish, chicken, veal	**
Cave Spring Cellars Estate Bottled Gewürztraminer	White	Tropical fruit, floral	Cheese, fruit, Asian	**
Cave Spring Cellars Estate Bottled Reserve Riesling	White	Fruity, minerally	Asian, shellfish	**
Cave Spring Cellars Gamay	Red	Jam, berry	Pizza, Asian, pork chicken, veal,	*
Cave Spring Cellars Off Dry Riesling	White	Floral, tropical fruit	Asian, cheese	*
Cave Spring Cellars Riesling Icewine	White	Floral, tropical fruit	Dessert	***
Château des Charmes Sec Méthode Traditionelle	Sparkling	Stone fruit, minerally	Pizza, shellfish	**
Château des Charmes Late Harvest Riesling	White	Floral, stone fruit	Cheese, dessert	**

Wine name	Style	Flavor/ Bouquet	Compatible Foods	Price Range
Château des Charmes Paul Bosc Riesling Icewine	White	Tropical fruit, waxy, floral	Dessert	***
Château des Charmes St. David's Bench Vyd. Cabernet Franc	Red	Berry, oaky	Beef, pork	**
Château des Charmes St. David's Bench Vyd. Chardonnay	White	Butter, oaky	Chicken, veal, fish	**
Cilento Late-Harvest Riesling	White	Tropical fruit, floral	Dessert	**
Cilento Reserve Cabernet Sauvignon	Red	Berry, oaky	Lamb, beef	**
Cilento Vidal Icewine	White	Nutty, tropical fruit	Dessert	***
Colio Late Harvest Vidal	White	Fruity, nutty	Dessert	**
D'Angelo Estate Select Late Harvest Vidal	White	Fruity, nutty	Dessert	**
Henry of Pelham Family Estate Cabernet/Merlot	Red	Earthy, berry	Beef, lamb	**
Henry of Pelham Family Estate Reserve Baco Noir	Red	Berry, earthy	Pasta, pork	**
Henry of Pelham Family Estate Reserve Baco Noir	Red	Jam, spicy	Pizza, pasta, pork	**
Henry of Pelham Family Estate Reserve Chardonnay	White	Butter, oaky	Chicken, fish	**
Henry of Pelham Family Estate Reserve Riesling	White	Floral, fruity	Asian, shellfish	**
Henry of Pelham Family Estate Riesling Icewine	White	Floral, tropical fruit	Dessert	***
Henry of Pelham Family Estate Select Late Harvest Vidal	White	Tropical fruit, nutty	Dessert	**
Henry of Pelham Family Estate Winery Barrel Fermented Chardonnay	White	Fruity, oaky	Fish, chicken	**
Hernder Estate Wines Baco Noir	Red	Fruity, spicy	Pizza, pasta, Asian	*
Hernder Estate Wines Barrel Fermented Chardonnay	White	Fruity, oaky	Fish, chicken	**
Hernder Estate Wines Cabernet Franc	Red	Berry, spicy	Beef, veal, pork	**
Hernder Estate Wines Icewine	White	Fruity	Dessert	***
Hernder Estate Wines Select Late Harvest Vidal	White	Nutty, fruity	Dessert	**
Hernder Estate Wines Select Late Harvest Vidal	White	Tropical fruit, nutty	Dessert	**
Hillebrand Estates Winery Glenlake Showcase Unfiltered Cabernet Sauvignon	Red	Earthy, berry	Lamb, beef	**
Hillebrand Estates Winery Harvest Riesling	White	Fruity, stone fruit	Cheese, Asian	**
Hillebrand Estates Winery Trius Chardonnay	White	Fruity, oaky	Chicken, veal, pasta, fish	**
ilento Barrel Fermented Reserve Chardonnay	White	Fruity, oaky	Fish, chicken	**
Inniskillin Wines Cabernet Franc	Red	Berry, complex	Beef, veal, pork	**
Inniskillin Wines Culp Vyd. Chardonnay	White	Stone fruit, vanillin	Fish, chicken, veal	**
Inniskillin Wines Founders' Reserve Pinot Noir	Red	Berry, spicy	Pizza, veal, pork	**
Inniskillin Wines Reserve Chardonnay	White	Butter, oaky	Chicken, fish	**
Inniskillin Wines Riesling Icewine	White	Floral, tropical fruit	Dessert	***
Inniskillin Wines Vidal Icewine	White	Nutty, tropical fruit, complex	Dessert	***
Joseph's Estate Wines Pinot Gris	White	Floral, minerally	Salads, shellfish, fish, chicken	**
Joseph's Estate Wines Vidal Icewine	White	Nutty, tropical fruit, floral	Dessert	***
Kittling Ridge Estate Wines Marechal Foch	Red	Berry, spicy	Pizza, pasta, Mediterranean	*
Konzelmann Estate Winery Late Harvest Riesling, Very Dry	White	Floral, stone fruit	Asian, cheese	**
Konzelmann Estate Winery Pinot Noir	Red	Berry, spicy	Chicken, veal	**
Konzelmann Estate Winery Riesling/Traminer Icewine	White	Fruity, spicy	Dessert	***
Konzelmann Estate Winery Select Late Harvest Vidal	White	Fruity, nutty	Dessert	**
Konzelmann Estate Winery Vidal Icewine	White	Tropical fruit, floral	Dessert	***
Lakeview Cellars Estate Winery Baco Noir	Red	Fruity, spicy	Pizza, pasta, Asian	*

Wine name	Style	Flavor/ Bouquet	Compatible Foods	Price Range
Lakeview Cellars Estate Winery Cabernet/Merlot	Red	Berry, toasty	Beef, lamb	**
Lakeview Cellars Estate Winery Chardonnay Musqué	White	Fruity, complex	Fish, chicken, pasta	**
Lakeview Cellars Estate Winery Vidal Icewine	White	Tropical fruit, floral	Dessert	***
Lakeview Cellars Estate Winery Vinc Vyd. Reserve Chardonnay	White	Butter, oaky	Fish, pasta, chicken	**
Magnotta Barrel Fermented Chardonnay	White	Fruity, oaky	Fish, chicken	**
Magnotta Harvest Moon Vidal	White	Fruity, floral	Cheese, fruit, dessert	**
Magnotta Limited Edition Cabernet Franc Icewine	Red	Berry, mint	Cheese, dessert	***
Magnotta Limited Edition Riesling Icewine	White	Floral, fruity	Dessert	***
Magnotta Limited Edition Sparkling Vidal Icewine	Sparkling	Fruity, complex	Dessert	***
Magnotta Select Late Harvest Vidal	White	Tropical fruit, nutty	Dessert	**
Magnotta Vidal Icewine	White	Tropical fruit, floral	Dessert	***
Malivoire Winery Dry Late Harvest Gewürztraminer	White	Tropical fruit, complex	Cheese, fruit, Asian	**
Malivoire Winery Gewürztraminer Icewine	White	Tropical fruit, floral	Dessert	***
Marynissen Estate Winery Cabernet Franc	Red	Berry, oaky	Beef, chicken, veal	**
Marynissen Estate Winery Merlot	Red	Berry, oaky	Beef, pork	**
Marynissen Estate Winery Riesling	White	Fruity, floral	Salads, Asian	*
Pelee Island Winery Cabernet Franc	Red	Berry, spicy	Veal, pork	**
Peller Estates Chardonnay	White	Fruity, butter	Fish, chicken	**
Peller Estates Founder's Series Chardonnay	White	Fruity, butter	Fish, chicken	**
Pillitteri Estates Winery Baco Noir	Red	Fruity, spicy	Pizza, pasta, Asian	*
Pillitteri Estates Winery Barrel Aged Chardonnay	White	Fruity, oaky	Fish, chicken	**
Pillitteri Estates Winery Family Reserve Cabernet Franc	Red	Berry, oaky	Veal, pork, pasta	**
Pillitteri Estates Winery Riesling Icewine	White	Floral, tropical fruit	Dessert	***
Pillitteri Estates Winery Select Late Harvest Riesling	White	Tropical fruit, floral	Dessert	**
Reif Estate Winery Off Dry Riesling	White	Floral, tropical fruit	Asian, cheese	*
Reif Estate Winery Reserve Chardonnay	White	Butter, oaky	Chicken, fish	**
Reif Estate Winery Riesling Icewine	White	Floral, tropical fruit	Dessert	***
Reif Estate Winery Select Late Harvest Vidal	White	Tropical fruit, nutty	Dessert	**
Reif Estate Winery Vidal Icewine	White	Tropical fruit, floral	Dessert	***
Southbrook Farms Lailey Vyd. Cabernet Sauvignon	Red	Berry, leather	Beef, lamb	**
Southbrook Farms Marechal Foch	Red	Berry, spicy	Pizza, pasta, Mediterranean	*
Southbrook Farms Pinot Gris	White	Floral, minerally	Salads, shellfish, Fish, chicken	**
Southbrook Farms Sauvignon Blanc	White	Citrus, floral	Antipasto, salads, cheese, pasta, fish	**
Southbrook Farms Select Late Harvest Vidal	White	Fruity, floral	Dessert	**
Southbrook Farms Triomphe Chardonnay	White	Butter, oaky	Chicken, veal, fish	**
Stonechurch Vineyards Pinot Noir	Red	Berry, spicy	Chicken, veal	**
Stonechurch Vineyards Vidal Icewine	White	Tropical fruit, nutty	Dessert	***
Stoney Ridge Cellars Barrel Fermented Gewürztraminer Icewine	White	Tropical fruit, complex	Dessert	***
Stoney Ridge Cellars Butler's Grant Vyd. Reserve Pinot Noir	Red	Berry, oaky	Veal, pork	**
Stoney Ridge Cellars Cuesta Old Vines Chardonnay	White	Fruity, complex	Fish, chicken, veal	**
Stoney Ridge Cellars Full Oak Chardonnay	White	Fruity, oaky	Fish, chicken, veal	**

Wine name	Style	Flavor/ Bouquet	Compatible Foods	Price Range
Stoney Ridge Cellars Lenko Vyd. Old Vines Chardonnay	White	Butter, fruity, complex	Fish, chicken, veal	**
Stoney Ridge Cellars Reserve Chardonnay	White	Butter, oaky	Chicken, fish	**
Stoney Ridge Cellars Reserve Pinot Noir	Red	Berry, spicy, oaky	Pork, chicken	**
Stoney Ridge Cellars Select Late Harvest Vidal	White	Tropical fruit, nutty	Dessert	**
Stoney Ridge Cellars Wismer Vyd. Cabernet Franc	Red	Berry, oaky	Chicken, veal, pork	**
Strewn Pinot Blanc	White	Stone fruit, minerally	Pasta, fish, chicken, veal	**
Strewn Riesling Sussreserve	White	Citrus, fruity	Shellfish	***
Strewn Select Late Harvest Vidal	White	Fruity, nutty	Dessert	**
Strewn Vidal Icewine	White	Tropical fruit, floral	Dessert	***
Thirty Bench Winery Reserve Cabernet Sauvignon	Red	Berry, oaky	Lamb, beef	**
Vineland Estates Gewürztraminer	White	Tropical fruit, floral	Asian, cheese	*
Vineland Estates Reserve Riesling	White	Floral, fruity	Asian, shellfish	**
Vineland Estates Semi-Dry Riesling	White	Tropical fruit, floral	Asian, cheese	*
Vineland Estates Seyval Blanc	White	Fruity, floral	Shellfish, fish, chicken	**

UNITED STATES OF AMERICA

Arizona

Callaghan Buena Suerte (cabernet sauvignon/merlot/cabernet franc)	Red	Plums, vanillin	Veal, pork, beef	**

Central Valley/California

Baron Herzog Lodi Zinfandel	Red	Berry, spicy	Pizza, beef, sausages	*
Baywood Cellars Lodi Vineyard Select Zinfandel	Red	Berry, spicy	Pizza, beef, sausages	*
Bella Vigna Lodi Vigna Antica Zinfandel	Red	Berry, spicy	Pizza, beef, sausages	**
Biff and Scooter Abroad/Livermore Valley Cellars Yolo County Orange Muscat	Sweet	Honey, floral	Dessert	*
Big White House Lodi Phillips Vineyards Carignane	Red	Spicy, earthy, jam	Pizza, beef, veal, pork	*
Big White House Lodi Ripken Vineyards Roussanne	White	Floral, melon	Shellfish, salads	**
Big White House Lodi Ripken Vineyards Viognier	White	Floral, fruity	Shellfish, fruits	**
Big White House Lodi Ripken Vineyards Viognier Ice Wine	Sweet	Sweet, honey, stone fruit	Dessert	**
Big White House Lodi Von Rueten Vineyards Syrah	Red	Berry, spicy	Pork, beef, veal	**
Bogle Vineyards California Chardonnay	White	Apples, buttery	Chicken, fish	*
Bogle Vineyards California Old Vine Cuvée Zinfandel	Red	Berry, spicy	Pizza, beef, sausages	*
Bogle Vineyards California Petite Sirah	Red	Berry, peppery	Pizza, pasta, beef	*
Bogle Vineyards Clarksburg Chenin Blanc	White	Floral, fruity	Shellfish, salads	*
Bogle Vineyards Colby Ranch Reserve Clarksburg Chardonnay	White	Butter, oaky	Chicken, fish, veal	*
Burgess Cellars Lodi Zinfandel	Red	Berry, spicy	Pizza, beef, sausages	**
Campus Oaks Lodi Old Vine Zinfandel	Red	Berry, spicy	Pizza, beef, sausages	**
Chouinard Lodi Mohr-Fry Ranch Zinfandel	Red	Berry, spicy	Chicken, veal, beef	**
Clayton Lodi Petite Sirah	Red	Berry, peppery	Pizza, sausages	**
Clayton Lodi Zinfandel	Red	Berry, spicy	Pizza, pasta, beef	**
Clos du Val Napa-El Dorado-San Joaquin Zinfandel	Red	Berry, oaky	Beef, pork	**
Delicato California Cabernet Sauvignon	Red	Plums, jam	Pizza, beef	*
Delicato California Merlot	Red	Plums, earthy	Chicken, beef	*
Delicato California Syrah	Red	Plums, spicy	Veal, beef, pizza	*

Wine name	Style	Flavor/ Bouquet	Compatible Foods	Price Range
Dry Creek Clarksburg Chenin Blanc	White	Floral, fruity	Shellfish, salads	*
Eola Hills Lodi Zinfandel	Red	Berry, spicy	Pizza, sausages, beef	*
Fenestra Winery Lodi Syrah	Red	Berry, spicy	Pizza, sausages, beef	*
Ficklin Madera NV Port	Fortified	Berry, sweet	Dessert, cheese	*
Ficklin Madera Vintage Port	Fortified	Berry, sweet	Dessert, cheese	**
Gnekow Family Winery California Symphony	White	Floral, fruity	Fruit, cheese	*
Indigo Hills California Merlot	Red	Plums, jam	Pizza, beef, veal	*
J. Lohr Lodi Cypress Zinfandel	Red	Berry, spicy	Pizza, sausages, beef	*
Jessie's Grove Lodi Fancy Quest Old Vine Zinfandel	Red	Berry, spicy	Sausages, beef	**
Jessie's Grove Lodi Reserve Westwind Old Vine Zinfandel	Red	Berry, complex	Beef, pork	**
Jessie's Grove Lodi Spenker Vineyard Royalty Old Vine Zinfandel	Red	Rich, toasty	Beef, pork, cheese	**
Kenwood Lodi Old Vine Zinfandel	Red	Berry, spicy	Pizza, sausages, beef	*
Lucas Lodi Chardonnay	White	Apples, minerally	Fish, chicken, pasta	*
Lucas Lodi Old Vine Zinfandel	Red	Berry, spicy	Pizza, sausages, beef	*
M. Cosentino California CigarZin Zinfandel	Red	Berry, oaky	Pork, beef	**
Oak Ridge Vineyards Lodi Classic Reserve Zinfandel	Red	Berry, spicy	Pizza, sausages, beef	**
Peirano Estate Vineyards Lodi Chardonnay	White	Apples, minerally	Fish, salads	*
Peirano Estate Vineyards Lodi Old Vines Zinfandel	Red	Berry, spicy	Pizza, sausages, beef	*
Phillips Vineyards California Symphony	White	Floral, fruity	Salads, fruits	*
Phillips Vineyards Lodi Cotes de Lodi Rhone Blush	Rosé	Fruity	Salads, shellfish	*
Phillips Vineyards Lodi Old Vine Carignan	Red	Earthy, spicy	Pizza, Mediterrerean	*
Phillips Vineyards Lodi Syrah	Red	Berry, jam	Pizza, chicken	*
Quady Madera Electra Fortified Muscat	Fortified	Floral, zingy	Fruit, Asian, cold meats,	*
Quady Madera Elysium Fortified Muscat	Fortified	Spicy, floral	Dessert, cheese	*
Quady Madera Essensia Fortified Muscat	Fortified	Fruity, tangy	Dessert	*
Quady Madera Starboard Port	Fortified	Berry, rich	Nuts, cheese	*
R. H. Phillips California Dunnigan Hills Night Harvest Sauvignon Blanc	White	Sweet, floral, honey	Cold meats, cheese, dessert	*
R. H. Phillips California EXP Dunnigan Hills Syrah	Red	Berry, licorice	Pizza, Mediterrerean	*
Ravenswood Lodi Zinfandel	Red	Berry, spicy	Pizza, sausages, beef	**
Rutherford Vintners Lodi Zinfandel	Red	Berry, spicy	Pizza, sausages, beef	**
Sable Ridge Vineyards Lodi Old Vines Zinfandel	Red	Berry, spicy	Pizza, sausages, beef	**
Spenker Family Winery Lodi Zinfandel	Red	Berry, spicy	Pizza, sausages, beef	**
St. Amant California Zinfandel	Red	Rich, plums, earthy	Pork, lamb, beef	**
St. Amant Lodi Barbera	Red	Berry, spicy, oaky	Pork, lamb, beef	**
St. Amant Lodi LBV Port	Fortified	Berry, rich	Nuts, cheese, dessert	*
St. Amant Lodi Mohr-Fry Ranch Old Vines Zinfandel	Red	Berry, earthy	Lamb, beef, pork	**
St. Amant Lodi/Amador Syrah	Red	Rich, spicy	Mediterrerean, nuts	**
Thomas Coyne California Viognier	White	Floral, minerally	Shellfish, salads	*
Turley Wine Cellars Lodi Spenker Vineyard Zinfandel	Red	Berry, rich	Cheese, lamb, dessert	***
Unalii Lodi Hillside Estates Zinfandel	Red	Berry, spicy	Pizza, sausages, beef	**
Vigil Lodi Mohr-Fry Ranch Old Vines Zinfandel	Red	Berry, spicy	Pizza, sausages, beef	**
Woodbridge Robert Mondavi Lodi Barbera	Red	Plums, spicy	Pizza, sausages, Asian	*

Wine name	Style	Flavor/ Bouquet	Compatible Foods	Price Range
Woodbridge Robert Mondavi Lodi Merlot	Red	Plums, licorice	Pizza, chicken, beef	*
Woodbridge Robert Mondavi Lodi Old Vine Zinfandel	Red	Berry, spicy	Pizza, sausages, beef	*
Woodbridge Robert Mondavi Lodi Sauvignon Blanc	White	Herbaceous, citrus	Shellfish, salads	*
Woodbridge Robert Mondavi Lodi Viognier	White	Floral, stone fruit	Fruit, salads	*
Colorado				
Colorado Cellars Merlot	Red	Plums, herbaceous	Lamb, beef	**
Plum Creek Cellars Cabernet Sauvignon	Red	Plums, vanillin	Beef, pork	**
Two Rivers Winery Cabernet Sauvignon	Red	Berry, herbaceous	Beef, lamb	**
Columbia Valley/Washington State				
Canoe Ridge Reserve Merlot	Red	Smoky, intense, plums, cloves	Beef, lamb	**
Chateau Ste. Michelle Reserve Merlot	Red	Rich, fruity, oaky	Beef, lamb	**
Columbia Crest Reserve Red (cabernet sauvignon/merlot/cabernet franc/malbec)	Red	Plums, cloves, spicy	Beef, lamb	**
Columbia Crest Reserve Syrah (syrah/grenache)	Red	Berry, spicy, oaky	Chicken, veal, pork	**
Columbia Winery Red Willow Sangiovese (piccolo sangiovese/grosso sangiovese)	Red	Berry, spicy, licorice, oaky	Chicken, veal, pork	**
Columbia Winery Sagemoor Cabernet Sauvignon	Red	Berry, herbaceous, complex, oaky	Beef, lamb	***
Dunham Cabernet Sauvignon III	Red	Berry, herbaceous, intense, oaky	Beef, lamb	**
Edgefield Columbia Valley Syrah	Red	Plums, smoky	Beef, lamb	**
Glen Fiona Columbia Valley Syrah (syrah/viognier)	Red	Berry, spicy, floral, elegant	Chicken, veal, pork	**
Mathews Cabernet Sauvignon Elerding Vineyard	Red	Berry, herbaceous, intense	Beef, lamb	**
Woodward Canyon Celilo Vineyard Chardonnay	White	Apples, buttery, vanillin	Chicken, fish	**
Woodward Canyon Merlot	Red	Berry, plum, oaky	Beef, lamb	**
Connecticut				
Chamard Vineyards Cabernet Franc	Red	Berry, spicy	Pork, beef	**
Chamard Vineyards Chardonnay	White	Apples, buttery	Fish, chicken	**
Sharpe Hill Vineyard Cabernet Franc	Red	Berry, herbaceous	Veal, pork, beef	**
Sharpe Hill Vineyard Select Late Harvest Stonington Vineyards Rosé	Rosé	Sweet, fruity, floral	Cheese, fruit, dessert	**
Idaho				
Camas Winery Hog Heaven White	White	Fruity, floral	Salads, shellfish	*
Camas Winery Tej Hopped Mead	Sweet	Sweet, honey, waxy	Dessert	**
Carmela Vineyards Barrel Ferment Chardonnay	White	Apples, toasty	Fish, chicken	**
Carmela Vineyards Blush	Rosé	Fruity, floral	Salads, shellfish	*
Carmela Vineyards Cabernet Franc	Red	Berry, herbaceous	Pork, veal	**
Carmela Vineyards Lemberger	Red	Fruity, spicy	Pizza, pasta	*
Carmela Vineyards Proprietor Grown Merlot	Red	Berry, herbaceous	Lamb, pork, beef	**
Carmela Vineyards Riesling	White	Floral, minerally	Shellfish	*
Carmela Vineyards Semillon	White	Floral, waxy	Fish, veal	*
Indian Creek Pinot Noir	Red	Berry, spicy	Fish, veal, pork	**
Koenig Vineyards Cabernet Sauvignon	Red	Plums, spicy	Pork, beef, lamb	**
Koenig Vineyards Pinot Noir	Red	Berry, spicy	Pork, beef, fish	**
Koenig Vineyards Zinfandel	Red	Berry, spicy	Beef, pork	**

Wine name	Style	Flavor/ Bouquet	Compatible Foods	Price Range
Pend d'Oreille Bistro Rouge Red Table Wine	Red	Fruity, jam	Pizza, pasta, pork	*
Pend d'Oreille Chardonnay	White	Apples, buttery	Fish, chicken	**
Pend d'Oreille Pinot Noir	Red	Berry, spicy	Fish, chicken, veal	**
Rose Creek Vineyards Johannisberg Riesling	White	Floral, minerally	Salads, shellfish	*
Sawtooth Cabernet Sauvignon	Red	Plums, earthy	Beef, lamb	**
Sawtooth Chenin Blanc	White	Fruity, floral	Salads, shellfish	*
Sawtooth Riesling	White	Floral, minerally	Shellfish, fruits	*
Sawtooth Semillon/Chardonnay	White	Apples, honey	Fish, chicken	**
South Hills/Hegy's Chenin Blanc	White	Fruity, floral	Salads, shellfish	*
South Hills/Hegy's Pinot Noir	Red	Berry, spicy	Fish, veal, pork	**
Ste. Chapelle Cabernet Sauvignon Winemaker's Series	Red	Plums, toasty	Beef, pork, lamb	**
Ste. Chapelle Chardonnay	White	Apples, minerally	Fish, chicken	**
Ste. Chapelle Chardonnay Winemaker's Series	White	Complex, oaky	Fish, chicken	**
Ste. Chapelle Dry Riesling Winemaker's Series	White	Floral, minerally	Shellfish, fish	**
Ste. Chapelle Idaho/Washington Cabernet Sauvignon	Red	Plums, spicy	Beef, pork, lamb	**
Ste. Chapelle Idaho/Washington Merlot	Red	Plums, herbaceous	Pork, veal, beef	**
Ste. Chapelle Merlot Winemaker's Series	Red	Plums, oaky	Beef, pork, lamb	**
Ste. Chapelle Reserve Syrah Reserve Series	Red	Berry, spicy	Sausages, beef, pork, veal	**
Maryland				
Basignani Winery Cabernet Sauvignon	Red	Plums, spicy	Beef, pork, lamb	**
Boordy Vineyards Seyval	White	Fruity, floral	Cheese, fruit, fish	*
Fiore Winery Caronte (merlot/cabernet sauvignon)	Red	Plums, herbaceous	Beef, pork, lamb	**
Massachussets				
Westport Vineyards Blanc de Noirs	Sparkling	Crisp, fruity	Fruit, Asian	**
Michigan				
Chateau Grand Traverse Ice Wine	Sweet	Sweet, rich, fruity	Dessert	**
L. Mawby Vineyard Sparkling Wine	Sparkling	Crisp, fruity	Fruit, Asian	**
Peninsula Cellars Chardonnay	White	Apples, minerally	Fish, chicken	**
St. Julian Wine Co. Semi-Dry Riesling	White	Honey, tropical fruit	Cheese, fruits, fish	*
Missouri				
Stone Hill Winery Norton	Red	Fruity	Pizza, Asian	*
Stone Hill Winery Seyval	White	Fruity, floral	Salads, fish	*
Monterey/California				
Anapamu Cellars Central Coast Chardonnay	White	Buttery, rich	Fish, chicken	*
Baywood Cellars Private Reserve California Port	Fortified	Berry, jam	Dessert, nuts	*
Baywood Cellars Vineyard Select California Symphony	White	Honey, floral	Salads, fruit	*
Baywood Cellars Vineyard Select Merlot	Red	Plums, jam	Pizza, beef, sausages	*
Bernardus Carmel Valley Marinus Meritage	Red	Rich, toasty	Lamb, beef, cheese	***
Bernardus Chardonnay	White	Rich, buttery	Fish, chicken, veal	***
Bernardus Sauvignon Blanc	White	Rich, citrus	Shellfish, fish, cheese	**
Big White House Arroyo Seco Vineyards Viognier	White	Floral, tropical fruit	Fish, salads	**
Bonny Doon Vineyards Ca del Solo Big House Red	Red	Plums, spicy	Pizza, pasta, beef, pork	**

Wine name	Style	Flavor/ Bouquet	Compatible Foods	Price Range
Bonny Doon Vineyards Monterey/San Luis Obispo Syrah	Red	Berry, spicy	Veal, pork, beef	**
Bonny Doon Vineyards Moscato Fior d'Arrancio Fortified Muscat	Fortified	Fruity, floral	Dessert	**
Bonny Doon Vineyards San Bernabe Vineyard Barbera	Red	Spicy, earthy	Pizza, pork, veal	**
Bonny Doon Vineyards Sangiovese	Red	Berry, spicy	Pizza, pasta, veal, pork	**
Boyer Arroyo Seco Syrah	Red	Berry, spicy	Pizza, veal, pork	**
Boyer Chardonnay	White	Apples, buttery	Fish, chicken	**
Boyer Pinot Noir	Red	Berry, spicy	Fish, pork, chicken	**
Cain Musque Ventana Vineyard Sauvignon Blanc	White	Complex, citrus	Shellfish, fish, salads	**
Calera Central Coast Chardonnay	White	Rich, tropical fruit	Fish, chicken	**
Calera Jensen Mount Harlan Pinot Noir	Red	Complex, berry, spicy	Fish, pork, cheese	***
Calera Mills Mount Harlan Pinot Noir	Red	Complex, berry, earthy	Fish, pork, cheese	***
Calera Mount Harlan Chardonnay	White	Elegant, floral	Fish, chicken, cheese	***
Calera Mount Harlan Viognier	White	Rich, floral, stone fruit	Fruits, Asian, fish	***
Calera Reed Mount Harlan Pinot Noir	Red	Complex, berry, spicy	Fish, pork, cheese	***
Calera Selleck Mount Harlan Pinot Noir	Red	Complex, berry, spicy	Fish, pork, cheese	***
Camelot California Chardonnay	White	Oaky, buttery	Fish, chicken	**
Carmel Road Chardonnay	White	Oaky, buttery	Fish, chicken	**
Case Pinot Noir	Red	Berry, spicy	Fish, pork, veal	**
Chalone Vineyard Chalone Chardonnay	White	Complex, rich	Fish, chicken	***
Chalone Vineyard Chalone Chenin Blanc	White	Floral, minerally	Shellfish, fish	***
Chalone Vineyard Chalone Pinot Blanc	White	Rich, nutty	Fish, chicken	***
Chalone Vineyard Chalone Pinot Noir	Red	Complex, berry, spicy	Fish, pork, cheese	***
Chalone Vineyard The Pinnacles Chardonnay	White	Rich, minerally	Fish, chicken	***
Chateau Christina Carmel Valley Russell's Vineyard Cabernet Sauvignon	Red	Plums, toasty	Beef, lamb	**
Chateau Christina Francioni Vineyard Pinot Noir	Red	Berry, spicy	Fish, chicken, pork	**
Chateau Julien Chardonnay	White	Apples, buttery	Fish, chicken	**
Chateau Julien Sangiovese	Red	Berry, fruity	Pizza, pasta, sausages	**
Chouinard Vineyards Petite Sirah	Red	Berry, peppery	Pizza, sausages, pork	**
Cloninger Cellars Cabernet Sauvignon	Red	Plums, toasty	Beef, pork, lamb	**
Cloninger Cellars Chardonnay	White	Minerally, oaky	Fish, chicken	**
Cloninger Cellars Pinot Noir	Red	Berry, earthy	Fish, chicken, pork	**
Cobblestone Arroyo Seco Chardonnay	White	Tropical fruit	Fish, chicken	*
Concannon Vineyard Arroyo Seco Late Harvest Viognier	White	Sweet, floral, honey	Dessert, fruits	**
Concannon Vineyard Central Coast Reserve Chardonnay	White	Apples, buttery	Fish, chicken	**
Concannon Vineyard Central Coast Selected Vineyard Cabernet Sauvignon	Red	Plums, vanillin	Beef, pork, lamb	**
David Bruce Central Coast Pinot Noir	Red	Berry, oaky, spicy	Fish, pork, veal	**
David Bruce Chalone Pinot Noir	Red	Berry, minerally	Fish, pork, veal	***
De Rose Cedolini Family Vineyard Cienega Valley Old Vines Zinfandel	Red	Berry, spicy	Pizza, beef, pork	**
Elliston Vineyards Cabernet Franc	Red	Berry, herbaceous	Veal, beef, pork	**
Estancia Pinnacles Chardonnay	White	Apples, toasty	Fish, chicken	**
Estancia Pinnacles Pinot Noir	Red	Berry, spicy	Fish, pork, Asian	**

Wine name	Style	Flavor/ Bouquet	Compatible Foods	Price Range
Fenestra Santa Lucia Highlands Merlot	Red	Complex, spicy	Lamb, beef, pork	**
Galante Carmel Valley Blackjack Cabernet Sauvignon	Red	Powerful, complex	Lamb, beef, pork	***
Galante Carmel Valley Rancho Galante Cabernet Sauvignon	Red	Rich, smoky	Lamb, beef, pork	**
Galante Carmel Valley Red Rose Cabernet Sauvignon	Red	Powerful, tannic	Lamb, beef, pork	***
Garre Vineyard and Winery California Grenache	Red	Fruity, spicy	Pizza, sausages	**
Georis Winery Carmel Valley Cabernet Sauvignon	Red	Powerful, tannic	Lamb, cheese	***
Georis Winery Carmel Valley Merlot	Red	Powerful, tannic	Lamb, cheese	***
Hahn Estates Cabernet Franc	Red	Plums, spicy	Pork, beef, lamb	**
Hahn Estates Merlot	Red	Plums, vanillin	Pork, beef, lamb	**
Hahn Estates Red Meritage	Red	Rich, oaky	Pork, beef, lamb	***
Heller Estate/Durney Carmel Valley Cachagua Cabernet Sauvignon	Red	Complex, earthy	Lamb, beef, cheese	***
Heller Estate/Durney Carmel Valley Chardonnay	White	Rich, minerally	Fish, chicken	***
Heller Estate/Durney Carmel Valley Chenin Blanc	White	Floral, minerally	Shellfish, fish	***
Heller Estate/Durney Carmel Valley Merlot	Red	Plums, toasty	Lamb, beef, pork	***
Heller Estate/Durney Carmel Valley Private Reserve Cabernet Sauvignon	Red	Powerful, elegant	Lamb, beef, cheese	***
Ivan Tamas Pinot Grigio	White	Floral, spicy	Shellfish, salads	*
J. Lohr Arroyo Seco Arroyo Vista Vineyard Chardonnay	White	Buttery, oaky	Fish, chicken	**
J. Lohr Bay Mist White Riesling	White	Floral, fruity	Fruits, shellfish	*
J. Lohr Chardonnay	White	Tropical fruit, buttery	Fish, chicken	*
J. Lohr Wildflower Valdiguié	Red	Fruity	Pizza, pasta	*
Jekel FOS Reserve Chardonnay	White	Tropical fruit, oaky	Fish, chicken	**
Jekel Syrah	Red	Berry, licorice	Pork, veal	**
Joullian Carmel Valley Cabernet Sauvignon	Red	Earthy, complex	Lamb, beef, cheese	***
Joullian Carmel Valley Merlot	Red	Plums, earthy	Lamb, beef, pork	***
Joullian Carmel Valley Sauvignon Blanc	White	Citrus, honey, toasty	Fish, pasta	**
Joullian Carmel Valley Zinfandel	Red	Berry, spicy	Pork, veal, pasta	**
Joullian Chardonnay	White	Rich, minerally	Fish, chicken	**
Kali-Hart Vineyard Chardonnay	White	Tropical fruit	Fish, chicken	***
Kendall Jackson Arroyo Seco Paradise Vineyard Chardonnay	White	Tropical fruit	Fish, chicken	**
Lockwood Cabernet Sauvignon	Red	Plums, toasty	Pork, beef, lamb	**
Lockwood Chardonnay	White	Fruity, oaky	Fish, chicken	**
Lockwood Merlot	Red	Plums, toasty	Pork, beef, lamb	**
Lockwood Pinot Blanc	White	Apples, toasty	Fish, chicken	**
Lockwood Syrah	Red	Spicy, oaky	Pork, veal	**
Lockwood Very Special Reserve Red Meritage	Red	Rich, oaky	Lamb, beef, cheese	***
Logan Sleepy Hollow Vineyard Chardonnay	White	Tropical fruit	Fish, chicken	**
Logan Sleepy Hollow Vineyard Pinot Noir	Red	Berry, toasty	Fish, pork	**
Mer et Soleil Central Coast Chardonnay	White	Rich, buttery, toasty	Fish, chicken	***
Mirassou Harvest Reserve Mission Vineyard Chardonnay	White	Tropical fruit	Fish, chicken	**
Mirassou Harvest Reserve Pinot Blanc	White	Apples, toasty	Fish, chicken	**
Mirassou Harvest Reserve San Vincente Vineyard Chardonnay	White	Tropical fruit	Fish, chicken	**
Mirassou Showcase Selection Harvest Reserve Pinot Noir	Red	Berry, toasty	Fish, pork	**

Wine name	Style	Flavor/ Bouquet	Compatible Foods	Price Range
Monterey Peninsula Winery Doctor's Reserve Sleepy Hollow Vineyard Chardonnay	White	Tropical fruit	Fish, chicken	**
Monterra San Bernabe Ranch Cabernet Sauvignon	Red	Jam, toasty	Pizza, pasta, beef	*
Monterra San Bernabe Ranch Chardonnay	White	Tropical fruit	Fish, chicken	*
Monterra San Bernabe Ranch Syrah	Red	Jam, vanillin	Pizza, pork	*
Morgan Chardonnay	White	Tropical fruit	Fish, chicken	**
Morgan Monterey/Sonoma Sauvignon Blanc	White	Melon, citrus, toasty	Shellfish, fish, salads, cheese	**
Morgan Pinot Gris	White	Floral, nutty	Shellfish, fish	**
Morgan Pinot Noir	Red	Jam, spicy	Fish, pork, duck	**
Morgan Reserve Pinot Noir	Red	Jam, oaky, rich	Fish, pork, duck	***
Paraiso Springs Santa Lucia Highlands Chardonnay	White	Apples, toasty	Fish, chicken	*
Paraiso Springs Santa Lucia Highlands Pinot Blanc	White	Melon, buttery	Fish, chicken	*
Paraiso Springs Santa Lucia Highlands Pinot Noir	Red	Berry, spicy	Fish, pork, cheese	**
Paraiso Springs Santa Lucia Highlands Port Souzao	Fortified	Caramelly	Nuts, cheese, dessert	*
Paraiso Springs Santa Lucia Highlands Reserve Pinot Blanc	White	Nutty, oaky	Fish, chicken	**
Paraiso Springs Santa Lucia Highlands Riesling	White	Floral, crisp, minerally	Shellfish, fish	*
Paraiso Springs Santa Lucia Highlands Syrah	Red	Spicy, smoky	Veal, pork, cheese	**
Pavona Vineyards Paraiso Springs Vineyard Pinot Blanc	White	Apples, nutty	Fish, chicken	**
Pavona Vineyards Paraiso Springs Vineyard Pinot Noir	Red	Jam, spicy	Fish, pork	**
Pietra Santa California Sasso Rosso Red Table Wine	Red	Rich, oaky	Pork, beef, lamb	***
Pietra Santa California Sassolino Sangiovese/Cabernet Sauvignon	Red	Rich, oaky	Pork, beef	***
Pietra Santa Cienega Valley Cabernet Sauvignon	Red	Rich, oaky	Pork, beef, lamb	***
Pietra Santa Cienega Valley Sangiovese	Red	Rich, oaky	Veal, pork	***
Pietra Santa San Benito Dolcetto	Red	Rich, oaky	Chicken, veal, pork	***
Pietra Santa San Benito Zinfandel	Red	Rich, oaky	Pork, beef	***
Robert Mondavi Coastal Monterey Merlot	Red	Plums, vanillin	Pork, beef, pizza	*
Robert Mondavi Coastal Monterey Syrah	Red	Berry, vanillin	Pork, beef, pizza	*
Robert Talbott Cuvée Cynthia Chardonnay	White	Apples, toasty	Fish, chicken	***
Robert Talbott Diamond T Estate Chardonnay	White	Tropical fruit, toasty	Fish, chicken	***
Robert Talbott Sleepy Hollow Vineyard Chardonnay	White	Tropical fruit, toasty	Fish, chicken	***
Savannah-Chanel Central Coast Pinot Noir	Red	Berry, oaky	Fish, pork	**
Scheid Vineyards Gewürztraminer	White	Spicy, floral	Fruits, Asian	*
Scheid Vineyards Pinot Noir	Red	Berry, spicy	Fish, pork, pizza	**
Scheid Vineyards San Lucas Chardonnay	White	Apples, minerally	Fish, chicken	**
Smith and Hook Baroness Reserve Masterpiece Cabernet Sauvignon	Red	Powerful, tannic	Lamb, beef, cheese	***
Smith and Hook Cabernet Sauvignon	Red	Plums, toasty	Lamb, beef, pork	**
Smith and Hook Viognier	White	Floral, honey	Shellfish, fruits	**
Taylor California Cellars Reserve Marsala	Fortified	Tangy, nutty	Nuts, cheese, dessert	*
Testarossa Chalone Chardonnay	White	Buttery, toasty	Fish, chicken	***
Testarossa Chalone Michaud Vineyard Viognier	White	Rich, honey, floral	Shellfish, fruits	***
Testarossa Santa Lucia Highlands Cuvée Niclaire Reserve Pinot Noir	Red	Berry, rich, spicy	Fish, pork, veal	***
Testarossa Santa Lucia Highlands Pisoni Vineyard Chardonnay	White	Tropical fruit, toasty	Fish, chicken, pasta	***

Wine name	Style	Flavor/ Bouquet	Compatible Foods	Price Range
Testarossa Sleepy Hollow Vineyard Pinot Noir	Red	Rich, berry, earthy	Fish, pork, cheese	***
Tria Vineyards Pinot Noir	Red	Fruity, vanillin	Fish, chicken, pork, pizza	*
Ventana Vineyards Barrel Fermented Dry Chenin Blanc	White	Crisp, citrus	Shellfish, chicken	*
Ventana Vineyards Cabernet Franc	Red	Fruity, herbaceous	Veal, pork, pizza	*
Ventana Vineyards Gold Stripe Chardonnay	White	Tropical fruit	Fish, chicken	*
Ventana Vineyards Merlot	Red	Plums, jam	Pizza, pork	*
Ventana Vineyards Monterey Rose	Rosé	Fruity	Salads, shellfish	*
Ventana Vineyards Riesling	White	Floral, fruity	Salads, shellfish	*
Ventana Vineyards Syrah	Red	Jam, spicy	Pork, chicken, pizza	*
Wente Brut Reserve Arroyo Seco Méthode Champenoise	Sparkling	Crisp, citrus	Fruit, Asian, shellfish	*
Wente Central Coast Sauvignon Blanc	White	Citrus, stone fruit	Shellfish, cheese	*
Wente Reliz Creek Reserve Arroyo Seco Pinot Noir	Red	Berry, spicy	Fish, chicken, pork	**
Wente Riva Ranch Reserve Arroyo Seco Chardonnay	White	Tropical fruit, minerally	Fish, chicken	**
Westover Vineyards Johannisberg Riesling	White	Floral, fruity	Fruit, shellfish	*
Westover Vineyards Santa Lucia Highlands Cabernet Sauvignon	Red	Plums, spicy	Lamb, beef, pork	**
New Jersey				
Sylvin Farms Chardonnay	White	Apples, buttery	Fish, chicken	**
Tomasello Winery Cabernet Sauvignon	Red	Plums, spicy	Beef, pork	**
Unionville Vineyards Seyval	White	Floral, grassy	Shellfish, salads	*
New Mexico				
Gruet Winery Blanc de Blancs	Sparkling	Crisp, nutty	Shellfish, cold meats	*
Hermann J. Weimer Vineyard Chardonnay	White	Apples, buttery	Fish, chicken	**
Hermann J. Weimer Vineyard Late Harvest Riesling	White	Sweet, floral, honey	Dessert	**
Hermann J. Weimer Vineyard Riesling	White	Floral, fruity	Shellfish, fruits	*
Lenz Winery Sparkling Wine	Sparkling	Crisp, citrus	Shellfish, Asian	**
Millbrook Vineyards & Winery Tokai	White	Sweet, floral, nutty	Dessert	**
Palmer Vineyards Merlot	Red	Plums, toasty	Lamb, beef, pork	***
Palmer Vineyards Pinot Blanc	White	Citrus, apples, vanillin	Fish, chicken	**
Paumonock Vineyards Assemblage (cabernet sauvignon/cabernet franc/merlot)	Red	Rich, oaky	Lamb, beef, cheese	***
Pellegrini Vineyards Cabernet Franc	Red	Plums, herbaceous	Veal, pork, beef	**
Pellegrini Vineyards Vintner's Pride Chardonnay	White	Apples, vanillin	Fish, chicken	**
Pindar Vineyards Cuvée Rare (Sparkling 100% Pinot Meunier)	Sparkling	Crisp, fruity	Shellfish, Asian	**
Shalestone Vineyards Legend (merlot/cabernet sauvignon/cabernet franc)	Red	Plums, spicy	Beef, pork, lamb	***
Standing Stone Vineyards Gewürztraminer	White	Floral, spicy	Asian, fruits	**
Treleaven Wines (King Ferry Winery) Barrel Fermented Chardonnay	White	Apples, toasty	Fish, chicken	**
Wolffer Estate/Sagpond Vineyards Chardonnay	White	Apples, buttery	Fish, chicken	**
Wolffer Estate/Sagpond Vineyards Merlot	Red	Plums, vanillin	Beef, pork, lamb	**
New York				
Anthony Road Wine Company Late Harvest Vignoles	Sweet	Sweet, fruity	Dessert	**
Bedell Cellars Cabernet Franc	Red	Plums, spicy	Pork, beef, veal	**
Bedell Cellars Eis (Riesling Dessert Wine) Clinton Vineyards Seyval	Sweet	Sweet, honey, floral	Dessert	***

Wine name	Style	Flavor/ Bouquet	Compatible Foods	Price Range
Page Mill Chardonnnay	White	Apples, minerally	Fish, chicken	**
Ridge California Montebello Meritage	Red	Complex, minerally	Lamb, beef, cheese	***
Ridge Montebello Chardonnay	White	Crisp, rich, minerally	Fish, chicken	***
Ridge Santa Cruz Mountains Chardonnay	White	Elegant, rich	Fish, chicken	***
Ridge Santa Cruz Mountains Merlot	Red	Complex, spicy	Lamb, pork, veal	***
Sarah's Vineyard Estate Chardonnay	White	Complex, elegant	Fish, chicken	***
Sarah's Vineyard Estate Merlot	Red	Rich, oaky	Lamb, beef, pork	***
Sarah's Vineyard Estate Pinot Noir	Red	Elegant, earthy	Fish, pork, cheese	***
Savannah-Chanel Cabernet Franc	Red	Powerful, oaky	Lamb, beef, cheese	**
Savannah-Chanel Carignane	Red	Berry, spicy	Pizza, pork, veal	**
Savannah-Chanel Chardonnay	White	Intense, spicy	Fish, chicken	**
Savannah-Chanel Late Harvest Cabernet Franc	White	Sweet, fruity, spicy	Dessert, cheese	**
Savannah-Chanel Zinfandel	Red	Berry, spicy	Pizza, pork, veal	**
Solis Winery Estate Sangiovese	Red	Berry, spicy	Pizza, pork, veal	**
Storr's Mann Vineyard Merlot	Red	Rich, fruity	Lamb, beef, pasta	***
Storr's San Ysidro Merlot	Red	Plums, toasty	Lamb, beef, pork	***
Storrs Ben Lomond Mountain Meyley Vineyard Chardonnay	White	Elegant, tropical fruit	Fish, chicken	***
Storrs Santa Cruz Mountains Christie Vineyard Chardonnay	White	Complex, tropical fruit	Fish, chicken	***
Storrs Santa Cruz Mountains Petite Sirah	Red	Powerful, tannic	Lamb, beef, cheese	**
Storrs Santa Cruz Mountains Vanamanutagi Vineyard Chardonnay	White	Tropical fruit, minerally	Fish, chicken	***
Sycamore Creek Johannisberg Riesling	White	Fruity, floral	Shellfish, salads	*
Thomas Fogarty Chardonnay	White	Apples, vanillin	Fish, chicken	**
Thomas Fogarty Gewürztraminer	White	Floral, spicy	Shellfish, Asian	**
Thomas Kruse Brut Méthode Champenoise	Sparkling	Crisp, citrus	Shellfish, Asian	**
Thomas Kruse Chardonnay	White	Citrus, toasty	Fish, chicken	**
Thunder Mountain Cabernet Sauvignon	Red	Powerful, earthy	Lamb, beef, cheese	***
Westover Vineyards Santa Cruz Mountains Eagles Nest Vineyards Chardonnay	White	Apples, toasty	Fish, chicken	**
Ohio				
Chalet Débonné Pinot Gris	White	Floral, nutty	Shellfish, fish	**
Firelands Wine Co. Pinot Grigio	White	Fruity, nutty	Shellfish, fish	**
Harpersfield Vineyard Gewürztraminer	White	Floral, spicy	Shellfish, Asian	**
Harpersfield Vineyard Riesling	White	Citrus, stone fruit	Shellfish, Asian	**
Markko Vineyard Riesling	White	Floral, fruity	Shellfish, Asian	**
Pennsylvania				
Allegro Vineyards Cadenza (cabernet sauvignon/cabernet franc)	Red	Plums, spicy	Beef, pork, lamb	**
Chaddsford Winery Merican (cabernet sauvignon/merlot)	Red	Plums, spicy	Beef, pork, veal	**
Chaddsford Winery Pinot Grigio	White	Floral, nutty	Shellfish, Asian	**
Chambourcin Presque Isle Wine Cellars Cabernet Franc/Petite Sirah	Red	Plums, spicy	Beef, pork, veal	**
Clover Hill Vineyards & Winery Concord	Red	Fruity, spicy	Pizza, pasta, sausages	**
French Creek Ridge Vineyards Cabernet Franc	Red	Plums, spicy	Veal, pork, beef	**
Naylor Vineyards & Wine Cellar Vidal Ice Wine	Sweet	Sweet, honey, floral	Dessert	***

Wine name	Style	Flavor/ Bouquet	Compatible Foods	Price Range
Bedell Cellars Merlot	Red	Plums, vanillin	Pork, beef, lamb	**
Dr. Frank's Vinifera Wine Cellars/Chateau Frank Riesling	White	Crisp, floral, citrus	Shellfish, Asian	*
Duckwalk Vineyards Reserve Merlot	Red	Plums, spicy	Pork, beef, lamb	***
Fox Run Vineyards Chardonnay	White	Apples, vanillin	Fish, chicken	**
Fox Run Vineyards Reserve Pinot Noir	Red	Berry, spicy	Fish, pork, veal	***
Gristina Vineyards Andy's Field Cabernet Sauvignon	Red	Complex, toasty	Lamb, beef, cheese	***
North Central Coast/California				
Bargetto Regan Vineyards Chardonnay	White	Apples, spicy	Fish, chicken	**
Bonny Doon Vineyards Clos de Gilroy Grenache	Red	Berry, spicy	Asian, fish, pizza	*
Bonny Doon Vineyards Le Cigare Volant California	Red	Jam, spicy	Pizza, beef, pork	**
Bonny Doon Vineyards Vin de Glacière California Muscat	White	Sweet, floral, complex	Cold meats, dessert	**
Burrell School Vineyards Cabernet Sauvignon	Red	Rich, earthy	Lamb, beef, pork, cheese	***
Burrell School Vineyards Chardonnay	White	Apples, oaky	Fish, chicken	**
Cinnabar Vineyards Cabernet Sauvignon	Red	Plums, toasty	Lamb, beef, pork	***
Cinnabar Vineyards Chardonnay	White	Apples, spicy	Fish, chicken	**
Clos Tita Cabernet Sauvignon	Red	Elegant, earthy	Lamb, beef, cheese	***
Clos Tita CV Chardonnay/Viognier	White	Elegant, complex	Shellfish, fish	***
Clos Tita Estate Pinot Noir	Red	Earthy, minerally	Fish, pork, cheese	***
Concannon Vineyard Limited Bottling Marsanne	White	Citrus, nutty	Fish, chicken	**
Cooper-Garrod Cabernet Franc	Red	Plums, toasty	Beef, pork, veal	**
Cooper-Garrod Chardonnay	White	Apples, toasty	Fish, chicken	**
Cronin Vineyards Alexander Chardonnay	White	Citrus, buttery, toasty	Fish, chicken	**
Cronin Vineyards Pinot Noir	Red	Berry, spicy	Pork, veal	***
David Bruce Vineyards Petite Sirah	Red	Peppery, oaky	Veal, pork, beef	**
Equinox Vintage Blanc de Blancs Méthode Champenoise	Sparkling	Citrus, yeasty	Shellfish, Asian	***
Fellom Ranch Montebello Ridge Cabernet Sauvignon	Red	Plums, earthy	Beef, lamb, pork	**
Guglielmo Private Reserve Petite Sirah	Red	Berry, peppery	Pizza, pork, veal	**
Hecker Pass Winery Petite Sirah Select	Red	Berry, spicy	Pizza, pork, veal	**
J. Lohr Cypress California Chardonnay	White	Apples, buttery	Fish, chicken	*
Jory Winery California Chardonnay	White	Apples, toasty	Fish, chicken	**
Jory Winery Syrah	Red	Berry, spicy	Veal, pork, chicken	**
Kathryn Kennedy California SHHH Chenin Blanc/Viognier	White	Fruity, floral	Shellfish, Asian	**
Kathryn Kennedy Estate Cabernet Sauvignon	Red	Elegant, powerful	Lamb, beef, cheese	***
Kathryn Kennedy Lateral Meritage	Red	Elegant, earthy	Lamb, beef, cheese	***
Kathryn Kennedy Maridon Vineyard Syrah	Red	Rich, tannic, spicy	Pork, veal, lamb	***
Martin Ray Mariage California Chardonnay	White	Apples, minerally	Fish, chicken	***
Mount Eden Santa Cruz Mountains Cabernet Sauvignon	Red	Powerful, elegant	Lamb, beef, cheese	***
Mount Eden Santa Cruz Mountains Chardonnay	White	Elegant, minerally	Fish, chicken	***
Mount Eden Santa Cruz Mountains Cuvée des Vielles Vignes Pinot Noir	Red	Earthy, rich, spicy	Fish, pork, veal, cheese	***
Mount Eden Santa Cruz Mountains Old Vine Reserve Cabernet Sauvignon	Red	Minerally, complex	Lamb, cheese	***
Mount Eden Santa Cruz Mountains Pinot Noir	Red	Rich, complex	Fish, duck, veal	***

Wine name	Style	Flavor/ Bouquet	Compatible Foods	Price Range
Rhode Island				
Sakonnet Vineyards Fumé Blanc (Vidal)	White	Fruity, floral	Shellfish, fish	**
Sakonnet Vineyards Samson Brut (chardonnay/pinot noir)	Sparkling	Crisp, rich	Shellfish, Asian	**
San Francisco Bay/California				
Big White House Byer Ranch Vineyard Zinfandel Port	Fortified	Fruity, rich	Dessert, nuts	**
Big White House Concannon Estate Vineyard Mourvedre	Red	Plums, spicy	Pork, beef, lamb	**
Big White House Fraser Ranch Chardonnay	White	Apples, buttery	Fish, chicken	**
Big White House Kurtzer Vineyard Syrah	Red	Berry, spicy	Beef, lamb, pork	**
Big White House Ruby Hills Vineyard Cabernet Sauvignon	Red	Plums, spicy	Beef, lamb, pork	**
Bonny Doon Vineyards Cardinal Zin Narly Old Vines Zinfandel	Red	Complex, spicy	Pizza, pork, veal	**
Bonny Doon Vineyards Old Telegram Mourvedre	Red	Powerful, earthy	Beef, lamb, cheese	**
Cedar Mountain Blanches Vineyard Cabernet Sauvignon	Red	Complex, minerally	Beef, lamb, cheese	**
Cedar Mountain Cabernet Royal Dessert Wine	Red	Sweet, fruity, rich	Dessert, nuts, cheese	**
Cedar Mountain Duet Cabernet Sauvignon/Merlot	Red	Earthy, fruity	Lamb, beef, pork	**
Cedar Mountain Estate Chardonnay	White	Crisp, rich, minerally	Fish, chicken	**
Cedar Mountain Library Reserve Cabernet Sauvignon	Red	Elegant, earthy	Lamb, beef, cheese	***
Chouinard Vineyards San Francisco Bay Cabernet Sauvignon	Red	Plums, spicy	Pork, beef, lamb	**
Chouinard Vineyards San Francisco Bay Palomares Vineyards Chardonnay	White	Citrus, apples, spicy	Fish, chicken	**
Cline Cellars Ancient Vines Zinfandel	Red	Rich, earthy, minerally	Lamb, beef, pork	**
Cline Cellars Cotes d'Oakley Vin Blanc	White	Fruity, floral	Shellfish, salads	*
Cline Cellars Cotes d'Oakley Vin Gris	Rosé	Berry, floral	Shellfish, cold meats	*
Cline Cellars Cotes d'Oakley Vin Rouge	Red	Fruity, peppery	Pizza, pasta, sausages	*
Cline Cellars Live Oak Vineyard Zinfandel	Red	Powerful, earthy	Lamb, beef, cheese	***
Cline Cellars Small Berry Mourvedre	Red	Powerful, spicy, mint	Lamb, beef, cheese	***
Concannon Vineyard California Selected Vineyards Petite Sirah	Red	Berry, peppery	Pizza, pork, beef	*
Concannon Vineyard Reserve Assemblage Red Meritage	Red	Plums, spicy	Veal, pork, beef	**
Concannon Vineyard Reserve Assemblage White Meritage	White	Citrus, honey, spicy	Shellfish, fish, chicken	**
Concannon Vineyard Reserve Petite Sirah	Red	Peppery, oaky	Pork, beef, lamb	**
Concannon Vineyard San Francisco Bay Selected Vineyards Sauvignon Blanc	White	Stone fruit, minerally	Shellfish, salads	*
Elliston Vineyards California Captain's Claret (merlot/cabernet franc/cabernet sauvignon)	Red	Plums, oaky, herbaceous	Lamb, beef, pork	**
Elliston Vineyards Pinot Blanc	White	Apples, nutty	Fish, chicken, nuts	**
Elliston Vineyards Sunol Valley Vineyard Pinot Gris	White	Floral, nutty	Shellfish, Asian	**
Fenestra Winery Semillon	White	Honey, waxy, citrus	Shellfish, fish, chicken	**
Fenestra Winery Semmonay (chardonnay/semillon)	White	Complex, fruity	Fish, chicken	**
Fenestra Winery Zinfandel	Red	Berry, spicy	Pizza, pork, veal	**
Garre Vineyard and Winery Merlot	Red	Plums, spicy	Pork, beef, lamb	**
Ivan Tamas Cabernet Sauvignon	Red	Plums, jam	Pizza, beef, chicken	*
Ivan Tamas Sangiovese	Red	Berry, licorice	Pizza, pasta, sausages	*
Ivan Tamas Trebbiano	White	Floral, nutty	Shellfish, Asian	*
Ivan Tamas Zinfandel	Red	Jam, spicy	Pizza, beef, chicken	*
Jackson Cellars Zinfandel	Red	Berry, spicy	Pizza, beef, pork	**

Wine name	Style	Flavor/ Bouquet	Compatible Foods	Price Range
Jacuzzi Reserve Zinfandel	Red	Rich, fruity, tannic	Lamb, beef, cheese	***
Jade Mountain Mourvedre	Red	Powerful, fruity, spicy	Lamb, beef, cheese	***
Kalin Cellars Semillon	White	Honey, waxy, citrus	Shellfish, fish, chicken	**
Livermore Valley Cellars/LVC Arcanum Red Table Wine	Red	Fruity, spicy	Lamb, beef, pork	**
Livermore Valley Cellars/LVC Chenin Blanc	White	Fruity, floral	Shellfish, Asian	*
Livermore Valley Cellars/LVC Graham Vineyard Zinfandel	Red	Berry, spicy	Pizza, pork, veal	**
Livermore Valley Cellars/LVC One Oak Vineyard Merlot	Red	Plums, spicy	Lamb, beef, pork	**
Livermore Valley Cellars/LVC Semillon/Chardonnay	White	Apples, nutty, spicy	Shellfish, fish, chicken	**
Murrieta's Well Red Vendemia Meritage	Red	Earthy, minerally	Lamb, beef, cheese	**
Murrieta's Well White Vendemia Meritage	White	Complex, minerally	Shellfish, fish, chicken	**
Murrieta's Well Zinfandel	Red	Berry, spicy	Pizza, pork, veal	**
Retzlaff Vineyards Cabernet Sauvignon/Merlot	Red	Elegant, earthy	Lamb, beef, cheese	***
Retzlaff Vineyards Chardonnay	White	Apples, minerally	Fish, chicken	**
Retzlaff Vineyards Sauvignon Blanc	White	Stone fruit, minerally	Shellfish, cheese	**
Retzlaff Vineyards Trousseau Gris	White	Floral, fruity	Shellfish, salads	**
Ridge Bridgehead Mataro	Red	Elegant, rich, fruity	Lamb, beef, cheese	***
Rosenblum Carla's Reserve Zinfandel	Red	Rich, fruity, spicy	Pizza, beef, veal, lamb	***
Rosenblum Chateau La Paws Cote du Bone Mourvedre	Red	Powerful, fruity	Lamb, beef, cheese	***
Stephen Kent Winery Folkhendt Vineyard Cabernet Sauvignon	Red	Rich, fruity, oaky	Lamb, beef, pork	***
Stony Ridge Malvasia Bianca	White	Apples, melon, minerally	Shellfish, salads	**
Stony Ridge Sangiovese Robusto Dessert Wine	Fortified	Fruity, rich	Dessert, nuts, cheese	**
Thackrey Pleiades VII Old Vines Red	Red	Fruity, rich, spicy	Chicken, veal, beef	**
Turley Duarte Zinfandel	Red	Powerful, spicy	Lamb, cheese, dessert	***
Viano Vineyards Martinez Zinfandel	Red	Earthy, minerally	Lamb, beef, pork	*
Wente Crane Ridge Reserve Merlot	Red	Plums, oaky, earthy	Lamb, beef, pork	***
Wente Vineyards Cabernet Sauvignon	Red	Spicy, toasty	Lamb, beef, pork	**
Wente Vineyards Charles Wetmore Reserve Cabernet Sauvignon	Red	Rich, elegant	Lamb, beef, cheese	***
Wente Vineyards Herman Wente Reserve Chardonnay	White	Complex, oaky`	Fish, chicken	***
Westover Vineyards Je t'aime Meritage	Red	Plums, spicy	Lamb, beef, pork	***
Westover Vineyards Kalthoff Vineyards Cabernet Sauvignon	Red	Rich, earthy	Lamb, beef, pork	***
Westover Vineyards Late Harvest Zinfandel	Red	Sweet, fruity, rich	Dessert, nuts	**
Westover Vineyards San Francisco Bay Palomares Vineyards Chardonnay	White	Apples, citrus, vanillin	Fish, chicken	**
Westover Vineyards San Francisco Bay Sunol Valley Vineyards Chardonnay	White	Rich, fruity, minerally	Fish, chicken	**
Westover Vineyards Thatcher Bay Merlot	Red	Plums, spicy	Lamb, beef, pork	**
Westover Vineyards Zinfandel	Red	Berry, spicy	Chicken, veal, pork	**
Sierra Foothills/California				
Black Sheep Amador Clockspring Vineyard Zinfandel	Red	Berry, spicy	Pizza, pork, veal	**
Black Sheep Calaveras Zinfandel	Red	Berry, spicy	Pizza, pork, veal	*
Black Sheep Sierra Foothills True Frogs Lily Pad White	White	Floral, fruity	Shellfish, salads	*
Boeger Winery El Dorado Barbera	Red	Plums, earthy	Pizza, pasta, chicken, pork	*
Boeger Winery El Dorado Merlot	Red	Jam, earthy	Veal, chicken, beef	*

Wine name	Style	Flavor/ Bouquet	Compatible Foods	Price Range
Boeger Winery El Dorado Muscat Canelli	Fortified	Floral, fruity	Dessert, nuts	*
Charles B. Mitchell Vineyards El Dorado Everyday Red	Red	Jam, spicy	Pizza, pork, veal	*
Charles B. Mitchell Vineyards El Dorado Malbec	Red	Plum, cloves	Chicken, veal, pork	**
Charles B. Mitchell Vineyards El Dorado Semillon	White	Waxy, honey, citrus	Shellfish, fish	**
Charles Spinetta Winery Amador Barbera	Red	Fruity, spicy	Pizza, pasta, pork	**
Charles Spinetta Winery Amador Primitivo	Red	Berry, spicy	Pizza, pasta, pork	**
Charles Spinetta Winery Amador Zinfandel	Red	Berry, spicy	Pizza, pork, veal	**
Chateau Rodin Winery El Dorado Barbera	Red	Plums, earthy	Pizza, pasta, pork	**
Coulson Eldorado Winery El Dorado Zinfandel	Red	Berry, earthy	Pizza, pasta, pork	**
Deaver Vineyards Amador Barbera	Red	Jam, earthy	Pizza, pasta, pork	*
Deaver Vineyards Amador Sangiovese	Red	Berry, spicy	Pizza, chicken, veal	*
Deaver Vineyards Amador Zinfandel	Red	Berry, spicy	Beef, pork, veal	*
Deaver Vineyards Golden Nectar 150-Year-Old Vine Zinfandel Port	Fortified	Fruity, rich	Dessert	**
Dobra Zemlja Amador Syrah	Red	Plums, spicy	Pork, beef, lamb	**
Dobra Zemlja Amador Viognier	White	Elegant, floral	Shellfish, fish, fruits	**
Domaine de la Terre Rouge Shenandoah Valley Sentinel Oak Vineyard Syrah	Red	Earthy, gamey	Lamb, beef, cheese	***
Edmunds St. John California Rocks and Gravel Rhone Red Blend	Red	Earthy, spicy	Chicken, veal, pork	**
Edmunds St. John El Dorado Matagrano Vineyard Sangiovese	Red	Complex, earthy	Beef, pork, veal	**
Edmunds St. John El Dorado Wylie-Fenaughty Syrah	Red	Powerful, minerally	Lamb, beef, cheese	***
Firefall Vineyards El Dorado Sangiovese	Red	Berry, spicy	Pizza, pork, pasta	**
Firefall Vineyards El Dorado Syrah	Red	Fruity, spicy	Beef, pork, veal	**
Fitzpatrick Winery El Dorado King's Red	Red	Berry, spicy	Beef, pork, veal	**
Fitzpatrick Winery El Dorado Petite Sirah	Red	Berry, peppery	Chicken, veal, beef	**
Fitzpatrick Winery El Dorado Zinfandel	Red	Berry, spicy	Pork, chicken, veal	**
Folie à Deux Shenandoah Valley Fiddletown Zinfandel	Red	Berry, oaky	Pork, beef	**
Gold Hill Vineyard El Dorado Cabernet Franc	Red	Plums, vanillin	Pork, veal, beef	**
Granite Springs Winery El Dorado Petite Sirah	Red	Berry, peppery	Pizza, pork, pasta	**
Granite Springs Winery El Dorado Zinfandel	Red	Berry, spicy	Pizza, pork, chicken	**
Jodar Vineyard and Winery El Dorado Cabernet Sauvignon	Red	Fruity, earthy	Lamb, beef, pork	**
Joel Gott Amador Dillian Ranch Zinfandel	Red	Rich, fruity	Pork, beef, veal	**
Karly Amador Pokerflats Zinfandel	Red	Rich, fruity, smoky	Lamb, beef, cheese	***
Karly Amador Warrior Fires Zinfandel	Red	Rich, fruity, smoky	Lamb, beef, cheese	***
Latcham Vineyards El Dorado Petite Sirah	Red	Berry, peppery	Pizza, pork, pasta	**
Latcham Vineyards El Dorado Zinfandel Reserve	Red	Berry, spicy	Pork, veal, beef	**
Lava Cap Winery El Dorado Barbera	Red	Earthy, fruity	Pizza, pork, pasta	*
Lava Cap Winery El Dorado Muscat Canelli	Fortified	Mandarin, honey, floral	Dessert, fruits	"
Madrona Vineyards El Dorado Cabernet Franc	Red	Plums, spicy	Beef, pork, veal	**
Madrona Vineyards El Dorado Gewürztraminer	White	Floral, spicy	Shellfish, Asian	**
Madrona Vineyards El Dorado Late Harvest Zinfandel	Red	Sweet, fruity, rich	Dessert, nuts	**
Montevina Amador Barbera	Red	Elegant, earthy	Pizza, pasta, beef, chicken, veal	*

Wine name	Style	Flavor/ Bouquet	Compatible Foods	Price Range
Montevina Amador Brioso Zinfandel	Red	Fruity, spicy	Pizza, pasta, beef, chicken, veal	*
Montevina Amador Sangiovese	Red	Berry, spicy	Pork, chicken, veal, pizza	*
Montevina Amador Terra d'Oro Barbera	Red	Earthy, spicy, oaky	Pork, veal, beef	**
Montevina Amador Terra d'Oro Deaver Ranch Vineyard Zinfandel	Red	Complex, rich, earthy	Lamb, beef, cheese	**
Montevina Amador Terra d'Oro Sangiovese	Red	Berry, oaky	Pork, veal, beef, pasta	**
Oakstone Winery El Dorado Cabernet Franc	Red	Plums, spicy	Pork, veal, beef	**
Oakstone Winery El Dorado Meritage	Red	Fruity, spicy	Beef, lamb, veal	**
Perry Creek Vineyards El Dorado Nebbiolo	Red	Licorice, jam	Pork, beef, lamb	**
Perry Creek Vineyards El Dorado Wenzell Vineyards Mourvedre	Red	Rich, fruity, earthy	Lamb, beef, cheese	**
Perry Creek Vineyards El Dorado ZinMan Zinfandel	Red	Berry, spicy	Pizza, pork, pasta	**
Renaissance North Yuba Cabernet Sauvignon	Red	Berry, herbaceous	Lamb, beef, pork	**
Renaissance North Yuba Muscat	Fortified	Spicy, floral, honey	Dessert, fruits	*
Renaissance North Yuba Sangiovese	Red	Berry, spicy	Pizza, pork, pasta	**
Renaissance North Yuba Sauvignon Blanc	White	Grassy, zingy	Shellfish, salads	**
Renaissance North Yuba Select Late Harvest Sauvignon Blanc	White	Sweet, zingy, fruity	Cold meats, dessert	**
Renwood Winery Amador Clockspring Vineyard Sangiovese	Red	Powerful, earthy	Pork, lamb	***
Renwood Winery Amador Colheita Vintage Port	Fortified	Fruity, rich	Dessert, cheese, nuts	***
Renwood Winery Amador D'Agostini Zinfandel	Red	Powerful, complex	Lamb, beef, cheese	***
Renwood Winery Amador Fred's Vineyard Chardonnay	White	Rich, oaky, fruity	Fish, chicken	***
Renwood Winery Amador Grandpère Zinfandel	Red	Spicy, rich, oaky	Lamb, beef, cheese	***
Renwood Winery Amador Ice Zinfandel Ice Wine	Sweet	Fruity, rich	Dessert	***
Renwood Winery Amador Linsteadt Vineyard Barbera	Red	Earthy, rich, oaky	Lamb, beef, cheese	***
Renwood Winery Amador Viognier	White	Tropical fruit, spicy	Fish, Asian	***
Renwood Winery Sierra Foothills Syrah	Red	Rich, oaky	Lamb, beef, cheese	***
Runquist Amador "Z" Zinfandel	Red	Berry, spicy	Pizza, pork, pasta	*
Santino Amador Moscato del Diavolo	White	Sweet, floral, fruity	Shellfish, salads, fruit	*
Savannah-Chanel Amador Muscat Canelli	Fortified	Mandarin, honey	Dessert, fruit	**
Shenandoah Vineyards Amador Cab-Shiraz	Red	Complex, earthy	Lamb, beef, pork	**
Shenandoah Vineyards Amador Sangiovese	Red	Berry, spicy, earthy	Pizza, pork, pasta, beef	**
Shenandoah Vineyards Amador Vintners Selection Zinfandel	Red	Powerful, spicy	Lamb, beef, pork	**
Shenandoah Vineyards Amador Zingiovese	Red	Fruity, spicy	Pizza, pork, pasta, veal	*
Sierra Vista Winery El Dorado Fleur de Montagne Rhone Red Blend	Red	Berry, spicy	Pizza, pork, veal	**
Sierra Vista Winery El Dorado Old Vines Zinfandel	Red	Spicy, earthy	Chicken, veal, pork	**
Sierra Vista Winery El Dorado Syrah	Red	Plums, spicy	Beef, chicken, pork	**
Single Leaf Vineyards El Dorado Zinfandel	Red	Rich, fruity, spicy	Chicken, veal, pork	**
Sobon Estate Shenandoah Valley Cougar Hill Zinfandel	Red	Complex, spicy	Lamb, beef, pork	***
Sobon Estate Shenandoah Valley Fiddletown Zinfandel	Red	Rich, fruity, spicy	Lamb, beef, pork	***
Sobon Estate Shenandoah Valley Orange Muscat	Fortified	Mandarin, honey, floral	Dessert, fruits	**
Sobon Estate Shenandoah Valley Rocky Top Zinfandel	Red	Complex, oaky	Lamb, beef, cheese	***
Sobon Estate Shenandoah Valley Roussanne	White	Grassy, melon, vanillin	Shellfish, fish, salads	**
Sonora Amador Story Vineyard Old Vine Zinfandel	Red	Berry, earthy, spicy	Chicken, veal, pork	**
Sonora Amador TC Vineyard Old Vine Zinfandel	Red	Berry, spicy	Pizza, pork, pasta	**

Wine name	Style	Flavor/ Bouquet	Compatible Foods	Price Range
Sonora Amador Winery & Port Works Old Vine Zinfandel	Red	Spicy, earthy	Chicken, veal, pork	**
Sonora Sierra Foothills Vinho Tinto	Red	Plums, spicy	Chicken, veal, pork	**
Sonora Sierra Foothills Vintage Port	Fortified	Fruity, rich	Dessert, nuts, cheese	**
Story Winery Amador Alitia Zinfandel	Red	Powerful, earthy	Chicken, veal, pork	**
Story Winery Amador Miss-Zin	Red	Fruity, spicy	Pizza, pork, pasta, chicken	*
Story Winery Amador Picnic Hill Zinfandel	Red	Berry, spicy	Pizza, pork, pasta, chicken	**
Story Winery Amador Sweet Mission	Sweet	Sweet, fruity, tangy	Dessert, nuts, cheese	*
Venezio Vineyard El Dorado Zinfandel	Red	Berry, spicy	Pizza, pork, pasta	**
Vino Noceto Amador Riserva Sangiovese	Red	Berry, earthy, spicy, oaky	Pork, veal, beef	**
Vino Noceto Amador Sangiovese	Red	Berry, jam, spicy	Pizza, pork, veal, pasta	*
Vino Noceto Frivolo Sparkling Malvasia Bianca/Muscat	Sparkling	Fruity, crisp	Shellfish, fruits, salads	*
Vino Noceto Rosato di Sangiovese	Rosé	Fruity, floral	Shellfish, salads	*
Windwalker Vineyards El Dorado Zinfandel	Red	Berry, spicy	Pizza, pasta, pork, chicken	**
South Central Coast/California				
Brewer-Clifton Sangiovese	Red	Powerful, spicy	Chicken, veal, pork, duck	***
Chouinard Cabernet Sauvignon	Red	Jam, spicy	Beef, pork, lamb	**
Chouinard Orange Muscat	Fortified	Floral, rich	Dessert	**
Foley Barrel Select Chardonnay	White	Rich, complex, oaky	Fish, chicken	***
Foxen Sanford & Benedict Vineyard Pinot Noir	Red	Complex, earthy, spicy	Fish, pork, duck	***
Gainey Limited Selection Pinot Noir	Red	Rich, earthy, spicy	Fish, pork, duck	***
Lincourt Pinot Noir	Red	Complex, spicy	Fish, pork, duck	**
Longoria Cuvée Blues Cabernet Franc	Red	Powerful, oaky	Lamb, beef, cheese	**
Mount Eden Edna Valley Macgregor Vineyard Chardonnay	White	Complex, oaky, tropical fruit	Fish, chicken, pasta	**
Ridge Zinfandel	Red	Powerful, oaky	Veal, pork, beef	***
Savannah-Chanel Laetitia Vineyards Chardonnay	White	Tropical fruit, oaky	Fish, chicken	**
Savannah-Chanel Zinfandel	Red	Berry, spicy	Pizza, pork, veal	**
Stephen Ross Bien Nacido Vineyard Pinot Noir	Red	Rich, earthy	Fish, pork, duck	**
Talley Chardonnay	White	Tropical fruit, oaky	Fish, chicken	**
Talley Rincon Pinot Noir	Red	Berry, smoky	Fish, veal, pork	***
Testarossa Santa Maria Valley Bien Nacido Vineyard Chardonnay	Red	Rich, fruity, oaky	Fish, pork, veal	***
Testarossa Santa Maria Valley Chardonnay	White	Buttery, citrus, smoky	Fish, chicken	***
Texas				
Fall Creek Vineyards Meritus (merlot/cabernet malbec)	Red	Plums, herbaceous	Beef, pork, lamb	**
Llano Estocado Cabernet Sauvignon	Red	Plums, spicy	Beef, pork, lamb	**
Virginia				
Barboursville Vineyards Pinot Grigio	White	Citrus, floral	Shellfish, Asian	*
Breaux Vineyards Madeleine's Chardonnay	White	Apples, buttery	Fish, chicken	**
Gray Ghost Vineyards Cabernet Franc	Red	Plums, spicy	Chicken, veal, pork	**
Horton Vineyards Dionysius (Touriga Nacional Blend)	Red	Berry, spicy	Veal, pork, beef	**
Horton Vineyards Norton	Red	Fruity, spicy	Pizza, pork, pasta	**
Horton Vineyards Viognier	White	Stone fruit, floral, minerally	Shellfish, fruits	***

Wine name	Style	Flavor/ Bouquet	Compatible Foods	Price Range
Ingleside Plantation Vineyards Merlot	Red	Plums, vanillin	Beef, pork, lamb	**
Jefferson Vineyards Fantaisie Sauvage (native yeast Chardonnay)	White	Complex, fruity	Fish, chicken	**
Linden Vineyards Cabernet Sauvignon	Red	Plums, toasty, herbaceous	Beef, pork, lamb	**
Oakencroft Vineyard & Winery Chardonnay	White	Apples, citrus, vanillin	Fish, chicken	**
Oasis Vineyards Cuvée D'Or (sparkling wine)	Sparkling	Crisp, citrus	Shellfish, Asian	**
Prince Michel Vineyards Chardonnay	White	Apples, buttery, minerally	Fish, chicken	**
Rockbridge Vineyards Meritage (merlot/cabernet sauvignon)	Red	Plums, earthy, spicy	Lamb, beef, cheese	**
White Hall Vineyards Cabernet Franc	Red	Berry, spicy	Veal, chicken, pork	**
White Hall Vineyards Soliterre (Vidal Dessert Wine)	Sweet	Sweet, honey, nutty	Dessert, nuts	**
Williamsburg Winery Gabriel Archer Reserve (cabernet sauvignon/cabernet franc/merlot)	Red	Plums, spicy	Beef, veal, pork	**
Walla Walla Valley/Washington State				
Andrew Will Pepper Bridge Cabernet	Red	Plums, toasty, rich	Beef, lamb	***
Cayuse Cobblestone Vineyard Syrah	Red	Plums, smoky, spicy, oaky	Beef, lamb	**
L'Ecole No 41 Barrel-fermented Semillon	White	Honey, waxy, toasty	Chicken, fish	***
L'Ecole Pepper Bridge Apogée (merlot/cabernet sauvignon/cabernet franc)	Red	Powerful, fruity, toasty	Beef, lamb	**
Leonetti Merlot	Red	Powerful, tannic	Beef, lamb	***
Sevenhills Merlot	Red	Plums, vanillin	Beef, lamb	**
Waterbrook Viognier	White	Floral, honey, stone fruit	Asian, fish	**
Woodward Canyon Charbonneau (merlot/cabernet sauvignon)	Red	Berry, herbaceous, oaky	Beef, lamb	**
Willamette Valley/Oregon				
Amity Pinot Blanc	White	Apples, citrus, vanillin	Fish, chicken	**
Archery Arcus Estate Pinot Noir	Red	Berry, jam, spicy	Chicken, veal, pork	***
Archery Premier Cuvée Pinot Noir	Red	Berry, spicy, oaky	Chicken, veal, pork	***
Argyle Reserve Riesling	White	Floral, fruity	Shellfish, fish	**
Beaux Frères Pinot Noir	Red	Berry, fruity, oaky	Veal, pork, beef	***
Bridgeview Dry Gewürztraminer	White	Spicy, floral	Asian, shellfish	*
Cameron Abbey Ridge Pinot Noir	Red	Berry, spicy	Fish, chicken, pork	**
Domaine Drouhin Cuvée Laurene Pinot Noir	Red	Berry, jam, vanillin	Veal, pork, duck	***
Domaine Drouhin Pinot Noir	Red	Berry, spicy, oaky	Chicken, veal, pork	***
Elk Cove Estate Reserve Pinot Noir	Red	Berry, spicy	Veal, pork	**
Evesham Unfiltered Wood Cuvée J Pinot Noir	Red	Berry, jam, complex	Chicken, veal, pork	***
Eyrie Pinot Gris	White	Honey, nutty, crisp	Chicken, fish	*
Eyrie Pinot Meunier	Red	Plums, berry, spicy	Fish, chicken, pork	**
Ken Wright Canary Hill Pinot Noir	Red	Berry, earthy, oaky	Veal, pork, beef	***
Ponzi Pinot Gris	White	Citrus, nutty, crisp	Shellfish, fish	**
Ponzi Reserve Pinot Noir	Red	Berry, spicy, toasty	Veal, pork, beef	***
Rex Hill Reserve Pinot Noir	Red	Berry, jam, vanillin	Veal, pork, beef	***
Sokol Blosser Redlands Pinot Noir	Red	Berry, earthy, spicy	Veal, pork, beef	**
Yakima Valley/Washington State				
Apex Ice Wine Gewürztraminer	White	Spicy, floral, tropical fruit	Dessert	**
Chateau Ste. Michelle Cold Creek Vineyard Riesling	White	Intense, floral, stone fruit	Asian, shellfish	**

Wine name	Style	Flavor/ Bouquet	Compatible Foods	Price Range
Delille Chaleur Estate Meritage blend (cabernet sauvignon/merlot cabernet franc)	Red	Berry, herbaceous, toasty, elegant	Beef, lamb	***
Delille Charleur Estate D2 (merlot/cabernet sauvignon/cabernet franc)	Red	Plums, herbaceous, vanillin	Beef, lamb	**
Hedges Red Mountain Reserve (cabernet sauvignon/merlot/cabernet franc)	Red	Fruity, oaky, rich	Beef, lamb	**
Hogue Genesis Cabernet Franc	Red	Plums, jam, toasty	Pork, beef, lamb	**
Kestrel Signature Series Syrah	Red	Plums, smoky	Beef, lamb	**
McCrea Boushey Vineyard Syrah Viognier	Red	Berry, floral, spicy	Veal, pork, beef	**
McCrea Ciel du Cheval Vineyard Viognier	White	Floral, honey, stone fruit	Asian, fish	**
Quilceda Creek Cabernet Sauvignon	Red	Berry, herbaceous, oaky	Pork, beef, lamb	**
Waterbrook Meritage Red Mountain (cabernet franc/merlot)	Red	Plums, jam, oaky	Beef, lamb	**

MEXICO AND SOUTH AMERICA

MEXICO/Baja California

Bodegas de Santo Tomás Cabernet Sauvignon	Red	Plums, spicy	Pork, beef, lamb	**
Cavas de Valmar Cabernet Sauvignon	Red	Plums, leathery	Beef, lamb	**
L. A. Cetto Petite Sirah	Red	Berry, spicy	Chicken, pork, beef	**
Monte Xanic Cabernet-Merlot	Red	Berry, plums, earthy	Veal, pork, beef	**

MEXICO/Mexico City

Casa Pedro Domecq Chateau Domecq Cabernet Sauvignon	Red	Rich, elegant	Beef, lamb	***

MEXICO/Parras Valley

Vinedos San Marcos Brut	Sparkling	Citrus, yeasty, crisp	Shellfish, nuts	**

MEXICO/San Juan del Río

Salva Uiva Brut	Sparkling	Citrus, nutty, crisp	Shellfish, nuts	**

CHILE

Anconcagua Valley

Errazuriz Don Maximiano Cabernet Sauvignon	Red	Licorice, spicy, earthy, complex	Beef, lamb	***
Errazuriz Don Maximiano Merlot	Red	Fruity, earthy, oaky, rich	Beef, lamb	***
Errazuriz El Ciebo Estate Cabernet Sauvignon	Red	Fruity, spicy, complex	Beef, lamb	***
Seña Red Table Wine	Red	Earthy, oaky, intense, elegant	Beef, lamb	***
Viña San Estaban Reserva Cabernet Sauvignon	Red	Berry, vanillin, rich	Chicken, veal, pork	*

Bío-Bío Valley

Viña Gracia Barrique-Fermented Chardonnay	White	Apples, buttery, oaky	Fish, chicken	**
Viña Gracia Chardonnay	White	Apples, minerally	Fish, chicken	**

Carico Valley

Miguel Torres Manso de Velasco Cabernet Sauvignon	Red	Fruity, minerally, herbaceous	Veal, pork, beef, lamb	**
Montes Alpha Cabernet Sauvignon	Red	Berry, oaky, rich	Beef, lamb	***
Montes Alpha Chardonnay	White	Stone fruit, buttery, vanillin	Fish, chicken	***
Montes Alpha M	Red	Berry, herbaceous, complex, rich	Beef, lamb	***
Montes Alpha Merlot	Red	Fruity, dill, rich	Veal, pork, beef	***
Montes Sauvignon Blanc	White	Grassy, melon, crisp	Shellfish, Asian	**
Montes Special Cuvée Merlot	Red	Berry, vanillin	Pizza, chicken	*

Wine name	Style	Flavor/ Bouquet	Compatible Foods	Price Range
Casablanca Valley				
Casa Lapostolle Cuvée Alexandré Chardonnay	White	Buttery, fruity, oaky	Fish, chicken	**
Concho y Toro Amelia Chardonnay	White	Buttery, toasty, tropical fruit	Fish, chicken	***
Concho y Toro Casillero del Diablo Chardonnay	White	Citrus, buttery	Shellfish, fish	**
Errazuriz Reserva Chardonnay	White	Tropical fruit, vanillin	Fish, chicken	**
Errazuriz Wild Ferment Chardonnay	White	Apples, buttery, complex	Fish, chicken	**
Santa Rita Medalla Real Chardonnay	White	Citrus, melon, toasty, crisp	Fish, chicken	**
Veramonte Cabernet Sauvignon	Red	Spicy, oaky, fruity	Pork, beef	*
Central Valleys				
Caliterra Chardonnay	White	Citrus, apples, crisp	Fish, chicken	*
Caliterra Merlot	Red	Fruity, tannic	Chicken, pork	**
Caliterra Reserva Cabernet Sauvignon	Red	Licorice, plums, minerally	Pork, beef	*
Carmen Gold Reserve Cabernet Sauvignon	Red	Berry, rich, oaky	Beef, lamb	***
Carmen Reserve Merlot	Red	Elegant, plums, herbaceous	Beef, lamb	**
Casa Donoso Reserve Cabernet Sauvignon	Red	Powerful, earthy	Beef, lamb	**
Casa Lapostolle Cabernet Sauvignon	Red	Fruity, spicy, delicate	Beef, pork	**
Casa Lapostolle Cuvée Alexandré Cabernet Sauvignon	Red	Spicy, toasty, oaky	Veal, pork, beef	**
Casa Lapostolle Cuvée Alexandré Merlot	Red	Fruity, oaky, rich	Pork, beef, lamb	**
Clos Robert Merlot	Red	Berry, spicy	Pizza, chicken	*
Concho y Toro Don Melchar Puente Alto Vineyard Cabernet Sauvignon	Red	Licorice, spicy, intense	Pork, beef	***
Cousino Macul Antiguas Reservas Cabernet Sauvignon	Red	Fruity, oaky, minerally	Beef, lamb	**
Cousino Macul Finis Terrae	Red	Minerally, licorice, toasty	Beef, lamb	***
Cousino Macul Limited Release Merlot	Red	Berry, earthy, leathery	Beef, lamb	**
De Martino Prima Reserva Cabernet Sauvignon	Red	Berry, oaky	Pork, beef	*
De Martino Reserva de Familia Cabernet Sauvignon	Red	Berry, vanillin, intense	Beef, lamb	***
Domaine Paul Bruno	Red	Complex, intense	Beef, lamb	**
La Palma Cabernet Sauvignon	Red	Fruity, spicy	Pizza, pasta	*
La Palma Gran Reserva Chardonnay	White	Apples, buttery, crisp	Fish, chicken	**
La Palma Gran Reserva Merlot	Red	Fruity, oaky	Veal, pork, beef	**
La Palma Reserva Cabernet Sauvignon	Red	Berry, spicy, toasty	Pork, beef	**
La Palma Reserva Merlot	Red	Fruity, rich	Veal, pork, beef	**
La Playa Claret Maxima	Red	Licorice, spicy, oaky	Veal, pork, beef	**
La Playa Estate Reserve Cabernet Sauvignon	Red	Berry, spicy, toasty	Chicken, veal	*
La Playa Estate Reserve Merlot	Red	Fruity, oaky, coconut	Chicken, veal, pork	**
Luis Felipe Edwards Carmenere	Red	Plums, berry, herbaceous	Beef, lamb	**
Luis Felipe Edwards Pupilla Cabernet Sauvignon	Red	Berry, plums, spicy	Pork, beef	**
Miguel Torres Santa Digna Brut	Sparkling	Crisp, citrus	Shellfish, nuts	**
Pionero Cabernet Sauvignon	Red	Fruity, spicy	Pizza, pasta	*
Pionero Merlot	Red	Berry, crisp, spicy	Pizza, pasta	*
Santa Alicia El Pimiento Gran Reserva Merlot	Red	Fruity, plums	Pizza, chicken	*
Santa Amelia Reserve Selection Cabernet Sauvignon	Red	Fruity, vanillin	Pork, veal, beef	*
Santa Amelia Reserve Selection Chardonnay	White	Grassy, citrus, crisp	Fish, pasta	*

Wine name	Style	Flavor/ Bouquet	Compatible Foods	Price Range
Santa Erna Reserve Cabernet Sauvignon	Red	Berry, spicy, oaky	Veal, pork, beef	**
Santa Erna Reserve Merlot	Red	Berry, oaky, coconut	Chicken, veal, pork	*
Santa Marvista Reserva Cabernet Sauvignon	Red	Fruity, herbaceous, austere	Chicken, veal	*
Santa Marvista Reserva Merlot	Red	Plums, zingy	Pizza, pasta	*
Santa Rita Casa Real Old Vines Vineyard Cabernet Sauvignon	Red	Intense, fruity, tannic	Beef, lamb	***
Santa Rita Medalla Real Special Reserve Cabernet Sauvignon	Red	Berry, herbaceous, tannic	Pork, beef, lamb	**
Undurraga Chardonnay	White	Apples, oaky	Fish, chicken	*
Undurraga Reserva Cabernet Sauvignon	Red	Fruity, berry, vanillin	Pork, beef, lamb	**
Viña Aquitania Cabernet Sauvignon	Red	Plums, spicy	Pork, beef, lamb	**
Viña Calina Cabernet Sauvignon	Red	Berry, licorice, earthy	Beef, lamb	**
Viña Calina Merlot	Red	Fruity, herbaceous	Pizza, chicken	**
Viña Calina Selección de las Lomas Cabernet Franc	Red	Fruity, toasty, elegant	Beef, lamb	***
Viña Calina Selección de las Lomas Chardonnay	White	Citrus, oaky	Fish, chicken	**
Viña Calina Selección de las Lomas Merlot	Red	Fruity, oaky, rich	Beef, lamb	***
Viña Calina Vicuña Vineyard Cabernet Sauvignon	Red	Intense, fruity, toasty	Beef, lamb	***
Viña La Rosa Cabernet Sauvignon	Red	Plums, earthy, oaky	Pork, beef	**
Viña Santa Carolina Reserva Merlot	Red	Berry, vanillin	Pork, veal, beef	*
Viña Tarapaca Zauala	Red	Earthy, minerally, oaky	Beef, lamb	***
Vista Sur Merlot	Red	Plums, spicy	Chicken, pork, beef	**
Colchegua Valley				
Château La Joya Gran Reserva Merlot	Red	Berry, oaky	Chicken, pork	*
Los Vascos Cabernet Sauvignon	Red	Berry, oaky	Pizza, chicken	*
Undurraga Merlot	Red	Berry, herbaceous, jam	Pork, veal, beef	*
Viña San Esteban President's Select Cabernet Sauvignon	Red	Fruity, herbaceous, vanillin	Pork, beef	**
Viu Manent Reserva Cabernet Sauvignon	Red	Berry, elegant, herbaceous	Veal, pork, beef	**
Viu Manent Reserve Chardonnay	White	Citrus, vanillin, elegant	Fish, chicken	**
Viu Manent Reserve Oak-Aged Malbec	Red	Berry, toasty, zingy	Pork, beef	**
Lontue				
Valdevisio Barrel Select Malbec	Red	Plums, spicy	Veal, pork, beef	**
Valdevisio Caballo Loco	Red	Complex, intense, oaky	Beef, lamb	**
Valdevisio Reserve Merlot	Red	Plums, earthy, oaky	Pork, beef, lamb	**
Viña San Pedro Castillo de Molina Reserva Cabernet Sauvignon	Red	Licorice, berry, oaky	Pizza, chicken	*
Rancagua Valley				
Santa Monica Tierra del Sol Reserva Cabernet Sauvignon	Red	Earthy, spicy	Pork, beef	**
ARGENTINA				
Cafayate				
Bodegas Etchart Arnaldo B Etchert Reserva	Red	Minerally, berry, herbaceous	Pork, beef, lamb	**
Bodegas Etchart Cafayate Chardonnay Barrel Fermented	White	Citrus, butter, toasty	Fish, chicken	**
Etchart Arnaldo Etchert Reserve	Red	Fruity, earthy, spicy	Beef, lamb	**
Maipu				
Correas Syrah-Sengiovese	Red	Berry, earthy, crisp	Pizza, chicken	*
Finca Flinchman Dedicado	Red	Berry, earthy, oaky	Beef, lamb	**

Wine name	Style	Flavor/ Bouquet	Compatible Foods	Price Range
Mendoza				
Alamos Ridge Malbec	Red	Berry, plums, spicy	Chicken, veal, pork	*
Altos de les Hormigas Malbec	Red	Berry, spicy	Pizza, beef	*
Balbi Chardonnay	White	Citrus, minerally, zingy	Shellfish, fish	**
Balbi Malbec	Red	Berry, spicy	Pizza, chicken	**
Barral y Roca Malbec	Red	Berry, herbaceous, spicy	Pork, beef	**
Bodegas Curton Tempranillo-Malbec	Red	Berry, spicy	Pizza, beef	**
Bodegas Etchart Rio de Plata Merlot	Red	Berry, spicy	Pizza, chicken	*
Bodegas Norton Privada	Red	Earthy, spicy	Beef, lamb	**
Catena Agrelo Vineyards Chardonnay	White	Fruity, oaky, butter	Fish, chicken	**
Catena Alta Malbec	Red	Complex, rich, earthy, oaky	Beef, lamb	***
Catena Lunlunta Vineyards Malbec	Red	Plums, fruity, rich, oaky	Beef, lamb	***
Grove Street Cabernet Sauvignon	Red	Berry, herbaceous, vanillin	Pizza, beef	**
Hos de Medrano Viña Hormigas Reserva Malbec	Red	Fruity, intense, toasty	Pork, beef, lamb	***
La Agricola Montepulciano	Red	Berry, earthy	Beef, lamb	*
Lavaque Cabernet Sauvignon-Merlot	Red	Berry, spicy, herbacous	Pork, beef, lamb	*
Mariposa Tapiz Reserve Malbec	Red	Berry, tannic	Beef, lamb	**
Norton Barbera	Red	Berry, spicy	Pizza, chicken	*
Putini Malbec	Red	Plums, spicy	Pork, beef	**
Q Tempranillo	Red	Rich, berry, spicy, dill	Beef, pork	**
Rafael Malbec-Tempranillo	Red	Rich, plums, berry, leathery	Chicken, veal, pork	*
Santa Julia Oak Reserve Cabernet Sauvignon	Red	Berry, spicy, leathery	Beef, lamb	*
Santa Julia Oak Reserve Malbec	Red	Berry, vanillin	Pizza, chicken	*
Santa Julia Tempranillo	Red	Berry, minerally	Pizza, chicken	*
Santa Silva Barbera	Red	Berry, spicy	Pizza, chicken	**
Trapiche Iscay Merlot-Malbec	Red	Rich, toasty, powerful	Veal, pork, beef	***
Trapiche Medalla Cabernet Sauvignon	Red	Berry, oaky, austere	Beef, lamb	**
Trapiche Medalla Chardonnay	White	Tropical fruit, toasty	Fish, chicken	**
Trapiche Medalla Merlot	Red	Berry, oaky, tannic	Veal, pork, beef	**
Trapiche Oak Cask Cabernet Sauvignon	Red	Fruity, oaky	Pizza, beef	*
Trapiche Oak Cask Malbec	Red	Berry, oaky	Chicken, pork	*
Tri Vento Malbec	Red	Berry, elegant	Pizza, chicken	*
Viñas de Medrano Cabernet Sauvignon	Red	Berry, plums, spicy	Pizza, beef	*
Viñas de Medrano Malbec	Red	Plums, earthy, spicy	Beef, lamb	*
Weinert Cabernet Sauvignon	Red	Berry, earthy, toasty	Beef, lamb	**
Weinert Cevas de Weinert Gran Vino	Red	Mushroom, earthy, austere	Beef, lamb	**
Weinert Malbec	Red	Berry, gamey, leathery	Pork, beef, lamb	**
Patagonia				
Infinitus Malbec-Syrah	Red	Rich, berry, spicy	Veal, pork, beef	***
Rio Negro				
Canale Malbec	Red	Berry, earthy	Pork, beef, lamb	**
San Juan				
Graffigna Barbera	Red	Berry, spicy	Pizza, chicken	**

Wine name	Style	Flavor/ Bouquet	Compatible Foods	Price Range
Graffigna Cabernet Sauvignon	Red	Plums, spicy, elegant	Chicken, pork, beef	**
Graffigna Malbec	Red	Berry, spicy	Veal, pork, beef	**
Graffigna Pinot Gris-Semillon	White	Floral, fruity, zingy	Shellfish, Asian	**
Grafigna Shiraz-Cabernet Sauvignon	Red	Berry, licorice, oaky	Pork, beef, lamb	**
Vinterra Chardonnay	White	Butter, waxy, apples	Fish, chicken	*
Vinterra Malbec	Red	Berry, vanillin	Pizza, chicken	*
San Rafael				
Covisan Syrah Artuel Valley	Red	Berry, mint, rich	Pork, lamb	*
Valentin Bianchi Elsa Malbec	Red	Berry, fruity, vanillin	Pizza, beef	*
Valentin Bianchi Famiglia Bianchi Cabernet Sauvignon	Red	Intense, earthy, spicy, toasty	Beef, lamb	***
Valentin Bianchi Malbec	Red	Powerful, earthy	Beef, lamb	**
Tupungato				
Trumpeter Merlot	Red	Plums, spicy, toasty	Pizza, beef	*

Glossary

a.b.v. "Alcohol by volume," the standard form of measuring the alcohol level in a wine, given as a percentage.

AC Initials of *Appellation Contrôlée*.

Acetic A tasting description for a usually unpleasant wine with a sharp, vinegary character caused by bacteria.

Acid The component of substances which gives them a sharp, tangy taste. Lemons, for example, are very acidic. Acidity, mainly in the form of tartaric acid, is a key component of wine.

Acidification The process of adding acidity to juice or wine to make it taste fresher and prevent damage from bacteria and oxygen.

Adega (Portuguese) A cellar or winery.

Aguardiente (Spanish) A popular high-proof grape spirit produced by the continuous still method.

Air-bag press A cylindrical press which works by expanding a rubber bladder under air pressure. As the bladder expands it squeezes the grapes in the press, producing juice.

Alcohol by volume *see* a.b.v.

Amphorae Traditional vessels used by the Greeks and Romans to store wine. These oval, earthenware vessels were often, themselves, stored by being pushed into the ground.

Amtliche prufungsnummer (**AP**) (German) The number which appears on every bottle of QbA or QmP wine. It signifies that the wine has passed the official taste tests.

Appellation A term used to describe a demarcated wine region, one where the boundaries of the region are mapped out. The term is originally French. *See also Appellation Contrôlée.*

Appellation Contrôlée (**AC**) (French) A demarcated wine region in France. For example, only wine made in the specifically defined area around Bordeaux can claim to be from the Bordeaux appellation. French appellation laws also prescribe various viticulture and winemaking practices for each AC.

Aromatic Literally a wine with a noticeable smell, but often used to describe wines with a very floral or spicy nose.

Artisanal Wine made by an artisan: the "crafted" result of small-scale (probably quite traditional) production.

Assemblage (French) The term used for the blending of still wines prior to a secondary fermentation which will produce champagne or sparkling wine.

Aszú (Hungarian) Botrytized grapes. Most often encountered as tokay aszú (tokaji), Hungary's most famous sweet wine.

Ausbruch (Austrian) A notable wine made from botrytized grapes and considered to be more opulent than wines from the Beerenauslese category.

Auslese (German) One of the *Prädikats* of German wine law, literally meaning "selected harvest." In practice, a wine with greater must weight than is normal for German wines, and probably with noticeable sweetness and a hint of botrytis.

Autolysis The process resulting from the decomposition of dead yeast cells following fermentation. It gives a creamy texture and yeasty aromas to wine. It is especially important for sparkling wine that has undergone second fermentation by the traditional method.

Autolytic characters The aroma and flavor characters resulting from autolysis in sparkling wines.

Balance The relationship among the factors that make up the structure of a wine—the acid, residual sugar, tannin, alcohol, weight, texture, and fruit intensity—when tasting it.

Barrel-aging The process of aging wine in a barrel (usually of new or newish oak) rather than in a large tank and/or the bottle.

Barrel fermentation The process of fermenting wine in small oak barrels rather than tanks or vats. The process imparts a richness and creaminess to the texture of the wine, but if all new oak is used, this can be overdone.

Barrica (Spanish) *see Barrique.*

Barrique (French) A term originally used in Bordeaux but now commonly used worldwide for a barrel of 225 liters (60 gallons).

Base wine The wine, fermented dry, that will undergo a second fermentation to become sparkling wine.

Bâttonage (French) The stirring of yeast lees in barrel. It encourages the uptake of lees flavors in the wine, and prevents some faults developing.

Baumé (French) One of the methods of quantifying sugar levels in grape juice; the others are brix and *oeschle*. This method is used in France, elsewhere in Europe, and Australia. One degree *baumé* is roughly equal to one percent of alcohol in the resulting wine.

Beerenauslese (BA) (German) One of the *Prädikats* of German wine law, literally "selected berries." This category implies the selection of botrytized grapes, to make intense and sweet wine.

Biodynamic A system of cultivation which is related to organic viticulture. It is based around viewing the soil as a living organism that should not be treated with inorganic substances. The system has a complex dogma, which is dismissed as superstition by some, but it has been adopted by some of the leading producers in France and elsewhere.

Bladder press *see* Air-bag press.

Blanc de Blancs (French) White wine from white grapes but attaches to champagnes made from 100 percent chardonnay grapes.

Blanc de Noirs (French) White wine from black (or red) grapes. In Champagne, it refers to wines made from pinot noir and/or pinot meunier, though there are not many. Bollinger's VVF is the classic example. It is possible to make white wine from these grapes as they, and almost all other "black" grapes, have "white" juice and pulp, the color of the wine eventually coming from skin content.

Bodega (Spanish) This word has many meanings: cellar, wine producer, merchant, store selling wine, tavern.

Bodeguero (Spanish) Proprietor of a bodega.

Botrytis The Latin term for fungus, encompassing all the rots that can affect grapes and damage the resulting wine. In one form, however—noble rot—it does not harm the grapes, but rather produces a complex and sweet wine, commonly referred to as "botrytized."

Botte (Italian) Barrel.

Bottiglia (Italian) Bottle.

Bottle shock The term for the impact of bottling on wine: the wine can become less aromatic or tasty in the few weeks after bottling.

Brix One of the methods of quantifying sugar levels in grape juice; the others are *baumé* and *oeschle*. Winemakers in the U.S. and New Zealand as one component of assessing grape ripeness use this method.

Brut (French) This term is used to denote dry or very dry champagne. Extra brut is even drier.

Cane The woody growth developing from vine shoots: it both produces the vine leaves and carries the bunches of grapes.

Canteiro (Portuguese) The eaves of the Madeira houses under which the island's great vintage wines must age for a minimum of 20 years in cask.

Cap The mixture of skins, stalks, and other matter which accumulates at the top of fermenting red must.

Carbonic maceration The process of starting to ferment juice in unbroken grapes, using enzymes rather than yeast; a full yeast fermentation follows once the alcohol level in the grapes reaches about 4 percent. It is traditionally used in Beaujolais, producing fruity wines with low tannin.

Casa Vinacola (Italian) A producer who buys in grapes and even wine, rather than a producer that grows their own grapes.

Cava Spanish sparkling wine made in a number of regions, especially Catalonia, by the traditional method.

Cepage (French) Grape varieties. *Encepagement* refers to the grape varieties that make up the blend of any wine. For example, the *encepagement* of a Bordeaux will include some or all of merlot, cabernet sauvignon, cabernet franc, petit verdot, and malbec.

Chai (French) Storage facilities for wine, usually above the ground.

Chaptalization The process of adding sugar to fermenting must to increase the resulting alcoholic strength of the wine.

Charmat A method of inducing the second fermentation, and thus creating sparkling wine, in large pressure tanks. This method reduces the production costs usually associated with the traditional method.

Château (French) Used in Bordeaux to describe wineries, which can be traditional and impressive, even majestic, or simple and basic.

Clairet Deep rosé wine that is produced in Bordeaux.

Classic When used on German labels, at the discretion of the producer, it indicates the wine is dry, officially under 1.5 percent residual sugar. The term has been used since 2000.

Classico (Italian) The designation for the best part of any DOC region. The best known is Chianti Classico, which has attained a DOC rating of its own.

Climat (French) A term used particularly in Burgundy for a vineyard site defined by its mesoclimate as well as by its soil.

Clone Propagation of vines from an original mother vine. Some varieties, especially pinot noir, may have hundreds of clones. They will have different uses. For example, one clone of pinot noir may suit the production of sparkling wine while another may be more suited to table wine. Most serious producers of a grape such as pinot believe that it is of benefit to the final wine for their vineyard to have a number of different clones.

Clos (French) A vineyard surrounded by a wall, though today, some of the walls may now be almost non-existent. Examples are Krug's Clos de Mesnil in Champagne and Clos Vougeot in Burgundy.

Cold stabilization The process whereby tartrate crystals are precipitated out of the wine (if not, they can leave small harmless crystals) by swift chilling.

Colheita (Portuguese) A tawny port, which is not a blend of different years but which is "dated," that is, from a single vintage.

Commune (French) A term often associated with the small subregions of Bordeaux. They can be appellations in their own right.

Concentration The intensity and focus of flavor in a wine.

Condition The state of a wine being drunk, whether or not it has any faults.

Cordon A permanent branch of a vine, usually trained along a wire.

Cork taint A wine fault caused generally by the interaction of mold (originating from the cork) with chlorine compounds, causing a loss of fruit flavor and—to a greater or lesser extent—a damp, hessian-like smell on the wine.

Crémant (French) This term was banned in Champagne in the early 1990's. Prior to that, it had been used to describe wines with a lesser degree of pressure (resulting in less fizz). These wines are still made in Champagne but each producer will provide the wine with its own name. The term is still used for sparkling wines made outside the Champagne district. Examples are Crémant de Loire and Crémant d'Alsace.

Crianza (Spanish) The term for aging, and for the youngest official category of a wood-matured wine (used particularly in Rioja, and some other regions, such as Ribera del Duero).

Crossing A new variety produced by adding the pollen of one variety to the flowers of another and planting the resulting grape seeds. Müller-thurgau is probably the most utilized crossing in the world. Note the difference between a crossing and a hybrid.

Cru (French) Literally "growth." Practically, this is difficult to translate, but usually it is used in a qualitative context, as in "premier cru"— "first growth"—which is a high-quality wine.

Cuvée (French) Derived from the term for a tank, this word now refers to a particular selection of wine. In Champagne it is the first selection of juice on pressing—the best for making sparkling wine.

Deacidification The process of reducing the acid level in wine, normally by malolactic fermentation or the addition of various compounds which cause acidity to deposit out.

Decanting The process of pouring a wine from the bottle into a decanter. This allows any sediment to be left in the bottle and also promotes the aeration of the wine. It normally occurs with older wines, though some advocate decanting even young whites. Whether or not to decant and how long before drinking should a wine be decanted will long remain debatable issues.

Demarcation The process of defining the exact geographical limits of a wine region. *See also* Appellation.

Demi-sec (French) A term used for sweet sparkling wine or champagne.

Denominazione di Origine Controllata (Italian) DOC equates to France's Appellation d'Origine Contrôlée laws. Over three hundred have been proclaimed. As with the French system, the laws govern the viticulture and winemaking practices permitted in each DOC. The wines also undergo chemical analysis and tasting under controlled conditions before they can be called DOC.

Denominazione di Origine Controllata e Garantita (Italian) DOCG is the quality level above the DOC wines. The regulations for these wines (there are more than twenty such regions) are stricter than those for DOC wines.

Disgorgement The action of expelling frozen yeast lees from a bottle of wine which has undergone second fermentation, to ensure that the wine is not cloudy.

DOC Initials of Denominazione di Origine Controllata.

DOCG Initials of Denominazione di Origine Controllata e Garantita

Domaine (French) Often used to denote a winery, commonly used in Burgundy. In Bordeaux, it is much more likely that they will be referred to as Châteaux. In southern France, the term, Mas, is often substituted.

Dosage (French) Just prior to corking, a small quantity of "*liqueur d'expedition*," of varying degrees of sweetness, is added to sparkling wines. This *dosage* will determine the final classification of sweetness of the wine.

Eau-de-Vie A spirit or brandy, usually clear and sometimes flavored, that is made from distilling wine or grape skins (known as pomace). Translated literally, it means "water of life." Where an eau-de-vie is particularly strongly flavored or powerful, it can be called a marc.

Einzellagen (German) Individual vineyard sites. The number of these sites in Germany is approaching 3,000. Germany's regions are divided first into *Berieche*, then *Grosslagen*, and finally *Einzellagen*.

Eiswein (German) An intensely sweet wine that is made from grapes which have been left to hang on the vine for an extended period of time. The production of *eiswein* is a risky business. The grapes are pressed while frozen and the tiny amount of juice that is extracted is extremely concentrated and high in acid. The wines, which will age for many years, are rare and very expensive because of this method of production. Canada also produces wines in this style, called ice wine.

En primeur (French) The first sale of wine in Bordeaux from each vintage, in which wine is sold to the customer while the wine is still in barrels in the cellars.

Enology The science of wine production.

Enrichment The process of increasing the alcohol level of the wine, usually by chaptalization, to modify its structure.

Estufa (Portuguese) The method of heating madeira which accelerates its development; it gives madeira its characteristic style by caramelizing the sugars in the wine.

Ethyl alcohol A scientific classification of the predominant type of alcohol in wine. Often popularly referred to as ethanol.

Extract The dry matter which would remain were you to evaporate the liquid from a wine. The higher the sugar-free extract, the more flavor, body, and phenolic components there are in the wine. However, over-extraction can cause a wine to be unbalanced, especially if it results in excessive phenolics.

Feinherb (German) A term denoting an off-dry wine.

Fermentation The chemical process involved in converting sugar to alcohol and carbon dioxide brought about by the activity of yeast.

Filtration The process of removing unwanted matter (even matter as small as bacteria or yeast cells) from a wine by various methods of straining.

Finesse The term used to describe elegant delicacy in a wine.

Fining The process of removing undesirable particles (usually proteins or phenolics) dissolved in the wine.

Flor (Spanish) The layer of yeast which forms on the surface of Fino and Manzanilla sherries during aging. It helps inhibit oxidation and also plays a role in contributing to the final flavor of the wine.

Fortification The addition of spirit (normally grape spirit) to wine. This is normally done during fermentation, to a point where yeast cells die and fermentation stops. Wines produced in this way are referred to as "fortified."

Foxy A description often applied to wine from native American varieties where the wine has a wild, earthy, gamey, grapey character. The term is most often applied disparagingly.

Fractional blending The process whereby when some wine is extracted from a cask for bottling it is replaced by wine from a more recent blend, which in turn may be replaced by a yet more recent blend, and so on until wine from the current vintage is added to the youngest blend. The process is used especially in the making of sherry.

Free run The juice that runs from the presses merely because of the weight of the other grapes and before any extra pressure has been applied. Often considered to be the very finest juice available for certain wines. Examples of these wines are champagne and young fresh whites such as rieslings.

Frizzante (Italian) Slightly sparkling wine, an example is prosecco.

Garrafeira (Portuguese) A wine which has been subject to additional aging—three years for red wine and one year for white—for that type of wine. Wines labeled "*Garrafeira*" are generally considered to be of better quality.

Generoso (Spanish and Portuguese) Fortified wine.

Glycerol A heavy liquid, which is related to alcohol, which may impart hints of sweetness to a wine.

Gran Reserva (Spanish) This term is used to denote a wine that has had extra aging. Specifically, this means two years in cask and three years in bottle for red wines, and rather less for whites.

Grand Marque (French) This denotes that a particular Champagne house is a member of an association of what was once perceived as the cream of the Champagne producers. The organisation is known as the Syndicat de Grandes Marques and works to ensure the highest standards are maintained in the region.

Grand vin (French) Literally "big wine": this can be interpreted as a great, serious, or important wine. Also used in Bordeaux for the main wine (not the second wine) made by a château.

Granvas (Spanish) Sparkling wine made by either the tank method or the charmat method.

Green harvesting The process of removing some bunches on a vine to reduce the yield and enhance the ripening process in the bunches which remain.

Guyot-trained A method of training a vine which uses a new cane or canes each year to provide shoots and ultimately fruit; it is unlike cordon training, which uses a permanent branch.

Halbtrocken (German) Literally "half dry": in practice, a medium dry wine.

Harmony The sense of integration and equilibrium one gets when tasting a wine that is in balance.

Herbaceous A wine which tastes rather herbal, or of dried grass. Sometimes used in a derogatory way.

Hybrid A new vine produced from two parents, generally one *Vitis vinifera* (which provides almost all the grape varieties used for making wine) and the other a native American species. This was done to combine the best aspects of both varieties, and to increase the vines' resistance to phylloxera (in Europe in the late nineteenth century), but the hybrids produced poor wine; only a few, such as seyval blanc and chambourcin, make acceptable wine.

IGT (Italian) Initials for *Indicazione Geografica Tipica*.

Imbottigliato all'Origine (Italian) Estate bottled wine. The grapes must also have been grown on the property.

Indicazione Geografica Tipica (IGT) (Italian) A category of wines considered to equate to France's *vin de pays*. There are well over one hundred IGTs, and they are subject to regulations that are less strict than those for DOC and DOCG wines. Super Tuscans such as Sassicaia and Tignanello are high-profile IGT examples.

Jeropiga (Portuguese) Grape juice prevented from fermenting by fortification. Usually used to sweeten fortified wines.

Joven afrutado (Spanish) A young wine made to emphasize overt fruity characters.

Jug wine U.S. wine of mediocre quality produced in bulk and sold cheaply.

Kabinett (German) The most basic of the *Prädikats* of German wine law, but still usually of higher quality than basic QbA wine. These are very light wines.

Keller (German) German wine cellar.

KWV Initials (from the name in Afrikaans) of the Cooperative Wine Growers' Association of South Africa.

Lagar (Portuguese) A shallow basin in which the grapes used for port can be trodden to release their juice and extract phenolics while fermentation takes place.

Late disgorgement A form of champagne which remains on its yeast lees in the bottle for many years. The champagne is then disgorged shortly before sale. The lees allow the champagne to age slowly, and may also impart further flavor complexity.

Lees The term literally means debris that falls out of wine (including skins, pips etc), but it is often used to refer to the dead yeast cells deposited at the end of fermentation, (also known as yeast lees). *See also* Autolysis; *Battonage.*

Legs Also known as tears, these are the small trickles of wine that form on the inside of a glass and slowly drain back into the wine. Despite popular belief to the contrary, the legs have nothing to do with the quality of a wine. Rather, they are the result of factors such as alcohol and glycerol levels. Hence, an old fortified will show considerably more "legs" than a young riesling.

Length The amount of time the taste of wine lingers in the mouth after it has been swallowed. A long wine is generally a wine of high quality.

Levada (Portuguese) An irrigation trench used in Madeira to take water to the vineyards.

Liqueur de Tirage (French) A blend of wine, sugar, and yeasts that is added to still wine, which the producer intends to be sparkling, to induce the second fermentation, hence providing the effervescence.

Liqueur d'Expedition (French) The wine which is used to top up a champagne bottle after disgorging and prior to final corking. It adds the *dosage*, which determines the final level of sweetness in the wine.

Low cropping Vines that are managed in order to produce lower yields and, theoretically, higher quality yields. Also called crop thinning.

Maceración carbonica (Spanish) *see* carbonic maceration.

Maceration The process of leaving must or wine with grape skins during or after fermentation in order to increase the taking up of phenolics.

Maderization A process by which wine is made to taste like madeira: oxidation is sped up by the addition of heat. The term is sometimes used pejoratively, to indicate excessive oxidation and consequent unpleasant taste.

Magnum A bottle containing 1.5 liters, twice the normal size.

Malolactic fermentation The conversion by bacteria of crisp malic acid into softer lactic acid, making the wine fuller. It is commonly used in making red wines, but only with discretion in whites.

Mercaptans A wine fault stemming from a sulfur compound that causes an unpleasant garlic-like smell, and which is impossible to shift.

Meritage (U.S.) A trademarked name for wine based on a blend of the traditional red Bordeaux varieties—primarily cabernet sauvignon, cabernet franc, and merlot. Most Meritage is made in California.

Méthode ancestrale (French) A traditional way of making sparkling wine which involves stopping the fermentation by chilling, leaving a wine that is fizzy, slightly sweet, and cloudy (from the yeast lees). It is mainly used for Blanquette de Limoux.

Méthode champenoise (French) The traditional method of making sparkling wine as utilized in Champagne.

Méthode traditionelle (French) *see* Traditional method.

Methyl alcohol A form of alcohol found in

wine, but is much less important than ethyl alcohol. It is more popularly known as methanol.

Método tradicional (Spanish) *see* Traditional method.

Millésime (French) A term used to denote a vintage wine in Champagne.

Minerally A tasting term used to describe wine flavors which are not fruity, oaky, or floral, but which may be more reminiscent of sucking on a pebble.

Mistelle (French) Grape juice which has been prevented from fermenting by fortification with spirit.

Moelleux (French) Sweet, but not luscious.

Monopole (French) A term used in Burgundy, which indicates that a vineyard is owned by one estate, and only they produce wine from it. La Tache, owned by the Domaine de la Romanee Conti, is an example.

Mousse The bubbles on the surface of a sparkling wine. The term is also used to describe the feel of the bubbles in the mouth.

Must The liquid that is fermenting—neither pure juice nor finished wine.

Muzzle The wire restraint that contains the cork of a sparkling wine.

Négociant (French) A wine merchant.

Nematodes Microscopic insects which may damage a vine or, more dangerously, carry a disease which will infect the vine.

New World In one sense, the term refers to methods of wine production that rely more on science than tradition, wherever they are used. When referring to New World countries, it is accepted that these are the non-European producers such as Australia, New Zealand, Chile, and the rest of South America, South Africa, and the U.S.

Noble A contraction of "noble rot," referring to wine which has undergone the beneficial effects of botrytis.

Nonvintage A wine made from more than one vintage. The majority of champagne is nonvintage. Some producers, such as Krug, prefer to use the term, "multivintage," which more correctly describes the wine. Outside of Champagne, most view nonvintage wines as of lesser quality.

Nose A term used to describe the smell of a wine.

Nouveau (French) Refers to a very young wine made for immediate drinking; Beaujolais Nouveau being the best known example.

Oechsle One of the methods of quantifying sugar levels in grape juice; the others are *baumé* and brix. It is commonly used by winemakers in Germany and Central Europe as one component of assessing grape ripeness.

Old World Those countries where wine originated and where, in a very general sense, the old and traditional methods of production still hold sway. They are the European and Mediterranean countries. "Old World winemaking" is using those traditional methods, even if carried out in a New World country.

Organoleptic An adjective referring to the process of tasting.

Oxidation The dulling of color, aroma, and flavor of a wine resulting from too much air contact.

Palate A term used to describe the taste of wine.

Pasada (Spanish) Describes sherry that has been well aged.

Passerillage (French) Concentrating the sugars in grapes by leaving them to hang on the bunches and partially dehydrate.

Passito (Italian) Wine made from half-dried grapes, which has the effect of concentrating them. The wine is almost always sweet.

pH. The scientific measurement of acidity and alkalinity. Water (which is neutral) has a pH. of 7. A pH. of less than that means a substance is acidic (at a pH. of 1 it would be very highly acidic), and a pH. above 7 means the substance is alkaline. Wine generally has a pH. between 2.9 and about 3.6 (sometimes a little higher).

Phenolics Substances extracted from the skins of grapes that provide the coloring (anthocyanins) and texture (tannins) for red wine.

Phylloxera An aphid, with nineteen lifecycles, which attacks and slowly kills the root system of a vine. There is no known cure and the only way to save the vineyards of Europe and many other countries in the nineteenth century was to graft the *Vitis vinifera* vines on to the rootstock of native American vines, from where the aphid originated. Otherwise, there would likely be no wine industry, as we know it today.

Power A tasting term referring to the combined weight and flavor intensity of the wine—and possibly the impact of its alcohol as well.

Prädikat (German) Literally a "distinction," given to QmP wines: essentially a marker of the sugar level and an indicator of the likely style of the wine. The term is used in both Austria and Germany.

Pumping over A method of increasing phenolic extraction from black grapes by pumping must from the bottom of a tank and spraying it over the cap at the top.

Punching down A method of increasing phenolic extraction from black grapes by pressing the cap down into the must, thus increasing contact between the cap and the liquid.

Qualitätswein bestimmter Anbaugebiete (QbA) (German) Literally "quality wine from a region": the most basic level of quality wine in Germany and Austria.

Qualitätswein mit Prädikat (QmP) (German) Higher in quality than QbA in Germany and Austria, QmP wines are defined using an additional categorization, which is based essentially on the wine's must weight (sugar level). *See also Kabinett; Spätlese; Auslese; Beerenauslese; Trockenbeerenauslese.*

Quinta (Portuguese) Strictly speaking means farm, but it can be used to indicate either a specific vineyard or a specific wine estate, the Port House of Quinta do Noval being a prime example.

Racking The process of moving wine from one container to another, generally leaving some deposit behind. Sometimes, though not invariably, some aeration is involved.

Recioto (Italian) A sweet wine made from dried grapes, most famously from the Soave and Valpolicella regions.

Reduction The process of maturing wine in an environment with no oxygen contact. As the oxygen dissolved in the wine is used up, further oxidation cannot occur. This environment helps preserve freshness in wine, but in certain environments off-odors can develop.

Remuage (French) The French term for riddling. It can be achieved by hand or by machines known as gyropalettes.

Reserva (Spanish) Red wine that has been aged for at least a year in cask and two years in bottle. White wines age for a shorter period. These wines are generally of higher quality than ordinary wines.

Residual sugar The sugar that remains in the finished wine after fermentation has been completed, giving some sweetness to it.

Riddling The process (in the traditional method) of slowly shaking the yeast lees to the neck of the bottle ready for disgorgement.

Rootstock The part of the vine which is planted in the soil. Different rootstocks can be used for different vines, as a grapevine does not have to grow on its own rootstock and can be grafted on to another. It was this ability which finally allowed producers to defeat the scourge of phylloxera. This was accomplished using resistant American rootstocks and grafting on to them *Vitis vinifera* vines.

Rosado (Spanish) Rosé wine.

Saignée (French) The process of "bleeding off" some red must at the start of fermentation in order to achieve a greater concentration of phenolics.

Sec (French) Although it literally means dry, if it appears on a champagne label, it means a wine that is slightly sweet, certainly sweeter than brut.

Second fermentation The means of adding the fizz (in the traditional method), by adding additional yeast and sugar to base wine in a bottle or tank, then capping it in order to trap the resulting carbon dioxide.

Second Wine Used by prestigious estates around the world to bottle and offer wine that does not make the grade for their very best. It is done to ensure the quality of the primary wine. Many Bordeaux estates now follow this practice, as do wineries in the New World. It is useful in lesser years and also for grapes from younger vines. Some wineries will market a second wine, which is merely different from their primary label and is a wine they do not wish to be seen as inferior in any way, but most fall below the major label. They can still be very fine wines in their own right.

Selection (German) A term for dry wine, under 1.2 percent residual sweetness, which can only be used where the label details the vineyard in which the grapes were grown. The term can be used at the maker's discretion.

Sélection de Grains Nobles (French) The term used in Alsace for wines made from very late harvested fruit, which has been affected by botrytis. The wines are intense and can be very expensive.

Set The point, after the vine has flowered, when the fertilized flowerheads begin to turn into minute berries.

Shy-bearing A vine which does not produce much fruit.

Skin contact The process of allowing the juice of crushed grapes to mix with the skins for a period of time. In red wine, this imparts color and tannins. It will also be used with certain white wines (some chardonnays, for example) to enhance complexity and flavor. Minimal skin contact with red grapes will lead to rosé wines.

Smaragd (Austrian) Refers to wines from the Wachau region of Austria that have attained a minimum of 11.3 percent alcohol. They equate to wines that would, elsewhere in Austria, be labeled as *Spätlese.*

Solera system A system of fractional blending, used mainly with sherry, which allows younger wine to gradually be blended with, and refresh, older wine.

Sommelier A specialized wine waiter. Most restaurants with serious wine cellars will employ a sommelier whose job is to maintain that cellar and assist customers in selecting the wine most appropriate to their needs. Often the butt of humor from those outside the wine world, good sommeliers can enhance any dining occasion.

Sorting tables Tables set up at harvest on which grapes can be sorted before crushing, to remove any of unacceptable quality. *See also triage.*

Sparkling wine Any wine with bubbles. The most famous and best known example is Champagne but other regions in France and most other wine producing countries also produce versions of sparkling wine. In Australia, sparkling red, usually made from shiraz, has developed a cult following.

Spätlese (German) One of the *Prädikats* of German wine law, literally "late picked."

Spritzig (German) Wine which has a prickle of carbon dioxide, without being fully sparkling.

Spumante (Italian) Sparkling wine, which has a poor reputation in many parts of the world but which can, in the better wines, be of good quality.

Stabilization The process of ensuring that wine has no components that may give rise to haze, deposits or further microbial activity once bottled.

Still wine The term used to describe any wine that is not sparkling.

Structure In tasting, the relationship between the elements sensed in the mouth (sugar, acidity, tannin, alcohol, bitterness, weight, and texture), as well as the flavor intensity of the wine.

Sulfur A naturally occurring chemical that has been used for preserving wine for centuries, mostly in the form of sulfur dioxide. It prevents bacterial spoilage, inhibits yeasts, aids in the prevention of oxidation, can prevent malolactic fermentation, and can stop alcoholic fermentation, which enables the winemaker to leave a wine with the required level of sweetness. Even though today's health conscious winemakers are careful to minimize the amount of sulfur used, a very small percentage of drinkers are allergic to it.

Super Seconds Denotes certain Bordeaux estates that were classified as Second Growths in the 1855 Classification and are now producing wine that, in some vintages, is comparable to that of the First Growths. There is no actual list and each person will consider different estates as worthy of the title.

Superiore (Italian) A quality designation often indicating extra aging of the wine, or possibly because it exceeds the minimum alcohol content.

Sur lie (French) Literally "on lees": a wine that has been matured for some time on its yeast lees.

Süssreserve (German) Literally "sweet reserve": unfermented grape juice or grape concentrate added to the wine before bottling to sweeten it.

Table wine In Europe, this is the legal classification of the most basic wine, which distinguishes it from "quality" wine. In some European Union countries, this can now refer to blended wines, called European table wines.

Tafelwein (German) *see* Table wine.

Tannin A phenolic compound that gives a textural character to (mainly red) wine—"furring" the teeth and gums in much the same way that stewed tea does. In balance within the wine, it is an essential part of the structure of red wine and crucial to its quality.

Tartrates If a wine has not been properly cold-stabilized, small crystals of tartaric acid can form and will sit at the bottom of the bottle. They are without taste or aroma but can affect the marketing of the wine. At one time, they were known as "wine diamonds."

Tastevin This is the small, shallow tasting vessel, often made from silver, which is used by sommeliers to assess wine prior to service. The dimples allow for contemplation of the wine's color. The tastevin is often considered by many to be a rather pretentious item.

Tenuta (Italian) Wine estate.

Terroir (French) There is no exact one-word English translation for this term that encompasses all factors making each vineyard unique. These include soil, climate, aspect, slope, environment, topography and sometimes goes so far as to incorporate the winemaking. While New World winemakers now generally agree that *terroir* is a valid concept, there is a belief among some that the Old World producers, especially the French, have used the concept as an innate, though not always substantiated, reason for the superiority of French wines.

Texture A tasting term for the tactile sensation of wine in the mouth: this relates particularly to tannin.

Toasting The process of charring the insides of a new barrel over an open fire, leading to the wine developing obvious oak flavors that are indeed toasty.

Traditional method The production of sparkling wine by the induction of a second fermentation in a bottle, which is then riddled and undergoes disgorgement.

Triage (French) The sorting of grapes during vintage to discard those of unacceptable quality. With botrytized wines, triage is used to delay the picking of grapes that have not yet adequately developed noble rot.

Trocken (German) Dry wines. The level of sweetness must not exceed 0.9 percent residual sweetness. It can be used for both Austrian and German wines.

Trockenbeerenauslese (TBA) (German) One of the *Prädikats* of German wine law, literally "selected dried berries": the name implies selection of botrytized grapes, to make very intense and sweet wine. This is the pinnacle of German and Austrian sweet wine, and commands extremely high prices.

Ullage The small gap between the bottom of the cork and the top of the wine (in a bottle standing upright) is known as the ullage. The greater the ullage, the more chance of oxidation of the wine.

Unfiltered Most wines, particularly if they are made in large quantities, are filtered before bottling to ensure no bacterial spoilage occurs later. There is a current trend to release wines that have not been filtered ("unfiltered" on a label is considered a marketing plus) as some winemakers and critics believe that filtering a wine may remove some of the flavor and character.

Varietal Refers to wine made primarily from, and named after a specific grape variety, for example, shiraz, riesling, or chardonnay. Each country is likely to have laws that determine the percentage (rarely 100 percent) of a grape variety that a wine must contain to be labeled varietal.

Vaslin press A cylindrical press that works by pulling together two plates from either end of the cylinder, thus squeezing the grapes contained between the plates.

Vendange (French) Harvest.

Vendange tardive (French) Late harvest. The term is used in Alsace, and equates to the German *spätlese*.

Vendemmia (Italian) The vintage; *Annata* is another term which is used.

Veraison (French) A critical stage in the ripening process, when black grapes start to attain their color and white grapes cease to be intense green and become translucent. From this point the grape size expands noticeably and the sugar content starts to increase dramatically.

Verband Deutscher Prädikats und Qualitätsweingüter (VDP) A German growers' association that requires its members to meet far higher production and quality standards than those demanded by the wine laws.

Vigna (Italian) Vineyard.

Vigor Vines may have more or less vigor. A certain amount implies a healthy vine, but excessive vigor may result in too much foliage, which shades grape bunches and may impede ripening. Some vines are naturally more vigorous than others.

Vin de pays (French) A category of table wine that is nevertheless allowed to state a region of origin. Its production—particularly its yield—is more controlled than that of table wine (although without the constraints imposed by the appellation system), in an attempt to produce better wine.

Vin doux naturel (French) Literally, "a wine that is naturally sweet," but used to describe a kind of fortified wine where spirit is added to grape juice rather than to wine. In various forms this is made across much of the south of France, either from grenache or muscat.

Vin Gris (French) Pale rosé wine, almost gray in color, hence the name.

Vino Bianco (Italian) White wine.

Vino da Tavola (Italian) The term used for basic, non-DOC table wine.

Vino joven afrutado (Spanish) Young, fruity wine.

Vino Rosato (Italian) Rosé wine.

Vino Rosso (Italian) Red wine.

Vintage The year in which the grapes used to produce wine were picked.

Vitis vinifera (Latin) Botanical classification for the wine vine. Almost all varieties used to make wine are members of this species.

Volatile acidity Commonly known as VA, if found in excess in a wine volatile acidity will give it a sharp, unpleasant character. It derives from the bacteria which produces acetic acid. In tiny quantities, it can be considered an enhancing and positive component.

Weight The apparent feeling of heaviness (or otherwise), which a wine gives when in the mouth. It is related to the alcohol content of the wine.

Weingut (German) German wine estate.

Winkler-Amerine heat summation scale A system of viticultural climate classification for California, based on the average environmental temperature. Growing zones are graded into regions (I–V) using monthly averages of temperatures over 50° Fahrenheit (10°C) during the vine's growing season. Daily temperature surpluses are averaged then multiplied by the number of days per month. Accumulations of heat are measured in degree days. The fewer the degree days, the cooler the region.

I. Less than 2,500 degree days: Bordeaux, Reims, Carneros, Edna Valley.

II. 2,501–3,000 degree days: Asti in Piedmont, Auckland, St. Helena in Napa Valley.

III. 3,001–3,500 degree days: Calistoga in Napa Valley, Ukiah in Mendocino.

IV. 3,500–4,000 degree days: Capetown, Florence.

V. More than 4,000 degree days: Perth, San Joaquin Valley.

Yield The amount of grapes produced by a vineyard, normally indicated by tons per acre/tonnes per hectare/ hectoliters per hectare. As a rule of thumb, high yields are considered to produce lesser wine than vineyards with low yields, but many other factors must be taken into account.

Index

Captions for the photographs in the introductory pages of each chapter

THE WORLD OF WINE

14–15: High above a Basque village in Spain, vines are planted along the contours of the mountain to reduce erosion.

FRANCE

42–43: Vineyards in Chinon, Loire valley. 45: Plowing with a horse in the Rhône Valley; Vineyards above the town of Tain, with the Rhône River in the background.

GERMANY

122–23: Picking Grapes above Zeltingen-Rachtig, Mosel. 225: Grape pickers, Mosel; Trittenheim, Mosel.

AUSTRIA

146: Fertilizing vines with old grape skins. 147: The historical association between the Church and wine-producing regions is highly visible in Austria.

SWITZERLAND

152: Vaud's Lavaux region on the slopes above Lake Geneva, where the vines are said to receive three suns—from the sky, reflected off the lake, and from stone walls. 153: Vineyard labor costs in Switzerland are probably the highest in the world. Pulley systems help at harvest time, but pickers often carry boxes of grapes up or down impossibly steep paths and stone steps between terraces.

ITALY

158–159: Terraced vines trained over ancient stone pillars. 161: Michelangelo's David (1504), Florence; Part of Tuscany's charm are the picturesque town's and villages dotting the countryside.

SPAIN

188–189: Tiny underground wine cellars, northwest Spain. 191: The Rio Vero in Aragón.

PORTUGAL

213: Winter pruning of over-long shoots encourages vines to grow in straight rows; Peso da Régua, a grape-growing area at the confluence of the Douro and Corgo rivers.

ENGLAND AND WALES

224: Vineyards and winery buildings in Wootton Vineyard, Shepton Mallett, Somerset; harvesting grapes, Wootton Vineyard.

CENTRAL AND EASTERN EUROPE

229: A sizeable Eastern European vineyard with new spring growth.

SOUTHERN EUROPE

238: Transporting an oak barrel, Achaia Clauff, Patras, Greece

SOUTH AFRICA

247: A harvest of sauvignon grapes at the Bouchard Finlayson vineyards in the Overberg.

AUSTRALIA

258–59: Hillstowe Wines's Adelaide Hills vineyards. 260: Penfolds's grand Kaiser Stuhl Winery in South Australia.

NEW ZEALAND

296–297: Brancott Estate vineyards, Marlborough. 299: Stonyridge is the source of New Zealand's most expensive red wine, Larose Cabernet; Vineyards at Hawkes Bay in New Zealand's North Island.

CANADA

326–327: Vineyards at Naramata in the Okanagan Valley, British Columbia. 329: Café in the old quarter, Québec

UNITED STATES OF AMERICA

340–341: Eberle vineyards, Paso Robles, California. 342: Discussing harvesting, Eberle vineyards. 343: Vines in full leaf.

MEXICO AND SOUTH AMERICA

396: Vineyard workers grafting cabernet sauvignon onto phylloxera-resistant rootstock. Casa Madero, Pajas Valley, Mexico. 397: Montevideo, Uruguay's picturesque capital at the mouth of the Rio de la Plata

CHILE AND ARGENTINA

402: Picking cabernet sauvignon grapes, Viña Los Vascos, Rapel Valley, Chile

Photographers

Glenn A Baker, Gilbert Bel-Bachir, Rob Blakers, John Borthwick, Ken Brass, Adam Bruzzone, Claver Carroll, Craig Cranko, Steven Elphick, Jean-Paul Gollin, Richard Humphrys, David Keith Jones, Brian Jordan, Ionas Kaltenbach, Mike Langford, Gary Lewis, Andre Martin, John McCann, David McGonigal, Craig Potton, Janet Price, Geof Prigge, Christo Reid, Don Skirrow, Ken Stepnell, Oliver Strewe, Jon Wyand

Produced by Global Book Publishing Pty Ltd, 1/181 High Street, Willoughby, NSW Australia 2068
Phone +61 2 09967 3100   Fax +61 2 9967 5891   Email globalpub@ozemail.com.au